Microeconomic Policy

To our wives, children and grandchildren
Mariel; Ann-Marie, Christopher; and Lucy Marie
Winifred; Adam, Lucy, Cecilia; Oliver, Matthew, Katie and Sophie

Microeconomic Policy
A New Perspective

Clem Tisdell

Professor Emeritus, School of Economics, The University of Queensland, Australia

Keith Hartley

Professor of Economics, Department of Economics and Director, Centre for Defence Economics, University of York, UK

University of Nottingham
Hallward Library

Edward Elgar
Cheltenham, UK • Northampton, MA, USA

Published by
Edward Elgar Publishing Limited
Glensanda House
Montpellier Parade
Cheltenham
Glos GL50 1UA
UK

Edward Elgar Publishing, Inc.
William Pratt House
9 Dewey Court
Northampton
Massachusetts 01060
USA

1005603875

A catalogue record for this book
is available from the British Library

Library of Congress Control Number: 2008926583

ISBN 978 1 85278 556 7 (cased)
     978 1 85278 561 1 (paperback)

Printed and bound in Great Britain by MPG Books Ltd, Bodmin, Cornwall

Contents

Preface

This book has its genesis in *Micro-Economic Policy* which was authored by K. Hartley and C. Tisdell and published in the 1980s by John Wiley. This previous book was widely used internationally as a textbook, and several users of it urged us to bring out a new edition. We were delighted when Edward Elgar expressed his interest in this enterprise. It took us, however, much longer to do this than expected. Furthermore, the changes turned out to be so substantial that it became evident that this book had to be regarded as a new book, even though it retains several significant features of the previous book.

Microeconomic Policy: A New Perspective has involved substantial additions to and revision of the earlier work so as to reflect changes in the direction and substance of microeconomic policy in recent decades as well as new developments in microeconomic analysis. The earlier book included policy implications of neoclassical microeconomics as well as extensions to take account of such factors as knowledge limitations, search, the costs of decision-making, principal–agent problems (features often associated with the New Institutional Economics) and aspects of the theory of games. While this emphasis has been retained and strengthened, greater consideration is given to the relevance of other approaches to microeconomic thought such as those associated with traditional institutional economics, behavioural economics and the Austrian School of Economics.

Very often microeconomic policies have to be considered from varied perspectives. For example, depending upon the policy issue being considered, different degrees and types of abstraction may be appropriate, dynamic rather than static models may be relevant, and diverse time-periods may need to be considered. Thus, different frameworks of microeconomic thought are likely to be required. While neoclassical microeconomics has its valuable uses for policy purposes, it is inappropriate for modelling all microeconomic policy issues, as will become apparent in this text. As pointed out by Joan Robinson, one usually has to adapt existing economic tools to apply these to policy formulation and to be selective in deciding on the type of economic analysis to apply. Judgement is needed because the world is complex and ever changing and consequently, ready-made solutions to policy issues are rarely available.

It is our hope that this text will make its users aware of varied perspectives on microeconomic thought, expand the range of microeconomic analysis that they can draw on in formulating and assessing microeconomic policies and above all, be an antidote to 'tunnel-vision'. Nevertheless, our text is necessarily selective, and additional perspectives can be obtained by further reading. In addition, it should be borne in mind that economic and social systems are continually undergoing change or evolution, and in time, this alters the applicability of existing microeconomic theories to policy formulation.

While the main features of the previous book (*Micro-Economic Policy*) have been retained in this book, new features have been added. For example, the new Chapter 3 is intended to enhance students' appreciation of different models of microeconomic thought and their consequences for business management and policy-making. New chapters have been included on issues of ownership (Chapter 10) and to emphasize the relevance of microeconomics to environmental policies of global relevance (Chapter 16). There is also a chapter dealing with defence, conflict and terrorism (Chapter 17). Elsewhere, other chapters have been modified, updated or revised completely (for example Chapters 7 and 14).

In the Reading and reference lists items suitable for selective reading by students have been highlighted by an asterisk.

In preparing this book, we have benefited from feedback from staff from many different universities. We are very grateful for the specific feedback received from Mohammad Alauddin, Peter Earl, Habibullah Khan, John Parker, Frank Staehl, Guido Van Huylenbroeck and Leopolodo Yanes who have voluntarily given of their time to help improve our manuscript. The final responsibility for this manuscript remains, however, with us.

We also wish to thank Genevieve Larsen for assisting with the scanning of some of our material used in the preparation of this book; Evelyn Smart (Queensland) and Kim Snedden (York) for their contribution in preparing the typescript; as well as the Universities of Queensland and York for their overall support. Once again we thank Mariel and Winifred for their patience and support.

Clem Tisdell
Brisbane, Australia

Keith Hartley
York, UK

September, 2007

Preface to earlier book

Students tend to find micro-economics one of the more difficult parts of the subject [of economics]: they regard it as abstract, unrealistic, and remote from 'real-world' problems. This was our starting point. We believe that micro-economics as the study of choice is *the* foundation of the subject and that economists have an obligation to show students how micro-economics theory can be used and applied.

Applied micro-economics embraces empirical work and policy issues, and our emphasis is on the latter. This book avoids the presentation of micro-economic theory in a 'vacuum'. It shows students how micro-economics can be applied to major issues of public policy. In the process, it is hoped to improve the understanding of both micro-economic *theory and policy*.

Micro-economics consists of price theory and welfare economics, embracing theories of consumer and firm behaviour, the operation of product and factor markets, the role of the state, and the 'desirability' of policy changes. We have tried to show the policy relevance of each of the major components of micro-economic theory. However, the emphasis is on general principles of micro-economic policy, rather than on providing a detailed account of any one nation's actual policies. Indeed, the different nationalities and backgrounds of the authors has contributed to the development of a text suitable for an international audience. The book is written for students interested in the application of micro-economics to policy issues in capitalist-type economies. Throughout, the emphasis is on analysis rather than description.

The book is designed for late first year and second year [as well as later] higher education students who have a basic knowledge of micro-economic theory. The aim is to learn through applications in a policy context. While nations will differ in the extent and form of state intervention within product and factor markets, the examples chosen are typical of the policy issues confronting many governments. Hence, our emphasis is on the *principles* of micro-economic policy: the objective is to provide students with a general 'tool-kit' which can be applied to any specific micro-policy problem.

In addition to applying *standard* theory, we have introduced students to some of the more recent developments in the subject. These include the economics of politics, bureaucracies, and public choice; the Austrian school of subjectivism; search behaviour among consumers and workers; the economics of population; managerial theories of the firm, multi-nationals, labour-managed firms, advertising, and regulation; employment contracts, human capital, and screening; energy and pollution; time–cost trade-offs, de-industrialization, and public sector micro-economics, including defence, alliances, nuclear weapons choices and the economics of conscription versus an all-volunteer force.

The book is divided into five parts. Part A considers how economists approach micro-policy issues and why governments need micro-economic policies, either as a means of contributing to society's welfare or to obtain votes. Part B is concerned with applications of demand, supply, and competitive market analysis. Imperfect markets, including models of firm behaviour, monopoly, and oligopoly are analysed in Part C. Factor markets in the form of labour, trade unions, and human capital markets are discussed in Part D, which concludes with a chapter on energy. Given the book's emphasis on public policy, it seemed appropriate to conclude with an analysis of the public sector (Part E). To assist students, each chapter has suggestions for further reading and there are questions for review and discussion.

Readers might be curious to know how the authors, located in Australia and England, could possibly have written a joint textbook. The enterprise was greatly facilitated by Clem Tisdell's visit to the United Kingdom when he spent the Autumn Term of 1979 located at the Institute of Social and Economic Research (ISER), the University of York. This allowed both authors to work together in planning, discussing, and writing each chapter, either in outline or in its first draft form. Each author was responsible for specific chapters and parts, but both commented and agreed on each other's chapters. We are indebted to Professor Jack Wiseman, ISER, for providing office accommodation, facilities, and an attractive research environment. John Hutton, Research Fellow at ISER, kindly read and commented on the manuscript. Others who have offered specific comments, contributions, and assistance, sometimes unknowingly, included Celia Bird, Michael Coombs, Tony Culyer, Douglas Dosser, Ted Lynk, Cecil Margolis, Alan Maynard, John Nash, Bernard O'Brien, Alan Peacock, Robin Shannon, and Alan Williams. Colleagues and students at the Universities of York and Newcastle, Australia, have always been willing teachers and listeners. Barbara Dodds, Elizabeth Williams, Wendy Amos-Binks, and Margaret Johnson had the unenviable task of typing their way through our handwriting. Finally, our families have been the victims of scarcity resulting from our writing. Our thanks to Winifred and Mariel for their patience, and to our children Adam, Lucy, Cecilia, together with Ann-Marie and Christopher.

January, 1981

KEITH HARTLEY
CLEM TISDELL

PART A

The methodology of microeconomic policy

1. How do economists approach microeconomic policy?

1.1 INTRODUCTION: MICROECONOMICS VERSUS MACROECONOMICS

Economics often seems to follow fashions. In the early twenty-first century, one current fashion focused on the emergence of a so-called 'new economy' or knowledge economy based on information technology, E-commerce and globalization. Questions arise as to whether this new economy has rendered obsolescent established economic models and requires a new economics. Other fashions in economics have centred on the relative importance of state intervention in the economy, ranging between the extremes of complete socialism and central planning on the one hand, and laissez faire capitalism on the other. The former Soviet Union is a good example as it attempts the transition from a centrally-planned economy to a private enterprise market economy.

Other current issues have emerged to attract the interest of both economists and governments. These included international terrorism and conflicts in Afghanistan and Iraq which were the focus of defence economics; the challenges to international competitiveness from the growth of both China and India which attracted the interests of industrial and trade economists; concerns about the economic impacts of pandemics (for example, bird flu) and global warming; the economics of enlarging the European Union; and international concerns about subsidies to agriculture in rich nations and major disagreements between the EU and USA involving subsidies for large civil jet airliners (Airbus and Boeing).

The debate about the relative importance of micro- and macroeconomics is a further example of fashions in economics. For many years after the Second World War, in most capitalist economies macroeconomics tended to dominate public policy. This is not to imply that microeconomic policies were totally neglected. Typical examples included agricultural price support schemes, monopoly policy, regional development, rent control and tariffs. Nevertheless, Keynesian macroeconomics had emerged and it appeared to be a well established and agreed part of economic theory. It had obvious appeals to economists interested in manipulating the system and to policy-makers seeking to avoid a repetition of the large-scale unemployment of the 1930s. Macroeconomics was attractive for two reasons. First, it seemed to be relatively simple, enabling the economy to be described with a few straightforward equations. Second, it gave policy-makers the opportunity of controlling the economy through the management of aggregate demand. But, in the 1970s macroeconomics became more controversial. Governments in capitalist economies were confronted with greater policy problems, particularly 'stagflation' associated with high and rising rates of both unemployment and inflation.

Economists became worried about describing complex economies and their microeconomic foundations with a few simple aggregate equations. Often, microeconomic behaviour was assumed rather than subjected to empirical research and the emphasis was on homogeneity rather than heterogeneity. Nor does it follow that government actions to regulate aggregate demand will be motivated solely by a concern for society's welfare. Votes might not be irrelevant to democratic governments. In other words, questions were being asked about the micro-foundations of macroeconomics. At the same time, governments have increasingly intervened at the microeconomic level. Subsidies have been used for regional developments and for the support of 'lame duck' and 'key' firms and industries. In some cases, the subsidies have been designed to preserve jobs, especially among large employers who would otherwise go out of business, with major multiplier effects in local economies. Elsewhere, subsidies have been used to promote the development of high technology industries such as aerospace, electronics and nuclear power (for example, Airbus). Governments have also intervened to change industrial structure through mergers and the nationalization of private firms and industries. Large firms, obtaining scale economies in research and production, are often believed to be 'essential' to compete in world markets. An alternative view believes that 'small is beautiful'. These are all examples of state intervention concerned with the supply side of the economy compared with the traditional Keynesian emphasis on aggregate demand management.

Increasingly, governments recognized the potential contribution of microeconomics to 'solving' some of their major policy problems. In recent years, policies have focused on structural adjustment involving less government in economic production (for example, the Reagan and Thatcher eras). Supply-side economics involves the use of policies aimed at increasing the aggregate supply of goods and services through measures such as lower income taxes, abolishing subsidies, promoting competition, privatization and creating an enterprise economy. Such policies aimed to make markets work better (that is, more efficiently by removing major market failures). In this form, supply-side economics focuses on microeconomics and its use in solving some of the major policy problems. For example, when confronted with unemployment, governments will need to know its causes: which economic theory best explains unemployment? The possibilities include 'excessive' union wage demands; or rigidities and restrictive practices in labour markets; or technical change (for example, E-commerce) resulting in new technology equipment replacing workers; or declining international competitiveness; or the level of state unemployment pay and welfare benefits.

Whilst microeconomics focuses on efficiency issues, governments might also be concerned about equity. Government might aim to ensure that everyone is protected from hardship and income deficiency due to circumstances beyond their control. Thus, social policy will provide assistance in cash and kind to those in 'need', such as the poor, unemployed, chronically ill and disabled. Microeconomics can contribute through enquiring whether theory offers any 'guidelines' for social policy and what might be the implications of alternative measures such as minimum wage legislation, equal pay, rent control, and 'free' health care.

Microeconomics can also be used to analyse new and topical issues which emerge unexpectedly and which governments might not be able to ignore. An example of a major shock effect for economics occurred in the late 1980s and early 1990s associated with the end of the Cold War and the collapse of communism. Events in Eastern Europe and the former Soviet Union around this time raised major doubts about the efficiency and performance of central planning, state ownership and collectivist solutions to economic problems. These changes provided opportunities for showing how microeconomics, with its focus on markets, could be applied to the study of economies attempting the transition from a centrally-planned to a market economy. At the same time, the end of the Cold War and the superpower arms race and its replacement with disarmament and the search for a Peace Dividend also created adjustment problems for the economies of the former Warsaw Pact and NATO. A Peace Dividend required that resources be re-allocated from the military-industrial complex to the civilian sector. But such adjustments involve costs in the form of unemployment of resources (labour, capital and land), and it takes time. Resource re-allocation is a microeconomics issue, involving analysis of how well and how quickly labour and other factor markets can adjust and clear following the shock of large-scale disarmament. It also involves analysis of the response of defence contractors to the loss of markets where firms will respond by reducing their work force, closing plants, merging, seeking export markets as well as diversifying into new civil markets. Faced with such major shocks to the economy, governments have to decide whether to intervene to assist resource reallocation from defence to civil activities and, if so, the form of state intervention. For example, should governments leave defence contractors to make commercial decisions about conversion (for example, swords to ploughshares; tanks to tractors) and diversification into civil markets?

The oil crises of the 1970s and 2005 are further examples of shocks, where governments were obliged to revise and rethink their energy policies. What is the appropriate response for an economy which depends upon imported oil? Microeconomics shows how taxes and subsidies can be used to influence the price of existing substitutes, such as coal and gas, as well as affecting the direction of search for new energy sources (for example, wind; nuclear power). Economists can also help to clarify some of the issues, pointing out potential conflicts in policies and the inter-temporal and inter-generational nature of using limited stocks of energy resources (see Chapter 16). These examples, and many others, form the subject matter of this book.

This chapter introduces some of the general concepts and methodology which are used throughout the book. Initially, the scope of microeconomics is outlined, emphasizing that it is the study of choice in a world of uncertainty. Controversy always exists and a framework is presented for identifying the sources of disagreement. Disputes often arise over policy objectives, the choice between alternative theories, and the selection of the 'best' policy measure. In reviewing these issues, it is difficult to avoid asking what it is that makes you believe some statements and not others. You should also ask who is likely to gain and who is likely to lose from the development of new economic theories and new economic policies (for example, established interest groups in the economics profession; consultants marketing new ideas; politicians seeking instant popularity).

1.2   THE SCOPE OF MICROECONOMICS

Microeconomics is the study of scarcity and choice. It focuses on individual and group decision-making in parts or sectors of the economy which are most conveniently described as markets. A market is any arrangement whereby individuals undertake voluntary exchange, the basic premise being that there are gains from voluntary transactions and trading. However, capitalist economies are characterized by a large number of interdependent markets. For example, the demand for oil depends not only on its price but also on the prices of coal, gas, electricity, cars, and on the prices of more distant substitutes such as refrigerators and television sets, as well as on the prices of factor inputs which will determine available incomes. The interdependence between markets forms the subject area of general equilibrium. This explores whether there exists a set of relative prices which will simultaneously clear all markets in an economy, with the result that each market will be in equilibrium. A perfectly competitive economy results in a general equilibrium. Having accepted interdependence, does it mean that we can only proceed by recognizing that an economy is complex, that interdependencies exist and are essential to understanding, and that we cannot avoid the fact that everything depends upon everything else? This is certainly a realistic approach which recognizes that economies are complex systems – a feature which policy-makers cannot ignore.

There is an alternative approach which seeks to simplify the complexities of general equilibrium. At the same time, this alternative *partial equilibrium* approach incorporates just enough variables to obtain sufficiently accurate answers. Partial equilibrium concentrates on equilibrium in a single market, with demand and supply analysis used as a starting point for explaining market behaviour and performance. An equilibrium or unchanged situation occurs when the plans of buyers and suppliers in a market are identical. Demand and supply analysis enables a complex issue to be simplified while providing explanations and predictions which have proved to be consistent with the facts. One technique for simplification incorporates a *ceteris paribus* assumption: 'other things' being equal or everything else in the economy is assumed to remain unchanged. As a result, demand and supply analysis provides a simple model for classifying and understanding price and output changes in markets. Its predictions are qualitative, relating to directions of change and not magnitudes. For example, a rise in the price of cars is usually expected to result in a fall in the quantity demand but, without data on demand curves, it is not possible to state by how much quantity demanded will decline. However, Austrian economists (for example, Hayek, Kirzner) are critical of the standard obsession with equilibrium, particularly general equilibrium and perfect competition. They believe that an emphasis on market equilibrium results in a failure to understand the actual market processes through which resources are transferred from lower- to higher-valued activities during *continuous market disequilibrium*. Actual markets are characterized by ignorance, uncertainty and continuous change.

Ignorance and uncertainty about the future creates opportunities for profits and it is the task of an entrepreneur to discover the opportunities for 'making money' before anyone else. Entrepreneurs will formulate plans on the basis of expectations about future prices and events and these are matters on which individuals have different views and subjective evaluations. Market experience as reflected in shortages, surpluses, profits and losses will reveal the correctness of different plans. Those who guess correctly will survive and those who make mistakes will pay. Austrian economists are critical of the text book model of competitive markets in which the entrepreneur is left with little actual decision-making (for example, given prices; identical products) simply because the model assumes away such real-world facts as uncertainty, innovation and entrepreneurship. However, both the Austrian and neoclassical approaches to microeconomics incorporate a major role for choice.

The Study of Choice

Since resources are scarce, choices cannot be avoided. Any economy, whether capitalist or socialist, has to solve a number of basic problems (choices). It has to decide:

1. What to produce – for example, cars, television sets, schools, hospitals, or weapons? Where an economy's resources are fully and efficiently employed, then all expenditure involves a sacrifice of alternatives (opportunity cost). For example, increased expenditure on defence involves a sacrifice of schools, hospitals and roads (for example, the classic guns versus social welfare trade-off).
2. How to produce goods and services – for example, should coal, oil, nuclear power or wind power be used to generate electricity?
3. Who receives the goods and services which are produced? This is a *distributional problem*. Should everyone receive the same incomes or should some receive more than others – if so, how are the lucky ones chosen? Should football stars receive more than nurses?
4. Who will choose? For many activities, society might agree to leave individuals to their own devices (private individualistic choices). But there will be some activities where democratic societies will agree to accept collective or *public choices*, with decision-making delegated to governments. In these circumstances, society has to determine the rules and institutions for reaching collective choices or ranking alternatives and the 'desirability' of the outcomes. It also means that voters (as *principals*) elect governments as their *agents* to make choices (principal–agent relations). Such issues are considered in Chapters 2 and 14.

Western economists are fond of using the competitive market model and such a model provides one economic system which 'solves' the choice problems outlined above. In a competitive system firms respond to consumer preferences (consumer sovereignty), and this determines *what* is produced. The question of *how* to produce will be solved by profit-seeking firms aiming to combine factors so as to produce efficiently. Total output or income will be *distributed* on the basis of resource endowment and the relative scarcity of different factors of production. In such an economy, individuals are assumed to be the 'best' or only judges of their welfare, and consumer sovereignty determines resource allocation. But economists are not only interested in how an economic system works; they are also concerned with how well it works. Does it give results which are 'socially desirable' or are there some faults, and can such failures be 'corrected' through government intervention? Are consumers well informed and are they really sovereign or are their preferences determined by 'big business' through advertising? These are obviously recurring themes throughout the book and some general criteria are presented in Chapter 2.

Economic Agents, Behaviour and Coordinating Mechanisms

Despite the complexities of markets, microeconomics simplifies analysis by concentrating on a few major elements in any economic system. These consist of decision-makers, their behaviour, and the coordinating mechanisms. A classification system is shown in Table 1.1. Broadly, economic agents consist of individuals and groups as represented by

Table 1.1   Agents, behaviour and coordination

Decision-makers	Activities	Aims	Relevant theory	Possible coordinating mechanisms
Households	a. Demand goods	Utility	Consumer choice	Prices
	b. Supply factors	Income	Distribution theory	Voting Barter
Firms	a. Demand factors b. Supply goods	Profits	Theory of the firm and market structures	Dictatorship Command
				Theft/Force (including military force) Persuasion
Governments	a. Demand factors b. Supply goods/services	Social welfare Votes	Public sector economics Public choice Welfare economics	Planning

decision-making households, firms and governments. To explain the behaviour of these economic agents, we have to know what motivates them. What are they trying to achieve? For private enterprise economies, it is usually assumed that firms and households are motivated by self-interest, guided by the price mechanism. Firms are often assumed to be profit-maximizers, although there are alternative models of behaviour, as outlined in Chapter 7. Households are both consumers and workers. As consumers they are assumed to be utility-maximizers (Chapter 5). As workers, they aim to maximize income or net advantages. Individual workers in their labour market and human capital context are analysed in Chapters 11 and 12, while their group or union behaviour is considered in Chapter 13. Finally, governments are assumed to be passive agencies, maximizing something called 'social welfare'; in a democracy, however, they might be vote-maximizers (see Chapter 14). Of course, the behaviour of all economic agents will be subject to *constraints*. Thus, income, resources, information, knowledge and the law all act as constraints. For example, laws affect economic behaviour, and economic behaviour generates the need for laws (for example, enforcement of contracts).

Decision-makers are only part of an economic system. Firms and households, for instance, are involved in buying and selling. Households demand goods and supply factors, while firms demand factors and supply products. Since the various agents are making separate decisions, some mechanism is required to bring them together. Prices are one possible coordinating and allocative mechanism. Others include voting procedures as determined by the constitution; queuing and waiting lists (for example, where the state provides 'free' health care); barter and bargaining; central planning and dictatorship; customs, gifts, inheritance, chance, persuasion and favouritism; together with allocation by force, fraud, deceit, and bribery, criminal action and wars. Many of these allocative mechanisms are present in any economy. Consider the arrangements for allocating resources in your household: pay, persuasion, bargaining, queuing, dictatorship and voting all exist in households.

Regardless of the method, the necessity for some allocative mechanism reflects scarcity. Resources, including time, are scarce and have many alternative uses and users. By choosing one thing, you are sacrificing the (subjective) satisfaction or utility which could have been obtained from alternative courses of action. Work involves the sacrifices of off-the-job leisure; space exploration requires a 'sacrifice' of schools, hospitals, roads and cars which could have been produced with the resources. This is what the concept of opportunity cost is all about: it focuses on the subjective evaluation of alternatives. And in considering alternatives, choices cannot be avoided. This is a simple proposition, but it is amazing the number of times that governments believe that their plans will not involve any sacrifices (for example, election manifestos).

1.3 CONTROVERSY AND THE METHODOLOGY OF MICROECONOMIC POLICY

Microeconomics abounds with controversy, although this is not apparent from a reading of the standard textbooks. This perhaps is one of the reasons why students often appear to have greater difficulty in understanding the relevance of microeconomics to real world problems. In this context, macroeconomics appears to be much more relevant and useful, especially since everyone has the opportunity of acting as Chancellor of the Exchequer or Treasury Minister! Yet most departments of government are organized on a microeconomic basis, handling parts of an economy. Usually there are separate departments responsible for sectors such as agriculture, consumer affairs, defence, education, energy, environment, health, industry, labour, and transport. All these departments provide massive opportunities for applying microeconomics.

Think of the controversies involving microeconomics. There are continuous debates about the proper role of government and market versus state solutions (see Chapters 2, 3, 4, 10 and 14). For example, is there a need for a national transport policy to 'coordinate' road, rail, air and sea transport? Why can the price mechanism not solve the 'problem'? Disputes occur about monopoly, oligopoly and competition, and the 'best' structure for an industry (Chapters 6 to 9). Consumers are not neglected, with controversy about whether they should be protected from dangerous drugs, unsafe cars and unhealthy food (Chapter 5). A concern with poverty and income distribution raises questions as to whether labour should receive a wage based on its productivity and whether improvements can be achieved through state action in the form of rent control, minimum wages and equal pay (Chapters 4, 11 and 12). A government concerned with income distribution and efficiency cannot ignore trade unions. Does economic theory offer any guidelines for a public policy towards unions and professional associations (Chapter 13)?

Economists will differ in their answers to these and other policy issues. Why? Disputes arise because economists and politicians will differ about the objectives of microeconomic policy, the relevance of alternative theories or explanations, and the choice of appropriate solutions. These sources of dispute provide a general framework for analysing any microeconomic policy issue. Disagreement is not, however, unique to economists. Doctors might disagree about a patient's symptoms, illness and appropriate treatment. Scientists disagree about the use of nuclear weapons while the record of designers of aircraft, high-rise flats and bridges provides plenty of evidence of their theories being refuted! Even laboratory experiments are not conclusive. After a major military aircraft crash due to the loss of a wing, the manufacturer claimed that its laboratory fatigue tests had shown no evidence of cracks in the wing spar: wreckage from the crashed aircraft provided the evidence which laboratory tests had failed to identify!

Methodology

The methodology of economic policy involves a three-stage approach to policy issues:

1. The objectives of microeconomic policy have to be identified. What is a government trying to achieve (that is, its objective or subjective function)?
2. The relevant theory has to be identified. Which part or parts of microeconomic theory 'best' explain the problems confronting policy-makers?
3. A policy solution has to be chosen from a range of alternatives. Once again, governments cannot avoid choices: they have to choose between different objectives, competing theories and alternative policy solutions.

Policy Objectives

Microeconomic targets can be regarded as the foundations of macroeconomic policy objectives. As such, they embrace product and factor markets and are concerned with possible employment, prices, balance of payments, growth, and income distribution objectives. At the micro-level, employment targets involve the location decisions of firms, labour mobility, restrictive labour practices, and the effects of wage increases. Price targets cannot ignore the determinants of prices, the relationship between factor and product prices, and the effects of monopolies on pricing behaviour. Balance of payments objectives lead to questions about why nations trade, the gains from trade, the operation of the foreign exchange market, and the reasons why firms export. A government aiming to raise the growth rate will need to know which factors of production, market structures and industries contribute to growth. Finally, distribution of income and wealth targets cannot ignore the determinants of wages and profits, the relevance and effects of private and state ownership of the means of production, and the likely impact of policy solutions, such as profit controls. Each of these objectives requires an understanding of basic causal factors. Why do firms change employment, prices, exports, imports, investment, wages and profits? Conflicts are also likely between objectives. For example, growth might result in the substitution of new technology and capital for labour and hence job loss; policies designed to protect consumers from unsafe products (for example, medicines) might adversely affect innovation; while wage controls might lead to industrial disputes and distort the allocation of labour. At this point, economic theory is required to identify the causes of policy problems and conflicts in objectives. But theory only provides a basic tool kit and a starting point for analysing facts: adjustments are often needed to fit specific cases.

Microeconomic Theory

A theory consists of a set of definitions and assumptions from which it is possible to make logical deductions about behaviour. There is, however, controversy as to whether a theory should be accepted or rejected on the basis of the 'realism' of its assumptions or its explanatory power and predictive accuracy. This debate is associated with Friedman (1953) who argued that theories should be tested by predictions only and not by assumptions. Indeed, he maintained that by design, assumptions are abstractions and simplifications of reality: the more unrealistic an assumption becomes, the more likely it will increase the general explanatory power of a theory. But what is meant by a 'realistic assumption'? Would we accept a theory which predicted accurately but which was based on an assumption which was not consistent with the facts? Two responses are possible. First, the advocates of more realistic assumptions can incorporate these into alternative theories, compare their predictions, and test to identify which is most accurate. Second, a less extreme view might recognize the need for testing, but insist upon using all opportunities for empirical verification, including the testing of assumptions. Nevertheless, problems remain. If theories are to be tested, what constitutes a satisfactory test of a theory? Are interview-questionnaires and sample surveys appropriate techniques or are statistical-econometric methods superior?

Economists have a great deal of enthusiasm for econometric techniques. They are quantitative and seem to provide convincing tests of hypotheses, especially since other relevant variables can be included and held constant in the estimation process. But much depends upon the reliability of econometric techniques. Often different econometric studies of a common problem reach conflicting conclusions. They might all be equally acceptable using standard statistical criteria, such as 'goodness of fit' (R^2), significant coefficients, and Durbin–Watson statistics. As a result, advocates of alternative positions obtain empirical support for their views. Furthermore, how many economists, econometricians and research assistants carefully check and re-check for data errors before accepting and publishing what appear to be 'very good results'? Mistakes and errors in data processing can have drastic implications for empirical results, possibly causing changes in the goodness of fit (R^2), in the significance of coefficients, and in their signs! Data are not always reliable: time-series data are subject to changing definitions (for example, industrial classifications change over time) and international cross-section data might be based on different definitions (for example, of defence expenditure). Nor can we ignore the role of 'playometrics' or 'one-upmanship' whereby professional prestige attaches to technical sophistication for its own sake: it provides an opportunity to demonstrate intellectual aerobatics. Equally disturbing is the fact that many econometric studies simply report significant results without any indication of the number of equations actually estimated. Austrian economists are even more critical of econometrics. They regard empirical testing as superfluous since they start from a true axiom (called the 'category of action' or choice) and all other propositions deduced from it must be true. Moreover, since choices are subjective: they exist in the minds of the choosers, which makes life difficult for empiricists!

What is the contribution of theory to microeconomic policy? Theory serves three functions:

1. It can explain the causes of policy problems. For example, if governments are concerned about prices and wages in, say, the car industry, theory can be used to explain

the determinants of these variables. However, choices are often needed between alternative theories. Again, there are fashions in economic theories with economists influenced by the 'conventional wisdom'. Examples include the debates between the Classical and Keynesian economists; the contributions of modern macroeconomics, monetarism, Marxist economics, institutional economics and the microeconomics of privatization and competitive tendering. More recently, there has been the widespread adoption of game theory with its analysis of strategic interactions involving small numbers (for example, duopoly and oligopoly markets; arms races and international conflict).

2. It can predict the likely consequences of government policy. For instance, it can tell us how firms and workers are likely to respond to price, profit and wage control or to a change from state to private ownership (privatization). In some instances, unexpected outcomes can be identified. Thus, a government restriction on the amount of advertising which firms can undertake is likely to result in an expansion of other (less efficient) selling methods, such as the use of more sales staff or mailing campaigns. In other words, policy-makers need to recognize that markets are highly flexible, with firms continuously searching for new profit opportunities and searching to overcome state regulatory constraints.

3. It can offer 'guidelines' for public policy. Here, economists often approach policy problems by asking whether economic theory provides any rules or guidelines for a public policy towards, say, consumer protection, energy, monopolies, takeovers or subsidies for 'lame duck' enterprises. This, of course, involves issues of normative as distinct from positive economics. But if there is a category of positive welfare economics, is this distinction always so clear-cut? For example, if the statement that more is bought at a lower price than at a higher price is accepted as part of positive economics, does the same status apply to the proposition that monopoly results in a lower level of economic welfare than competition (where monopoly, competition and welfare are clearly defined)?

The Choice of Policy Solutions

Having used theory to explain the causes of a problem or to offer policy guidelines, it is then possible to deduce and construct policy solutions. Usually, a set of alternative solutions will be indicated. For example, an excess demand problem, such as a local shortage of skilled manpower, could be removed by acting upon supply, demand or wages. The balance of payments can be improved through exchange rates (fixed or floating), tariffs and quotas, a domestic deflation, or subsidies to domestic firms. Private monopoly can be controlled through state ownership, by breaking up the monopoly, by lower tariffs and by regulating aspects of the monopolists behaviour (for example, prices; profits; non-price behaviour). An optimum allocation of resources can be achieved with private competitive markets or socialism. Once again, governments must choose. They have to choose between conflicting policy objectives, competing theoretical explanations, and a variety of policy solutions.

One approach to policy choices, developed by Tinbergen (1952), focuses on targets and instruments. Recognizing the existence of conflicts between objectives, it suggests that policy-makers require at least as many instruments as there are objectives. For instance, a state agency might support mergers and industrial re-structuring for balance of payments objectives, but an additional policy instrument is required for controlling any resulting monopoly and its consequences. Similarly, if wage controls are used for price stability objectives, some other instrument such as legislation will be required for industrial relations objectives and a further measure, such as subsidies, will have to be used for improving the allocation of labour. This is a technocrat's approach, where policy-makers are assumed to have a clearly specified objective function and use policies, like a set of levers, to achieve targets. However, this approach ignores the political, bargaining and institutional framework within which decisions and choices are made. How is a government's objective function formulated? Presumably, it is the outcome of bargaining between groups and actors such as a President, a Prime Minister, a Cabinet, departmental heads, and bureaucrats. Within this framework, individuals and departmental representatives will have only limited information and knowledge. They will tend to seek coalitions of 'like-minded' interest groups and their choice of objectives and instruments will be constrained by the political market place (for example, the constitution and voting rules). In such a bargaining environment, governments might be 'satisficers' rather than maximizers. After all, objective functions are not acquired without costs. As a 'satisficer', a set of targets will be selected which satisfy different interest groups, such as the Treasury, together with the Departments of Agriculture, Defence, Education, Health Industry and Labour. The targets are likely to be revised downwards if they cannot be achieved at reasonable cost (including potential vote losses).

1.4 CONCLUSION

This chapter has outlined some of the general concepts and examples which form the material for this book. Many of the points will recur in subsequent sections. The main features of microeconomics have been reviewed, although a summary treatment cannot do justice to the immense richness and fascination of the subject. It has many applications, some of them unusual and unexpected, such as the family, marriage, suicide, political parties, bureaucracies, crime, police protection, wars and terrorism. Even churches are not immune, and useful insights into their behaviour can be obtained by analysing them as non-profit firms combining resources of land, buildings, priests, and lay-people to produce a variety of outputs which straddle an individual's life-cycle (for example, births, marriage, sickness, death and the care of souls). Further examples and ideas can be obtained from the suggested readings and questions which are found at the end of each chapter.

Consideration has also been given to methodology. Why do we believe some statements and not others? Do you believe because you have seen it with your own eyes, directly, in a book or on television? Do you accept something because it is consistent with your other beliefs, you are unable to think of any convincing objection, and it comes from a professor? And if you require supporting evidence, would you accept an exchange of personal experiences, casual empiricism, or would you insist upon controlled experiments? Imagine that you are a member of the jury in a court of law: what would determine the way you would vote in a murder trial?

Finally, microeconomics is of continuing relevance to policy-makers. Labour mobility, regional unemployment, relative wages, house prices, education, health and poverty, together with monopoly, competition, microelectronics, and industrial performance in 'key' industries are only a few examples. The major issue of capitalism versus socialism is ever present. Critics of capitalism claim that it results in pollution, destroys the environment, benefits monopolies, creates massive inequalities of income, and exploits the working classes. However, none of this 'proves' that socialism is 'superior'. Admittedly, capitalism and private markets might fail to work 'properly' and this might provide an economic justification for state intervention. But here, analysts distinguish the *technical issues*, involving the causes of market failure, from the *policy issues*, concerned with the choice of the most appropriate policy solutions. Why do governments intervene at the micro-level and what determines their selection of policies? This question will be considered in Chapters 2 and 3 (and 14). The rest of the book follows the general format of any standard microeconomic theory textbook. Policy applications involving markets, consumers and supply are covered in Part B. The behaviour of private firms and policy towards imperfect markets and ownership occupy Part C. Factor markets and policy towards labour, human capital and trade unions are considered in Part D. In view of the book's emphasis on policy, Part E addresses public choice and some of the microeconomics of the public sector. Part F concludes with global applications, namely, environmental issues, conflict and terrorism.

READING* AND REFERENCES

*Blaug, M. (1980), *The Methodology of Economics*, Cambridge Surveys of Economic Literature, Cambridge: Cambridge University Press.
Boettke, P.J. (ed.) (1994), *The Elgar Companion of Austrian Economics*, Aldershot, UK and Brookfield, US: Edward Elgar.
Friedman, M. (1953), 'The methodology of positive economics', in M. Friedman *Essays in Positive Economics*, Chicago: University of Chicago Press.
Kirzner, I.M. (1979), *Perception, Opportunity and Profit*, Chicago: University of Chicago Press (this book also contains references to the work of Hayek and Austrian economics).
*Kirzner, I.M. (1997), *How Markets Work: Disequilibrium, Entrepreneurship and Discovery*, Hobart Paper 133, London: Institute of Economic Affairs.
*McCloskey, D. (1983), *The Rhetoric of Economics*, London: Harvester Wheatsheaf.
Rowley, C. and A.T. Peacock (1975), *Welfare Economics*, London: Martin Robertson.
Stewart, I.M.T. (1979), *Reasoning and Method in Economics*, London: McGraw-Hill.
Tinbergen, J. (1952), *On the Theory of Economic Policy*, Amsterdam: North-Holland.
Wiseman, J. (1989), *Cost, Choice and Political Economy*, Aldershot, UK and Brookfield, US: Edward Elgar.

Note: *shows recommended reading.

QUESTIONS FOR REVIEW AND DISCUSSION

1. Are actual socialist economies different from actual capitalist economies? Explain. Which do you regard as preferable and why?
2. Is predictive accuracy the best criterion for choosing between alternative theories? Give examples from microeconomics, specifying how you would test your examples. Do you believe that econometric techniques are superior to questionnaire methods? Explain.

3. How are resources allocated in (a) your household, (b) your college or university? Do you regard the results as satisfactory? Explain.
4. What is the Austrian approach to microeconomics? What would persuade you to accept or reject it? What are the microeconomic policy implications of the Austrian approach?
5. Which parts of microeconomics have the greatest relevance to public policy? Explain your choice. How are your chosen parts used in policy formulation?

2. Why do governments need microeconomic policies?

2.1 INTRODUCTION

As pointed out in the previous chapter, economics, particularly microeconomics, is primarily concerned with studying the reasons for the existence of scarcity, and the impacts of different social mechanisms for resource use or the extent, distribution and nature of scarcity. The study of these social mechanisms includes the use of market mechanisms and these are given the greatest attention by microeconomists. The focus of microeconomics implies that some of its major objectives are to find policies that will minimize scarcity and to predict in a social context the implications of government policies for scarcity. For example, a government policy that subsidizes the production of one commodity and reduces its scarcity may add to overall scarcity because it reduces the supply of other valued commodities that are forgone. An opportunity cost is incurred in a fully employed economy; the opportunity cost being the supply of other commodities forgone. However, it should be borne in mind that scarcity reduction is not the only goal of government policy and that human values often include additional considerations.

Different economic systems impinge on social relationships in different ways. If an economic system results in less scarcity than another it may be rejected by some individuals because in their view it has other negative consequences. For example, libertarians (such as some members of the Austrian School of Economics, see Chapter 3) may reject some scarcity-reducing economic policies because these policies restrict the liberty or perceived rights of individuals, for example in their choices about their use of private property. This can make libertarians very reluctant to accept policies involving government intervention.

In some cases, policies that are scarcity-minimizing may accord with or support other non-economic social values of some groups in society. For example, libertarians frequently argue that an economic system based on free markets is not only supportive of libertarian values but is also likely to be efficient in reducing economic scarcity, or is at least the most efficient workable mechanism available for scarcity reduction taking into account both economic allocation and growth perspectives. On the other hand, socialists are less convinced and do not see individual liberty as an absolute virtue. They are more likely to favour intervention in the market system to achieve particular social objectives.

For some social groups, other values may influence their social choices. For example, some conservationists may believe that human choices should be constrained by the rights of other species to exist (see Chapter 16). Animal rights supporters may believe that the economic use and treatment of animals should be subject to constraints. However, even within these constraints, an economic problem continues to exist, namely how to meet the constraints and minimize scarcity. Also one has to consider what are likely to be the economic costs of these constraints and decide on appropriate mechanisms to achieve these. Even when social values differ from those traditionally assumed by mainstream economists, the scarcity problem remains relevant.

The purpose of this chapter is to provide an overview of microeconomic policy questions and the role of microeconomics in policy-making. It outlines mainstream economic approaches to scarcity and to scarcity reduction as well as alternative points of view, and their limitations. As pointed out, microeconomic policy advice may either be of an idealistic or of a technical nature. Both types of policy advice may be relevant to the basic economic problem of reducing scarcity. But there are difficulties in deciding on what constitutes a reduction in scarcity in a social context. Two criteria for resolving these difficulties, Pareto's criterion and the Kaldor–Hicks criterion, are outlined and their limitations discussed. This leads to a consideration of the requirements which must be met by the operations of an economy if it is to minimize scarcity, namely to achieve a Paretian ideal allocation of resources.

The requirements are first outlined for the simplest economy, a Robinson Crusoe (single person) economy, and this is also used to show how specific government policies can prevent the attainment of the Paretian ideal, that is add to scarcity. The Paretian requirements for minimizing scarcity are then considered for a normal economy. It is claimed, and further details are given, that Paretian optimality requires:

1. economic efficiency in production;
2. economic efficiency in consumption; and
3. an optimal conformance between production of different commodities and the desires of individuals for these commodities.

In theory, in an economy in which knowledge is not a constraint, Paretian optimality might be achieved either by the operation of perfectly competitive markets or by direct commands, as in a collectivist or centralized economy. But in practice both means are found to be imperfect for this purpose.

An Edgeworth–Bowley box is introduced to demonstrate that there are *several* Paretian ideal allocations of resources. The Paretian ideal allocation varies with the distribution of income or ownership of resources. The greatest stumbling block to determining *the* socially ideal allocation of resources is the problem of deciding on what is *the* ideal distribution of income. The Edgeworth–Bowley box is also used to illustrate the benefits of free trade or exchange and the possible costs of different types of government interference in free trade. This, however, is not to suggest that government interference in free trade cannot be justified on Paretian and on Kaldor–Hicks grounds in certain circumstances, for example, where traders are ill-informed.

Various microeconomic policies and possible reasons for introducing them are reviewed according to whether they are designed:

1. to strengthen the operation of market forces, for example, measures to increase the mobility of resources;
2. to modify or supplant market forces, for example, policies to correct for environmental spillovers and to establish or control monopolies; or

3.   to ensure public supply or a socially optimal supply of goods that are not marketable, that is public goods such as defence.

These apparently 'opposed' policies may be effective in different circumstances in reducing scarcity. One of the functions of a microeconomist is to specify these circumstances.

   It would, however, be a folly to believe that government policies are always based upon idealism. In most cases, actual policies are the outcome of political rivalry between groups in society, involve compromise, and may indeed not satisfy the ideals of any group, let alone the ideals of an economist. In tendering policy advice one has to accept that there are social and economic constraints on the implementation of policies and these limit the type of economic policies that can be introduced. Imperfections in political and bureaucratic mechanisms of resource allocation restrict the type of policies that can be *effectively* implemented, just as there are market imperfections which cannot be eliminated by any practical means. As is stressed in this book, in considering and in giving policy advice, there is a need to take into account imperfections in all of these areas. Economists in the past have tended to concentrate on market perfection and imperfection and to neglect the other mechanisms of resource allocation.

2.2   NATURE OF MICROECONOMICS AND POLICY

Microeconomics is concerned with the universal problem of scarcity. Microeconomists have used their tools of analysis to suggest various measures to reduce scarcity or shift its impact and to predict the effects of such policies as wage, price and income controls, and regulations on market competition. Given the central importance of relative scarcity (that is, that more commodities or valued possibilities are desired than can be produced or provided, given the available limited resources of the world) most governments need to assess the relevance of alternative microeconomic policies and choose between the alternatives.

   Microeconomic studies concentrate on the individual parts of the economy and the interdependence of these components in the working of the economy. Microeconomics deals with the decisions of individual actors such as firms, workers, consumers and investors and in more recent studies with family decisions, political decisions, and the behaviour of non-profit organizations such as schools, hospitals and charitable organizations, and the way in which these shape the pattern of industries and the allocation of resources through the aims and objectives of agents and the external market environment. One set of microeconomic theories explores the consequences, for example, of utility maximization by consumers and by voters, of profit maximization by firms, and of vote maximization by political parties, a subject discussed in Chapter 14.

Questions Raised by Scarcity

Because resources are scarce, two important questions arise. One is a positive question: how *are* resources allocated between alternative possibilities? The other is a normative question: how *should* resources be allocated between alternative possibilities? Microeconomists have had a great deal to say about both questions. Each question poses further questions such as how are and how should resources be allocated between individuals (both those alive now and those expected to be born in the future), between different productive units such as firms, between regions, between the production of different products, and between the current consumption of resources and their conservation for the future? Resource allocation and microeconomic issues are involved in such diverse policy matters as how best to conserve non-renewable resources such as oil, how best to reduce greenhouse gas emissions, the desirability of government subsidies or aid for production or employment in depressed regions, and the desirability of protecting selected products or industries from foreign competition or giving them government assistance. However, the list does not stop there. It also includes the effect of taxes, the best means to provide relief to the needy and poor, the allocation of public expenditure, and the influence of unemployment benefits or dole payments on the willingness of the unemployed to seek work.

Mechanisms for Deciding the Use of Resources

The social customs and mechanisms in any country or region influence the decisions of its inhabitants about the use of its resources. In societies such as our own, relying on a mixture of market mechanism and state intervention, the price mechanism plays a considerable role in determining the allocation of resources. Each individual is free to acquire private property (resources) for productive purposes and each is free, within limits, to pursue his or her own self-interest in trading in resources and in using those resources which he or she owns. The resulting pattern of resource use may be very different from that which occurs when resources are centrally allocated by a planning body in conformity with its priorities.

Government Interference and Microeconomic Policy

We should not exaggerate the extent to which private decisions determine the use of resources in our society. Governmental interference in the use of an economy's resources is widespread. The public sector is not only a large purchaser and supplier of commodities but it interferes to a considerable extent with the private sector. Typical types of interference are as follows: in foreign trade, restrictions on imports (such as tariffs and quotas on imported goods) are common; there is legislation to protect consumers, some of which specifies that products should meet certain minimum standards; various restrictive trade practices such as collective business agreements to maintain prices are banned; and subsidies may be given to particular regions to encourage new industries or support declining ones. Furthermore, some services are made available free to consumers or are heavily subsidized, such as education and medical attention; social services such as unemployment benefits and disability and aged pensions are provided by the government; some industries obtain subsidies for their production or other incentives (although this may be less common than it used to be) and minimum levels of wages often must be paid by industries. There is a considerable amount of interference by government in the private sector of the economy and the type of interference which occurs is influenced by political factors and mechanisms.

These types of interference raise microeconomic policy questions. What are the costs and benefits associated with each of the above types of intervention? Is it possible to obtain the desired economic change at lower cost by using a different policy? Economists need to consider such questions. An improved knowledge of the consequences of alternative policies may sway policy-makers to adopt policies that are more likely to achieve their objectives. The proponents of policies may be wrong in assessing the effects of their policies because remote consequences may be ignored and they may be mistaken about the immediate consequences of their policies. Microeconomic knowledge can help resolve such important issues. However, we need to consider the role of microeconomics in policy and the role of a policy-adviser more carefully.

2.3   AIMS OR OBJECTIVES OF MICROECONOMIC POLICY AND THE ROLE OF AN ECONOMIC ADVISER

Economists may involve themselves in microeconomic policy advice because they wish to foster policies in support of their own ideals or they may be employed by politicians or other policy-makers including business managers, to provide advice on how best those policy-makers can achieve their aims – aims which may not parallel those of the economist. These alternatives might be described as:

1.   An idealistic or utopian approach based upon general philosophical considerations. Pareto's approach, to be discussed below, is of this type because Pareto wished to support the ideals underlying his theory by policy suggestions.
2.   A 'technical' approach in which the aims of the policy are specified by an individual or some group of individuals, for example, a group of politicians. In this approach, the policy adviser does not question the aims (unless these are internally inconsistent) of the individual or group hiring him or her but devises policies to achieve their objectives if this is possible. Privately, of course, an economist may or may not have the same aims as his or her employer.

Both possibilities involve normative and positive economics, but in the first case the norms are supplied by the economist whereas in the latter case they are supplied by the employer. Positive economics is involved in both cases since it is necessary to know what microeconomic relationships in fact exist to identify the policies which best meet the proposed aims.

Reduction in Scarcity as an Ideal and the Means of Achieving this Reduction

One *idealistic approach* to microeconomic policy (one to which the majority of economists currently subscribe and one accepted by many policy-makers) begins from the proposition that the main aim of microeconomic policy is to reduce scarcity and/or more fairly share its burden, for example, by altering the distribution of income. Measures to reduce scarcity or shift its burden include those designed to:

1.   improve economic efficiency in the use of resources;
2.   maintain full employment (an aim which can be seen as a part of the problem of maintaining economic efficiency; see Chapter 11);
3.   foster a desirable pattern of economic growth; and
4.   improve the distribution of income.

Many economic policies affect scarcity. Listing these under the above four headings, they include policies affecting *economic efficiency in the allocation of resources*, such as:

- freedom of trade and production and openings for trade and production;
- the payment of subsidies on the production of particular goods or on production in particular regions;
- limitations on international trade such as those resulting from tariffs on imported commodities or quotas on the quantity to be imported of particular commodities;
- measures to protect consumers such as restrictions on maximum prices and constraints on acceptable qualities of goods to be traded;

those affecting *employment*, such as:

- wages, prices and profit policies; subsidies for employment in depressed regions;
- measures to increase the mobility of workers such as the payment of relocation subsidies to the unemployed;
- schemes to provide more information about job opportunities to the unemployed and to employers seeking employees;

those influencing *economic growth*, such as:

- schemes to influence the adoption of superior techniques of production;
- measures to encourage the development of new techniques and products through subsidies for research and development expenditure;
- education policies to encourage individuals to be innovative and to make it easier for them to adjust to a changing world;

those altering the *distribution of income*, such as

- social welfare benefits;
- taxation; and
- aid to less developed countries.

Most of these specific policies have implications for all the main influences on scarcity. Freedom of trade, for instance, not only affects the efficient allocation of resources but also has consequences for employment, influences economic growth, and alters the distribution of income.

Difficulties in Deciding what Constitutes a Reduction in Scarcity

Even if we accept that it is ideal for microeconomic policy advisers to suggest policies to minimize or reduce scarcity, it is difficult to decide what constitutes a reduction in scarcity. This is especially so when an economic reform makes some individuals better off and others worse off, because interpersonal comparisons of welfare need to be made to decide whether the reform increases social welfare. There have been two main responses to this problem by economists – that by Pareto and that by Hicks and Kaldor.

Pareto's Criterion

Pareto's response is to concentrate on the *necessary* conditions for minimizing scarcity. According to Pareto, scarcity is only minimized if it is impossible to make any individual better off (in his/her own estimation) without making another worse off (in his/her own estimation). For Pareto, policies satisfying this condition are ideal and it is seen as the task of the economist to identify these policies. Given Pareto's criterion, no policy can be ideal from the point of view of minimizing scarcity if it is possible by altering it to make someone better off without making another worse off.

Pareto believed that as far as reform is concerned any economic change preferred by at least one individual and not less preferred by any to the status quo can be regarded as increasing the efficiency of the economy in satisfying wants. Such a reform reduces scarcity and is desirable in his view. The change is called a Paretian improvement. In practice, however, there are likely to be few policies which make at least one individual better off in the individual's estimation without making any other individual worse off. Furthermore, if policies must conform to this Paretian criterion, it is clear that they will differ depending upon the initial status quo. Policies of this kind tend to be constrained by the status quo. For example, the initial distribution of the ownership of resources limits the range of policies available.

Kaldor and Hicks proposed a criterion which allows more scope for economic reform than the Paretian criterion. They suggest that an economic change is socially desirable if the gainers from the change can more than compensate the losers, that is, if a *potential* Pareto improvement is possible. But this brings one face to face with the income distribution question. If compensation is not in fact paid to the losers, is the distribution of income worsened and, if so, is the deterioration sufficient to offset the benefits otherwise of the change? But for the moment let us concentrate on Pareto's criterion and its policy implications and return to the Kaldor–Hicks criterion later.

The Nature of the Paretian Ideal

In practice, and as already mentioned, policy recommendations based upon Pareto's criterion have usually been ones aimed at achieving *maximum* economic efficiency, a situation where it is impossible to make any individual better off without making another worse off. These recommendations have been concerned with the ideal, an ideal which it is necessary to fulfil no matter what is the distribution of income, if scarcity is to be minimized. The economic relationships which *need* to be satisfied to meet the ideal hold whether the economy is a socialist one, a capitalist one, or one organized along other lines.

Conditions to be Satisfied for a Paretian Ideal

Given that the economic world (preferences for commodities and production relationships) has *a particular set of characteristics*, economists have shown that the allocation of resources must satisfy certain conditions in order to yield a Paretian optimum. For instance, under the *normally* assumed circumstances (which include certain convexity conditions to be satisfied by the production and consumption relationships), the composition of the output of products should be such that the rate at which products can be technically transformed into one another is equal to the rate at which consumers are willing (given their tastes) to substitute one for the other.

Paretian Ideal Production and Consumption in a Robinson Crusoe Economy

The necessity of this condition is easily illustrated for a Robinson Crusoe economy in which the appropriate convexity conditions are satisfied by production and consumption relationships. As will be shown, even this simple model can be used to illustrate policy problems in real economies, and the model brings out the importance of both individual preferences and technical production possibilities in the scarcity problem.

Given Robinson Crusoe's resources and the amount of effort that he wishes to put into productive activity, assume that the curve ABC in Figure 2.1 represents his production possibility frontier. Given his technical knowledge, his limited resources prevent him from producing a combination of products to the right of this curve which is his scarcity constraint. Robinson Crusoe's choice problem is to maximize his utility or preferences for consuming wine and bread subject to his limited production possibilities. To specify his best choice, let us represent his tastes or preferences for bread and wine by a set of indifference curves.

The indifference curves marked $I_1 I_1$ and $I_2 I_2$, for example, help indicate Robinson Crusoe's tastes or preferences for bread and wine. Any combination along an indifference curve is just as much desired by him as any other on the same curve.

Combinations on higher indifference curves are preferred to those on lower curves. Therefore, given the economic situation shown in Figure 2.1, it is optimal for Robinson

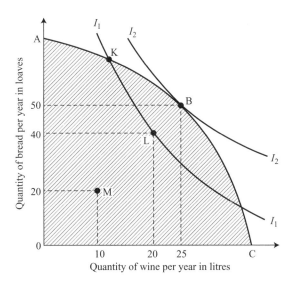

Figure 2.1   *Given Crusoe's production possibilities as represented by the hatched area and his wants or desires as represented by his indifference curves, it is optimal for Crusoe to produce and consume the amount of bread and wine represented by combination B. Point B is on his production possibility frontier and conforms to the best possible extent with his preferences*

Crusoe to produce the quantity of bread and wine corresponding to point B. At point B the (marginal) rate of technical substitution between bread and wine equals Crusoe's (marginal) rate of indifferent substitution between these. Any other attainable production combination is on a lower indifference curve than B. For example, the production possibility at point K is on a lower indifference curve than B and therefore is less preferred than B. Similarly, production possibility combinations below the production possibility frontier, such as at point L, do not satisfy Crusoe's wants to the greatest extent possible. Crusoe may, for example, produce a production combination below the frontier because he does not use the best (most productive) techniques of production available to him.

Policies Preventing the Attainment of a Paretian Ideal in a Crusoe Economy

Let us use this Crusoe example to identify policies which can prevent the attainment of a Paretian optimum. Suppose that Robinson Crusoe is discovered by a neighbouring kingdom, and his land annexed, but he is left on his island alone except for occasional visits by the King's authorities to see that the King's laws are being obeyed. The King is opposed to the drinking of wine and believes that it is immoral for Crusoe to consume 25 litres annually. He decrees that Crusoe is not to produce and consume more than 12 litres of wine annually. By rationing Crusoe's supply of wine, the King moves Crusoe in terms of Figure 2.1 from position B to K. Crusoe is made worse off in his own estimation, that is made poorer by this policy. Similarly, in real world economies, when governments restrict the production of particular commodities by quotas, taxes or other means, they are liable to reduce economic welfare.

The King, however, may feel that from an administrative point of view the best way to limit Crusoe's consumption of wine is to restrict his production possibilities. The main reason for Crusoe's large production of wine may be his discovery of an effective grape press. Seeing this, the King might order the destruction of the press and forbid the building of a new one with the aim in mind not only of limiting Crusoe's wine consumption, but also of reducing the risk of the spread of knowledge of the invention to other parts of his Kingdom where it is unknown. The King may fear that the spread of this knowledge would raise wine consumption, generally, and increase leisure time, so making it harder for him to maintain law and order. However, the effect as far as Crusoe is concerned is to restrict his production possibilities to a level below his production possibility frontier and he may reach a new constrained optimum at a position such as point M. As a result of this policy, Crusoe now enjoys 20 loaves of bread and 10 litres of wine per year and is much worse off than before he was regulated. In real economies, measures to restrict the introduction of new techniques (such as is sometimes favoured by particular industries or unions) can keep scarcity greater than it need be and all may suffer in the end.

Or to give another example, suppose that the King decides that grapes can only be grown on that part of the island which is relatively least suitable for their production. He sees that this will also restrict the amount of wine available to Crusoe. This policy also results in Crusoe's optimal restricted position becoming one like M, that is one within the interior of his production possibility boundary. Crusoe is made poorer as a result of this policy. In real economies, the community can similarly be made poorer by policies which encourage production of commodities in relatively less productive regions by subsidizing such production or by taxing or placing limitations upon the production of commodities in areas which relatively suit their production. This occurs, for instance, in some regional policies and in some agricultural policies.

It ought to be noted that the King in this hypothetical example does not share Pareto's ideal. For one thing he believes either that the individual is not the best judge of his own self-interest or that the preferences of individuals, at least in some respects or to some extent, are unimportant compared to the King's. An economist, however, can point out some of the economic costs of the King's policies.

Conditions for Pareto Optimality in Normal Economy

In a normal economy involving many producers and consumers, the conditions which must be satisfied to ensure Pareto optimality (a resource allocation for which it is impossible to make some individual better off without making another worse off) are more complex. However, the basic conditions to be satisfied are simple and are as follows:

1. *Economic efficiency in production.* It must be impossible, given available techniques, to increase the production of any valued commodity without reducing that of another by altering the allocation or use of resources. This implies that production must be on the production possibility frontier of an economy.
2. *Economic efficiency in consumption.* Commodities must be allocated between consumers in a way which makes it impossible by re-allocating commodities to increase the satisfaction of any consumer (place him or her on a higher indifference curve) without reducing that of another.
3. There must be *an optimal conformance* between the quantities supplied of different commodities and the desires of individuals for the various commodities. The composition of production must be such that it is impossible by altering its composition (by increasing the supply of one commodity at the expense of another) to make any individual better off without making another individual worse off. In the Crusoe case, point B in Figure 2.1 represents a composition of production which optimally conforms with desires.

While the above Robinson Crusoe model illustrated some of the conditions which need to be satisfied in an economy if it is to achieve maximum efficiency in production and an optimal conformance between production and the desires of individuals for the different commodities which can be produced, it does not illustrate economic efficiency in the exchange and consumption of commodities. However, the model to be introduced shortly, based on the Edgeworth–Bowley box, does. It illustrates how trading of commodities internationally or nationally can increase economic welfare (that is in this case bring about a Paretian improvement) and how restrictions on trade, such as tariffs on imports or rationing, can have the opposite effect. Furthermore, the model lends emphasis to the point that the Paretian criterion is unable to prescribe an optimal distribution of income. But before outlining the Edgeworth–Bowley box model, it should be pointed out that economists have focused their attention on two broad social means for achieving Pareto optimality.

Alternative Means of Attaining Paretian Optimality – Markets or Direct Controls

Under suitable conditions which include the possession of adequate knowledge by decision-makers, a Paretian optimal allocation of resources can be achieved by:

1. the operation of perfectly competitive markets (for instance, in a private enterprise economy); or
2. direct controls or commands (for example in a collectivist or centralized economy) intended to achieve a Paretian optimal position by ensuring that the required production and consumption conditions are satisfied.

The Paretian optimality of either economic system (given the assumed theoretical sufficiency of knowledge on the part of the economic decision-makers) can be shown by mathematical means. These theoretical considerations have sometimes led economists to recommend that actual policy efforts should be made by the government to foster perfectly competitive markets or that governments in centrally directed economies should strive to direct their economies towards a Paretian optimum since there are no real obstacles to achieving the optimum by direction. But in both instances the suggested policies are based upon theoretical assumptions which are unlikely to be satisfied in practice. For one thing, perfectly competitive markets are not likely to occur because information is imperfect. Perfect central direction of the economy is also likely to be impossible because the knowledge possessed by central planners is very imperfect.

As strongly maintained by most members of the Austrian School of Economics (see Chapter 3), the different sets of information possessed by individuals in society about their wants and technological production possibilities are more likely to be used with greater efficiency in a free market economy in allocating resources than in a centralized economy. This is because the limited capacities of central planners prevent them from obtaining and comprehending adequately all this information possessed by different individuals in society. In essence, it is claimed that even imperfect free-market systems are likely to be more efficient in resource allocation (scarcity reduction) than imperfect centralized economic planning systems; and the former are usually more consonant with the maintenance of individual liberty. Furthermore, free market systems may be more effective than centralized economies in fostering economic growth, because, for example, they are more conducive to research and business innovation (Schumpeter, 1954), which Schumpeter claimed might reach its zenith under some forms of imperfect market competition (see Chapters 8 and 9).

Even if it is granted that perfect competition can occur in practice, it results in a Paretian optimum only if production and consumption relationships satisfy a range of assumptions. Given the absence of externalities, the absence of significant ranges of increasing returns to scale in production, and the fact that all goods are private goods, perfect competition can lead the economy to a Paretian optimum. However, in practice market failures do occur, and the ideal of attaining a Paretian optimum by the operation of perfectly competitive markets cannot be achieved. Market failures, which will be explored later in this chapter, may call for government intervention in the economy and microeconomic policy advice is needed in this regard.

Paretian Optimality in Exchange and the Income Distribution Problem Illustrated by the Edgeworth–Bowley Box

There is a further problem with the Paretian criterion. It gives the policy-maker no guide to the ideal distribution of income. Different allocations of resources are Paretian ideal depending upon the distribution of income or rights of individuals to resources. This can be illustrated by means of an Edgeworth–Bowley box, shown in Figure 2.2. This diagram will also be used to illustrate the advantages of trade and the drawbacks of policies restricting trade.

Imagine that there are two individuals, A and B, and that two commodities, petrol and bread, are available to them. The total number of loaves of bread and number of litres of petrol available to both in any year is fixed. Any other two commodities can of course be taken as an example, or one may wish to consider petrol as a surrogate for travel and bread as a surrogate for food. Other examples can be easily constructed such as rice versus wine, or access to computers and the Internet versus recreational travel. The question is how to allocate the total available quantity of these commodities between the two individuals so as to achieve Paretian optimality.

The optimal allocation depends on the preferences of the individuals for petrol compared to bread, which can be specified in an Edgeworth–Bowley box like that in Figure 2.2. The height of this box represents the total number of loaves of bread available in a year and its width indicates the total number of litres of petrol available in a year. The

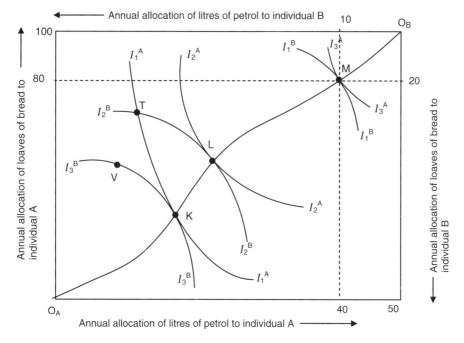

Figure 2.2   An Edgeworth–Bowley box. It shows that a number of different allocations of resources can be Paretian optimal. In this case any allocation of resources along the contract curve $O_A KLMO_B$ is Paretian optimal

indifference curves marked $I_1^A I_1^A$, $I_2^A I_2^A$ and $I_3^A I_3^A$ indicate individual A's preferences for bread and petrol. The allocations to individual A are measured away from the origin O_A. The allocations of petrol and bread to individual B are measured away from the origin O_B and the indifference curves $I_1^B I_1^B$, $I_2^B I_2^B$ and $I_3^B I_3^B$ represent individual B's preferences.

An allocation of petrol and bread corresponding to point M (this allocates 40 litres of petrol and 80 loaves of bread to individual A and 10 litres of petrol and 20 loaves of bread to individual B) is Pareto optimal. Any movement away from this allocation, once it is achieved, places at least one individual on a lower indifference curve. Similarly, the allocation at point K is Pareto optimal. Indeed any allocation of petrol and bread corresponding to a point of tangency of the individuals' indifference curves is Pareto optimal. All the points along the (contract) curve, $O_A KLMO_B$, are points of tangency between the individuals' indifference curves and represent Paretian optimal allocations. While it is clear that there are always allocations on the contract curve preferred to those not on it (for instance any allocation on KL is preferred to the allocation at point T), the Paretian criterion gives us no way of ranking the social desirability of different allocations along the contract curve. Indeed, the Paretian criterion is unable to rank social changes in which one party is made better off and another worse off. Just as the relative social desirability of K and L cannot be compared, neither can that of V and T be compared by using the Paretian criterion.

The Need for a Social Welfare Function and its Non-uniqueness

It is impossible to select the ideal economic allocation of resources in the absence of a social welfare or ordering function of the alternative possible distributions of wealth or income, for there is no way of choosing between allocations which make some better off and others worse off. However, there is no agreement about how such a social welfare function can be scientifically obtained and whether or not there ought to be one such function. Hence, for the economic adviser or technician, the relevant social welfare function is specified by the party or parties hiring his/her services and reflects their value judgements. While the relevant social welfare function may vary from individual to individual, between politicians and political parties, most such functions might be expected to satisfy Pareto's criterion, that is a change making at least one individual better off (in the individual's own estimation) without making any other worse off is a social improvement. If this criterion is satisfied by the social welfare function then, as will be shown, this implies that the social optimum lies upon the utility possibility frontier of the economy, and in turn this implies the necessity of Paretian efficiency in production and exchange, and an optimal conformance between production and consumption. This can be illustrated from Figure 2.3.

Let the hatched area in Figure 2.3 represent the utility possibilities for individuals A and B given the opportunities and preferences shown in Figure 2.2. Points on the utility possibility frontier, DEH, are in one-to-one correspondence with those along the contract curve in Figure 2.2. Thus, point E on the utility possibility frontier may correspond to point (allocation) L on the contract curve, and vice versa. The optimal allocation of resources can be determined using the utility possibility set and the relevant social welfare function. For example, suppose that the relevant social welfare function reflects a very

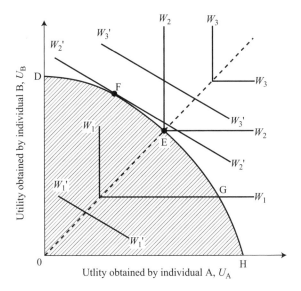

Figure 2.3   *The social welfare function is not unique. The social welfare indifference curves corresponding to two possible social welfare functions are shown. One social welfare function implies that the social optimum occurs at point E on the utility possibility frontier and the other implies that it occurs at point F. In both instances, Pareto's necessary conditions for a social optimum must be satisfied*

strong desire for equality of income so that the social welfare indifference curves corresponding to it are like the right-angled ones marked W_1W_1, W_2W_2 and W_3W_3 in Figure 2.3. In this case the highest attainable level of social welfare occurs at point E when both individuals are judged to obtain equal utility. In turn, position E corresponds to L on the contract curve in Figure 2.2 and implies that the allocation of commodities must be the one corresponding to L if this social optimum is to be achieved.

Or to take another example, suppose that the relevant social welfare function reflects favouritism for individual B in the distribution of income. The social welfare indifference curves corresponding to it might be like the straight-line indifference curves $W_1'W_1'$, $W_2'W_2'$, and $W_3'W_3'$ in Figure 2.3. In this case, the social optimum occurs on the utility possibility frontier at point F and, in turn, this implies an allocation of commodities on the contract curve, such as that at point K in Figure 2.2.

As can be seen, the two different social welfare functions imply different optimal allocations of resources. One implies the allocation at L in Figure 2.2 and the other implies an allocation such as K. Nevertheless, in both cases the *necessary* conditions for a Paretian optimum are satisfied. Indeed, these conditions must always be satisfied for a social optimum if the social decision-maker believes that any change which makes at least one individual better off without making any other worse off is a social improvement. In these circumstances, satisfaction of the Paretian conditions is *necessary but not sufficient* for a social optimum. The mere fact that the necessary conditions are satisfied does not ensure maximization of social welfare, as can be seen from Figure 2.3. The Paretian conditions are satisfied if G on the utility possibility frontier is reached, but for neither of the social welfare functions represented in Figure 2.3 is G a social optimum.

The Need for a Social Welfare Function and its Non-uniqueness

At this stage, it is worthwhile drawing some further policy implications from the
Edgeworth–Bowley box introduced in Figure 2.2. The model introduced there can be used
to illustrate how free trade can result in a Paretian optimum and how policies restricting
trade can prevent the attainment of a Paretian optimum or rule out an otherwise possible
Paretian improvement. To avoid cluttering Figure 2.2 let us redraw and modify it as in
Figure 2.4.

In Figure 2.4 the contract curve is shown as $O_A LO_B$ and the Paretian optimal conditions for allocation are only satisfied along this curve. Trade can be mutually beneficial if
the individuals have an initial allocation of petrol and bread away from the contract curve
such as the allocation at point J. In this case, if individual A exchanges petrol with individual B for bread, the parties can move to position L where both are better off than before
trade. If both parties are well informed about the characteristics of the commodities, free
trade can only make both parties better off.

But suppose that the government decides that the distribution of goods corresponding
to J is fair and forbids trade in the goods. This prevents the parties from obtaining a
Paretian optimum. For instance, they are prevented from moving from J to a position such
as L and both are worse off than they could be through trade. The government's solution
fails to take account of the fact that individual B has a relatively greater preference for
petrol than individual A.

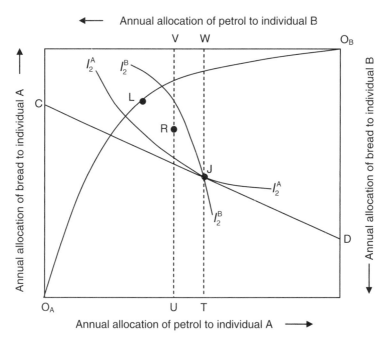

*Figure 2.4   Policies restricting or limiting trade or exchange can prevent the attainment of a
               Paretian optimum. This is so if the allocation of commodities corresponds to point J, for
               example, and trade is only allowed at an exchange rate indicated by CD*

Again, although exchange may not be forbidden, it might only be allowed at an exchange rate which makes trade unprofitable to the parties or rules out the attainment of an optimum. For instance, assume that trade is only permitted at the exchange rate indicated by the price line CD. Then no trade will occur because individual A receives too little bread in exchange for petrol. All permissible trading opportunities along CD are such that they would make one party worse off and hence no trade will occur. The restriction on the exchange rate results in parties remaining at J and forgoing a possible Paretian improvement such as would occur if they were not prevented by policy from moving to position L. In the real world, a government could achieve this distortion of price ratios by imposing a tax on the exchange of petrol (a tax payable in the example by bread). An excise or sales tax could have this effect. Or again, A might be the resident of a foreign country and B a national, in which case the government can distort the price ratio by placing a tariff (tax) on the import of petrol. All such restrictions on trade can prevent a Paretian optimum from being achieved or rule out an otherwise possible Paretian improvement.

Another possibility is that the government uses quotas to restrict trade or exchange. Suppose that the government restricts individual A to exchanging a maximum of UT of petrol or, in the case of imports, limits individual B to importing this much petrol. If no other restrictions apply, trade will occur. After trade, parties will achieve an allocation along UV between the two indifference curves through point J. For instance, the new allocation may be at point R. While both are better off than at J, point R is off the contract curve and both could be made better off by further trade if it happened to be allowed. Quotas imposed by the government or by agreements between suppliers limiting domestic supplies or limiting imports are likely to prevent the attainment of a Paretian optimum and stand in the way of a Paretian improvement.

The Kaldor–Hicks Criterion – a Potential Paretian Improvement

In practice, it is difficult to find policies which ensure a Paretian improvement. Most policies, while benefiting some individuals, are detrimental to the interests of others. However, much of cost–benefit analysis skirts around this problem by adopting the Kaldor–Hicks criterion. This criterion regards any social change as an improvement if gainers from the change can compensate the losers (*irrespective of whether they do*) and be better off than before the change. It is sometimes argued that the application of this criterion is justified because when all policies are considered the gains and losses to individuals tend to cancel out. However, they are not certain to cancel out. Consequently, the rider is sometimes added that a social change satisfying the Kaldor–Hicks criterion is a social improvement provided that it is judged not to worsen the distribution of income.

The Importance of Non-economic Variables in Policy-making

The above idealistic changes are judged purely by reference to economic variables. But economic changes can alter social and political relationships in society. For instance, if economies of scale are important, it may be possible to achieve a Kaldor–Hicks improvement by merging firms and fostering the growth of a few large firms in the economy. But by virtue of their increased size, these firms may be able to wield greater political influence, and indeed they could become sufficiently powerful to restrict the liberty of others. Economists such as Rowley and Peacock (1975) argue that such possibilities need to be taken into account before recommending an economic reform. Again measures designed to move an economy towards Paretian optimality may have unwanted sociological effects. While mobility of labour may be judged to be necessary for economic efficiency, great mobility may interfere with the cohesiveness of groups and families, and create psychological stress. Just how much weight should be put upon these non-economic effects is a moot point, but in an ideal solution they need to be taken into account.

There are some theories of welfare not in the main economics stream which assert that welfare depends upon the difference between material wealth and other characteristics attained or attainable and those aspired to. Welfare falls if aspirations move too far ahead of that which can be realized or obtained. Marcuse (1964) suggests, for example, that welfare may not actually rise in developed economies with material wealth because advertising by companies pushes aspiration levels well above what can be achieved and increases dissatisfaction. This point of view will be discussed in Chapter 5.

Policy Advice at a Technical rather than an Idealistic Level

There is another level at which microeconomic policy advice may be valuable. It may be useful at the *technical* level. For instance, would a tariff on imports be effective in increasing the local production of a particular commodity? What level of tariff is needed to increase local production by 10 per cent? Is there an alternative means of achieving this 10 per cent increase in production? What are the alternative means? Advice at this level is concerned with positive relationships between economic variables.

Again it is a matter for positive economics to determine whether economic aims or objectives can be met and whether there are conflicts. Formulated aims may be internally inconsistent or economic constraints may make it impossible to achieve all aims simultaneously. For instance, it may be impossible to minimize the degree of inequality of income and maximize the level of production of commodities simultaneously. This would be so if the relationship between production and income inequality happened to be like that shown in Figure 2.5.

In this case, the level of output is assumed to be a function of the degree of inequality of income. This could occur if the inequality arises as a result of rewards for effort which provide incentives to individuals to raise production. On the other hand, it might be argued that in some cases the causation runs the other way. Less income inequality may occur at higher levels of production because there is less involuntary unemployment when production is high and there may be a greater demand for labour relative to other factors. But no matter which way the causation flows, or whether a more sophisticated theory is needed to take account of the relationships, one cannot simultaneously maximize production and minimize income inequality if the relationship is as in Figure 2.5.

Many other examples of unrealistic objectives can be given. A policy aimed at maximizing economic growth and guaranteeing employment to individuals no matter where they reside or wish to reside would be unrealistic and/or costly. The last-mentioned objective conflicts with the first. It is an important task of an economic policy adviser to specify the possible trade-offs. For instance, there is usually a trade-off between regional assistance and economic growth. Other examples of necessary trade-off will be given throughout this text.

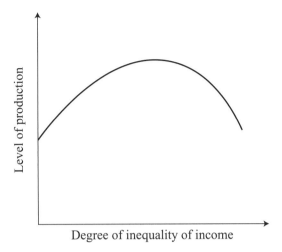

Figure 2.5   *It may be impossible to minimize the degree of inequality of income and simultaneously maximize the level of production. This would be so if the relationship between the inequality of income and level of production happened to be as shown*

2.4   GENERAL MICROECONOMIC POLICIES FOR ATTAINING OBJECTIVES

Microeconomic policies appear to fall into three broad categories:

1. those policies designed to strengthen the operation of market forces;
2. measures intended to modify or supplant the operation of market forces; and
3. policies adopted in circumstances where market forces are incapable of operating.

Policies to Strengthen the Operation of Market Forces

Microeconomic policies designed to strengthen the operation of market forces in allocating resources are often predicated on the view that perfect competition is socially optimal. Consequently, measures may be taken to foster perfectly competitive conditions. Such measures may be designed to improve the flow of information to participants in the economy and to facilitate the mobility of resources such as labour. Legislation may be passed to outlaw restrictive trade practices, and collusion between businesses may be banned in order to encourage greater market competition. In some instances, the operation of market forces may be strengthened by altering property rights, for example by converting open-access resources (available to individuals in common and without restriction) to private property. Thus, for instance, the enclosure of common grazing land and its assignment as private property strengthens market forces because individuals' returns from the land depend upon their own effort and are not interfered with by the efforts of others. However, in the case of some natural resources which are common property, such as fish and whales on the high seas, these cannot be economically made private property and their conservation requires international agreement.

Not all policies aimed at strengthening the operation of market forces are motivated by the view that perfect competition is socially ideal. Special interests sometimes support such policies in order to gain from them. At other times, they may gain support because it is believed that some degree of competition (but not a perfect degree) is socially optimal and that actual competition should not diverge too much from the perfectly competitive ideal. Supporters of this view may also couple it with the opinion that private control of resources is preferable to public control because private individuals and organizations are likely to be better informed about future economic wants and costs than public organizations.

However, even when commodities can be marketed, markets may fail to work perfectly enough for them to ensure a social optimum. They may fail because of imperfect knowledge on the part of market participants, because of spillovers in production or consumption, because some traders have market power, or because of constraints on the behaviour of firms when decreasing average costs of production occur. Furthermore, some commodities cannot be marketed at all even though they have economic value (see Chapter 14 and below). Market failure occurs in these cases and failure of this type will be illustrated below. But it does not follow that these failures will be eliminated under public control of markets. Public or civil servants, for instance, are also likely to have imperfect knowledge.

Policies to Control or Modify Market Forces

Where markets work, but work imperfectly, the government may adopt policies to modify, control or supplant the operation of markets in order to achieve a Kaldor–Hicks type of gain. Gains of this type may be realized:

1. when individuals or groups of traders in a market have market power, as is the case of a monopoly or monopsony, and exercise it; or
2. when important externalities or spillovers occur.

Consider the externality case first.

Control of Externalities or Spillovers

When an economic activity by one party harms another and no compensation is paid to the damaged party or when the activity benefits another and no payment is made by the beneficiary for this benefit, an externality or spillover occurs. The former involves an unfavourable externality and the latter a favourable one. Thus, a factory which emits air pollutants and damages the health and property of nearby residents without its owners compensating them for these damages is creating a harmful or unfavourable externality or spillover. Actual examples include the emission of fluorides from aluminium plants, of lead in vapour from lead refineries, and of sulphur dioxide and corrosive gases from factories and power generating plants burning high sulphur coal. Or the spillover may take the form of water pollution with biological and chemical wastes from industry being dumped into waterways or be in the form of noise pollution. Activities involving spillovers are unlikely to be conducted on a socially optimal scale and in a socially optimal manner if these activities are determined by market forces. A Kaldor–Hicks gain can usually be obtained as a result of government intervention in such cases.

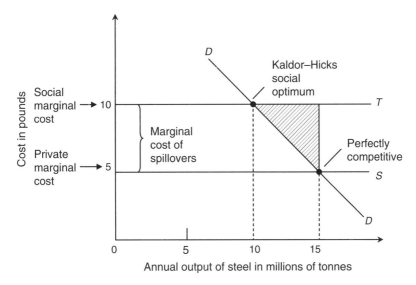

Figure 2.6   Market failure can occur as a result of unfavourable externalities or spillovers. The area of the hatched triangle indicates the extent of the social loss occurring under perfectly competitive conditions given an unfavourable spillover of £5 per tonne of steel produced

For instance, consider the case illustrated in Figure 2.6. Suppose that steel is produced by a perfectly competitive industry and that it costs each firm £5 to produce a tonne of steel. The private supply curve of steel (reflecting the costs borne by the producer) is the horizontal line marked *SS* in Figure 2.6. Given that the market demand for steel is as indicated by the curve marked *DD*, the market equilibrium supply of steel is 15 million tonnes annually. However, suppose that each tonne of steel produced causes £5 worth of damage to individuals (in terms of increased ill-health, damage to the fabric of their residences, deterioration in their gardens and the freshness of their air) for which they are paid no compensation by producers. This spillover may occur because the steel industry is using high sulphur coal to smelt its steel. The marginal spillover cost of steel is £5 and the social marginal cost of producing steel is £10, that is, equal to its costs to steel producers plus spillover costs, and is indicated by the horizontal line marked *TT* in Figure 2.6. Clearly, a Kaldor–Hicks gain can be made by reducing the annual output of steel from 15 million tonnes to 10 million tonnes, that is to the level where the marginal *social* costs of producing steel equal the demand for it. The community gains by the difference between the fall in total social costs (£10 × 5m. = £50 million) and the value placed on the lost output by consumers (£5 × 5m. + £5 × 2.5m. = £37.5 million). The net benefit of reducing the production of steel to 10 million tons annually is £12.5 million and is indicated by the shaded triangle in Figure 2.6. Assuming that restricting the quantity produced of steel is the only policy option for reducing the level of pollution from steel production, a Kaldor–Hicks social optimum occurs for the output for which the social marginal cost of producing steel equals the demand for it, that is the level of output for which the benefits and costs to society of steel production are equal at the margin.

There are, however, a number of different measures which a government can take to ensure that externalities are taken into account in resource allocation. In the case of unfavourable spillovers, the government can, for example, impose suitable taxes and in the case of favourable externalities pay a suitable subsidy on production. A suitable tax is one sufficient to equate private marginal costs of production with social marginal costs. In the example given in Figure 2.6, the imposition of a tax of £5 per tonne of steel produced would ensure the production of 10 million tonnes of steel annually, a socially optimal amount, because it results in the after-tax marginal costs borne by producers being equal to social marginal cost. There are also other policy means available to the government such as quotas on production that can be used to achieve the same level of production. In other circumstances, policies might be introduced to ban harmful activities or change property rights and allow courts to determine compensation for victims of spillovers (see Chapter 16). Microeconomic policy-makers must consider the benefits and limitations of alternative policies to deal with spillovers. Is it preferable to impose a tax on output rather than a quota? Is it more efficient to tax emissions of pollutants rather than the output of the product? These issues will be discussed in Chapter 16. It will be shown there, for instance, that more economical (efficient) means often exist for regulating pollution than restricting the quantity produced of a commodity causing pollution (the case illustrated by Figure 2.6). But observe from the above simple example that usually it is not socially optimal to reduce pollution to zero. At the socially optimal level of output, pollution remains – spillovers are not eliminated.

Control of Market or Monopoly Power

Market power can also be a source of market failure. When individual traders in a market have market power and exercise this, a social loss in the Kaldor–Hicks sense may occur. It may be possible for the government to 'perfect' markets in this case, for instance by banning collusion by traders and by outlawing restrictive trade practices, or by ensuring that there are many producers of a commodity by breaking up monopolies. A situation in which a Kaldor–Hicks gain is possible is illustrated in Figure 2.7.

The curve *DD* represents the weekly demand for water in an area. Suppose that the supply of water for this area is provided by a stream and that the supplies naturally available from this stream are well in excess of 20 million litres weekly, the quantity demanded of water when it is freely available. Since the costs of supplying water are assumed to be zero and since its available supply exceeds demand, a social optimum is achieved when water is a free good. But suppose that the stream, the sole source of water supply in the area, falls into the hands of a single owner intent on maximizing his/her profit. A non-discriminating monopolist is able to maximize his profit by charging a price of £1 per litre for water. This restricts the consumption of water from 20 million litres weekly to 10 million litres weekly. A supply of 10 million litres maximizes the monopolist's profit since his/her marginal cost of supply is zero, and therefore marginal revenue equals marginal cost when marginal revenue equals zero. (At that level of supply, the price elasticity of demand is unity.) As a result of his restriction of supply, the monopolist makes £10 million in profit weekly. However, a return to the consumption of 20 million litres of water weekly (at a zero price) would result in a Kaldor–Hicks improvement. After paying the monopolist £10 million, (as compensation for profit forgone and as a bribe to act benevolently) consumers would be better off than in the restricted situation by an amount equivalent to the area of the hatched triangle in Figure 2.7. This represents the additional

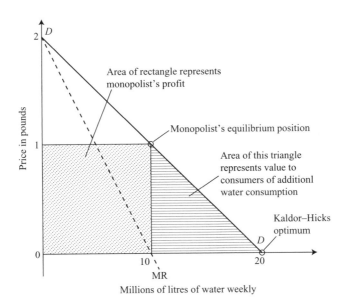

Figure 2.7   When market or monopoly power is exercised, the government may be able to intervene in the market to bring about a Kaldor–Hicks gain. A monopoly leads to a Kaldor–Hicks loss as represented by the hatched triangle

consumers' surplus to be obtained from the extra water consumption and is equal to £5 million weekly in this case.

The government may adopt a number of different policies to deal with the monopoly. It may place the ownership of different parts of the stream in many different hands thus promoting competition; it may regulate the maximum price of water; or it may itself take over the ownership of the resource and make it freely available. Microeconomic policy-makers need to consider the benefits and limitations of these alternative policies. Difficulty arises in particular when the cost per unit of supplying a commodity declines with the volume of its supply, and per-unit costs of production of a commodity are minimized when one firm supplies the whole market. A natural monopoly is said to exist. In this decreasing cost case, a Kaldor–Hicks loss may result from government policies designed to ensure that a large number of suppliers produce the commodity. A profit-maximizing monopoly, even though not socially optimal, may (in this case) result in less economic scarcity than when many suppliers supply the commodity. This and related issues will be discussed in Chapter 8 dealing with monopoly.

Non-marketability – the Case of Pure Public Goods

As mentioned above, sometimes markets are unable to operate at all to supply commodities. This is so when it is impossible or impractical to make the availability of a commodity to individuals conditional upon their payment for the commodity. In particular, a commodity cannot be marketed when its supply ensures its availability to all, none of whom can be excluded from using it and none of whom experience decreased satisfaction from jointly consuming the good. Such goods are called pure public goods. In other words, in the case of pure public goods *exclusion* is impossible and there is *non-rivalry* in the consumption of the goods. Examples of *pure* public goods include:

1. The destruction of mosquito larvae in swamps or of other pests having considerable mobility and range (for example, locusts).
2. Flood mitigation.
3. The provision of peace, defence and military alliances (for example, NATO).
4. The retention of wilderness areas so as to keep options (the option of visiting such areas) available to potential users.
5. The reduction or elimination of disease 'reservoirs', such as the elimination of small-pox and reduction in sources of other communicable diseases as is being achieved by the World Health Organization and other public bodies.
6. The supply of basic knowledge or principles for use in science.
7. The provision of public regulations or laws which benefit all.
8. Measures to prevent the entry of exotic diseases into a country such as quarantine measures.
9. Reduction in international pollution such as measures to reduce greenhouse gas emissions.

Unless collective or government action is taken to supply it, a smaller quantity of a pure public good is likely to be supplied than is socially optimal, or it may not be supplied at all. This can be illustrated by the following example.

Take the case of a military alliance. Suppose that two countries in a region are jointly threatened by an attack from an outside power. They are able to buy protection or deterrent power by military expenditure. The marginal cost (incremental cost) of obtaining protection or security in the region is indicated by the curve marked MC in Figure 2.8. Suppose that each fall of 0.1 in the probability of being attacked is valued by each nation at £10 million. Hence, both nations together (each benefits jointly) value each fall of 0.1 in the probability of attack by £20 million and their combined marginal valuation of protection is as indicated by the line marked ΣMV. It is collectively optimal to raise the degree of security by 0.2, that is to increase the likelihood of not being attacked from 0.5 to 0.7. At this level, the marginal cost of increasing security equals the combined marginal value of doing so.

The alliance, however, faces the problem of ensuring that each nation contributes £10 million to defence preparations. If one nation believes that the other member of the alliance will spend £5 million on defence (choosing security level 0.6 where MC = MV), it gains by not undertaking defence spending. In this case, the marginal cost to the nation uncommitted to defence expenditure of increasing security by 0.1 – that is, of increasing the likelihood of not being attacked from 0.6 to 0.7 – is £15 million (the area of the square plus the triangle indicated in Figure 2.8 for the range 0.6 to 0.7) and exceeds its incremental gain (£10 million). Consequently, one nation may free-ride and not contribute to military expenditure in its region. Or if both nations believe that the other will spend on defence, neither may undertake military expenditure. In either case the amount of security provided in the region is less than socially optimal. Collective coordinated action in which both nations share the military expenditure of £20 million is needed. This then raises the question of how the burden should be shared. Should, for example, contributions be based

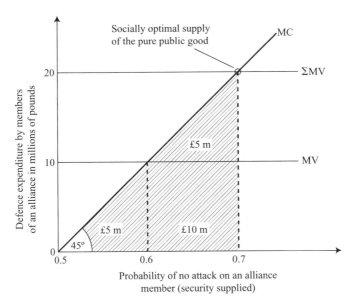

Figure 2.8   Collective or government action is usually required to ensure a socially optimal supply of a pure public good. For example, in the case of a military alliance between countries (such as NATO) it is necessary to have binding agreements on levels of defence expenditure by individual members. Otherwise some members may try to free-ride

on ability to pay? Should progressive or proportional income taxes be used to fund the public expenditure involved.

Merit Goods and Income Redistribution as a Rationale for Government Interference in Markets

Not all government action to supply goods is intended to provide pure public goods. Some such action is for the purpose of supplying or encouraging the supply of merit goods, that is goods which the government believes deserve or merit greater consumption than in fact occurs. In this case, the government acts to impose the preferences of one group in society upon others. Three different circumstances are worthwhile distinguishing. These are:

1. The philanthropic case where a group desires to subsidize from its own pocket the consumption by others *of particular* goods, such as housing and medical services for the poor, or education. In this case, there is an earmarked or tied subsidy or assistance for the purchase of particular goods rather than a cash payment which can be spent at the recipient's discretion. The government may facilitate the transfer of this subsidy from the philanthropic group, for example by supplying tied foreign aid or giving subsidies for particular charities.
2. The selfish case in which an interest group represents a product for which it has a high preference as a merit good and seeks a subsidy from the community as a whole. But it has to offset the benefits it receives against the cost to it of lobbying. The particular group may thereby benefit at the expense of the whole community. Examples of

policies of this kind might include subsidies for the arts and for cultural activities, for some types of scientific research, for the development of advanced technology such as space technology or technology for nuclear fusion.

3.   The altruistic case in which individuals are believed not to be aware of their own best interests. Interference is intended to alter their behaviour, for instance their consumption of goods, so that the pattern of consumption by individuals accords more closely with others' perceptions of their best interests. Examples include measures to deter individuals from smoking cigarettes, policies to restrict the availability of various drugs, and campaigns to encourage individuals to eat foods that reduce the risk of heart and other diseases.

Governments also interfere in the operation of markets to alter the distribution of income, even though economists sometimes argue that this is an inefficient method of altering the distribution of income. Concession rates for pensioners on public transport provides an example of this although they are of no benefit to non-travelling pensioners. Minimum wage legislation provides another example even though this may reduce the employment of those it is intended to help. Microeconomic policies of this type need to be assessed to see whether or not they have undesirable side-effects and whether or not the aims of the policies can be attained more efficiently.

2.5   THE IDEAL AND THE POLITICALLY ATTAINABLE

The aim of much literature on microeconomic policy is to state necessary conditions and formulate policies to attain a socially ideal or optimal allocation of resources. This, for instance, is the guiding goal of Paretian welfare economics. But in the actual world these conditions and policies may be of limited relevance because of constraints (political, institutional and otherwise) which prevent the ideal conditions being put into effect. Thus, the important policy issue arises of what is the best policy given the existence of constraints which rule out a Paretian ideal solution.

Second Best Policies

This matter has been considered by some economists under the title of *second best* policies, (Lipsey and Lancaster, 1956–57). It has been shown that when it is impossible to satisfy some of the conditions for a Paretian optimum, it is usually not optimal to adopt policies which ensure that the remaining Paretian conditions are satisfied. Thus, if there is a section of the economy in which perfect competition can be fostered, such as the agricultural sector, and Paretian conditions satisfied there, the existence of imperfect competition in another sector, such as the manufacturing sector may make it socially undesirable to foster perfect competition in the agricultural sector. Because imperfect competition prevents Paretian optimality conditions being satisfied in the manufacturing sector and assuming that the policy-maker cannot change this situation, it is unlikely to be optimal to foster perfect competition in the agricultural sector (unless the links between the two sectors are weak). For example, a second best solution might be to create imperfect competition in the agricultural sector by government intervention in it. Second best optimal policies and conditions must be worked out from first principles in these cases, taking into account existing institutional, technical or political constraints, and these conditions are *all* likely to differ from the 'first' best conditions (those in the absence of political or institutional constraints). If the second best constraints are policy-created, it may be possible to alter policy. However, second best theory indicates that policies based on a partial Paretian improvement may, in fact, not result in a general Paretian improvement.

The Stress of Economic Theory on Equilibria

Traditional neoclassical economic theory has also been criticized on the grounds that it takes inadequate account of time. Because it concentrates on equilibria and alternative possible equilibria (that is, comparative statics) traditional theory pays little attention to the time-paths and uncertainties of economic change and disequilibria. While this criticism, (often made by members of the Austrian School of Economics, see Chapter 3, and others) seems justified, equilibria and alternative equilibria are important in dynamic models (those taking explicit account of time). Hence, comparative static models are a first step to these more complex models which an economic policy adviser may have to construct to analyse a particular economic problem, for example to provide advice on floating exchange rates compared to fixed ones.

2.6 CONCLUDING COMMENTS

Economic policy advisers are likely to be called upon to give governments advice which takes account of political and institutional constraints. These constraints may be made known to economic advisers by politicians. Microeconomic principles and optimality conditions need further development in this area. Microeconomic policy advisers must be aware of the need to modify existing theories and develop new ones to reflect the particular policy problem under consideration. At the same time, there is a role for idealistic theories which ignore short-term political and institutional constraints, since these can become a basis for long-term political and institutional reform. In both cases, existing microeconomic theory contains tools likely to assist in the shaping of new theories and the modification of existing ones to fit particular complex policy problems, for instance questions about the social optimality of choosing nuclear power stations rather than conventional power stations using coal or oil.

READING* AND REFERENCES

*Cohen, S.I. (2001), *Microeconomic Policy*, chapter 1, London and New York: Routledge.
*Gravelle, H. and R. Rees (2004), *Microeconomics*, 3rd edn, chapters 13–14, Harlow, Essex: Prentice Hall.
*Lipsey, R.G. and A. Chrystal (2004), *Economics*, 10th edn, chapter 19, Oxford: Oxford University Press.
Lipsey, R.G. and K. Lancaster (1956–57), 'The general theory of the second-best', *Review of Economic Studies*, **24**, 11–32.

Marcuse, H. (1964), *One Dimensional Man*, London: Routledge and Kegan Paul.
*Nicholson, W. (2005), *Microeconomic Theory: Basic Principles and Extensions*, 9th edn, chapter 12, Mason, Ohio: South-Western.
*Pashigian, B.P. (1998), *Price Theory and Applications*, 2nd edn, chapter 18, New York: Irwin/McGraw Hill.
*Perloff, J.M. (2005), *Microeconomics*, 3rd edn, chapter 10, New York and London: Pearson Addison Wesley.
*Pindyck, R.J. and D.L. Rubinfeld (2005), *Microeconomics*, 6th edn, chapter 6, Upper Saddle River, New Jersey: Pearson Prentice Hall.
Rowley, C. and A. Peacock (1975), *Welfare Economics*, chapters 1 and 2, London: Martin Robertson.
Schumpeter, J. (1954), *Capitalism, Socialism and Democracy*, 4th edn, London: Allen and Unwin.
*Varian, H.R. (2006), *Intermediate Economics: A Modern Approach*, 7th edn, chapters 31–33, New York, London: Norton.

QUESTIONS FOR REVIEW AND DISCUSSION

1. Why are there difficulties in deciding what constitutes a reduction in scarcity? Outline Pareto's criterion and the Kaldor–Hicks criterion and consider the limitations of both as a means of choosing policies to reduce scarcity.
2. Distinguish between an idealistic approach and a technical approach to policy-making. Can these approaches coincide? Are both approaches needed? To what extent do both rely on positive economics?
3. List according to their prime influence on scarcity (via economic efficiency, employment, economic growth and the distribution of income) microeconomic-type policies affecting scarcity. Show that some of these policies have a multiple effect, for example, affect income distribution primarily but also influence economic efficiency.
4. Explain using the Robinson Crusoe model the economic conditions that must be satisfied for Paretian optimality.
5. Using an Edgeworth–Bowley box, show how free trade leads to mutual gains by traders. Is it possible for this gain not to occur in certain circumstances? Using this box, illustrate types of government interference in trade which can prevent the attainment of a Paretian optimum.
6. 'The Paretian ideal allocation of resources, including the optimal supply of products, varies with the distribution of income or ownership of resources.' Illustrate by using an Edgeworth–Bowley box.
7. What is meant by saying that satisfaction of the Paretian conditions is necessary but not sufficient for a social optimum? Use social welfare indifference curves to illustrate your answer.
8. Show why a Kaldor–Hicks gain *might be made* as a result of government intervention in each of the following cases:
   (a) Where unfavourable environmental spillovers occur in production
   (b) A monopoly exists
   (c) A product is a public good
   Illustrate your answer.

9. Is there a role for idealistic economic theories? To what extent (and in what ways) should policy or economic policy advice take account of the politically and bureaucratically attainable?
10. Discuss the view that because of knowledge constraints, economic scarcity is likely to be less in free market systems than in centrally directed economic systems.
11. Explain the economic concept of the second best and indicate its potential policy implications.

3. Relevance to business management of microeconomics and microeconomic policy

3.1 INTRODUCTION

Knowledge of microeconomics and of microeconomic policy develops the capabilities of business managers, and can help them improve the performance of their businesses. It provides a basis for understanding the economic implications of production decisions within a business, and is a means for assessing the economic implications for the firm of changing environments external to the firm, such as alterations in the demand for commodities and variations in government microeconomic policy.

Figure 3.1 provides a simple schematic representation of how knowledge of microeconomics and microeconomic policy can assist managerial decision-making in business.

However, it needs to be recognized that there are different approaches to microeconomic modelling. They differ in the factors that they take into account in modelling the economic operations of businesses and the economy. They often vary in their degree of abstraction from reality and in the range of influences that they deem to be important in explaining, analysing or predicting economic phenomena. They provide different ways for looking at the actual complex world. Each provides a partial picture of the

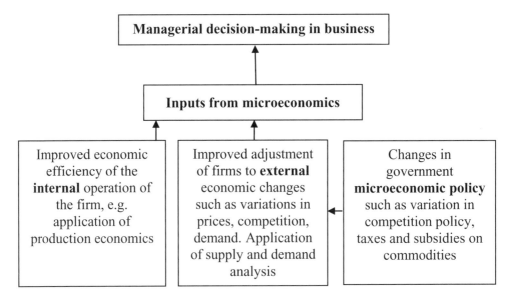

Figure 3.1   A schematic representation of how a knowledge of microeconomics can assist business decision-making

world and depending on the issue to be considered, judgement is required to select the most relevant model or models and adjust these as needed to best fit the problem under consideration.

Microeconomics is able to provide insights into how different types of institutional arrangements can affect the economic performance of businesses. For example, how is the economic performance of a firm with a unitary pyramid-type of management structure likely to differ from that with a multidivisional decentralized management structure? If the ownership and management of business are separated, as is the rule for most public companies, how might this affect their economic performance? In the early development of neoclassical economics, these were not features given significant attention because during the early period of its development, firms tended to be small and public companies were only starting to evolve. However, they have been given more attention in recent developments of microeconomics.

Early development of neoclassical economics did not entirely ignore institutional structures. For example, in relation to markets, neoclassical economics gives particular attention to how different types of industry structures can affect the operations and economic performance of markets. It emphasizes the importance of institutional factors such as the number of firms in an industry and the ease of entry by new firms (and exit of existing firms) as major influences on the degree of market competition in an industry or market and in turn, the impact of market structure on prices, supplies and the type of competitive strategies adopted in industry. These institutional or structural characteristics are important considerations also for governments and industry stakeholders in predicting the effects of changes in government microeconomic policies.

With this background in mind, this chapter considers how different approaches to microeconomics relate to business management, then considers how one might choose between different economic perspectives before considering the applicability of microeconomic policy to business management and subsequently concluding.

3.2 THE RELEVANCE TO BUSINESS MANAGEMENT OF DIFFERENT APPROACHES TO MICROECONOMICS

In contrast to macroeconomics, which concentrates on the study of economic performance using broad aggregates of economic variables, microeconomics focuses on the individual participants in the economy, their individual economic decisions, and how these decisions combine to determine economic outcomes in the economy, particularly in different industries of the economy. Although the focus here is on microeconomics and microeconomic policy, it should also be noted that knowledge of macroeconomics and macroeconomic policy can be relevant to business decisions and performance. Business prospects are usually affected by the general performance of an economy, and some industries and firms are more sensitive to macroeconomic variations than others.

Microeconomic Knowledge not Fixed

It is important to realize that microeconomic knowledge is not fixed but is continually evolving. This is partly a result of accumulating and improving knowledge. However, it also reflects the fact that the structure and nature of economies and societies alter with the passage of time. While some economic principles may retain their long-term applicability, structural or institutional changes in society often mean that new economic issues arise which cannot be effectively addressed by pre-existing microeconomic theory. As a result, new or modified microeconomic theories are then required to provide a better understanding of new economic phenomena or relationships. Consequently, microeconomic thought involves a continual process of development and evolution.

Figure 3.2 can be used to illustrate ways in which the body of economic theory or perspectives alters. Let the rectangular figure in the top half of Figure 3.2 represent the set A of economic phenomena in a stationary economic world. Initially three theories, or idealized perspectives, may exist providing insights into three sets of phenomena identified by the points marked 1, 2 and 3, and possibly some knowledge about phenomena in the neighbourhood of these points. However, many types of economic phenomena remain unaccounted for by these three theories. Subsequently, additional theories may be developed. For example, theories may develop to explain economic phenomena in the region indicated by the crosses identified by 4 and 5. Thus even in a stationary world, new economic theories and perspectives on economic phenomena are liable to arise.

However, economic systems do not remain stationary. Over long periods of time, some existing institutional structures disappear and new ones emerge. Thus in the large rectangular set (consisting of subsets A, B and C) in the lower half of Figure 3.2, economic phenomena in the subset A might disappear, those in subset B might remain, and a new subset, C, of economic phenomena may emerge. Thus if points 1 and 2 represent existing theories,

(a) A stationary economic world

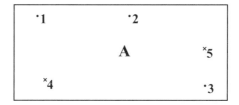

(b) An evolving and altering economic world

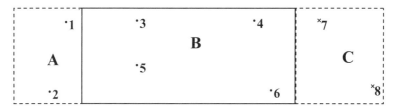

Figure 3.2   Microeconomic models evolve and their relevance varies with institutional and other changes that occur with the passage of time. In case (a), models 4 and 5 are added to existing models (1, 2 and 3) to explain economic phenomena. In case (b), economic phenomena in set A become irrelevant with the passage of time but a new set C becomes important and adds to the relevant set B

these theories become irrelevant for explaining or predicting current microeconomic phenomena, the theories represented by points 3 to 6 continue to be relevant but new theories or perspectives are needed to address new economic phenomena in subset C. For example, new theories represented by 7 and 8 may emerge. Thus there are several reasons why the body of microeconomic theory alters, and is likely to continue to do so.

The following may help to illustrate the situation envisaged in Figure 3.2. In Anglo-Saxon countries beginning in the 1930s, new economic theories modelling imperfect competition (for example dealing with monopolistic competition, monopoly, oligopoly, see Chapters 7–9) became an increasing focus of interest in economics and supplemented existing theories of perfect competition. They added a set like C in Figure 3.2(b). This was a reflection of the growing importance of imperfect competition in industrial economies. On the other hand, interest in the labour theory of value has waned in recent times and, in practice, this theory has virtually become a part of set A in Figure 3.2(b).

Neoclassical Economics and Different Perspectives on Microeconomics

Figure 3.3 provides an overview of different perspectives on economic thought of relevance to microeconomics and for business management. Neoclassical economics, which developed in the nineteenth century and still evolves, has been the main influence on the development of microeconomic theory. A central hypothesis of neoclassical economics is the assumption that economic actors (individuals) are perfectly rational and that their behaviour can be typified by that of an abstract individual, rational economic man. Economic man is assumed to be a well informed individual and to pursue his/her self-interest consistently. Self-interest is supposed to result in consumers maximizing their utility and in businesses maximizing their profits.

The main purpose of neoclassical economists is to provide simplified theories of how market systems work, given that individuals pursue their own economic self-interest. Decisions by individual buyers and sellers are the basis of this economic theory of markets. Thus this approach is atomistic in nature. Market demand and supply is envisaged as the aggregate result of self-interested decisions by individual buyers and sellers. The analysis of how market systems work can, according to this view, be unravelled by examining how individual entities make their economic decisions. Furthermore, the total result is revealed by studying the individual components of the economic system in isolation and summing the individual relationships. Therefore, this approach is a reductionist one.

A further hallmark of neoclassical economics is that most of its modelling is static and it simulates dynamic variations by means of comparative statics. As a result of this approach, its prime focus has been on market equilibrium and changes in equilibrium. Basic changes in market conditions, such as changes in consumers' tastes or preferences, are normally considered to be exogenous (outside) influences in neoclassical economics.

Neoclassical economics provides simplified theories of how markets work. It provides a series of market models, each of which is an idealized type and which can provide useful benchmarks of how actual markets work. Such knowledge about markets can be useful to business managers for predicting market conditions likely to be faced by their companies.

Note that, traditionally, neoclassical economics has not focused on using economics to improve the internal management of businesses nor on improving the ability of business managers to take account of external economic changes. Application of microeconomics to

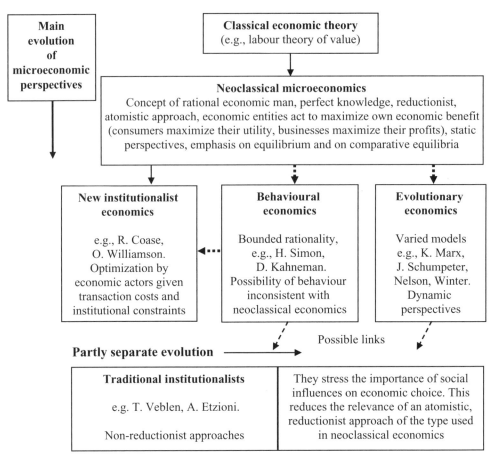

Figure 3.3   *A representation of some different perspectives on microeconomics. All the perspectives have different types of applications to business management. Note that not all perspectives are represented; for example, that attributed to the Austrian School of Economics is not*

management is a relatively recent development. Its application is illustrated in textbooks on managerial economics (for example, Salvatore, 2004; McGuigan et al., 2002), by the content of tertiary-level courses and on managerial economics. Coverage includes such topics as applications of economic demand analysis (see Chapter 5): production and cost analysis (see Chapter 6): strategies and tactics for engaging in market competition taking into account economic models of market competition, (see for example, Chapters 8 and 9): the economic impacts of government regulation on businesses: and economic considerations that should be taken into account in long-term investment decisions and risk analysis.

New and Traditional Institutional Economics

At the same time as traditional neoclassical economics continued to develop in the twentieth century, another line of thought (New Institutional Economics), closely connected with neoclassical economics, but taking into account some factors that it had regarded as unimportant, began to emerge in the 1930s. New Institutional Economics recognized that economic dealings with others are rarely costless. They usually involve transaction costs. These costs (discussed in more detail later) include searching for suppliers or buyers, negotiations of terms of exchange, and monitoring and policing of contracts or business agreements. These costs have implications for the nature of institutions such as whether or not firms exist and their size (Coase, 1937) and for the ideal managerial structures of firms (Williamson, 1975). Furthermore, these costs are important in considering the efficiency of market operations (Tisdell, 1996, Chapter 6).

A further feature of New Institutionalist Economics is its consideration of how the separation of the ownership and management of businesses affects the economic performance of firms. The importance of this separation has increased in modern times with the growing prevalence of public companies in which the managers are separated from the owners consisting of many shareholders. Shareholders are unable to exercise much power over the actual management of their companies because the cost to the individual shareholders of exercising their control of managers normally exceeds their expected benefits – their transaction costs are too high. This gives rise to a set of issues described as principal-and-agent problems. In this particular case, the principals are the shareholders and the firm's managers are their agents.

The separation of ownership and management in businesses raises the possibility that business managers will not act to maximize their firm's profit (the presumed aim of shareholders) but will, to some extent, pursue their own objectives. Therefore, account must be taken of managerial objectives in considering how businesses will behave in the market place when the ownership and management of firms is separated (see Chapter 7). Thus New Institutionalist economists have proposed new theories (for example Williamson, 1964) of how some markets work given the evolution of new business institutions.

In general, New Institutionalist Economics retained the rationality assumption of traditional neoclassical economics that individuals try to maximize their economic benefit. However, it recognized that the behaviour of individuals is constrained by transaction costs, which are partially a consequence of institutional arrangements.

Transaction costs are the organizational costs incurred merely from engaging in economic processes involving more than one individual or legal entity. These organizational costs can arise from the exchange of commodities (market transaction costs), from organizing economic production involving several individuals, and in the use of agents to discharge economic functions on behalf of others, the principals. The latter are agency costs.

A distinction is usually made between new economic institutionalism and old or traditional economic institutionalism. New institutionalists tend to retain the basic axiom of neoclassical economics that individuals act in accordance with their own self-interest but new institutionalists suppose that their behaviour is constrained by transaction costs and the costs of decision-makers generally. On the other hand, old or traditional economic institutionalists, such as Veblen (1934), Commons (1951) and Myrdal (1958), emphasize the importance of social values for the behaviour of individuals. They argue that culture and existing institutions help shape social values which in turn influence the values and behaviour of individuals, and therefore, their economic and social choices. Their perspectives overlap significantly with those of sociologists.

In the view of most traditional institutional economists, one must study the culture, institutions and their evolution of a society to understand the working of its economic system. It is also recognized that social values and institutions are not static but are liable to alter, particularly in the long-term. Therefore, the social dynamics involved in those variations are also of interest. In this respect, 'two-way' or mutual causation is often considered likely. For example, changes in the economic system are liable to alter social values and institutions. However, variations in social values and institutions can also change economic systems. There are differences of opinion about the relative influence of these forces. Karl Marx (1930) for example, argued that economic systems are the dominant force in determining institutions and social values whereas Myrdal (1958) sees institutions and social values as being much less influenced by economic systems. The interest of some traditional institutionalists in social dynamics may have led them to develop evolutionary economic theories, for example, Marx (1930).

Behavioural Economics

Interest in behavioural economics began to gather momentum in the 1950s. Assumptions about human behaviour play a critical role in neoclassical economics and most economic theory. In the second part of the twentieth century, several writers with training in psychology began questioning the behavioural assumptions underlying neoclassical economics as embodied in the concept of rational economic man. They included Herbert Simon (1957) and Kahneman and Tversky (1979, 2000, Chapter 1).

Simon proposed that the concept of 'economic man' be replaced by that of 'administrative man' as far as business management is concerned (Simon, 1961). In fact, he thought human behaviour was not best modelled as optimizing behaviour but rather as behaviour based on aspiration levels. In his view, this involves a search to achieve aspiration levels with satisfactory outcomes being acceptable to the individual. Thus Simon thought that optimizing behaviour of the type envisaged in neoclassical economics would be atypical and that satisficing behaviour would be normal. This, in his view, is particularly so when account is taken of the fact that decision-making is not costless and that individuals have limited capacities for collecting, sorting and processing information.

Not only do decision-making costs and the limited capacities of individuals favour satisficing behaviour, they often result in the adoption of rules of thumb and encourage habitual types of behaviour. In developing his views about economic behaviour, Simon drew on psychological theories of human behaviour, as have most contributors to the development of behavioural economics.

However, some writers point out that the type of behaviour described by Herbert Simon is similar to that predicted by optimizing theories when account is taken of the cost of search (Stigler, 1961) or by optimizing models that take into account decision costs generally (Baumol and Quandt, 1964). In other words, they claim that the observed behaviour suggested by Simon can be predicted, or approximately predicted by supposing that human behaviour is based on the objective of optimizing provided account is taken of the costs of decision-making and transaction costs. This is a theme developed by some contributors to New Institutionalist Economics, such as Oliver Williamson (see, for example, Williamson and Masten, 1999).

Simon's emphasis on bounded rationality raises several questions. In what ways is human behaviour bounded? How bounded is it? How rational are individuals? To what extent do individuals vary in these respects? Economists differ in their answers to these questions and in their responses in their development of theories. Neoclassical economists did not believe human rationality and knowledge limitations to be sufficiently important as to call for modifications of their theories. While writers such as Oliver Williamson, belonging to the new institutionalist stream of economics, have retained the neoclassical assumption of economic rationality (optimizing by economic man), they suppose that costs and constraints on decision-making, including transaction costs, are taken into account by decision-makers. Their position is a compromise. On the other hand, Simon (1957, 1961) suggests that bounded rationality may be so considerable that it is likely to be misleading to model human behaviour as if it is optimizing behaviour. In any case, it is now clear that human behaviour is more bounded in its rationality than typically assumed by neoclassical economists. Neoclassical economic theories represent just one point in the spectrum of theoretical possibilities.

However, many behavioural economists are convinced that individuals are less rational in their economic behaviour than both neoclassical economists and supporters of theories of bounded rationality claim. Some predictable and persistent economic behaviours do not seem to be rational. Kahneman and Tversky (2000), drawing on psychology and observed behaviours, have done much to promote this point of view. For example, it has been found that new entrants to industries consisting of small firms grossly overestimate their chances of business success, that the care taken in spending funds depends upon how they were obtained, and that individuals often display a status quo or endowment effect when they acquire assets. This makes them reluctant to sell or dispose of assets even when the opportunity cost of not doing so is high. Effects of this type can influence the way markets operate and the economic valuations that individuals place on commodities. New textbooks on microeconomics (for example, Bowles, 2004) have appeared that take into account these types of phenomena, and some coverage can be found in Varian (2006, Chapter 30).

Behavioural economists frequently conduct experiments to test whether individuals act or choose as predicted by economic theories. These are usually controlled experiments conducted under laboratory conditions. Not all economists accept the validity of this approach. It has been said that 'some economic theorists, especially the Austrian school, reject the entire concept of economic empiricism, since they reach their conclusions strictly by deduction (from opinions arrived at introspectively)' (Anon c, no date, p. 3).

It is also a feature of neoclassical economics that it assumes homogeneity of behaviour by human beings or supposes that microeconomic situations can be satisfactorily modelled by concentrating on the behaviour of 'representative' economic agents, (for example, consumers or firms). However, while there often are similarities in the behaviour of individuals and economic entities, there may also be differences, for example, in the extent to which individuals engage in rational behaviour and variations in their beliefs about the world. While this variety may, in some circumstances, be so small as to be immaterial from an economic point of view, in other cases this is not so (Tisdell, 1996) and one needs to consider the distribution of behaviours, not just the central tendencies involved. This is increasingly recognized by behavioural economists and is, for instance, relevant to the marketing of commodities.

Many behavioural economists (for example, Etzioni, 1988) are also interested in how beliefs about the world and values are influenced by social and cultural interaction. In this respect, their interests overlap with those of the 'traditional' or 'old' institutionalists, such as Veblen (1934), who adopt a non-reductionist approach. As discussed above, old institutionalists believe that the economic objectives of individuals and their beliefs about the world are largely shaped by the institutional framework and the cultural environment that surrounds them. Given such surrounds, the 'free' economic choice of individuals is limited. Therefore, one must study institutions and cultures and their dynamics to appreciate how economic systems operate and evolve.

Evolutionary Economics

As mentioned earlier, neoclassical economics does not focus on the evolutionary changes in economic systems. Because economic systems appear to be changing continually, many economists see this lack of attention to the change and 'development' of economic systems as a serious limitation of neoclassical economics. Consequently, a variety of evolutionary economic models have been proposed. Some are deterministic, others are stochastic, and still others open-ended.

For example, Marx's theory of economic development is deterministic as far as the various successive stages of development are concerned (Marx, 1930). So also are some of the early theories predicting that business competition will always favour profit-maximizing firms and that the more efficient profit-maximizers will be the ones likely to survive. This form of social Darwinism hypothesizes that the fittest will survive in the economic world and these are likely to be those maximizing their profits or, generally, their own selfish gains. Nelson and Winter (1982) claim that firms are characterized by customary behaviours or relatively settled forms of behaviours. These are analogous to the genes possessed by individual biological organisms. As the external environment changes, some firms are able to adapt better to these changes than others, or their settled behavioural patterns become more (or less) suited to their survival in their altered environment. Thus a selection process akin to that in ecology occurs and determines the rise and fall of businesses.

Joseph Schumpeter (1942) was critical of the lack of attention given in neoclassical economics to processes of the creation of new knowledge, innovation and technological change. He saw such changes as a more telling form of business competition than capitalism based on the more efficient use of existing knowledge, given techniques and resources; the main focus of neoclassical economics. He recognized that innovations are uncertain although they are capable of altering the economic structure of societies. His work stimulated research into the economics of research and innovation and led to the widespread recognition that research and development by businesses and innovation is an extremely important form of business competition in modern times.

The Austrian School of Economics

The views of Joseph Schumpeter are associated with the Austrian School of Economics. The origin of this school of economic thought is usually identified as being the publication in 1871 of Carl Menger's *Principles of Economics*. Whereas neoclassical economics focuses on equilibria as important phenomena to take into account in explaining how economies operate, most members of the Austrian School see the study of processes of change and disequilibria as more important. They are also sceptical about how precisely processes of change can be modelled mathematically.

As in neoclassical economics, behaviour by individuals is seen by the Austrian School as the building block for economics. Their emphasis on individualism distinguishes their approach from that of traditional institutionalists who see individual values as being greatly influenced by social phenomena. Unlike neoclassical economists, followers of the Austrian School of Economics stress the limited economic knowledge of individuals in a changing world, the search of economic agents for social mechanisms to reduce their uncertainty and to find ways in which the most beneficial use can be made of the limited but different sets of knowledge that individual entities possess.

Politically, most followers of the Austrian School of Economics favour a decentralized economic system with a small government sector that interferes little in the economy. They are highly critical of the economic value of centralized economic systems, a view forcefully presented by Hayek (1944, 1948). There are several reasons for this. First, centralized systems do not use the available knowledge that different economic entities have in society in as effective a way as in decentralized market systems. Secondly, centralized economic systems suppress spontaneous experimentation and innovation by individuals, therefore, they fetter economic development. Furthermore, centralized systems are seen as a threat to the preservation of human rights.

The emphasis of the Austrian School of Economics on processes means that their views overlap to some extent with those of evolutionary economists. However, most followers of the Austrian School are sceptical about the extent to which these processes can be modelled mathematically. The emphasis of the Austrian School on knowledge and knowledge imperfections also provides some overlap with New Economic Institutionalism. However, the latter tends to be more mathematically formalistic with less emphasis on dynamic processes than the Austrian approach. Nevertheless, the Austrian approach is more diverse than is often portrayed.

Oskar Morgenstern has been identified as a member of the Third Generation of the Austrian School (Anon a, no date) but in conjunction with the mathematician von Neumann, developed applications of the theory of games to economic behaviour (von Neumann and Morgenstern, 1944). The theory of games makes considerable use of mathematics, relies heavily on equilibrium concepts and assumes a high degree of rationality and knowledge on the part of economic entities (see Chapter 9).

Nevertheless, at its core, game theory is concerned with how knowledge affects human behaviour, the problems of coordinating interdependent human behaviour, and allowing for the uncertain actions of others. These are recurring interests of economists belonging to the Austrian School of Economics.

In reality, different approaches to studying economics overlap to some extent and expositions of different schools of thought vary with the focus of the presenter. Short expositions of concepts and views that have been widely associated with the Austrian School of Economics are readily available on the web: see for example Anon a (no date), Anon b (no date) and Walker (2002). They do, however, give the impression that the School is more unified than it actually is. For more in-depth considerations of the Austrian School of Economics see Boettke (1994).

3.3 BUSINESS MANAGEMENT AND THE CHOICE OF MICROECONOMIC PERSPECTIVES

Given that there are so many perspectives or schools of thought about microeconomics, one may be left wondering which one is the most relevant to business managers. Furthermore, even within these different approaches to microeconomics, there are different models of economic phenomena. Therefore, a wide range of perspectives exist.

In practice, all the perspectives can be relevant depending on the purpose for which the economic modelling is to be used. Judgement is required to decide which perspective or perspectives best capture an economic situation which needs examination or consideration. In some circumstances, it may be necessary to consider the matter from several perspectives. Furthermore, analysis of a microeconomic situation will require consideration of the applicability of different available microeconomic models. How applicable are they? Do they need to be modified and how?

Economic models are not designed to replicate all aspects of reality. If they did, they would be too complex and unmanageable to be useful for decision-making. They are intended to provide tractable representations of important facets of reality. Microeconomic analysis only provides an input, method or tool for managerial decision-making. Judgement is required about whether a microeconomic model is relevant to a particular case, whether it needs to be adjusted and how.

The ability of business managers to use and apply microeconomic theories and concepts successfully depends on three factors:

1. their formal knowledge of microeconomic thought;
2. their experience with and knowledge of the economic business situation being considered; and
3. their creativity, intelligence and wisdom, that is, their personal abilities.

Strengths in one area with a deficiency elsewhere is liable to result in poor decisions. For example, an excellent knowledge of microeconomics combined with lack of empirical knowledge of an industry does not ensure sound decision-making about the economic prospects of the industry. An appropriate balance of capacities in the three above-mentioned areas is necessary to ensure sound managerial decisions about economic matters. For example, creativity and intelligence are needed to decide what aspects of microeconomic thought are relevant and how to adjust microeconomic theories and data sets so as to increase their relevance to the decision to be made.

Nevertheless, many business decisions involve enterprise or entrepreneurship. The outcomes of enterprise (involving relatively novel situations) are not very predictable and can even be highly uncertain. While knowledge of microeconomics may assist entrepreneurs in their business decision-making, it cannot provide complete guidance in situations involving new entrepreneurial initiatives. The importance of the uncertainty aspect of entrepreneurship has been stressed by most members of the Austrian School of Economics. One should, therefore, have limited expectations about the contribution that microeconomics can make to business decision-making.

3.4 THE RELEVANCE TO BUSINESS MANAGEMENT OF KNOWLEDGE ABOUT MICROECONOMIC POLICY

Business managers can benefit from a knowledge of government microeconomic policy and its economic effects in several ways. They may, for example, be able to predict how the economic fortunes of their own business or their industry may alter as a result of a change in microeconomic policy, for instance, with the withdrawal or reduction in tariffs or subsidies protecting their industry.

Secondly, many countries have policies outlawing particular trade practices. In certain circumstances, governments may ban mergers of companies or acquisitions of companies if these are likely to reduce competition in an industry substantially, or create a monopoly. It is necessary for businessmen to be familiar with this legislation and this calls for some knowledge of microeconomics. It can also be advantageous for business managers to be aware of economic arguments that might provide a defence for a business acquisition or merger if it is challenged by government authorities.

There are, of course, many other areas of government economic policy where knowledge of microeconomics is helpful. These include economic aspects of science and technology policy, particularly the economics of intellectual property rights. Intellectual property rights include patents, registered trade marks and designs, copyrights and plant variety rights. Public policies to regulate the use of the environment and shared natural resources have become more common, and these usually have an economics rationale. Microeconomic consequences of industrial relations policies and international trade and investment policies as well as public finance issues often have important implications for the economic fortunes of businesses.

Knowledge of microeconomics may also help a business or industry to decide whether it is likely to be economic for it to lobby for or against a particular microeconomic policy. Using microeconomics, it may be possible to estimate the economic loss or gain to a business or industry if a particular change in microeconomic policy is made. Of course, in deciding on whether it is likely to be economic for a business to lobby, business management will also have to take into account the cost of political lobbying as well as the probability of its success.

Business managers may find some microeconomic policies more acceptable if they are aware of social economic reasons for their adoption. There is, therefore, an advantage in knowing the rationale behind particular microeconomic policies.

Again, institutional structures are of major importance for business operations. Government policies, legislation, and its administrative machinery play a major role in maintaining and developing the institutional structure of society. For example, government policies significantly influence the extent to which members of the community respect private property and other forms of property; and the extent to which individuals and other economic entities feel compelled to meet their economic obligations promptly and fully, for instance, in relation to contracts or sale of goods.

As claimed by institutional economists, the structure of institutions affects economic efficiency, economic growth, the distribution of income, the availability of opportunities for individuals and the distribution of power in society. Furthermore, in the long-term, institutions influence widely-held beliefs and values in society. Consequently, public policies that alter the institutional structure of society can have wide-ranging, long-term consequences.

While economic reforms are capable of modifying, and altering, social values and beliefs in the long run, the scope for socially acceptable economic reform is restricted to some extent by existing cultural values and institutional structures. Consequently, microeconomic reforms that are acceptable and effective in one society may not be workable in another with a different set of traditions and a different cultural background. They may at least have to be modified and introduced using different timetables in unlike societies. While economic globalization may be fostering worldwide convergence of institutions and cultural values, divergent social and cultural values still occur, and these differences cannot yet be ignored when economic policy proposals are considered.

3.5 CONCLUDING COMMENTS

Although orthodox neoclassical economics has dominated textbooks on microeconomics and managerial economics, it provides only one possible perspective on microeconomics and microeconomic policy. Depending on the economic issue being considered, it is useful to take into account other perspectives. For example, while neoclassical microeconomics and New Institutional Economics (which is often regarded as an extension of neoclassical economics) may be effective in addressing short-term economic issues or considering economic effects in relatively stationary economic conditions (as may also some aspects of behavioural economics), long-term economic change may require consideration of the types of matters raised in traditional institutional economics and in some strands of behavioural or experimental economics. However, given the fundamental importance of entrepreneurship in business, it would be too optimistic to expect microeconomics to provide a complete guide to business decision-making no matter which approach is used. Nevertheless, a knowledge of microeconomics does make for more informed managerial decision-making.

The main emphasis in this book is on neoclassical microeconomics and the critical assessment of its applications. However, concepts and theories from New Institutionalist Economics and some behavioural theories are also considered, and issues involving traditional institutional economic perspectives are raised when relevant.

It can be concluded that both knowledge of microeconomics and of microeconomic policy can improve business management. However, the contribution of microeconomics is to provide concepts and methods of thinking about business issues involving economics rather than providing off-the-shelf solutions to these. Business managers need to know what types of microeconomic analysis can assist them and to consider any required modifications of the analysis to better deal with the particular economic problems faced by them. Apart from knowledge of microeconomics, this calls for experience and creativity. It is hoped that this book will provide a useful microeconomic basis for those who have an interest in business management as well as in broader economic and social issues.

READING* AND REFERENCES

*Anon a (no date), 'The Austrian School', http://cepa.newschool.edu/het/schools/austrian.htm, accessed 30/11/2006.

*Anon b (no date), 'Austrian School', http://en.wikipedia.org/wiki/Austrian_School, accessed 30/11/2006.
*Anon c (no date), 'Experimental economics', http://en.wikipedia.org/wiki/Experimental_ economics, accessed 30/11/2006.
Baumol, W. and R. Quandt (1964), 'Rules of thumb and optimally imperfect decisions', *American Economic Review*, **54**, 23–46.
Boettke, P. (1994), *The Elgar Companion to Austrian Economics*, Aldershot, UK and Brookfield, US: Edward Elgar.
Bowles, J. (2004), *Microeconomics: Behaviour, Institutions, and Evolution*, Princeton, NJ: Princeton University Press.
Coase, R.J. (1937), 'The nature of the firm', *Economica*, **4**(16), 386–405.
Commons, J.R. (1951), *The Economics of Collective Action*, New York: Macmillan.
Etzioni, A. (1988), *The Moral Dimension: Towards a New Economics*, New York: The Free Press.
Hayek, F.A. von (1944), *The Road to Serfdom*, London: Routledge.
Hayek, F.A. von (1948), *Individualism and Economic Order*, Chicago: The University of Chicago Press.
Kahneman, D. and A. Tversky (1979), 'Prospect theory: an analysis of decisions under risk', *Econometrica*, **47**, 263–91.
Kahneman, D. and A. Tversky (2000), *Choices, Values, and Frames*, Cambridge, UK: Cambridge University Press.
Marx, K. (1930), *Capital*, translated from the 4th German edition, London: Dent.
McGuigan, J.R., R.C. Moyer and F.H. deB Harris (2002), *Managerial Economics: Applications, Strategy and Tactics*, 9th edn, Mason, Ohio: South-Western.
Myrdal, G. (1958), *Value in Social Theory: A Selection of Essays in Methodology*, New York: Harper and Brothers.
Nelson, R. and S. Winter (1982), *An Evolutionary Theory of Economic Change*, Cambridge, Mass: Harvard University Press.
Neumann, J. von and Morgenstern, O. (1944), *Theory of Games and Economic Behavior*, Princeton, NJ: Princeton University Press.
Salvatore, D. (2004), *Managerial Economics in a Global Economy*, 5th edn, Mason, Ohio: South-Western.
Schumpeter, J.A. (1942), *Capitalism, Socialism and Democracy*, 2nd edn, New York: Harper Brothers.
Simon, H. (1957), *Models of Man*, New York: John Wiley.
Simon, H. (1961), *Administrative Behavior*, New York: The Macmillan Company.
Stigler, G.J. (1961), 'The economics of information', *Journal of Political Science*, **69**, 213–25.
*Tisdell, C.A. (1996), *Bounded Rationality and Economic Evolution*, chapter 1, Cheltenham, UK and Brookfield, US: Edward Elgar.
*Varian, H.R. (2006), *Intermediate Microeconomics*, 7th edn, chapter 30, New York and London: W.W. Norton and Company.
Veblen, T. (1934), *The Theory of the Leisure Class: An Economic Study of Institutions*, New York: Random House.
Walker, D. (2002), 'Austrian economics', *The Concise Encyclopaedia of Economics*, http://www.econlib.org/library/Ene/AustriaE.economics.html, accessed 30/11/2006.
Williamson, O.E. (1964), *The Economics of Discretionary Behavior: Managerial Objectives in a Theory of the Firm*, Englewood Cliffs, NJ: Prentice Hall.
Williamson, O.E. (1975), *Markets and Hierarchies: Analysis and Anti-Trust Implications*, New York: Free Press.
Williamson, O.E. and J.E. Masten (1999), *The Economics of Transaction Costs*, Cheltenham, UK and Northampton, MA, USA: Edward Elgar.

QUESTIONS FOR REVIEW AND DISCUSSION

1. Why in general can it be useful for business managers to have some knowledge of microeconomics and microeconomic policy?

2.   The body of microeconomic knowledge changes and evolves. Explain and indicate why this happens.
3.   A major component of modern microeconomics is based on neoclassical economics. What are the main assumptions underlying neoclassical economics? What is its prime purpose? What is its main method of analysis? How can it be relevant to business management?
4.   Neoclassical economics has some important limitations. Outline some of these. To what extent and in what ways does new institutional economics address these shortcomings? Is new institutional economics more relevant to business management than neoclassical economics? Why?
5.   How does the perspective of traditional institutional economics differ from that of new institutional economics and neoclassical economics? To what extent can the perspective of traditional institutional economics be relevant to business management?
6.   There are different types of evolutionary economics involving different degrees of predictability. Discuss. Indicate how some of the existing evolutionary economic models and its concepts are relevant to business management.
7.   Views of members of the Austrian School of Economics vary but there is a common element. Explain. In doing so, indicate some of the differences between members of this school and identify the element they have in common. Are there features of this school of thought that are particularly relevant to business management? What are they and why are they relevant?
8.   One needs more than a knowledge of microeconomic theory to apply it successfully to business management. Explain and discuss.
9.   How can a knowledge of microeconomic policy be of value to business managers?
10. As a business manager, it is advantageous to be aware of and to draw on different schools of economic thought in making decisions. A multiple perspective is needed. Discuss.

PART B

Demand, supply, markets and policy

4. Competitive markets and price regulation

4.1 INTRODUCTION

Spillovers or externalities can result in a social (Kaldor–Hicks) welfare loss, even under perfectly competitive conditions, and as pointed out in Chapter 2, may call for government intervention in markets. But actual government intervention in competitive markets is not limited to correcting market operations to allow for externalities. There is considerable government interference in competitive markets even when externalities do not occur. *The purpose of this chapter is to consider how and why governments interfere in competitive markets even when externalities are absent and to outline the economic effects that such intervention has.* Government policies to maintain, to limit, or to stabilize product or factor prices, and government regulation of prices in international markets are examined.

Before considering the effects of such intervention, it is worthwhile to digress and clarify the meaning of different types of market competition. This is because this chapter concentrates on government intervention in perfectly competitive and purely competitive markets; intervention which in the absence of externalities is liable to result in a Kaldor–Hicks social welfare loss.

Defining the state of competition in an industry and in markets generally is not as straightforward as it may appear at first sight. It is likely to depend on the ease of entry of new firms into the industry, the number of producers in the industry, and the ease with which other products can be substituted for those of the industry. An industry tends to be more competitive the easier entry is into it, the larger the number of producers are in the industry, and the more nearly other products substitute for those of the industry.

Defining Competition

Two broad approaches to defining the state of competition in an industry are found in the economics literature. One approach defines competition in an industry by reference to its *structure* and the other defines it by reference to the *performance* of the industry. The traditional approach is the structural one. The state of competition in an industry is defined by the number of producers in an industry, conditions of entry into the industry, the degree or absence of collusion between market participants, and the degree to which their products are identical or differentiated. Thus a *purely competitive industry* is one in which there are many sellers and buyers (so many that the supplies or purchases of any individual do not influence the price of the commodity), commodities are homogeneous, and therefore perfect substitutes, and entry and exit in the long run is easy. Markets for fish and vegetables are usually of this type. In a *perfectly competitive market*, these characteristics are satisfied, but in addition, traders in the market have perfect knowledge of the relevant economic variables.

At the other end of the competition spectrum is pure *monopoly*. This is characterized by a single seller of a product with no close substitutes and the absence of possible entry by other firms. Posts and telecommunications in many countries used to be a state monopoly. Often inventors of new products, such as a new medicine or a veterinary product, can obtain a patent from the state which gives them an exclusive right to the inventions' use for a limited number of years. This legally established monopoly is often justified on the grounds that it provides an incentive for research and development effort.

Oligopoly is a market situation in which there are few sellers. The supply of motor fuel, cement in some regions, air travel, and man-made fibres is oligopolistic. A *monopsony* is said to exist when there is a single buyer of a commodity and an *oligopsony* arises when there are few buyers of a commodity. With the growth of supermarket chains, the retail trade has increasingly become concentrated in the hands of a few companies in some countries, and their suppliers may be faced with an oligopsonistic market in which larger retail chains exercise considerable market power (Smith, 2006). Each of these circumstances has implications, or likely implications, for the degree of competition in an industry. This chapter concentrates on purely competitive and perfectly competitive markets, but other market structures will be considered in later chapters.

Stock Characteristics of Perfect Competition and of Monopoly

It is useful now to summarize the 'stock' characteristics of perfect competition and monopoly and compare these using Table 4.1. Assuming that market participants have perfect knowledge, the structural characteristics stated in the top part of this table give rise to the performance characteristics mentioned in the lower part of the table. In assessing markets, some economists and lawyers have concentrated on the structural characteristics of industries but others have been more concerned about the performance characteristics of markets.

Performance Definitions of Competition Compared to Structural Characteristics

Differences in the performance and structural approaches to assessing economic competition in an industry are summarized in Figure 4.1. Performance definitions of competition pay little attention to market structure but concentrate on the question of whether the performance of an industry is similar to that which might be expected under pure competition. If there is little divergence between the price charged for a product and the marginal cost of producing it, an industry might be regarded as workably competitive by this approach. This may be given further support if long-term profits in the industry are not excessive, if technological progress and innovation occur at a socially desirable rate, and if avoidable waste and inefficiency do not occur in the running of businesses in the industry. Given this approach, it is feasible for an industry which is structurally oligopolistic to be workably competitive. If it is shown that an industry is workably competitive (despite its structure), this is sometimes used to argue that the market situation is socially acceptable.

There are possibly no markets in practice which are perfectly competitive and few are purely competitive. The degree of perfection of knowledge and mobility of resources required for the operation of perfect competition is so great that it can only be

Table 4.1   'Stock' characteristics of perfect competition and monopoly

Characteristics	Perfect competition	Monopoly
Structural		
Number of firms	Large	One
Size of firms	Small relative to industry output	Sufficiently large to produce all of industry output
Entry	Free (in long run)	Barriers to entry
Product	Homogeneous	Homogeneous – lack of close substitutes
Performance		
Pricing and resource allocation	Price equals marginal cost – therefore, allocation of resources is Pareto optimal	Price exceeds marginal costs – therefore, allocation of resources is not Pareto optimal
Profit	Normal (average) in the long run	Above normal in the long run
Organizational slack or X-inefficiency	Absent	May be present
Diffusion of technology	Rapid	Rate of adoption uncertain
Rate of technical progress and innovation	Uncertain	Uncertain

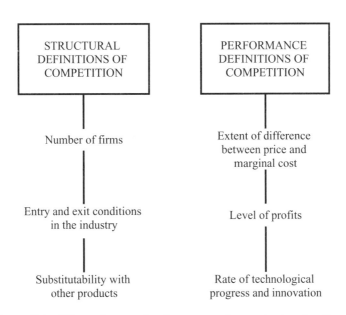

Figure 4.1   Some of the different factors taken into account in structural and performance definitions of competition

approached. But the perfectly competitive model provides an ideal or a benchmark as a basis for welfare judgements and comparison. The model is useful in a similar way to Euclidean geometry. Both refer to limiting cases but both have applications to the actual world because the degree of approximation is sufficiently close for some purposes.

There has been a political shift in favour of market systems and economic liberalism in the last few decades (see Chapter 10). This means that there is less government regulation of the operation of economies than was common in the 1950s and 1960s and most of the 1970s. However, the speed at which different countries have moved to deregulate the operation of their economies and open them to international competition has varied in timing and in extent. Australia, for example, started on this path in the second half of the 1970s (King, 1997; Tisdell, 2005) whereas India delayed this switch in policy until the beginning of the 1990s. China embarked gradually on such a course beginning in 1979. Then it began to move from a centralized relatively closed economic system towards a market system increasingly open to the outside world. As a result of such changes, there is less government regulation of purely competitive markets than used to be the case. For example, in Australia, milk prices are no longer regulated by governments and entry into milk production is no longer controlled by governments (Edwards, 2003).

Many markets for agricultural products and for fish either satisfy or nearly satisfy the conditions required for pure competition. Nevertheless, in many countries, there is still considerable government interference in the operations of these markets. In Japan, for example, rice production is heavily subsidized. In the EU, Japan and USA, imports of many competing agricultural products are restricted. While capital movements and foreign exchange markets were commonly controlled by most governments in the past, this is not usually the case now. In several countries, minimum wages for work are specified, for example, in the UK by the Low Pay Commission and in Australia (in 2007) by the Australian Fair Pay Commission, which replaced the Australian Industrial Relations Commission in 2006. Local governments also limit market competition by restricting the purposes for which land can be used. The regulations, for example, often restrict the type of business that can be conducted in a particular area.

4.2　WHY DOES THE STATE REGULATE COMPETITIVE MARKETS?

Why is there so much government intervention in markets that are purely competitive or nearly so? This may be explained by idealistic considerations or by the economics of politics. One idealistic reason for intervention, as mentioned in Chapter 2, is to allow for externalities or spillovers. But the government may also intervene in markets to 'improve' the distribution of income, for example, by subsidizing medical care, or to foster the supply of merit goods. Its aim in such cases may be to increase the political support of, or *votes* for, the party in power, and its policies may be a response to demands from particular political *pressure groups*. While state intervention in markets can be based on idealistic social welfare considerations, this intervention is sometimes (maybe often) based upon political realities of a non-idealistic nature, can add to scarcity, and, despite intentions to the contrary, may injure those whom it is designed to assist. Let us consider in more detail some of the reasons why governments interfere in competitive markets.

Information Failure (due to Externalities or Spillovers)

As mentioned in Chapter 2, externalities or spillovers such as those caused by polluting economic activities may give a government scope to intervene and bring about a Kaldor–Hicks improvement in the economy. Within the EU and in Japan, it has been claimed that agriculture in some cases produces environmental amenities, such as desirable landscapes (Durand and Huylenbroeck, 2003). This has been used to argue that farmers are deserving of public financial support in such cases. Externalities in the supply of information may provide another reason for government interference with markets. Less information may be collected and disseminated by individuals than is collectively of value. Individual search for information may be much more risky than collective search and individuals may not be able to sell all information which they collect or discover at its full value to others. For instance, suppose that there is a piece of information or knowledge worth £10 each to 100 individuals but that it costs £12 to collect or discover it. Once one individual discovers the information, suppose that all can share it at no extra cost. Collectively the information is worth £1000 and far exceeds its cost of discovery of £12. But the information may not be able to be sold because once one individual discovers it and acts on it, all become aware of the information. In the absence of government intervention, the information is unlikely to be collected because any collector loses £2. The government may solve this problem by subsidizing the collection and provision of information (for instance, it may subsidize basic research) or by making the information the exclusive private property of the discoverer in appropriate cases so that it becomes marketable, as are certain inventions, for example, under patent law.

Pressures from Producers for Government Enforcement of Cartel-like Arrangements

Producers in most competitive markets stand to gain if they can jointly restrict their supplies to a market. By doing this, as a rule they raise the price of their product and their profits above competitive levels. Existing producers in an industry also stand to gain if they can restrict the entry of new competitors into their industry. But in industries where the number of producers is large and entry barriers are few, producers face many difficulties in jointly restricting their supplies and jointly raising barriers to entry to their industry. Difficulties (such as organizers providing benefits to free-riders) arise in forming associations of producers and in ensuring that individual producers do in fact restrict their supplies to the market. Moreover, the more successful any association or cartel is in raising profits in its industry the greater is the incentive for new firms to enter the industry, expand supplies, and push profits down again. A cartel, once formed, is threatened by conflicting interests of its own members and from potential entrants to the industry, and the threat is greater the greater its success in raising prices. Where the number of suppliers in the market is large, suppliers therefore may lobby the government to help police cartel-type rules for the industry.

The conflict between the individual interest of suppliers and their collective interest in limiting supplies to a market is illustrated in Figure 4.2. For simplicity, the short-run situation is taken in which entry into the industry is impossible. Crude oil supplies are taken as the example in this case but markets for agricultural products provide other possible illustrations, as could the supply of taxis, medical practitioners and lawyers in some countries.

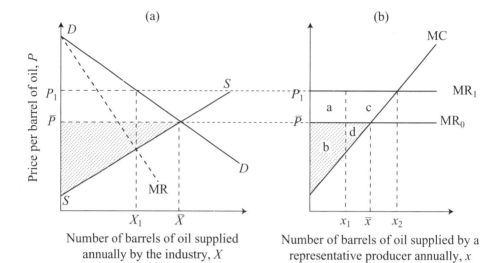

*Figure 4.2   Illustration of the incentive for individual suppliers to break an agreement limiting their
supplies even though restriction is in their collective interest. For this example, the
higher the agreed price in a cartel, such as OPEC, the greater is the incentive of
individual suppliers to undercut the price and/or exceed their supply quotas*

Let DD in Figure 4.2(a) represent the market demand curve for crude oil and the broken line
MR represent the marginal (additional) revenue obtained by the industry from selling oil.
Given the industry supply curve SS, market equilibrium *under competitive conditions* would
be established at a price of $\bar{P}$ per barrel and for an annual supply of $\bar{X}$. Assuming that curve
SS represents marginal costs in the industry, the profit obtained by all members collectively
in the industry is represented by the shaded triangle in Figure 4.2(a). The corresponding
profit for a representative supplier is as indicated by the shaded triangle in Figure 4.2(b), it
being assumed that the curve marked MC is the supplier's marginal cost curve.

Suppose that suppliers of crude oil agree to restrict their supplies of oil and reduce the
annual supply of oil by the industry from the market equilibrium one of $\bar{X}$ to X_1. In the
absence of the entry of new oil producers into the industry, the price of oil rises from $\bar{P}$
to P_1 per barrel and the profitability of oil production increases. But as can be seen from
Figure 4.2(b), each individual producer faces a dilemma. Suppose that the agreed production quota or limit for the producer considered in Figure 4.2(b) is x_1. If all abide by
their agreement collectively to restrict production to X_1, the profit of the producer considered in Figure 4.2(b) is equal to the area of the rectangle immediately surrounding a
plus the area of the quadrilateral immediately surrounding b. The producer's profits are
higher than in the absence of agreement, that is they exceed the area of the shaded triangle. But the producer has a strong incentive to break the agreement and not restrict his/her
production. If the producer expands his/her production to x_2 and the others keep to the
agreement, he/she increases his/her profit by the area of the triangle consisting of the area
of the quadrilateral immediately surrounding c plus the area of the triangle immediately
surrounding d. Indeed, no matter whether others in the industry keep or break the agreement, (for example, supply X_1 or $\bar{X}$ of X) the individual supplier has an incentive to

produce more than x_1 and thereby increase its profit. But if all producers act in this way, collective output will not be limited, all will fail to make gains, and the cartel will be ineffective. On the other hand, if all suppliers feel morally obliged to honour the agreement (a result by no means assured), profits in the industry are raised and this may encourage new firms to enter the industry. Such entry (together with the increased use and development of substitutes such as coal, wind and solar energy and nuclear fuel instead of oil) will reduce the profitability of action by existing suppliers to limit production and is likely to lead to the breakdown of the cartel.

Thus an oil cartel, such as OPEC, is under constant threat of collapse. To the extent that it raises the market price of crude above its equilibrium level, individual OPEC members have an incentive to accept a slightly lower price, and the search for new oil reserves and substitutes for oil increases in non-OPEC countries. While short-term gains may be made by the cartel, its profitability and viability may diminish with the passage of time.

Because an industry consisting of a large number of suppliers faces considerable difficulty (that is, costs in enforcing cartel-type arrangements among its members and in restricting entry of new suppliers to its industry) it is likely to seek government regulation if it aims to restrict competition or modify market behaviour. It may, for instance, aim to raise or maintain incomes of suppliers already in the industry either by limiting the number of new entrants to the industry or by restricting the supplies of existing producers. The government may restrict entry, for example, by requiring all producers to be licensed, and issue licences to existing producers but not to new firms or only to new firms in special circumstances. Production of suppliers may be limited by specifying maximum quantities to be sold or by limiting the use of productive resources in the activity, for example, the area of land that can be sown with sugar beet may be restricted. In the airline industry, national governments tend to restrict supply by licensing the routes available to international aircraft operators. In many cities, taxis have to be licensed and their number is restricted.

Stabilization of Incomes and Prices in an Industry

Another purpose of governmental regulation of a competitive industry is sometimes to stabilize incomes or prices in the industry. In particular, the prices of primary products tend to be very unstable, and governments sometimes intervene to stabilize these. One means of reducing price fluctuations is by the use of buffer stocks. During periods of low demand or those in which price would otherwise be lower than average, the government or its agency buys the commodity whose price is to be stabilized and stockpiles it. It thereby pushes up the market price of the commodity. During periods of high demand or those in which price would otherwise be higher than average, the agency releases supplies to the market from its stockpile, thereby keeping the price closer to its average level. Income stabilization schemes operated in the past in Australia for wool and wheat but with the introduction of Australia's microeconomic reforms they have been discontinued (Tisdell, 2005). Government-backed stabilization schemes may fail to stabilize incomes and may be used to subsidize incomes of producers. The need for government involvement in those activities is reduced by the presence of private futures markets. Trading in futures markets for commodities (such as on the Chicago Futures Exchange) can provide a hedge against fluctuations in commodity prices obtained by primary producers or traders in commodities generally. For example large wholesalers of Australian grains use future exchanges to cover their trading risks.

Pressure from Participants on the Competitive Side of a Market to Regulate Prices on its Less Competitive Side

Occasionally, competitive sellers or buyers in a market are faced by buyers or sellers, respectively, with market power. Consequently, competitive market participants may seek government control of the prices paid by buyers or those prices charged by sellers having market power. If those on the competitive side of a market are successful in obtaining government regulation of prices, the distribution of income moves in their favour and the allocation of resources *may be* improved in the Kaldor–Hicks sense.

If there are many suppliers selling to a single buyer (a monopsonist), the monopsonist's purchases are likely to influence the price of a traded commodity. By reducing his/her quantity of purchases, the monopsonist may lower the price of the commodity to his/her advantage. The government, by setting a suitable minimum price for the commodity, can ensure that sellers receive a higher price than otherwise and sell a greater quantity than otherwise. Similarly, if many buyers face a single seller (a monopolist) the government may be able to improve the economic position of buyers by setting an appropriate maximum price for sales of the product. In the United States, for instance, the government sets maximum prices for household gas and electricity which are supplied by private monopolies.

Having pointed out some of the reasons why the state regulates competitive markets, let us now consider specific examples of regulation of competitive product, factor and international markets. In doing so, we shall consider why there is regulation in specific cases and examine its effects, including possible undesirable side-effects.

4.3   PRICE REGULATION IN PRODUCT MARKETS: SOME EXAMPLES

The prices of some products are regulated by governments 'to improve' the distribution of income or to aid 'disadvantaged' groups. When the maximum allowable price for a commodity is less than its equilibrium market one, demand exceeds supply at this price and shortages occur. Price is not allowed to carry out the function of allocating supplies to potential buyers. Other methods of matching demand and supply are then necessary or come into play, such as the issue of rationing cards or coupons by the government, the establishment of priorities for different types of buyers by the government, or the decisions about priorities may be left to sellers and they may, for instance, adopt a first-come-first-served philosophy and/or impose purchasing limits on their customers. Black markets (illegal trading in the regulated commodity) at prices higher than the equilibrium one are also likely to spring up.

Maximum Prices – Rent of Dwellings

Given the widespread adoption of economic liberalism, it is becoming difficult to find cases in which governments prescribe maximum prices that may be charged for products

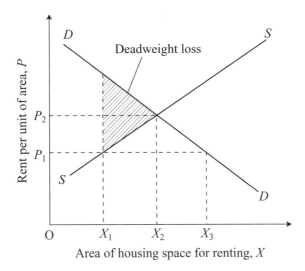

Figure 4.3   Excess demand results from decreeing a maximum price for a commodity less than its equilibrium price. Means other than price alone are then used to allocate supplies to buyers. In the above case, a rent ceiling of P₁ results in the demand for housing space for renting exceeding the available supply by X₃ − X₁. The deadweight or Kaldor–Hicks loss of rent control is shown by the hatched triangle

traded in purely competitive markets. However, this practice was common for a part of the twentieth century. For example, maximum rents of dwellings were regulated by governments in the UK and Australia for a considerable period following World War II. Such policies raise several economic issues, which can be illustrated by Figure 4.3.

Suppose that the decreed maximum rent (price) for housing space is less than the market equilibrium rent. In Figure 4.3, the market equilibrium rent is P_2, but suppose that a maximum rent of P_1 is decreed. The available space for renting falls from X_2 to X_1 and the quantity of space demanded for renting rises from X_2 to X_3. The gap between the quantity of space available at P_1 and that demanded (the excess demand) is $X_3 - X_1$. The problem, then, is how to allocate the quantity available to the individuals demanding it, since price is not permitted to perform this function. As pointed out above, ration coupons and ad hoc methods may be used for this purpose. In the latter case, it is not certain that the 'disadvantaged' will be favoured. Furthermore, there are often legal ways to circumvent the spirit of the law. For instance, the practice arose in Britain of letting houses with 'furnishings', and the rental of furnishings was adjusted upwards to allow for the shortfall on house rent which was regulated.

The purpose of setting a maximum price for a commodity may be to bring the commodity within reach or more easily within reach of families with lower incomes. But at the lower price, they may find it more difficult to obtain supplies (because total supply falls, as did housing space for renting in the above example) and it can be argued that there are more effective means of dealing with poverty, such as by cash payments. However, we cannot conclude that price controls with rationing by government are never a socially and politically acceptable solution. This depends on the relevant social welfare function. But all methods of rationing are not equally efficient in satisfying wants. Methods which do not allow trading of ration quotas or coupons by those initially allocated them are not efficient. This is clear, for example, from Figure 2.4 (an Edgeworth–Bowley box) where if individuals A and B are allocated coupons for an equal amount of petrol and bread but are not permitted to trade them, this is inferior to trading, as was discussed.

An alternative method to rent control for assisting the disadvantaged or poor with housing is for governments to supply them with a rental subsidy or rebate. This is now (2007) used in Australia to assist some recipients of social welfare payments. It has the advantage compared to rent control of not restricting the availability of dwelling space. In fact, it indirectly provides a subsidy to landlords for the provision of more housing space. Nevertheless, there are still likely to be handicapped persons who cannot afford to pay much commercial rent at all. Their assistance with housing would call for a large subsidy.

The general effect of a rental subsidy for the disadvantaged can be illustrated by Figure 4.4. There the line SS represents the supply of housing space, and in the absence of a rent subsidy, DD indicates the demand for this space. If, however, a rental subsidy is provided to the disadvantaged, this raises the demand for housing space, for example to the level indicated by line D_1D_1 in Figure 4.4. Given normally sloped demand and supply curves, the equilibrium rent and supply of housing will increase. However, the rent will normally increase by less than the rental subsidy (particularly if the proportion of tenants eligible for it is low). Hence, those tenants eligible for the rental subsidy will still benefit and the somewhat higher rents will stimulate landlords to increase housing stock. Rents rise from P_2 to P_3 and the supply of housing space increases from X_2 to X_3.

Another alternative means to assist the disadvantaged is via the provision of public housing. Usually, however, because rents for public housing are below market prices and the stock of such housing is limited in relation to demand, long waiting lists develop for those eligible for such housing. Allocation is dependent on administrators who may be in

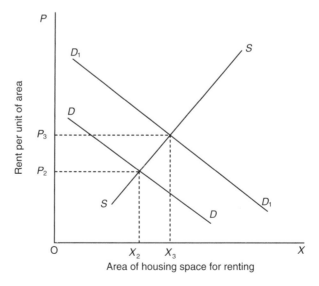

Figure 4.4   An illustration of some economic consequences of the government providing the disadvantaged with a rental subsidy

a position to favour personally some applicants relative to others. Questions inevitably arise about whether such housing is efficiently provided and managed. The social processes involved are more supply driven than demand driven. This means that the public housing provided may not be well adjusted to meeting the demands of tenants.

Public Intervention in the Provision of Education Generally

The provision of education can be entirely market determined. However, in most countries, governments play a major role in the provision of education. For example, the state often supplies education through state-owned schools and other educational institutions, regulates its content to some extent (for example, all schools, whether private or state-owned, may be required to cover a similar basic curriculum) and the purchase of education may be subsidized, or even be 'free' when supplied by state-owned institutions. Furthermore, consumers' choices about education are often limited by the state. For example, children between certain ages in most countries must attend state-approved schools.

The provision of education fulfils multiple purposes in society and the reasons for state intervention in its supply are varied and often complex. In evaluating educational policy, it is important to realize that the provision of education has both private economic benefits as well as additional social or public economic benefits. Much of the discussion about the extent to which the government should regulate and subsidize the provision of education depends on the views about the extent to which the private economic benefits of education diverge from the social economic benefits obtained from its supply. Economic analysis suggests that if the social economic benefits from education exceed its private economic benefits, there is a case for subsidizing its provision. The extent of the relevant subsidy will tend to be higher the greater is the extent to which the social benefits of education exceed the private benefits.

The social benefits of primary education are considered by many to be high relative to its private benefits and there is widespread support for the view that all should be provided with at least free primary education. A goal of the United Nations is to try to achieve universal primary education (globally) and thereby widespread literacy.

A second economic benefit of education is that it reduces social transaction costs, including the costs involved in economic transactions. It reduces the costs and widens the possibilities for communication and exchange by facilitating social networks and networking. It lowers the cost of social administration. This is especially evident with the development of computer technology and the worldwide web. As a result, computer literacy reduces the costs of social transactions, including economic transactions.

Also education helps to transmit social and cultural values and is a vehicle for socialization. This can foster social cohesiveness in society and social stability (education for citizenship). In turn, these features can have economic value. A politically unstable society is likely to be hampered in its economic progress. Therefore, one of the reasons why governments may interfere in the provision of education is to ensure that educational systems are supportive of social cohesion and not socially disruptive.

Apart from this, educational systems have many other functions. They provide knowledge which can increase enjoyment of the educated and raise their productivity. They also act as significant sorting or screening devices. For example, one of their functions is to sort the intellectually more able from the less able. How well and how economically they do this is sometimes controversial. Possibly also this sorting is not purely reflective of intellectual ability but also indicates whether the individuals sorted are able to complete required educational and other tasks punctually and discipline themselves effectively in other ways. These may be important attributes in the workplace (see Chapter 12).

Opinions differ about the extent to which higher education should be subsidized. One view is that individuals capture most of the economic benefits from their higher education and therefore, they should pay for most of its cost. On the other hand, those who favour highly subsidized tertiary education often believe that its social spillover benefits are high or that it is justified on the grounds of providing equality of opportunity to the intellectually gifted. There are often concerns that gifted children from less well-off households will be unable to obtain tertiary education unless it is free or offered at low cost. That could, however, be overcome to some extent by offering scholarships to those who are intellectually gifted, especially those from less well-off families. Possibly, the intellectually gifted will generate the largest positive external benefits for society as a result of their education.

Another policy mechanism to support tertiary education is for the government to offer loans to students to help them finance their higher education. Such a scheme operates in Australia for university fees for Australian students enrolling for the first time in undergraduate degrees (Chapman, 2001). They pay a part of the cost of their tuition. The loan is repaid after their graduation based on their income tax returns. In some countries, for example Canada, some tertiary students rely on bank or similar loans to finance their university studies. However, the capital market for financing education is imperfect and gifted students from poorer families may not want to take the risk that such a loan involves (the risk of not succeeding academically) and they or their parents may not be able to offer enough collateral or security to the potential private lenders. Private capital market failures of this type are one reason why public loans are available to cover the university fees of Australian students (also see Chapter 12).

Subsidies for University Education and Regulation of Fees

In many countries, the state is a major supplier of university facilities and regulates the fees charged by universities that are either state-owned or dependent to a significant extent on financing from the state. In countries such as Britain and Australia, domestic university undergraduate students do not pay the full cost of their tuition, and the fees that 'state' universities can charge to domestic students are regulated. A subsidy is provided to state universities to cover the differences between their expected costs of providing education and their income from student fees. Assuming that only domestic students are enrolled at universities, some of the policy issues that arise can be illustrated by Figure 4.5. In Figure 4.5, the line DD represents the demand for university places and SS indicates the supply of such places.

In the absence of state regulation, market equilibrium would be established at E with the level of fees being P_3 and with X_2 students enrolled. Suppose, however, that the state fixes the university fee at P_1 for students, and pays a public subsidy of $P_2 - P_1$ per student to universities for each student enrolled. Universities, therefore, provide X_1 places but students demand X_3. There is a shortfall in available places of $X_3 - X_1$. This has at least two

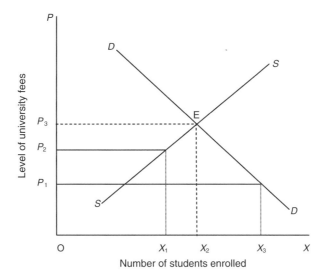

Figure 4.5   Regulation of university fees results in 'excess' demand for university places and political pressure for expansion of such places

consequences. First, the universities have to ration available places and may, for example, allocate these on the basis of school grades. Secondly, because there is a gap between the demand for and supply of available university places, this generates political pressure for the expansion of universities or for higher state subsidies for them.

Education, however, is a complex commodity. Because it serves multiple functions in society, it is doubtful whether access to it should depend merely on ability to pay. Certainly, if degrees or awards depended only or mostly on just paying for them, they would be without economic value because they would no longer signal adequate qualifications and sort individuals by intellectual merit.

In some countries, education has become an important earner of foreign exchange and universities are free to determine their own fees for foreign students. Because their net fees from foreign students are higher than from domestic students, many universities have concentrated on expanding enrolment of foreign students rather than domestic students. Whether or not domestic students are disadvantaged as a result is unclear.

Expenditure on health care, as for education, is usually a major component of outlays by most governments. Frequently, medical services are free or subsidized as in the UK, Germany and Australia. It therefore often happens that the demand for medical services exceeds their supply, and queuing for these services occurs (Hall, 2001). This has happened, for example, in Australia for hospital care in public hospitals. Such care is free or available at a low cost to patients. Because long waiting lists emerge for operations in public hospitals and public hospital beds, the admission of patients has to be prioritized. The problem can be illustrated by Figure 4.6.

In Figure 4.6 the demand for public hospital places is shown by line DD and in the short run, the supply of those places is shown by line SS. If the use of public hospitals is free, the demand for places, X_2, exceeds their supply, X_1. Excess demand is equal to $X_2 - X_1$ and mechanisms other than price have to be used to allocate the available places. In public

Demand, supply, markets and policy

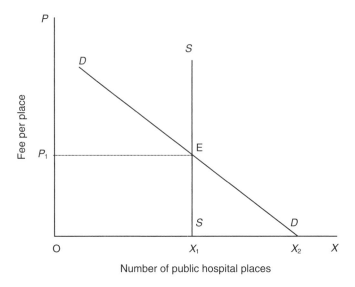

Figure 4.6   Free public hospital services typically result in excess demand for public hospital places and queuing occurs as indicated by waiting lists for admissions

hospitals, for example, those judged to be in most urgent need of hospitalization may be given priority. This usually means that some of the needy do not get hospital services or do so only after a long delay. Some may, as a result, turn to private hospitals and pay for the hospital services they need. Consequently, even though they help pay for the national health scheme, their benefits from it are limited.

A feature of the provision of free or subsidized hospital services provided by public hospitals is that the public continually criticizes the government for not providing enough of those services. Expansion in the supply of such services is usually insufficient to close the gap between demand and supply.

It is also not uncommon for governments to subsidize visits by patients to medical practitioners. In Australia, for example, the government refunds a standard fee or percentage of this to patients for a medical consultation. This is equivalent to a subsidy for medical consultation. The economic impact of such a subsidy can be examined by means of Figure 4.7.

Assume that each patient receives a flat amount as a rebate from the government for each medical consultation. In Figure 4.7 the amount is equivalent to the vertical distance between line $D_1 D_1$ and that marked DD, where the latter represents the demand for medical consultations in the absence of the government rebate, and $D_1 D_1$ is the demand when the government gives a rebate for medical consultations. If the available supply of medical consultations is as indicated by line SS, the market equilibrium shifts from E_1 to E_2 as a result of the rebate scheme. The fee for consultation rises from P_2 to P_3 and the number of consultations increases from X_1 to X_2. Note that the cost to a patient does not fall by the full amount of the rebate, which is equivalent to $P_3 - P_1$ in this case. Because the prices of consultations rise, the cost to patients of consultations after rebate only falls by $P_2 - P_1$. This is said to be the incidence of the subsidy on consumers. Some of the economic benefits of the subsidy go to medical practitioners. The incidence of the subsidy

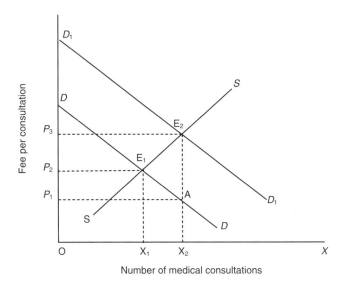

Figure 4.7   An illustration of economic consequences of public subsidies for medical consultations

from their point of view is equal to $P_3 - P_2$. The increase in income received by medical practitioners as a result of the whole scheme is equivalent to the area of a trapezium $P_2E_1E_2P_3$. This is an addition to their producers' surplus. There is also an increase in consumers' surplus for those demanding medical consultations. This is equivalent to the area of trapezium $P_1AE_1P_2$. Consumers' surplus represents the maximum amount which patients would be willing to pay over and above what they actually pay for the extra number of consultations.

Note that the incidence of the subsidy depends on the relative slope of the supply and demand curves. If the supply curve is relatively elastic compared to the demand curve, purchasers of the subsidized commodity will be the main beneficiaries. If the opposite is so, then suppliers will be the main beneficiaries. Hence, if the supply of medical consultations is relatively inelastic and less so than demand, consultation fees can rise almost to the full extent of the subsidy and are accompanied by little expansion in the supply of medical consultations. This is a distinct possibility in the short run. However, because of rising incomes of medical practitioners, demand to enter the profession is likely to rise. More individuals may want to study medicine, and doctors may want to migrate to countries with subsidized health schemes. On the other hand, medical associations are likely to do their utmost to counteract this tendency by raising requirements for entry to the profession, for example, requiring a longer period of training for new entrants and discounting foreign qualifications.

Note that while the subsidy for medical consultations in the normal case improves the economic situations of medical practitioners and those demanding economic consultations, there is an economic opportunity cost not accounted for by the above discussion of Figure 4.7. The subsidy results in the supply of medical services being expanded at the expense of alternative services such as, possibly, engineering services. An opportunity cost is involved in expanding medical services. In an economic system involving free choice, the demand curve DD in Figure 4.7 would represent the extra value that consumers place on extra medical consultations, and the line SS represents the extra or marginal costs of such consultations. The latter is an indicator of marginal opportunity cost. Thus, from a social point of view and given the existing distribution of income, the extra consumer benefits of increasing the number of consultations from X_1 to X_2 is less than the extra opportunity cost. Therefore, given the distribution of income, a social loss occurs as a result of the subsidy which can be roughly measured by the area of triangle E_1AE_2. If this is so, it raises the question of why access to medical services is widely subsidized.

One reason could be a social feeling (social value) that no individuals should be denied medical care because of inadequate income. Thus, in a sense, medical care is considered to be a merit good. Therefore, social values tend to override the individualistic values represented by the traditional economic analysis based on Figure 4.7. Nevertheless, society still needs to recognize that an opportunity cost is involved in subsidizing the supply of a merit good.

Europe's Common Market Agricultural Policy (CAP) and the Support of Farm Incomes

In many countries, governments provide economic support for agriculture, and the extent of this support is substantial in industrialized countries or communities, such as Japan, the USA and the European Union. Such support may be sustained by various factors such as political lobbying by farming groups, income redistribution considerations and a feeling that agriculture could merit special consideration because of the public good functions it provides besides supplying food and fibre. There are a variety of ways in which governments can support agriculturalists and these have differing economic consequences.

Agricultural support represents a large but declining proportion of public expenditure by the European Commission. In 2005, this support amounted to about 44 per cent of the Commission's budget. It financed Europe's Common Agricultural Policy (CAP). CAP came fully into operation in 1962 as a follow up to the Treaty of Rome (1957) which established the Common Market. The original six member states agreed in 1958 (at the Conference of Stresa) to harmonize their agricultural policies and transfer responsibilities for agricultural policies to the European Community level, subsequently the EU level. In the 1970s the budgetary cost of the CAP as well as its distortion on the world agricultural markets became of increasing concern. Consequently, CAP was reformed in stages, with 1992 being a turning point because then it was decided to shift from mere production-related support towards income support (Swinbank, 2002). Another major change was agreed to in 2003 when the income support was decoupled from production and the rural development policy was given increased emphasis. Not only was the original system increasing in cost to EU taxpayers but it resulted in large storage costs for excess agricultural production and disrupted sales on foreign markets because exports were often at prices well below the cost of production. The system relied on tariffs to exclude or reduce imports of competing agricultural products to the EU, support prices for particular agricultural products, and subsidies based on the area of land used for the cultivation of specified crops. One of the reasons initially advanced for CAP was that it would encourage Europe to become self sufficient in food production. On the other hand, it also resulted in more expensive food in the EU than would have been available with less restriction on international trade. These effects can be illustrated by economic analysis.

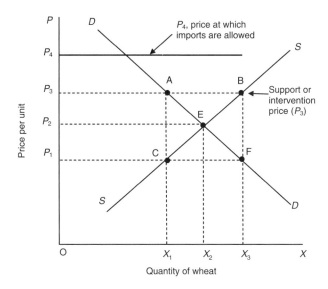

Figure 4.8   An illustration of the economic consequences of the EU's Common Agricultural Policy based on pre-1992 policies. After 2003, CAP changed substantially and there were also some reforms in the preceding decade

A *simplified* analysis of the pre-1992 CAP system (vestiges of which continued until early 2005 despite reforms) is provided by Figure 4.8. Assume that the line DD represents the demand for wheat in the EU and that the line marked SS is its supply from EU agriculture. P_3 is the internal intervention price for wheat (or support price) within the EU. European farmers are assured of this price. In the case shown in Figure 4.8, this is above the EU equilibrium wheat price of P_2. Imports of wheat to the EU are assumed to be excluded because the target price for allowing imports is supposed to be P_4.

As a result of the support or intervention price, EU farmers produce X_3 units of wheat. However, at the support price P_3, there is an excess of wheat supply in comparison to demand of $X_3 - X_1$. The EU in the past either stored the excess or sold it below cost of production abroad. EU consumers of wheat are disadvantaged by such a policy. Firstly, they are denied the possibility of importing cheaper wheat from abroad. Second, the price they must pay for wheat is higher than the free market price, P_2, which would prevail in the EU in the absence of wheat imports. EU consumers pay P_3 per unit of wheat purchased rather than P_2 per unit.

The incomes of European wheat growers increase as a result of the market intervention. Compared to the situation which would prevail in the EU in market equilibrium in the absence of wheat imports, the income of EU wheat growers rises by an amount equivalent to the area of the trapezium P_2EBP_3. On the other hand, the surplus of EU consumers of wheat falls by an amount equal to the area of P_2EAP_3. Furthermore, there is a burden on EU taxpayers if the wheat surplus is disposed of at a price below P_3. For example, if the wheat surplus is sold abroad at a price per unit of P_1, the loss which is equivalent to area of rectangle CFBA has to be met from the public finances of the EU. The economic benefits to farmers of the scheme will be greater for larger rather than for smaller EU producers of wheat, and the disbenefits to consumers higher for those more inclined to consume wheaten products.

As a result of the first major reform in 1992 of the original CAP system, high price support levels were reduced and were partly replaced by direct income support in 2003 when further fundamental changes were agreed to in the operation of the EU's CAP. While earlier reforms to CAP reduced surpluses of basic foodstuff in the EU, lowered the quantity of food in public storage (so called 'food mountains') and resulted in a decline of the total outlay of the EU on agricultural import subsidies, it was agreed in 2003 that further reforms were needed (see Leguen de La Croix, 2004, pp. 9–11). These further reforms are partly a response to pressure from the World Trade Organization (WTO) (arising from criticism of CAP by agricultural exporting countries outside the EU) and the changing relative power of political lobby groups within the EU. The political power of farm lobby groups may have declined, for instance, relative to that of social groups interested in the environment, food safety and animal welfare.

Two major changes to CAP involved (1) so-called 'decoupling' and (2) the introduction of 'cross compliance' (Leguen de La Croix, 2004, p. 7). Decoupling was intended to make public support of farm income independent of subsidies for agricultural production. Income support is paid as a lump sum single farm payment. This payment, however, can be reduced if a farm fails to comply with cross compliance regulations concerning animal welfare, nature and environmental protection, food quality requirements and so on. By early 2007, all states in the EU had adopted the changed agricultural policies, the operation of which will continue until 2013 with a mid-term review in 2008.

Aspects of the new policies which also support rural development generally and the multifunctionality of agriculture are discussed for example, by Durand and Van Huylenbroeck (2003) and Van Huylenbroeck et al. (1999). The rationale behind cross compliance can be illustrated by Figure 4.9 which focuses on agriculture and environmental quality. The cross compliance component of the new CAP is intended to address perceived market failures.

Agricultural production results both in environmental amenities (pleasant landscapes in some cases) and environmental disamenities, such as loss of biodiversity and pollution. These involve economic externalities or spillovers and farmers have no private economic incentive to take them into account in their decision-making. For example, the curve ABCDF in Figure 4.9 might represent the relationship between agricultural production and an index of environmental quality. This indicates that some growth in agricultural production adds to environmental amenity (expansion from zero to X_1) but that further expansion in agricultural production is at the expense of environmental quality. If both environmental quality and agricultural production are desired commodities, a scale of agricultural production of at least X_1 is socially desirable. However, X_3 of agricultural output may, for example, be produced if farmers do not take into account environmental externalities. This level of agricultural production is likely to be greater than the social optimum. For example, given the socially desired trade-off between environmental quality and agricultural production, the highest attainable social iso-welfare curve might be as indicated by W_1W_1. This implies that a level of agricultural production of X_2 rather than X_3 is socially optimal.

It should, nevertheless, be borne in mind that Figure 4.9 involves considerable simplification. It does not, for example, consider alternative techniques of agricultural

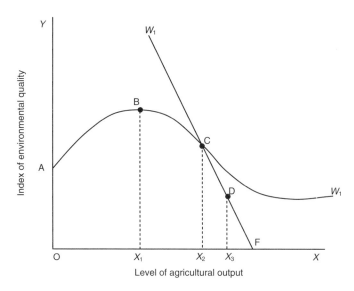

Figure 4.9   *A hypothetical relationship between environmental quality and the level of agricultural output given the amount of resources available in agriculture. Adjustments in the level of agriculture production (and in techniques used in agriculture) may be required to bring about a socially acceptable outcome. The reforms of 2003 to the Common Agricultural Policy were intended to take this into account*

production. The socially optimal outcome is likely to require some control of the techniques used in agricultural production because different techniques usually generate differences in external effects. Techniques used may need to be regulated as well as the level of agricultural production. Consequently, the public regulation of agriculture could become quite complex. The economic costs (transaction costs) involved in the public administration of such complex policies would need to be taken into account in assessing their social desirability. There is also a danger that agriculture's environmental benefits and costs may not be carefully measured and that the perception of these could be subject to possibly undesirable political influences.

Note that although income support for European farmers by means of public financial transfers has been decoupled from the levels of agricultural production, barriers to agricultural imports to the EU remain. These have the same types of consequences as those analysed later using Figure 4.14. European agriculture is not yet fully exposed to global free market competition. Furthermore, even the present decoupled income support for farmers is likely to maintain the *long-run* supply of agricultural products in aggregate in the EU by retarding the exit of farmers from agriculture. From this viewpoint, the new CAP is not market neutral but creates a distortion in favour of agriculture and rural exports. Therefore, the price mechanism is unable to function perfectly in re-allocating resources. It is anticipated nevertheless, that in the period 2007–2013, real financial support for individual farmers will decline in the EU as support for farmers in new member states of the EU increases (Leguen de La Croix, 2004, p. 29). While the new CAP still involves shortcomings in terms of scarcity minimization, it involves less of an economic burden on non-farm entities (such as intermediate sectors and consumers) in the

EU than its predecessors. It is also possible that the new CAP's propensity to increase or maintain agricultural output could be (is) reduced by its cross compliance rules. However, this may not occur to such an extent as to completely offset its positive impact on the level of the EU's agricultural production.

4.4 PRICE REGULATION IN FACTOR MARKETS: SOME EXAMPLES

Regulation of prices of the factors of production is not uncommon and the resources of labour and capital appear to be more often the subject of such regulation than land. However, this does not imply that there are no regulations affecting the market for land. In fact there are many regulations, for instance the zoning of the use of land in urban areas, affecting the price of land.

Minimum Wage Rates

Minimum wage rates are set by regulatory bodies in some countries. When the minimum wage rate for a particular type of labour *is less than* the equilibrium wage rate and perfect competition occurs, the price control has no effect on the level of employment of this type of labour and wages obtained. But if there is some ignorance among labourers, the regulation could reduce the likelihood of a labourer receiving a wage well below the equilibrium rate. In the example shown in Figure 4.10, a minimum wage rate of w_1 (since it is less than the equilibrium wage rate) does not affect the amount of employment of women.

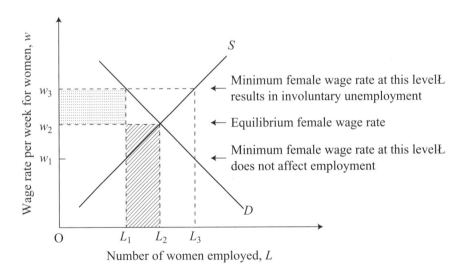

Figure 4.10   *A minimum wage rate in excess of the equilibrium wage rate leads to involuntary unemployment if markets are competitive. In this case, a minimum wage rate of w_3 for women results in the involuntary unemployment of $L_3 - L_1$ of women and in fewer women (L_1) being employed than in the absence of intervention (L_2)*

But the minimum wage rate may be set by a wage-regulating authority at a level in excess of the equilibrium rate in an effort on income distributional grounds to assist those who would normally earn lower pay, or a strong trade union may be able to negotiate an above-equilibrium award in the industry with the same aim in mind and the possible additional aim of increasing the total wage bill. If there is monopsony, oligopsony, or collusion between hirers of labour, this policy on wage regulation *can* be effective in achieving its objectives and in raising total employment of the group concerned. But if the hiring side of the labour market is competitive, the policy has the adverse side-effect of reducing employment in the industry or among the group 'protected' by such wages. As for the total wage bill, this will fall if wage rates are at levels on the elastic (upper) portion of the demand curve for labour and will only go up if wages are in the region of the inelastic (lower) portion of the demand curve.

These effects can be illustrated by means of Figure 4.10, which considers the employment of women. The argument might apply where the rule of equal pay for women would result in a wage rate for women above the equilibrium rate for the employment of women. In the example shown in Figure 4.10, the fixing of a minimum weekly wage rate for women of w_3 (that is a wage rate in excess of the equilibrium level) leads to a fall in the employment of women in comparison to the unregulated position. This fall is equal to $L_2 - L_1$. If employment is an important consideration, the regulation may be regarded as injurious to the interests of women. Also at the minimum wage rate of w_3, involuntary unemployment occurs among women in the sense that more women wish to work, L_3, than can find employment, L_1. At a wage rate of w_3, the difference between the number of women seeking work and those able to find work is $L_3 - L_1$. Furthermore, in this case, the regulation reduces the total wage bill paid to women because the loss shown by the hatched area exceeds the gain as shown by the flecked area. This happens because wage rates are on an elastic part of the demand curve for the employment of women.

Regulated Rates of Interest, Dividends and Profits

The rates of interest on loans are sometimes controlled by governments. In some countries, the government specifies a lower than normal maximum rate of interest for loans for particular purposes. Regulations may result in interest rates on loans for the purchase of first homes being at a maximum rate below the normal and loans for rural investment may be available at reduced interest rates. Interference of this type may stem from income redistribution considerations (for example, the desire to assist families to purchase a first home) and from political considerations such as the desire to win votes in rural seats. The effect of such regulations is likely to reduce the supply of funds for the purposes in question and make it necessary to ration the available supply by some means other than price.

This is illustrated in Figure 4.11. Given the supply and demand curves indicated there, the equilibrium rate of interest is r_2 and the equilibrium quantity of loanable funds supplied and demanded is K_2. Suppose that the maximum rate of interest on funds is set at r_1, that is at a level below the equilibrium rate. The effect is to reduce the available quantity of loanable funds to K_1 and increase the demand for funds to K_3. Consequently, the demand for funds exceeds the supply of funds by $K_3 - K_1$. Thus, for instance, first-time house buyers whom it is intended should be assisted by such policies may find that fewer funds are available to them and there is keener competition for available funds. Some means other

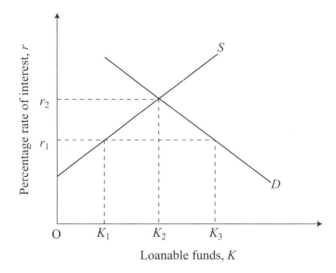

Figure 4.11   Controls on the maximum rate of interest lead to a shortage of available funds if the maximum rate is less than the equilibrium one. In this case, a ceiling on the rate of interest r_1 of results in an excess demand for funds of $K_3 - K_1$ and in less loanable funds being supplied than in a free market

than the rate of interest must be used to distribute the relatively limited funds. In these circumstances, the government may provide lending institutions with guidelines or priorities to be followed in their lending. For instance, borrowers may be expected to find a higher proportion of a house's price from their own savings and loans may not be available on established houses. Consequently, funds will not be allocated in the most efficient manner if this is determined by willingness to pay, and income distribution effects can be the opposite to those intended. The wealthier members of the community (especially if collateral and deposits are a consideration) may be favoured in the queue for funds.

In a competitive world, controls on the maximum level of dividends payable can reduce the amount of funds supplied by investors to companies and reduce capital formation, but the position is complex. If high dividends are a consequence of unappropriated rents (low royalties being paid to the government, for example, for the use of minerals), controls on dividends up to a point may not reduce the available supply of risk capital. The complexity of the situation is clear from the fact that less-developed countries tend to treat foreign direct investment in different ways. Some limit the remission of profits and dividends to parent companies (this is less common than in the past) and others provide for tax concessions and in effect subsidize dividends in order to attract foreign capital.

4.5 PRICE REGULATION IN INTERNATIONAL MARKETS: SOME EXAMPLES

International markets for goods, for factors of production, and for currencies are subject to a number of restrictions. In many countries, some imported goods are subject to tariffs (taxes) or to quotas limiting their quantity. International movements of labour are

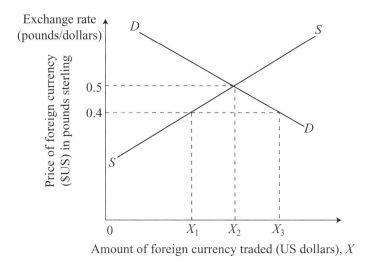

*Figure 4.12   A foreign exchange market in which equilibrium occurs when the US dollar costs 50p.
Suppose, however, that the Bank of England fixes the exchange rate at 40p to the
dollar. The pound is then overvalued in relation to the dollar and the demand for dollars
for foreign exchange purposes exceeds their supply by $X_3 - X_1$. Some mechanism
(such as priorities for different purposes for which foreign exchange is required) is
needed to ration out the reduced supply of dollars*

restricted by the immigration requirements of many countries. Some countries regulate
dealings in foreign currencies, usually in order to maintain a more stable exchange rate
between the domestic currency and foreign currencies, but this has become less common
now with the widespread introduction of policies that favour market liberalism.

Fixed Exchange Rates

Consider the regulation of foreign exchange markets using Figure 4.12 for illustrative purposes. This figure shows the exchange market for pounds sterling and a foreign currency,
say US dollars, where *DD* indicates the demand for dollars by those wishing to exchange
pounds sterling for dollars and *SS* indicates the supply of dollars by those wishing to
obtain pounds sterling in return for dollars. The UK's demand for US dollars reflects the
UK's demand for US imports (these have to be paid for in dollars), the demands of
holders of sterling for US dollars for investing in the US and their desire to have US
dollars for other purposes such as currency speculation. The supply of US dollars in relation to pounds sterling depends on the demand of Americans for imports from the UK,
their desire to invest in the UK and to have pounds sterling for other purposes such as
currency speculation. The equilibrium rate of exchange in this case is 50p to the dollar.
At this rate of exchange, the balance of payments of the United Kingdom and the United
States is in equilibrium. But suppose that the UK government controls the exchange of
pounds sterling for dollars and fixes an exchange rate of 40p to the dollar. (One of the
reasons for regulating or fixing the exchange rate may be to reduce the uncertainty of firms
and individuals engaging in international trade. For instance, if a UK exporter is to be

paid by a US importer at an agreed dollar price on delivery of the exports, the UK exporter runs the risk if the exchange rate is floating that the value of the pound will appreciate so that he/she receives a lower payment after converting his/her dollar receipts in pounds than originally expected.) At this exchange rate of 40p to the dollar, the demand for dollars exceeds their supply by $X_3 - X_1$. The limited supply of dollars (to be exchanged for sterling) may be rationed and a black market may arise in the exchange of dollars. In some less-developed countries, regulation of exchange rates, in the past, was accompanied by rationing of available foreign currencies, foreign exchange black markets, and illegal entry of foreign currency.

   Countries which attempt to maintain a fixed exchange rate or a relatively fixed exchange rate frequently make use of a buffer stock type of approach to maintain exchange price stability. This approach can be illustrated by the example given in Figure 4.13. Suppose that fluctuations in the exchange rate between pounds sterling and US dollars are due to variations in the demand for dollars and for half of the time the demand is as indicated by D_1D_1 and for the remainder of the time as indicated by D_2D_2. In the absence of regulation, the exchange rate fluctuates between P_1 and P_3. Suppose now that the UK government sets the exchange rate at P_2 and the central bank (the Bank of England) or its agents are in charge of all foreign currency transactions involving sterling. The central bank adds $X_2 - X_0$ dollars to its reserves when demand is D_1D_1 and draws an equal amount from reserves, $X_4 - X_2$, when demand is high. It is therefore possible for the central bank to use its reserves, provided that low and high levels of demand occur in suitable sequence, to stabilize the exchange rate. But there is no guarantee that the sequence of demand variations will be satisfactory in practice. Furthermore, levels of demand and supply curves may alter unpredictably and make stabilization difficult to achieve because reserves are insufficient to maintain the rate at which the exchange rate is pegged. This can

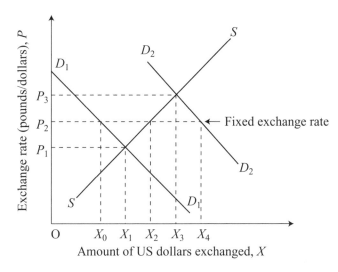

Figure 4.13   *Stabilization of the exchange rate by the use of (buffer stock) reserves of foreign currency. In this case, a buffer stock system enables the exchange rate to be stabilized at the fixed exchange rate of* P_2. *In the absence of intervention the exchange rate fluctuates between* P_1 *and* P_3

lead to periodic crises of confidence and speculation about the exchange rate, thus creating considerable uncertainty if a change in the pegged rate of exchange appears imminent. It has been suggested that this type of uncertainty might be more damaging to trade than that which occurs when exchange rates are flexible because, under a flexible exchange rate scheme, exchange rates may be continually adjusted by small amounts.

Most governments operated fixed or pegged exchange rates from 1944 to the early 1970s under the Bretton Woods system. Subsequently, managed flexible exchange rates were the rule for most countries. Exchange rates were managed only to the extent that central banks intervened to smooth out what appeared to be very short-term gyrations in the rates of exchange. Otherwise, rates were free to find their own level as a result of the operation of market forces. Nowadays, floating or flexible exchange rates are more common. China, however, and a few other countries still retain a fixed exchange rate system.

Tariffs and Quotas on Imports

Consider now the effects of restrictions on imports of goods by means of tariffs or quotas. These may be imposed by the government in an attempt to maintain domestic employment, to improve the profitability of the operations of domestic producers, and to raise revenue for the government's use. Take yarn as an example and suppose that the domestic demand for yarn is as indicated by $D_H D_H$ in Figure 4.14 and that the domestic supply

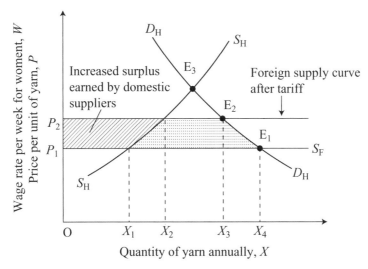

Figure 4.14   An example of the effect of a tariff on imports, assuming perfect competition in the domestic industry. The tariff raises the price of yarn in the domestic market, expands its local production, reduces imports, and increases the surplus earned by domestic suppliers. In contrast, as discussed below, domestic production may fall when a tariff or import quota is imposed if the domestic industry is imperfectly *competitive. In the above case, imports fall after imposition of the tariff by $(X_2 - X_1) + (X_4 - X_3)$, local production rises by $X_2 - X_1$, and the surplus of domestic suppliers rises by the hatched area. But if this gain in producers' surplus is offset against the loss in consumers' surplus, the net social loss (in the Kaldor–Hicks sense) from the imposition of the tariff amounts to the flecked area*

is as indicated by $S_H S_H$. In the absence of international trade, the domestic price of yarn and the equilibrium quantity traded correspond to E_3, assuming that the market for yarn is perfectly competitive. But suppose that yarn can be imported at a price of P_1 per unit and that the supply from abroad is perfectly elastic as indicated by S_F. Under free-trade conditions the price of yarn in the domestic economy falls to P_1 so that X_1 of yarn is produced at home, and $X_4 - X_1$ is imported. Suppose now that the domestic government imposes a tariff of $P_2 - P_1$ upon each unit of yarn imported in order to protect local yarn producers and increase domestic employment in yarn production. This tariff alters the equilibrium trading conditions in the domestic market from E_1 to E_2. Imports of yarn fall from $X_4 - X_1$ to $X_3 - X_2$, domestic production rises by $X_2 - X_1$, and employment in yarn production increases. The profits of firms producing yarn in the domestic economy rise by the equivalent of the hatched area in Figure 4.14, and the government raises $(P_2 - P_1)$ $(X_3 - X_2)$ in revenue from the tariff. Consumers are worse off as a result of the tariff. The price of yarn is raised and the consumption of yarn falls. But domestic producers of yarn, suppliers of capital and labour for yarn production, benefit because protection from imports results in greater profits, increased domestic employment, and possibly higher wages for them. Domestic firms producing yarn may therefore lobby for protection. They are likely to be supported by yarn labour unions in this lobbying since the tariff results in greater employment of yarn workers and could raise the wage obtained by them. Interested parties, however, will need to weigh the costs of lobbying against its expected benefits to them.

Nevertheless, it should be noted that the loss in consumers' surplus as a result of imposition of the tariff (equal to the hatched plus the flecked area in Figure 4.14) exceeds the gain in the surplus of domestic producers (the hatched area) by the flecked area. This means that consumers could in principle bribe producers not to press for the tariff by paying them an amount equal to the hatched area in Figure 4.12 and be better off than without the tariff. But such bribes cannot be organized because there are large numbers of consumers and each one has an incentive to free-ride. Indeed, most consumers may fail to perceive that the tariff exists and that they are damaged by it. Each consumer might lose only a small amount of consumers' surplus (for example £1 annually) so it may not pay an individual (given that search is not costless) to search for the determinants of the price of yarn even though, if there are 50 million consumers, the total loss in consumers' surplus is £50 million annually.

The above are the usual effects of a tariff in competitive markets. In markets where competition is *imperfect*, a tariff can lead to a reduction in local production and employment rather than a rise as in the competitive case because producers take advantage of their enhanced monopoly position to restrict supplies. Nevertheless, in this case, as the result of the imposition of a tariff, the profits and prices of local producers of the protected product are still likely to rise and imports can be expected to fall if foreign supply is not perfectly inelastic.

Imperfect Competition Modifies Predictions about the Effects of Tariffs

Let us be more specific about the type of modifications that must be made to predictions about the effects of tariffs when imperfect competition rather than perfect competition exists. Consider the position assuming a *domestic* monopoly in the supply of a product X.

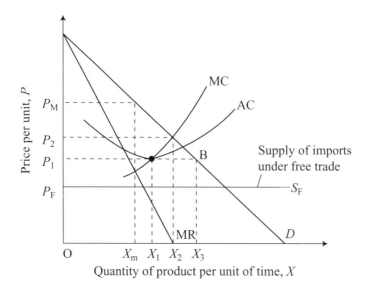

Figure 4.15   A diagram to illustrate the impact on the behaviour of a domestic monopolist of tariffs on the import of competitive products. Depending upon the circumstances discussed above, the tariff can lead either to an increase or a decrease in the monopolist's level of output whereas under perfect competition an increase in the tariff on a product can normally be expected to result in an increase in its level of domestic production

Suppose that the demand, marginal revenue, average costs, and marginal costs faced by the monopolists are as shown by the appropriately identified curves in Figure 4.15. In this figure the supply curve of product X from abroad is represented by the horizontal curve marked S_F.

The domestic monopolist clearly needs a minimum tariff on imports of X of $T_1 = P_1 - P_F$ if the firm is to survive. At this level of tariff, the price of X is P_1 and the monopolist supplies X_1 to the domestic market and $X_3 - X_1$ is imported because the demand curve faced by the monopolist after the tariff is P_1BD. If a higher tariff is imposed but which is still less than $T_2 = P_2 - P_F$ (where P_2 corresponds to the intersection point of the monopolist's marginal cost of production curve and the domestic demand curve for X), the monopolist's output and employment rise. But if a still higher tariff is imposed, the monopolist takes advantage of his/her protection from imports to raise his/her profit by reducing his/her output and employment and increasing the scarcity of his/her product. The domestic monopolist finds that this policy increases his/her profit and thus, in this region, a higher rate of tariff reduces domestic output and employment in producing X. This pattern holds until the tariff becomes high enough to enable the monopolist to charge the maximum monopoly price P_M without fear of competition from imports. Should the tariff exceed this level, $T_M = P_M - P_F$, the monopolist will not decrease the firm's output and employment further, but leaves these unchanged.

The relationship between output and employment, the level of imports, and the profits earned by the domestic monopolist are indicated in Figure 4.16. This shows that both the domestic monopolist and the workers (or their union) in industry X have a common interest (as in the perfectly competitive case) in raising the tariff to level T_2, but (unlike the

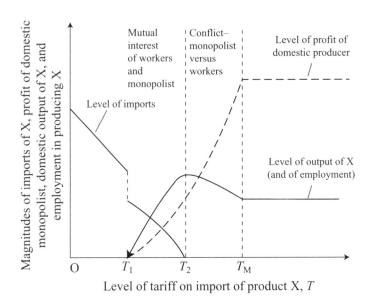

Figure 4.16   Relationship between various economic magnitudes and the level of a tariff on a product, assuming that domestic supply of the product is in the hands of a monopoly. Specifically, assuming the monopoly-type situation shown in Figure 4.16, general relationships for the following are shown as a function of the level of tariff imposed on the imports of X: the level of imports of X, the profit of the domestic monopolist, the quantity of output of X produced by the monopolist, and the level of employment in the production of X

perfectly competitive case) a higher rate of tariff (one between T_2 and T_M) is damaging to the interest of workers in X in terms of their level of employment and possibly level of wages, even though it improves the level of profit earned by the monopolist. Workers in a particular industry do not always benefit from protection of that industry by a tariff, and employment can sometimes be increased by lowering tariffs.

Import Quotas

An import quota can be used to achieve similar effects to a tariff. In the competitive example shown in Figure 4.14, a quota limiting the annual import of yarn to $X_3 - X_2$ units would result in the equilibrium trading conditions being achieved which correspond to E_2. The supply curve of yarn for the domestic economy after the imposition of the quota is equal to S_H plus the import quota at prices equal to or above P_1. At prices below P_1, no yarn is imported and the supply curve from domestic production alone applies. In contrast to a tariff, however, import quotas yield no revenue to the government unless they are auctioned to importers. In the absence of auctioning, some method of rationing quotas among importers is needed. Those lucky enough to obtain a quota obtain a windfall gain. Together importers benefit in the above example by increased profit of $(P_2 - P_1)(X_3 - X_2)$ if quotas are not auctioned. Income is therefore not only redistributed in favour of domestic producers of yarn but also in favour of merchants importing yarn.

4.6 CONCLUDING COMMENTS

Regulation of competitive markets (product, factor and international markets) still occurs but is less frequent than it used to be because market-based economic liberalism is now more widely accepted as being desirable than in the decades following World War II. Competitive markets are regulated for varied reasons and by diverse means. But policy-makers do not always obtain the results that they aim for through regulation, and their policies can give rise to undesirable (and in some cases unforeseen) side-effects, such as those pointed out in this chapter. The chapter also underlines the point that it is necessary to pay considerable attention to political self-interest as a factor influencing the extent and type of regulation of competitive industries (see Chapter 14).

READING* AND REFERENCES

Anon (no date), 'Common Agricultural Policy', *Wikipedia, the free encyclopedia*, http://en.wikipedia.org/wiki/Common_Agricultural_Policy. Accessed 19/12/2006.
Chapman, B. (2001), 'Australian higher education financing: issues for reform', *Australian Economic Review*, **34**, 195–204.
*Cohen, S.I. (2001), *Microeconomic Policy*, chapters 2, 4 and 5, London and New York: Routledge.
*Durand, G. and G. Van Huylenbroeck (2003), 'Multifunctionality and rural development: a general framework', in G. Van Huylenbroeck and G. Durand (eds), *Multifunctional Agriculture: A New Paradigm for European Agriculture and Rural Development*, Aldershot, UK and Burlington VT, USA: Ashgate Publishing, pp. 1–16.
Edwards, G. (2003), 'The story of deregulation in the dairy industry', *Australian Journal of Agricultural and Resource Economics*, **47**, 75–98.
*Gravelle, H. and R. Rees (2004), *Microeconomics*, 3rd edn, chapter 14, Harlow, UK: Prentice Hall.
Hall, J. (2001), 'Health, healthcare and social welfare', *Australian Economic Review*, **34**, 320–31.
King, S.P. (1997), 'National competition policy', *Australian Economic Review*, **34**, 320–31.
*Leguen de La Croix, E. (2004), *The Common Agricultural Policy Explained*, Brussels: European Commission, see also: http://ec.europe.eu/agriculture/publi/capexplained/cap_nl.pdf.
*Lipsey, R.G. and K.A. Chrystal (2004), *Economics*, 10th edn, chapters 19–20, Oxford: Oxford University Press.
*Mansfield, E. and G. Yoho (2004), *Microeconomics*, 11th edn, chapters 8–9, New York: Norton.
Smith, R.L. (2006), 'Australian grocery industry: A competition perspective', *Australian Journal of Agricultural Economics*, **50**, 33–50.
Swinbank, A. (2002), 'The Common Agricultural Policy', in J. Gower (ed.), *The European Union Handbook*, 2nd edn, London and Chicago: Fitzroy Dearborn, pp. 164–79.
Tisdell, C.A. (2005), 'Australia's economic policies in an era of globalization', in C. Tisdell (ed.), *Globalisation and World Economic Policies*, New Delhi: Serials Publication, pp. 151–66.
Van Huylenbroeck, G., A. Coppens and M. Whitby (1999), 'Introduction to research on Countryside Stewardship Politics', in G. Van Huylenbroeck and M. Whitby (eds), *Countryside Stewardship: Farmers Policies and Markets*, Amsterdam: Pergamon, pp. 1–19.

QUESTIONS FOR REVIEW AND DISCUSSION

1. Outline two broad approaches to defining the state of competition in an industry. Distinguish between monopoly and perfect competition in terms of stock characteristics.

2. 'It seems surprising that there should be so much state regulation of competitive markets considering that perfectly competitive markets are often claimed to allocate resources efficiently.' Discuss, and give general reasons why the state has intervened in competitive markets and outline general ways in which it has intervened.

3. Illustrate the type of difficulties which a cartel (such as OPEC) faces both from its members and from external sources.

4. Should the government supply housing for the poor, homeless and the disadvantaged? What problems can arise if this housing is made available at very low rent? Is it more desirable for the state to provide this housing rather than subsidize the rent of needy tenants? If the rent of needy tenants is subsidized, will the rent paid by these tenants fall after deducting the subsidy by the full amount of the subsidy?

5. Why does the state interfere in the provision of education when it could be left entirely to market forces?

6. Do you agree with the view that while basic education should be free, students should pay for higher education? What market failures might occur if students have to pay for higher education? How might these economic failures be reduced?

7. Discuss the case for and against 'free' hospital services. Using supply and demand analysis and assuming that the government finances hospitals, show how demand for hospital services could well exceed their supply and consider the difficulties that then arise in allocating this limited supply between consumers.

8. What effect is the subsidization of fees for medical consultations likely to have on the supply of those services? To what extent are patients and medical practitioners likely to benefit from such a subsidy?

9. The Common Agricultural Policy (CAP) has been a burden on EU food consumers and on EU taxpayers. Explain. Why has the policy been reformed? Do you think the reforms are desirable? Why?

10. 'Minimum wage rates may fail to assist those they are intended to help.' Illustrate, but also consider cases in which these policies been assist employees, for instance, where information is imperfect or monopsony exists.

11. Explain how a fixed international exchange rate may be maintained and indicate circumstances in which such a scheme will fail.

12. Consider the effects on domestic supplies, profits, imports and prices of a commodity of the imposition of a tariff on imports, assuming that the domestic industry is perfectly competitive in structure. Show that a Kaldor–Hicks loss occurs. What effect may the tariff have on other industries? Repeat this exercise for an import quota. Does a quota differ in its effects from a tariff?

13. 'When a domestic industry is imperfectly competitive some of the general economic effects of a tariff (or of an import quota) are the same as under perfectly competitive conditions, but other effects differ.' Explain.

5. Consumers and policy

5.1 INTRODUCTION

Consumer demand plays both an important normative and positive role in policy-making. As pointed out in Chapters 2 and 4, it is important in determining the welfare gains from economic activity (for example, for a Paretian optimum, there should be an optimal conformance between what consumers want and the composition of production) and, indeed, economists since Adam Smith have tended to stress the point that consumption is the end-purpose of all production. Economic systems are often judged by how well they meet the demands of consumers.

But demand relationships are important *positive* components of many policy decisions. If a tax or import tariff, for instance, is to be imposed on a particular commodity the government will need to know the demand function for that commodity (and the supply function) if it wishes to predict the effect of the tax on the quantity consumed of the commodity and aims to estimate its tax revenue. A large firm which hopes to influence the sales of its products needs to be familiar with the factors determining this demand. A government which engages in 'international resource diplomacy' or adopts policies for the conservation of resources needs to take account of demand relationships.

Both positive and normative aspects of demand theory are considered in this chapter. The main positive areas covered are the testing and predictive accuracy of demand theories and elasticities of demand with policy applications. The normative parts of the chapter deal with consumer welfare and sovereignty in terms of traditional and new theories, and with market failure, for instance, as a result of imperfect information on the part of the consumer and the need or otherwise for consumer protection.

5.2 PREDICTIVE ACCURACY AND TESTING OF DEMAND THEORY

Traditionally economic theory has stressed the influence of prices and incomes on the demand for commodities. In so doing, economists have not denied that other influences such as social interdependence, tastes, advertising and ignorance can be of importance but have felt the study of these forces might more appropriately be undertaken by other academic disciplines such as psychology and sociology. But carried to extremes, such rigid demarcations are of limited value when policies are being formulated.

Development of Demand Theory

The introduction of the concept of a demand curve for a commodity, implanted in the mainstream of economic thought by Alfred Marshall (1890) in the nineteenth century, helped to specify the relationship between the quantity demanded of a commodity and its price with considerable accuracy and improved the predictive potential of economic theory. One main principle emerged: the quantity demanded of a commodity usually increases as its price is lowered, other things held constant. In other words, the demand curve for a commodity is normally downward sloping when expressed as a function of the price of the commodity. Marshall assumed that *consumers maximize their utility* in purchasing commodities with their limited incomes and argued that consumers eventually obtain *diminishing marginal utility* if they increase their consumption of any commodity. It is basically diminishing marginal utility which is the prime cause of downward sloping demand curves. In the twentieth century, John Hicks (1946), using indifference curve analysis, increased the precision of this theory, following in the wake of advances by a number of theoreticians. The use of indifference curves strengthened the basic theory since they made it unnecessary to assume cardinal (measurable) utility as in the Marshallian case. Hicks' theory of demand still concentrates on the influence of price on the quantity demanded of a commodity but the effect of a price change is divided into two parts: an income effect and a substitution effect.

The income effect, which was ignored in Marshall's analysis, occurs because a fall in the price of a commodity increases the real income of the consumer and the substitution effect arises because a fall in the price of a commodity reduces the commodity's price relative to the price of other commodities. The substitution effect always increases (other than in exceptional circumstances when it is zero) the quantity demanded of a commodity whose price has fallen, all other things constant. This effect always tends to make for a downward sloping demand curve. The income effect may reinforce the substitution effect, so ensuring a downward sloping demand curve. It does so (and this is considered to be the *normal* case) if the consumption of the commodity rises with income, other factors constant. On the other hand, if the consumption of the commodity falls with increased income (if the commodity is *inferior*), the income effect operates against the substitution effect (the income effect tends to reduce the quantity demanded of the commodity subject to the decrease in price), but *only in exceptional cases* is it likely to more than counteract the substitution effect and result in a demand curve which is upward sloping over at least a part of its range. When this exceptional case occurs, the good is said to be a Giffen good (Hicks, 1946). Possibly potatoes and sausages are two such goods in western countries and rice is such a commodity in Asia.

Indifference Curves, Substitution and Income Effects: a Policy Application

Consider a possible application of Hicks' theory to population policy. A government wishes to stimulate population growth and to do so intends to pay parents a subsidy or allowance which rises with the number of their children. Will this subsidy lead to families of greater size? This can be analysed using Figure 5.1. The indifference curves in Figure 5.1 (indicated in the usual way) represent the preferences of a couple for income for themselves and for numbers of children.

But children are not costless. For simplicity assume that the price line or trade-off between the income enjoyed by the couple and the number of their children is linear. Let

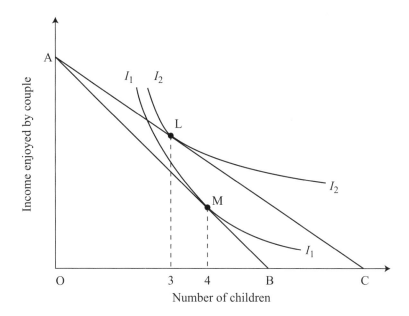

Figure 5.1   The payment of a bonus to parents rising with the number of their children may reduce rather than increase the size of families. In this case, the negative income effect of the subsidy more than offsets the substitution effect

us suppose that given their income possibilities it is AB. Then the optimal number of children for this couple is four and they achieve equilibrium at position M.

Now consider the effect of a government subsidy on the number of children which swings the price line around to AC. The couple reach a new equilibrium at position L and their optimal number of children falls to three. The subsidy therefore reduces population growth, if this couple is typical, rather than increases it as hoped. Children are 'inferior goods' in this case; fewer are wanted as income rises, and the income effect more than counteracts the substitution effect.

On the other hand, the income effect of the subsidy may reinforce the substitution effect. Independent evidence might indicate that in the country concerned the number of children in families tends to rise with the income of households. If this is so, Hicks' theory predicts that the subsidy will be effective in raising the size of the family. In this case, the income effect and the substitution effect operate in the same direction and reinforce one another.

If evidence suggests that family size falls with income, further information will be needed to predict the effect of the family allowance or subsidy. Only if the negative income effect is large enough, relative to the substitution effect, will family size fall rather than increase after the introduction of a subsidy based on the number of children. Hicks' approach pinpoints the information needed for greater accuracy in prediction, that is the required evidence on the magnitudes of the income effect and the substitution effect.

Limitations of Hick's Theory, Social Effects on Demand, Imperfect Knowledge

But even Hicks' advanced theory does not account for all the influences on demand which may need to be taken into account for predictive purposes in different circumstances. Social influences such as the bandwagon effect, snob effect, and Veblen effect are not, for example, taken into account. When the bandwagon effect applies to a commodity, the quantity of the commodity purchased by each consumer rises, other things being equal, as more of it is purchased by others. The opposite is the case for the snob effect. The possibility also cannot be ignored that the price paid for a commodity is sometimes of social significance. The price paid may act as a signal to others, for instance the price paid for perfume. When the apparent price paid impresses others and the purchaser deems this consequence to be important, the Veblen effect is said to operate, and this effect may cause a demand curve to slope upwards over a range. In some circumstances, as pointed out by Gabor (1977), consumers take the price of a product as an indicator of its quality, that is in a world of imperfect information consumers may use price as a signal of higher quality.

Lancaster – Characteristics and Demand

Lancaster (1966) believes that traditional demand theory, by concentrating on the demand for commodities per se, has less predictive ability than can be achieved by considering the demand for commodities in terms of the characteristics inherent in them. He developed a theory based upon the demand for characteristics or attributes of commodities. While his theory is not without limitations (the availability of a characteristic is assumed to be *proportional* to the quantity of a product and relevant characteristics can be difficult to identify) it can be used to predict the likely demand for new products combining known characteristics. For instance, an attempt has been made to use it to predict the demand for characteristics in new cars such as fuel economy, roominess and power, and thus the overall demand for cars containing these characteristics in different degrees.

Price is only one of the Factors Influencing Demand

In all the above-mentioned theories, the price of a commodity is considered to be an important determinant of the demand for it. Is its significance over-stressed? Are economists ignoring other variables of predictive importance? Some available evidence suggests that this is so, especially as far as new products are concerned. J. Udell (1964), for instance, found in a survey of 200 American firms that half of them did not consider pricing as one of the five most important decision variables influencing their marketing success. For individual firms, factors such as advertising and promotion, presentation of product, novelty of product, location of outlets, and reputation of the firm may be more important determinants of demand than the price of its product.

A firm may be restricted by the nature of market competition in the amount of profitable use it can make of price to influence the demand for its product. In particular, in oligopolistic markets (markets having few sellers) firms may be restricted to charging the established or conventional price for a product because any lower price is matched or more than matched by competitors. This assumption underlies the 'kinked' demand approach to analysing oligopolistic markets (see Chapter 9). Oligopolistic firms, therefore, may concentrate on other avenues for competition such as advertising and product differentiation.

The range of variables which can influence the demand for a product is wide and depends upon the time-period for which demand is to be estimated and on the product involved. One or more of these variables, other than price, may need to be incorporated specifically in the demand model. Variables such as the size of the population and its ethnic and age composition, the level and distribution of income in the community, available leisure time, the available range of commodities and their prices, the degree of unemployment and inflation, expectations about prices, new products and replacement patterns of durable goods may need to be taken into account. Developments in the technology of consumption can, for instance, greatly transform demands for products as has the introduction of the personal computer. No simple mechanical demand model ('off the hook') is adequate for predicting demand for all commodities. Models have to be modified or constructed to meet the situation in hand. Failure to do this may result in misleading predictions with dire policy consequences. Nevertheless, standard demand models do introduce important variables and illustrate pitfalls in estimating and predicting demand. Consider these pitfalls.

Estimation of Demand Curves – Time-series Method

Demand curves may be estimated by using data from time-series, cross-sectional data, or information obtained from experience or interviews. Consider the case where the demand for a product is believed to depend principally on its price. Suppose that a series of past market prices and quantities sold of the product are available. In special circumstances, this series identifies a demand curve for the product, or in other circumstances, identifies a supply curve for the product, or may identify neither a supply nor a demand curve. A demand curve for the product is identified when:

1. the only price subject to variation is the price of the product;
2. other determinants of demand are constant;
3. the supply curve alone is subject to variation; and
4. the observed prices and quantities traded of the product are equilibrium.

For instance, suppose that the prices and quantities of sale of the product are observed for the years indicated in Table 5.1 and the conditions just mentioned apply. These

Table 5.1   Observed prices and quantities sold of a hypothetical product, X. Do they identify the demand curve for the product?

Year	Price in pounds	Quantity sold in millions
2006	1	4
2007	3	2
2008	2	3
2009	4	1

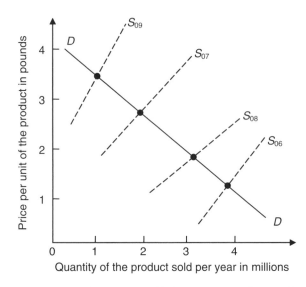

Figure 5.2   *The observed prices and quantities sold of a product, X, during a four-year period,*
shown by the solid dots, identify a demand curve in this case. The supply curve is shifting
and the demand curve is stationary

quantities identify the demand curve marked *DD* in Figure 5.2 and the observed price
and quantities are located at the intersection points of the demand curve and the (hypothetical) supply curves, appropriately labelled and represented by the broken lines in
Figure 5.2.

But past price and traded quantity observations for a product may fail to identify its
demand curve. If the conditions mentioned above apply and the demand curve for the
product is subject to variation and the supply curve is stationary, price–quantity observations identify the supply curve for the product. The reader may wish to illustrate this in
the same way as was done for a demand curve in Figure 5.2, remembering that the observations (in this case usually) fall along a positively sloped curve.

On the other hand, if the price and quantity observations are disequilibrium ones, *or if*
both the supply curve and demand curve for the product are subject to shifts, the past
observations may identify neither a demand curve nor a supply curve for the product. The
latter case is illustrated in Figure 5.3. The same price–quantity observations apply in
Figure 5.3 as in Figure 5.2, but the supply and the demand curves for the product, as
appropriately labelled, shift in each of the years in which observations are made. The line
LL linking the price–quantity observations in this case identifies neither a supply nor a
demand curve.

The identification problem is not limited to demand models based on price as a determinant of demand. It can also, for instance, arise in models emphasizing advertising
expenditure as an important determinant of demand. For instance, if a company's supply
of funds for advertising is a fixed proportion of its sales receipts, the time-series of the
value of its past sales and its levels of advertising expenditure may identify this supply
curve, rather than consumers' expenditure on the company's product as a function of the
company's level of advertising expenditure.

Figure 5.3   The observed prices and quantities sold of a product, X, during a four-year period, shown by the solid dots, fail to identify either a demand or a supply curve in this case. Both the supply curve and the demand curve are shifting

Other Methods for Estimating Demand – Cross-sectional Data

Cross-sectional data provides another possible means for estimating demand curves. If there are regional variations in the price of the product, purchases per head in the different regions may be used as data to estimate demand for the product as a function of its price. However, systematic differences between regions can make the results misleading. For instance, suppose that the data *indicates* that the demand per head for a product is $p = 10 - 0.2x$ where p represents its price and x indicates the quantity demanded. If the lowest prices for the product occur in regions where individuals also have the lowest incomes, the cross-sectional data will reflect the influence of both income and prices on demand. The actual demand curve might be more responsive to price variations than appears to be the case from the estimated demand curve because income variations have not been allowed for in the estimates.

Consumer clinics and focus groups are also used by some market analysts to gauge the demand for a product (McGuigan et al., 2002, p. 128). These involve the selection of a sample of potential buyers of the product and the use of laboratory experiments and observations to help determine the demand for the product. The value of these methods depends on how representative the sample of potential buyers is and on the design of the laboratory experiment.

Experimentation and Surveys to Estimate Demand

Experimentation in stores provides another possible means of estimating a demand curve. For instance, the commodity under consideration might be made available to consumers at some stores at different prices over a period of time and the varying quantities of their purchases recorded and the data used to estimate demand per head as a function of the price of the commodity. In other words, a new product can be trial-marketed and a per capita demand curve estimated. The further step might then be considered of assuming that this per capita curve applies to the whole population. But whether or not the last inference is justified will depend upon how representative the sample of stores is of the whole population and on how well the experimental situation replicates that of the actual world.

Another possibility is to use a survey method to obtain demand data. A sample of consumers may be asked to indicate their likely quantity of purchases of the commodity (under consideration) at various prices and the data used to estimate the market demand curve. This method runs foul of the same difficulties as the last method and in addition there is the problem of whether the responses are reliable. The situations posed are hypothetical, and therefore anticipated reactions by respondents could be unreliable. Furthermore, respondents may deliberately understate their demand at high prices in order to induce price-setters to charge lower prices. Bias in responses is a problem.

Alternative Models of Demand – Replacement and Product Cycle Models

Many other models for predicting demand exist. These include replacement models and product cycle models. Replacement models are relevant for durable consumer goods such as cars, computers and refrigerators and take the expected economic life of such products into account. Product cycle models are based upon typical patterns of market penetration by new products.

A typical pattern for sales for a successful new product is like that shown in Figure 5.4. There is an initial introduction stage followed by a fast growth stage if the product is successful, a mature phase in which maximum market penetration is achieved, and then a

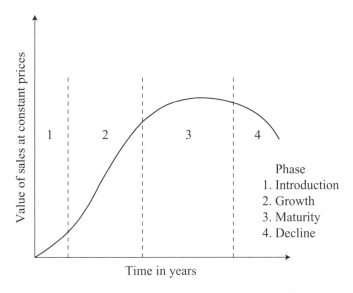

Figure 5.4   A typical product cycle pattern of sales revenue for a successful new product. The quantity sold of the product can be expected to follow a similar pattern

decline in sales as new products replace the old. The elongated S-shape of the product cycle may reflect the following:

1. *Learning* curves. Individuals (consumers) may need a number of exposures or trials of a product before they learn about or accept its superiority, and individual learning curves tend to be of an S-shape.
2. *Diffusion* of knowledge takes time and some patterns of diffusion give rise to this logistic-type curve.
3. The distribution of innovators and laggards. The propensity to try the novel (or take a risk) may be normally distributed and this can give rise to a logistic curve of this type.

Thus, the typical product cycle pattern appears to reflect the fact that we live in a world of imperfect information in which *learning and search* take time and are of great importance.

The problem for a company marketing a new product is to estimate the precise form of its product cycle if it adopts this representation of demand, which incidentally is a rather crude one because it does not take account of specific influences on demand such as price. The degree of prediction using this method may, however, be improved by segmenting the population of potential purchasers into groups of similar individuals, predicting the product cycle for each group and combining these to obtain the overall time-pattern of sales.

The product cycle relationship has been used by Vernon (1966) to predict the flow of international trade and changing patterns of specialization of countries in the production of new products. Vernon suggests that new products tend to be first produced and sold in large, developed economies and then production spreads to other developed countries. In the stage of a worldwide decline in demand, production tends to become concentrated in less-developed countries with little production remaining in developed countries. The production of television sets has followed this pattern (Gao and Tisdell, 2005). For countries engaging in industrial policy designed to influence technical progress in their domestic industry, the product-cycle model raises the question of when it is likely to be best for a nation's producers to enter the product cycle of a new product. Will a nation benefit most by being a leader in technology, a close follower, or a laggard? Further microeconomic knowledge is needed to answer this question. But the following are some of the factors that need to be considered: the first entrant obtains a monopoly but this could be temporary and it could be costly to establish the market. Learning may be costly in terms of mistakes. A later entrant may be able to learn from the mistakes of others but could find it difficult to obtain market share because early entrants are established and have raised market entry barriers. This has led one group of economists to speculate that a nation (or a firm) is likely to gain most from producing a new product as an *early follower* rather than a leader. But the issue is complex.

5.3 CONSUMER WELFARE: HOW IS IT TO BE TAKEN INTO ACCOUNT?

Consumers, since the time of Adam Smith, have been given a central role in the theory of economic welfare. Indeed, many economists have come to judge economic systems by how well they serve the needs of consumers. Systems in which consumers are sovereign (systems responsive to the expressed needs of consumers) are the most desirable ones in the opinion of many economists. For example, as pointed out in Chapter 2, if a Paretian optimum is to occur it is necessary for there to be an optimal conformance between production and the desires of consumers for different commodities, that is for the rate of product transformation to be made equal to the rate of indifferent substitution. Furthermore, economic policy advice often hinges on the extent to which alternative policies increase consumer welfare, for instance as measured by rises in consumer surpluses.

The mainstream of economic theory makes a number of fundamental assumptions about consumer welfare as far as consumer sovereignty and non-satiation are concerned. Not surprisingly these assumptions have been subjected to challenge or criticism in recent years.

Criticism of Traditional Views of Consumer Behaviour and Welfare

Consumer sovereignty
The view that an economic system should respond to the wishes of consumers has been challenged by some socialist writers on the basis that individuals are not always the best judge of their own self-interest. Other writers, such as Marcuse (1964) and Galbraith (1967), claim that in corporate economies consumers' preferences are manipulated through advertising and promotion by corporations so that consumers' preferences no longer reflect their basic desires. Again consumers' preferences may not be independently determined but may in part be shaped by the social setting of consumers as suggested by old institutionalists (see Chapter 3). Furthermore, the consumer-orientated view of humankind is claimed to be too narrow because the welfare of individuals should be judged in relation to all of their roles in society, including their role as workers and as political and social participants.

Strong rationality assumptions and perfect knowledge
Neoclassical economic theory assumes that consumers have perfect knowledge of the attributes of commodities and their prices, know what they want, and act with logical consistency to maximize their utility from their purchases given their income constraints. They are never disappointed with their actual purchases after they have chosen them. To some extent, these consumers are a theoretical type because few, if any, consumers will meet these conditions. Hicks (1946) suggests that such a theoretical type may be representative of consumers as a whole even if no individual exactly conforms with this type. Also as pointed out by Tisdell (1996, Chapters 2 and 3), the neoclassical rationality and knowledge assumptions are stronger than is necessary for individuals to act with perfect rationality. Nevertheless, consumers do not always act with the degree of rationality supposed by the theory, and their knowledge is frequently inadequate to ensure perfect choices and requires consumers to engage in search behaviour. Economic theory can be extended by taking such situations into account and as will become evident in this chapter, they have policy consequences.

Behavioural economists (for example, Bowles, 2004; Camerer et al., 2003) have argued on the basis of observations that consumers do not always choose in a logically consistent manner and that they can be significantly influenced by the way in which alternative choices are presented to them. Furthermore, the limited capacities of individuals to store, recall and process information may mean that consumers make choices based on a restricted set of alternatives rather than on comprehension of the full range of relevant alternatives. Advertising, for example, may alter the limited set considered. Consequently, consumers may sometimes make poor choices because of their limited comprehension of possibilities. Varian (2006, Chapter 30) provides a short outline of behavioural economics.

New institutionalists emphasize the importance of limited knowledge available to consumers, the costs involved in choosing, in searching for exchange possibilities and the transaction costs involved in exchange. These factors all influence the behaviour of consumers and have several policy implications, as is pointed out in detail in this chapter.

Furthermore, much economic theory (including neoclassical economic theory), does not allow for significant differences in the behaviour of consumers. For example, the extent to which consumers act in a rational manner could vary in a population; some may be proactive in their choices of health care whereas others are reactive. The mixture of types may have important social implications. It is even possible that the behaviour of the same individual could be different in different market situations. Diversity of behaviours can have important policy implications and is worthy of more study.

Non-satiation and dependence of welfare on quantity of commodities consumed

Established economic theory maintains that consumers cannot be satiated by commodities as a whole. In other words, greater quantities of *some* commodities always raise the welfare of a consumer, even though the consumer may be satiated by other commodities. An implication of this is that if a narrow view is taken (in which possible environmental trade-offs are ignored) consumers prefer more income to less. Furthermore, it justifies the preoccupation of economists with policies to reduce scarcity by increasing the supply of available commodities.

A variety of objections have been raised. Some writers claim, in contradiction of the traditional view, that consumers can be readily satiated in affluent economies. This is so, notwithstanding the fact that most consumers are observed to desire higher incomes and levels of consumption in such societies. These desires are said to be 'false'. They are fostered by corporate advertising, foisted on individuals, and mask their own self-interest. For example, individuals may be encouraged to desire more and richer food with subsequent deleterious effects on their health and fitness – effects contrary to their own self-interest. This raises the question of whether consumers should be protected by public policy and whether or not they can be protected. These matters are discussed later in this chapter.

Critics of traditional demand theory argue that it unduly concentrates on the availability of marketed commodities (or at least marketable ones) as influences on welfare, and over-emphasizes the importance of personal income for welfare, thereby neglecting the importance of non-marketable goods, such as public goods. Consequently in traditional economic theory, for example, the importance of non-traded commodities of an environmental kind (such as the provision of attractive landscapes, clean air, parks) tends to be ignored, as was discussed in Chapter 2 and as is considered further in Chapter 16.

Does Consumer Welfare Depend on Aspiration Levels? An Unorthodox Application of Indifference Curves

Doubts have been expressed about the proposition that consumer welfare depends solely on the quantity of commodities enjoyed by the consumers. One view, for instance, is that welfare depends upon the *expected* level of consumption (or the level aspired to) by a consumer and the actual level. The relationship may take various forms. But it may be most common for consumer utility to rise with actual income and with the excess of actual income over that aspired to: .

$$U = f(Y, Y - A) \qquad \left(\frac{\partial U}{\partial Y} > 0, \frac{\partial U}{\partial (Y - A)} > 0 \right)$$

where U represents the utility obtained by a consumer, Y is the actual level of income of the consumer, and A is the level of income aspired to by the consumer.

Figure 5.5 illustrates two possibilities using indifference curves. The set of horizontal indifference curves corresponds to the traditional view – utility depends only on the level of income. Utility is independent of aspirations in the traditional model. The downward sloping set of indifference curves, on the other hand, corresponds to a situation in which both actual income and aspirations about income are important determinants of utility obtained by an individual. This set of curves indicates that at any income level, a consumer's utility is higher the lower the level of income aspired to by him or her, that is, the greater is $Y - A$. Utility can be influenced by manipulating actual income or the level of

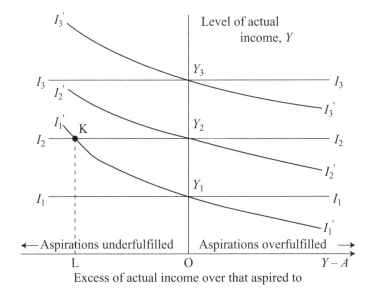

Figure 5.5   The horizontal indifference curves correspond to a situation in which a consumer's level of utility is independent of his/her aspirations about income whereas the downward sloping set corresponds to one in which utility is not independent of such aspirations. In the latter case, if aspirations rise and actual income remains constant, utility falls

income aspired to. It is possible that, as income falls, the slope for such a trade-off may be reduced and the indifference curves in Figure 5.5 may tend towards horizontal ones. This model illustrates how traditional concepts, in this case indifference curves, can be used to construct new or modified theories.

Policy Implications of Aspiration-welfare Theory

If aspirations are an important determinant of welfare, this opens up new policy possibilities. The government and companies can influence welfare by influencing aspirations. The possibility should also not be overlooked that aspirations may affect the level of effort and production of individuals. Policy can be designed to influence production through variations in aspirations or targets. But governments and companies have to face the possibility that if production targets are set too high in relation to what is possible, this may breed intense dissatisfaction and result in less production than if targets had been more realistic.

Marcuse (1964) claims that under corporate capitalism levels of consumption aspired to by consumers outrun those that are possible. This is because of advertising pressure by corporations designed to raise their sales. As a result dissatisfaction is manufactured among consumers and income earners. Certainly, if the downward sloping indifference curves shown in Figure 5.5 apply, inflated aspirations reduce consumer utility. Suppose that the consumer's actual income is OY_2 but that the consumer is persuaded to aspire to consumption requiring an income of $OY_2 + OL$. If the consumer's aspirations accorded with his/her income, he/she would be placed on indifference curve $I_2'I_2'$ but given the higher aspirations, the individual's combined outlook places him/her at position K on the lower indifference curve $I_1'I_1'$. If one accepts *this point of view*, there is a case for limiting the amount of advertising. But all advertising does not have the same effect. Some is informative and there is also a possibility that it yields utility in other ways which are discussed later in this chapter.

Scitovsky (1976) argued that dissatisfaction among consumers in affluent societies occurs for other reasons. He agrees that income and utility are not positively related but argues that this arises because dissatisfaction occurs for those who are materially well off (for example, the middle-aged couple with 'everything') because of lack of variety, challenge, uncertainty, novelty and change in their consumption possibilities. However, the problem may be one arising from the social insularity of the individuals involved because many opportunities exist for the affluent to obtain novelty and challenges in the modern world in their leisure time by pursuing relevant hobbies, sport, tourism and other recreational opportunities.

Determinants of welfare are more complex and wide ranging than those taken into account in traditional neoclassical consumer theory. While for some problems traditional theory may capture the most important influences on welfare, for other problems aspiration theories suggest it is inadequate. Policy-makers need a range of welfare theories in their tool kit.

Observations about Consumer Behaviour and Welfare Based on Traditional Institutionalism

Traditional institutional economics is quite varied in its content but stresses the importance of social influences and institutional structures on economic behaviour. In an earlier section of this chapter, the influence of snob, bandwagon and Veblen effects on market demand curves was mentioned. There is further discussion of these social influences in Tisdell (1972, Chapter 6). However, traditional institutionalism also deserves to be considered in a broader way.

Veblen (1934) suggests that the demand for non-necessities may be to a large extent socially determined. This means that a significant portion of the discretionary expenditure of those on higher incomes (or even lower incomes) may be largely determined by social considerations which may in modern societies be heavily influenced by advertising by companies (Galbraith, 1967). The demand for luxury items may be to a large extent socially determined and the consumption of these items may often be used as markers of social status. In some cases, the prime reason for the consumption of luxury items is to display social status. Veblen (1934) suggested that the taking of leisure time and involvement in particular leisure activities may be used by these on higher incomes to indicate their higher social status.

The type of commodities that indicate high social status may vary with the passage of time but some commodities, such as diamonds and precious jewels, have a long history of being used as status symbols. The value of such items may vary from society to society. For instance, while jade is treasured in China as a precious item, this is less so in the West. Also suppliers of status-type commodities need to keep these commodities 'rare' and can benefit from promoting their social image. This provides a rationale for the diamond cartel, said to be controlled by De Beers.

Social pressures may 'obligate' individuals to purchase commodities they really do not want personally. Furthermore, some sections of the community may try to keep up with the Joneses' and suffer a reduction in their welfare. For example, pressure to earn extra income to buy luxury items for status purposes may mount and add to family pressures. Some individuals and families may become burdened by debt in their attempts to maintain or improve their social status. In some cases also, the luxury items involved have adverse environmental effects, such as golf courses in some locations. When individual demands for commodities are socially influenced, these demands may be an unreliable guide to human welfare and individual welfare. This is at odds with the neoclassical analysis of economic welfare. In such cases, social value judgements (outside the realms of neoclassical economics) seem to be essential for deciding on whether the willingness of consumers to pay for a commodity is a satisfactory guide to the utility they obtain from consuming it.

Consumers' Surplus – a Practical Tool for Piecemeal Policies?

If policy-makers are concerned with a range of options or alternatives limited to a small part of the economy, they may be able to compare the effects of the alternatives on consumers' welfare by using consumers' surplus. This approach, however, assumes that consumers are able to determine accurately the value of commodities to them and that the institutionalist dilemma mentioned above is not relevant. Consumers' surplus takes account of the willingness of the consumers to pay for a commodity. More precisely, using Alfred Marshall's approach, consumers' surplus is the difference between the maximum amount consumers would have been willing to pay for the quantity purchased of a commodity and the amount they actually pay. It can be approximated by the appropriate area under the demand curve.

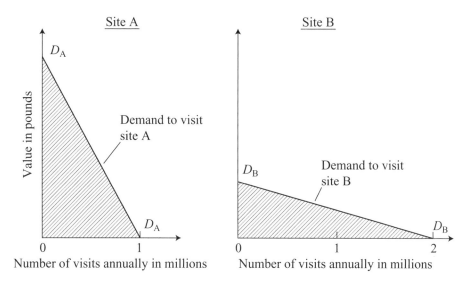

Figure 5.6   *An application of the concept of consumers' surplus to social choice. If a choice has to be made between two sites for a national park, admission to which is free, site A is more highly valued by consumers than site B, even though site B would be more frequently visited than site A*

For example, suppose that a decision has been made to establish a national park in a region but that a choice has to be made between two sites or areas involving equal opportunity cost. The decision between the two sites is to be made solely on the relative value to recreational users of the area. If the demand curves for visits to the alternative sites can be determined, these may be used to estimate the value of potential users of the alternative sites. The demand curve for visits to site A might be as shown on the left-hand side of Figure 5.6 and that for visits to site B might be as shown on the right-hand side. If entry to the park is free, a greater number of visits (2 million per year) will be made to site B than to site A where there will be 1 million visits per year. But the value placed by visitors on site A as indicated by consumers' surplus is much higher for site A than for site B. The hatched area under the demand curve for visits to site A is much greater than the hatched area under the demand curve for visits to site B. This indicates that the appropriate economic choice is site A rather than site B.

Consumers' surplus has many other policy applications. Consider another example. Suppose that a free public road connects two points and that DD in Figure 5.7 represents the demand to travel between these two points using this road. Suppose that initially the cost of each trip (fuel and other vehicle costs) is C_2 per trip. The number of trips made per period is then X_1. However, the road could be upgraded and the cost per trip reduced to C_1. Consequently, X_2 trips per period would be made on the road. As a result, the consumers' surplus of travellers will increase by an amount equivalent to the area of trapezium ACHG. This is also equal to the total cost savings on existing trips (X_1) and is equivalent to the area of rectangle ABHG plus the stemming benefit from extra trips (X_2-X_1) which is equal to the area of triangle BCH. If the stream of benefits from the upgrading represented by the increased levels of consumers' surplus (suitably discounted)

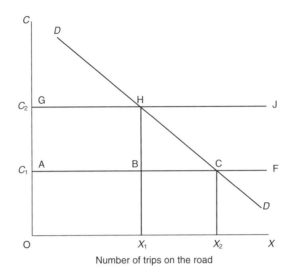

*Figure 5.7   Changes in consumers' surplus can be used to decide whether upgrading of a public road
is economic as is illustrated by this case*

exceed the cost of the upgrading of the road, then the upgrade provides a net economic
benefit.

However, the use of consumers' surplus in policy-making is not without limitations.
More advanced analysis indicates that a number of different conceptions of consumer
surplus are possible. Several of the alternatives are outlined in Perman et al. (2003,
Chapter 12) who also consider some of their different policy consequences. For example,
the minimum sum of money which individuals would be willing to accept to forgo an economic opportunity is an alternative measure of its economic worth and can be compared
with the amount they would be willing to pay to keep the economic opportunity. Usually,
the former sum exceeds the latter. Therefore, this influences cost–benefit results (Knetsch,
1990). Behavioural economists, such as Knetsch (1989), argue that the difference cannot
be fully explained by neoclassical economic theory and in fact the difference involves a
psychological factor dubbed the endowment or 'status quo' effect (Kahneman et al.,
1991). It is also the case that consumers' surplus is based upon prevailing or projected
demands. These reflect the existing or projected income distribution and tastes. If these
distributions or tastes are regarded as socially unacceptable, recommendations based
upon consumers' surplus will also be unacceptable.

5.4   MARKET FAILURE, IMPERFECTIONS AND CONSUMER PROTECTION

In orthodox demand theory, as for instance presented by Hicks (1946), consumers are so
well informed that they always dispose of their income in the best possible way from their
point of view. They are never disappointed about the bundle of commodities they purchased and could not be made better off by another available set. But in practice

consumers do not have such perfect knowledge about the prices of commodities and their characteristics.

Examples of Consumer Protection Policies

Because of this imperfection of knowledge, most countries have introduced policies to protect consumers. Policies take a number of forms. These include:

1. The fixing of maximum prices in some instances with the idea in mind of protecting individuals from 'overcharging'.
2. Requirements that commodities meet minimum standards prescribed by the government, for example, food such as milk and meat, drugs and motor vehicles.
3. Requirements that the composition or possible effects of commodities be disclosed to consumers, for instance on labels or in advertising, as in the case of tobacco products, poisons and some foods.
4. Education by the government about the possible effects of different commodities either in schools or through the media to the general public.
5. Prohibition of the sale of various goods such as drugs of different kinds.
6. Restrictions on persons permitted to supply certain services or commodities such as those involving qualifications and registration requirements for medical practitioners, lawyers and teachers.
7. Compulsory and/or subsidized consumption of some commodities such as education for children.
8. Requirements about honesty in advertising and in claims for products, for instance about the weight of goods.
9. In some countries, there is also a period of time in which a consumer can renounce an agreement to purchase a commodity, for instance if the buyer has been subjected to sales pressure by a door-to-door salesperson.

Are the above restrictions on freedom of choice justified? They might be if the consumer is not the best judge of his/her own self-interest or if these measures sufficiently and economically reduce the consumer's cost of searching for an optimum choice. Schemes for consumer protection are as a rule not costless and need to be subjected to cost–benefit analysis. Sometimes on closer analysis they are found to be means to protect special producer groups rather than consumers. Let us consider ways in which consumers may be damaged or may benefit from consumer protection policies.

Costs of Consumer Protection – Quality Restrictions

If consumers are reasonably well informed, minimum quality standards may reduce the welfare of consumers and increase the rent of those firms and resource-owners in a position to supply higher quality products at a profit. Take the simplest case in which consumers alone are damaged. Let us suppose that there is a continuum of qualities of a product, that the cost per unit of production of each quality is constant in relation to the quantity produced of that quality, but the cost per unit of production is higher for production of better quality goods. The cost per unit of production as a function of quality

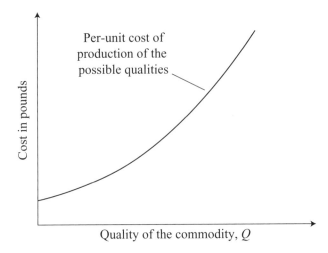

Figure 5.8   Per-unit costs of production of each quality of a product are constant but per-unit costs are higher for the production of a better quality product in this example

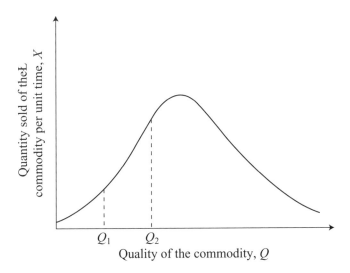

Figure 5.9   Distribution of quantity sold of various qualities of the commodity, assuming that each quality is sold at its per-unit cost of production

might rise in the way indicated in Figure 5.8, and the distribution of sales of the various qualities of the product, assuming that each quality is sold at its cost of production, might be as shown in Figure 5.9.

Suppose that in order to 'protect' consumers against products of shoddy quality the government passes a regulation banning the sale of commodities of a quality less than Q_2 (Figure 5.9). If consumers are reasonably well informed, consumers purchasing commodities of lower quality than Q_2 are damaged by the government regulation. Take the case of a consumer who would normally buy only quality Q_1 of the commodity and

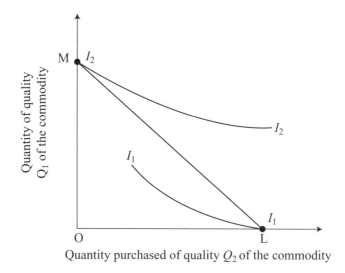

Figure 5.10   Protection of the consumer from a low-quality product reduces the consumer's welfare in this case. If quality Q_1 is banned, the consumer is shifted from equilibrium M to L in this case

allocates a fixed budget to purchasing the commodity. Suppose further that, if the consumer is denied quality Q_1, it is optimal for him/her to spend his/her earmarked budget on the lowest available quality of the product, Q_2. Figure 5.10 can be used to illustrate the effect on the consumer of not allowing the sale of a quality less than Q_2.

The budget line LM indicates the quantities of the commodity with quality Q_1 and Q_2 which the consumer can purchase from his/her earmarked budget for the commodity. In the absence of protection, the consumer reaches equilibrium at point M and purchases only quality Q_1 of the commodity and reaches the indifference curve I_2I_2. But if the consumer is protected by the minimum approved quality being Q_2, the consumer reaches a new equilibrium at point L and is placed on a lower indifference curve, I_1I_1. The quality regulation, far from assisting this consumer, reduces his/her welfare.

In some instances, consumer protection protects particular producer groups – the producers of 'better quality' products. It is, for example, not unknown for domestic producers to claim that imports of competing products are of inferior quality and to try to have these imports restricted ostensibly to protect domestic consumers. In reality, however, their prime motive is often their own protection, and domestic consumers may not benefit.

Benefits from Consumer Protection given Search Costs

Nevertheless, consumers can benefit from some forms of protection. Measures to ensure honesty or accuracy in the labelling and description of commodities often confer, as will be shown below, a net benefit on consumers. Uncertainty about characteristics, weights, qualities, and so on, of commodities offered for sale can reduce consumer welfare. Policies to protect exclusive rights to trademarks may be justified on this basis. Regular checks by public authorities on scales and measures and on specified weights and claims about products may be justified. It may be more economical for the government to assume this policing function than for each buyer to try to protect his/her own self-interest by checking. Individual checking or search involves duplication of effort by many individuals and the government may be able to achieve economies of scale in protecting consumers.

How much is it worth to a buyer to have the characteristics or quality of the commodity he/she is purchasing accurately specified? Naturally this will vary from commodity to commodity, but the value of increased accuracy will not be unlimited. Take a particular example. Suppose that a consumer is planning to purchase a particular quantity of a commodity X, which the consumer believes is most likely of quality Q_2. If it is of quality Q_2, the value to him/her of the purchase is £100, but in his/her view there is only a 0.5 probability of its quality being Q_2. There is a 0.25 probability of the quality being Q_1, in which case the value of the purchase is £40, and also a 0.25 probability of the quality being Q_3, in which case the consumer values the purchase at £110. Thus, given the degree of uncertainty that exists, the expected value of purchase is

$$E(V) = 0.5 \times £100 + 0.25 \times £40 + 0.25 \times £110 = £87.50$$

Thus, if the quality of the product could be accurately identified as Q_2, on average the consumer would be prepared to pay £100 − £87.50 = £12.50 for this or would value the information by this much.

Presumably the consumer could carry out a test or pay for a test to be made to determine the quality of product with accuracy. But this test might cost him/her more than £12.50, in which case it would not be worthwhile. On the other hand, the supplier might find it more economical to determine accurately the quality of the product. He/she will be producing many batches and may obtain economies of scale in testing and measurement. But the consumer needs to be reasonably sure that the supplier's claims are reliable. This *a consumer may learn* from experience. However, learning can be costly to the buyer for a reliable producer may not be found at first. Furthermore, new suppliers are disadvantaged even if they are honest because they have to prove themselves before buyers purchase their products in quantity. This restricts competition by favouring established firms. On the other hand, if a public authority actively takes measures to ensure that claims made by suppliers are accurate, this is an advantage to buyers and to new honest suppliers.

Yet we must not be too hasty in accepting the social desirability of detailed and accurate descriptions of goods. There are limits to the extent to which it is socially worthwhile and economical to describe accurately goods offered for sale. An increase in detailed description of goods should, if a Kaldor–Hicks loss is to be avoided, be carried to the point where the expected marginal value of this greater information to consumers is equal to the extra cost to suppliers. To proceed beyond this amount of information is to impose a Kaldor–Hicks loss on society. Nevertheless, it is clear that public policies requiring honesty and accuracy in description and trading of goods *can* (but need not) confer a net social benefit, and public rather than private enforcement of the appropriate regulations may be socially optimal.

To illustrate the last point, consider a dishonest supplier who indicates that the quality of his/her product in the above example is Q_2 when in fact it is Q_1. The unwary purchaser in the above example suffers an effective loss of £60. His/her remedy is legal action against the supplier. But this can be uncertain and even if the purchaser succeeds (and receives £60 in compensation), the actual proceedings will take time and he/she may, after allowing for this time, be out of pocket by, say, £80. Therefore, the purchaser may not take action on this petty claim and the supplier goes on cheating others and creating uncertainty in his/her trade. The *social* value of arresting the cheat's behaviour may well be considerably in excess of the cost to an individual of attempting to stop it because of the externalities involved. A case for public action exists because of collective or group benefits.

Observe also that state laws requiring honesty in trading can assist not only consumers but also honest sellers. Consider an example. Suppose that one lot of producers makes a shoddy product and the remainder a superior product but that buyers find it difficult to differentiate between these items by inspection. The superior products cost £15 each to manufacture and the inferior products cost £10 each to make and sell. At these prices, half the buyers prefer the superior product and half want the inferior product. Those choosing the superior product are assumed to value it at £20 and the inferior one at £12. However, some sellers of the inferior product claim that it is of superior quality. Those who would like to buy the superior product believe that there is a 75 per cent chance that the products on sale and claimed to be superior are in fact inferior. If this is so, they will not buy products claimed to be superior because the expected value to them of such products is only £20 × 0.25 + £12 × 0.75 = £12. Thus only the product of lower quality will have a market. The market for the superior product collapses because of cheating by some suppliers. Producers of the superior product are disadvantaged and prospective consumers of the superior product are denied an economic benefit. Deception has resulted in the bad product driving out the good product and a social loss clearly occurs. This has been termed 'adverse selection' (Varian, 2006, Chapter 37).

Of course, even in the absence of state laws to promote honesty in trading, evolution in social arrangements occurs which reduces the extent of deceitful trading. Where buyers do repeat buying over a period of time, they are likely to learn about how honest different sellers are and can avoid the less reputable ones. Reputable traders will develop goodwill and obtain respect in business. While money-back guarantees may help to differentiate honest from less honest traders, their worth depends on how readily the seller honours the guarantee or whether the seller is in a financial position to do so.

To overcome the phenomenon of adverse selection, makers of superior new products may trade their products through middle merchants who have an established good reputation with the public. Some large retailing chains have such a reputation and some even offer 'money back if not fully satisfied' to customers. In the case of defective products, these chains can usually claim against their suppliers and can penalize such suppliers in future purchasing. Nevertheless, despite the scope for natural social (institutional) adjustments, some state laws and enforcement to promote honesty and transparency in trading are likely to be of social economic benefit.

Another possible institutional means of addressing the economics of adverse selection is by a trader becoming a member of a trade or professional association that maintains the standards of its members. This requires potential buyers to have faith in the ability and willingness of the association to maintain the standards of its members. Sometimes such associations fail to act against their wayward members or do so only after a buyer expends a lot of effort to obtain action. Another possibility is for a seller to have his/her product accredited by a private agency or a non-governmental body. The value of this depends upon the reputation of the accrediting body and its zeal in sustaining its reputation. Alternatively, a government body may act as an accrediting authority in particular cases.

New challenges for consumer protection have arisen with the growth of Internet trading. While Internet trading can reduce significantly the transaction costs involved in market exchange, it also increases the scope for deceptive claims and fraudulent behaviour by sellers. Since the communications involved often come from offshore, national governments usually only have limited powers to protect the local traders involved. Similarly, credit card protection involves many challenges as do most transactions based on electronics. Companies offering such services on a regular basis normally try to protect their clients against fraud in using these services. Another problem with Internet and electronic trading is that consumers may be readily manipulated and enticed into making a transaction before they have had time to consider its consequences adequately. There is usually no 'cooling off' period, and the buyer may pay 'instantly' by credit card.

An interesting example of public protection of traders is in relation to currency. The government itself takes considerable trouble to guard against counterfeiting of currency. At an earlier time when coins contained precious metals, the practice of clipping coins was banned and coins were produced with rolled (milled edges) as a protection to traders. This considerably reduced transaction costs – that is, the need for individuals to test coins given in exchange on every occasion. Government action conferred a net social benefit.

It might be held that consumer associations are adequate to protect the consumer. They provide information for a joining fee. However, they are limited in the information they are able to provide (they give information for a sample) and the costs of their checking the qualities or characteristics of products rather than suppliers can be higher. There is also the possibility of their information being passed on to non-members, in which case non-members obtain a free-ride and legally, the activities of the consumer association may be more restricted than is socially optimal.

New products can create special problems for consumer protection since all their effects may not be known at their time of development. In the case of new drugs or pesticides, for example, governments may require considerable testing of these before they are released for sale to the public. The benefits forgone by delaying the introduction of a possibly superior drug must be weighed against the risk of its having unforeseen ill effects. Should the consumer be allowed to choose between the risks? Is paternalistic intervention justified? If the individual is given all the known facts, is it not reasonable for him/her to decide on his/her own risks to take? Paternalists might argue that some individuals cannot understand all the facts or that individuals should be restrained from being 'foolhardy', but a liberal would not be likely to adopt this view. On the other hand, if unfavourable externalities are likely to be imposed on others (for example the individual may become dependent on others, an invalid, or his or her children may suffer deformities) a liberal would consider that there may be a case for government intervention.

One problem encountered in government protection of consumers in relation to new products is that in fact superior products may not be developed because of the uncertainty of government approval, or the products may be excluded from the market for a socially excessive time. For instance, policies to delay the introduction of new drugs until side-effects are thoroughly explored do provide a benefit by reducing the risk of the introduction of drugs with crippling side-effects, but on the other hand, they also slow down the introduction of drugs with no such effects and this imposes a cost in terms of prolonged suffering and deaths, which might have been avoided by speedier use of the drug. Both benefits and *costs* must be weighed up in considering when a new product should be made available to consumers.

Digression on Search by Consumers

The above analysis recognizes that consumers do not have perfect knowledge but search and learn. Search may take many forms, but as the drug case just mentioned indicates, these can involve great risks when consumers learn by doing or by trying, and the effects of such trials may not be fully reversible.

Search and the gathering of information are not costless (as New Institutional Economics stresses) and this must be taken into account in optimizing any welfare function. In general, it is only economic to pursue these activities up to the point where their marginal expected benefit is equal to their marginal cost. This means as a rule that it is most economic to terminate search and information gathering before perfect knowledge is attained. If economic gain is to be maximized, it is usually rational not to seek perfect knowledge.

The above optimal search rule has several implications:

1. It provides one explanation of why different suppliers can charge somewhat varying prices for the same product and all obtain sales as pointed out by Stigler (1961). Consumers do not search until they find the lowest available price.
2. It helps explain why richer individuals tend to be more ignorant of the prices of basic food items than those on lower incomes, according to Gabor (1966). The cost of search or keeping track of this information in terms of *alternatives forgone* may be greater for the rich, and the marginal utility of extra real income obtained as a result of attention to relative prices is possibly smaller for the rich than the poor.
3. It accords with the observation that consumers expend more search effort when purchasing more expensive items, for instance durable items involving a large outlay, such as a house or car (Katona, 1960). The expected benefits from search and the initial degree of ignorance can be expected to be high in such cases and so the optimal search level is high, other things being equal.

But even if individuals do undertake an optimal amount of search and information gathering from their point of view, this does not mean that this activity is optimally organized from a social point of view. While a private firm (or a consumer association) could sell information about products (some do), there is likely to be market failure because the information gathered cannot be perfectly marketed. Some consumers are likely to gain access to the information (a public good) without paying for it, for instance by having it passed on by others who have purchased it. Therefore, a private market may undersupply information about commodities. Again, if externalities or spillovers from the consumption of products are important, this could call for government intervention in their consumption.

Waterson (2003) has pointed out that consumer search and switching behaviour is weak for some types of commodities. He provides evidence that this is so for motor insurance, current account banking and electricity supply. Waterson outlines several reasons for this. These include habit, inertia, immediate switching costs, the need for a quick decision because of prevarication (for example, some individuals leave their renewal of compulsory third party vehicle insurance until the last minute) or because of an emergency (for instance, towing of a vehicle in the case of a road accident). Waterson argues that these types of consumer behaviour limit business competition in some industries, and can therefore have important policy implications.

Externalities and Intervention in Consumption

Various types of externalities may provide a basis for government intervention in consumption. In nearly all countries, there are restrictions on the amount of noise which can be emitted by automobiles. In the absence of regulations on noise, some automobile purchasers would be inclined to buy noisier vehicles if this reduced their private cost of operating them.

Figure 5.11 illustrates the type of policy decision that may have to be made between the saving of fuel and the toleration of noise pollution. The curve passing through ABC represents the trade-off between fuel used in cars and the noise pollution caused by them. In the absence of controls on pollution, individuals economize on fuel and cause pollution corresponding, say, to A. But suppose that the social welfare trade-off between pollution

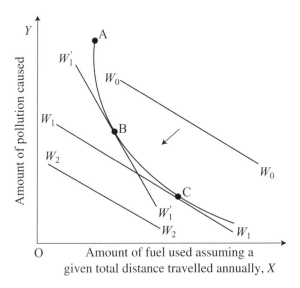

Figure 5.11   *Because of externalities, excessive noise pollution from cars may occur in the absence of government control. But if the cost of less noise pollution is greater fuel consumption, this should be taken into account in a social decision. If the value of fuel rises relative to the value of a clean environment, it may be optimal to allow greater pollution to save fuel. In the case shown, the social optimum shifts from C to B as the relative value of fuel rises*

and fuel used is as represented by the indifference curves W_0W_0, W_1W_1, and W_2W_2. Since greater pollution and greater use of fuel can be regarded as yielding disutility, that is as 'bads', welfare increases as the quantities of both are lowered. Thus greater social welfare corresponds to lower social indifference curves rather than to higher ones as in the normal case. The socially optimal (pollution, fuel consumption) combination is at C and policies need to be introduced by the government to guide consumers to this position. But what would be the effect of a rise in the price of fuel? If the price of fuel rises *relative* to the value of environmental quality, government policy needs to be modified to permit more pollution to save fuel. If the indifference curves tilt so that $W_1'W_1'$ becomes a relevant one, the new optimum corresponds to position B.

Externalities in practice result in significant government intervention in consumption. For example, in many countries, governments adopt measures to encourage vaccination against communicable diseases. Vaccination may be free or heavily subsidized. The more individuals vaccinated against a communicable disease, such as poliomyelitis, the less chance there is of infection of others. This is a positive externality. In relation to adverse externalities, considerable restrictions on smoking tobacco in public places now apply in many countries. This is to reduce the adverse externalities that arise from 'second hand' smoke. Restrictions are also placed on the consumption of alcohol. For instance, in most countries it is an offence to drive under the influence of alcohol, mainly because of risks to other persons.

Economists have recognized that some wants of consumers cannot be catered for through the market system but can only be met through the political system because exclusion from supplies is impossible. These goods, *pure public goods*, include items like defence and some environmental amenities. They are given in-depth consideration later in this book. As mentioned in Chapter 2, public goods may not be supplied or may be supplied in smaller quantities than is socially optimal unless collective action is taken. Their supply is affected by market failure, and government action is needed to direct their supply and level of consumption.

Advertising and Consumer Welfare

While some of the possible effects of advertising have already been mentioned in this chapter and more detailed discussion occurs in later chapters, especially Chapter 9, there are some aspects which are worth briefly noting now. Advertising has been a matter for controversy among economists. The controversial views of Galbraith (1967) and Marcuse (1964) about advertising have already been mentioned. Occasionally, social reformers claim that advertising wastes resources and misleads and confuses consumers. What should be the policy of the government towards advertising?

A case would seem to exist for government enforcement of honesty in advertising on the same grounds as that suggested above for accuracy in specifications of commodities. But even if advertising is accurate, resources used in advertising may be wasted from a Kaldor–Hicks social point of view. Take an oligopolistic market for instance. A supplier may try to increase his/her market share by raising his/her expenditure on advertising only to find that other oligopolists follow suit and market shares remain unchanged. If the overall demand for the product is inelastic, producers in the oligopolistic market become trapped in a high-cost advertising campaign in which no one benefits (except advertising agents). It is not clear what the government should do, if anything, to reduce the waste.

The government might act as an arbitrator for the parties in the hope that they will agree to cut their advertising expenditure by common consent. In some countries, as a result of greater business competition being allowed between universities (particularly those that are state universities), universities have become major spenders on the promotion of their services by advertising. To some extent, advertising expenditure by one university is counteracted by promotional expenditure of the other universities and the size of the university market may hardly increase. Thus, much of the promotional expenditure by universities could be a social economic waste.

In imperfect markets, advertising can be important in creating barriers to the entry of new firms. Thus, it can result in reduced competition. Consequently, prices may be kept higher than otherwise to the detriment of consumers. This matter is discussed in detail in section 9.3.

The psychological associations (for example, lifestyle messages) fostered by much advertising are often more important than the overt message communicated. This, for instance, was reasonably clear in the case of advertisements for cigarette smoking. The danger exists that such 'psychological' advertising will cause a consumer to act against his/her own self-interest. However, it need not do this and associations can be valued. Advertised associations, for instance in the case of perfumes, could easily increase the perceived value of the product to the consumer and be 'beneficial'. While some advertising is valued by consumers and is socially valuable because it is informative, some non-informative advertising is socially valued because its images are valued. Furthermore, there could be occasions on which the means justifies the ends, risky though such an approach to policy is. In order to induce consumers to try a superior new product, it may be necessary to catch the consumer's attention by other than informative means.

Thus, the welfare effects of advertising are complex and varied. A dogmatic government policy towards advertising would appear difficult to justify since advertising can take a variety of forms and serve different purposes.

Political Power of Consumers

Not only market power but also political power is important in the allocation of resources and the functioning of economies. Writers such as Downs (1957) argue that the political power of consumers is small compared to that of producers. The gain to any individual consumer from political action is likely to be small compared to the possible gain by a producer, and on the basis of cost–benefit analysis, the consumer is not likely to take political action. Indeed the consumer may even fail to notice that his/her interest is damaged. For instance, suppose that protection of a domestically produced product is under consideration and that a company stands to benefit by a £1 million annual increase in profit if the protection is approved. Consumers are disadvantaged by £1 each per year and if there are 50 million of them their combined loss is £50 million annually. The company standing to gain can spend a considerable sum to ensure introduction of the protection and still benefit. On the other hand, no individual consumer is likely to find it worthwhile to oppose the scheme politically since the cost of his/her opposition is likely to exceed his/her possible benefit. Indeed, a consumer may not even find it worthwhile to find out (search involves costs) the extent to which he/she is disadvantaged, since it may cost more than £1 to do so; therefore consumers rationally remain ignorant.

While collectively consumers have an incentive to oppose the introduction of protection, they usually have to be organized into a political pressure group to do this effectively. But this is not easily achieved because each consumer has an incentive to free-ride: to enjoy the benefits of political action without contributing to its cost. The benefit from political action (reversal of the protection decision) is of the nature of a pure public good. No consumer can be excluded from the benefit of reversal because he/she failed to contribute to the political campaign for reversal and this is why free-riding is a problem. Again, transaction costs and risks are involved in trying to form political pressure groups representing consumers. These costs may fall heavily or disproportionately on those trying to form such groups, so that it becomes unprofitable for any individual or small group of individuals to foster the formation of a pressure group.

Despite this, associations of some consumers have been formed and legislation has been passed that helps to protect consumers. This includes legislation against restrictive practices and against monopolization. But whether or not the main political force behind such measures has been consumers or competitive business people adversely affected in their own business by the restrictive trade practices of other businessmen, remains an open question.

5.5 ELASTICITIES OF DEMAND AND POLICY

The above discussion concentrated on normative policy matters. It is worthwhile balancing the discussion by considering some positive policy applications of simple demand elasticity concepts. Let us briefly consider policy applications of own-price elasticities, income elasticities, and cross price elasticities to such matters as sales taxes, pollution taxes, government planning of an economy's infrastructure, public policy on the regulation of monopoly, and decision-making about urban transport systems. Applications of each of the concepts are outlined in turn.

Own-price Elasticities of Demand – Policy Applications to Sales Tax and to Pollution Control

The own-price elasticity of demand for a commodity is an indicator of how responsive the quantity of sales of a commodity is to small variations in its price. It specifies the percentage of change in the quantity demanded of a commodity in proportion to and resulting from a small percentage change in its price, for example, a 1 per cent variation in its price. This ratio normally has a negative value. Its values usually range from zero (perfectly inelastic) to $-\infty$ (perfectly elastic). When its value falls in the range of zero to -1 (but not including -1), demand is said to be inelastic, and to be elastic when it has a greater negative value than -1. When its value is equal to -1, demand is said to have unitary elasticity. Conventionally in economics the minus sign is often not specified for this elasticity but is understood to apply. Although elasticities are simple concepts, they have many applications to economic policy.

Using own-price elasticities of demand, consider the impact on government revenue of a sales tax on a commodity. The revenue obtained by the government is greater, the smaller is (varies inversely with) the own-price elasticity of the commodity on which the

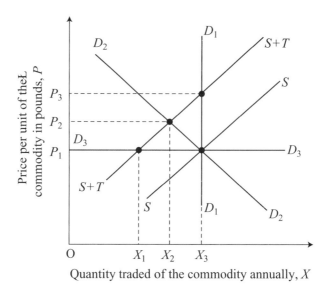

Figure 5.12   *The more inelastic is the demand for a commodity, the greater is the revenue obtained by the government from a sales tax on the commodity. The figure is also used to illustrate the point that the more elastic the demand curve, the more effective is a pollution tax on production in reducing pollution, assuming a given normal supply curve*

tax is levied, that is the more inelastic is the own-price elasticity of demand for the commodity, other things being equal. This can be illustrated by the example shown in Figure 5.12, where *SS* represents the supply curve of the commodity on which the government is considering the imposition of a sales tax (or excise tax) of *T* per unit of sales. The line identified by *S + T* is the supply curve after imposition of the tax. The vertical distance between this line and the supply curve before tax, *SS*, is equal to the rate of tax, *T*. Assume that the problem is to estimate the tax revenue which will be obtained by the government. If the demand curve is completely inelastic as indicated by D_1D_1, the government's tax revenue will be TX_3, for the market will reach a new equilibrium at (X_3,P_3) because the after-tax supply curve is $SS + T$. But if demand is more elastic, the equilibrium quantity demanded falls. If the demand curve is D_2D_2, for instance, the equilibrium quantity traded after imposition of the tax falls to X_2 and government tax revenue is therefore less. It is even less if the demand curve is perfectly elastic, as shown by D_3D_3 in Figure 5.12. Thus, the more elastic the demand for the commodity, the smaller is the government revenue. It may be no coincidence that commodities such as alcohol for which demand is relatively inelastic are also often subject to high government sales taxes. Note that the more inelastic is the demand curve the greater is the increase in equilibrium price resulting from the imposition of the sales tax, and therefore, the greater is the incidence of the tax on consumers. The incidence of a sales tax on consumers varies inversely with the elasticity of demand for the commodity on which it is imposed.

The effects of a pollution tax levied on production can also be considered in terms of Figure 5.12. Suppose that *SS* represents the private marginal cost of supply of the commodity and the line indicated by *S + T* represents its social marginal cost of supply. To bring the private marginal social cost of supply of the commodity into line with its social marginal cost, the government may decide to impose a pollution tax of T on each unit of the commodity produced. Do the polluters (producers) pay the tax? What effect does the tax have on the amount of pollution? The answer to these questions, assuming a given normal supply curve, depends upon the elasticity of demand for the commodity. If the demand for the commodity is perfectly inelastic as shown by D_1D_1, the level of production of the commodity is unaffected by the pollution tax and the price of the product rises by the whole per-unit amount of the tax. On the other hand, if the demand for the commodity is perfectly elastic as shown by D_3D_3, the full burden of the pollution tax falls on producers, production of the commodity falls from X_3 to X_1, and therefore there is a considerable reduction in pollution. If the demand curve has an elasticity between these extremes, the burden of the pollution tax partially falls on producers and partially on consumers and there is some reduction in pollution. The burden of the tax on producers and the reduction in pollution is greater, the more elastic is demand for the commodity.

For example, suppose that in order to reduce greenhouse gas emissions, a substantial increase in the sales tax on motor fuel is proposed. How effective will it be? The demand for motor fuel is known to be relatively inelastic in the short to medium term. This means that a considerable increase in the sales tax on motor fuel would be needed to bring about a significant reduction in the use of motor fuel. In addition, the burden (incidence) on buyers is likely to be high. Therefore, politically, this policy may be unpopular because it reduces the real incomes of consumers considerably in the short term. One of the reasons, for example, for reduction in political support in Germany for the Green Party at the beginning of this century may have been its support for higher taxes on motor fuel as a way of reducing greenhouse gas emissions. However, it is also the case that the demand for motor fuel is more elastic in the long run than in the short run. In the long run, for example, buyers of motor fuel tend to switch to more fuel efficient vehicles, and suppliers have an economic incentive to improve the fuel efficiency of their motor vehicles. There are also likely to be economic incentives to develop alternatives to carbon-based fuels if these are the only fuels subject to the sales tax.

The slogan is sometimes heard that the polluter (meaning the producer) should pay. But as we have seen, if a pollution tax is levied on a polluter's production, this (or a part of it) may be passed on to consumers. However, it can be claimed that consumers are just as responsible for the pollution as the actual producer if they demand products whose production necessarily causes pollution, and that both consumers and producers should be forced to take the social consequences of their choices into account. Incidentally, the above analysis leaves the question open of compensation for those damaged by pollution. Should the revenue obtained from the pollution tax by the government be used to compensate those damaged by the production activities causing pollution? How should it be used?

Observe also that elasticities have several applications to business policy or management. For example, suppose that a company is considering whether it should increase the price of its product. If the own-price elasticity of demand for the company's product is elastic; an increase in the price of the company's product will reduce its total revenue but will increase its total revenue if the demand for the company's product is inelastic. In the former case, the percentage reduction in the quantity sold of the company's product is greater than the percentage increase in the product's price, whereas the opposite is the case when the demand for the company's product is inelastic. Furthermore, if the company has separate markets for its commodity and demand is more inelastic in some than in others, it can increase its revenue by engaging in price discrimination between the markets; that is by charging higher prices for its product in markets where demand is more inelastic (see Chapter 8).

Income Elasticities – Applications to Planning the Supply of Public Facilities and Development of Export Markets

The income elasticity of demand for a commodity specifies the percentage change in the quantity demanded or sold of a commodity as a proportion of a small percentage increase in the income of buyers, other things being equal. Usually this indicator is positive but it is not always the case. An increase in income leads to a rise in demand for normal goods, such as housing space, but a decline in demand for inferior goods, such as food of low quality. Some commodities appear to have a high income elasticity of demand (in excess of unity) such as the demand for recreational and leisure travel and for 'designer' clothing and footwear.

Income elasticities of demand for commodities can be useful for planning by government and by business. For instance, they are useful to the government in planning public facilities such as roads, outdoor recreational facilities and national parks. If the income elasticity of demand for motor cars is known and the expected percentage rises in income can be predicted, this provides an estimate of likely car numbers in the future. This likely number in turn may influence the government's plans for providing roads and highways. Similarly, if the income elasticities of demand for outdoor recreational facilities and for national parks are known to be high and income is expected to rise, allowance can be made for this in the government's plans to provide such facilities.

Income elasticities of demand are useful in predicting the likely growth in demand for particular products. For example, income per head is rising significantly in China and in India. The demand for commodities that are positively responsive to rising income is likely to rise relative to those for which demand is less responsive to income. Thus, in China one might expect the demand for automobiles, domestic appliances and higher quality meat to grow but the demand for rice not to increase very much, if at all. Such information can be used by exporting countries and companies, and by businesses involved in foreign direct investment to identify market opportunities. For example, as a result of rising incomes in China, the demand for quality beef by the Chinese is likely to increase and provide extra opportunities for beef exports to China by Australia and some South American countries.

The relationship between the per capita level of consumption of a commodity and the per capita level of income is called an Engel curve. Note that the responsiveness of the consumption of a commodity can vary along an Engel curve. For example, at low or intermediate levels of income, the demand for beef may be income elastic but at higher levels of income it may be inelastic. The distribution of income also needs to be considered in determining the demand for a commodity. For example, although the average level of income is low in India, a large number of Indians have high incomes and provide a market for luxury goods.

Cross price Elasticities of Demand – Applications to Public Regulation of Monopolies and to Urban Transport Policies

The cross elasticity of demand for a commodity, A, in relation to another, B, is the percentage change in the demand for A which occurs as a result of a small change in the price of B divided by the percentage change in the price of B. The cross price elasticity of demand between two commodities indicates the extent to which they are substitutes or complements. If the cross elasticities are *negative*, the products are *complements*, and if they are *positive*, the products are *substitutes*. Thus in the case illustrated in Figure 5.13, commodity A is a substitute for commodity B if the demand curve for A as a function of the price of B has a positive slope like $D_1 D_1$ and a complement if it has a negative slope like $D_2 D_2$.

Cross elasticities of demand have applications to a variety of public policies. In considering whether public action ought to be taken to deal with a private monopoly, the extent to which other products are substitutes for the monopolist's product needs to be taken into account. The mere fact that a firm is a single seller (monopolist) in a market does not confer on it monopoly power. If the degree of substitutability of the monopolist's product for other products is high, the monopolist has little market power and little may be gained by attempting to control this monopoly. Intense competition from substitutes may restrain the monopolist from raising the price of his/her product to any extent above the marginal cost of its production (see Chapter 8).

Cross elasticities are also relevant to some urban transport policies. Suppose that roads in a city are congested by private cars and the government operates buses and electric trains in the city. The government is considering subsidizing its bus and rail services so that low bus and rail fares can be charged to encourage private motorists to use these facilities rather than their own cars. The success of the policy will depend upon the degree of

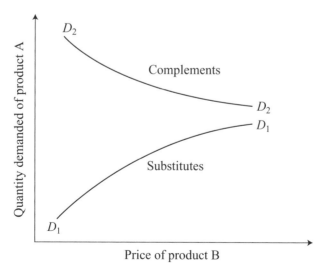

Figure 5.13   The cross price elasticities of demand for substitutes are positive and for complements are negative

substitutability between private and public transport. Evidence indicates that the cross elasticity of demand between public and private transport is low but positive. Thus, lower fares on public transport may do little to relieve traffic congestion in the city. On the other hand, high fees for city car parking or high electronic tolls for private cars in the city may lead to greater use of public transport.

5.6 CONCLUSION

This discussion has illustrated that microeconomics can be usefully applied to a variety of normative and positive policy decisions involving consumers. While standard analysis can sometimes be used for this purpose, in most instances standard analysis must be modified and extended to deal with the particular problem under consideration. But even when extension of the analysis is necessary, standard analysis frequently supplies useful concepts and tools for this purpose, as for instance was illustrated by the application of indifference curves in those theories in which aspirations are considered to be an important component of welfare. By simplifying and organizing our view of the world in terms of general concepts, microeconomic theory enables us to better comprehend the complex effects and alternative possibilities of economic policies and thereby (given our limited capacities and abilities to understand and deal with the world) can and does help us in problem-solving. But it would be naive of us to believe that the best conceptions (however defined) and tools have already been developed or that the existing ones are best for dealing with every microeconomic problem. While using and recognizing the value of current microeconomic tools in policy, we need to remain rationally sceptical and be on the lookout for more satisfactory perceptions.

READING* AND REFERENCES

Bowles, S. (2004), *Microeconomics: Behavior, Institutions, and Evolution*, Princeton, NJ: Princeton University Press.
Camerer, C.F., G. Lowenstein and M. Rabin (2003), *Advances in Behavioral Economics*, Princeton, NJ: Princeton University Press.
*Cohen, S.I. (2001), *Microeconomic Policy*, chapter 4, London and New York: Routledge.
Downs, A. (1957), *An Economic Theory of Democracy*, New York: Harper and Row.
*Earl, P.E. (1995), *Microeconomics for Business and Marketing*, chapter 3, Aldershot, UK and Brookfield, US: Edward Elgar.
Gabor, A. (1977), *Pricing: Principles and Practices*, London: Heinemann.
Galbraith, J.K. (1967), *The New Industrial State*, London: Hamish Hamilton.
Gao, Z. and C. Tisdell (2005), 'Foreign investment and Asia's, particularly China's rise, in the television industry: the international product lifecycle reconsidered', *Journal of Asia-Pacific Business*, **6**(3), 37–61.
Hey, J.D. (1979), *Uncertainty in Microeconomics*, Oxford: Martin and Robertson.
Hicks, J.R. (1946), *Value and Capital*, Preface and chapters 1 and 2, Oxford: Clarendon Press.
Kahneman, D., J.L. Knetsch and R.H. Thaler (1991), 'The endowment effect, loss aversion and status quo bias', *Journal of Economic Perspectives*, **5**, 193–206.
Katona, G. (1960), *The Powerful Consumer*, New York: McGraw-Hill.
Knetsch, J.L. (1989), 'The endowment effect and evidence of non-reversible indifference curves', *The American Economic Review*, **79**, 1277–84.

Knetsch, J.L. (1990), 'Environmental policy implications of disparities between willingness to pay and compensation demanded', *Journal of Environmental Economics and Management*, **18**, 227–37.

Lancaster, K. (1966), 'A new approach to consumer theory', *Journal of Political Economy*, **74**, 132–47.

*Lipsey, R.G. and K.A. Chrystal (2004), *Economics*, chapters 4, 6 and 7, Oxford and New York: Oxford University Press.

*Mansfield, E. and G. Yohe (2004), *Microeconomics*, chapters 3 to 5, New York and London: Norton.

Marcuse, H. (1964), *One Dimensional Man*, London: Routledge and Kegan Paul.

Marshall, A. (1890), *Principles of Economics*, 1st edn, London: Macmillan.

Mayer, R.N. (1999), 'Consumer protection', in P.E. Earl and S.Kemp (eds), *The Elgar Companion to Consumer Research and Economic Psychology*, Cheltenham, UK and Northampton, MA, USA: Edward Elgar, pp. 121–8.

*McGuigan, J.R., R.C. Moyer and F.H. de B Harris (2002), *Managerial Economics: Applications, Strategy and Tactics*, chapter 4, Cincinnati, Ohio: South-Western.

Perman, R., Y. Ma, J. McGilvray and M. Common (2003), *Natural Resource and Environmental Economics*, 3rd edn, chapter 12, Harlow, Essex: Pearson Education.

Scitovsky, T. (1976), *The Joyless Economy*, Oxford: Oxford University Press.

Stigler, G.J. (1961), 'The economics of information', *Journal of Political Economy*, **69**, June, 213–25.

Tisdell, C.A. (1972), *Microeconomics: The Theory of Economic Allocation*, Sydney, New York, London and Toronto: John Wiley.

Tisdell, C.A. (1996), *Bounded Rationality and Economic Evolution*, Cheltenham, UK and Brookfield, USA: Edward Elgar.

Udell, J. (1964), 'The role of price in competitive strategy', *Journal of Marketing*, **28**, 44–8.

*Varian, H.R. (2006), *Intermediate Microeconomics: A Modern Approach*, 7th edn, chapter 37 and chapters 2–6, New York and London: Norton and Company.

Veblen, T. (1934), *The Theory of the Leisure Class: An Economic Study in the Evolution of Institutions*, New York: The Macmillan Company and London: Macmillan and Co. Ltd.

Vernon, R. (1966), 'International investment and international trade in the product cycle', *Quarterly Journal of Economics*, **80**, May, 190–207.

Waterson, M. (2003), 'The role of consumers in competition and competition policy', *International Journal or Industrial Organization*, **21**(2), 129–50.

QUESTIONS FOR REVIEW AND DISCUSSION

1. How does Hicks' theory of demand (which relies on indifference curves) differ from Marshall's? What are the main limitations of Hicks' theory?

2. Suppose that in an effort to stem the rate of population increase, a government is considering imposing a tax on parents which is to rise with the number of their children. Using indifference curves and distinguishing between income and substitution effects, illustrate circumstances in which the tax leads to larger families and others in which it leads to families of reduced size.

3. What factors other than price may influence purchases of a product?

4. Outline four general means that can be used to estimate demand curves and give limitations of each.

5. 'Time-series data may identify a supply curve rather than a demand curve or neither curve.' Explain and illustrate.

6. Why might the product cycle curve of market sales or market penetration of a new product have a logistic form? To what extent is this curve a consequence of ignorance on the part of consumers?

7. Discuss the following views: (a) Consumers *should not* be sovereign and *are not* sovereign in the market system. (b) A consumer's utility does not continually rise with the level of his/her optimal consumption of commodities but may also depend on his/her aspirations.

8. Television stations frequently rate different television programmes in terms of *their relative number* of viewers. When consumers' surplus is considered, there is a serious limitation in this evaluation method. What is the limitation? Illustrate by means of a diagram.

9. Try to draw a diagram to illustrate how the optimal level of search effort might be determined. You will need a marginal expected benefit curve as a function of the level of search effort and a marginal cost curve as a function of such effort. Explain how shifts in these curves may alter the optimal level of search effort.

10. 'While consumer protection can benefit consumers, it can also damage consumers.' Discuss and explain.

11. Explain the phenomenon of adverse selection in markets. How can it result in a social economic loss? What means may be used to avoid adverse selection?

12. 'Spillovers or externalities from consumption may call for government interference in choice by consumers.' Discuss and illustrate.

13. Taking account of the views of Marcuse and Galbraith as well as *other* views, show how advertising can lead to a social loss. Explain carefully what you mean by a social loss. Also outline circumstances and types of advertising that could be socially beneficial.

14. 'Consumers are a weak political pressure group.' Explain.

15. Outline one policy application of each of the following: (a) the own-price elasticity of demand for a product, (b) income elasticities of demand, and (c) cross price elasticities of demand.

6. Costs, supply and policy

6.1 INTRODUCTION AND OVERVIEW

Every national policy decision or choice involving the use of resources requires a consideration of costs, usually in terms of opportunity costs. Opportunity costs are measured by the value of alternatives forgone as a result of choosing one possibility rather than alternative possibilities. The relevant cost of choosing one alternative from a set of possible choices is the value of the best alternative forgone.

The purpose of this chapter is to explain and illustrate policy applications of the concept of opportunity costs, to consider other cost concepts such as sunk costs, which are important for policy purposes, and to examine cost and supply relationships typically experienced by firms and industries and consider their implications for microeconomic policy.

The discussion deals first with the concept of opportunity costs and then illustrates how (private) opportunity costs are automatically taken into account by firms in a perfectly competitive market system. In some circumstances, this results in a Paretian optimum. But perfectly competitive markets can fail to achieve this result if marginal social opportunity costs diverge from the marginal private opportunity costs experienced by individual decision-makers (for example, firms), for instance as a result of environmental spillovers, as was illustrated in Chapter 2. This may call for government intervention in the operations of the economy. But as will be pointed out, governments and government bureaucrats may fail to take proper social account of marginal social opportunity costs. When government intervention is contemplated on the grounds of market failure, it is necessary to weigh carefully the social costs of likely *government failure* against the social costs of *market failure.*

As is illustrated below, proper account is often not taken of sunk costs or historical expenses in decision-making. They ought to be regarded as *bygones* and should not affect current decisions (except, of course, one should learn from mistakes). Bureaucrats and other policy-makers may sometimes make strategic use of sunk costs in order to increase the size of their budgets. On projects of doubtful economic worth, they may try to sink as much money (resources) into these as early as possible so that future funding then only becomes dependent upon the *added* net benefits to be achieved by bringing the project to completion. Another important concept that is introduced in this chapter is user costs.

Subsequent discussion in this chapter considers policies for accelerating the replacement of machinery, such as modernization schemes. These are often ill conceived because inadequate account is taken of opportunity costs. It is also emphasized that traditional economic theory does not allow for X-inefficiency (sometimes called X-efficiency) as an element influencing the cost levels achieved by firms and bureaucracies. X-inefficiency can be an important influence on costs when management has discretion not to maximize profit, for instance. This can occur when shareholders have limited control over the managers of their company as is often the case for large public companies. In general, when principals (for instance, owners) have limited control over the actions of their agents in an organization, such as their managers, their agents have scope not to pursue fully the objectives of their principals. A *principal-and-agent problem* is said to occur. It arises basically because the costs (transaction costs) to principals of closely controlling the actions of their agents are too high.

Furthermore, the forms of per-unit cost curves of production and supply curves are considered and it is suggested that the U-shaped per-unit cost curve may not be typical of several industries. Applications of this to government policies to eliminate excess capacity in industries and to policies to promote merger by firms are explored. Learning by experience, a neglected element in traditional theories of costs, but one which can be important, is taken into account and is shown to be relevant, for instance, to policies to encourage infant industries.

6.2 COST AS AN OPERATIONAL CONCEPT

The opportunity costs of choosing one alternative rather than others are the opportunities forgone. All economic choices involve an opportunity cost because they result in valued alternatives being forgone by decision-makers. Indeed, an economic problem and the subject of economics only exist because choice about the use of resources is not costless. Pleaders for greater public provision of particular goods, such as defence, health and roads (including bureaucrats in the civil service who have a personal interest in expansion of their activities), frequently fail to specify the costs of their proposals in terms of other economic possibilities forgone, such as forgone leisure time, private goods, or goods such as education.

Perfect Competition, Opportunity Costs and the Duality Theorem

In a market system, private opportunity costs are taken into account by economic agents following their own self-interest and, in the absence of market failure, the process results in a Paretian optimal level of economic welfare if perfect competition exists. Assuming a given amount of resources, the production possibility frontier represents the necessary trade-off in production of commodities. If we take a particular company producing TV sets and computers and employing a particular amount of resources, its production possibility set might be like the hatched area OABC in Figure 6.1. The opportunity cost of producing more TV sets is the number of computers forgone, but from the company's point of view (assuming that it is a profit-maximizer) opportunities forgone are valued in terms of profit forgone.

Because of its given employment of resources and thus the company's fixed outlay for these, the company maximizes its profit by maximizing its revenue subject to its production possibility constraints. The company's profit-maximizing production of computers and TV sets can be determined from Figure 6.1. Its revenue possibilities can be represented by a series of iso-revenue (equal revenue) curves like those marked R_1R_1, R_2R_2 and R_3R_3 in Figure 6.1. The iso-revenue lines identified by subscripts of a higher number

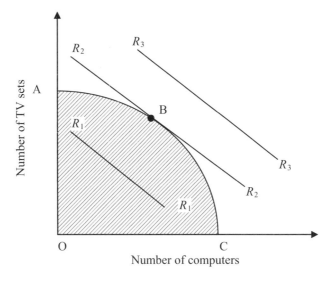

Figure 6.1   At point B, the production (marginal) opportunity cost of producing TV sets rather than computers equals the relative value placed upon TV sets and computers by consumers. Under perfect competition, a firm will produce combination B

correspond to higher levels of total revenue. As a result of movements in a north-east direction in Figure 6.1, the company's total revenue rises. The iso-revenue curves are straight lines in this case because their slope depends on the relative prices of TV sets and computers and the prices of commodities are constant for firms operating under perfect competition. Perfect competition is assumed here. In this case, the profit-maximizing output of computers and TV sets corresponds to point B. At this point, the slope of the firm's product transformation curve, that is, the rate of its product transformation (representing its marginal production trade-offs), equals the slope of an iso-revenue line, that is, the relative prices of TV sets and computers (representing the firm's marginal revenue or marginal profit trade-offs).

In a perfectly competitive market system in equilibrium, the production combination at point B is also optimal from the point of view of consumers, because at this point, the rate at which consumers are *willing* to substitute the commodities in consumption (as indicated by the slopes of their indifference curves), which in turn shows the relative value that consumers place on each of the products, equals the rate at which they have to substitute them in the production process. At point B, the rate of indifferent substitution equals the rate of product transformation of TV sets and computers, a necessary condition for a Paretian welfare optimum. This equality is brought about because all consumers face the same set of trading prices that producers face. Price parity is satisfied. As shown, producers equate their rate of product transformation to these relative prices in order to maximize profit. In order to maximize utility subject to their income constraint, consumers must equate their ratio of their indifferent substitution to this *same* set of relative prices. Hence, the self-interest of all parties leads to rates of product transformation and rates of indifferent substitution being equalized. Given the distribution of income, the perfectly competitive system ensures that there is no alternative allocation of resources (opportunities forgone) that is more highly valued by consumers. Thus this example has illustrated the *duality theorem* – the theorem that perfect competition automatically results in a Paretian optimum.

However, perfectly competitive systems are theoretical constructs, and in reality the conditions for their occurrence are only likely to be partially satisfied in practice. Consequently, actual market systems do not ensure exact fulfilment of the duality theorem nor achievement of Paretian optimality. Nevertheless, as discussed in Chapter 3, market systems, even if they fail to take adequate account of social opportunity cost, for example, may still be powerful systems (but imperfect systems) for reducing economic scarcity. Furthermore, governments are imperfect and can also fail to allow adequately for social opportunity costs. This can be emphasized by considering some examples.

Opportunity Costs and Government and Bureaucratic Failure

Take the case of a government able to allocate a limited budget between public provision of health services and income transfers to the poor. Both may be considered very worthy causes, but the amount that can be provided for each cause is restricted by the limited government budget. The trade-off frontier for the alternatives may be like ACF in Figure 6.2. This frontier indicates that as more funds are allocated for public health services, the incremental increase in these services declines or an increase in public health services becomes relatively more costly in terms of the *amount* of income support for the poor which has to be forgone to provide these services. Health services may be relatively inelastic in supply and become more so as the amount supplied increases.

Suppose that the government's aim is to achieve a particular level of 'healthiness' in the community and that public provision of health services and income support are strategies contributing to healthiness. Combinations of income support and public health provision

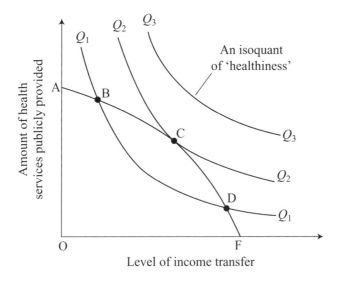

Figure 6.2   The required trade-off between income transfers and quantity of public health services (given a limited budget) is indicated by curve ACF. Health services, like other commodities, are not costless in terms of alternatives forgone

along curve Q_1Q_1 might meet this standard, where Q_1Q_1 is an *isoquant* showing the inputs of public health services and income support required to produce a given level of health-iness in the community. The shape of this isoquant indicates that *substitutability* between the inputs is possible. Other isoquants defining the production possibilities such as Q_2Q_2 and Q_3Q_3 exist. The higher ones correspond to higher levels of healthiness. Assuming that the whole of the limited budget is to be allocated, the *required standard* can be met either by the allocation at D or B, but in the absence of further information, there is no basis for choosing between these alternatives using the above criterion. The Health Department, however, is likely to favour position B and the Social Security Department position D, since in the former case the Health Department is larger and in the latter case the Social Security Department is larger than it would otherwise be.

If the government wished to *maximize* the healthiness of the community (rather than achieve the satisfactory level or standard indicated by Q_1Q_1) the allocation at position C in Figure 6.2 would be optimal relative to the government's allocative possibilities. But it is possible that the Health Department would not support the allocation at C because although this allocation maximizes healthiness, it results in fewer health services being provided, than, say, would be needed at B. Bureaucrats in the Health Department may wish to maximize their power over resources by maximizing their budget or supply of ser-vices. This department may be in a position to muster enough votes in the cabinet to ensure the choice of B rather than C. Consequently, the public interest is not promoted. If the allocation of the available budget does not correspond to point C, it is possible to increase the healthiness of the population be reallocating the available budget.

But should opportunities forgone be evaluated by the government merely on the basis of their effect on healthiness? Income transfer itself may have some value placed on it by the government apart from its effects on health. The relative value of this income redis-tribution consideration needs to be taken into account. Consequently, considering the government's alternatives and given its new preference function in which a weight is placed both on income redistribution and on healthiness, its optimal choice is likely to be on the trade-off frontier to the right of position C. Hence, once trade-offs and values rel-evant to the problem are *fully* considered, the government's welfare function supports some reduction in the attainable health of the community for the sake of greater income support.

Science Policy Example – Care Needed in Evaluating Opportunity Costs

The importance of carefully considering required trade-offs or opportunity costs can be illustrated by another hypothetical example from science policy. Suppose that a nation (for instance, China) is using a given amount of resources for its scientific effort to produce ideas at home and to import ideas from abroad. The allocation of scientific resources for the home production of ideas and their import can be varied, and consequently, changes the number of ideas imported and the number produced domestically. The production possibility set of ideas (given the quantity of resources used for scientific effort) might be as indicated by the hatched area OABCD in Figure 6.3. The shape of this set indicates that along the boundary AB, the import of ideas complements home production of ideas and along the boundary DC, home production of ideas complements the import of ideas. In the former case, the import of ideas stimulates local inventiveness and in the latter case

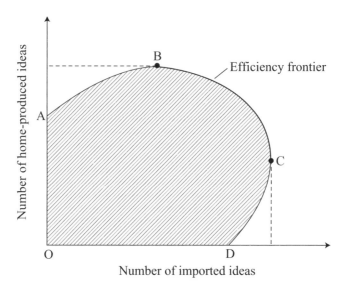

Figure 6.3   *While the production of many commodities is strictly competitive, that of others can be complementary up to a point, as in the above case. Unless production possibility frontiers are adequately explored, serious policy errors can be made. For instance, a policy which aimed to maximize the number of ideas produced at home by concentrating all resources on home production of ideas and allocating no resources to the transfer of ideas from abroad would lead to production at point A and fail in its objective, given the above relationship*

local inventiveness (minimum skill or knowledge about science) facilitates the import of ideas. From this relationship, it is clear that the extremely nationalistic goal of maximizing the output of home-produced ideas will not be achieved if the concentration of resources on home production of ideas is too restrictive of the import of ideas, for then the number of ideas may fall along AB of the boundary of the production possibility set. Provided that more ideas are more highly valued than fewer, the only efficient allocations of scientific resources are those corresponding to the boundary of the production possibility frontier between B and C. This is the efficient set or frontier of possibilities. The optimal choice in this set depends upon the relative valuation placed upon home-produced and imported ideas.

Sunk Costs and Opportunity Costs

Sometimes opportunity costs are not correctly evaluated because sunk costs are not ignored in decision-making. Sunk costs are historical outlays which cannot be recovered. They are bygones. Thus if I purchase a piece of machinery for £1000 and it costs £500 to install it, the historical cost of this equipment is £1500. If after it is installed the best price (net) that can be obtained for it is £100 (maybe for scrap), the *sunk* cost is £1400 and its opportunity cost after installation is £100. Prior to purchase, however, its opportunity cost (profit disregarded) is £1500. Historical and sunk costs are irrelevant to decisions about the future *operation* of the machine. Thus if the net operating profit per year from the machine turns out to be £8 per year and the best rate of interest is 10 per cent, profit can be increased by selling the machine for £100 if it has been installed, and investing the £100 at the going rate of interest. On the other hand, if the net operating profit happens to be £15 annually, profit would be maximized by continuing to operate the machine rather than by selling it and investing the money at the going rate of interest. Historical and sunk costs in no way affect the optimal use decision.

Sunk Costs and the Economics of Bureaucracy and Politics

While this is clear, the principle is not always taken into account. Sometimes it is argued that the mere fact that so much has already been outlaid on a project is a good reason for it to continue, otherwise all the earlier investment may be lost. But this or much of this past expenditure may already be a sunk cost and if further expenditure is not likely to be recovered, this will merely add to the magnitude of the loss. On the other hand, the fact that a large amount of costs is already sunk is not a reason for discontinuing a project. If a positive return can be obtained from further expenditures on the project after allowing for their opportunity costs and for the realizable value of resources already committed (for instance the scrap value of equipment), it is profitable to continue the project even though sunk costs are considerable. Hence, the longer that cancellation of a project is delayed, the more worthwhile it is to complete the project. Thus, the more specifically assets are already committed to a project and therefore the less the scope for using them elsewhere, the lower is their recoverable cost and, other things being equal, the greater the likelihood of continuation of a project being optimal once it has commenced. If, furthermore, the flexibility of committed resources becomes less as a project develops, the probability that it will be optimal to complete the project increases. So for bureaucrats interested in the completion of a project, it is optimal for them to delay its review as long as possible and to commit resources as inflexibly as possible to the project as quickly as possible. Consequently, to increase their own budgets, bureaucrats may promote and carry through projects which have high opportunity costs.

Consider another case involving *asset specificity*. Some contracts result in 'lock-in' of the seller and the buyer and may be performed in stages over a period of time. The further the performance of the contract proceeds, the more difficult it becomes for either party to avoid the contract. Contracts to complete buildings are often of this nature. Even if the buyer is not very satisfied with the early performance of the builder, it is difficult to avoid the contract. A dissatisfied buyer may delay progress payments but the builder in retaliation may delay construction. The dispute results in costs to both parties. In the end, the buyer might treat the past performance of the seller as a sunk cost, particularly if the contract is to some extent open and the cost of legal action high and uncertain. In such cases, it is a matter of the buyer adopting the action that minimizes his/her cost and accepting some costs as sunk costs.

Plant Modernization or Replacement Policies that Fail to Take Account of Social Opportunity Costs

The importance of opportunity costs and of disregarding sunk costs can be seen from another policy context. Policies to subsidize or encourage the replacement of old machines may result in economic waste, as illustrated in Figure 6.4. Suppose that all

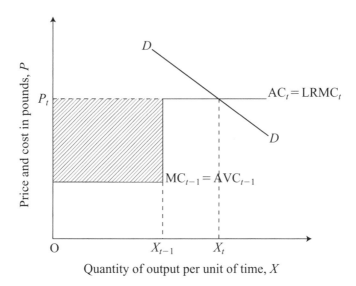

Figure 6.4   *Policies to encourage rapid modernization of an industry by replacing plants embodying old techniques with those embodying new techniques can fail to take account of opportunity costs and add to scarcity. In this example, the deadweight cost of replacing existing plants producing X_{t-1} by modern ones is represented by the hatched area*

existing machines or plants in an industry are one period (for example, a decade) old and incorporate or embody the techniques of the early period and have no alternative use except in the industry concerned (and no scrap value). If the marginal cost of operating these plants up to full capacity is constant, the opportunity cost of operating them is their total *variable* cost of operation. Suppose that a new technique is discovered and embodied in plants that can be purchased in the current period t. Average *total* cost of production arising from the new plants incorporating the new technique are lower than for new plants incorporating the old technique. So if any new plants are to be installed, it is more profitable to install those incorporating the new technique. If *DD* in Figure 6.4 represents demand in period t and X_{t-1} is the output accounted for by old plants working at full capacity and having a marginal cost of operation MC_{t-1}, and if AC_t represents the average costs of production with new plants embodying the new technique (equals the *long-run* marginal costs of introducing new plants since long-run average cost is constant), it is *optimal to install* sufficient modern plants to supply $X_t - X_{t-1}$ of the product. At this level of supply, long-run marginal costs are equal to the value of the last unit of output supplied.

It is not socially optimal to replace the existing plants. To do so would add to the total costs of producing X by the equivalent of the hatched area. This is so since the opportunity cost of new expenditure is equal to itself whereas the only opportunity costs involved in operating existing machines are total *variable* costs. Policies such as tax concessions and subsidies for the replacement of old plants or machinery incorporating old-fashioned techniques *can* add to scarcity rather than reduce it. Technological efficiency and economic efficiency are not the same.

Importance of Marginal Costs in Policy-making

In considering costs, economists tend to emphasize the importance of marginal costs of production (the additional cost of producing an extra unit of output of a commodity) as an important cost consideration to be taken into account in profit maximization. Indeed, profit maximization by a firm requires that its level of production be such that its marginal cost of production equals its marginal revenue from selling its output. Furthermore, marginal costs represent opportunity costs at the margin of a firm's operations.

An advantage claimed for the marginalist approach to optimization is that it economizes on the amount of information needed to determine an optimum. While the output necessary to maximize profit could in theory be found by enumerating the profit corresponding to every output possibility, this can be time-consuming and could be costly to the firm if it tried to determine its complete profit function by trial and error. Mathematically, the marginalist search for a maximum of profit considers only variations of profit in the neighbourhood of critical values, namely those quantities of output for which marginal cost equals marginal revenue. One problem, however, is that an actual firm may not know the relevant mathematical functions. But this knowledge is often unnecessary in practice because in many situations a firm can proceed by trial and error to an optimum. A firm can observe the marginal change in its revenue and in its costs by experimentally altering its output and use this information to guide it to its optimum without its having to enumerate *all* possibilities. It can engage in optimal search procedures relying on marginalist principles.

Nevertheless, as discussed in depth in Chapter 7, economists such as Hall and Hitch (1939) have expressed doubts about whether actual firms do use marginalism to determine an optimum. Their empirical study indicates that firms engage in full cost pricing, that is, base their price for products on average costs of production at normal capacity plus a profit mark-up. Some writers have argued from this that firms are not profit-maximizers and that prices are determined on the basis of costs rather than demand. It has been pointed out by Machlup (1967), for instance, that in some circumstances the above approach is consistent with profit maximization. Some econometric evidence, however, tends to support the traditional view that both demand and costs are important long-term determinants of prices, even though prices appear to be relatively stable or inflexible in the short term.

Neglect of Marginalism in Policy Decisions – Preference of Bureaucrats and Erroneous use of Cost–benefit Analysis

Serious error can be made in optimization problems if marginal opportunities are not explored and major alternatives are not taken into account. This can be illustrated by a research and development (R&D) problem involving a trade-off between cost and time. Assume that a decision has been made to launch an R&D project to provide a technical breakthrough in a particular field, for example, a method for safe disposal of nuclear wastes, landing a man on Mars, setting up a new type of space shuttle. The cost of achieving this breakthrough is likely to be greater the more quickly the breakthrough is desired, so that the cost function for a breakthrough is like that shown in

Figure 6.5 by the curve marked *CC*. To determine the optimal expenditure on R&D in relation to the delay factor, the (discounted) benefit of a breakthrough after any span of time must be considered. The curve marked *BB* in Figure 6.5 might, for instance, be the total benefit in this case. While this benefit might rise with delay at first, it is shown to fall eventually. It might eventually fall because others (other nations, other firms) are more likely to make the breakthrough with the delay. The benefits and costs represented by *BB* and *CC* are assumed to be appropriately discounted to the start of the project.

The optimal time in which to aim for a breakthrough is t_m, assuming that net benefits are to be maximized, and this implies an optimal discounted expenditure on research of E_1. For the breakthrough time t_m, the marginal benefits of waiting equal the marginal costs of waiting. At this point, the marginal reduction in research costs as a result of delay is equal to the marginal fall in benefits caused by this delay, as indicated by the equal slopes of the tangents to the total cost and total benefit curves at t_m.

However, bureaucrats desiring to maximize their expenditure and their control of resources may argue for speedier development, for instance for development within a time-span of t_1 with an expenditure of E_2. Indeed, they might even employ cost–benefit analysts to reinforce their wishes. A cost–benefit analyst can show that the discounted benefits of the project equal the discounted cost at t_1 and that if the rate of interest represents the alternative use of the investment, the project is worthwhile proceeding with at an expenditure level of E_2. But as already pointed out, this leaves out of consideration those time and cost–benefit trade-off possibilities which can raise net benefits even further, such as those in the neighbourhood of t_m.

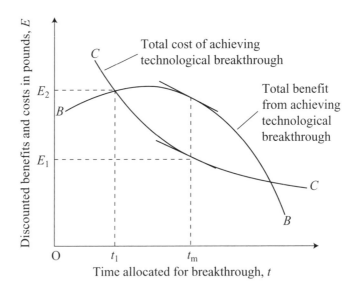

Figure 6.5   *The optimal breakthrough time for this research project is* t_m, *being the span for which the marginal savings in cost of delay equals the marginal fall in benefits as a result of delay. Although benefits exceed cost after* t_1, *speedier breakthrough than at* t_m *is not optimal*

User Costs

Sometimes greater use of a resource now results in its availability being reduced in the future and thus a loss of economic benefits from its future use. This reduction in future economic benefits as a result of the current use of a resource is the opportunity cost of its current use and is called user cost. An optimal rate of use of the resource is achieved when the marginal net benefit from its current use is equal to its marginal user cost (see Chapter 16). For example, oil used now is not available for future use. The user cost of utilizing it now is the future benefit forgone by not conserving it for the future.

Failure to take into account user costs can add to future economic scarcity and contributes to a lack of economic sustainability. Sometimes user costs are not adequately allowed for in market systems because of market failures such as those associated with some environmental spillovers and open access to the use of resources. A company that does not adequately allow for its user costs earns less profit in the future than it would do otherwise.

X-inefficiency as an Element in Costs

The per-unit cost curves normally used in microeconomics to show a firm's cost of producing its possible levels of output represent the minimum attainable costs of producing each of its alternative levels of output. Thus, the firm's average cost curve of production used in microeconomic analysis is usually the lower boundary of its attainable average costs given the known techniques of production. This is represented in Figure 6.6 by the curve marked SAC. A firm's actual average cost of production, however, may lie above this in the hatched area. This may occur because its managers fail to use the available

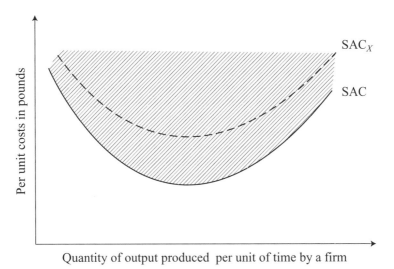

Figure 6.6   The curve marked SAC represents the type of a firm's short-run average cost curve normally used in microeconomic analysis and indicates that its costs are minimized at each level of output. Per-unit costs may in fact fall in the hatched area due to X-inefficiency

cost-minimizing technique or because management and employees fail to make the effort and take the *necessary* action to minimize cost. Production involves effort and the need for decisions to be made by a range of employees, all of whom have some discretion in the decision process about production. There is room for variation in the conscientiousness and ability with which employees fulfil their roles (as agents) because their actions cannot be completely regulated and *contracts* cannot be exactly specified and fully enforced with profit. Thus, due to this factor, variations occur in per-unit costs between firms and countries using exactly the same techniques of production and producing the same levels of output.

Leibenstein (1966) describes inefficiency (other than technological inefficiency) resulting in per-unit costs in excess of the attainable minimum (for each level of output) as X-inefficiency. Even though the firm uses the best technique, X-inefficiency can cause its actual short-run average cost curve to be like the broken line marked SAC_x in Figure 6.6. Because contracts cannot completely specify and determine the behaviour of individuals employed by a company, there is scope for variation in their conscientiousness, for attention to detail, and for organizational slack. As Leibenstein (1966) puts it:

> for a variety of reasons people and organisations normally work neither as hard nor as effectively as they could. In situations where competitive pressure is light, many people will trade the disutility of greater effort, of search, and the control of other people's activities for the utility of feeling less pressure and of better interpersonal relations.

Individuals usually enjoy some on-job leisure. One effect of this can be that inputs are not combined efficiently so that on the cost side, it can be difficult to disentangle allocative inefficiency and X-inefficiency. It is also true that organizational slack can result in technological inefficiency because effort is not made to install new techniques even when their installation is profitable. Organizational slack can cause both allocative and technological inefficiency. Note that if a certain degree of organizational slack is the social norm, X-inefficiency need not disappear even in a purely competitive economic system.

6.3 THE NATURE OF SHORT-RUN AND LONG-RUN COST AND SUPPLY CURVES

The U-shaped Cost Curve

Economists have assumed that typically firms have U-shaped average cost of production curves. While this relationship might be typical in agriculture, it appears to be less common for manufacturing industry and some tertiary industries. The assumed typical (Marshallian) average cost relationships are illustrated in Figure 6.7. This figure shows a selection of three short-run average cost curves marked SAC_1, SAC_2 and SAC_3 and a corresponding long-run average cost curve marked LRAC which is the envelope (lower boundary) of all the possible short-run average cost curves. The minimum efficient scale of plant or long-run optimum size of firm (the one minimizing the firm's per-unit costs of production) corresponds to an output of $\bar{x}$.

Under perfectly competitive market conditions and in the long run, firms are forced to adopt the scale of plant which minimizes the long-run average cost of production,

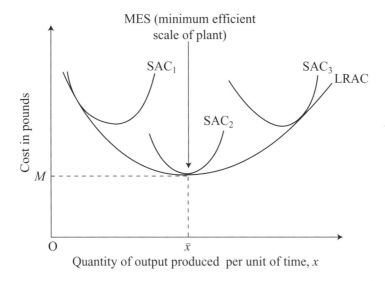

Figure 6.7   Economists have assumed that typically short-run and long-run average cost curves for production are U-shaped like those shown. In the above case, the minimum efficient scale of plant is that corresponding to SAC_2

otherwise they make a loss and fail to survive. Under perfect competition and in the long run, the price of the product produced by a firm becomes equal to its minimum long-run average costs of production. Because of contractual arrangements, profit is a residual for the firm. If in the short term, a firm earns above normal profit this is because entry of new firms is impeded. To the extent that a firm's source of short-term above normal profit is its access to superior factors of production (such as superior management) which in the short term are not paid their long-term rent, competition from other firms in the long run for these factors will force up their prices until no firm has a cost advantage in this regard. Under perfect competition and in the long run, all perfectly competitive firms operate a minimum efficient scale plant at minimum cost, but, as will be discussed later, this need not occur under imperfect competition. Furthermore, it only applies under perfect competition in the long run.

Doubts about U-shaped Short-run Cost Curves

Economists such as Johnston (1960) have claimed that the short-run per-unit costs of firms are better characterized by the cost curves shown in Figure 6.8 than by U-shaped ones. This cost relationship implies that the firm's short-run supply curve is of a reversed-L shape. The firm's average variable cost is constant and equal to its marginal cost until its production utilizes the full capacity of existing plant. To increase production beyond this full capacity level is virtually impossible or prohibitively expensive, given the existing plant. Average total cost is represented in Figure 6.8 by the downward sloping curve marked ATC.

In this reversed-L model, firms may be in short-term equilibrium when they have excess capacity and their average total cost is falling. The demand for the output of the industry

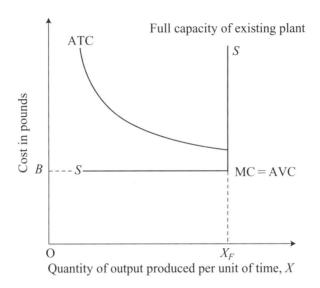

*Figure 6.8   The supply curve of a manufacturing firm may be characterized by a reversed-L supply
curve like that marked SS. Its average variable cost of production is constant and equal
to its marginal cost up to its full capacity level of output, X_F*

may, for instance, have fallen from D_1D_1 to D_2D_2 as indicated in Figure 6.9, in which the
industry supply curve is shown as *SS*. The lower branch of this curve is equal to average
variable cost, OB. In this case, total excess capacity equivalent to $X_F - X_2$ develops.

Political pressure may be put on the government by firms and unions in the industry in
such a case to grant a subsidy on sales. Firms may point to excess capacity and point out
that their per-unit costs will be lowered if this capacity is utilized, and trade unions may
point to the employment-raising impact of the subsidy. Suppose that a subsidy of AB is
granted. This subsidy will result in a Kaldor–Hicks deadweight loss, indicated by the
hatched area in Figure 6.9. This loss occurs because D_2D_2 represents the value to consumers of additional production of X and short-run marginal cost is represented by OB
because average variable costs are constant. This marginal cost indicates the marginal
value to consumers of resources (used in producing X) if employed alternatively in producing other products. Furthermore, if demand has permanently fallen to D_2D_2, then *in
the long run*, it is optimal to reduce the number of plants in the industry and eliminate
excess capacity by doing so. It is possible, however, that some transitional public assistance could be justified to relieve the economic hardships involved in market adjustment.

**Optimal Industry Structure and Long-run Average Costs – Empirical Evidence on
Economies of Scale**

The nature of long-run cost curves is particularly important for economic efficiency when
there is only room on economic efficiency grounds for a few firms or plants in an industry.
If long-run average cost declines with production, it is possible for an industry consisting
of a few firms to reach an equilibrium in which all firms are operating below minimum
efficient scale and hence production of the industry is achieved at greater per-unit cost than

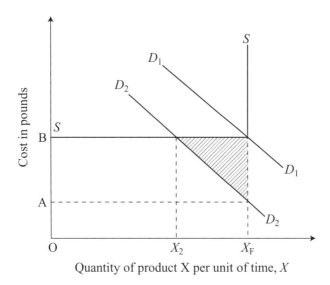

Figure 6.9 *If the short-run supply curve of a manufacturing industry supplying product X is as indicated by* SS *and demand is* D_2D_2, *excess capacity occurs in the industry. Although a subsidy on supplies designed to achieve full capacity lowers average total costs (the subsidy excluded), it results in the long run in a deadweight economic loss, represented by the hatched triangle*

would be the case if that production were shared by fewer firms. Economies of scale in the production of some manufacturing products are such that the whole output of an industry can be most economically supplied by one or a few plants, that is, by a monopoly or an oligopoly. One or a few plants operating at minimum efficient scale may be able to satisfy the whole demand for the product of an industry. This is illustrated in Table 6.1, which sets out the (maximum) number of plants needed a few decades ago to supply UK output at minimum per-unit cost. The table also gives the increase in costs which would occur if UK minimum efficient scale output happened to be equally shared by twice the number of plants needed to minimize cost. As indicated, four plants or less would minimize the costs of producing the UK output of some manufactured goods, for instance chemicals, cars, diesel engines and dyes.

Doubts about U-shaped Long-run Average Cost Curves

Note that Table 6.1 gives the *maximum* number of plants consistent with minimizing the cost of UK output. A smaller number of plants could also minimize unit costs of production. This is because in manufacturing industry the long-run average cost curve as suggested by Bain (1972) may have a horizontal minimum segment like AB in Figure 6.10 and then turn up like that marked $LRAC_1$ or even remain horizontal like $LRAC_2$. Only in the case where the long-run average cost curve is U-shaped is the number of plants needed to minimize the cost of producing an industry's output uniquely determined. Both Bain (1972) and Pratten (1971) found no evidence to support the contention that U-shaped long-run average cost curves are the general rule in manufacturing industry.

Demand, supply, markets and policy

Table 6.1   *Maximum number of plants needed in the UK to produce the UK output of selected products at lowest per-unit costs and the percentage rise in cost resulting from a doubling of the number of plants*

Product	Maximum number of plants needed to produce UK output at minimum cost	Percentage rise in costs as a result of doubling the number of plants in the previous column if output is equally divided
Turbo-generators	1[a]	5[b]
Aircraft	1[a]	20[b]
Electronics (radar, computers)	1[a]	8–10[b]
Machine tools	1[a]	5[b]
Dyes	1	22
Refrigerators, washing machines	2	8
Electric motors	2	15
Diesel engines	2	4
Cars	2–3	6
Chemicals	3–4	9
Steel	3–12	5–10
Cement	9–14	9
Oil refining	10	5
Bicycles	12	Small
Bread	100–200	15
Bricks	200	25
Footwear	500	2

Notes:
[a] A single plant would not reach minimum efficient scale.
[b] Approximation based upon percentage increase in unit costs at 50% MES (minimum efficient scale) compared with unit costs at MES.

Sources: Pratten (1971) and Cmnd 7198 (1978)

Indeed, their empirical evidence suggests that it is more likely that long-run average costs continually decline with output and approach a constant limit or become constant. This may also be so for many tertiary industries. There is no strong evidence to indicate that they typically turn up after a point. Consequently, as suggested by Joan Robinson (1933), it might typically be the size of the market and other factors which limit the size of the firm and/or its rate of growth.

An Excessive Number of Plants or Firms in an Industry in Equilibrium

In practice, the number of plants in manufacturing and other industries can exceed the number needed to minimize the cost of producing the output of these industries. An excessive number of plants from this point of view may occur because adjustment to long-term equilibrium can take a considerable amount of time or the state of competition in an industry may permit an excessive number of plants to exist in the long run. In a monopolistically competitive industry, as is pointed out in the next chapter, firms may

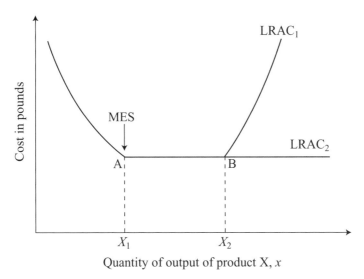

Figure 6.10   *Long-run average costs for a manufacturing plant may typically have a horizontal*
segment such as AB and not be U-shaped with a unique minimum. In the above case,
the minimum efficient scale corresponds to an output of x_1

operate in long-run equilibrium at less than minimum efficient scale and with excess capacity. While unit costs (and prices) exceed minimum unit costs in this case, it is possible that consumers are prepared to pay higher prices for greater variety. However, there are competitive circumstances in which consumers clearly lose as a result of an excessive number of plants and a Kaldor–Hicks gain can be made by reducing the number of plants.

Consider the following example. Assume that all firms in an industry and all entrants have the same long-run average cost curves and that the industry produces a homogeneous (that is non-differentiated) product. Furthermore, suppose that demand for the product is equally divided among suppliers (since consumers are indifferent about suppliers), all of whom charge the same price. Each firm regards its demand curve as 1/nth that for the industry where n represents the number of firms in the industry. Thus if the industry demand curve is

$$p = a - bX$$

where p is the price of the product and X is the quantity demanded, each individual firm considers its demand curve to be

$$p = a - b/nX$$

and sets a price for its product which equates its marginal revenue $(a - \frac{1}{2}b/nX)$ to its long-run marginal cost. The same price will be set by all firms. If above-normal profit occurs this will induce entry (in the absence of significant entry barriers) of new firms to the industry. Entry will continue (if there are many firms) until long-term equilibrium is achieved in which the demand curve faced by each firm is tangential to its long-run

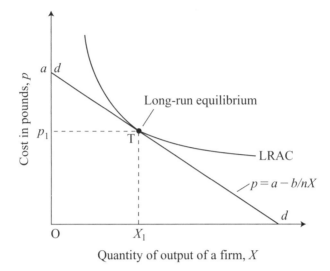

Quantity of output of a firm, X

Figure 6.11   As a result of entry, the demand curve faced by a firm rotates on a point a until it is tangential, as shown at point T, to the long-run average cost curve. Even in an industry producing a homogeneous product firms may come into equilibrium at a point such as T. They operate at less than MES and a social loss occurs

average cost curve as in Figure 6.11. Because the demand curve faced by each firm is downward sloping, each attains long-term equilibrium on the downward sloping part of its long-run average cost curve. Consequently, in the long-run, plants in the industry operate below minimum efficient scale, a deadweight loss occurs, and the output of the industry is produced at greater cost than is necessary.

Let us specifically identify the deadweight loss that occurs as a result of the duplication of firms or plants in a decreasing cost industry. Take the above model and assume for simplicity that in long-term equilibrium there are two firms in the industry just able to earn normal profit. Thus, if in Figure 6.12, *DD* represents the market demand curve for the industry's product, *dd* (half-way between *DD* and the Y axis) is the hypothetical demand curve faced by each firm. Each firm is in equilibrium at a point such as T so each produces X_1 of the product and $2X_1 = X_2$ is supplied to the market and is sold at a price of P_1.

Given the cost and demand conditions in the industry, the Paretian optimal level of supply for the industry is X_4, the level of supply for which long-run marginal cost equals demand, and can only be achieved if one firm alone supplies the market and supplies this amount. The deadweight loss due to duplication consists of two components, or the Kaldor–Hicks gain of shifting from a situation in which both firms produce X_1 to one in which one only supplies the market and produces X_4 consists of two components. The total Kaldor–Hicks gain is as follows:

1. $(p_1 - G_1)X_2 = (p_1 - G_1)2X_1$, the total cost saving as a result of X_2 being produced by one firm rather than production being equally shared, *plus*
2. the hatched area in Figure 6.12, which is the difference between the additional value of extra production and its marginal cost.

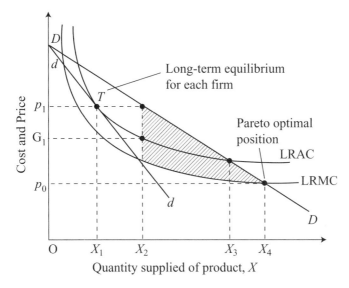

Figure 6.12   Long-term equilibrium in the large group (monopolistically competitive) decreasing cost case occurs at a point like T where all firms just earn normal profit. As explained in the text, duplication of firms under decreasing cost conditions can lead to large Kaldor-Hicks welfare losses

As can be seen, a substantial deadweight loss may occur as a result of duplication given that the products supplied are homogeneous. It might, of course, be held that marginal cost pricing is not practical in the decreasing cost case because the monopolist would make a loss. But even if the monopolist were to adopt average cost pricing, that is, charge a price equating long-run average cost and demand, the deadweight loss of duplication would still be substantial. It would be equal to the cost saving indicated in item 1 above *plus* the hatched area described in item 2 *less* the area of the hatched triangular-type figure bounded by LRMC between X_3 and X_4.

The previous argument that Kaldor–Hicks losses arise from duplication of plants or firms if costs are decreasing also applies in the kinked demand curve oligopolistic case (see Chapter 9) in which rivals match any cut in price below the 'customary' level which equates their long-run marginal cost and marginal revenue (based upon their proportional share of industry demand) but do not follow any increase in price above this level. A Kaldor–Hicks loss occurs in this 'small' group case, and Figure 6.12 can be easily modified to show this.

The possibility of firms operating in an industry at less than minimum efficient scale, even in the long term, raises the question of whether or not it may be desirable for a government to foster mergers in an industry. Depending upon the circumstances, mergers may enable greater plant economies to be obtained because the number of plants can be reduced, multi-plant economies may be reaped, and greater distribution and selling economies and financial economies may be obtained. Mergers may also reduce the business risks of the firms merging and increase their market power. It is possible for X-inefficiency to increase under the protective umbrella of greater market power and the rate of technical progress may taper off. Though it may be possible for merged firms to earn greater profit by taking advantage of economies of scale, such benefits do not appear to be realized, at least in the medium and short term. Most studies indicate that the profitability of companies tends to fall after a merger, even though merged companies may grow at an increased rate, and there is little evidence to suggest that economies of scale are the main reasons for business mergers. Managerial considerations such as the desire for increased security, market power and growth may play a larger role in merger decisions. The significance of these motives for the theory of the firm will be discussed in Chapter 7.

6.4   LEARNING, EXTERNALITIES AND POLICY

Evidence on the Importance of Learning by Doing

On the whole, neoclassical microeconomic analysis has neglected learning and experience as an influence on costs and supply. Especially in new and complex manufacturing, it has been observed that productivity improves with practice and experience. Arrow (1962) has called this 'learning by doing'. Significant studies of this phenomenon in the aircraft industry have been completed by Hartley (1965) in the United Kingdom and by Alchian (1950) in the United States. Both economists find that labour productivity in building air-frames rises with the *cumulative* number built. Hartley's evidence is that an 80 per cent learning curve applies. As the (cumulative) total output of airframes is doubled, direct labour input per aircraft declines by 20 per cent. Consequently, direct labour used in producing aircraft varies in the way indicated by curve AL in Figure 6.13. Curve AL shows direct labour used *per* aircraft as a percentage of labour required to produce the first aircraft. The curve declines at a decreasing rate as cumulative aircraft output rises (learning becomes of less significance) and approaches a limit.

Similar results have since been obtained for shipbuilding, the production of radar equipment, and the manufacture of metal products. As pointed out by Baloff (1966), these improvements in productivity may not be due solely to increased manual skill, but can also reflect an improvement in managerial and engineering skills with experience. Furthermore, beyond some limit to cumulative output, no further increases in productivity can be expected since learning and experience has reached its limit, and the life-cycle of machinery may also influence productivity progress (Tisdell, 1996, Chapter 7).

Policy Implications of Learning by Doing

Learning by doing has a number of policy implications. As a result of learning by experience, a firm's unit costs of producing any level of output may fall with its cumulative output to date, at least until its cumulative output reaches some limit. In other words, a firm's static-average cost curve as a function of its current output may *shift* down (nearer to the X axis showing current output levels) with increases in past output or experience with production. If this is so, a country introducing a new manufacturing technique from abroad or the manufacture of a new product may find that it can keep its costs of production at the lowest level by initially restricting use of the techniques to one or a few firms. This enables these firms to obtain a larger volume of sales and greater experience

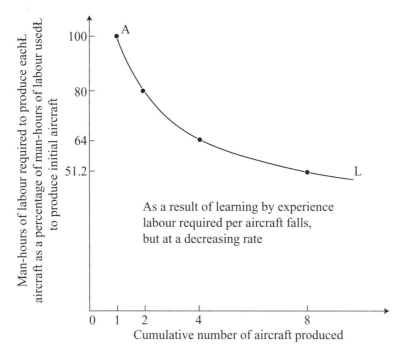

As a result of learning by experience labour required per aircraft falls, but at a decreasing rate

Figure 6.13   Labour required to produce each aircraft declines with experience or learning as the cumulative number of aircraft produced rises. As a result of a doubling of cumulative aircraft production, labour requirements may typically fall to 80 per cent of their original level per aircraft, as indicated above

than otherwise, so rapidly lowering their production costs. As the demand for home production rises and once initial entrants have built up experience, other firms may be permitted to embark on production. So the introduction of the new technique is phased or sequenced.

Japan has used a sequencing policy, but the drawback of the policy is that it gives initial entrants a temporary domestic monopoly. The policy also leaves the government with the problem of deciding which firms will be permitted to be early entrants, though in principle this could be solved by firms bidding for this privilege.

The learning phenomenon also implies that countries commencing production early using new technology are likely to be at a cost advantage compared to latecomers, even though latecomers have no natural disadvantage. Thus an innovative country such as the United States, with a large domestic market, obtains a competitive advantage by being a leader in the use and introduction of new technology. Apart from its learning advantage, it also obtains early economies of scale (Vernon, 1966). In a large economy, such as that of the United States, the large *current* output of a new product yields substantial economies of scale, *and* a high cumulative output achieved early means that the per-unit cost curve as a function of current output is shifted down quickly and would be much lower than that for a country embarking on production of the new product at a later stage. Late entrants (countries or firms) can be initially placed at a severe cost disadvantage because of their lack of experience in producing new products. Nevertheless, as the international product cycle indicates, shifts do occur as time passes in the geographical location of production of many products that were once new (Gao and Tisdell, 2005). This is because the length of experience with the production of a product is just one of several influences on its cost of production.

The learning effect has been suggested as a reason for temporarily protecting infant industries in countries not in the forefront of technological advance. The protection may enable local firms in a technologically lagging country to learn and build up experience by supplying a protected market. This may eventually allow firms to lower their unit cost below that of competitors if the country in question has a comparative natural advantage in supplying the temporarily protected product. Protection is then no longer necessary. The problem from a policy point of view, however, is that it is not always possible to tell whether an infant industry will become viable and how long this is likely to take.

External Economies as a Source of Falling per-unit Costs and as Reason for Market Failure

A firm may experience economies from its own expansion or from the growth of its whole industry (or complementary industries). If a firm experiences economies from expanding its own output, its unit costs fall and *internal economies* are said to be present. If its unit costs fall, other things being equal, as a result of the expansion of the whole industry *external economies* are said to occur. If the opposite effects are present, internal diseconomies and external diseconomies are respectively to occur. Mathematically suppose that a firm's average cost of production, AC, is a function of its own output, x, and that of the whole industry, X. Thus $AC = f(x,X)$. If $\partial f/\partial x < 0$, internal economies occur. If $\partial f/\partial X < 0$, external economies are present. A reversal of these inequalities implies internal diseconomies and external diseconomies, respectively.

If external economies can be reaped from the expansion of the whole industry, this may, but need not, result in the failure of markets to attain a social optimum. Markets adjust by localized private reactions (by each firm maximizing its own profit and each consumer his/her own utility) and in certain cases these reactions reinforce external economies so that a social optimum does eventuate as a result of participants following their own blind interest. But this does not always happen.

To illustrate this, take an extreme case. Suppose that the productivity of a resource depends solely upon the number of units of the resource present in a region or area. Let Y represent the total quantity of the product produced by the resources. Assume that the production function of the resources in area 1 is as represented by OBC in Figure 6.14 and the production function in area 2 is as indicated by OBD.

Suppose that each unit of X receives a return equal to its average productivity. Now if X increases from zero, its average productivity will initially be highest in area 2 and development is likely to take place there. However, if the quantity of resource X increases beyond X_1 it is optimal to locate all of X in area 1. But because units of X may be under the control of many individuals (and the production function in area 2 may not be known with certainty) there is no simple mechanism to encourage a shift of resources from area 2 to area 1 once the quantity of X exceeds X_1. Thus, even when the quantity of X increases beyond X_1, this resource may still continue to concentrate in area 1. In a manner similar to this, industries may continue to grow in regions where they initially developed, even

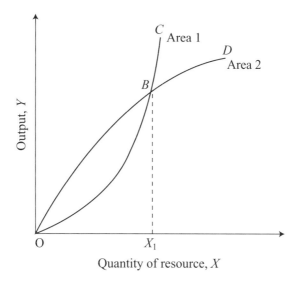

Figure 6.14 The average productivity of resource X *is highest in area 2 when its quantity is less than* X_1 *but greater in area 1 when it exceeds* X_1. *Initially all of the resource may locate in area 2 and there may be no self-correcting mechanism to alter this location once* X *expands beyond* X_1

though this is no longer the most productive location. Similarly, existing cities or towns (which are to a large extent productive units) may continue to attract individuals and other resources and expand, even though this is no longer the most productive location for the resources. In some countries this has influenced regional policy. Governments have established new cities by intervention, have given subsidies to firms locating away from major cities, or have taxed firms at higher rates locating in major cities.

Spillovers and the Divergence of Social and Private Marginal Costs

Another possible cause of market failures are spillovers or externalities in the production of commodities. These cause the marginal social costs of supplying commodities to diverge from the private marginal costs of their supply. From a policy point of view, it is important to consider what is the best means to ensure that such externalities are taken into account by producers. In this regard let us compare a tax on the emission of pollutants from an industry with a quota on these emissions.

Imagine that the marginal spillover or external cost imposed by the emission of a pollutant from an industry is a function of the total level of emission by the industry. Spillovers of the industry have a global rather than a localized impact. Let the curve marked ABC in Figure 6.15 represent the marginal spillover costs imposed by emissions from a particular industry and let the curve DBF represent the marginal cost to firms in the industry of controlling the level of emissions. In the absence of any control, the industry emits a quantity E_2 of a pollutant. However, the socially optimal level of pollution is E_1, where the marginal costs of controlling emissions equal the marginal costs of spillovers.

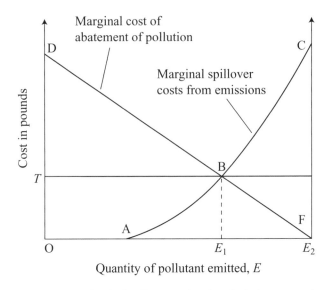

Figure 6.15   *The socially optimal level of pollution is that for which the marginal spillover cost of emissions equals the marginal cost of abatement. This occurs for a quantity of emissions of* E_1 *and can be achieved as a result of a per-unit tax of* T *on emissions*

The level of emission of E_1 could be achieved by the government imposing a tax of T on each unit of the pollutant emitted. Weighing the tax against the marginal cost of reducing emissions, producers find it profitable to reduce their collective emission of the pollutant by $E_2 - E_1$. The uniform tax also ensures that the reduction in emissions is distributed between producers in a way which minimizes the costs of the reduction in pollution achieved. Each firm reduces its level of emission of pollutants until the marginal cost of its abatement equals the tax rate on emissions. Because the tax rate on emissions is the *same* for all firms, their profit-maximizing behaviour results in each firm abating its pollution until the marginal costs of abatement are equal for all. Thus a necessary condition for minimizing the costs of pollution abatement in the industry is satisfied, namely that each firm reduces its level of pollution until the marginal cost of abatement is equal for all. Firms with lower marginal costs of abatement will reduce their pollution levels by more than those with high marginal costs.

If a tax on emissions is used, the government does not have to impose special restrictions on firms as far as pollution is concerned, since, given the global pollution, firms automatically share the burden of reducing pollution between them in an efficient (cost-minimizing) way. In comparison, if quotas are used to restrict pollution and if the marginal cost of pollution abatement varies between firms, quotas or limits on emission have to be determined by the government for each firm. To allocate quotas in a way which minimizes the cost of abating pollution, the government needs a considerable amount of information. It needs to know each firm's marginal cost of pollution abatement. To collect this information would be difficult and costly. The taxation approach to controlling pollution can be regarded as a pricing approach. Firms are required to pay a price (in this case a uniform tax) for polluting and the optimal price (tax) is set to equate the marginal social value of pollution abatement with the marginal cost of abatement.

Another policy approach to pollution control (discussed in Chapter 16) is to adopt a tradable pollution permit system. This is a market-based approach which allows firms to trade (market) their allowable quotas for levels of pollution emission. Like the taxation method outlined, it encourages firms to adopt innovations to reduce their levels of pollution emissions. In practice there is an even wider range of policy options for allowing for or regulating externalities, each of which has its advantages and disadvantages. Some of these options are discussed in more detail in Chapter 16.

6.5 MARKET TRANSACTION COSTS AND MARKET EXTENSION AS A SOURCE OF COST REDUCTIONS

Market Transaction Costs

The process of using markets to bring about exchange of commodities is now widely recognized as involving transaction costs. These costs can be significant. Until recent decades, market transaction costs were given little attention in microeconomics.

Market transaction costs vary with the type of transaction being undertaken but they include the cost of finding suitable buyers and sellers, drawing up agreements or contracts when required and ensuring compliance with these. For example, the hiring of employees may involve considerable transaction costs. Costs involve advertising the positions, checking the qualifications of the applicants, drawing up employment agreements, and monitoring the performance of those hired. Government charges on market transactions, such as sales taxes and tariffs, also add to market transaction costs.

Economic changes that result in a reduction in market transaction costs normally reduce economic scarcity and result in a social economic benefit. This can be appreciated by considering Figure 6.16. In Figure 6.16, the line AS represents the market supply curve for product X in the absence of market transaction costs. The line marked DD is the demand relationship for product X. In the absence of market transaction costs, market equilibrium is established at E_1. However, suppose that a constant level of market transaction cost per unit sold of X is incurred so that after market transaction costs incurred are taken into account, the market supply curve for X is as indicated by $BS + T$. The market equilibrium in this case corresponds to E_2.

Consider now the economic benefit that would be obtained if market transaction cost could be eliminated. Similar changes in economic benefit will occur if market transaction costs are reduced but not eliminated. In the case shown in Figure 6.16, elimination of market transaction costs results in a shift of market equilibrium from E_2 to E_1. This involves a reduction in the price of product X from P_2 to P_1 and an expansion in the amount traded from X_1 to X_2. The social economic benefit obtained is indicated by the area of quadrilateral AE_1E_2B. This benefit can be decomposed into two parts: the cost savings on the previous volume of X traded, that is X_1, and the stemming benefit from extra trading in X, an extension in market trading from X_1 to X_2. The cost saving component is equal to the area of parallelogram ACE_2B and the stemming benefits are equal to the area of triangle CE_1E_2. Both consumers of X and producers of X benefit from this reduction in market transaction costs. Consumers find that the price of the product falls from P_2 to P_1 and this increases their surplus by the equivalent of the area of quadrilateral $P_1E_1E_2P_2$.

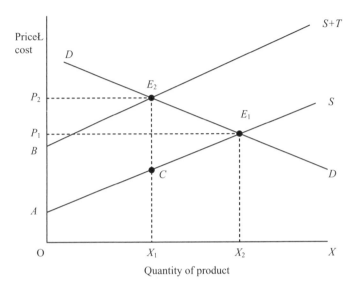

Figure 6.16   *An illustration of how a reduction in market transaction costs can reduce economic
scarcity and increase social economic benefits. The benefits consist of two components:
cost savings on existing market transactions plus stemming benefits from market
extension*

Producers' surplus for suppliers of X also rises because the area of triangle AE_1P_1 exceeds
the area of triangle BE_2P_2.

As a rule, policies, as well as technological and institutional changes which reduce
market transaction costs, reduce economic scarcity and confer an economic benefit. Such
policies can include reduced government taxes and encumbrances on trading and technological change. The latter include, for example, reductions in costs made possible by
new information technology. On the institutional side, marketing agents may help to
reduce market transaction costs because of their specialization. Many tertiary businesses
are facilitators of market transactions, such as banks and financial institutions. To the
extent that they reduce market transaction costs, they confer a social economic benefit.

Some other Aspects of Costs and Market Extension

In section 6.4, the possibility was raised that an expansion in market demand for a product
might result in reduced scarcity because of external economies from expansion of the
whole industry. Adam Smith for example argued, particularly in relation to manufacturing industry, that the expansion of the demand for a product could result in a fall in per-
unit cost of production. He ascribed this mostly to the increased scope which it gave for
the division of labour. Alfred Marshall developed this theme further, suggesting that the
expansion in the market for some industries could result in their costs of production
falling because greater specialization might emerge among producers in the industry and
those supplying the industry. Other factors could also contribute to this result. For
example, learning may proceed at a faster rate if it depends on the level of output of the
industry and market transaction costs per trade may fall with greater trading.

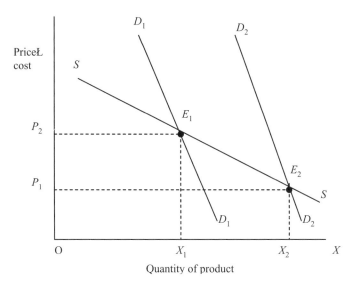

Figure 6.17   A case in which market expansion leads to reduced scarcity of a product because of external economies from expansion of the industry as a whole. This effect will be reinforced if market transaction costs also fall

The effect of an expansion in demand for the product of a decreasing cost industry can be illustrated by Figure 6.17. Here curve SS represents the long-run supply curve of the industry. If the demand for product X is initially as shown by the demand curve marked D_1D_1, market equilibrium is established at E_1. Should, however, market demand shift so that demand curve D_2D_2 applies, the market equilibrium becomes E_2. The cost of production of the product falls, its market price falls from P_2 to P_1 and its supply increases from X_1 to X_2. For some industries, expansion in the size of the European common market (EU) will have increased their market size and reduced their per-unit costs because they are decreasing cost industries. Note also that a reduction in market transaction costs has a beneficial economic effect in the case shown in Figure 6.17 because this shifts the industry supply curve downwards.

6.6   CONCLUDING COMMENTS

The importance of adequately considering costs in microeconomic decision-making has been demonstrated. Emphasis was placed on opportunity costs as an important consideration in decision-making by governments and business. Unless economic opportunity costs are appropriately taken into account by economic decision-makers, economic scarcity is greater and economic welfare is lower than can be achieved given the limited resources available. While a market system can, in particular competitive cases, ensure that full account is taken of opportunity costs and Paretian optimality is achieved, market failures do occur because of externalities and other factors.

In allocating their budgets, governments should take account of opportunity costs. However, bureaucratic failures can occur which result in opportunity costs not being taken into account in a scarcity-minimizing manner. Care is needed in evaluating opportunity costs. For example, sometimes up to a point resource-use can involve complementary rather than competitive possibilities as illustrated by a case involving science policy. It was shown how sunk costs and user costs can be considered within the framework of opportunity costs. Taking into account sunk costs, it was shown that it is not always economic to replace existing business plant by more modern and technologically advanced plant. It was also pointed out that complete evaluation of opportunity costs usually requires, not only total costs to be taken into account, but also marginal costs.

As a precursor to considering the nature of the production costs incurred by a firm, the notion of X-inefficiency was introduced. Traditional microeconomics assumes that X-inefficiency will be absent under competitive market conditions or if firms pursue profit maximization. In practice, this may not occur for reasons which were mentioned. By reducing X-inefficiency, it is possible to reduce economic scarcity.

The types of short-run and long-run cost curves that seem to be faced by business people were considered and their supply and efficiency implications were examined. The implications for the restructuring of industries were discussed. Traditional microeconomics theory has tended to neglect the importance of learning by doing for the economic performance of business. This aspect was considered along with some of its policy implications as were aspects of economic externalities.

Implications of market transaction costs for economic welfare were explored. Reductions in such costs widen the market for products and reduce the amount of resources used in market exchange. Policies which reduce market transaction costs tend to increase economic welfare. In addition, as discussed, market extension can have beneficial effects on costs and economic welfare in the case of decreasing cost industries.

Thus this chapter makes it clear that cost considerations should play an important role in economic decision-making and microeconomic policy proposals. Furthermore, it is apparent that costs must be considered in relation to demands or the relative valuation of the objectives sought.

READING* AND REFERENCES

Alchian, A. (1950), *Reliability of Progress Curves in Airframe Production*, Rand, RM-260-1.
Arrow, K.J. (1962), 'The economic implications of learning-by-doing', *Review of Economic Studies*, **29**, 155–73.
Bain, J.S. (1972), *Essays on Price Theory and Industrial Organization*, Boston: Little Brown.
Baloff, H. (1966), 'The learning curve: some controversial issues', *Journal of Industrial Economics*, **14**, June, 275–82.
*Cohen, S.I. (2001), *Microeconomic Policy*, chapter 5, London and New York: Routledge.
Cmnd. 7198 (1978), *A Review of Monopolies and Mergers Policy*, London: HMSO.
Gao, Z. and C. Tisdell (2005), 'Foreign investment and Asia's, particularly China's, rise in the television industry: the international product lifecycle reconsidered', *Journal of Asia-Pacific Business*, **6**(3), 37–61.
*Gravelle, H. and R. Rees (2004), *Microeconomics*, 3rd edn, chapters 5 and 6, Harlow, Essex: Prentice Hall.
Hall, R.L. and C.J. Hitch (1939), 'Price theory and business behaviour', *Oxford Economic Papers*, **49**, May, 12–45.
Hartley, K. (1965), 'The learning curve and its application to the aircraft industry', *Journal of Industrial Economics*, **13**, 122–8.

Johnston, J. (1960), *Statistical Cost Analysis*, Wiley.

Leibenstein, H. (1966), 'Allocative efficiency vs. X-efficiency', *American Economic Review*, **56**(3), June, 394.

*Lipsey, R.G. and K.A. Chrystal (2004), *Economics*, 10th edn, chapters. 1, 8 and 9, Oxford and New York: Oxford University Press.

Machlup, F. (1967), 'Theories of the firm: marginalist, managerial, behavioural', *American Economic Review*, **57**, 1–33.

*Mansfield, E. and G. Yohe (2004), *Microeconomics*, chapters 6–7, New York and London: Norton.

Pratten, C.F. (1971), *Economies of Scale in Manufacturing Industry*, London and New York: Cambridge University Press.

Robinson, Joan (1933), *The Economics of Imperfect Competition*, London: Macmillan.

*Tisdell, C. (1996), *Bounded Rationality and Economic Evolution*, chapter 7, Cheltenham, UK and Brookfield, USA: Edward Elgar.

*Varian, H.R. (2006), *Intermediate Microeconomics: A Modern Approach*, New York and London: Norton.

Vernon, R. (1966), 'International investment and international trade in the produce cycle', *Quarterly Journal of Economics*, **80**, May, 190–207.

QUESTIONS FOR REVIEW AND DISCUSSION

1. 'The duality theorem depends upon the price parity principle and economic agents seeking their self-gain (that is firms maximizing profits and consumers their utilities). The theorem shows that under perfect competition, social opportunity costs are (in Pareto's sense) taken into account in the market system.' Explain, qualify and discuss.

2. Indicate at least two reasons why decisions by politicians or bureaucrats may fail to take proper account of social opportunity costs. Illustrate your answer with actual or hypothetical cases.

3. What are sunk costs? Why in terms of opportunity costs are they irrelevant for current and future decisions? Explain why a bureaucrat who is interested in seeing a project fully funded and brought to completion may aim for the greatest possible level of sunk costs in the project as quickly as possible.

4. How could contracts involving 'lock-in' result in sunk costs?

5. 'Policies designed to subsidize the replacement of manufacturing plants or machinery (modernization programmes) may fail to pay attention to opportunity costs and may not be socially optimal.' Explain and discuss.

6. Explain how marginal cost concepts can reduce the costs involved in the decision-making process. Are marginalist concepts important in decision-making by firms?

7. What are user costs? What sort of opportunity costs do they involve?

8. Explain the concept of X-inefficiency. How does its presence affect the per-unit cost curves of a business?

9. Some economists doubt whether U-shaped short-run and U-shaped long-run average cost curves are typical in manufacturing (and tertiary) industries. What alternatives have been suggested? What policy implications may the alternative long-run average cost curves have for the optimal number of firms in an industry?

10. 'An excessive *equilibrium* number of firms in a decreasing cost industry is possible. Markets do not always have an in-built mechanism that ensures a socially optimal number of firms.' Illustrate and discuss.

11. On what factors does learning by doing depend and how does it affect input require-
     ments as the cumulative level of production rises? What factors may help to explain
     the cost advantage of the United States in producing some new products?
     Distinguish between economies of scale and economies due to learning.

12. 'The learning phenomenon may mean that it is socially optimal to phase in the pro-
     duction of a new product (or use of new technique) by limiting it to few firms in a
     country when it is introduced from abroad. But there are also difficulties in pursu-
     ing such a policy.' Discuss.

13. Distinguish between external economies for a firm and internal economies. Using
     these concepts explain why there may be no in-built mechanism in the economy to
     ensure optimal-sized cities. What types of policies have been introduced to deal with
     this problem? What are the dangers associated with such interventionist policies?

14. 'If spillovers exist, marginal social costs are likely to diverge from marginal private
     costs, but a tax such as a pollution tax can be used to bring these costs into equality
     and create a social optimum. At this social optimum, a spillover may continue to
     exist. The tax approach to control is more efficient than allocating spillover quotas
     to polluters.' Discuss carefully.

15. What are market transaction costs? Give some examples. Outline the economic
     benefits that may be obtained from a reduction in market transaction costs. What
     modern developments have helped to reduce market transaction costs? How can
     governments help reduce market transaction costs?

16. In some circumstances, increased demand for a product increases its market price in
     long-run equilibrium and in other cases this price may fall. Illustrate. What factors
     may cause per-unit cost of production to fall in the latter case?

PART C

Imperfect markets

7. The behaviour of firms

7.1 INTRODUCTION

The firm is one of the foundations of microeconomics. It acts as both a buyer and seller. Firms buy factors of production and combine them to produce goods and services. They can be privately or publicly owned, large or small in size, operating in different market structures. This does not mean that economic models of the firm are restricted to private firms in agriculture, manufacturing and services plus state-owned industries providing goods and services for sale to consumers. Other private and state organizations can be analysed as firms. Examples include banks, charities, churches, cooperatives, political parties and trade unions, together with government bureaucracies, state agencies, hospitals, schools, military bases, museums, prisons, sports centres and universities. Some of these will be non-profit organizations. Even households have elements which act as firms: they provide child production and child rearing activities as well as partnership and family support activities.

Economists need to know whether the market environment, the form of ownership, and the incentives facing the managers of an organization affect the behaviour and performance of firms. To economists, firms are represented by a set of cost and revenue schedules and an objective function. This analytical framework is used to explain the behaviour of firms as reflected in their demands for labour, capital and technology and their decisions about prices, outputs and product quality. Such decisions also determine the size of firms. Traditionally, economists have analysed firms as profit-maximizers, but modern theories allow the pursuit of other aims such as sales, growth and staff, or even 'satisfactory' performance. It is often believed that in private markets, departures from profit maximization are only possible under imperfect competition. This chapter provides a link between the previous sections which analysed competitive markets under profit-maximizing assumptions and the following parts which consider product market imperfections, factor inputs in the form of labour and human capital, as well as the micro-economics of the public sector (for example, bureaucracies). The analysis will be largely confined to private firms. Once again, the aim is to provide a framework which can be used to analyse a multitude of policy issues.

Consider the sheer extent of government policies towards private firms. There are taxes and subsidies on both factor inputs and outputs. For example, governments subsidize capital (physical and human investments), labour, research and development, and the subsidies might be restricted to one firm, an industry, or to all firms located in a certain region. How will firms respond to such subsidies? Similarly, a concern with inflation requires an understanding of the determinants of prices at the firm and industry level, and the likely effects of cost increases (for example, wages). Worries about the balance of payments require a knowledge of the determinants of a firm's export performance and whether, for example, a buoyant home market is 'good' for overseas sales. There is also a need to predict how firms will respond to a government-promoted expansion of demand. Will they increase output and take on more labour, so helping the achievement of employment targets? Also, governments often intervene in specific markets through restructuring and regulatory policies. In such circumstances, it is necessary to know whether mergers and regulation will affect firm behaviour and, if so, what the likely results might be for prices, output, employment, profits, technical progress and efficiency. Sometimes policy measures which seem attractive can produce unexpected and undesirable outcomes. For instance, a policy to control advertising might lead firms to search for alternative, less efficient and equally undesirable substitutes (for example, more sales people). Thus, models are required to explain and predict firm behaviour. Governments need to know how firms will respond to policy measures. In particular, policies which are introduced on the assumption that firms are profit-maximizers might be ineffective if enterprises pursue other goals.

Clearly, it is necessary to know the circumstances under which firms might pursue other objectives and the likely effects on their behaviour and performance. This chapter starts by outlining some of the central ideas in the development of theories of the firm. An explanation is required for the existence of firms, after which alternative objectives will be considered, together with their policy implications. Two policy issues will be addressed in detail. First, the economic logic of subsidy policy and second, whether governments need an industrial policy.

7.2   THE DEVELOPMENT OF THEORIES OF THE FIRM

This is not a text on the history of economic thought. Nevertheless, the development of ideas provides a fascinating study in methodology. In this respect, theories of firm behaviour can be most usefully presented in an historical context. Why, at any moment in time, is a particular theory rejected and a set of new ideas accepted? Does the history of economic thought show that theories of the firm have been rejected because of 'unrealistic' assumptions or because of a failure to offer accurate predictions? How, in fact, were our theories tested in the past? Today, there are sophisticated econometric techniques which can be applied through computers. In the past – before the Second World War – economists had to use graphs and plotted observations over time, always assuming that data were available. Official statistics were not as well developed or were non-existent. Or, tests were based on simple observations of the 'casual empiricism' type. Alternatively, in the 1930s, questionnaire and interview techniques were a popular method used by the Oxford group of business economists. They simply asked business people what they were doing, how they behaved, and why.

When questions are asked as to why some theories are accepted and others are rejected, more general issues are raised about technical progress in ideas and the nature of the knowledge market. The point to be stressed here is that very little is known about the production function for economic knowledge and scientific progress. Economists frequently analyse industrial structure, conduct and performance; they analyse industrial R&D, invention, innovation and technical progress in firms and industries. While they are fond of asking these questions about the economy, they are more reluctant to apply the same analytical framework to their own knowledge market. How scientists operate in seeking to establish knowledge is largely shielded from analytical and empirical study. The history of economic thought can make a major contribution to understanding technical progress in the knowledge market. Were new models of the firm developed by individual economists working alone or were they part of a larger research team studying common problems? Were there rivals working in similar areas and how far were the new ideas developed through private correspondence, seminars and publications? In other words, economists can be regarded as firms, working as one-man or multi-person research teams in different market environments (see Chapters 8 and 9).

The next task is to trace the development of ideas on the firm and this will be presented in the form of a story, linking some of the ideas of the key actors, such as Marshall, Chamberlin, Robinson and Coase on the theory side; and Berle and Means, together with Hall and Hitch, on the empirical side. Inevitably the approach is superficial, the aim being to select a few key names which help to clarify developments in this field.

Marshall and the Representative Firm

Marshall introduced the representative firm and the biological life-cycle. He drew an analogy between the trees in the forest and the birth, growth and inevitable decline of the typical business firm. Marshall's (1890) trees of the forest analogy went like this:

> the young trees of the forest . . struggle upwards through the shade of their older rivals. Many succumb on the way and a few only survive; those become stronger every year; they get a larger share of light and air with every increase of their height and at last they tower above their neighbours and seem as though they would grow for ever. But they do not; sooner or later age tells on them all; the taller ones gradually lose vitality; and one after another they give place to others which have on their side, the vigour of youth.

This biological life-cycle approach resembles a model of the growth and decline of firms, incorporating change and dynamics rather than a static equilibrium. Examples include the rise and fall of firms in industries such as aircraft, computers and motor cars (for example, Airbus and the US civil jet aircraft companies; IBM and Microsoft; Ford and Volkswagen). Using this model, Marshall replaced the idea of long-run equilibrium and the marginal firm with the concept of a representative firm. This is *neither* a new entrant nor a well-established firm, but it is a firm with average access to internal and external economies. For Marshall, equilibrium in an industry is where the representative firms earn normal profits. He defined a representative firm as 'in a sense, an average firm; it has had a fairly long life, and fair success, which is managed with normal ability and which has normal access to internal and external economies'.

There are obvious difficulties in giving any operational meaning to the concept of the representative firm. What, for example, is a 'fairly long' life and 'fair' success? However, two developments were emerging in this period:

1. There was the growth of the joint-stock company and limited liability, which raised the possibility of a permanent business firm which could outlive, and have a separate existence from, its entrepreneurial founder and owner. Marshall recognized this, so that by 1910, he had modified his trees in the forest analogy: 'As with the growth of

trees, so it *was* with the growth of businesses, before the great recent development of vast joint-stock companies which often stagnate but do not readily die.'

2. Economists were becoming more troubled by the existence of increasing returns to scale. How was it possible to reconcile increasing returns with competitive equilibrium? Here it should be remembered that the standard Marshallian view was that the theory of competition, together with the theory of monopoly, completed the economist's 'box of tools' for analysing the structure of modern industry. And in the competitive model, it was decreasing returns to scale which limited the size of firms: demand formed no limit to size, since it was perfectly elastic at the ruling price.

This brings us to the inter-war period, and the years of high theory in microeconomics. It was not solely a period of revolution in macroeconomics; Edward Chamberlin and Joan Robinson provided a 1930s revolution in microeconomics.

Chamberlin and Robinson: Theory in the 1930s

Edward Chamberlin's book *The Theory of Monopolistic Competition* and Joan Robinson's *The Economics of Imperfect Competition* were both published in 1933. Mention must also be made of Sraffa (1926) who contributed to the development of ideas which suggested that with increasing returns to scale and many firms competing against each other, the size of the firm would be limited by downward sloping demand curves. Chamberlin and Robinson were the pioneers of the marginal approach to the theory of the firm and the notion that profit maximization requires the equality of marginal cost and marginal revenue. Chamberlin, in particular, introduced product differentiation and brand loyalties in markets consisting of large numbers of firms, with free entry and each firm faced with a downward sloping demand curve. In other words, there could be competition without horizontal demand curves and there could be downward sloping demand curves without monopoly. The result was monopolistic competition, with possible examples being garages, shops and taxi-cabs. One of the implications of Chamberlin's model was his tangency solution. This predicted firms with excess capacity in the short run and unexploited economies of scale (see Chapter 6 and Figures 6.11 and 6.12). Thus, there would be too many firms in the industry, each of less than optimal size. Policy-makers often use these features as an argument for re-structuring an industry through state-supported mergers creating larger firms.

Evidence in the 1930s

The 1930s was also important for empirical work. In 1932, there was the pioneering work of Berle and Means which found US evidence of the divorce or separation between ownership and control in the large firm. It was argued that control had passed into the hands of the salaried management (for example, the Managerial Revolution). With managerial control the possibility arises that managers might pursue their own objectives which could differ from the profit-maximizing concern of the shareholders (a principal–agent problem).

Against this background, there was a major attack on profit maximization by two Oxford economists, Hall and Hitch (1939). As a result of talking to businessmen, Hall and Hitch argued that firms do not attempt to maximize profits. For example, they have no idea of marginal cost, marginal revenue and the elasticity of demand. Instead, prices are based on the *full cost* principle. With this principle, prices are determined by estimating average direct costs (constant over a large output range) plus an allowance for overheads and a profit margin (see Figure 7.7).

Change since 1945

Criticisms of profit maximization have led to the development of alternative objective functions. Managerial theories of the firm consider the implications of maximizing sales (Baumol, 1959), growth (Marris, 1964), or a more general utility function (Williamson, 1964). Such models operate within the constrained maximization framework. An alternative approach has been developed by the organization-behavioural theorists (Cyert and March, 1963; Simon, 1966). On this view, firm behaviour cannot be separated from its internal organization. Firms are coalitions of different interest groups, including shareholders, workers, unions and managers of various departments (for example, production, finance, sales). Information is not freely available, and each group is likely to pursue different and conflicting policy objectives, with the result that firms will 'satisfice' rather than maximize. Objectives are specified as targets or aspiration levels: they are likely to be revised upwards if easily achieved and downwards if they are difficult to attain. Further theoretical developments have attempted to model the behaviour of labour-managed firms or worker cooperatives in which labour hires capital (Meade, 1972; Vanek, 1975).

Critics have also concentrated on the market environment within which firms operate and the static, partial equilibrium approach. The analysis of monopolistic competition and the tangency solution have also been criticized. For example, what is the meaning of an *industry's* demand curve for different products (for example, motor cars); indeed, what is an industry in this model? What prevents firms forming a cartel to produce the industry's output in a smaller number of plants exploiting scale economies and earning abnormal profits? There is also the fundamental methodological issue of whether the monopolistic competition model yields alternative predictions from the theories of competition and monopoly. Chicago economists have argued that if models are judged by predictions rather than assumptions, then perfect competition plus some monopoly when required performs as well as, or better than, monopolistic competition. Other economists claim that monopolistically competitive situations are more appropriately analysed as oligopoly markets. For example, three petrol stations on a road form an oligopoly in the relevant local market. But, as will be shown, economic models of oligopoly are far from satisfactory.

Achievements and Problems

Any survey must consider what has been achieved and what are the remaining unsolved problems. A comparison between Marshall and a modern textbook shows technical sophistication. Partly as a result of the efforts of Chamberlin and Robinson, economic models of the firm are now presented both geometrically and mathematically. Marginalism and calculus are used to present a clear, unambiguous model of the firm pursuing a variety of objectives. Economists can use this 'tool kit' to analyse firm behaviour in different industrial situations (for example, car, chemicals, footwear and textile firms). More recently, developments in game theory enable analysis of oligopoly markets where there is strategic interdependence between firms. Also, new developments in experimental economics enable economists to test their theories in laboratory conditions. Even so, are economists missing something?

An obvious deficiency is the general lack of empirical work on firm behaviour and the predictive accuracy of alternative models. Often this reflects the impossibility of obtaining sufficiently comprehensive and accurate data for individual firms. In addition, economists might be missing something by concentrating upon equilibrium. Models of the firm are usually static, equilibrium constructs. But real firms operate in a dynamic world of uncertainty. Markets are always changing and the future is uncertain. In these circumstances, firms are likely to be in permanent disequilibrium, always adapting to, and adjusting to, change. This emphasis on firm behaviour under uncertainty and doubts about the traditional emphasis on the firm in equilibrium has been reflected in *subjectivism*, associated with some Austrian economists (for example, Hayek; Mises). This school focuses on the behaviour of individuals and groups in a world of uncertainty – in a world where individuals and firms do not have perfect information and knowledge, and markets are not in long-run equilibrium. There is a further problem which is basic to this subject area and which was raised by Coase (1937). How can economists explain the existence of firms?

7.3   WHY DO FIRMS EXIST?

Transaction costs are a central part of any answer. Even in markets, transactions and exchange are not costless. Firms economize on transaction costs, where these include the costs of search, acquiring information, negotiating, bargaining and reaching contractual agreements. Paradoxically, in capitalist economies, firms can be viewed as islands of central planning where market exchanges are eliminated and replaced with an entrepreneur who monitors and directs production. Within a firm, workers are directed by rules and orders, not by wages. But why are prices, markets and exchange used for transactions between firms and with consumers, but not for transactions *within* firms? There are two reasons:

1. Teamwork is more productive: there are gains from specialization, including economies of scale.
2. Firms economize on transactions with the suppliers of resources, particularly labour.

The advantages of teamwork can be seen by envisaging its absence. Consider the possibility of independent individuals each specializing in a specific task, then selling their output to another individual producer who undertakes a further part of the job, and so on, to a final individual who sells the finished product. As an example, think of car assembly. One individual could manufacture part of the car and then sell the part to another individual who would add a further part towards the assembly of the car. On this basis, a long assembly line under one roof would not be required and the separate activities in car production could be done individually and coordinated through prices. Firms achieve this 'coordination' without the price mechanism. Why?

One reason is that teamwork is more productive. In many activities, a larger output can be obtained from a team than from separate outputs produced by independent individuals. A team allows beneficial specialization of tasks, with individuals as painters, electricians, assemblers, clerks and managers. The possibility of managerial economies for large-scale outputs has led some organizationalists to claim that with appropriate management techniques no firm is too large to manage. They point to examples such as the Catholic Church and the size of armies in the Second World War. On this view, factors other than management limit the size of firms, for otherwise an economy would consist of only one firm. However, costs cannot be ignored. While teamwork is often more productive, it also has to be worthwhile. The larger team output compared with separate individual production has to exceed the costs of organizing and disciplining members of the team. With teams, problems arise because there can be shirking and 'free-riding'. In contrast, independent production means that an individual who produces less bears all of the costs of extra leisure. In a team, the costs of an individual's preference for more on-the-job leisure are not borne by the worker alone: some are shifted onto the group and the share of costs borne by the 'free-rider' is likely to be smaller with a large group. One solution to shirking and 'free-riding' is to hire a monitor to discipline the team. Sports teams use managers and coaches; factories hire managers, foremen and supervisors; while schools have headteachers. But who monitors the monitor? One possibility is to make the monitor the residual claimant, receiving what is left after paying the team members their contractually agreed price. In this way, the monitor bears the risks. Traditionally, in capitalist firms, capital hires labour, but in worker cooperatives the risk-bearing roles are reversed and labour hires capital.

The contractual arrangements for sharing the residual affect behaviour and performance within the firm. Such matters cannot be ignored by policy-makers. Where all the workers share in the residual, as in labour-managed enterprises, there are greater incentives for the monitor to shirk. It has been suggested that, in such circumstances, the losses from greater shirking by the monitor will exceed the benefits of less shirking by a large number of residual-sharing workers. In capitalist enterprises, much depends on the type of firm. With an owner-managed unit, a single person receives all the profits and there is no sharing. Alternatively, self-policing through profit-sharing might be used in small teams such as partnerships. Companies or corporations appear to be similar to large labour-managed firms in that shirking and free-riding is likely where profits are shared among a large number of shareholders and liability is limited. However, rather than incur the costs of trying to control and improve management decisions, a dissenting shareholder can readily 'escape' by selling his shares. As a result, managerial shirking in companies with large numbers of shareholders will be policed by competition from new groups of potential managers, either from outside the firm (takeover) or from within the enterprise. In contrast, in non-profit enterprises such as charities, mutual associations and state-owned enterprises, including hospitals and schools, there are no shareholders with private property rights in the activity. As a result, any potential profits are 'consumed' within the enterprise in such forms as luxury offices, on-the-job fringe benefits, and expense accounts.

This explanation for the existence of firms relies upon teamwork being worthwhile with a monitor, or his appointed agent, acting as a 'dictator'. It is the monitor who hires, fires, promotes and allocates labour within the firm. In other words, within the firm there is a hierarchy in which workers and managers can be regarded not as antagonistic, but as complementary, members of the team. Everyone willingly agrees to accept the decisions of a monitor. As a result, a firm resembles a command economy in which coordination is achieved not by prices but by issuing orders and commands to workers. However, the hierarchy is a voluntarily agreed and mutually advantageous contractual relationship. The transaction advantages and costs of this contractual relationship need to be explained.

For simplicity, let us return to our imaginary world of no firms, with production undertaken by separate individuals. In principle, it would be possible to combine the resources owned by many different persons through *a multilateral contract* between the individuals. Such a contract would specify for each individual the type and quantity of resources to be supplied to the productive process, the time of supply, and the price of the transaction. But such a complex contract would be costly to negotiate and costly to enforce. Firms reduce these transaction costs. They obtain the advantages of team production with the much lower cost method of a *bilateral contract.* Each individual does not have to deal separately with every other agent in the productive process; instead each individual deals only with a single entity, the firm. The firm substitutes a single incomplete contract – an *employment agreement* – for many complete contracts. In this way, it economizes on the costs of negotiating separate contracts. And the employment agreement is usually expressed in general terms, which allows the firm to adapt and adjust to changing market conditions.

Various forms of contractual relationships exist between workers and firms both within and between enterprises. These might offer a wage for a clearly specified task, a salary contract providing a fixed income for an agreed period, a profit-sharing arrangement, or an apprenticeship which provides training in return for a given length of service. *Employment contracts are a crucial determinant of firm behaviour and performance in both the private and public sectors* (see Chapters 10 and 14). The firm has to devise and negotiate contracts which police factor productivity and offer incentives and rewards for achieving organizational goals. The actual form of the employment contract, and the costs of policing and enforcing it, will determine the opportunities for discretionary behaviour and on-the-job leisure, as reflected in X-inefficiency. Problems arise because no top manager, particularly in a large organization, has the knowledge and the time to monitor everyone. Self-interested individuals will seek opportunities for hoarding and distorting information to their benefit. Firms will respond by searching for contracts and internal organizational arrangements which will reduce opportunities for discretionary behaviour and result in the pursuit of the organization's goals. Internal monitoring devices and incentives include payment by results, promotion, supervision and fringe benefits as well as threats in the form of firing for poor performance. Personnel departments can provide information on workers and managers: they can search for, and screen, new recruits and ascertain their motivation through, say, the use of references, certificates, selection tests and probationary appointments. However, internal monitoring is costly. In competitive markets, pressure from rivals will provide external policing. Interestingly, some large firms try to simulate external competitive policing through changes in their form of organization, although there might be trade-offs through the effects on scale economies. Large companies can be organized as unitary or multidivisional firms. The unitary form (U-form) company is organized by function such as development, production, finance, marketing and sales. Since divisional heads will aim to maximize their own function, there is a greater probability that goals other than maximum profits will be pursued. The multi-divisional form (M-form) consists of a set of semi-autonomous operating divisions organized, say, on a product basis. This form promotes competition in product markets and creates an internal capital market with each division bidding for scarce funds. On this basis, Williamson (1975) has suggested that the M-form favours goal pursuit and least-cost behaviour more nearly associated with profit maximization than does the U-form. There is support for this hypothesis, with the M-form showing superior profit performance.

The argument can be summarized. The standard analysis assumes that firms can be represented by a set of revenue and efficient cost schedules in which a manager has the simple task of maximizing profits. In this form, some of the interesting problems, insights and aspects of firm behaviour are assumed away. Internal organization is ignored. Firms lack perfect information and knowledge about the motivation of their workers and the profit-maximizing combinations of factors. They respond with an employment contract for the efficient organization of team production. In executing and enforcing this contract, the firm becomes a privately-owned information market with specialist knowledge on the productivity of its owned and hired factors of production. In the circumstances, it has been argued that transactions and transaction costs rather than technology determine the choice of organizational form for exchange. The shift of transactions from market exchange to hierarchy is largely explained by economies in transactions costs. Having explained the existence of firms, attention must now be given to alternative models of behaviour and their policy implications.

7.4 ALTERNATIVE MODELS OF FIRM BEHAVIOUR

Three developments led to a reappraisal of the traditional profit-maximizing postulate. First, evidence seemed to show that firms did not maximize profits: the theory appeared to be based on unrealistic assumptions about marginal cost and revenue. Second, the separation of ownership and control was believed to allow managers opportunities for pursuing their own goals rather than those of the shareholders. This is the principal–agent problem where shareholders as owners of the firm desire their managers as agents to maximize profits rather than to pursue some other managerial objectives (for example, a quiet life; higher salaries unrelated to performance). Third, discretionary behaviour and the pursuit of managerial goals was believed to be more likely in imperfect markets. The result was the development of models in which firms maximize sales, or growth, or a utility function containing such variables as staff, managerial emoluments and organizational slack. Such managerial theories and profit maximization can be regarded as a general class of utility-maximizing models, where there are differences in the variables which enter the utility function. With profit maximization, profits are the only element in the entrepreneur's utility functions: this can be represented by a set of horizontal indifference curves, as shown in Figure 7.1(a). In contrast, the inclusion of other variables besides profit can be represented by more conventional downward sloping indifference curves, as shown in Figure 7.1(b), where X represents some other variable (for example, managerial emoluments). Where other elements only enter the decision-maker's utility function (as in

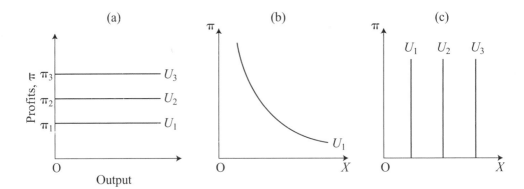

*Figure 7.1   Utility-maximizing firms. Indifference curves are shown by U_1, U_2, U_3 where utility U_2
exceeds U_1, and so on. A higher level of satisfaction or utility is preferred. In diagrams
(b) and (c), X can represent any other non-profit variable in the utility function,
e.g. size, growth, staff*

non-profit organizations), the result is a set of vertical indifference curves, as shown in
Figure 7.1(c).

Separation of Ownership and Control: a Principal–agent Problem

In addition to its possible implications for firm behaviour, this particular issue
involves questions about the distribution of economic and political power within capitalist economies. Have managers and the technostructure replaced the traditional
capitalist class and, if so, how might this affect an economy's performance? Moreover, if
governments wish to raise their economy's growth rate, would it be desirable to support
growth-maximizing firms? If so, under what conditions are such firms likely to emerge?

Without some qualifying conditions, the mere fact that ownership and control are
separated does not necessarily mean that managers fail to maximize profits. Much
depends on the costs and form of the employment contract negotiated between top
managers and shareholders. Presumably, the argument about the separation of ownership and control means that a manager's departures from the interests of shareholders
are less likely to be discerned and 'policed'. This principal–agent argument is not wholly
convincing. If some managers are pursuing their own ends, then rivals are always likely
to emerge either from within or outside the firm. Indeed, the internal organization of
firms can be regarded as a private competitive market in labour and capital as individuals and groups compete for top jobs and scarce funds and managers cannot ignore the
impact of poor performance on their reputations (that is, marketability). Also, if managers exercise discretionary behaviour which is attractive to others, there is likely to be
competition for such jobs, so that wages will reflect the *net* advantages of the work (see
Chapter 11). Similarly, if shareholders are aware of some of the opportunities for managerial slack and shirking, then they will make corresponding adjustments to monetary
contracts. On this view, widely dispersed shareholding does not necessarily imply lower
wealth for shareholders compared with firms where ownership is less dispersed
(Alchian, 1977).

The Role of Market Structure

General opinion suggests that a firm's objective function will depend upon *market structure*. Under competition, profit maximization is required for survival, whereas imperfect markets allow the pursuit of other objectives. However, which is the relevant market: for goods or factors, including managers? Even where product market competition is absent, competition in capital markets will ensure that profit-maximizers find it profitable to take over companies which are pursuing other aims. Competition in capital markets will allocate monopoly rights to those who can use them most profitably. Thus, governments concerned with efficiency in resource allocation might find it useful to concentrate their policies on the proper functioning of *capital markets* (that is, by correcting failures in capital markets). It is, however, possible that monopoly firms might be unwilling to maximize profits through fear of government intervention to regulate 'excessive' rates of return! Nor is it necessarily the case that competitive firms must be profit-maximizers. If entrepreneurs prefer 'independence' they might be prepared to pay for it by accepting a rate of return which is below the competitive level (for example, self-employed business people and shopkeepers): hence, general utility maximization could be possible under competitive conditions. Such a conclusion is also consistent with a subjectivist interpretation of firm behaviour and choices.

Subjectivists regard equilibrium as a special case in the analysis of dynamic markets which are characterized by disequilibrium and continuous entrepreneurial adjustment to constant change. Within such dynamic markets, firms operate under uncertainty where costs are never fully measurable by anyone other than the individual incurring the costs and assessing alternative courses of action. Faced with uncertainty and limited knowledge of the available options, individuals will have different views and valuations about the alternatives open to them. Errors are likely and markets exist to compare subjective evaluations and correct errors. Such an interpretation has major implications for both theory and public policy. Subjectivists maintain that costs are subjective rather than objectively measurable outlays: they exist in the mind of the decision-maker or chooser, so that they cannot be measured by anyone else, including economists and econometricians (who only have access to outcomes rather than *ex ante* data). It is accepted that in full, timeless, certain, general equilibrium, subjective costs can be represented by money outlays, but subjectivists claim, convincingly, that the real world is never in such an equilibrium. Their analysis of choice as non-predictable decisions requires the abandonment of much of standard equilibrium economics with its mathematical rigour and predictability of outcomes (see below and Wiseman, 1980). The policy implications of this approach are equally devastating. It is argued that empirical work and economic policy based on conventional models assuming certainty and full equilibrium may well be wrong in many cases. For example, if costs are subjective, what is the meaning of a government instructing the managers of state-owned enterprises to make price equal to marginal cost? Whose interpretation of marginal cost is being used? In these circumstances, marginal cost is whatever the manager says it is! This is most pertinent since under state or public ownership the costs of any choice are less fully thrust upon the decision-maker than under private ownership (Alchian, 1977).

Profit Maximization and other Models

The alternative models of firm behaviour raise a fundamental methodological issue and one which is relevant to policy formulation. Should economists choose between the alternatives on the basis of the realism of assumptions or their predictive accuracy? Consider the alternatives which result in determinate outcomes. Sales maximization associated with Baumol (1959) was believed to be typical in oligopoly markets. Firms maximize sales revenue subject to a minimum profit constraint. Larger sales might give managers satisfaction from greater size and its associated prestige and security; their salaries might also be related to sales performance rather than profits. An example is shown in Figure 7.2 where the sales-maximizer's price-output decisions can be compared with a profit-maximizer. It can be seen that, *ceteris paribus*, sales maximization results in a lower price and a larger output than under profit maximization. Obviously, the minimum profit constraint is crucial to sales maximization. It is defined as the amount which just satisfies shareholders. But what determines this minimum acceptable level? With competitive product and capital markets, this amount would coincide with the maximum profit position.

An alternative model, due to Marris (1964), assumes that firms are growth-maximizers subject to the desire to avoid being taken over. In this model, firms have a valuation ratio which is the ratio of the stock market value of the enterprise to its accounting or book-value. The relationship between the valuation ratio and the growth rate is shown by the valuation curve which reflects the relationship between growth and profitability and the present value of shareholders' dividends (profits) and capital gains (growth). After a point, increased growth will reduce the valuation ratio. As this ratio falls (substantially below 1.0), the stock market valuation becomes less than the book-value of the firm's assets and a takeover becomes more likely. In other words, this model incorporates a role

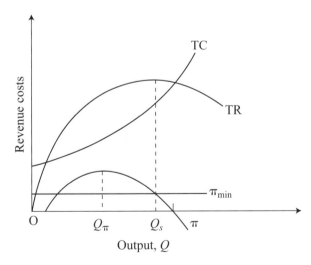

Figure 7.2   Sales maximization. A sales-maximiser will aim to obtain the maximum total revenue (TR), subject to the minimum profit constraint (π_{min}). Actual profit possibilities are shown by π which represents the difference between total revenue and total cost (TC). In this example, the sales-maximizing output is Q_s (it could be less with a greater minimum profit constraint). A profit-maximiser produces output Q_π

for the capital market as a mechanism for 'policing' firm behaviour. An example is shown in Figure 7.3 where the firm maximizes a utility function showing that satisfaction depends on growth and the valuation ratio, subject to the constraints of the valuation curve and the desire to avoid a takeover. In this model, managers desire the power, prestige, status and possibly salary associated with growth (g). They also derive utility from their company's standing in the stock market and the security from takeover (v). Shareholders will prefer the maximum market value (position P) and, in a growth context, this is interpreted as the profit-maximizing solution since it maximizes the present stock market value of the company. In contrast, utility-maximizing managers will aim at a higher growth rate and a correspondingly lower valuation ratio (position G). Since this model depends upon the threat of takeover, some insights into its empirical validity can be obtained by considering the role of the stock market as a disciplinary and policing mechanism. Evidence shows that, at least for large firms, the stock market does not compel such enterprises to maximize profits in order to reduce their chances of being taken over.

Capital market discipline appears to be weak, which might provide tentative support for non-profit-maximizing models of firm behaviour. This is reinforced by evidence which shows that mergers are often associated with a *decline* in profitability. As for the growth maximizing model, it seems that the valuation ratio is not a 'good' discriminator between acquired firms and companies not taken over. However, evidence on the apparent inefficiency of the capital market has to be treated with some caution. The evidence is *ex post*, whereas firm behaviour is based on *ex ante* subjective assessments which are in the minds of decision-makers and which are likely to differ from actual results. Moreover,

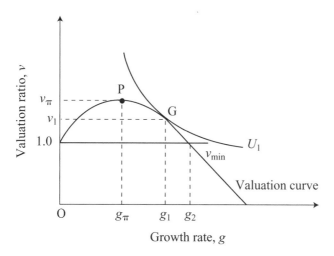

Figure 7.3   Growth maximization. The valuation curve shows the relationship between the valuation ratio (v) and the growth rate (growth of assets, g). Utility depends on v and g and the growth-maximiser is in equilibrium at G, compared with the shareholders' or profit-maximizing equilibrium at P (which maximizes the present stock market value of the company). An alternative position is shown where growth only is maximized, subject to a minimum valuation ratio located at 1.0; this corresponds to vertical indifference curves and results in growth rate g_2

information is not freely available and it is costly to search the capital market for all potential candidates for takeover; hence transactors might discriminate between takeover candidates on the basis of less costly and subjective criteria. Such an interpretation would be acceptable to subjectivists, although it creates problems for empirical work and policy-makers! For example, if it is believed that the facts about the capital market support state intervention to promote mergers and re-structuring for greater efficiency, what 'improved' decision-making criteria will be used by the government, especially in dynamic situations characterized by ignorance and uncertainty and government behaviour determined by voters?

A more general utility-maximizing model of firm behaviour has been constructed by Williamson (1964). In this model, managers have a preference for expenditures on staff, managerial emoluments and discretionary investment expenditures, subject to the need for reported profits to be at some minimum 'acceptable' level. This is a formal expression of the satisfaction and prestige which managers obtain from the number of staff under their control, luxury offices, company cars, expense accounts and other fringe benefits. In the general utility-maximizing case, managers have discretion and this will result in higher staff expenditures and greater managerial slack than for a profit-maximizer. Two examples are shown in Figure 7.4. In the staff model, the firm maximizes a utility function containing both profits and staff expenditures. Predictably, utility maximization results in a larger staff and smaller profits (position A) compared with profit maximization (position P), as shown in Figure 7.4(a). Another variant assumes that the firm derives satisfaction from profits and managerial emoluments. These are discretionary additions to salary and other expenditures or 'corporate personal consumption', which are not required for profit

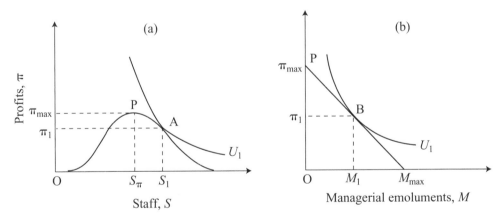

Figure 7.4   *Utility maximization. Diagram (a) shows the staff model where* $U = U(\pi, S)$ *and the 'hump'-shaped curve is a profit frontier showing the profit levels associated with different staff expenditures. Profit maximization occurs at P and utility is maximized at A, with a larger staff. Diagram (b) shows the managerial emoluments model where* $U = U(\pi, M)$; *the preferred combination is position B compared with the profit-maximizing solution at P. In this diagram, actual profits equal maximum profits minus actual managerial emolument (for example* $\pi_1 = \pi_{max} - M_1$*). A profits tax results in a downward shift of the budget line, pivoting around* M_{max} *(which is unaffected by the profits tax)*

maximization. Firms will be constrained by a budget line linking the extremes of maximum profits or diverting all profits to spending on managerial emoluments. With satisfaction derived from both profits and managerial emoluments, firms will obviously prefer more discretionary expenditures than a profit-maximizer, as shown by positions B and P, respectively, in Figure 7.4(b).

Do the Different Models Yield Alternative Predictions?

As outlined above, there are a variety of different models of firm behaviour. How do we choose between them? For example, observations of actual product prices cannot be used to distinguish between the different models. The fact that a car is priced at £x, y or euros z does not confirm that firms are profit-maximizers or anything else (such data does not indicate marginal cost or marginal revenue). In these circumstances, economists use a comparative statics methodology. This considers the price-output responses of different types of firms to changes in demand and taxation. Various types of taxation are analysed, namely a profits tax, a lump sum tax (or any increases in fixed costs), and a sales tax which will shift marginal cost upwards. The aim is to use different taxes to change average and marginal, fixed and variable costs and to predict the effects on the firm's prices and output. To illustrate both the methodology and its policy relevance, consider a government which is contemplating raising the demand for an industry's products. This could be achieved through government procurement policy or, indirectly, through a general expansion of aggregate demand or through changes in the price and availability of consumer credit for 'selected' goods (for example, loans for cars). Alternatively, a government might be considering subjecting an industry to a profits tax or a lump sum tax or an increase in tax rates. How might firms with different objectives react to such policy changes?

Demand and Taxation Policy

Three models of firm behaviour will be compared, namely profits, sales and utility maximization. For simplicity, the comparisons will be restricted to the *output* response of firms to the policy changes. The results of the exercise are summarized in Table 7.1, where the output responses have been derived by making the appropriate shifts in the demand and cost schedules facing each type of firm. The taxes can be considered either as the introduction of a new tax or an increase in rates, the lump sum tax being equivalent to a rise in fixed costs. For an increase in demand, all three models give the same qualitative predictions – that is, an expansion of output, and if employment depends on output, there will be an associated increase in jobs. However, the firms have different output responses to higher taxation. Profit-maximizers will not change output in response to higher profits

Table 7.1   Comparative statics: output responses of firms

Model	Increase in demand	Increase in lump sum tax	Increase in profits tax rate
Profit maximization	+	0	0
Sales maximization	+	−	−
Utility maximization	+	−	+(?)

and lump sum taxes (at least in the short run). Both sales- and utility-maximizers reduce output in response to the introduction of, or increase in, a lump sum tax. However, this only distinguishes between profit maximization and the other models. Alternative predictions for each type emerge in response to a profits tax. Sales-maximizers will reduce output and utility-maximizers are likely to raise it. In the utility-maximizing model, a profits tax probably raises expenditure on managerial emoluments and leads to a greater preference for staff: if so, the increased staff will be associated with a higher output (output and staff are positively associated). Of course, in empirical work, it might not be possible to obtain the required data to hold constant other relevant variables affecting changes in output (for example, home and export demand; changes in technology and costs). Nor might there be many examples of the required tax changes.

7.5 POLICY APPLICATIONS

Models of firm behaviour can contribute to policy formulation in two ways. First, they can help to explain the facts which might be matters of concern to governments. Second, they can be used to predict the likely implications of alternative policy measures, so helping governments to select their preferred option. This section will illustrate both these contributions by examining two sets of policy problems, namely the export performance of firms and subsidies. Exports have been chosen because of the frequent concern of governments with balance of payments targets. A model is required to explain why firms export and whether, for example, a high pressure of demand in the home market is 'good' or 'bad' for exports. Subsidy policy is an extensive area and emphasis will be given to its economic logic and to the employment effects of labour subsidies and the reactions of firms to recessions and regulation. Of course, governments might be reluctant to subsidize private firms. They might prefer to support the formation of worker cooperatives. If so, a model is required to explain and predict the behaviour of labour-managed firms. Nationalized industries are discussed in Chapter 10.

Exports and the Pressure of Domestic Demand

Governments often claim that in order to increase exports to achieve their balance of payments targets, home demand has to be reduced to free resources for an expansion of overseas sales. Broadly, this hypothesis asserts that, in the short run and with a fixed exchange rate, exports are affected by domestic demand, with a high pressure of demand in the economy adversely affecting its export performance. It is argued that a deflation of domestic demand will have both 'push and pull' effects on the export performance of firms and industries. A deflation will release goods and resources from supplying the home market, so allowing firms to increase their exports: they will be 'pushed' into overseas markets. Also, if a deflation means that firms can no longer sell their products in the home market, they will be encouraged to search for foreign markets (the 'pull' effect). At this point, it is necessary to ask what contribution theory can make to identifying the circumstances under which a domestic deflation will improve exports; and, are there any exceptions? Clearly, a model of firm behaviour is required which incorporates both home and overseas markets.

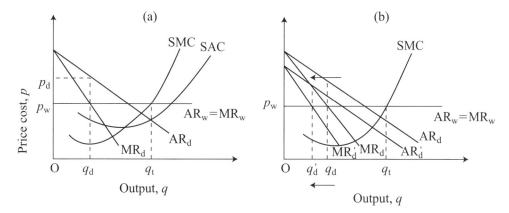

Figure 7.5   Exports and domestic demand. Average and marginal revenue and short-run cost schedules are shown by AR, MR, SAC and SMC; subscripts d and w refer to domestic and world markets, respectively. With two markets, profit maximization requires equality between MC and the combined MR curve. Initially in diagram (a), total output is q_t with $q_d q_t$ for export. A domestic deflation leaves total output unaffected (diagram b), but domestic sales fall and hence exports rise. Shifts in the firm's domestic demand curve will be associated with variations in its domestic prices, but export prices will remain unchanged

Consider a profit-maximizing firm producing a single product as a monopolist in the home market and faced with a competitive world market. Effectively, the firm acts as a price-maker or searcher at home and a price-taker abroad. For a profit-maximizer, home and export markets simply represent possible opportunities for profits. The short-run price-output decisions of this firm and the allocation of its total output between the two markets can be analysed in the same way as a discriminating monopoly. An example is shown in Figure 7.5. A profit-maximizer will produce an output of Oq_t, with Oq_d domestic sales and the rest for export (Figure 7.5a). The home market price of the product will exceed its export price. Similarly, profits per unit of domestic output will exceed the unit profitability of exports. Now, if a deflation of domestic demand in the economy leads to a decrease in the firm's home market demand, the result will be a rise in output exported. In other words, this simple model predicts an inverse relationship between a firm's exports and the pressure of home demand (Figure 7.5b).

The model can be modified to allow the firm to act as a price-maker in both home and overseas markets (that is downward sloping demand curves in each market). For such a profit-maximizing firm, the predicted short-run effect on exports of a change in domestic demand will depend upon its cost conditions. Depending on whether the firm is subject to increasing, decreasing or constant marginal costs, different short-run relationships can be predicted between exports and the pressure of domestic demand. Increasing marginal costs are required for an inverse relationship between a firm's exports and home demand. Other cost conditions give different predictions, as shown in Figure 7.6. Decreasing marginal costs result in a positive relationship: a reduction in a firm's home market sales will be associated with a fall in exports and such a relationship is often claimed to be characteristic of volume producers, such as motor car manufacturers (Figure 7.6a). With constant marginal costs, a change in the firm's domestic demand conditions will have no effect on its exports (Figure 7.6b).

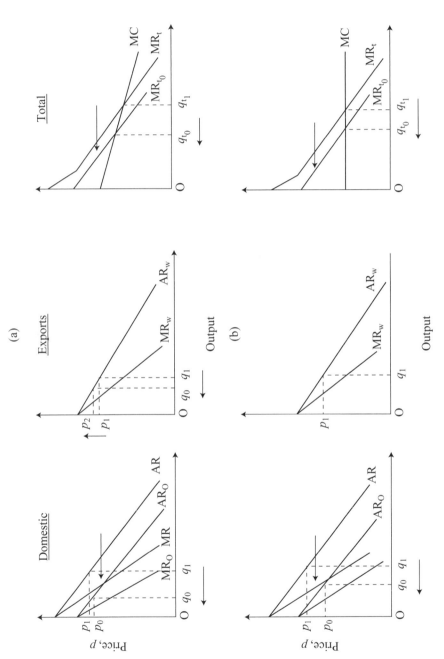

Figure 7.6 Exports and different cost conditions. The discriminating monopolist is a price-maker in both home and export markets. The total market shows the combined marginal revenue curves before and after a deflation. Decreasing costs are shown in diagram (a), with a deflation reducing exports. Constant marginal costs are shown in diagram (b), where exports are unaffected by a deflation

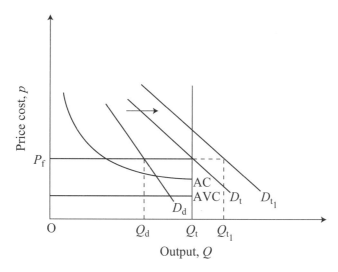

Figure 7.7   Full-cost pricing. The full-cost price is P_f estimated on the basis of average cost (including average variable cost) plus a profit mark-up. Capacity output is Q_t. Assume that initially the total demand D_t for the product results in the firm being able to sell the whole of its output at P_f. With given costs, prices will be the same in both home and export markets, with Q_d sold at home and the rest for export. An increase in domestic demand will shift the total demand curve to Dt_1, creating excess demand of $Q_{t1} - Q_t$ at the ruling price

The fact that the profit-maximizing model has predicted all the possible short-run relationships between exports and domestic demand might be regarded as sufficient for analytical purposes. Critics of profit maximization have suggested that benefits other than profits might be obtained from exporting. Firms sometimes claim that exports provide benefits in the form of prestige, security through market diversification, and the possibility of expansion which might be impossible to achieve at home. It is not at all obvious that these alleged benefits are inconsistent with profit maximization and consistent with some other aim (which?). However, some critics have proposed the full-cost principle as an alternative explanation of business behaviour. As such, the principle is really an explanation of pricing which implies that firms might be pursuing objectives other than maximum profits, but it fails to specify these objectives. Basically, it is a supply-side or cost hypothesis of pricing in which product prices depend on average variable costs plus a costing margin which includes an allowance for overheads and a profit mark-up. An example is shown in Figure 7.7, where the firm is working at capacity, supplying both home and export markets. Consider the effect on exports of an increase in home demand. With strict full-cost pricing, the immediate result is excess demand at the ruling price, as reflected in order books, lengthening delivery dates, and waiting times. The initial effect on exports will depend on the firm's criteria for determining priorities in a queuing situation. For example, overseas sales are likely to be adversely affected if domestic firms lengthen the delivery dates for their exports at a faster rate than their foreign competitors. Subjectivists, however, would be especially critical of the full-cost pricing principle simply because it is based on measured (realized) outlays which in disequilibrium cannot be accurate representations of opportunity costs.

Analysis shows that predictions about the short-run relationship between exports and domestic demand are related to the firm's objectives, together with its market and cost conditions. In fact, a decrease in the home demand for a firm's products can be associated with an increase, or a reduction or no change in overseas sales. Predictions can be obtained on domestic and export prices, queuing, and the relative profitability of home and overseas sales. Empirical work at the firm and industry level in the United Kingdom has shown a diversity of experience in the relationship between exports and domestic demand not only between industries but also between different overseas markets for the same industry. Such a finding makes life difficult for policy-makers! Moreover, a substantial amount of interview-questionnaire evidence now exists, showing that product prices are determined on the basis of estimated costs modified for market conditions (for example, competition, market research, prices of existing products): such findings refute the simple supply-side version of the full-cost hypothesis (Cooper et al., 1970).

Subsidy Policy: some General Issues

There are two approaches to subsidy policy. First, there is a need to consider the economic logic of subsidy policy: does economic theory offer any policy guidelines? Second, what are the likely impacts of various subsidies on firm behaviour? Economic theory suggests that if a nation wishes to achieve an optimum allocation of resources, there are two criteria for subsidies. First, subsidies are required whenever marginal cost pricing is applied in a decreasing cost activity. An example is shown in Figure 7.8, where a subsidy is necessary to cover the losses associated with marginal cost pricing (assuming no price

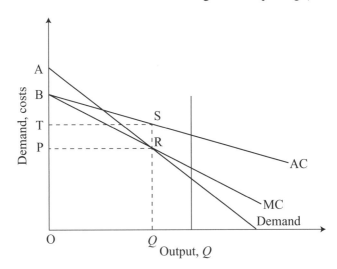

Figure 7.8   Marginal cost pricing and subsidies. Decreasing average and marginal costs are shown by AC and MC, respectively. Marginal cost pricing is based on the intersection of the demand and MC schedules, at position R. As a result, there are losses of PRST. The welfare maximum at R is represented by the net surplus ARB. At R, the potential gainers could overcompensate private firms for sacrificing profit maximization and operating at R

discrimination). Second, subsidies are required whenever there are substantial social benefits such that private firms left to themselves would provide less than the socially desirable output. This argument is often used to justify many activities which governments claim to undertake in the 'national interest'. Thus, subsidies might be rationalized on the grounds of jobs, regional employment, defence, high technology, the balance of payments, and the 'shortcomings' of the capital market (see Chapters 4 and 14). Many of these alleged benefits require critical evaluation, concentrating upon their analytical and empirical basis. Rarely is attention given to whether the resources would yield greater social benefits if they were used elsewhere in the economy. For example, would resources in the subsidized sector create more jobs or more exports if they were used elsewhere in the economy?

Increasingly, governments in developed nations, such as the European Union, are stressing the 'need' to subsidize high-technology industries. It is believed that the future competitiveness of European industry will depend on its ability to 'mobilize new technologies', especially in 'key' R&D industries such as aerospace, computers, electronics, nuclear power and telecommunications. Research and development is regarded as a 'key' element in innovation and it is characterized by high risk, long-term rather than immediate returns, and technical 'spillovers' to the rest of the economy. Such arguments for state support have some analytical basis. Competitive markets will tend to underinvest in research. This market failure can arise because of the risks and uncertainties of research, the costs of establishing complete property rights in marketable ideas, and increasing returns in the use of information (that is both beneficial externalities in the form of technology spin-offs and decreasing marginal costs). Critics of such market failure analysis have shown that a free enterprise economy is likely to result in the 'correct' or optimal adjustment to risk and uncertainty once it is recognized that such adjustments are not costless. Nor is the issue of property rights unique since the 'theft' of all information cannot be eliminated at reasonable cost; and this applies to any valuable asset. Even if the market failure analysis is accepted, it does not necessarily constitute a case for state support of a specific industry, such as aerospace or microelectronics. Governments cannot avoid choices about the allocation of scarce resources between alternative research activities and institutions in the public and private sectors, and between manufacturing and the rest of the economy.

An example of controversy about subsidy policy occurred in 2005/06 with the international dispute between Airbus and Boeing over allegations about subsidies received for their large civil jet aircraft (for example, Airbus 380; Boeing 787: Hayward, 2005). Both the European Union and the USA have submitted their cases for resolution by the World Trade Organization (WTO) unless a bilateral agreement is reached. Prior to this dispute, the 1992 US–EU bilateral agreement allowed governments to provide support for the development of airframes for large civil aircraft to 33 per cent of total development costs (paid as repayable Launch Investment in the EU) or to provide indirect support subject to a maximum of 4 per cent of annual commercial sales of a company or 3 per cent of industry-wide commercial sales in each country (indirect support affected the USA). Resolution of the controversy by the WTO will require that subsidies be defined and valued and that proof of damage to either or both Airbus and Boeing will have to be established. The controversy also raises economic principles related to the operation of private capital markets.

Are private capital markets able and willing to finance all development costs for large civil aircraft or are there genuine capital market failures preventing the availability of significant amounts of project risk-sharing finance at the launch stage? If there are market failures, why do they arise, how can they be removed and at what cost? The economics of new large civil jet aircraft and engine projects involves high development costs, lengthy development periods, substantial technical and commercial risks (for example, Airbus A380; Concorde) and long-term returns. Unlike the motor car and pharmaceuticals industries, such projects are relatively few and each represents a large proportion of the enterprise value of the companies involved in such programmes (Airbus; Boeing; General Electric; Pratt and Whitney; Rolls-Royce). There is evidence that the aerospace industry experiences difficulties in attracting risk-sharing finance for new projects at their early development stage; but difficulties in the provision of private capital may or may not constitute a capital market failure. Provision of finance at 'too high' a price is not necessarily evidence of capital market failure: it might reflect the view that there are more profitable opportunities for its funds in sectors other than aerospace.

Capital markets have arranged some solutions to this aerospace financing problem including capital raising at the company level (compared with the project level) and supplier financing where suppliers provide risk capital and are risk-sharing partners. Nonetheless, there remain a range of factors which might explain the pattern of capital markets' provision of finance to the civil aerospace sector. These include uncertainty and risk aversion of investors; the small number of programmes and asymmetric information; possible short-termism; the dependence upon single companies; and the availability of government financial support for civil aircraft in Europe, Japan, North America and elsewhere (that is, government failure). It is also possible that aerospace companies are unable to capture all the benefits from their investments, especially where there are beneficial externalities in the form of technology spin-offs (for example, spin-offs from military aerospace R&D to civil aerospace projects; Formula 1 racing cars). The question is which of these factors, if any, is a genuine market failure and are any such failures specific to aerospace or do they generally affect all sectors?

Subsidy Policy: Firm-level Issues

Governments often subsidize labour to achieve employment targets, either at the regional or national level. Models of firm behaviour can be used to predict the employment effects of a labour subsidy. An example for a profit-maximizing firm is shown in Figure 7.9. A labour or job subsidy results in both substitution and scale effects.

The substitution effect leads to the substitution of labour for capital. Also, if the subsidy reduces the firm's marginal costs, prices will fall and output rises, so that there is a scale effect. If both labour and capital are normal factors, the scale effect will reinforce the substitution effect and further increase employment.

Job subsidies appear attractive since they have an immediate impact and they seem to 'save' on state unemployment payments. But appearances are no substitute for analysis and evidence. Labour subsidies are likely to have 'displacement effects' in that employment preservation in subsidized firms is purchased at a cost of jobs lost in non-subsidized enterprises. Also, when assessing the quantitative impact of job subsidies, care is required to ensure that the number of jobs 'saved' in subsidized firms are *net* additions, directly

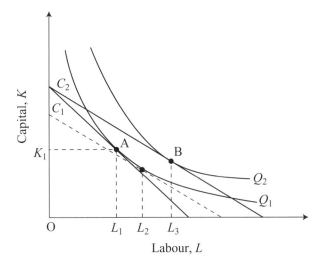

Figure 7.9 *Job subsidies. The firm is initially in equilibrium at position A where the isocost line* C_1 *is tangential to the isoquant* Q_1. *A labour subsidy leads to a new isocost line at* C_2, *a higher output* Q_2, *and a new equilibrium at position B. The substitution effect raises employment from* L_1 *to* L_2; *the scale effect further increases employment from* L_2 *to* L_3

attributable to subsidies rather than other influences. Nor are subsidies necessarily conducive to efficient performance: they might be used to finance existing or even higher levels of organizational slack (X-inefficiency). Consider a firm receiving a lump sum subsidy. A utility maximizer, enjoying profits and managerial emoluments, would use the subsidy to increase both these preferred 'goods'. However, the government might respond by imposing profit controls on the recipients of subsidies (for example, to prevent extra profits being earned at the taxpayer's expense). As a result, the firm is likely to 'consume' even more managerial perks, as shown in Figure 7.10 (see Chapter 15, Figure 15.1). Subsidized firms subject to profit controls could also have a reduced incentive to resist wage increases. Indeed, the existence of state subsidies might induce firms to become subsidy maximizers, seeking revenue from governments and bureaucrats rather than private consumers!

Utility Maximization and Recessions

The inefficiency aspect of subsidies suggests an alternative policy option. Governments sometimes claim that a recession is required to 'shock' firms into improved efficiency, so reducing organizational 'slack'. Such a policy might be appropriate for utility-maximizers and satisficers, and where governments aim to raise technical efficiency. For example, faced with a dramatic decline in demand, utility-maximizers are likely to make drastic reductions in their staff compared with profit-maximizers, as shown in Figure 7.11. Thus, the managerial discretion model predicts substantial adjustments in staff during adversity. There is some empirical support for this hypothesis. In addition, studies show that firms respond to adversity by reducing such discretionary expenditures as company cars, chauffeurs and office spending.

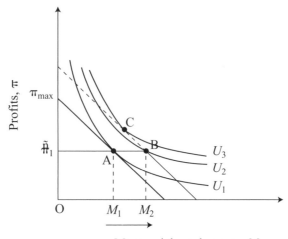

Figure 7.10   Utility-maximizers and subsidies. The firm is initially in equilibrium at position A. It now receives a lump sum subsidy but is unable to increase its profits above π₁. The result is a 'corner solution' at position B where the firm consumes more managerial perks, M₂, than with its preferred position at C

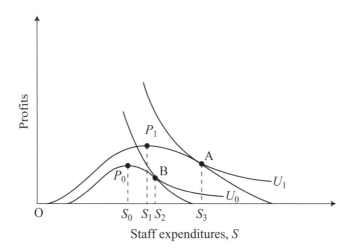

Figure 7.11   Utility maximization and adversity. A utility-maximizer will respond to adversity by making the adjustment from position A to B and the profit-maximizer adjusts from P₁ to P₀

Worker Cooperatives

Rather than subsidize private capitalists, governments might prefer to support worker cooperatives or labour-managed firms. It is believed that worker control will remove the traditional conflict between labour and capital (for example, industrial disputes, strikes, restrictive labour practices), and raise the productivity of individual workers and

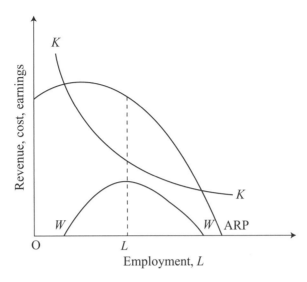

Figure 7.12 *A labour-managed firm. The diagram shows a LMF in long-run competitive equilibrium. The average revenue product of labour is ARP. Capital is the only other factor, and its fixed rental results in a capital cost per worker represented by a rectangular hyperbola,* KK *. Average net earnings are the difference between the ARP curve and* KK*, represented by the curve* WW*. Average net earnings are maximized at employment* L*. Of course, if the LMF is maximizing a utility function containing both earnings and employment, it will employ more than* L *workers*

managers. What is likely to happen if workers hire capital instead of capitalists hiring labour? Some answers are provided by economic models of labour-managed enterprises.

In a model associated with Meade (1972), a worker cooperative or labour-managed firm (LMF) is assumed to maximize the net earnings or income per worker. Capital and other inputs would be hired and the cooperative would sell its products at market prices. Risks would be borne by labour, with surpluses and losses distributed between the workers according to an agreed sharing system (for example, equality or sharing based on skills). As a result of a change in ownership, incentives are likely to differ between LMFs and profit-maximizing firms (PMFs) in capitalist economies. It is believed that in worker cooperatives, the sense of participation in decision-making may be greater. Self-policing is also expected, since any extra profits due to improved productivity will accrue to the workers as owners. The former Yugoslavia was an example of a self-managed economy, but other instances occur in capitalist systems, particularly with professional groups such as accountants, doctors, lawyers and orchestras. A model of the LMF in long-run equilibrium is shown in Figure 7.12.

The LMF is assumed to be a price-taker, aiming to maximize average net earnings. In a perfectly competitive economy, both LMFs and PMFs will, in the long run, result in an efficient (Pareto optimal) allocation of resources. Both will employ the same quantity of labour, *ceteris paribus*. The PMF will equate the marginal value product of labour with the ruling wage which will be the same as that paid by the cooperative. However, while the final outcome is identical, the short-run adjustment process differs. In competitive markets, a rise in products prices will cause PMFs to *increase* output and employment.

But in the short run, a LMF will respond by *reducing* employment and output, so as to continue maximizing average net earnings. Such a short-run response by a LMF might not be the reaction desired by a government committed to raising employment. Of course, in the long run, new and existing PMFs will compete away any abnormal profits and labour will be attracted to high-wage sectors. Similarly, in a self-managed economy, above-average earnings will lead to the formation of new worker cooperatives in the high-earnings industries.

The model of the LMF is not without its critics. Conflicts might arise in determining the rules for sharing surpluses and losses between labour of different skills. Similarly, the cooperative will have to determine rules for admitting new workers and the property rights of leavers. There might also be difficulties and costs of internal 'policing', especially in large LMFs where individual preferences for income and leisure will differ and where there are opportunities for 'shirking and free-riding'. Moreover, models of the LMF might not be appropriate where policy-makers wish to expand the opportunities for industrial democracy without changing ownership. Within Europe, for example, there is support for some form of worker representation on the boards of directors of private firms. It is argued that industry's future ability to adjust to change will depend upon the approval and support of its work force and that those affected by decisions must be involved in the decision-making process (for example, closures, new machinery, redundancy). Clearly, this is a subject area where there are opportunities for further analytical and empirical work. What are the likely implications of different forms of industrial democracy for firm behaviour and performance? Will industrial democracy raise or lower productivity and have adverse or favourable effects on investment and inflation? Indeed, issues of industrial democracy, worker cooperatives and subsidy policy raise wider issues about whether governments need an industrial policy.

7.6   INDUSTRIAL POLICY

De-industrialization

Governments often express concern about de-industrialization or the decline of their national manufacturing industrial base. One version of the de-industrialization hypothesis maintains that the public sector and government spending preempt resources, both of capital and labour, forcing a contraction in manufacturing industry. The result is 'too few' producers to the detriment of industry's, and hence the economy's, investment and export performance. Higher government spending might 'crowd out' private expenditure. If the 'crowding-out' occurs in private sector investment, particularly in manufacturing, then it is possible that the size of the public sector as reflected in state spending will adversely affect manufacturing investment (Bacon and Eltis, 1978). In this form, the de-industrialization hypothesis was offered as an explanation of the UK's economic performance in the 1960s and 1970s. If valid, it suggests that improved economic performance can be achieved through a public policy which expands the market sector by cutting public spending, including subsidies to both nationalized and private industries.

The public sector version of the de-industrialization hypothesis has been extensively criticized, both analytically and empirically. To its advocates, the main problem appears to be the relative decline in a nation's manufacturing industry. But this might be due to 'other causes', such as a long-run decline in both price and non-price international competitiveness. Similarly, a relatively poor investment record in manufacturing might reflect a lack of demand rather than the supply of funds. Critics have also suggested that the public sector might have been expanded to achieve full employment, in which case labour and resources would not have been attracted from manufacturing. Moreover, if the public sector is 'too large', what is its optimum size? And what are the implications of a smaller public sector? For example, which items of government expenditure are to be reduced? Are these items being provided inefficiently or is there no demand for them, and, if no demand exists, why were they ever provided? This raises questions about how society expresses its relative valuations of government services. An analytical framework is required to clarify some of these issues.

Part of the controversy can be represented as a debate about the shape of an economy's production possibility frontier and its actual position in relation to both the boundary and society's welfare function. An example is shown in Figure 7.13. The production possibility frontier has ranges showing a positive relationship between public sector and manufacturing output. This reflects the possibility that, up to a point, increases in government production might favourably affect manufacturing output. Also, the largest manufacturing output is unlikely to be associated with a zero-sized public sector (and vice versa). For an economy located within its boundary (for example, point S), an expansion of the public sector can be achieved without any sacrifice of manufacturing goods (and vice versa).

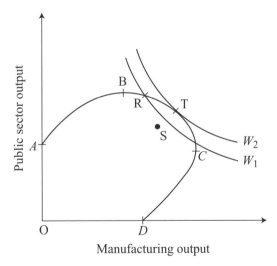

Figure 7.13   *The public sector and manufacturing. The production possibility boundary is represented by ABCD and society's preference functions by W_1 and W_2, with $W_2 > W_1$. Over the ranges AB and DC there is a positive relationship between output in the public sector and manufacturing. The range BC shows the more conventional trade-off between the two outputs. The postulated frontier also shows that the maximum manufacturing output is associated with a positive-sized public sector. The shape of ABCD can be determined by empirical testing. Position T is society's preferred combination, located on the highest welfare function. Point R, associated with a larger public sector than at T, gives lower welfare. Point S is located within the frontier*

Society's preferred combination of public sector and manufacturing goods is located at position T in Figure 7.13. In this sense, the combination shown at R results in a public sector which is 'too large'. However, some explanation is required of why a society might be located at R, a point which is neglected by the existing public sector versions of the de-industrialization hypothesis. One explanation is provided by the economics of politics and bureaucracies, and particularly by the models of bureaucracy (see Chapter 14). Such models also highlight some of the problems likely to be encountered in controlling bureaucracies and cutting the size of the public sector. But if society prefers a smaller public sector and more manufacturing goods, does this mean that the state requires an industrial policy?

Do Governments need an Industrial Policy?

Answers to this question can be approached with the standard methodology of economic policy which seeks to identify the policy problem, its causes and the range of alternative solutions. What is de-industrialization, why does it occur, and what can be done about it? Policy-makers often view the problem as de-industrialization or the relative decline of industry, especially the manufacturing sector, and the need to reverse this decline. A typical official policy view is that the health of manufacturing is of vital importance to national economic performance and that manufacturing has failed to respond adequately to changes in the pattern of world demand and suffers from structural rigidities, some of which are reflected in bottlenecks.

At the outset, any analyst requires a clear, unambiguous statement of the policy problem. If, as alleged, industry has not responded 'adequately', what would an 'adequate' response be and why has it failed to respond 'adequately'? If 'structural rigidities' are the answer, what are they, where do they exist, and why? Structural rigidities are supposed to be reflected in 'bottlenecks', although the term is rarely defined. If it means excess demand at the ruling price or wage, what is preventing relative prices from adjusting upwards and clearing markets? Imperfections are a possible cause. In which case, it is necessary to know whether the imperfections are policy-created through, for example, government restrictions on prices and incomes or entry barriers created by government procurement policy. There are more fundamental worries about bottlenecks. The illusion that bottlenecks can be removed completely resembles the nirvana approach to economic policy, where scarcity no longer exists and costs can be ignored. Nor is it possible to neglect uncertainty. Policy-makers cannot accurately predict the future: today's bottlenecks might be tomorrow's surpluses! Uncertainty will always exist about future changes in demand and supply in both domestic and world markets. Consumers' preferences are not static with, for example, air travel replacing surface travel and television being substituted for newspapers as well as for 'live' cinema, theatres and sports performances. Supply-side changes are caused by new entrants, lower-cost sources of supply, and technical progress (for example, computers, microelectronics, nuclear power). In other words, the comparative advantages and disadvantages of a nation's industries are not fixed forever.

Doubts, however, have arisen about whether the paradigm of comparative advantage based on factors of production provides an adequate explanation of world trade patterns. Critics point to much of world trade taking place between advanced industrial nations with similar factor endowments and they point to trade between different national subsidiaries of multinational firms. It is also recognized that assumptions of comparative advantage theories are unrealistic. The assumptions of no scale economies, identical technologies and competitive industries fail to conform to a world of scale economies, technology gaps, differentiated products, world markets dominated by duopoly and oligopoly suppliers (for example, Airbus and Boeing in large civil aircraft) and the globalization of firm and industries. One response to these changes suggests that any new theory needs to start by recognizing that competition is dynamic and not static, that innovation and technology are central elements of any new paradigm and that competition is characterized by a perpetual state of change and not by equilibrium. In his study of *The Competitive Advantage of Nations*, Michael Porter focuses on the importance of five competitive forces (Porter, 1990). These comprise the threat of new entrants, the threat of substitute products and services, the bargaining power of buyers and sellers and rivalry amongst existing competitors. Such competitive forces determine industry profitability. Porter uses his theory to identify the important long-term issues facing a nation's firms and government in upgrading competitive advantage in both industry and the national economy. He concludes that national competitive advantage is not a zero-sum game: innovation and change make the pie bigger so that national competitiveness is not a contest where some nations win at the expense of others. On this view, all nations can innovate faster and upgrade the productivity of labour and capital (Porter, 1990, pp. 682–4).

Where a government's industrial policy involves 'picking the winners', it cannot avoid choices under uncertainty. Which are likely to be the new growth sectors and job creators over the next ten or twenty years? To economists the issue involves the choice of the most appropriate institutional and policy arrangements for coping with, and responding to, uncertainty. Private markets with governments correcting any major failures are one possibility. It is argued that among large numbers of firms, with different views about the future and risking their funds, some are more likely to guess the future more accurately, and there are always opportunities for new entrants and exits. An alternative solution would be a single, centralized government decision-making body. But a single body could have a great chance of being wrong! Also, the economics of politics and bureaucracies suggests that decision-making by such a body will be strongly influenced by interest groups of bureaucrats and producers. In this situation, firms might be induced to seek revenue from governments rather than private consumers, with subsidies and protection blunting incentives. If the central body is 'wrong', the impersonal committee can be blamed and the taxpayer finances the costs of failure.

Why is there an Industrial Problem?

Once the policy problem has been clearly specified, its causes have to be identified. Compared with other countries, the relatively poor performance of a nation's manufacturing industry might be due to government policy and to significant failures in factor and product markets. The hypothesis that the public sector has preempted resources to the detriment of industry's investment and export performance has already been outlined. Factor markets, embracing capital and labour, might also be sources of relatively poor industrial performance. It is often alleged that private capital markets 'fail' to give priority to the 'needs' of industry, allocating funds to housing and 'speculative ventures'.

Sometimes, such views reflect a potential misunderstanding about the operation of private capital markets. If capital markets fail to allocate funds (at the ruling prices) to high-risk projects of the Concorde-type, this might be evidence that the market is, in fact, working properly and believes that there are more profitable alternative users of its funds. This is not to claim that all private capital markets are 'counsels of perfection'. Instead, it suggests that convincing evidence of market failure has first to be identified, after which consideration can be given to the causes of any failure.

Labour markets can also be a cause of relatively poor industrial performance. Shortages of skilled labour and relatively low labour productivity might reflect 'inadequate' consultation, overmanning, restrictive practices, industrial disputes, 'poor' management, and immobility. Once again, there is a danger of emphasis being given to *effects* rather than *causes*. What would be adequate consultation and why do restrictive practices and strikes occur? Why is management poor? Is it, and what is the evidence? It might be that a lack of competition in product markets allows firms to be relatively inefficient, pursuing aims other than maximum profits. Whatever the explanations of poor industrial performance, questions arise as to what contribution, if any, public policy can make to solving these problems.

One view maintains that left to themselves private markets will fail to improve a nation's economic performance. Supporters of the model of a 'cumulative and circular chain of causation' maintain that once a nation starts to decline, it will continue to contract and experience a vicious downward spiral (Myrdal, 1957). Difficulties arise in determining whether a nation is following such a vicious downward spiral or whether equilibrium economics is relevant and the economy is experiencing the resource re-allocations resulting from changing demands and comparative advantages in world markets. The model can be further criticized.

A concern with de-industrialization usually leads to a policy emphasis on manufacturing. This is reputed to be the dynamic sector of the economy, with the greatest potential for productivity growth through technical progress and increasing returns to scale. In other words, the underlying growth model postulates that a nation's growth rate depends on the growth of its manufacturing sector. However, a policy emphasis on production tends to neglect services and other non-manufacturing activities as well as technology (for example, agriculture, mining, oil and gas). Also, it might be that some of the beliefs about the relative lack of technical progress in non-manufacturing activities reflects the difficulties of measuring productivity and output in these sectors. But if governments require an industrial policy, what form should it take?

Some Policy Options

A distinction can be made between the technical issues concerned with the causes of market failure and the policy issues involving the choice of the most appropriate solution. Controversy usually arises over the form of industrial policy. Left-wing governments favour extending public ownership and greater state intervention aimed at re-structuring industry through mergers and using subsidies to support lame ducks. Right-wing governments prefer market solutions, with a smaller public sector, lower personal taxation to increase incentives, and competition policy for removing imperfections and improving efficiency in product and factor markets. Such solutions involve some state intervention through, for example, regulatory agencies for identifying market imperfections and subsequently enforcing and policing competition policy. Both sets of views reflect an increased emphasis on microeconomic policies, including the efficiency of supply, compared with the more traditional approach whereby economic policy was dominated by macroeconomics and the management of aggregate demand. However, the greater emphasis on microeconomic 'solutions' requires some criteria for the selection of specific markets and industries for policy action. For example, market-type solutions require competition to be defined as an operational concept. An alternative approach involves the selection of 'key' industries.

One policy designed to reverse de-industrialization aims to remove obstacles to the growth of some of a nation's 'key' industries. Economic analysis offers no guidelines for identifying a 'key' industry. Indeed, general equilibrium models stress the interdependency of product and factor markets within an economy. Nevertheless, policy-makers have used various criteria to define 'key' industries. They can be defined in terms of size, such as employment, output or export performance. Or, they might be industries whose performance is 'important' to the rest of the economy (for example, components suppliers), or industries which, on the basis of past performance, are likely to be successful. Or, they might be high technology sectors which are expected to provide the next generation of new highly-paid jobs (for example, aerospace; computing; electronics). Of course, the criteria for selecting 'key' industries will emerge in the political market and will be influenced by vote-sensitive governments, budget-conscious bureaucrats, and income-maximizing producer groups.

Even if policy can identify the 'winners' and 'losers', as well as those with potential for success, what should be done, particularly in a world of uncertainty? Should the already progressive and growing industries be stimulated and supported? But these might be at their peak. Or should help be given to industries which are lagging behind? But these are already declining sectors where state support might be costly in terms of opportunities forgone. Moreover, if the capital market is working properly, doubts arise about some of the proposals for assisting firms and industries which show potential for success. Nevertheless, where state assistance is required, choices have to be made between aid in cash or kind. Financial assistance requires further choices between loans and subsidies (to firms or investment or labour?). In this way, subsidy policy together with policies towards competition, regulation and ownership form elements of an industrial policy.

7.7 CONCLUSION

This chapter has explained why firms exist and has outlined alternative models of behaviour. For policy purposes, one of the fundamental issues concerns the appropriateness of alternative theories of the firm. Consideration has been given to the relationship between objectives, on the one hand, and ownership and market structures, on the other. For example, will a change from public to private ownership, together with greater competition, improve economic efficiency? Some models, such as satisficing, seem to provide accurate descriptions. The firm is viewed as a coalition of different interest groups, with entrepreneurs making 'side payments' for the cooperation of the various groups. But is descriptive accuracy the 'best' or only criterion for choosing between alternative theories? Another criterion would be alternative predictions and their empirical validity. Here, it is interesting to note that there are a number of circumstances where alternative models result in similar qualitative predictions. In this situation, policy advisers might find that the basic profit-maximizing postulate continues to provide an adequate *starting point* for analysis.

READING* AND REFERENCES

Alchian, A. (1977), *Economic Forces At Work*, Indianapolis: Liberty Press.
Bacon, R. and W. Eltis (1978), *Britain's Economic Problem: Too Few Producers*, London: Macmillan.
Baumol, W.J. (1959), *Business Behavior, Value and Growth*, New York: Macmillan.
Baumol, W.J. (1990), 'Entrepreneurship: Productive, unproductive and destructive', *Journal of Political Economy*, **98**(5), 893–921.
Berle, A.A. and G.C. Means (1932), *The Modern Corporation and Private Property*, New York: Harcourt Brace.
Blume, L. and S.N. Durlauf (2008), *The New Palgrave Dictionary of Economics*, 2nd edn, London: Macmillan, forthcoming.
Chamberlin, E.H. (1933), *The Theory of Monopolistic Competition*, Cambridge, Mass: Harvard University Press.
*Coase, R.H. (1937), 'The nature of the firm', *Economica*, November, vol. **4**, 386–405.
Cooper, R., K. Hartley and C. Harvey (1970), *Export Performance and the Pressure of Demand*, London: Allen and Unwin.
Cyert, R.M. and J.G. March (1963), *A Behavioral Theory of the Firm*, Englewood Cliffs, N.J.: Prentice-Hall.
Foss, N.J. (1994), 'The theory of the firm: The Austrians as precursors and critics of contemporary theory', *Review of Austrian Economics*, **7**(1), 31–65.
Foss, N.J. and P.G. Klein (2004), '*Entrepreneurship and the economic theory of the firm: any gains from trade?* DRUID Working Papers 04-12, Copenhagen Business School, Aalborg University, Denmark.
Hayward, K. (2005), 'Trade disputes in the commercial aircraft industry: a background note', *Aeronautical Journal*, **109**(1094), Royal Aeronautical Society, London.
King, J. (ed.) (1980), *Readings in Labour Economics*, Part 2, Oxford: Oxford University Press.
Kirzner, I.M. (1979), *Perception, Opportunity and Profit*, Chicago: University of Chicago Press.
Marris, R. (1964), *The Economic Theory of Managerial Capitalism*, London: Macmillan.
Marshall, A. (1890), *Principles of Economics*, 8th edn (1920), pp. 315–18, London: Macmillan.
Meade, J. (1972), 'The theory of labour-managed firms and of profit-sharing', *Economic Journal*, **82**, March (supplement).
Myrdal, G. (1957), *Economic Theory and underdeveloped Regions*, London: Duckworth.
*Porter, M.E. (1990), *The Competitive Advantage of Nations*, London: Macmillan.
Robinson, J. (1933), *The Economics of Imperfect Competition*, London: Macmillan.
Simon, H.A. (1966), 'Theories of decision-making in economics and behavioural science' in *Surveys of Economic Theory*, vol. III Royal Economic Society, London: Macmillan.
Sraffa, P. (1926), 'The laws of returns under competitive conditions', *Economic Journal*, December, vol. **36**, 535–50.
Wildsmith, J.R. (1973), *Managerial Theories of the Firm*, London: Martin Robertson.
*Williamson, O.E. (1964), *The Economics of Discretionary Behavior: Managerial Objectives in a Theory of the Firm*, Englewood Cliffs, N.J.: Prentice-Hall.
Williamson, O.E. (1975), *Markets and Hierarchies: Analysis and Anti-Trust Implications*, New York: Free Press.
Wiseman, J. (1980), 'Costs and decisions', in D. Currie and W. Peters (eds), *Contemporary Economic Analysis* Vol. 2, London: Croom Helm.
Vanek, J. (ed.) (1975), *Self-Management: Economic Liberation of Man*, Harmondsworth: Penguin.

QUESTIONS FOR REVIEW AND DISCUSSION

1. Why do firms exist? What are the policy implications of your analysis?
2. Does the full-cost pricing principle explain the behaviour of firms in:
   (a) the motor car industry:
   (b) commercial banking; and
   (c) the distributive trades?
3. Predict the effects of a domestic deflation on a firm's export performance. How would you test your predictions?
4. Do employment contracts explain the behaviour and performance of firms in the public and private sectors? What are the implications of your analysis for state subsidies to private firms?
5. Are costs subjective or objective? What are the policy implications of these alternative interpretations?
6. What is the policy relevance of firms pursuing non-profit objectives? Explain and give examples.
7. What would be the effect on a nation's manufacturing industry if all firms became workers' cooperatives? Does a knowledge of welfare economics enable you to determine whether such firms are 'desirable'?
8. Critically evaluate the theoretical and empirical basis of X-inefficiency. What are the public policy implications of your conclusions?
9. 'Changes in the internal organization of firms have mitigated capital market failures by transferring functions traditionally imputed to the capital market to the firm instead' (Williamson, 1975). Evaluate this statement showing the implications of your analysis for empirical work on the efficiency of the capital market and for public policy.
10. Consider the subsidy dispute of 2005/07 between Airbus and Boeing. What are the central economic issues in this dispute and what are the possible policy solutions?

8. Monopoly: Consequences, regulation and prevention

8.1 INTRODUCTION

As was illustrated in Chapter 2, monopoly in a market can result in an economy not achieving a Paretian optimum. A Kaldor–Hicks loss occurs because in order to maximize its profit a monopolist raises the price of its product above its marginal cost of production. A monopolist fosters scarcity of the monopolized good in order to increase its profit. Consumers (buyers) are economically disadvantaged as a result. Economists have traditionally argued that economic scarcity will be greater under monopoly than if greater market competition is present. More specifically, it is often argued that monopoly will result in greater economic scarcity than if perfect competition prevails. But as will be seen in this chapter, monopoly *may be* superior to perfect competition in stimulating economic growth and thereby reducing scarcity. Also a monopoly may be advantageous when decreasing costs of production occur. In this case, demand for the product could be met at least cost by one supplier.

Just as perfect competition is an ideal or abstract market type, so too is monopoly. The difficulties of defining monopoly and measuring monopoly power and the pitfalls of various measures are discussed in this chapter. The traditional profit-maximizing model of monopoly, assuming the *absence of entry*, is outlined first and the consequences of a monopolist's behaviour for consumers' surplus are explored. The extent of losses in consumers' surplus as a result of monopoly compared to the alternative of perfect competition is shown in a static setting to depend on the inelasticity of the demand for the monopolized product and on the inelasticity of marginal cost. This leads on to a discussion of the relative benefits of monopoly and perfect competition in a dynamic setting involving technological change and to a consideration of 'X-inefficiency' under monopoly and the possible social costs of this compared to 'allocative' inefficiency. The possibility of non-profit-maximizing behaviour on the part of a monopolist (previously discussed in Chapter 7) is then allowed for, and some of the effects and welfare consequences of this are analysed.

Entry conditions are extremely important in determining whether and for how long a monopoly lasts and these conditions influence the behaviour of 'incumbent' monopolists. Consequently, in any discussion of monopoly behaviour, it is important to take potential entry into account. In this chapter, account is taken of *barriers to entry* such as absolute cost barriers (for instance arising from patenting and learning differences between businesses), legal barriers, and economies of scale such as those stemming from features of technology or advertising and marketing.

Once models of monopoly behaviour have been outlined and explored in this chapter, the discussion considers government regulation of monopolies, government action to prevent the formation of monopolies, and the seemingly inconsistent policy of public encouragement of the formation of monopolies, for instance by fostering mergers of firms. Issues discussed include the following: are public monopolies the answer to problems and difficulties of regulating or preventing private monopolies? What patterns of behaviour can be expected from bureaucrats managing public monopolies and how are politicians likely to influence the behaviour of such enterprises? Is there a significant separation of ownership and control or management of public enterprises? What consequences does this have? Is government failure to be expected in operating public monopolies and how does this compare with likely private market failure? These issues are given further attention in Chapter 10.

Subsequently, this chapter assembles empirical evidence on the size of the deadweight loss due to monopoly, and the consequences of monopoly for the amount of research and development, patenting, and invention and advertising. This is followed by an analysis of aspects of price discrimination, bundling and full-line forcing practices which imply a degree of market power by a seller, and by some discussion of predatory pricing.

8.2   THE NATURE OF MONOPOLY

Monopoly as an Ideal Type

Monopoly is a market situation in which there is only a single seller of a commodity. It is traditionally regarded as the polar opposite of perfect competition. The *traditional* relationship of different types of competition in the selling of commodities is represented by the spectrum shown in Figure 8.1. However, a number of assumptions, such as impossibility of entry of competitors, have to be made to ensure that a monopoly situation is in fact the polar opposite of perfect competition.

Just as few markets are perfectly competitive, few involve absolute monopolies in the sense that the seller does not have to take account of actual or possible competition from other commodities or the threat of potential entrants to its industry. Nevertheless, this does not mean that predictions based on the 'ideal' types are valueless. Some markets approach the ideal type of monopoly sufficiently for the predictions of the monopoly model to apply.

Factors Resulting in the Creation of Monopolies

Monopolies can arise in several ways. In the past, the state was instrumental in creating many monopolies. Under the mercantilist system, the sovereign often granted monopolies to individuals in return for a fee. For example, in ancient China local monopolies for the supply of salt were granted by the Emperor. In more recent times, the state under the patent system grants temporary monopolies to inventors of new products, such as new drugs.

Monopolies may arise naturally in cases where an industry experiences falling per-unit costs of production, and duplication of supply facilities, such as distribution networks, would add to per-unit costs of supply. It was common in many countries, for example the UK, for decreasing cost industries (for example, railways, telecommunications, post,

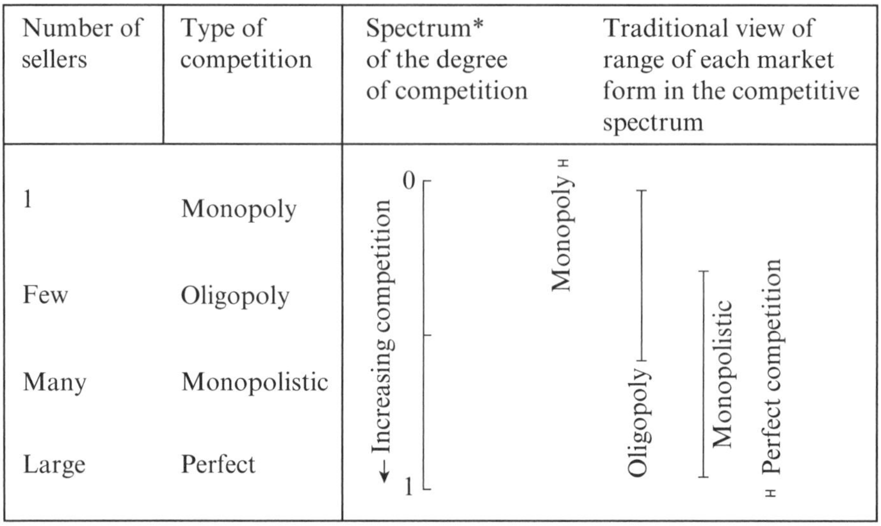

Number of sellers	Type of competition	Spectrum* of the degree of competition	Traditional view of range of each market form in the competitive spectrum
1	Monopoly		
Few	Oligopoly		
Many	Monopolistic		
Large	Perfect		

*Hypothetical measure

Figure 8.1   A characterization of the traditional spectrum of types of competition in the selling of the commodities. Notice that there is some overlap between oligopoly and monopolistic competition in terms of the degree of market competition

electricity and gas supply, water supply) to be state monopolies in the 1970s and into the early 1980s. However, changes in social attitudes towards state enterprises as well as technological changes, particularly in telecommunications, have resulted in privatization of many of these state enterprises.

Private individuals or firms can also engage in behaviour intended to create monopolies. A dominant firm in an industry may engage in price cutting in different localities, one after the other, to drive competitors out of business. This can be described as predatory pricing. Or a company may merge with or take over another, not because this will reduce costs but because it will create an enterprise with monopoly power – power which can be used to increase the profits of the merged businesses.

The Market Power of a Monopolist

The economic consequences of a monopoly in a market depend (1) on the market power of the monopolist and (2) on its market behaviour, that is, on the extent to which the monopolist exercises this power. The latter is likely to depend upon the monopolist's objective function. The mere fact that a firm is the sole seller of a product does not mean that it has, or significantly has, monopoly or market power, that is, the ability to raise its price profitably above the marginal cost of production of its product. As will be recalled, under perfect competition price equals the marginal cost of production of a commodity and a firm has no ability to sell at a higher price. It is a price-taker. The power of a monopolist to raise the price of a product above its marginal cost of production (or more generally to raise the price of a commodity above its supply price – the minimum price needed to call forth a particular level of supply) depends upon

1. the inelasticity of demand for the commodity which in turn depends upon such factors as the availability and closeness of substitutes for the commodity; and
2. the ease with which new suppliers can enter the industry, that is, the costs or barriers to their entry.

In contemplating the possible public control of a monopoly, consideration needs to be given to both of these elements. If the demand for a monopolist's product is very elastic and if entry of new firms or suppliers (for example, from abroad) is easy (which implies that the monopoly is highly contestable), the case for public regulation of a monopoly may be weak because the monopolist has little scope to raise its price above its marginal cost of production and is threatened if lower-cost sources of supply emerge.

Measuring Monopoly Power

Various measures of monopoly power have been suggested. These include:

1. *The Lerner index.* The Lerner index (Lerner, 1934) measures the degree of monopoly power by the extent to which the price of a product diverges from its marginal cost of production in relation to its price. The Lerner index is obtained from the formula

$$L = (P - MC)/P$$

where P is the price of the product and MC represents its marginal cost of production. Under perfect competition, $P = MC$ and so $L = 0$. But under monopoly $P > MC$ and so $L > 0$. As will be explained in section 8.3, an excess of price over marginal cost is liable to result in a misallocation of resources. Under monopoly conditions, the Lerner index will be greater the more inelastic is the demand for a monopolist's product and the lower is the threat of entry.

From a practical point of view, several difficulties are involved in using the Lerner index as a measure of monopoly power. Marginal costs are not always known and are not always easy to estimate. Also one must consider whether or not the index is to be based upon monopoly power exercised or upon potential power. If the monopolist is a profit-maximizer, these will not differ, but if the monopolist charges less than its profit-maximizing price, the index based upon its actual price will be less than that based upon its potential price. Furthermore, it is necessary to consider the time-period involved. A firm may have great monopoly power in the short term, but little in the long term because new substitutes may be developed by rivals, and buyers or consumers have a greater ability to economize and to switch to substitutes in the long term compared to the short term. For these reasons, the Marshallian long-run demand curve can be expected to be more elastic than a short-period one and consequently the Lerner index is lower in the long run.

2. *Excess returns as a measure of monopoly power.* Under perfect competition, firms (at least in the long run) only earn a normal or average return on capital invested, but under monopoly above normal or average returns may persist, even in the long run. Some economists have therefore used the level of returns or profit as an indicator of monopoly power. Harberger (1954), for instance, did this in his study of monopoly.

However, monopolists may not choose to maximize their profit (they may, for example, try to maximize revenue) and this limits the value of the level of returns as a measure of monopoly power. Again in applying this measure consideration needs to be given to the *time-period* for which returns can be maintained. Can returns be maintained for one year, five years, or ten years above the levels which would prevail under perfect competition? Even perfectly competitive firms can earn abnormal profit in the short run if demand for their product suddenly increases. This is because it takes time to adjust supplies and for new firms to enter the industry. Therefore, it is important to assess the performance of a monopoly in a dynamic setting as suggested by several Austrian economists. Empirical studies that attempt this are reviewed by Lipczynski and Wilson (2001, pp. 179–83).

3.   *Concentration ratios or market share as a measure of monopoly power*. A relatively crude measure of monopoly power is the size of a firm's share of its market. The larger this share, the greater is its presumed market power. Once again, however, concentration ratios can change over time. If there is considerable variation in these ratios with the passage of time, this may indicate that despite a high degree of business concentration, an industry is highly competitive.

General Effects of Monopoly

In general, the effect of a monopoly depends upon the monopolist's market power and its behaviour. Market power is a necessary but not sufficient condition for monopoly to result in a misallocation of resources because a monopolist may choose not to exploit its monopoly power, as, for instance, illustrated below in discussing Figure 8.6.

Consider the four main possible effects of monopoly. These are:

1.   Its impact on the *allocation of resources*. If a monopolist has market power and exercises it to raise the price of its product above its marginal cost of production, resources are misallocated. Resources are misallocated in the sense that the value consumers place on extra production of the commodity (as indicated by the price they are willing to pay) exceeds the additional cost of producing an extra amount of the commodity. Consequently, as pointed out in Chapter 2, a deadweight social loss occurs.

2.   A monopolist can influence the *distribution of income*. By exercising its monopoly power, a monopolist may earn above average profit and so redistribute income in its favour. Consequently, the monopolist obtains abnormal profit by creating an artificial scarcity.

3.   The impact of monopoly on *economic growth*, compared to alternative market forms. As we shall see, there is a difference of opinion among economists on whether monopoly promotes or retards economic growth in comparison to alternative market forms.

4.   Greater potential *political interference* of a monopolist compared to participants in a more competitive market environment. A monopolist, other things being equal, is likely to have a greater incentive to lobby on behalf of its industry than would a supplier in a more competitive industry because the monopolist appropriates all the benefits to suppliers in the industry from 'assistance' to the industry, whereas in a competitive industry a supplier must share the gains with other suppliers. Thus a

monopolist is likely, for instance, to find it more profitable to mount a campaign for tariff protection for its industry from imports than would a supplier in a more competitive industry. Again, a monopolist is likely to find it more profitable to be better informed (than a large number of competitors) about any factor affecting its industry, including political measures which may affect it, and to take action to alter the course of events if this is in the monopolist's interest.

In order to assess the possible economic impact of monopoly and of policies to control it, it is necessary for us to consider the behaviour of monopolists.

8.3 BEHAVIOUR OF MONOPOLISTS AND ITS CONSEQUENCES GIVEN NO ENTRY AND THE TRADITIONAL PROFIT-MAXIMIZING MODEL

Economists traditionally have assumed that monopolists, like other firms, maximize their profit. Let us outline some implications of this assumption, assuming that entry is impossible into the industry being considered. We shall then discuss some alternative behavioural models and subsequently allow for potential entry.

Deadweight Loss from Monopoly

In order to maximize its profit a monopolist must equate the firm's marginal cost of production to the firm's marginal revenue from sales of the product. In the absence of price discrimination, this results in a price for the product which exceeds its marginal cost of production. As explained in Chapter 2, this leads to a deadweight (Kaldor–Hicks) social loss. In the constant average cost case shown in Figure 8.2 where the curves are identified by obvious abbreviations, this deadweight social loss amounts to the area of the triangle marked d. The question arises of why this potential gain is not 'captured' if all *could* be made better off by the monopolist changing from a policy of producing a quantity which equates marginal revenue and marginal cost to one of equating average revenue or market demand and marginal cost. The problem basically seems to be one of how consumers can be organized to pay the monopolist a bribe to alter its behaviour. Costs would be involved in organizing the bribe and some consumers may try to free-ride. In this case, transaction costs of considerable magnitude provide barriers to the formation of politically effective consumer groups.

Extent of Loss of Consumers' Surplus from Monopoly

Figure 8.2 enables some predictions to be made about the extent to which consumers may suffer as a result of a traditional monopoly. Assume that perfect competition is a possible alternative to monopoly, and that in this alternative situation the linear demand curve *D* is the same as that for the industry and that the competitive supply curve for the industry is equivalent to the line marked MC. Then the equilibrium market quantity and price under perfect competition are X_c and P_c, respectively, and consumers' surplus is equivalent to the combined areas of the triangles immediately surrounding a, b, c, and d. Under

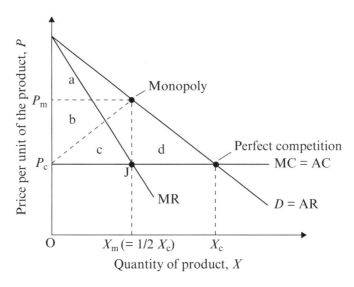

Figure 8.2   Consumers' surplus under monopoly amounts in this case to the area of triangle
a whereas under perfect competition it amounts to the combined area of
triangles a, b, c and d, four times as much as under monopoly. *The dead weight*
social loss from monopoly in this case is equivalent to the area of the triangle
surrounding d

monopoly, supply is X_m (equals half that under perfect competition) and price is P_m so that consumers' surplus is equal to the area of the triangle marked a. Since the four triangles surrounding a, b, c, and d can be shown to be congruent, monopoly in this linear constant cost case reduces consumers' surplus to a *quarter* of that under perfect competition.

Loss in Consumers' Surplus as a Result of Monopoly depends on Inelasticity of the Marginal Cost Curve

If the marginal cost curve is upward sloping and passes through point J in Figure 8.2, the loss in consumers' surplus as a result of monopoly is less than when the supply curve is perfectly elastic. Indeed, in the extreme case where this cost curve is vertical, there is no loss in consumers' surplus from monopoly and no difference between its effect and that of perfect competition. *The more inelastic is supply the smaller is the loss in consumers' surplus as a result of monopoly* and also the smaller is the deadweight loss. (The reader may wish to draw a couple of alternative supply curves through point J and consider their comparative effects.)

Loss in Consumers' Surplus as a Result of Monopoly depends on Inelasticity of Demand

As a rule, the magnitude of the loss in consumers' surplus and of the deadweight loss resulting from monopoly is greater (when compared to perfect competition) the more inelastic is the demand for the monopolized product, other things being equal. This is illustrated in Figure 8.3.

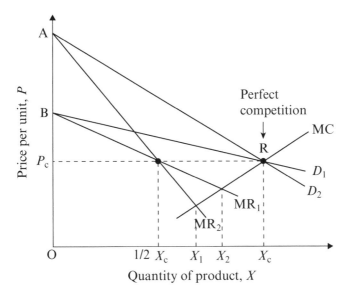

*Figure 8.3   When the demand curve is more inelastic (D_2 compared to D_1) the loss in consumers'
surplus as a result of monopoly is greater. Thus if MC is the supply curve, output falls
by X_c-X_2 if D_1 applies and by X_c-X_1 if D_2 applies and monopoly occurs. The loss in
consumers' surplus is greater in the last case*

In this example, two demand curves marked D_1 and D_2 are shown. Assuming that industry equilibrium under perfect competition corresponds to point R, D_2 is relatively more
inelastic than D_1 in this equilibrium. A greater loss in consumers' surplus occurs if D_2 rather
than D_1 is the case and the competitive supply curve (equals marginal cost for the monopolist) is not perfectly inelastic. Consider first the simple case in which the competitive supply
curve (equals marginal cost) is constant and passes through R. On the basis of the argument just considered above, the loss in consumers' surplus as a result of monopoly is three-
quarters of the area of triangle BP_cR when D_1 is the case and three-quarters of the area of
triangle AP_cR when D_2 is the case. This loss is clearly much larger in the more inelastic case,
that is, for the last-mentioned one. The deadweight loss is equal to one-quarter of the area
of these triangles. In this particular case, output by the monopolist is the same in the inelastic and elastic case. But if marginal cost is increasing (but not vertical) as indicated by the
curve MC in Figure 8.3, the reduction in supply by the monopolist compared to the quantity supplied under perfect competition is greater the more inelastic is demand. Also, as
before, the rise in price under monopoly is greater the more inelastic is demand. In Figure
8.3, supplies fall by only $X_c - X_2$ as a result of monopoly if the more elastic demand curve
D_1 applies, but fall by $X_c - X_1$ if the more inelastic curve D_2 applies. Consequently, since
$D_2 > D_1$ in this range, the *loss in consumers' surplus is considerably higher when demand is
more inelastic. Thus consumers are likely to suffer a greater loss from the presence of a monopoly the more inelastic is the demand for the commodity, other things being constant.*

Hence, given the traditional monopoly model, the damage to consumers from monopoly as measured by the loss in consumers' surplus compared to consumers' surplus under
perfect competition tends to be greater (1) the more elastic is the marginal cost curve, and

(2) the more inelastic is the demand for the product. In assessing the effect of monopoly, policy-makers need to take both these aspects into account.

Note that these static comparisons between the economic consequences of monopoly compared to perfect competition assume that the industry demand is the same for both of the market situations, and that the industry supply curve under perfect competition coincides with the marginal cost curve under conditions of monopoly. Whether or not this hypothesis is able to be or is satisfied in practice is subject to debate. For example, there might be more X-inefficiency under monopoly than perfect competition, or the rate of technological progress under perfect competition might differ from that under monopoly so that cost conditions diverge between the market forms, or the monopolist may promote its product to a greater extent than under perfect competition so industry demand diverges from that under perfect competition. Therefore, one should be wary in generalizing about the economic consequences of monopoly compared to perfect competition based on the above static models.

Monopoly versus Perfect Competition if the Rate of Technical Change is Different

Consider the view that the type of comparison between monopoly and perfect competition outlined in Figures 8.2 and 8.3 is illegitimate because the rate of technical progress under perfect competition differs from that under monopoly. Schumpeter (1954), for example, argued that more rapid technical progress is likely to occur under monopoly (and oligopoly) than under perfect competition. This may occur because:

1. A monopolist appropriates a greater proportion of the return from an invention or innovation in its industry than does a company sharing a market with many competitors who may imitate the invention or innovation without payment or full payment to the inventor/innovator. By virtue of its dominant market position, a monopolist retains its effective property rights in any of its inventions or innovations. This makes it more profitable for a monopolist to invent and innovate than for a competitive firm.
2. A monopolist usually earns excess profit which provides it with funds for investment and these funds may be used in fostering technical progress.
3. Innovation may be less risky for a monopolist than for those in an industry consisting of many firms. For instance, a monopolist is likely to find it more profitable to purchase or obtain more information about the market prospects of a potential innovation than would a single firm among many in the same market.
4. It may also be true, as Schumpeter believed and as was argued by John Maurice Clark (1940), that a monopoly is not safe from long-term competition. Competition may come from new products and new sources of supply and the business of a monopolist may only survive if the monopolist is technically progressive.

On the other hand, some economists argue that technical progress is likely to be slower under monopoly because competitive pressures are weaker than in more competitive markets in which firms have less market power. According to Lipczynski and Wilson (2001, p. 263), empirical evidence about this matter is inconclusive.

Even if technical progress is more rapid under monopoly than under perfect competition, this does not ensure that consumers are able to buy the products involved at a lower

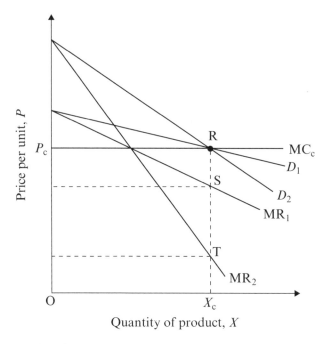

Figure 8.4 Greater technical progress under monopoly compared to perfect competition does not guarantee consumers a lower price for a product than under perfect competition. If the demand curve happened to be D_1, per-unit costs would need to fall below S for the monopoly price to be less than the perfectly competitive price P_c

price under monopoly. For the price of a product to be actually less under monopoly than would occur under perfect competition with less technical progress, the monopoly must result in a substantial reduction in per-unit costs of production. This can be seen from Figure 8.4.

Suppose that the curve identified by D_1 represents the demand curve for the product of the industry and that MC_c represents the supply curve under perfect competition. Under perfect competition, the equilibrium quantity supplied is X_c and the equilibrium price is P_c. If monopoly is to result in a higher output than X_c and a lower price than P_c, the monopolist must introduce techniques which lower per-unit costs of production by more than RS. Any smaller reduction in per-unit costs of production will not benefit purchasers of product X. Faster technical progress under monopoly is not sufficient to ensure gains to the purchasers of the monopolized product.

The more inelastic is the demand for a product, the greater must be the reduction in per-unit costs of production achieved by a monopolist, if consumers are to enjoy a lower price for the product than under perfect competition. This can also be seen from Figure 8.4. The demand curve D_2 is more inelastic than D_1 relative to position R, the perfectly competitive equilibrium. But if D_2 applies, per-unit costs must fall under monopoly by more than RT if the price of X is to be lower under monopoly. This illustrates the point that the more inelastic is the demand for a product the greater must be the comparative rate of technical progress under monopoly to ensure that prices are lower than they would have been under perfect competition. Conversely, the more elastic is demand, the smaller needs to be the extent of technical progress under monopoly to ensure a price reduction in comparison to perfect competition. Thus, the degree of elasticity of demand can be an important consideration in deciding whether monopoly in a particular instance is advantageous or disadvantageous to consumers.

X-inefficiency again

As discussed in Chapters 6 and 7, monopolists may choose not to maximize profit and can be X-inefficient in the sense of not using resources efficiently to produce whatever output is produced at minimum cost. Instead of making an effort to minimize cost by attending fully to the direction and coordination of employed resources, a monopolist may decide to avoid friction with individuals within its business and 'take it easy'. Given this in-built inefficiency in the operation of the business, the monopolist may still, however, maximize profit *subject to it*. Thus, although costs are not minimized and profit cannot therefore be absolutely maximized, profit may be maximized *subject* to a certain degree of in-built X-inefficiency. Consumers suffer by higher prices as a consequence of the in-built inefficiency and it can be argued that there is a waste of resources because the costs of production are higher than they need be. Hence, more resources are used in supplying output than is necessary. For instance, in the example shown in Figure 8.5, MC_E might represent marginal cost when the monopolist operates so as to minimize cost and MC_I might be his marginal cost given its in-built degree of X-inefficiency. As a result of this 'in-built' inefficiency, the price of the product is P_I rather than P_E and output is X_I rather than X_E. Due to the presence of the X-inefficiency, there is a loss in consumers' surplus represented by the dotted area. Furthermore, X-inefficiency wastes resources in the sense that it adds the equivalent of the hatched rectangle to the cost of producing, that is it adds to the per-unit *cost* of production.

   The loss of consumers' surplus as a result of X-inefficiency is greater the more inelastic is the demand for the product relative to the perfectly competitive equilibrium, position C. (You may wish to draw a steeper demand curve through C and observe the effect.) But note also that in this constant cost case the loss in consumers' surplus due to X-inefficiency is much smaller than that due to the restrictive allocative impact of monopoly on supply. As shown above, the restrictive (allocative) impact of monopoly (its raising of price above marginal cost) leads to a loss of three-quarters of consumers' surplus compared to that under perfect competition, that is to a loss of three-quarters of the area of triangle ABC. The additional *loss due to X-inefficiency*, the dotted area, is less, and indeed cannot exceed the area of triangle AP_EL, that is a quarter of the area of triangle ABC. The X-inefficiency loss of consumers' surplus becomes relatively more important, however, if marginal cost is increasing. Nevertheless, a priori, it does not appear to be as great as might have been imagined at first sight. We shall discuss this again when Harberger's (1954) findings are considered.

   It might also be recalled, as discussed in Chapter 6, that increased X-inefficiency may offset potential gains from the merger of firms. Even though economies of scale may be possible, the potential of these for reducing per-unit costs may be more than offset if greater X-inefficiency occurs.

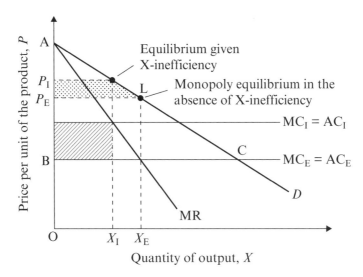

Figure 8.5   X-inefficiency may occur under monopoly. It results in a loss of consumers' surplus and 'a waste' of resources, in the sense that the per-unit costs of producing output are higher than under competitive conditions where X-inefficiency is more likely to be absent or less. In the above case the Kaldor–Hicks loss due to X-inefficiency ($MC_I > MC_E$) consists of the loss in consumers' surplus shown by the dotted area plus excess costs shown by the hatched area

Non-profit-maximizing Behaviour

While the presence of X-inefficiency implies non-profit-maximizing behaviour on the part of a monopolist, at least in relation to the internal control of the firm, non-profit-maximizing behaviour can be more pervasive because the monopolist may not strive to maximize its profit in selling to buyers. The occurrence of and the scope for non-profit-maximizing behaviour by firms has already been discussed in Chapter 7. As a rule, a monopolist has considerable scope for engaging in non-profit-maximizing behaviour because it lacks market rivals, and in the case of a company, there may be failure in the capital market. The monopolist may, for example, act in the manner suggested by Baumol (1967), that is, try to maximize the value of the sales of its product subject to some satisfactory rate of return. The monopolist may do this because sales give business prestige and it may wish for a 'quiet life'; one not made difficult by angry buyers. Behaviour of this type is likely to lead to greater supplies by the monopolist and to a smaller deadweight loss than otherwise. This can be illustrated by Figure 8.6.

In Figure 8.6, the demand and cost curves facing a monopolist are indicated in the usual way and MR is the marginal revenue corresponding to the market demand curve *D*. The line *RR* indicates the minimum level of average revenue needed to achieve the target return of the monopolist. It is assumed that subject to meeting its target rate of return, the monopolist aims to maximize its revenue. In this case, the monopolist produces X_N and sells it at P_N compared to X_M sold at P_M if the monopolist maximizes profit. The deadweight social loss amounts to the hatched area and is much smaller than would be the case for profit maximization. In the profit-maximizing case, the deadweight loss amounts to

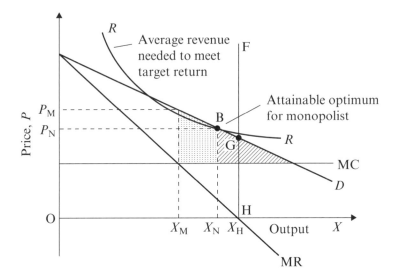

Figure 8.6   *A monopolist may aim to maximize his/her value of sales subject to a target rate of return. On average this results in less restriction of output than if profit maximization is the monopolist's aim. It also results in a smaller deadweight loss than otherwise. In the above case, the deadweight loss is shown by the hatched triangle. Note that total revenue reaches a maximum when the quantity of the monopolist's sales is X_H (MR=0 for X_H). If RR only cuts the demand curve above or at G, the monopolist's optimum output corresponds to the lower intersection point (B in the above case) and is constrained by the profit target. However, if RR cuts the demand curve below G, the monopolist's optimum output is constrained to X_H by its sales revenue aim*

the hatched area plus the dotted one. A sales-maximizing monopolist may, therefore, not distort the allocation of resources as much as a profit-maximizing one. On the other hand, the monopolist could spend a socially excessive amount on product advertising. This will be discussed later.

8.4   MONOPOLY BEHAVIOUR TAKING POTENTIAL ENTRY INTO ACCOUNT

A monopolist may alter its market behaviour or strategy if faced by the threat of entry of a competitor even though the monopolist continues to try to maximize its profit. The monopolist may try to raise barriers to the entry of competitors and lower its prices to deter potential entrants. Barriers to new entrants may (as specified by Bain, 1956):

1. be legal ones, that is, they could occur because of restrictions to entry resulting from statutes;
2. be absolute per-unit cost disadvantages which may come about because the monopolist controls the least-cost technology, for instance through patent protection or secrecy, or obtains resources such as minerals or energy from the government or its agencies at a privileged low price;

3. stem from economies of scale in production and/or distribution;
4. arise from large advertising and promotion campaigns of branded products of the monopolist; or
5. be obtained because the monopolist has product protection via patents or other forms of intellectual property rights established by law.

The effect of the threat of entry on a monopolist's pricing behaviour depends not only on the height of barriers to entry but also on the expected behaviour by the monopolist's rivals after entry. A variety of different types of behaviour are possible after entry. An entrant or entrants may allow the established firm to be the price-leader if the established firm has the lowest per-unit costs, or if there are many entrants, the market may tend towards a perfectly competitive one after entry. Another possibility is that the established firm will continue after entry to supply and sell the same quantity of supply as before entry. The remainder of market demand after entry is then supplied by entrants. This is the Sylos postulate (Modigliani, 1958).

Whether or not a new firm or firms will enter an industry and challenge an established monopoly, depends not only on the barriers to its entry but also on how the incumbent monopolist is expected to behave after entry. A further consideration that a potential entrant needs to take into account is how much of its costs of entry will be sunk if its entry bid should fail. When these sunk costs are likely to be high, the monopoly is less contestable.

The Sylos postulate assumes relatively passive or habitual type of behaviour on the part of the incumbent monopolist should entry to its industry occur. In fact, the incumbent monopolist may engage in aggressive competitive behaviour to rapidly drive out a firm which attempts entry. This may involve temporarily flooding the market to cause heavy losses for a challenging entrant or predatory pricing, discussed later in this chapter. The threat of this type of behaviour if believed to be credible by potential entrants will help to deter entry. It will, therefore, be economically advantageous to the incumbent monopolist if it is able to create a perception that punishing retaliatory competitive action will follow should attempted entry occur. There may, however, be circumstances in which the incumbent monopolist is unable to engage in effective retaliatory action. For example, the potential entrant might be a subsidiary of an asset-rich multiproduct company and in a strong position to withstand any competitive actions by the incumbent monopolist to drive it out of the industry should it enter. Many of these types of situations can be illustrated by the use of game theory (see for example, Gravelle and Rees, 2004, pp. 433–43). However, the possibilities are considerable. In some instances, an incumbent monopolist may even accept an entrant and reduce its level of output to adjust to the entry. Varian (2006, pp. 516–18) provides a simple outline of the possibilities using the framework of a sequential game.

Whether or not game theory can adequately capture all the complexities involved is debatable but it does highlight the strategic aspects of the situation. A useful coverage of strategic and other aspects of business entry can be found in Cabral (2000, Chapters 14–15) and in Church and Ware (2000, Chapters 13–17). When strategic aspects are taken into account, the entry forestalling price of an incumbent monopolist can differ from that indicated by the application of the Sylos postulate. Nevertheless, the Sylos postulate does provide useful insights into the importance of entry barriers for the behaviour of monopolists, and the strong unbounded rationality assumptions often used in game theory limit its applicability (Tisdell, 1996, Chapter 8).

Effect of Absolute Barriers

The effect of absolute barriers to entry, if the Sylos postulate applies, can be seen from Figure 8.7. Let D represent the demand curve for product X and the line marked MC_E represent the marginal cost and average cost of production experienced by the established firm. In the absence of any threat of entry, the established monopolist would find it profitable to produce X_M of the product and sell it at P_M. But suppose that a potential rival has per-unit costs as indicated by MC_R. The potential rival finds it profitable to enter the market if the established firm supplies less than X_R to the market. Thus, taking this entry element into consideration, the marginal revenue curve of the established firm consists of the heavy lines shown in Figure 8.7. Since the marginal cost of the established firm passes through the discontinuous part of this modified marginal revenue curve, the most profitable policy of the established firm is to supply X_R to the market at a price of P_R, the entry-forestalling price. *Unless* the entry-forestalling price (a limit price) exceeds that which maximizes profit in the absence of possible entry (P_M in this case), the most profitable policy for the established firm is to charge the entry-forestalling price and supply all demands at this price. This is an example of limit pricing.

But if the entry-forestalling price P_R exceeds the absolute monopoly profit-maximizing price of P_M, then the established firm maximizes its profit by charging P_M, that is a price

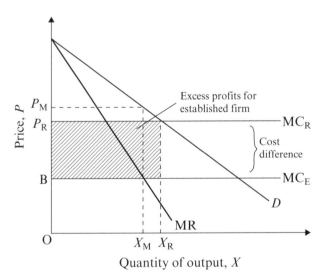

Figure 8.7   Because of the risk of entry, a monopolist may find it most profitable to charge an entry forestalling price, a price lower than otherwise. The greater the per-unit cost disadvantage of its potential rival, the higher is the most profitable price for the established firm to charge and the greater its profit. Given the cost difference shown by $MC_R - MC_E$, the established firm can charge P_R without inducing entry and makes abnormal profits, indicated by the hatched area

less than P_R. Note also that until $P_R > P_M$ the entry-forestalling price and the profit-maximizing price of the established firm rises with the per-unit costs of production of the potential rival. Furthermore, if $P_R < P_M$, the excess profits of the profit-maximizing established firm, as indicated in Figure 8.7 by the hatched rectangle, is higher the larger is the per-unit cost disadvantage of the potential entrant.

Rapidly Increasing Economies of Scale as a Barrier to Entry

Apart from differences in the per-unit costs experienced by established firms and the expected per-unit costs of entrants (absolute cost difference), economies of scale can be entry barriers. These barriers depend not only on the size required for the minimum efficient scale (MES) of operation of the firm but also on the rapidity with which average costs fall with the firm's volume of production. The steeper (that is, the faster the rate of decline of) the average cost curve of production, the greater, other things being equal (including MES), can be the price charged by established firms without provoking entry. Also this price tends to be higher the larger is the minimum efficient scale.

The last-mentioned effect can be illustrated by a simple example. Assume that the minimum scale of operations of a firm is unique and results in per-unit costs of production of 0B and a level of output of $\bar{x}$, as illustrated in Figure 8.8. The larger is $\bar{x}$ the greater the price charged by established firms can be without provoking entry if the

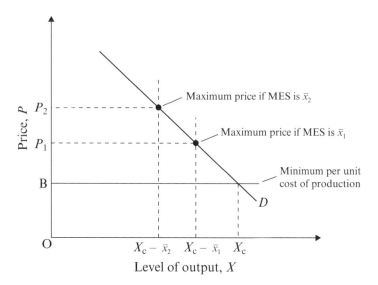

Figure 8.8   *The maximum price which an established firm(s) can charge without provoking entry tends to be greater the larger is the minimum efficient scale of operations. This maximum price is P_1 if the (unique) MES is $\bar{x}_1$. At P_1 it is just profitable for a new firm to enter, add $\bar{x}_1$ to industry output, and so lower the price of the product to OB. At the larger scale $\bar{x}_2$ it is only just profitable to enter and add $\bar{x}_2$ to industry supply if $P = P_2$. Note that X_c corresponds to the output of a perfectly competitive industry in the absence of scale barriers*

Sylos postulate applies. If $\bar{x} = \bar{x}_1$, established firms can charge up to P_1 for product X without triggering entry if the market demand curve is as indicated by curve D in Figure 8.8. If the required scale is greater, say $\bar{x} = \bar{x}_2$, an even higher price, P_2, can be charged without enticing entry.

Figure 8.9 illustrates the impact of a speedier fall in per-unit costs with scale. The curve C_2C_2 represents per-unit costs for the *same* minimum efficient scale as C_1C_1. The minimum efficient scale occurs in both instances for an output of $\bar{x}$. Per-unit costs fall more rapidly in the first case and in this case of rapidly increasing economies of scale, established firms can charge up to P_2 without encouraging entry. If costs fall more slowly with scale as indicated by C_1C_1, established firms cannot charge more than P_1 without provoking entry. Rapidly decreasing economies of scale may therefore enable established firms to charge higher prices than otherwise without provoking entry, if MES is constant.

To appreciate that a higher maximum entry-deterring price, P_2, is possible if C_2C_2 applies rather than if C_1C_1 is the case consider the following: if C_2C_2 applies and price is P_2, a new entrant would just find it profitable to enter and add AF to the quantity of the product supplied by the industry. If C_1C_1 applies and price is just equal to P_1, a new entrant would just find it profitable to enter and add BE to the quantity of the product supplied by the industry. P_2 and P_1 are located by 'sliding' the per-unit costs of each plant to the left until tangency is achieved with the industry demand curve at N and M respectively. Each of these prices then corresponds to the intersection point with the demand curve of the vertical from the left-hand end-points of the respective cost curves. K corresponds to the intersection point for C_2C_2 and L that for C_1C_1.

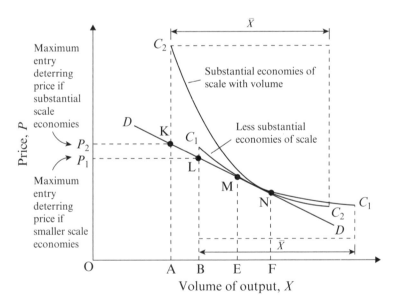

Figure 8.9   *If economies of scale substantially increase with volume (if per-unit costs of production fall rapidly with volume) established firms may be able to charge higher prices than otherwise without provoking entry. Thus, for* C_2C_2, *the maximum entry-deterring price* P_2 *exceeds that for* C_1C_1, P_1

Advertising expenditure can be one source of substantial economies of scale. Many types of advertising require a large fixed outlay and this implies a rapid decline in per-unit selling costs with volume of sales. Thus a firm trying to enter an industry in which advertising expenditure by established firms is considerable (such as detergents, and some soft drinks) may find this advertising a major barrier. This barrier may protect established firms and enable them to charge a higher price than otherwise without initiating entry. One reason why established firms may maintain high levels of expenditure on advertising and promotion is to deter potential entrants.

A government may be in a position to reduce the market power of a monopolist by making entry or potential entry of new firms or new sources of supply easier. For example, imports of commodities which may compete with a monopolist's product may be permitted to enter at a reduced tariff, and where restrictive legislation such as licensing laws limits possible entry of competitors these may be relaxed. Sometimes, however, by interfering in monopoly-like market situations governments add to restrictions on entry rather than reduce these since the regulatory body established for an industry can become a captive client of established firms. The economics of politics and bureaucracy suggests that established firms in an industry may be the major pressure group affecting the behaviour of the regulatory body. Therefore, there is a risk that the regulatory body will act to restrict entry rather than encourage it.

The behavioural relevance of barriers to entry of monopolized and oligopolistic industries has gained considerable empirical support (Lipczynski and Wilson, 2001, Chapter 5). Furthermore, barriers to entry have also been shown to be an important consideration in determining business strategies adopted by firms possessing market power (Smiley, 1992). As pointed out by Gravelle and Rees (2004, pp. 433–43), the theory of games can be used to model some aspects of business behaviours taking into account barriers to entry, but is not applied here. The theory of games is applied to other aspects of imperfect competition in the next chapter.

8.5 PUBLIC ACTION TO REGULATE AND PREVENT MONOPOLIES

Public action to regulate the activities or restrict the formation of monopolies may be based on one or more of the following considerations:

1. *The allocative loss* caused by a profit-maximizing monopolist raising the price of its product above its marginal cost of production.
2. *The redistributive effect* from a profit-maximizing monopolist earning above normal profit.
3. *Possible economic growth consequences* of monopoly because it *may* impede technical progress.
4. The *possible X-inefficiency* in the management of a monopolized business.
5. The extent of political *power of a monopolist.*

Public concern about monopolies is likely to be considerable when they supply commodities that are inelastic in demand and are necessities or near necessities. In such cases, their income redistribution impact can be large. Also there is likely to be political concern when mass media are monopolized or are in few hands. This is not to say that the other potential consequences of monopolies are unimportant.

General Measures to Control Monopoly

At least three general types of policy may be used to regulate monopoly. These are:

1. Measures to prevent the formation of monopolies. These may include bans on mergers or takeovers of firms where these are likely to create a monopoly or near monopoly. In addition, predatory pricing and other market behaviour intended to create a monopoly by eliminating competitors may be banned.
2. The break up of a monopoly may be pursued where this is deemed to be in the public interest.
3. The behaviour of existing monopolies may be regulated by, for example, placing limits on the maximum prices they may charge for their products.

Examples of Means to Control Monopolies

Within the European Union, collusive business practices which restrict or prevent competition are illegal. These include agreements on price-fixing and on the sharing of markets unless it can be demonstrated that the benefits to consumers of the agreement outweigh its cost. Benefits which can be taken into consideration include speedier technical progress and economies of scale.

Abuse of market power is also an offence in the EU. If a firm has 40 per cent or more market share, and engages in monopoly pricing, predatory pricing or price discrimination, it can be investigated and penalized.

There are also provisions for investigating business mergers in the EU in cases where the merger might lead to a dominant market position for the newly formed firm. The EU's investigations of a merger concentrate mainly on whether the merger will establish a dominant market position in a geographical area or product market for the newly established firm. Furthermore, possible public benefits from the merger are weighed against its effect in reducing market competition. Even if the merger reduces competition, it may be decided that the economic benefits of the merger are likely to outweigh the costs of reduced competition.

These measures apply only to firms which trade between EU countries. Those firms that confine their trade to one country are not subject to these rules. They are, however, subject to national legislation, for example, the Competition Act 1998 in the UK. Lipczynski and Wilson (2001, p. 367) state that this act is intended to harmonize UK competition policy with that of the EU.

In a few instances, monopolies have been dismantled by law. This has happened in the United States. Nevertheless, in most cases once a monopoly is in existence, governments opt to regulate their behaviour rather than break them up. This tends to be so particularly for utilities such as electricity and water supplies. In the United States, regulators determine the maximum price of a commodity supplied by a utility so that the price gives a 'fair' rate of return on capital to investors in the utility. Therefore, the price of the commodity equals the per-unit cost of supplying it plus sufficient mark-up to give a fair rate of return on the capital invested. In determining the 'fair' return, it is considered that the maximum allowable price should be high enough to be able to attract additional investment from shareholders and that it should be adequate to enable updating and replacement of equipment as it depreciates.

A criticism of the rate of return approach adopted in the United States is that it does not provide an incentive to a utility company to reduce its cost because its rate of return is guaranteed. It is also possible that a close relationship may develop between the regulators and the regulated so that the regulators become 'captured' by the regulated, who significantly influence their decisions.

In the United Kingdom, a related but different approach is used to regulate the prices charged by private suppliers of utilities. Many of these utilities were previously supplied by public enterprises. There is an initial price cap (maximum price) for the commodity supplied. This is adjusted periodically for the rate of inflation using the retail price index and a fraction is deducted for expected productivity gains. Therefore, the maximum allowable price of the commodity should fall with the passage of time. This puts pressure on utility suppliers to increase their productivity.

How a realistic target productivity factor can be accurately estimated is unclear. Furthermore, costs are not only affected by productivity gains. For example, the price of raw materials used by the utility may alter. It will therefore be necessary to revise the price formula periodically. There is also no guarantee in the UK system that the regulators will not be subject to influence by the regulated. Regulation of monopolies is therefore subject to imprecision as discussed further below.

Where a monopoly exists due to the presence of networks, governments may split portions of the enterprise into those that are contestable and can be competitive and those that cannot. For example, rail tracks form a fixed network. The owner of the rail tracks may be forced to make the tracks available to all those who wish to use them for operating trains. Consequently, this part of the rail system becomes competitive in principle. The regulator may only regulate the prices that the owner of the network (that is of the rail lines) charges for access to their use.

However, it is not always the case that the government is eager to prevent business mergers or the formation of monopolies and to regulate their behaviour. In some instances, governments have promoted or allowed the formation of monopolies and business mergers. Arguments that have been used to support this policy include:

1. It increases economic efficiency because firms obtain a fall in per-unit costs of operation by expanding their size. A natural monopoly exists.
2. It fosters economic growth by speeding up technical progress and investment.
3. It is necessary if the domestic industry is to compete more effectively in international trade and investment and to maximize its gains from international trade and direct investment overseas.
4. It improves the coordination of the economy and makes government planning more effective by reducing uncertainty about the operation of the economy.

Within the EU, the first three of these arguments can provide possible grounds for allowing a business merger.

8.6   PRIVATE VERSUS PUBLIC MONOPOLIES

Difficulties in Regulating Private Monopolies

Public regulation of private monopolies involves several difficulties. For instance, a public body regulating the maximum price to be charged by a monopolist may be unable to determine the price which will equate the demand for the monopolist's product with its marginal cost of production. The actual marginal cost and demand curve indicated in Figure 8.10 may be unknown to the authority and it may not be able to obtain information to eliminate its ignorance. If it knew these curves, the optimal maximum price would be P_R, which would induce the monopolist to produce X_R of the product. This regulated price would be optimal from a Kaldor–Hicks point of view in the absence of externalities and second-best considerations. As a result of the regulation, the monopolist's marginal revenue curve would be discontinuous, as indicated by the solid lines, which means that the monopolist supplies X_R of the product rather than X_M.

It might be thought that the regulatory authority could discover the optimal regulated price level by trial and error. A myopic profit-maximizing monopolist would fail to supply all demands for its product if the regulated price happened to be set below P_R, the value for which marginal cost equals demand. The problem might then appear to be one of the authority raising the ceiling price until all demands are *just* met. But a monopolist would not need to be very clever to thwart this approach. It would pay the monopolist to maintain an artificial scarcity until the authority raised the regulated price to P_M. Consequently, the regulating authority could be manipulated to set the regulated price equal to the monopoly price.

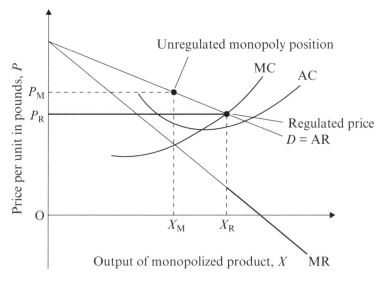

Figure 8.10   *A case in which price to be charged by a monopolist is regulated so as to equate marginal cost and demand. Because of ignorance on the part of the regulating body, marginal cost pricing may not always be practical. Given the regulated price P_R, the monopolist's effective demand curve is the one indicated by the heavy lines*

A further difficulty is that marginal cost pricing is not always compatible with the continued existence of a firm. When average costs of production decline with the volume of production, marginal cost pricing causes a firm to make a loss and the firm will go out of existence unless it obtains a grant to cover this loss. The firm makes a loss in these circumstances because when average costs are falling, marginal cost is below average cost. For instance, in the case illustrated in Figure 8.11, if the regulated price is set at P_R and *if* the firm produces X_R, it makes the loss shown by the hatched area and it would need a lump sum grant of this amount to remain in existence. The danger in the government underwriting the loss of the firm, however, is that this may encourage the firm to become inefficient since it has some assurance that its losses will be covered.

To avoid the necessity of paying the monopolist a subsidy, the government may deter-mine a ceiling price which would result in the monopolist supplying an output equating its average cost of production with demand for the product. In the case shown in Figure 8.11, this is a price of P_A. However, the regulating authority may have insufficient infor-mation about costs and demand to determine this price accurately. This may provide man-agers of regulated industries with an incentive to inflate their costs, for instance by following policies for their own personal gain in the expectation that the regulated price will be altered to cover the inflated levels of cost. The policy may also encourage X-inefficiency. Revenue-maximizers, for instance, may aim for a *regulated price* which ensures the level of sales for which their marginal revenue equals zero. They may engineer this by inflating their per-unit costs to the level of this *desired* regulated price. Of course, this also applies to managers of public enterprises.

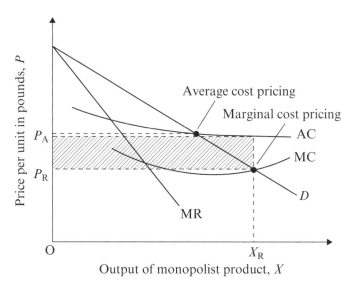

Figure 8.11   *Marginal cost pricing leads to a loss for the monopolist if average cost falls with the volume of output. In the above instance if price is regulated to P_R and X_R is supplied (so equating marginal cost and demand) the loss shown by the hatched area is incurred by the monopolist*

Public Ownership as a Means of Overcoming Difficulties of Regulating Private Monopolies

While public ownership of monopolies may appear to be a way of overcoming the information problems involved in controlling private monopolies, it is not necessarily a solution. Public enterprises have their own identity; their managers foster the interests of these enterprises as they see them and may make information available selectively to other branches of government and the public. The information problem is not overcome though it could be reduced in some instances. The annual reports which public enterprises make to Parliament contain selected and insufficient information to enable a careful and detailed assessment of their performance to be made.

Members of the general public frequently do not find it worthwhile to bring pressure to bear upon public enterprises through the political process to improve their economic efficiency. The gain of any individual agitator is likely to be small in relation to the cost of the effort to him/her, since other individuals who also stand to gain may free-ride on the agitator's efforts. Politicians of the government may also (especially if they are members of the board of the public enterprise or a minister nominally responsible for the public enterprise) be sympathetic to the public enterprise's own managerial position. Opposition politicians may be critical from time to time of performance, but are likely to be hampered by a lack of information about the public enterprise. Thus the political forces regulating a public enterprise in the general interest may be weak. This may encourage allocative and X-inefficiency by public enterprises, and members of the management of public enterprises may be tempted to follow policies based upon their own (possibly narrow) perceptions and interests. Perfection is not guaranteed by public operation of enterprises since the political process does not appear to make for the presence of powerful watchdogs. Significant principal–agent problems exist (Gravelle and Rees, 2006, chapter 20).

Because of the difficulty faced by Parliament in keeping itself informed about public enterprises and the role that they are performing, it has been suggested that when a public enterprise is formed it should be stipulated that it will go out of existence in a specified number of years unless it can justify its continued existence to Parliament before that time. This has been called the sunset principle by US politicians and is indicative of the problem of regulating public enterprises. The question of whether private or public ownership of utilities and similar enterprises is to be preferred is given attention in Chapter 10.

8.7 EMPIRICAL EVIDENCE ON THE IMPACTS OF MONOPOLY

Empirical Evidence about the Extent of Monopoly Losses

Ambitious attempts have been made to measure deadweight losses due to monopoly. Harberger (1954) concluded on the basis of data on the US manufacturing industry for 1924–1928 that the annual *actual* total deadweight or Kaldor–Hicks loss from monopoly in the United States amounted to about one-tenth of 1 per cent of its GDP. His estimate of this allocative loss is based upon the special assumptions of constant long-run average costs of production and a unitary elasticity of demand for products.

This estimated loss is lower than many economists may have expected. But the low relative loss could reflect the unwillingness of monopolists to exploit their monopoly power fully and their restriction of price levels to deter potential entrants. The result does not prove that there is no need to be concerned about monopoly. Monopoly power may be exploited in particular instances and can result in a considerable Kaldor–Hicks loss.

Again, it needs to be remembered that the allocative loss *as measured by Harberger* is only part of the possible social loss from monopoly. For instance, monopoly *may* result in greater X-inefficiency and slower technical progress than, say, under conditions of oligopoly.

Research and Development, Patenting and Innovation

If monopoly accelerates technical progress, this may provide a social argument in its favour. Schumpeter (1954) suggested on theoretical grounds that monopoly, oligopoly and big business *might* speed up technical progress compared to industries dominated by small firms and low levels of concentration. However, as will be emphasized in Chapter 9, Schumpeter qualified his hypothesis by suggesting that very large firms may become bureaucratic and not be conducive to research and innovation.

Little direct evidence is available about the impact of monopoly on the level of research and development expenditure and its effect on the volume of inventive output. While the major proportion of industrial R&D expenditure in developed countries is accounted for by a few large firms, research intensities (the proportion of R&D expenditure to sales, for instance) tend to rise as the size of the firm increases and *then fall off* at very large sizes according to the findings of Mansfield (1979) and of Scherer (1965). But of course one should not only take the input to R&D effort into account but also the value of inventive output. On the basis of his study of the chemical, steel and petroleum industries in the United States, Mansfield concluded that the inventive output per dollar of R&D expenditure seems to be lower for the largest firms in these industries than for medium-sized firms. Mansfield's result is not inconsistent with Freeman's (1974) finding that large firms (those with more than 1000 employees) are responsible for most innovations and that the proportionate share of medium and large firms (200 and over employees) is in excess of their proportionate share of employment and output. But firms can of course be large without monopolizing an industry.

On the other hand, Geroski (1994) concluded using UK data that there was little support for Schumpeter's hypothesis that monopoly tends to stimulate technical progress. This is probably not surprising because market structure is likely to be just one of the factors influencing technical progress in an industry. Further consideration is given to this matter in the next chapter.

Note that the patent system provides an interesting example of the creation of monopolies by government intervention. On the payment of a fee to the government, an inventor is granted exclusive property rights in its invention for a specified period of time. Various arguments have been put in favour of such a grant. For instance, it has been suggested that the monopoly profit which may be obtained through a patent may provide inventors with greater incentive to invent and innovate, thus speeding up technical progress. The question to be considered, then, is whether the allocative and other losses from granting a temporary monopoly are less than the benefits obtained from speedier technical progress, for example, in the form of lower prices and the speedier introduction of products with new qualities.

Advertising and Monopoly

In assessing the welfare effects of monopoly, one may also wish to take account of its effects on the level of advertising. Kaldor (1940–41) and Telser (1964) have suggested that monopoly can lead to a socially excessive level of advertising. Dorfman and Steiner (1954) have theorized that, other things being equal, advertising intensities are likely to be higher the more inelastic is the demand for a product. Thus, other things being equal, advertising intensities could be higher when monopolies are present than when an industry has a low level of concentration. Monopolists may also use advertising as a barrier to entry of new firms. Nevertheless, as discussed in the next chapter, advertising intensities may be highest in oligopolistic industries.

8.8   PRICE DISCRIMINATION AND BUNDLING

Under perfect competition, each unit of a commodity commands the same price. Price discrimination is impossible. However, under imperfect competition, price discrimination is sometimes possible. If a commodity cannot be resold and traded easily by customers, or by an identifiable group of customers, a monopolist is able to engage in price discrimination. Price discrimination is clearly impossible if customers can easily resell a commodity, as those who are able to purchase lower-priced units from a monopolist can resell these at a profit to customers forced to pay higher prices. This will tend to equalize prices.

First Degree Price Discrimination

Different types of price discrimination can be identified. At one extreme, a monopolist may theoretically vary price so that each customer pays the full additional value, to the monopolist, of each unit purchased. With a downward sloping demand curve, this means the price to the customer *of each additional unit* purchased is lowered, but by an amount such that the customer is left with no consumer's surplus.

Take the case shown in Figure 8.12. Assume the monopolist wishes to sell x_3 of a product to a customer. Assuming that the customer's demand for the product is *dd* (and the real income effect is zero), the monopolist might charge the same price p_1 for all units and obtain total receipts from the customer equivalent to the rectangle Ox_3Kp_1. However, by charging p_4 for the initial unit and lowering the price of additional units along the curve *dd* until p_1 is reached, the monopolist increases total revenue by the area of the hatched triangle p_1Kp_4. Thus the consumer is left with no consumer's surplus and the monopolist increases profit. This is a case of *first degree price discrimination*.

Second Degree Price Discrimination

It is seldom practical to vary price with quantity purchased in such a fine way that all consumers' surplus is appropriated by the monopolist. A more likely pattern is discrete

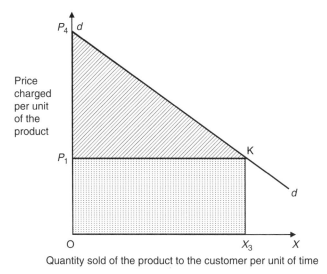

Figure 8.12   *An illustration of first degree price discrimination*

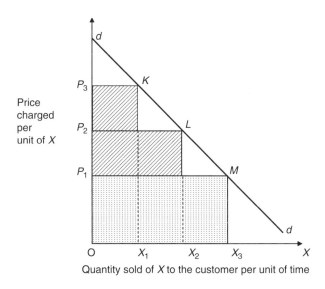

Figure 8.13   *An illustration of second degree price discrimination*

variations in price. An example of this is given in Figure 8.13. The customer is charged p_3 on each of the first x_1 units purchased, p_2 on each of the next $x_2 - x_1$ units used and p_1 on the remainder. The total receipts of the monopolist from this customer equal the dotted area plus the black hatched areas. Revenue and profit are greater than if a uniform price of p_1 is charged, but the consumer is still left with some surplus. This is sometimes called *price discrimination of the second degree*. It is commonly employed in charging for products such as electricity and gas.

Third Degree Price Discrimination

Price discrimination of the third degree arises when a monopolist finds it profitable to charge different prices for his product in different markets. For discrimination of this type *to be possible*, the markets must be separated, otherwise, *arbitrage* will equalize prices in the markets. Arbitrage will occur if traders find it profitable to buy in the low-priced market and resell in the higher-priced market. Consequently, prices will tend to fall to the level in the area where the monopolist charges the lower price. Markets may be physically separated, as in the case of a doctor's services (operations cannot be traded between buyers), or artificially divided by government tariffs or embargoes on imports, as in the case of some domestic and overseas markets.

Differences in elasticities of demand in separable markets form the basis for profitable price discrimination. This is highlighted by Figure 8.14, which provides a simple illustration of third degree price discrimination. Suppose that a domestic producer is producing X_N of product X, that the demand for this product in the domestic market is as indicated by demand curve D_H, and that demand overseas is as shown by the horizontal line D_F. Demand is more inelastic in the domestic market than in the foreign market, where, in fact, it is perfectly elastic.

If the monopolist does not discriminate between these markets in product pricing, all output is sold at a price of P_F, which is the overseas price. In this case, all of the monopolist's output of X_N is sold on the domestic market. However, the monopolist's marginal revenue K in the domestic market is consequently lower than in the overseas market, where it corresponds to T. The monopolist, therefore, is not maximizing total revenue (and in this case profit) by using this strategy. To do this, he or she should only supply X_H of

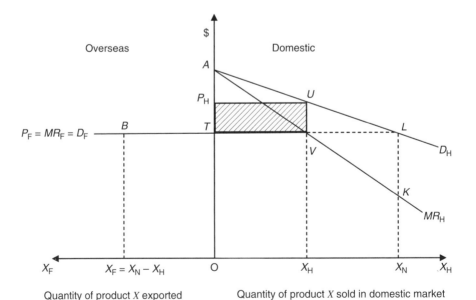

Figure 8.14   A monopolist finds it profitable to charge different prices for a product in separate markets if the elasticity of demand is not the same in these markets

output to the domestic market and should sell the remainder overseas, thereby equalizing marginal revenue from the markets. If the monopolist does this, the domestic price of the product will be increased to P_H, and X_F of the product will be sold abroad. The product's price is higher in the market where demand is most inelastic and the monopolist raises its total revenue by the equivalent of the area of the hatched rectangle. Note, however, that although the domestic supplier gains by this policy, domestic consumers suffer. They lose an equivalent of the area of the quadrilateral $TP_H UL$ in consumers' surplus and there is deadweight economic (Kaldor–Hicks) loss in the domestic economy equal to the area of the triangle UVL.

Social Implications of Price Discrimination

Consider some of the social implications of price discrimination. The technique increases profit and *may* lead to a Paretian (social) ideal level of production and can result in an improvement in social welfare if the potential Paretian improvement criterion is used. However, compared to the alternative of no discrimination, price discrimination can result in an income distribution which is less acceptable than its absence. Taking this into account, a Paretian optimal point with price discrimination *may* be regarded as socially inferior to an alternative, non-Paretian optimal point. This is illustrated by the example of first degree price discrimination in Figure 8.15.

The curves in Figure 8.15 are indicated by the usual notation. In the absence of price discrimination, the monopolist charges P_1 for each unit sold and produces X_1 units. Consumers reap a surplus indicated by the area of triangle P_1LA. However, a Paretian ideal level of output is not attained. Now, suppose that discrimination of the first degree

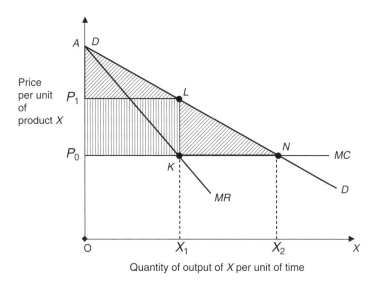

Figure 8.15   First degree price discrimination can result in a Paretian optimum (in the above case, the supply by a monopolist of X_2 rather than X_1), but such efficiency is purchased through a substantial redistribution of income from consumers (buyers) to the monopolist

is possible and is practised. The demand curve is consequently the monopolist's marginal revenue curve and he/she maximizes profit by expanding production to X_2. A Paretian ideal level of output is attained and, under these circumstances, it is not possible to make any market participant better off without making another worse off. But note the other consequence. Consumers' real incomes are thereby reduced. They pay for the extra value of the additional output and lose the surplus they previously enjoyed. Consequently, the income distribution aspect needs to be considered in deciding whether a social improvement results.

However, sometimes all parties may prefer some price discrimination under monopoly to no price discrimination. For example, in the case illustrated in Figure 8.15, a non-discriminating monopolist would produce X_1 of a product and sell it at P_1. But suppose that the monopolist does discriminate, using discrimination of the second degree, and in fact charges P_1 on the first X_1 units and P_0 on the remainder. Compared with the no-discrimination position, consumers' surplus rises by an amount equivalent to the area of triangle KLN and the above-normal profit of the monopolist remains unchanged. In this case, price discrimination results in a Paretian improvement – some parties are made better off and none are made worse off.

Price discrimination of the third degree *can result* in a type of 'Robin Hood' income distribution from the rich to the poor in the population. For example, if the demand of the poor for the service or product is relatively elastic compared to that of the rich (as may be the case for medical services), price discrimination between these two groups results not only in a relatively lower price of the commodity for the poor, but also in an absolutely lower price if their demand for the commodity is not perfectly elastic. This, however, is a by-product of the monopolist's continuing quest for profit, not a result of any overriding compassion for the poor. Indeed, the redistribution of income works in the opposite direction if the demand of the poor for the product or service provided by the monopolist is inelastic relative to that of the rich.

Note that, in some circumstances, price discrimination is essential for the production of a commodity. When the average cost curve for the production of a commodity lies above the demand curve, it is unprofitable to produce this commodity if price discrimination is not possible. If price discrimination *is* possible, this raises the total revenue from producing any output and *may* do so by enough to cover total cost, and so make production of the product possible.

Bundling, Full-line Forcing and Predatory Pricing

Bundling is the practice of a seller making the purchase of a commodity dependent upon the buying of an additional commodity or commodities supplied by the seller. Full-line forcing is a similar practice. In this case, the seller requires the buyer to purchase a full range of the seller's products if the buyer purchases one or more. As in the case of price discrimination, it usually reduces the buyer's economic surplus from exchange. For example, it will do so if the buyer could buy one or more of the commodities in the bundle elsewhere at a lower price.

If one of the commodities in the bundle is unique, or nearly so, and the seller therefore has a monopoly on it, the package or bundle of commodities will most likely be marketable and add to the profit of the seller. However, this practice may also be used as a restrictive trade practice. By including in the bundle a commodity or commodities that could be supplied by competitors or potential competitors, their market is undermined and the barriers to entry of new competitors increased. Therefore, this practice may be illegal in some jurisdictions.

In order to create or retain a monopoly, a business may engage in predatory pricing. Because, for example, of its superior asset position, a business may engage in price cutting to ruin its competitors or potential competitors. It is able to survive because of its superior financial assets. Once competitors have been eliminated, the victorious firm can then engage in monopoly pricing.

This practice can take at least two forms. Prices may be slashed everywhere for a time until competitors are eliminated or prices may be reduced selectively by geographical regions or in other areas where some separation of markets is possible, for example, in circumstances where third degree price discrimination is possible. Competitors may then be eliminated serially from each of the sub-markets. However, observe that their behaviour is not based on third degree price discrimination. In a sub-market, prices may be pushed lower than would be most profitable in a static meeting. This is done to drive out business competitors and establish a monopoly. Predatory pricing is illegal in many jurisdictions. In practice, however, it can be difficult to distinguish between intentional predatory pricing by a business and non-predatory pricing designed to meet growing market competition. The situation can become problematic when the intentions of the players have to be taken into account in deciding whether or not pricing behaviour is predatory.

8.9 CONCLUSION

To assess the social consequences of monopoly merely in terms of its static allocative effects is likely to be misleading. The social consequences of monopoly are likely to vary with the particular situation facing a monopolist, for example whether the threat of entry is important.

One needs also to take account of other consequences of monopoly, for instance its influence on the rate of technological change and its implications for the distribution of income and for the working of the political system. One should be sanguine about idealistic public attempts to regulate private monopolies and to establish state monopolies to guard against the shortcomings of private monopolies. In both cases, government and bureaucratic organizational failures (some of which cannot be eliminated because humans have *limited abilities*, for instance, to collect and to process information) may mean that idealistic policies cannot be fulfilled. Beginning in the 1980s, privatization of public monopolies became popular. In many instances, this process has been accompanied by considerable state regulation of the privatized undertakings. Such regulation involves additional bureaucratic controls with extra costs, and cannot be perfect for some of the reasons mentioned above. Goldstein (2006, p. 211) argues, however, that the ills associated with privatization of state-owned enterprises have been exaggerated and that in most cases consumers and end-users have benefited in terms of choice, quality and prices.

One cannot judge the economic consequences of a monopoly by merely considering the market share of a firm. While 100 per cent market share indicates that *potentially* the monopolist has market power, it is necessary to investigate further. Factors such as competition from substitutes or potential substitutes and the threat of entry must be taken into account. Furthermore, the behaviour of a monopolist (this may differ from the profit maximizing case) and the actual economic performance of a monopoly need to be assessed. Because the circumstances surrounding a monopoly can vary considerably, hasty generalization about the economic consequences of monopoly should be avoided. While some monopolies have had bad economic effects, this is not true of all. Most legislation designed to control the formation of monopolies and to regulate monopolies takes this into account.

READING* AND REFERENCES

Bain, J.S. (1956), *Barriers to New Competition*, Cambridge, MA: Harvard University Press.
Baumol, W.J. (1967), *Business Behavior, Value and Growth*, 2nd edn, chapters 6–8, New York: Harcourt Brace.
*Cabral, L.M.B. (2000), *Introduction to Industrial Organization*, chapters 14–15, Cambridge, MA and London, England: The MIT Press.
Church, C. and R. Ware (2000), *Industrial Organization: A Strategic Approach*, chapters 13–17, New York: McGraw-Hill.
Clark, J.M. (1940), 'Towards a concept of workable competition', *American Economic Review*, **30**, 241–56.
Dorfman, R. and P.O. Steiner (1954), 'Optimal advertising and optimal quality', *American Economic Review*, **44**, 826–36.
Freeman, C. (1974), *The Economics of Industrial Innovation*, London: Penguin.
Geroski, P.A. (1994), *Market Structure, Corporate Governance and Innovative Activity*, Oxford: Clarendon Press.
Goldstein, A. (2006), 'State-owned enterprises, privatization and industrial policy', in B. Bianchi and S. Labory (eds), *International Handbook of Industrial Policy*, Cheltenham, UK and Northampton, MA, USA: Edward Elgar, pp. 198–214.
*Gravelle, H. and R. Rees (2004), *Microeconomics*, 3rd edn, chapter 9 and pp. 433–43, Harlow, UK: Prentice Hall.
Harberger, A.C. (1954), 'Monopoly and resource allocation', *Proceedings of the American Economic Association*, (**44**), 77–87.
Kaldor, N. (1940–41), 'Economic aspects of advertising', *Review of Economic Studies*, **18**, 1–27.
Lerner, A.P. (1934), 'The concept of monopoly and the measurement of monopoly power', *Review of Economic Studies*, **1**, 157–75.
Lipczynski, J. and J. Wilson (2001), *Industrial Organisation: An Analysis of Competitive Markets*, Harlow, England: Prentice Hall.
*Lipsey, R.G. and K.A. Chrystal (2004), '*Economics*', 10th edn, chapter 11, Oxford: Oxford University Press.
*Mansfield, E. and G. Yohe (2004), *Microeconomics*, 11th edn, chapter 10, New York: Norton.
Mansfield, E. (1979), *Microeconomics*, chapter 10, London: Norton.
Modigliani, F. (1958), 'New developments on the oligopoly front', *Journal of Political Economics*, **66**, 215–32.
*Perloff, J.M. (2007), *Microeconomics*, 4th edn, chapter 11, Boston, MA: Addison Wesley.
*Pindyck, R.S. and D.L. Rubenfeld (2005), *Microeconomics*, 6th edn, chapter 10, Upper Saddle River, New Jersey: Prentice Hall.
Scherer, F. (1965), 'Firm size, market structure, opportunity and the output of patented inventions', *American Economic Review*, **55**, December, 1110–20.
Schumpeter, J.A. (1954), *Capitalism, Socialism and Democracy*, London: Allen and Unwin.
Smiley, R. (1998), 'Empirical evidence on strategic entry deterrence', *International Journal of Industrial Organization*, **6**, 167–80.
Telser, L.G. (1964), 'Advertising and competition', *Journal of Political Economy*, **72**, 537–62.

Tisdell, C. (1996), *Bounded Rationality and Economic Evolution*, Cheltenham, UK and Brookfield, USA: Edward Elgar.
*Varian, H.R. (2006), *Intermediate Economics*, 7th edn, chapters 24 and 25, New York: Norton.

QUESTIONS FOR REVIEW AND DISCUSSION

1. Outline measures of monopoly power and carefully state the limitations of each. How could cross price elasticities be an important consideration in deciding whether a monopolist has monopoly power? What other considerations are important in deciding whether monopoly power exists?

2. 'Market power is a necessary but not sufficient condition for monopoly to result in a misallocation of resources.' Explain. In what sense might monopoly result in a misallocation of resources? What other general social effects might a monopoly have?

3. 'Profit-maximizing behaviour by a monopolist results in a loss of consumers' surplus compared to that under perfect competition.' Explain. How great may this loss be? On what factors does the size of the loss depend? What implications might this have for deciding whether or not government interference with a monopoly is desirable?

4. 'While monopoly may lead to a faster rate of technical progress and innovation than perfect competition, this does not ensure lower prices than under conditions of perfect competition.' Discuss.

5. What is X-inefficiency? Show that the Kaldor–Hicks loss from X-inefficiency under monopoly consists of two components.

6. Does non-profit-maximizing behaviour by a monopolist *necessarily* result in a smaller deadweight loss than profit-maximizing behaviour? Illustrate your answer.

7. 'The effect of the threat of entry on a monopolist's pricing behaviour depends on the expected behaviour by the monopolists rivals after entry.' Explain. What is the Sylos postulate? Do you believe that it is realistic?

8. 'The effect of the threat of entry on a monopolist's pricing behaviour depends on the height of barriers to entry.' Explain and illustrate for absolute cost barriers and barriers created by economies of scale.

9. The policies of governments in relation to monopoly are *seemingly* inconsistent. On the one hand there are policies to regulate monopolies and prevent their formation, and on the other hand policies exist that favour the formation of monopolies. Why do these different policies exist and to what extent are they inconsistent?

10. The method of regulating prices charged by utilities in the United States differs from that adopted in the United Kingdom. Explain and discuss the merits and limitations of those policies.

11. Suppose that a government wishes to regulate the behaviour of a private monopoly so that its production is brought into line with that required for a Pareto optimum. What policies could it adopt? What would be the main obstacles to the government achieving its objective?

12. 'A government is more likely to be able to achieve economic efficiency and a Paretian optimum through a public monopoly than by attempting to regulate a private monopoly.' Discuss.

13. 'Evidence about the effect of monopoly on the rate of technical progress is inconclusive as is that about the impact of monopoly on advertising.' Explain and discuss, taking account of the possible welfare effects of both of these activities.
14. Distinguish between different types of price discrimination. In what circumstances is price discrimination (a) possible and (b) likely to be profitable? Does price discrimination add to economic scarcity? Why is it often opposed on social grounds?
15. Outline the concepts of bundling and full-line forcing. What consequences can these practices have for buyers and for market competition?
16. Outline the processes of predatory pricing. Explain why predatory pricing and the economic theory of third degree price discrimination differ. Why is it sometimes difficult to determine whether a business is engaging in predatory pricing?

9. Oligopoly and policy-making

9.1 INTRODUCTION

Oligopoly is a frequent market form in present-day industrial economies. It describes a market situation in which there are few sellers of a commodity or closely competitive commodities. Each seller usually holds a sizeable share of the market. Commodities in the hands of few sellers may be homogeneous or differentiated. A characteristic of oligopolistic markets is that sellers recognize that their individual decisions about marketing their commodities, such as changes in their prices or in their level of advertising effort, not only influence their own volume of sales but also significantly alter the sales of their competitors. Strong market interdependence exists between competitors. Consequently, competitors (rivals) may react by altering their marketing programme in response to an alteration in market strategies by an oligopolistic competitor. Thus, expected variations in the marketing behaviour of rivals need to be taken into account by an oligopolist contemplating a change in his/her market behaviour.

The presence of oligopoly depends on the size of the market. At the international level, one can expect more competitors than at a national level, and more at a national level than at a regional level. A range of important products are oligopolized. Most high technology products, such as advanced computerized equipment and jet airliner production (on a worldwide scale), are controlled in their supply by oligopolists. Supplies of alumina and aluminium, refined copper, petroleum products, tractors, trucks, computer software in many cases, cigarettes, detergents, to give a few examples are oligopolized. Within national markets, banking is sometimes, as in Australia, in the hands of an oligopoly. Often, firms operating in oligopolistic industries are limited liability public companies in which ownership and management are separated. These institutional arrangements (as discussed in Chapter 7) may alter the behaviour of firms and this may be especially important in oligopolistic industries.

This chapter discusses some of the difficulties involved in modelling oligopolistic behaviour, the policy implications of the models, and the possible effect of oligopoly on the volume of advertising and its likely influence on the rate of technical progress. In the penultimate section organizational and institutional arrangements, such as those discussed by Galbraith (1967) and associated with the emergence of large oligopolistic firms are considered. Do we in fact have a dual economy (as suggested by Galbraith) with one part of it organized by small firms and markets and another part controlled by oligopolies and monopolies in which planning rather than market forces is the dominant feature? If so, what policy implications does this have? In addition, in this section implications of growing economic globalization for multinational companies and for oligopolies are considered.

9.2   MODELLING OLIGOPOLISTIC BEHAVIOUR

Modelling of oligopolistic behaviour is difficult. This is because the reactions of oligopolistic competitors can be so varied. Nevertheless, several models are available to assist in
the understanding of typical oligopolistic markets. Kinked demand curve models, price
leadership models, and cartel models, as well as models based on game theory, have all
proven to be of value for understanding the operation of oligopolistic markets, and these
will be outlined here. All of these models indicate ways in which oligopolists cope with
the uncertainty arising from their close interdependence. There may be a strong desire on
the part of the management of oligopoly to reduce uncertainty in their market environment and this may explain why the following models help to explain the operation of oligopolistic markets.

Kinked Demand Curve Model

Markham (1951), Sweezy (1939) and Hall and Hitch (1939) observed that prices of commodities sold in oligopolistic markets tend to be 'sticky'. They remain stationary for
significant time-intervals and alter discretely so that when price levels are graphed against
time they tend to form a stepped function. One possible explanation of this is based upon
the theory that an oligopolist may face a kinked demand curve for his/her commodity.

The kink in this demand curve arises because of the possible reaction of market rivals
to the marketing behaviour of an oligopolist. If attention is restricted to pricing as the
relevant marketing variable, an oligopolist may face a demand curve for his/her product
like the kinked one marked by d in Figure 9.1. The kink occurs at a conventional or acceptable price, P_A, for the commodity. It is an acceptable price in the sense that if the oligopolist charges this price or a higher one his/her rivals do not alter their marketing
arrangements, for instance they do not alter their prices. But if the oligopolist under consideration should happen to charge a price less than the conventional one, P_A (general circumstances in the industry not having altered), rivals do react in an attempt to retain their
share of the market. For instance, they may lower their prices to match that of the oligopolist or lower these by a greater amount, thereby sparking off a 'price-cutting' war. If
it is assumed that rivals react by matching an oligopolist's price-cut below the conventional price, the oligopolist's demand curve below P_A may look like the lower end of curve
marked by d in Figure 9.1. The lower portion is steeper than the upper portion of the
demand curve for the oligopolist's product because matching behaviour by rivals only
occurs when the oligopolist lowers his/her price below P_A.

Because of the kink in the demand curve for an oligopolist's product, the associated
marginal revenue relationship (identified by MR in Figure 9.1) is discontinuous, as
indicated by the two heavy lines in Figure 9.1, and the discontinuity occurs directly below
the kink in the oligopolist's demand curve. If the oligopolist's marginal cost of production or of supply passes through the gap in these marginal revenue lines, his/her profit-
maximizing strategy is to charge the acceptable or conventional price, P_A, and meet all
demands at this price. In the case illustrated, all demands can be met by supplying X_1 of
the product. On the other hand, if an oligopolist's marginal cost of supply should pass
through the upper branch of the marginal revenue curve, he/she would maximize his/her
profit by charging a price higher than the conventional one; should it pass through the

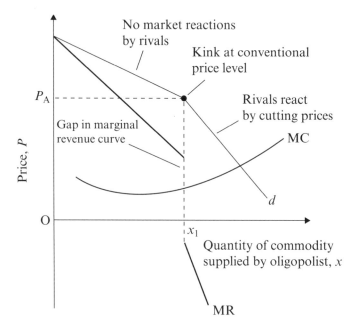

Figure 9.1   A kinked demand curve for an oligopolist's product and associated discontinuous marginal revenue curves. This can arise because of the market responses of rivals

lower branch, he/she *may* make the greatest profit by charging less than the conventional price. But in the latter case, the oligopolist may face the risk of a price war.

In the kinked demand curve case, there is a high probability that the firm's optimal pricing strategy for maximizing its profit is similar to that for maximizing its value of sales. Sales maximization and profit maximization can result in the same price and supply level for an oligopolist faced by a kinked demand curve. This is so if the conventional price maximizes the firm's profit and if the branches of its marginal revenue curve do not intersect the X-axis, and so MR is negative for $x \geq x_1$. In the example given in Figure 9.1, the price P_A and the supply x_1 maximize both the firm's profit and the value of its sales. If the kinked demand curve applies, *substantial variation* can occur in the demand *for a firm's product* or in its *cost of production* and the firm does *not* find it *profitable to alter* the price of its product from the conventional level. This is illustrated in Figure 9.2. If the demand curve d_1 and corresponding marginal revenue curve MR_1 applies, a rise in the firm's marginal cost of supply from MC_1 to MC_2 leaves its profit-maximizing price unaltered at P_A.

Similarly, a rise in the demand for the firm's product which shifts its demand curve to d_2 and its marginal revenue to MR_2, leaves its profit-maximizing price unchanged at P_A because the marginal cost curves continue to pass through the gap in the marginal revenue curves.

This model provides one possible explanation of why oligopolists may maintain stable conventional prices even though their *individual* costs or demand conditions change appreciably. On the other hand, an alteration in the cost or demand conditions facing *all oligopolists* in a market is liable to lead to a change in the conventional or acceptable price level. The kinked demand curve model, the characteristics of which do *not* require overt *collusion* between oligopolists, has two other important implications:

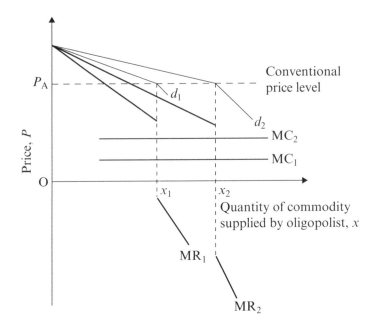

*Figure 9.2   The demand for an individual oligopolist's product may vary considerably, and so too
may his/her per-unit costs of production, and yet it may not be profitable for the
oligopolist to alter the price of his/her product from the conventional level. In the above
case, the conventional price P_A maximizes profit even if there is an alteration in the
demand curve from d_1 to d_2 or a change in marginal costs from MC_1 to MC_2*

1. Wage increases or improvements of conditions of work need not result in reduced
    employment, especially if the increases apply to one or a few firms. Although mar-
    ginal cost may rise, the MC curve may continue to pass through the gap in the MR
    curve.
2. There is *no price competition* between oligopolists so market competition must take
    other forms. Non-price competition is likely to be important in an oligopolistic market.
    This occurs via advertising, product differentiation, quality variations, product variety
    and other means.

Nevertheless, the theory raises the question of how conventional or acceptable price levels
are determined and altered. They may be set by a price-leader; there may be customary
rules for altering established prices such as their upward variation to pass on all general
cost rises; manufacturers or wholesalers may 'recommend' prices to retailers; or there may
be some consultation between firms as to their intentions when general cost rises occur so
that a consensus emerges. New acceptable prices may fall in a range, for instance a 20 to
30 per cent price rise might be acceptable as a result of a 25 per cent rise in general costs
but a 10 per cent rise might not be acceptable because it implies 'chiselling'. Any firm
increasing its price by such a small amount and persisting in such behaviour might expect
retaliatory action from its rivals. This is a matter which would benefit from further study.

   Note that the kinked demand curve model of oligopoly can also be envisaged using
the theory of games (von Neumann and Morgenstern, 1944). The above oligopolistic

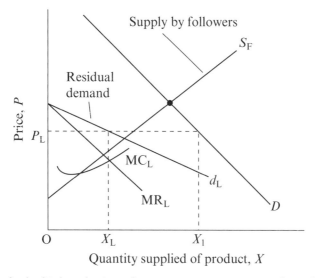

Figure 9.3   Price leadership by a dominant firm aiming to maximize its profit. In the case shown, the price-leader sets the market price at P$_L$ *and supplies* X$_L$ *of market demand*

situation can be modelled as a non-zero sum repetitive game in which the players (the oligopolists) adopt a tit-for-tat policy if any oligopolist charges less than the customary price, general economic conditions remaining stationary. This tit-for-tat policy ensures the stability of the strategy of each oligopolist charging not less than the customary price.

Price Leadership Models

As suggested above, the conventional price in a kinked demand curve situation may be set by a price-leader. However, there is not a single form of price leadership but a range of forms. The barometric and dominant firm models of price leadership are of particular interest.

In the *barometric case* one firm or supplier, not necessarily the lowest cost or largest producer, acts as the barometer for the whole industry and alters its price when conditions alter in the whole industry. The leader is recognized as having a 'good feel' for industry conditions and its leadership may be reinforced by past behaviour in the industry. In the past, Bethlehem Steel was reputed to be the price-leader in the US steel industry but US Steel was the largest producer. Bethlehem's lead was traditionally followed by other steel producers.

In the *dominant firm case*, a firm may be the price-leader because it is financially stronger than the others in the oligopolistic markets or has lower per-unit costs of production. The predictions of this model are relatively precise if the following conditions are satisfied: other firms charge the same price as the price-leader, the leader aims to maximize profit and aims to satisfy that part of market demand which would not be met by rivals. This is illustrated by Figure 9.3. Assuming a homogeneous product, let the curve marked *D* be the market demand for the product and let *S*$_F$ represent the supply of followers at alternative prices set by the leader. The difference between *D* and *S*$_F$ gives the demand for the leader's supply and is shown by the line marked d_L. The marginal revenue curve corresponding to d_L is indicated by MR_L. If the leader aims to maximize his/her profit and MC_L is his/her marginal cost of production, the most profitable price from the leader's viewpoint will be P_L. Other firms follow this lead. The leader supplies X_L of the product to the market and the remainder of demand, $X_L - X_L$ is met by followers. In this dominant price-leadership case, the price of the product is liable to be higher and its supply less than under perfect competitive with the reverse being so compared to the alternative of a monopoly or a profit-maximizing cartel. Hence, in a market where dominant price leadership exists, a loss in consumers' surplus is likely compared to the alternative of pure competition, but the loss is smaller than if monopoly or a profit-maximizing cartel exists. If the price leadership involves overt collusion, it may result in prosecution of the businesses for engaging in restrictive trade practices. If, on the other hand, the price leadership occurs 'spontaneously' without any explicit collusion, conviction for collusion does not seem possible.

This model implies (other things being equal) that the price-leader adjusts the price charged by him/her upwards if his/her marginal costs of production rise or if the demand for his/her supplies increases. This may happen if the market demand for the product expands or if the costs of inputs rise generally. There is no reason to expect the price-leader to be hesitant about passing on inflationary cost rises. Indeed, he/she may adjust price in anticipation of future inflationary cost rises if price alteration is restricted to discrete intervals, and this could speed up the rate of inflation.

The dominant price leadership case can also be envisaged as involving a non-zero sum repetitive game in which the price leader retains his/her leadership by adopting a tit-for-tat policy. If financially weaker firms do not follow the price-leader in their pricing behaviour, they face the prospect that the price-leader will slash the price of his/her product and inflict economic losses on them. If this threat is really likely to be carried out, this tit-for-tat policy makes for stability of the price leadership economic conditions in the industry stationary.

As time passes, however, the relative economic dominance of firms in an industry can alter and new firms may enter. Hence, a new dominant leader may emerge or the pattern of market competition in the industry may alter. When a struggle for dominance emerges, the market may become unstable for a time (it is thrown into disarray) until the new pattern of dominance is established or the old pattern is confirmed. There has been little study of these critical points or periods in market transformation even though they are an important part of the process of market competition.

Cartel Models

The possibility was discussed in Chapter 4 of cartels (associations of suppliers) forming and aiming to maximize their joint profit or increase their profit by a common policy, for instance by each restricting its supply. If a cartel happens to agree on a policy of maximizing the joint profit of its members, it is relatively easy in principle to determine its optimal pricing and supply policy. The cartel should adopt the same policy as a multi-plant monopolist. Total quantity supplied of the commodity and its price should be adjusted so that marginal revenue in the market and marginal cost in the industry are equal and production should be allocated between plants or firms so that the marginal costs of production of all operating plants are equal. The effects of cartels on economic welfare are similar to those associated with monopoly (see Chapter 8) and this type of collusion is usually prohibited.

However, it is not certain that cartel members will agree to policies to maximize the joint profit of members because of conflicts between its members about sharing their joint profit. A firm may resist the allocation of a small production quota even though the firm has high per-unit costs of production and this allocation would maximize collective profit. The firm may succeed by political means in the cartel organization in obtaining a higher quota at the expense of collective profit. Political in-fighting over the share of collective profits is likely to rule out a pure monopoly-type solution. This problem, however, is reduced if the companies involved merge, although it is not certain to be eliminated if units within the company have separate identities.

A well-known international cartel is OPEC (Organization of Petroleum Exporting Countries). OPEC consists of a group of major oil-exporting countries which have agreed to quotas on their levels of output of oil, presumably with the aim in mind of maintaining or increasing their monopoly profits from oil exports. Multinational companies sourcing their oil from OPEC countries must charge a price to buyers at least sufficient to cover the oil export tax of OPEC countries plus their costs of production. Adelman (1972) has claimed that multinational petroleum companies are essential to the success of the scheme because in their absence 'chiselling' and secret discounts would be more common and this would undermine the cartel. OPEC claims that one of its functions is to help stabilize the price of oil but its success in this regard may be limited.

As pointed out in Chapter 4, cartels are under constant threat from within and from without and OPEC is no exception. Individual members can profit from marginally undercutting others in price but if all do this the cartel fails. Similarly, new entrants to the industry are encouraged by increased profits, and non-cartel members producing oil (such as Norway, Russia and the United Kingdom) may have no incentive to limit supplies. Nevertheless, it has been suggested (see next reference) that Norway, Bolivia, Mexico, Syria and Sudan could join OPEC. Angola joined OPEC at the beginning of 2007, bringing its membership to 12 nations. It was estimated that in 2005 OPEC members held about two-thirds of the world's oil resources and that their production was almost 42 per cent of world production (http://en.wikipedia/org/wiki/OPEC. Accessed 19/4/2007).

IATA (the International Air Transport Association) has also been claimed to be a cartel. IATA's aim in the past has been to determine common international air fares on principal routes and it has been aided in this policy by governments. On the other hand, IATA claims that one of its functions is to maintain airline and travel standards. But IATA has had to face both internal and external threats. Some of its members have offered 'extras' such as lower than normal hotel rates, low internal air fares, finance for tours at lower than normal interest rates, or cheap car hire to win business. An external threat has also been posed by some charter operators, by non-IATA operators and cut-price operators such as Ryanair. With a political swing in favour of economic liberalism and the fact that many governments have divested themselves of ownership of airlines, governments appear to have become less sympathetic to the operations of IATA. The operations of IATA are being more carefully scrutinized in the EU and the USA (http://wikipedia.org/wiki/International_Air_Transport_Association. Accessed 19/4/2007).

Other Models of Oligopolistic Behaviour

Other models of oligopolistic behaviour include those by Cournot (1838), Bertrand (1883), von Stackelberg (1952), and those stemming directly from the 'theory of games'. Cournot's model is an interaction model of the follower-follower type. In the duopoly case, each duopolist adjusts his/her output to maximize his/her profit on the assumption that his rival's output of the last period is unaltered. Both do this until an equilibrium is reached. A problem of the model is that neither duopolist learns that in fact the assumption of unchanged output by the rival does not hold except in equilibrium. The Bertrand model is similar to the Cournot model. In Bertrand's model, duopolists alter prices charged by them rather than their supplies.

Von Stackelberg's model covers a broader range of possible behaviours than either Cournot's or Bertrand's. Apart from follower-follower types of situation, it examines leader-follower types. Leader-follower types assume that one oligopolist or duopolist is the leader and that others follow. In deciding on the best policy from his/her point of view the leader takes account of the reactions of other suppliers to his/her policies. But if more than one firm tries to lead, the von Stackelberg model gives no solution. In some such instances, the theory of games may be able to predict an outcome even though it too is limited in its powers of prediction.

The theory of games has been increasingly applied to the modelling situations of economic and social conflict and behaviour following the publication by von Neuman and Morgenstern of *Theory of Games and Economic Behaviour* (1944). Predictions of the theory appear to be most reliable for situations of pure conflict which are often modelled by *two-person zero-sum games*. Two-person zero-sum games involve two parties or players and the gain of any party from the game equals the loss of the other so that *gains* of all players *add to zero*. But most oligopolistic situations are non-zero sum, that is the gain of one party or set of parties is not equal to the loss of the other ones. Non-zero sum games also provide useful economic insights as has already been observed in this chapter. Applications of the theory of games, to advertising, to product differentiation and to innovation are outlined below.

Oligopolistic Competition through Variables other than Price, and Non-profit Maximization

Many microeconomic texts stress the importance of price as a variable in competition between firms. This may be because price is an important variable or could be because price is a variable which can readily be measured in building economic models. Model-building is highly regarded by most economists and this could influence their choice of variables. A study by Udell (1964) indicates that price may be a less important variable in marketing than it is sometimes thought to be. He found from a survey of 200 American firms that half did not consider price to be among the first five most important decision variables influencing their market success. But even if price is not an important variable, managers need to take account of *price* and non-price variables as *alternative* possible methods of competing with rival firms, and models based upon price as a variable may throw light upon behaviour associated with other variables. Advertising expenditure, for instance, is one means of competing. But in an oligopolistic industry a firm increasing its advertising intensity needs to take account of its effects of this on its rivals. If the firm's intensity of advertising increases beyond a customary or acceptable level, rivals may react by increasing their advertising intensity to a similar extent and a *kinked demand* relationship occurs.

Oligopolists are frequently suppliers of a range of products and apart from competing by means of price may compete by means of:

1. variations in their terms of credit;
2. advertising, promotion, and presentation of products, as packaging;
3. the variety and range of products supplied and available such as in the case of supermarkets;
4. services provided such as after-sales service on durable products, assistance if problems arise in the use of the product, and widespread availability of support services; and
5. through the development and supply of new products or improvements in existing products as a result of R&D effort and search by the companies concerned.

Some of these competitive means such as advertising, product differentiation and R&D effort are discussed later in this chapter. The major emphasis in this chapter is on forms of non-price competition used by oligopolists.

Most of the oligopolistic models mentioned above assume that the aim of the firm is to maximize its profits. As discussed in Chapter 7, firms need not have this objective, for instance because of the separation of ownership and management. To the extent that non-profit maximization is important, profit-maximizing theories of oligopoly are restricted in their application.

9.3 ADVERTISING AND OLIGOPOLY

One criticism sometimes made about oligopoly is that it results in a socially excessive level of advertising. But the critics do not always provide a clear guide to their criterion for a social optimum. In *some* circumstances, oligopoly results in a socially excessive level of advertising in the Kaldor–Hicks sense but not always. Sometimes informative advertising may be inadequate under oligopoly in the sense that a Kaldor–Hicks gain might be made by increasing its level or by its altering its nature. These aspects will be discussed presently.

Advertising Intensity and Market Structure

Empirical evidence suggests that advertising intensities (the ratios of advertising expenditure to the value of sales) tend to be highest in oligopolistic industries, lower under monopoly, and least under competitive conditions. Sutton (1974) found that the relationship between advertising intensity and concentration ratios tended to be approximately of the inverted U-shape shown in Figure 9.4. This relationship indicates that advertising intensities reach a maximum of around 2.9 per cent for a concentration ratio of about 64 per cent, fall to zero at 19 per cent or smaller concentrations, and to about 1 per cent under complete monopoly. But these results are based upon a narrow sample of UK consumer goods and the study did not include producer industries.

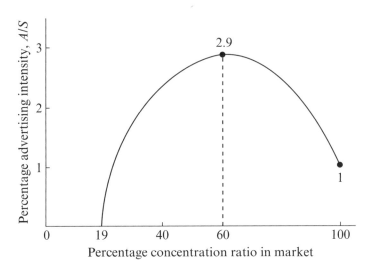

*Figure 9.4   The empirical relationship between advertising intensity and market concentration
suggested by Sutton (1974)*

Advertising intensities could be higher under oligopoly than under alternative market forms for a number of reasons:

1. Price competition may not be prevalent under oligopoly (as suggested, for example, by the kinked demand curve) and advertising may provide an alternative means of competition.
2. More new products and products of a complicated type *may* be introduced by oligopolists than by suppliers in other types of markets so that a greater amount of informative and 'awareness'-type advertising may be required.
3. Oligopolists may be prone to a competitive advertising trap (to be discussed below) which locks all of them into high levels of advertising expenditure.
4. The greater the concentration of supplies in the industry, the greater may be the incentive of the dominant firms to engage in advertising designed to deter entry.

An Advertising Trap and Applications of Theory of Games

Consider the possibility of oligopolists becoming trapped into high advertising intensities. This could occur if each either (1) aims to maximize its profit or (2) attempts to maximize its market share. The trap is easily illustrated by applying the theory of games.

Take the profit maximization case first. This involves a non-zero game. For simplicity assume duopolists (that is, an industry consisting of two sellers) with two available strategies each, namely to employ low advertising intensities (L) or high intensities (H). The available strategies of each are shown in the matrix in Figure 9.5. The profits of the firms depend upon the strategies jointly employed by them and the hypothetical figures in the body of the matrix shown for each strategy, the profit received by firm 2 and firm 1, respectively. Thus if firm 2 adopts a low advertising intensity and firm 1 a high intensity, the profit for firm 2 is 6 units and for firm 1 is 12 units, as shown by the entry (6, 12) in Figure 9.5.

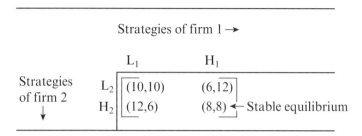

Strategies of firm 1 →

		L₁	H₁
Strategies of firm 2 ↓	L₂	(10,10)	(6,12)
	H₂	(12,6)	(8,8) ← Stable equilibrium

Figure 9.5 If each firm tries to maximize its own profit, each will choose a high intensity of advertising. Consequently, the profit of each will be lower than if both had adopted a low advertising strategy

This matrix indicates that whatever strategy is adopted by firm 2, firm 1 makes the most profit by adopting strategy H. Similarly, it can be seen that whatever strategy firm 1 adopts, firm 2 makes the most profit by adopting strategy H. In order to maximize its profit each is liable to choose H, a high advertising intensity, and this choice forms a stable equilibrium (a Nash equilibrium). In this non-zero sum non-cooperative game, both firms become trapped in this Nash equilibrium. The outcome corresponds to that of prisoner's dilemma problem of game theory. This is a Nash equilibrium because neither firm (player) has any incentive to adopt unilaterally any other strategy than the one involving a high level of advertising. Assuming that the game is a repetitive game, each firm could earn greater profit if each agreed to switch to a low advertising intensity but they would need to cooperate and to trust one another for this agreement 'to work'.

Duopolists or oligopolists concerned primarily with market share can also become trapped into high levels of advertising expenditure which benefit none of them. This can be illustrated by means of a *zero-sum* game such as that shown in the matrix in (Figure 9.6). In a zero-sum game what one player gains the other loses (the sum of their gains is zero) and consequently, there is no scope for their cooperation. As before, assume the existence of a duopoly and that each firm has two alternative strategies, a high intensity (H) and a low intensity (L) one. The body of the matrix shows the market share (proportion) obtained by firm 1 when the indicated joint strategies are adopted. For instance, if firm 1 adopts a high intensity of advertising H₁ and firm 2 a low intensity L₁, firm 1 obtains 0.8 of the market. This market share may also be regarded as having been lost by firm 2. Whatever share firm 1 gains firm 2 loses, and vice versa. Hence, the zero-sum nature of the game.

If both firms wish to maximize their market share, they are in conflict. Assuming both to be rational and well informed, each would be wise to suppose that the other will try to minimize the gain of the opponent. Thus firm 1 would be wise to assume that firm 2 will attempt to minimize firm 1's share of the market. Therefore, firm 1 (to do the best it can in the circumstances) should adopt the strategy which maximizes the minimum gain associated with each of its available strategies. Its minimum gain associated with L₁ is 0.2 and with H₁ is 0.5. Hence, its maximin choice is H₁, Similarly, firm 2 will try to minimize its maximum loss. This occurs when it chooses H₂, its minimax strategy. Thus, both firms are led to adopt strategies of high intensity advertising and their choice forms a stable equilibrium. However, note that their market shares are no different to those which would have eventuated if *each* had adopted a low intensity of advertising. They have become trapped

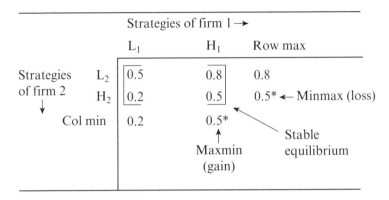

		Strategies of firm 1 →		
		L_1	H_1	Row max
Strategies of firm 2 ↓	L_2	0.5	0.8	0.8
	H_2	0.2	0.5	0.5* ← Minmax (loss)
	Col min	0.2	0.5*	

Maxmin (gain)

Stable equilibrium

Figure 9.6   If duopolists aim to maximize their market share a two-person zero-sum game emerges, the outcome of which is likely to be a high intensity of advertising by both firms. In the above case, strategies H_1 and H_2 are the solution for the game

into a high level of advertising by their own competitiveness and this is a very stable outcome. Once again, it is a Nash equilibrium.

Benefits and Costs to Buyers of Advertising

Such competitive advertising behaviour need not benefit consumers or buyers. They may know the qualities of the advertised product well and may gain no image satisfaction nor social benefit from the advertising. The sole impact of the advertising may merely be on the way that a comparatively fixed aggregate sales of a relatively homogeneous product is shared between firms. The advertising primarily keeps buyers 'evenly' aware of all sources of supply. In these circumstances, a Kaldor–Hicks gain could be made by firms reducing the intensity of their advertising. Possibly advertising of major brands of coke fits this case.

However, we need also to consider generally the type of benefits that advertising activity may have for buyers or consumers. It is also interesting to speculate about the effect of advertising expenditure on price levels.

Advertising may reduce the cost to a buyer of searching for or obtaining information about products. It can be less costly for sellers to provide information in this way than for buyers to seek required products by advertising or similar means. In supplying information by advertisement, sellers tend to undersupply it from a social point of view. Profit-maximizers will disseminate information until their marginal profitability from this activity is zero. But at this level of dissemination, the marginal value to buyers or consumers of information may still remain positive. Hence, from a social point of view, greater dissemination of information would be socially worthwhile. This does not occur because sellers cannot appropriate all the gains from *additional* information. This problem is illustrated in Figure 9.7. The curve indicated by MPS is the marginal profitability to sellers of providing information, and that indicated by MSV is the marginal social value of disseminating information which equals MPS plus the marginal value of information to buyers (MVB). Sellers disseminate Q_1 of information but a social optimum would be achieved by supplying Q_2 of information. Although consumers gain from the provision

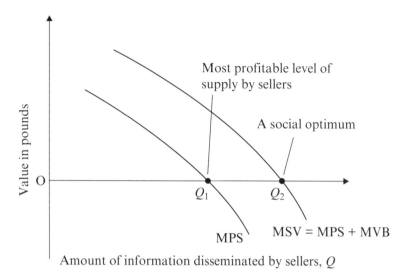

Most profitable level of
supply by sellers

A social optimum

Value in pounds

O

Q_1

Q_2

MPS

MSV = MPS + MVB

Amount of information disseminated by sellers, Q

*Figure 9.7   While sellers may play a useful social role in providing information through advertising,
their supply of information is likely to be less than socially optimal since they do not
appropriate all marginal gains from the supply of information*

of information by sellers, gains are not maximized by the policy of sellers. There is under-provision of information from a social point of view.

Other aspects of advertising are difficult to evaluate but nevertheless warrant mention. Sometimes advertising messages are forced on individuals (as joint consumption, for example, in conjunction with television programmes and Internet use) and are considered to be repulsive and an intrusion. On the other hand, these messages can be highly valued and may provide a product with an image which is desired by the buyer. Furthermore, advertising can also increase demand for products, the consumption of which is detrimental to the apparent interests of buyers. For instance, should cigarette smoking and the taking of drugs be encouraged by cigarette and drug advertisements? Should the advertisement of 'junk' foods that contribute to obesity be restricted, particularly when the target is children?

The effect of advertising on price levels can vary and is not known with certainty. When advertising increases demand for a product, the marginal cost of which rises with its production, it is likely to result in a rise in its price, but if its marginal cost of production is falling, this may lead to a fall in the price of the advertised product. However, even in the last case, it is necessary to be cautious because if monopolistic large-group competition prevails, advertising may result in higher prices, even if per-unit costs are decreasing. This is illustrated in Figure 9.8. There the costs of a representative monopolistically competitive firm are shown. The curve indicated by AOC is its average operating costs, and its average total cost curve includes average operating costs plus average advertising costs. In the absence of advertising in the industry, the firm might come into a long-term tangency equilibrium at a point such as C. But if advertising is a practice common to all firms, the firm reaches a long-term equilibrium at a point such as B (where its average total cost curve is tangential to its demand curve after advertising) and only makes normal profit.

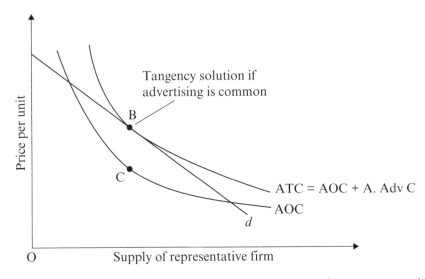

Figure 9.8   Under conditions of monopolistic large-group competition, advertising may result in a higher price for the advertised product than in its absence. In the case shown, the equilibrium of the representative firm is reached at point B rather than at C

The price of the product in equilibrium B is higher than in case C and in both instances price exceeds marginal cost. However, it cannot be concluded solely from this, that consumers are worse off as a result of the advertising even though they might be. Consideration would be needed of the nature or content of the advertising.

As one might expect, empirical evidence about the impact of advertising on prices is inconclusive. However, there is some evidence from the USA that advertising of professional services in states where it is allowed reduces prices and the variation in prices charged by suppliers (Lipczynski and Wilson, 2001, pp. 213–17). This may be because the type of advertisements involved provide increased information to consumers, thereby making the markets more competitive. The economic impacts of advertising appear to vary with the nature of the advertising undertaken. The economic impacts of advertising are complex.

Public Policies and Advertising

Despite ambiguities about the economic impact of advertising, public policies have been adopted and contemplated to influence it. For instance, in many countries the advertising of cigarettes and tobacco products is restricted. Advertisements must carry a health warning and are not permitted by means of some media, such as television. The rationale for the interference is that individuals, especially the young, may be influenced to smoke against their long-term health interests, and the habit may become addictive. The judgement is made that if advertising is unregulated, some individuals will be unable to choose what is in their best long-term interest. Their choice may also have external repercussions in the long term, for instance if they become sick and dependent on others. There is also danger to the health of non-smokers from inhaling 'second-hand' smoke. Nevertheless, restricting the flow of information to individuals in their own long-term interest can be problematic. For example, it is not always certain that others are better judges of this interest. Furthermore most of us value the right to be wrong in our decisions, and many resent restrictions on freedom of choice.

Occasionally some forms of advertising are banned on the grounds that they cause 'environmental pollution', unfavourable externalities. In some cities, neon and billboard advertising is restricted by local governments. Programmes of the BBC and the Australian Broadcasting Corporation carry no advertising – a feature appealing to many viewers and listeners.

Restrictions on advertising often have a displacement effect. For instance, as a result of the restriction on television advertising, cigarette companies initially increased their relative expenditure using other media until this was also banned in many countries. Furthermore, by increasing their sponsorship of televised sporting fixtures, they continued to have indirect access to television coverage.

The intensity of advertising varies considerably between industries, and according to Sutton's (1974) study, is least in industries consisting of many firms with little concentration of market power. Consequently, consumers might be less aware of the value of products supplied in competitive markets than those supplied by oligopolies. This may mean that consumers do not make the type of choices they would make if they had a more 'balanced' view of the available products. Their choice may be slanted too much in favour of products supplied by oligopolists. If this is so, one remedy might be to take collective action to increase information about products supplied in competitive markets. On the other hand, it is possible that consumers are more familiar with products supplied mainly in competitive markets than those supplied by oligopolies. Products produced by oligopolies could on the whole display greater novelty due to a higher rate of innovation.

In many countries, there is legislation against false and misleading advertising. One of the functions of the Australian Competition and Consumer Commission (ACCC) is to protect consumers from such advertising. While this legislation is designed to protect consumers, it may indirectly benefit honest competitive sellers. The pros and cons of such interference were discussed in Chapter 5.

9.4   PRODUCT DIFFERENTIATION

What is the likely effect of oligopoly on the available variety and differentiation of products? Hotelling (1929) suggested that oligopolistic firms tend to minimize product differentiation, locate together, and supply similar products. Their similar products are designed to satisfy buyers with *median* tastes.

Principle of Minimum Product Differentiation

This principle holds if products are able to be differentiated solely by a single characteristic. For theoretical purposes, let this attribute be measured by lambda (λ) which might represent, for example, the degree of whiteness or degree of sweetness of the product. In addition, this theory assumes that consumers purchase the product having the characteristic closest to their preferred degree of the characteristic. Furthermore, the theory

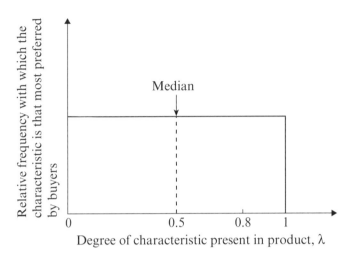

*Figure 9.9   Given Hotelling's assumptions and the above distribution of preferences, duopolists will
supply identical products containing a characteristic in the degree most preferred by the
median buyer, namely λ = 0.5 in this case*

supposes each firm finds it profitable to supply the product only in one degree of the characteristic but can supply any of its degrees at the same per-unit cost; and aggregate demand is relatively fixed.

This theory can be illustrated by an example for a duopoly. Let the degree of the characteristic, λ, present in the products of the duopolists be measured on a scale from zero to one and assume that the relative frequency with which each of the possible degrees of the characteristics are most preferred by buyers forms a rectangular distribution as in Figure 9.9. The median buyer prefers a product containing 0.5 of λ. Thus, both duopolists will supply a product containing 0.5 of λ. No product differentiation occurs and each duopolist obtains 50 per cent of the market. If any duopolist were to diverge from λ = 0.5, he/she would run the risk of obtaining less than 50 per cent of the market. For instance, given the distribution in Figure 9.9, if one duopolist chooses λ = 0.8, and the second duopolist supplies a product with attributes λ = 0.5, the second obtains 65 per cent of the market. The second duopolist obtains all customers preferring λ ≤ 0.5 plus all preferring 0.5 ≤ λ ≤ 0.65, given that customers purchase the product with the nearest available quality. On the other hand, if the rival supplied a product of λ = 0.79, he/she would gain 79 per cent of the market, that is the custom of all buyers preferring a quality of λ < 0.8.

It could be argued that consumers' tastes would be more fully satisfied if one duopolist supplied a product of λ = 0.25 and the other a product of λ = 0.75. In that case, each would still obtain 50 per cent of the market. But this is not a stable solution because one firm can obtain a greater share of the market by moving closer towards the type of product produced by his/her rival.

Minimum Product Differentiation Illustrated by a Zero-sum Game

The theory of two-person zero-sum games is possibly the most satisfactory means by which to see that the median outcome is the most likely solution. It forms a stable

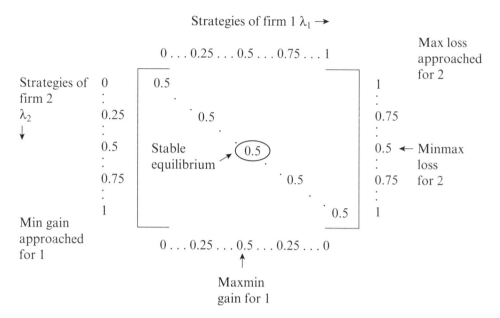

Figure 9.10 *The pattern of a zero-sum game used to illustrate the principle of minimum product differentiation assuming that each of the suppliers of a product wants to maximize its marker share*

equilibrium (Nash equilibrium) in terms of game theory. In matrix form, 'the game' involving the duopolists may be represented in the way shown in Figure 9.10. There λ_1 represents the choice of degrees of the characteristic available to firm 1 and λ_2 represents the choices available to firm 2. Their market shares depend upon their joint choices. Entries in the matrix show the share of the market obtained by firm 1. Some of the diagonal entries are shown. All diagonal entries (for both diagonals) would be 0.5, indicating that for these joint strategies the duopolists would share the market equally. Minimum gains by firm 1 approach the figures shown at the foot of the matrix. For $\lambda_1 < 0.5$, these figures are given by λ_1 and for $\lambda_1 > 0.5$ are given by $1 - \lambda_1$. The maxmin gain for firm 1 occurs for $\lambda_1 = 0.5$. The *maxmin gain* is the maximum of possible minimum gains. Similarly the minmax loss for firm 2 occurs for $\lambda_2 = 0.5$. The *minmax loss* is the minimum of possible maximum losses. Hence, both duopolists reach a *stable equilibrium* by producing a product with a characteristic of $\lambda = 0.5$, catering for the median preference. For this choice, the maxmin gain of firm 1 equals the minmax loss for firm 2. If either unilaterally alters its choice of strategy it will be worse off than otherwise. Hence, if each caters for the median taste of customers, a Nash equilibrium occurs.

The minimum gain available to firm 1 is shown in Figure 9.11 as a function of λ_1 by the solid lines, and reaches a maximum for $\lambda_1 = 0.5$. The maximum possible loss for firm 2 is shown in Figure 9.11 as a function of λ_2 by the broken lines, and reaches a minimum for $\lambda_2 = 0.5$. These results confirm the above insights that a stable solution occurs when both firms produce a product with characteristic $\lambda = 0.5$ to satisfy the median preference.

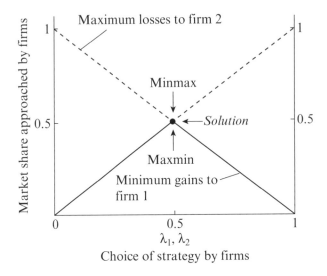

Figure 9.11   *A diagrammatic illustration of a zero-sum game solution resulting in minimum product differentiation by duopolists. As Hotelling points out, this principle may also help to explain the similarity of party platforms in a two-party political system*

Applications of Hotelling's Principle

Hotelling suggested that his theory might have an application outside economics; for example, that it might help to explain why the election platforms of major parties tend to be similar and aimed at the voter with the median preference on major issues (see Chapter 14). Hotelling's theory has been used to help justify public supply or supplementary supply of broadcasting and television by public corporations such as the BBC (British Broadcasting Corporation) and the Australian Broadcasting Corporation (ABC). It has been suggested that commercial stations and television channels will supply relatively undifferentiated programmes aimed at the median listener or viewer and that the interests of better educated individuals will be neglected. Government supply or supplementary supply, it is argued, add to the available variety of programmes.

However, the BBC is also required to produce some 'popular' shows (probably to bolster political support for it) as well as items that would not normally be supplied by commercial broadcasters. In addition to the ABC, Australia has the government-owned Special Broadcasting Service (SBS). Its role, according to its website, is 'to promote multi-lingual and multicultural radio and television services that inform, educate and entertain all Australians and, in doing so, reflect Australia's multicultural society'. It contributes to diversity in broadcasting by providing services that would not normally be provided by commercial broadcasters.

Qualifications to Hotelling's Principle

One must be careful about pressing Hotelling's hypothesis too far. The assumptions needed for the theory to hold do not always apply. Consumers may not buy or may buy

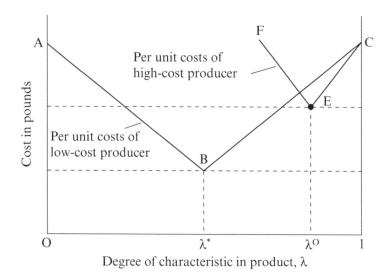

Figure 9.12   *In order to survive, a high-cost producer may have to differentiate his/her product sufficiently from that of the low-cost producer. If the low-cost producer in the above case chooses λ*, the high-cost producer can maximize his/her market share by choosing to supply λ°, that is, a well-differentiated product*

in lower quantities a product that is not of the type most preferred by them and the per-unit cost of production of suppliers can be different. The last mentioned difference favours product variety because producers with a high cost per unit need to differentiate their products from those with low costs in order to survive.

If a low-cost producer has transport costs which rise as he/she attempts to sell to buyers further away from his/her primary location or to buyers seeking a product with a characteristic further away from his or hers, a high-cost producer may be able to survive by catering for demands on the fringe. This is illustrated in Figure 9.12. Suppose that a low-cost producer locates at λ* and has per-unit production costs of λ*B. When transport or selling costs are added to this, the low-cost producer's per-unit total cost of reaching buyers at the different locations is shown by the relationship ABC. A high-cost producer with per-unit production costs, say, of λ°E could not survive by locating near λ*. But assuming the location of the low-cost producer to be fixed and the overall per-unit costs of the high-cost producer to be as shown by FEC, the high-cost producer could survive by locating at λ° and thus supplying a product well differentiated from that of his rival. In countries with high per-unit costs of production but having non-median tastes, local producers may survive in competition with low-cost imports catering for worldwide median tastes by producing a differentiated product aimed at local tastes.

The available evidence is insufficient to conclude that, in general, oligopoly leads to a lowering in the degree of product differentiation. Indeed it has been argued by some by reference to the monopolistic competition model that oligopoly in some markets results in excessive variety from a social point of view. Furthermore, Marris (1964) in his theory of managerial capitalism suggests that oligopolistic management-dominated firms have considerable incentives to promote a variety of products. Marris argues that oligopolistic firms are typically multi-product suppliers, that their management places a high value on the growth of the firm, and that this growth may be fostered by developing and adding a greater variety of products to the firm's range. Thus, the issues of the general effect of oligopoly on product differentiation and what is the optimal degree of product differentiation are not as yet settled.

9.5 TECHNICAL PROGRESS AND INNOVATION AS A COMPETITIVE STRATEGY

The likely general impact of oligopoly on the rate of technical progress is uncertain. In part, this is because the rate of technical progress has several dimensions and is therefore difficult to measure unambiguously. Factors which need to be taken into account when considering the rate of technical progress include:

1. levels of research and development effort and expenditure;
2. the level of inventive output and the value of this output;
3. the rapidity of innovation (for example, commercial application of inventions); and
4. the rate of diffusion and application of new techniques.

Superior performance by a market structure or market form in one of these dimensions may be offset or more than offset by an inferior performance in another of these dimensions.

Market Structure and Rate of Technical Progress

Parker (1974, pp. 62–78) has expressed the view that technical progress is likely to be faster under oligopolistic conditions than for any other market form. This is because sufficient competition exists between firms in an oligopoly (compared to monopoly) to induce them to develop and apply new techniques, but competition is not as intense as under perfect competition. Such intense competition may slow technical progress since cost-reducing techniques and successful innovations may be rapidly copied by rivals (property rights are not available or cannot be easily protected), thus leaving little profit for inventors and innovators. Furthermore, perfectly competitive firms have no *excess* profit in the long run for investment in research and development and to cushion them against the risks of research and development and innovation. Again, some types of research are 'lumpy' and require large outlays for success. Consequently, they exceed the financial capacities of small firms.

More attention may also be given to research and development under conditions of oligopoly than under other market forms since, as discussed earlier in this chapter, non-price competition tends to be more important in oligopolistic markets than price competition. If one accepts Parker's hypothesis, the index of the rate of technical progress as a function of the intensity of competition in a market would be of an inverted U-shape. R&D intensities and aggregate inventive output may be higher and the rate of innovation faster under oligopolistic market conditions than under alternative market forms.

Figure 9.13 illustrates Parker's hypothesis. Under pure monopoly, little or no market competition is present whereas under pure competition market competition is intense.

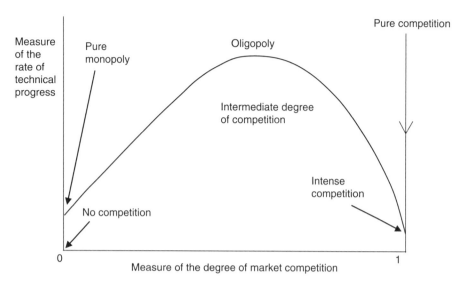

Figure 9.13   An illustration of Parker's (1974) thesis that oligopoly is the market form likely to result in the fastest rate of technical progress. In practice, the relationship is likely to be fuzzy or imprecise because market competition is not the only factor influencing technical progress

Under oligopoly, there is an intermediate degree of market competition. However, in practice, one would expect the relationship shown in Figure 9.13 to be quite fuzzy because factors additional to the degree of market competition in an industry affect its rate of innovation and technical progress. Figure 9.13 assumes that these other factors are held constant.

Empirical evidence about the effect of the nature of the competition on technical progress is limited. However, private research intensities do tend to be lower in industries consisting of many small competitive firms, such as in agriculture. But much research and development of relevance to agriculture, for instance for genetically modified organisms (GMOs), tractors and pesticides, is done by secondary industry which sells producer goods to farmers. Research intensities tend to be high in markets which are typically oligopolistic such as aircraft supply, electronics, chemicals, pharmaceuticals and transport equipment. But it is not clear that oligopoly is the sole cause of such high intensities. The industries may be ones which give a high return on R&D effort and the high intensities might be observed even if monopoly existed in these industries. In the United States and in the United Kingdom and some other nations, these high research intensities are also heavily influenced by government contracts for defence research and development and defence equipment.

Size of a Firm and Rate of Technical Progress

More evidence is available about the likely impact of the size of a firm on technical progress. Galbraith (1957) claims in *American Capitalism* that modern industry consisting of *large firms* is an almost perfect instrument for bringing about technical change. But the available evidence does not support the view that the bigger a firm is in an industry the greater is its rate of technical progress.

Both Scherer (1965) and Mansfield (1979) found in their study of American industry that R&D intensities of the largest firms in the *oligopolistic* industries studied tended to be lower than for medium- to large-sized firms. The evidence suggests that within an industry R&D intensities may bear an inverted-U relationship to the firm-size variable. Mansfield also found that average productivity of research and development (inventive output) rises with firm size and then declines for firms very large in size. Alexander et al. (1995) came to a similar conclusion as a result of their study of the pharmaceutical industry. While larger firms may speed up innovation if large amounts of capital are required for an innovation, many innovations are within the financial capacity of small to medium firms. However, it is possibly *in this area of innovation* that *larger firms tend to have an advantage over smaller ones* as originally suggested by Schumpeter (1954). Nevertheless, it is clear that very large firms are not the perfect instruments for technical progress in *all* industries and the extent to which they are socially optimal or the best socially feasible instrument for technical progress in any industry is not settled.

Schumpeter's Hypothesis

Schumpeter (1954) emphasized that in present day economies, product innovation is a more important source of market competition than price variations. He was also of the view that an economy consisting exclusively of purely competitive small firms would achieve less technical progress than one comprised of some industries containing larger firms experiencing imperfect market competition. Thus, he rejected the traditional view that economic scarcity would be minimized if an economy was comprised exclusively of perfectly competitive industries. This is not to say that no technical progress can be achieved by small firms. Clearly, during the Industrial Revolution in Europe, significant technical progress was achieved by individual entrepreneurs and small businesses. However, with economic development, reliance on this source alone became less productive. To some extent, the views of Schumpeter seem to reflect evolving economic conditions in more developed countries.

The view has been ascribed to Schumpeter that 'highly concentrated industries and large firms are more likely to invest in research and development than industries with low concentration and small firms' (Lipczynski and Wilson, 2001, p. 255). It is, however, debatable whether Schumpeter claimed this exactly. In fact, it seems that his position may be more akin to that of Parker (1974) as illustrate in Figure 9.13. There is little evidence to suggest that he thought technical progress would be a continually declining function of the degree of market competition. Secondly, he was not of the opinion that technical progress and innovation would continually rise in intensity with the increased size of firms. In fact, Schumpeter (1954) warns that large firms are liable to become bureaucratic and stifle invention and innovation. He believed that economic success and growth of an innovative firm might in the end prove to be its undoing. Schumpeter's view is therefore consistent with the observation that in any particular industry the intensity of innovating activity of firms tends to bear a reversed U-shaped relationship to their size. Note also that some large companies 'spin-off' small subsidiary companies in the hope that they will be less bureaucratic and innovative than their parent. This adds further weight to Schumpeter's point of view.

Can Technical Change be too Rapid?

Even economists can be easily lulled into believing that a faster rate of technical progress is desirable. This is not only because technical progress has brought clear advantages to mankind since the Stone Age but because we live in a society containing strong pressure groups favouring greater technical progress for it. If a Galbraithian outlook (Galbraith, 1967) on modern society (to be discussed in section 9.6) is accepted, technocrats in big companies (engineers, scientists, managers directing them) desire high rates of technical progress to support the growth of their companies and for self-fulfilment (utility maximization), and these technocrats dominate modern society, greatly influence government bureaucrats, the government, and even universities and academic endeavours. Business managers and scientists, including academic scientific pressure groups and government bureaucrats, cooperate in pressing for greater scientific and technical change. In these circumstances, the costs of technical change may not be taken into consideration or adequately considered.

Technical change can, as a rule, only be purchased at a cost. For instance, greater expenditure on research and development effort is likely to be at the expense of other alternatives forgone such as improved hospitals, schools and roads. The marginal sacrifice needs to be taken into account but is difficult to evaluate since the results of research and development are so uncertain. The rate of innovation and replacement of techniques can also be too rapid from a social point of view. For instance, as pointed out in the discussion relating to Figure 6.4, government schemes to subsidize acceleration of the replacement of machinery may lead to a social loss. Barzel (1968) has claimed, for example, that innovation may be more rapid under oligopoly than is socially desirable. Environmentalists have also expressed concern about the types of technical changes that have occurred in modern societies and many believe that insufficient attention has been given to the environmental spillovers associated with the use of new technologies such as nuclear power and genetically modified organisms (GMOs).

Game Theory and Innovation by Oligopolists

Competition between oligopolists can result in their innovating at a faster rate than would maximize their profits, and in some circumstances, this rate may result in a net social economic loss. This can be illustrated by the matrix shown in Figure 9.14. It is assumed for simplicity that a duopoly exists in the market and that each firm has three alternative strategies: no innovation, a moderate rate of innovation or a rapid rate of innovation. These are respectively indicated in Figure 9.14 by α_1, α_2 and α_3 for Firm 1 and by β_1, β_2 and β_3 for Firm 2. The entries in the body of the matrix represent the payoffs (in terms of units of profit) for Firm 1 and Firm 2, respectively.

It can be seen from Figure 9.14 that if both duopolists were to engage in a moderate degree of innovation, their collective gains would be greatest. However, this situation is not stable. Each of the players has an incentive to adopt a rapid innovation policy given the other is planning on a moderate innovation policy. Therefore, both are liable to opt for a

			Firm 2's innovation rates		
			Zero β_1	Medium β_2	High β_3
Firm 1's	Zero	α_1	(3,3)	(0,9)	(0,7)
innovation	Medium	α_2	(9,6)	(6,6)	(2,8)
rates	High	α_3	(7,0)	(8,2)	(1,1)

Figure 9.14   A theory of games matrix illustrating a case in which duopolists (oligopolists) as a result of market competition engage in an excessive rate of innovation

rapid innovation policy. This results in the joint set of strategies (α_3,β_3). Consequently, the payoffs to each are less than if they had both adopted the moderate strategy or had even opted for a policy of no innovation. The strategy set (α_3,β_3) is stable because no player can increase his/her payoff by unilaterally diverging from it. It is a Nash equilibrium.

It has been suggested (Perloff, 2007, Chapter 3) that Airbus and Boeing (producers of large aircraft) have engaged in excessive innovation from their point of view. Their competition has been intensified by European subsidies to Airbus and the financial support of the United States for Boeing mainly via defence contracts. Not only might the profits of these companies be diminished by their competitive innovatory strategies but the general public could suffer an economic welfare loss as a result of government financial support for this type of competition.

Why, in this case, are the subsidies paid? The reasons are probably complex. First, the development of new high-profile aircraft seems to be a matter of national and regional prestige, for example, the pride of the EU versus that of the USA. In addition, the technological and managerial factors proposed by Galbraith and Veblen (discussed in the next section) may play a role. Furthermore, international technological superiority frequently results in enhanced global political power. To a large extent, the global political power of Western countries has been based on their superior technologies. Subsidies for research and development and innovation by Western governments may partly be motivated by their desire to retain this political power or increase it.

Again, another reason for subsidizing the technological progress of oligopolists or monopolists may be the prospect that a nation or region will obtain large monopoly profits as a result of international trade and investment if it can obtain a technological lead on other nations or regions. The monopoly-profit thesis may hold, namely that an innovating country or firm (if it has market power or can establish this) will make above-normal profits from successful innovation by exploiting its (temporary) global advantages in trade and investment. Usually, however, to retain these advantages continuing innovation is needed. Therefore, the whole monopoly-profit system involves a treadmill-like situation. Early proponents of the monopoly-profit thesis (sometimes called the new technology theory of international trade) and of its links with international trade include Posner (1961), Hirsch (1972) and Gruber et al. (1967). This subject will be discussed further in the penultimate section of this chapter.

Note that in some circumstances government subsidies for development and innovation may be justified on economic grounds because of the existence of market failures. For example, the results of basic scientific research cannot as a rule be patented. Therefore, private property rights in such results cannot be established. Although the results may have many economic applications and considerable economic value, there is no commercial incentive to engage in this research unless it complements other areas in which an enterprise can obtain a patent or some property rights. Results stemming from basic research have the attributes of a pure public good and thus market failure occurs (see section 2.4, Chapter 2).

9.6 INSTITUTIONAL ASPECTS OF OLIGOPOLY AND OF INDUSTRIAL SOCIETIES

The danger always exists in discussing economic problems in detail that we may fail to see the woods for the trees. Institutional arrangements within society as a whole affect its microeconomic operations, and as these arrangements evolve or alter with the passage of time, the functioning of the economic system may alter. For instance, the increased importance of the limited liability company, of non-agricultural sectors, and of management separated from ownership indicate that our economy now operates in a different manner to that of the nineteenth century and that the economic theories developed in that period may be less applicable to this century (see Chapter 3). This institutionalist view has been championed by Galbraith (1967), Marris (1964), and others.

Galbraith's Overview of Present Capitalistic Industrial Societies

Galbraith's (1967) overview of present-day industrial economies has the following main features:

1. Sellers (firms) in the economy belong to a *dual economic system*. One sector of the dual system consists of small competitive firms dominated by the operation of markets. The other sector consists of large oligopolistic or monopoly-like firms not dominated by markets but in a position to control or manipulate markets, input prices and government policies. This is the industrial planning sector and in the United States consists of the 500 or so largest companies in the manufacturing sector.
2. Technocrats (the managerial, scientific and technical class) are the dominant group in present-day society and are the dominant decision-making force in the industrial planning sector. The American economist, Veblen (1924), predicted this trend in society.
3. Shareholders have no or little effective power over management, as was observed by Berle and Means (1932). Thus, management has considerable scope to pursue its own objectives.
4. Technocrats in the private planning sector have strong links with government and the government bureaucracy. Movements and contacts between government and private bureaucracies are frequent. But, more importantly, on the basis of the theory of Downs (1957), larger firms find it more profitable to lobby than smaller ones. The industrial planning sector is likely to have much more political influence and involvement in government than the competitive market sector.

5. Technocrats have a high desire for the growth of their corporations and use their power to inflate demand for goods produced by the planning sector (the sector dominated by large imperfectly competitive firms). They concentrate on developing new products and markets and on advertising and promotion, and this fosters overconsumption of products supplied by the planning sector. Elements of this view are to be found both in the writings of Marris (1964) and of Marcuse (1964).

Galbraith's view is a caricature but should not be dismissed just because of this. It is important to try to test and where necessary qualify the hypotheses involved. There are limits to the extent to which business managers and technocrats can manipulate demand, but what are these limits? Large companies sometimes fail in their bids to market new products and make considerable losses. Large companies may not be as 'powerful' as Galbraith claims. How great is the political influence of technocrats, say, compared to pressure groups of farmers? Furthermore, as pointed out earlier in this chapter, the very largest firms in industries do not appear to put as much effort into technical progress as Galbraith suggests.

Given his view of industrial market economies, Galbraith believes that it is an idle dream to aim for a completely competitive market system. Rather he claims that a more realistic and effective aim is to encourage countervailing economic groups where imperfect competition exists, to foster unionism and socialization of some sectors of the economy, to subsidize the competitive market sector, and to introduce price controls to push up prices in the competitive market sector consisting of small firms. A case *might* be made out for such policies on second best grounds and *feasible* income redistribution grounds. Although Galbraith recommends greater government interference in the market sector as a means of improving the operation of the economy, he does not closely examine the prospects for this and the likely effects of his proposals.

Beginning in the 1970s, microeconomic policies have evolved along different lines to those suggested by Galbraith. Governments have increasingly tried to foster competitive market systems and restrict market collusion, including some types of collusion that could be seen as representing countervailing power, such as trade unions. Such policies have been partly motivated by the view that they are necessary for maintaining national and regional economic competitiveness in a world that has become more globalized economically. Greater globalization has occurred because of fewer restrictions on international trade and investment and reduced transport and communication costs. Possibly, the process of economic globalization has been favourable to many large firms engaged in imperfect competition, particularly those with multinational operations. While they may be faced with somewhat greater market competition as a result of growing globalization, they are subject to less countervailing power and have new global economic opportunities for marketing and investment.

Multinational Firms, Globalization and Oligopolies

Multinational companies epitomize the rise and importance of large industrial corporations. They are involved in the international use and administration of resources, often by non-market means. Such companies are *common in high technology oligopolistic industries* and frequently these are industries with substantial barriers to entry and economies of scale. This is not to say that all multinational companies are involved in imperfect competition. Markusen (2002, Chapter 1) usefully summarizes important factors that are associated with the occurrence of multinational enterprises.

Multinational business operations provide a means for the expansion of companies into new markets and the international transfer of technology by non-market methods. It is claimed that multinational companies have grown in importance because they are an efficient means for companies to appropriate gains from new technology developed by them (Parker, 1974, p. 206). Alternatively, the companies concerned could license their technology to overseas firms. But overseas local companies may not have sufficient management expertise or, if they do, they could eventually improve on the licensed technology to the detriment of the licensor. Furthermore, the growth of the licensee could make it more difficult for the licensor to enter the relevant overseas market at a later stage, if this is contemplated.

Multinational corporations are also likely to increase the international flow of commercial information (between their branches), for instance information about market possibilities. Since information is a valuable resource, these flows may be an added benefit for multinational companies. There is no economic reason why companies should find it most profitable to stop their economic operations at national borders. Diversification and horizontal and vertical integration extending beyond national borders can yield economies and increase the profitability of a company's operation. National borders are artificial constructions.

The benefits received by host countries from the presence of multinational companies can vary from little or no benefit to a substantial one. Where a multinational company is mining in a host country using imported management and skilled labour and has sufficient political influence to pay low royalties and export the mineral, the host may receive little benefit. But in other cases where the development of local skills and management expertise are stimulated by the presence of a multinational corporation, the host country might obtain much greater benefit. The assessment of multinational companies is complicated since assessments are liable to be tinged with feelings of nationalism and doubts about where the national loyalties, if any, of such corporations lie. Do these corporations pose a challenge to the state and to nationalism? If so, is this a bad thing?

Several microeconomic questions are raised by the process of growing economic globalization (Tisdell and Sen, 2004). Has it resulted in an increase in the incidence of multinational firms? Has it meant that oligopolies have changed their nature or have been forced to alter their behaviour? Has it reduced the occurrence of imperfectly competitive markets, including the incidence of oligopolies and monopolies?

Concerning the first matter, there has been a reduction in recent decades to barriers to foreign direct investment. Other things being constant, this favours multinational operations by firms. On the other hand, barriers to international exchange of commodities have also declined, so access to many foreign markets is less dependent on direct investment in these. Tariff walls are lower so it is less necessary for business to produce behind these to access some local markets. Furthermore, international transport costs have declined in real terms. International economic theory indicates that this tends to reduce the profitability of having a multinational enterprise, particularly if decreasing costs of production are important (Krugman, 1995). The net effect of these two trends (that for barriers to international direct investment and that for international trade) is unclear.

The overseas operations of some multinational companies are designed to take advantage of the international product cycle (Vernon, 1966). A pattern of such companies based in more developed countries was to begin production of new commodities or to introduce new procedures in developed countries and then with the efflux of time, to begin production in lower income countries, eventually phasing out production in developed countries. Now as a result of growing globalization, production using innovations made by companies from the more developed world may move offshore more quickly than previously to lower income countries, such as China and India. Furthermore, growing technological competition fostered by growing globalization may have reduced the length of typical product cycles. The net result may be that greater profits can be earned from successful innovations by oligopolists or monopolists. However, these above-normal profits may persist for a shorter period of time based on the original innovation. Therefore, pressure for continuing innovation might be increased by growing globalization.

Coming to the second question, in theory growing globalization should reduce the incidence of monopolies and oligopolies in markets. However, it is not certain to eliminate these market forms. In some industries, there may be few competitors internationally so global extension of the market makes little difference to the state of competition. Some markets (such as the credit card market, the software industry and petroleum distribution) appear to remain oligopolistic despite growing globalization. Economies of scale in networks, advertising and promotion and, up to a point, research development and product design may make some industries naturally oligopolistic even on a world scale. A few might even be global natural monopolies.

According to Bianchi and Labory (2007), globalization has resulted in many imperfectly competitive industries in more developed countries intensifying their innovatory effort to meet growing marked competition from emerging industrial giants such as China and India. As indicated above, such firms are hoping for at least temporary monopoly-profits from this policy as a result of international trade or investment, as well as economic gains in their home markets. However, as illustrated in section 9.5, such competitive strategies are not costless and are not bound to result in economic gains for innovating firms.

Those firms that survive and even prosper as a result of growing globalization may reap significant economic gains from the process because the process appears to be accompanied by weakening of the type of countervailing forces mentioned by Galbraith (1957). Although regulations against anti-competitive trade practices and marked collusion have been strengthened in many countries, in some cases, market manipulation requires no collusion.

9.7   CONCLUDING COMMENTS

Oligopolistic markets are varied and complex in their nature, even though all are characterized by strong economic interdependence between suppliers. Consequently, no single model typifies all cases, and in practice, economic models need to be adjusted and supplemented to fit many actual cases. Modern economic theory emphasizes the importance of non-price competition in the operation of oligopolistic markets. In this chapter, considerable attention has been given to advertising and promotion, product differentiation and innovation as important parts of the non-price competitive strategies of oligopolists.

This chapter raises the following query: does the occurrence of oligopoly add to economic scarcity or reduce it compared to a market situation that approaches perfect competition? It appears that in some circumstances, oligopoly results in less economic scarcity than the hypothetical market alternatives of pure competition and monopoly. For example, economies of scale can be substantial and sometimes make for natural oligopolies, and Schumpeter's hypotheses may also apply. That is not to say that oligopoly is necessarily an ideal economic form nor that it is always superior to other market forms from the point of view of reducing economic scarcity. We can, however, conclude that it is not the case that a single market type such as pure competition is superior (as a means of scarcity reduction) for every industry compared to the alternative possible market forms. For this reason, a circumstantial approach to regulatory policies affecting market competition is required. Economic systems are complex in practice and theories need to be adapted to actual situations when formulating microeconomic and industrial policies. Many judicial systems for regulating market competition allow for the particular circumstances of the cases to be decided. In doing so, the varied nature and consequences of imperfect competition are recognized.

READING* AND REFERENCES

Adelman, M.A. (1972), *The World Petroleum Market*, Baltimore: Johns Hopkins University Press.

Alexander, D.L., J. Flynn and L. Linkins (1995), 'Innovation and global market share in the pharmaceutical industry', *Review of Industrial Organisation*, **10**, 197–207.

Barzel, Y. (1968), 'Optimal timing of innovations', *Review of Economics and Statistics*, **50**, 348–55.

Berle, A.A. and G.C. Means (1932), *The Modern Corporation and Private Property*, New York: Harcourt Brace.

Bertrand, J. (1883), 'Theorie mathematique de la richesse sociale', *Journal des Savants*, Paris, pp. 499–508.

Bianchi, P. and S. Labory (2007), 'From 'old' industrial policy to 'new' industrial development policies', in P. Bianchi and S. Labory (eds), *International Handbook of Industrial Policy*, Cheltenham, UK and Northampton, MA, USA: Edward Elgar, pp. 3–27.

Cournot, A. (1838), *Researches into the Mathematical Principles of the Theory of Wealth*, New York: Macmillan.

Downs, A. (1957), *An Economic Theory of Democracy*, New York: Harper Row.

Galbraith, J.K. (1957), *American Capitalism*, London: Hamish Hamilton.

Galbraith, J.K. (1967), *The New Industrial State*, London: Hamish Hamilton.

*Gravelle, H. and R. Rees (2004), *Microeconomics*, 3rd edn, chapter 6, Harlow, UK: Prentice Hall.

Gruber, W., D. Mehta and R. Vernon (1967), 'The R&D factor in international trade and international investment of United States industries', *Journal of Political Economy*, **75**, 20–37.

Hall, R. and C. Hitch (1939), 'Price theory and business behaviour', Oxford Economic Papers, No. 2, pp. 20–37.

Hirsch, S. (1972), 'The United States electronic industry in international trades', in L.T. Wells Jr. (ed.), *The Product Life Cycle and International Trade*, Boston: Harvard University, pp. 39–52.

Hotelling, H. (1929), 'Stability in competition', *Economic Journal*, **39**, 41–57.

Krugman, P. (1995), 'Increasing returns, imperfect competition and the positive theory of international trade', in G.M. Grossman and K. Rogoff (eds), *Handbook of International Economics*, Vol.3, Amsterdam: Elsevier, pp. 1243–77.

Lipczynski, J. and J. Wilson (2001), *Industrial Organisation*, Harlow, UK: Prentice Hall.

*Lipsey, R.G. and K.A. Chrystal (2004), *Economics*, 10th edn, chapter 12, Oxford: Oxford University Press.

Mansfield, E. (1979), *Microeconomics*, chapter 12, New York: Norton.

*Mansfield, E. and G. Yohe (2004), *Microeconomics*, 11th edn, chapter 12, New York: Norton.

Marcuse, H. (1964), *One Dimensional Man*, London: Routledge and Kegan Paul.

Markham, J.W. (1951), 'The nature and significance of price leadership', *American Economic Review*, **41**, 891–905.

*Markusen, J.R. (2002), *Multinational Firms and the Theory of International Trade*, chapter 1, Cambridge, MA and London, England: The MIT Press.

Marris, R. (1964), *The Economic Theory of Marginal Capitalism*, London: Macmillan.

Neumann von, J. and O. Morgenstern (1944), *Theory of Games and Economic Behaviour*, Princeton: Princeton University Press.

Parker, J.E.S. (1974), *The Economics of Innovation*, London: Longman.

*Perloff, J.M. (2007), *Microeconomics*, 4th edn, chapter 13, Boston: Addison Wesley.

*Pindyck, R.S. and D.L. Rubinfeld (2005), *Microeconomics*, 6th edn, chapter 12, Upper Saddle River, NJ: Prentice Hall.

Posner, M.V. (1961), 'International trade and technical change', *Oxford Economic Papers*, **13**, 323–41.

Schumpeter, J.A. (1954), *Capitalism, Socialism and Democracy*, London: Allen and Unwin.

Stackleberg, H. von (1952), *The Theory of the Market Economy*, New York: Oxford University Press.

Sutton, C.J. (1974), 'Advertising, concentration and competition', *The Economic Journal*, **84**, 56–59.

Sweezy, P. (1939), 'Demand under conditions of oligopoly', *Journal of Political Economy*, **47**, 568–73.

Tisdell, C.A. and R.K. Sen (2004), 'An overview of economic globalisation: its momentum and consequences examined', in C. Tisdell and R.K. Sen (eds), *Economic Globalisation: Social Conflicts, Labour and Environmental Issues*, Cheltenham, UK and Northampton, MA, USA: Edward Elgar, pp. 3–23.

Udell, J.G. (1964), 'The role of price in competitive strategy', *Journal of Marketing*, **28**, 44–8.

*Varian, H. (2006), *Intermediate Microeconomics*, 7th edn, chapters 27–29, New York: Norton.

Veblen, T. (1924), *The Theory of the Leisure Class*, London: Allen and Unwin.

Vernon, R. (1966), 'International investment and international trade in the product cycle', *Quarterly Journal of Economics*, **80**, 190–207.

QUESTIONS FOR REVIEW AND DISCUSSION

1. What is oligopoly? Is it common in particular sectors of the economy? Why is it important for an oligopolist to take account of the behaviour of his/her rivals?

2. Does the kinked demand curve help to explain price rigidities and price stability in oligopolistic markets?

3. How might the theory of repetitive games of business strategy help to explain the kinked demand curve phenomenon in oligopolistic markets and dominant price leadership?

4. The continued effective operation of a cartel is usually under a twin threat. What are these threats? Take an actual cartel and give some evidence of the threats.

5. Apart from the kinked demand curve, price leadership and cartel models, there are several other models of oligopolistic behaviour. Why is there such a variety of models?

6. What forms can non-price competition by oligopolists take? How important is non-price competition in oligopolistic markets compared to price competition?

7. How are advertising intensities under oligopoly likely to compare with those under other market forms. What are the likely effects of differences in advertising intensities between markets?

8. 'Oligopolists can become caught in an advertising trap and this can result in a Kaldor–Hicks loss in social welfare.' Explain.

9. What factors would you want to take into account in assessing the social benefits and costs of advertising by oligopolists?

10. Outline public policies (actual or proposed) to control advertising and the supply of information. What is the rationale behind such policies? What dangers may they pose?

11. Outline the principle of minimum product differentiation and give a simple proof of it in terms of game theory. What limitations and applications does it have?

12. The general effect of oligopoly on product differentiation is not as yet settled. Why? Are there competing theories? Should governments try to influence the extent of product differentiation?

13. 'It is common to speak about the rate of technical progress as though it is easily measured. But the rate of technical progress has several dimensions, not easily combined in a single index.' Explain.

14. Outline Parker's hypothesis (and his reasons for holding it) that the rate of technical progress is likely to be higher under oligopoly than any other market form. Would you want to qualify the hypothesis?

15. Show that innovation can occur too rapidly from various economic points of view. Also show how the theory of games can be used to illustrate the possibility that duopolists (oligopolists) can get trapped into excessive innovatory effort.

16. Critically discuss Galbraith's view that large firms are almost the perfect instruments for bringing about technical progress.

17. Outline Galbraith's perspective on current capitalist industrial economies. Do you believe that his view is realistic? Should countervailing power be encouraged or discouraged by government policy?

18. Why do multinational firms exist and what functions do they perform? How might their presence be beneficial to host countries and how could their presence impose costs on host countries?

19. 'Economic globalization has not reduced the market power of all oligopolists. It may have increased the power of some.' Discuss.

20. 'In some industries, oligopolies result in less economic scarcity than alternative market forms'. Explain why this may occur and consider its relevance to industrial competition policy.

10. Ownership of enterprises: Public or private?

10.1 INTRODUCTION: DOES OWNERSHIP MATTER?

There has been a continuing controversy about the role and relevance of ownership as *the* major determinant of the performance of firms, industries and economies. Left-wing political parties often prefer state ownership of the means of production, which enables governments to intervene to determine prices, outputs, wages and employment throughout the economy. In contrast, right-wing political parties favour private ownership as a means of achieving efficiency objectives. They criticise state ownership for its inefficiencies, financial losses, crowding-out effects and its poor record on innovation. The implication is that these adverse economic effects will be removed under private ownership.

The debate between state and private ownership raises the general question of whether ownership is an important determinant of economic performance. This question needs answering in two stages. First, consideration needs to be given to whether economic theory offers different predictions about the impact of ownership on economic performance; and second, empirical work is needed to determine the accuracy of these predictions.

Consider the following 'story'. After the privatization of previously state-owned enterprises it is observed that both productivity and profitability rise dramatically. The official explanation offered is that employees have become shareholders in the newly-privatized companies and that they want their companies to succeed; that their companies have been released from the detailed controls of central government and given the freedom to manage their companies; and that they have been exposed to the commercial disciplines of the customer and the rivalry of other competitors. This 'story' suggests a model in which improved economic performance depends not only on ownership but on other variables (that is, a model: $P = P(O,Z)$ where P is enterprise performance; O is ownership; and Z is other relevant influences). These other relevant variables include competition and managerial freedom in the form of internal organization and employment contracts as well as any 'shock effects' such as the withdrawal of subsidies. Some of these issues can be simplified into a two-variable model showing the impact of ownership and market structure on efficiency. A framework is shown in Table 10.1 where the following hypotheses on enterprise performance can be formulated:

1. D is superior to A, where D represents private ownership and a competitive product market.
2. D is superior to C: neoclassical economics favours competition over monopoly.
3. D is equal to, or superior to, B: does ownership matter, with some evidence suggesting that under competition, private firms are likely to be superior.
4. B is superior to A, reflecting the role of competition.

Table 10.1   Ownership and market structure: a taxonomy

	Monopoly	Competition
Public Ownership	Potential for allocative efficiency ($P=MC$) Lack of competition means technical inefficiency No threat of bankruptcy Government interferes with decision-making **A**	Potential for allocative efficiency Rivalry promotes technical efficiency No threat of bankruptcy Government interference with decisions **B**
Private Ownership	Shareholders exert efficiency pressures on managers Threat of bankruptcy No government intervention in decisions **C**	Allocative and technical efficiency Shareholder pressure Threat of bankruptcy No government intervention in decisions **D**

5. C is superior to A, reflecting the policing and monitoring role of private capital markets.
6. B could be superior, inferior or equal to C. The outcome is inconclusive, depending on the relative strengths of competition and ownership.

10.2   PUBLIC OWNERSHIP OR NATIONALIZATION

Governments offering subsidies to private firms are often faced with a further policy choice as to whether such firms should be taken into public ownership. Distributional judgements enter into such a choice. After all, it might be thought that if society is financing a private firm, it would be equitable to share in any resulting wealth-creation. Also, with private firms, there might be substantial transactions costs in negotiating and monitoring subsidies. Public ownership or nationalization is not, however, the only policy option. There are alternatives, such as the creation of worker cooperatives or the state requiring an equity in private firms receiving subsidies. Each alternative will involve different costs and benefits. For instance, private firms in competitive markets might be technically more efficient than enterprises in a nationalized industry, but governments might believe that subsidies to state-owned units are less costly to administer and monitor, and that such enterprises can be compelled to conform to economic planning targets and wider policy objectives (for example, job-preservation and hence votes).

There are other general arguments for state ownership. These are:

1. The desire to plan and control the 'commanding heights' of the economy (for example, steel?).
2. The control of private monopoly power, including the technical monopoly case. Or, public enterprises might be used to provide competition for private monopolies and oligopolies.

3. To enable *social* costs and benefits to be incorporated into decision-making.
4. To preserve defence industries and promote high technology (for example, aerospace).
5. To improve industrial relations and extend worker participation and industrial democracy.
6. To provide a source of independent information for the government (for example, Australian Commonwealth Bank).

As emphasized throughout this book, there are alternative solutions to policy problems. An economy can be controlled through macroeconomic policy rather than via the so-called 'commanding heights' (wherever those might be!). Private monopolies might be controlled through price or profit regulation or through lower tariffs, without creating a *public* monopoly. Similarly, social costs and benefits can be incorporated through tax-subsidy policy or through changes in legislation to re-define property rights. Questions also arise about the extent to which nationalized industries have been successful in improving industrial relations, extending industrial democracy and allowing for social costs and benefits. Furthermore, state ownership creates a set of problems. Objectives have to be specified, pricing and investment rules are required, and performance has to be assessed and monitored.

Pricing and investment rules are related and cannot be divorced from the objectives of state-owned enterprises. A concern with optimum resource allocation requires prices equal to long-run marginal cost which will also be a point on a short-run marginal cost curve. Such a pricing 'rule' is not without its difficulties. Marginal cost has to be defined and measured, and will differ between the short- and long-run. Lumpiness could mean that the extra cost of another passenger on an empty aeroplane is almost zero; for a full aircraft, the marginal cost is the price of another plane (similarly for a bus, train, bridge or tunnel). Further problems with marginal cost pricing arise because of technical inefficiency, distributional considerations, externalities and second best solutions:

1. Where state industries are monopolies, there are no alternative cost yardsticks nor competitive pressures against which governments and society can assess true marginal opportunity costs. In such a market structure, there are substantial opportunities for discretionary behaviour and organizational slack.
2. Increasing or decreasing costs result in surpluses or losses, respectively (see Figure 10.1). Each has distributional implications between society and consumers of the state enterprise's output. However, losses due to marginal cost pricing under decreasing costs are consistent with an economically-efficient solution and are not an indication of inefficiency.
3. External economies and diseconomies cannot be ignored in assessing the marginal benefits and costs of a nationalized industry's output. State-owned coal mines which deposit waste in beautiful countryside and on holiday beaches are minimizing the enterprise's costs and not society's!
4. Since the conditions required for an optimum allocation are unlikely to be achieved throughout the economy, the second-best pricing rule for a public enterprise is likely to involve a departure from strict marginal cost pricing. In the case of substitute prod-

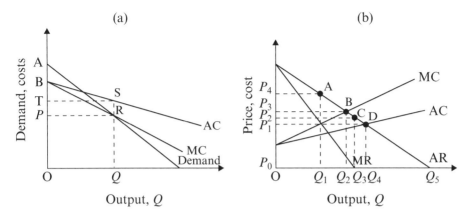

Figure 10.1 *(a) shows marginal cost pricing under decreasing costs with losses of PRST. Figure 10.1 (b) shows alternative pricing rules under increasing costs. Point A shows the profit maximization position with no price discrimination; point B is the marginal cost pricing solution; C is the sales revenue-maximizing position; D is where price equals AC (break-even); and Q_5 is the zero price position. A similar analysis can be applied to the cases of constant and decreasing costs*

ucts, if prices elsewhere exceed marginal costs, then, the appropriate rule might be for price to exceed marginal cost in the state enterprise.

Alternative pricing rules exist. Public enterprises could be instructed to act as profit-maximizers or they could be required to 'break even', charging a price equal to average cost. Alternatively, they could act as sales revenue-maximizers or adopt zero pricing. Each alternative has different price, output, employment, investment and financial implications. An example is shown in Figure 10.1(b). Under increasing costs, marginal cost pricing leads to surpluses, while the break-even rule results in a lower price and greater output (cf. decreasing costs), and zero pricing gives the maximum consumer surplus, but at considerable cost. Given such predictions, governments can choose the pricing solution which best achieves their policy objectives.

10.3 PRIVATE OWNERSHIP

A Classification System

Privatization was actively pursued by the nations of Western and Eastern Europe in the 1980s and 1990s. In some states, it was associated with the transition from a centrally-planned to a market economy. Such transitions raised questions about how to introduce markets into a non-market system, where and how to start and how rapidly to proceed (for example, a rapid transition or 'shock-effect' or a gradual transition over a period of years). Within Europe, the UK was an early pioneer of privatization. UK examples included the privatization of utilities such as gas, electricity, telecommunications and water as well as enterprises such as British Airways, British Aerospace, Jaguar,

Rolls-Royce, the National Freight Corporation, UK shipbuilding yards, the Royal Ordnance Factories (manufacturer of ammunition and tanks) and Short Brothers (an aerospace company based in Northern Ireland). Also, a number of UK markets were deregulated, thereby reducing or removing barriers to new entry. Examples included bus services, opticians, allowing building societies to offer banking services and the emergence of Mercury as a rival supplier of telecommunications services. Furthermore, a range of UK services provided by central and local government were exposed to rivalry. Competitive tendering allowed private contractors to bid for work previously undertaken 'in-house' by public producers. Examples included catering, cleaning and laundry services, refuse collection, street cleaning and the management of local sports facilities (Buxton et al., 1998). But privatisation became an international movement and was not confined to the UK (Ott and Hartley, 1991).

There are various definitions and aspects of privatization. These embrace the transfer of assets from the state to the private sector (denationalization) as well as competitive tendering or contracting-out and deregulation (market liberalization). Furthermore, asset transfers take various forms including the public issue of shares in the newly-privatized enterprise, or a direct sale of an organization to the private sector or a management buyout. Table 10.2 presents a classification system for privatization based on the distinction between government (public) and private *finance* and *provision*. This classification system provides a starting point which allows the rival advocates of public and private ownership to contemplate horizontal, vertical and diagonal movements between the boxes. Inevitably, Table 10.2 is only a broad classification system. For instance, some state-owned enterprises receiving private finance might also receive state finance and there are privately-owned and privately-financed schools and hospitals.

Table 10.2   A classification system

		FINANCE	
		Public state	Private
PROVISION	Public (state)	Defence Education Health Roads	UK examples: Post Office BBC TV and Radio
	Private	Competitive tendering *Australian examples* Many local government services e.g. refuse collection *UK examples:* Health and local government services	*Australian examples* Telstra (telecommunications) Commonwealth Bank Toll roads *UK examples:* British Airways British Gas British Telecom

Nor is there a simple privatization versus state ownership distinction. Instead, there are various organizational forms ranging from the extremes of owner-managed firms in the private sector to government departments in the public sector. Government departments are the most 'political' body directly under the control of ministers who are accountable to Parliament for the actions of their departments. The private sector extreme is the sole trader or owner-manager with unattenuated rights to profits. Between these extremes, there are other public and private sector organizations such as quasi-government agencies (for example, trading funds) and public corporations as well as public joint stock companies and ultimately owner-managed firms in the private sector. Also, between the extremes, there are 'hybrids' which seem to straddle the public and private sector divide. Examples include not-for-profit organizations such as trusts, clubs, charities and churches, as well as cooperatives. Property rights and public choice theories predict that the performance of an organization improves as its status is changed from state to private, ranging from government departments through public corporations to joint stock companies and ultimately, owner-managed firms (Dunsire et al., 1991; Ott and Hartley, 1991, Chapter 2).

Economic Theory of Privatization

Does economic theory offer any guidelines for a public policy towards privatization? Critics of state-owned firms and industries claim that they are monopolistic, inefficient, loss-making organizations characterized by bureaucracy, by a failure to innovate and by their unresponsiveness to consumer demands. State-owned industries are also subject to damaging political interference and are dominated by powerful trade unions with decisions made on political rather than commercial criteria. Vote-conscious governments often determine price, investment, location and employment decisions (for example, loss-making plants may be kept open in marginal constituencies). Nor are state-owned firms subject to capital market threats of bankruptcy: they have access to unlimited taxpayers' funds (that is, soft budget constraints). Overall, state ownership is claimed to be associated with inefficiency, losses, poor productivity and management-organization structures which are bureaucratic and have failed to adjust to new technologies and changing markets.

In contrast, privatization aims to promote competition and improve efficiency. Privately-owned companies are reputed to offer benefits to consumers in the form of more rivalry, greater choice, increased efficiency and more innovation. Further economic benefits of privatization include a smaller public sector, a source of state funding and reduced public sector borrowing, the end of state funding of loss-making activities, wider share ownership and reductions in the monopoly power of public sector trade unions. Some of these objectives are in conflict. For example, maximizing returns to the national exchequer might require that state-owned enterprises be sold as private monopolies, leading to a transfer of monopoly from the public to the private sector. Critics might also claim that governments sell off public assets (the 'family silver') so as to boost their budgets and use the extra cash flow to their advantage for their limited time in power. Sometimes, public assets are sold below their market value and to favoured buyers, as in some of the former communist countries.

Economic theory provides a basis for analysing these claims about privatization. As a starting point, efficiency needs to be defined. Here, a distinction is needed between technical and allocative efficiency. Technical efficiency focuses on the least-cost solutions

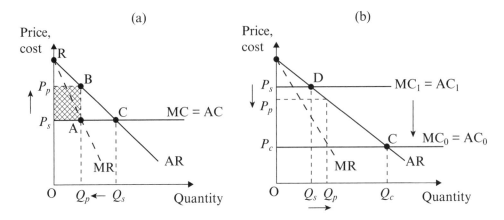

Figure 10.2   Ownership and efficiency. In Figure 10.2(a), state-ownership leads to marginal cost pricing at Op$_s$. Welfare is maximized with consumer surplus of P$_s$RC. Privatization means profit-maximization at price P$_p$; a lower output, monopoly profits of P$_s$P$_p$BA (hatched area) and a deadweight loss of ABC. A state regulatory agency can impose price constraints at P$_s$. Figure 10.2(b) shows state-ownership leading to major technical inefficiency (MC$_1$ compared with MC$_0$). Privatization results in improvements in technical efficiency achieving the lowest-cost solution (at MC$_0$), with lower prices of P$_p$ and a greater output of OQ$_p$. Competition can lead to a Pareto optimal solution at price P$_c$ and output OQ$_c$.

for a given output whilst allocative efficiency requires technical efficiency and then focuses on the socially-desirable output (that is, where price equals marginal cost). The standard neo-classical case against monopoly and in favour of competition can be applied to the arguments about privatization. Figure 10.2(a) shows that, in principle, a state-owned enterprise by adopting marginal cost pricing and acting as a benevolent monopolist can be allocatively efficient (including achieving efficiency losses: see Figure 10.1(a)). In these circumstances, privatization appears to be socially undesirable. It leads to a misallocation of resources reflected in higher prices, a lower output, monopoly profits and a deadweight loss of consumer surplus (with price greater than marginal cost). This suggests that the economic case for privatization has to be based on additional criteria related to regulation, technical efficiency and competition.

Where privatization involves a transfer of monopoly from the public to the private sectors, the monopoly power of the privatized firm can be controlled by a state regulatory agency. Such an agency might seek to ensure that the newly-privatized firm acts as a benevolent monopolist charging prices equal to marginal costs. In this case, the choice is between a state-owned benevolent monopolist and the equivalent privately-owned benevolent monopolist subject to state regulation. But regulatory agencies lack perfect information about a firm's production possibilities and future market conditions and they are liable to be 'captured' by producer interest groups. Regulatory failures also arise where agencies impose profit ceilings which lead regulated firms to substitute spending on non-profit activities to avoid profit-constraints (for example, spending on capital or managerial salaries: see Chapter 7). However, the UK introduced a regulatory regime based on the principle of price capping rather than controlling the required rate of return on capital. The UK's price capping formula which was applied to the utilities was based on RPI − X where RPI is the retail price index and X is a percentage figure representing efficiency savings which are passed onto consumers.

The case for privatization might also be based on substantial technical inefficiency under state-ownership (as shown in Figure 10.2(b)). Here, privatization of a state monopoly might lead to major improvements in technical efficiency which are then reflected in lower prices and greater output, even though there remains a misallocation of resources (with price greater than marginal cost: see Figure 10.2 (b)). Such a misallocation can then be removed by opening up the product market to competition allowing new entrants or the threat of entry, so leading to the socially-desirable output (a Pareto optimum where price equals marginal cost). However, it is far from clear that a private monopoly will have incentives to achieve substantial internal cost savings and much will depend on the operation of private capital markets as monitoring mechanisms.

The case for privatization has been developed further with arguments about property rights, public choice and government failure. On this view, property rights matter and alternative systems of property rights affect incentives, behaviour and economic welfare. Property rights determine the control of assets and how they might be used or transferred and the ownership of any income generated from their use. The property rights literature emphasizes the distortion of efficiency incentives associated with attenuated property rights which arise under public ownership. Monitoring arrangements for state-owned enterprises are dependent on government ministers, taxpayers and voters being able to control managerial discretion: such arrangements are poor substitutes for private shareholders. In contrast, private markets allow transfers of ownership to achieve a more efficient use of resources, and monitoring by shareholders is more efficient than relying upon monitoring by the political process. The public choice literature reinforces the case for privatization by showing that government failure reflecting the influence of bureaucracies, interest groups and the lack of competition for public producers results in allocative inefficiency. Moreover, the potential for government failure casts doubts on the traditional market failure case for state intervention (see Chapter 14).

Capital markets are central to the case for privatization. They provide a policing and monitoring mechanism for controlling and assessing the efficiency with which private-sector managers use scarce resources. Private firms are subject to the threat of takeovers where managers lose their jobs and the ultimate threat of bankruptcy (that is, private firms are subject to hard budget constraints). But private capital markets often work imperfectly. With the separation between ownership and control, managers are likely to pursue their own interests (for example, for higher salaries or an easy life: see Chapter 7). Shareholders are often subject to limited information on the efficiency of their company's managers (a principal–agent problem) and there are transaction costs of trading in shares, especially for small shareholders. Care must also be taken to avoid the methodological problem of comparing an actual imperfect state-owned firm with an idealized privately-owned company. Overall, where the economic arguments for and against privatization and state-ownership remain inconclusive, then it is necessary to resort to empirical testing.

Empirical Results

Testing hypotheses about the effects of ownership and market structure on enterprise performance and efficiency is not without its problems. Indicators are required to measure enterprise performance and, ultimately, economic efficiency. Some simple indicators are readily available such as financial data on profitability and losses, labour productivity, employment changes and exports as a measure of international competitiveness. Tests can then be undertaken to determine whether performance improves following a change from public to private ownership, *ceteris paribus*. Other relevant factors cannot be ignored. For example, an increase in profitability might reflect the exercise of market power by a newly-privatized monopolist and higher labour productivity could reflect increased investment in new plant and equipment (here, total factor productivity measures are superior to labour productivity data). Typically, tests of the impact of ownership on performance focus on technical efficiency rather than the more difficult to measure concept of economic efficiency (which requires data on prices and marginal costs although customer complaints are a useful proxy). Furthermore, empirical tests of performance before and after a change of ownership need to allow for the counter-factual: what would have happened to enterprise performance without a change of ownership? Leads and lags cannot be ignored: for example, performance might improve in anticipation of privatization or there might be lags or delays with performance improving a considerable time after privatization. Analysis is further complicated by the possibility that the transfer of ownership will result in the pursuit of different objectives (for example, profit maximization under private ownership compared with public interest obligations under state ownership).

A UK study examined the performance of 11 organizations which were privatized before 1989. Four performance indicators were used, namely, labour productivity, total factor productivity, value-added per employee and profitability. It concluded that overall, it was not possible to 'reject the null hypothesis that there is no difference between the performance of publicly and privately-owned companies' and that 'the overall picture reveals little evidence of any systematic improvement in performance' (Martin and Parker, 1997, pp. 215–16). Elsewhere, an early study of two Australian airlines – one government-owned and the other privately-owned – found the private firm to be substantially more efficient (Davies, 1971); but a similar study of Canadian railways found no evidence of inferior performance by the government-owned railroad (Caves and Christensen, 1980). A survey of more than 50 studies from the 1970s and 1980s considered the relationship between performance and ownership for matched public and private firms where output was not priced by competition. The survey concluded 'that after controlling for a wide variety of factors, large industrial mixed enterprises and state-owned enterprises perform substantially worse than similar private corporations' (Boardman and Vining, 1989, p. 26). Finally, another UK study of ten UK organizations concluded that tests of performance using productivity, employment and financial ratios against change in ownership status, competition and internal management 'failed in most cases to support the thesis that change in ownership improves enterprise performance' even where ownership change is accompanied by increased competition and improved managerial incentives (Dunsire et al., 1991, p. 21).

Other performance indicators might show a more convincing case for privatization. Examples include improvements in the quality of service following privatization and dynamic benefits through innovation in new products. Privatization also led to new forms of industrial organization, especially in the utilities sector where the extent of natural monopoly was re-defined. National networks for electricity, gas and telecommunications were identified as natural monopolies with policy focusing on allowing new entrants access to these national networks. In some cases, technical progress reduced constraints on the entry of competitors (for example, mobile phone services as rivals to landlines). Also, competition resulted in the formation of new diversified utility companies offering a range of services supplying electricity, gas and phone services (compared with the previous organization where one firm specialized in supplying each of these services). Privatization policy also embraces competitive tendering for a range of public services.

Competitive Tendering

Competitive tendering is also known as contracting-out or contractorization. It covers the possible use of private contractors for supplying a whole range of public sector services. In this form, it is concerned with national, regional or city governments *financing* services which could be *provided* or supplied by private contractors (see Table 10.2). Examples include refuse collection, street cleaning, training and security guarding. Traditionally, the public sector would undertake these and other activities 'in-house' effectively acting as a public sector monopoly. But how can the efficiency of such public sector monopolies be assessed? Direct labour departments and 'in-house' units are usually monopoly suppliers of services, protected from possible public and private sector rivals. The absence of competition from rival government departments and from private contractors means that there are no alternative sources of information and no alternative cost yardsticks to assess the efficiency of a public provider. Efficiency is defined to embrace technical and allocative aspects, both of which are central to arguments about competitive tendering. Technical efficiency requires competitions for a *given* level of service (for example, daily street cleaning) whilst allocative efficiency is concerned with selecting the *optimal* level of service (that is, where marginal costs and benefits are equal). Selecting the optimal level of service requires that there be a competition for different levels of service, thereby revealing data on the marginal costs of alternative levels of service provision (for example, the extra costs of cleaning the streets twice or three times daily). Here, the aim is to generate sufficient cost data to determine whether the existing level of service is worthwhile or whether a different level is preferred or socially desirable.

Competitive tendering is an aspect of public procurement policy since it involves the public sector purchasing goods and services from the private firms. As such, the debate about competitive tendering and contracting-out is not new. Governments in capitalist economies often buy products such as computers, defence equipment, office furniture, railway networks and pharmaceuticals from private suppliers; they also purchase buildings such as hospitals, schools, roads, bridges and military bases, as well as a range of services such as accountancy, financial, legal and management consultancy (see also Chapter 15).

Competitive tendering is seen as a solution to the problem of public sector monopolies which are often criticized as inefficient bureaucracies responding to the wishes of producer groups rather than consumers. To its supporters, competitive tendering or even the threat of rivalry (contestability) means improved efficiency and cost savings. Private firms are seen as better managed, more innovative and able to change to new technology and new market opportunities. Successful firms in a competition are also subject to the incentives and penalties of a fixed price contract so that there is a threat of bankruptcy: hard budget constraints mean that there is no open-ended financial commitment as can arise with public providers.

Critics and opponents of competitive tendering claim that it results in a poor quality and unreliable service. Examples are given of dirty streets, hospital wards and schools, of penalty clauses imposed on defaulting contractors and cases of contractors failing because of bankruptcy. Private contractors are believed to be less reliable than public providers with claims that they are less able to respond to emergencies, they are liable to default and bankruptcy and that the award of a contract to a private firm leads to industrial relations problems and strikes. Critics also claim that any cost-savings are short-lived. Low bids can be used to buy into an attractive new contract and eliminate the public provider so that the public agency loses its bargaining power. As a result, it becomes dependent on a private monopoly which in the long-run means higher prices, a lack of dynamism and a poor quality service (and a return to the status quo with a private monopoly replacing a public monopoly). Nor is competitive tendering costless: it involves substantial transaction costs which are often ignored by the supporters of contracting-out. For example, contracting-out can add to transaction costs and reduce the knowledge and expertise of public procurement agencies (hence, transaction costs are relevant). Furthermore, critics claim that any cost savings from competitive tendering are achieved at the expense of the poorly-paid members of society so that there are equity versus efficiency issues in determining whether the policy is socially desirable.

The arguments for and against competitive tendering provide extensive opportunities for critical analysis and evaluation. Some of the arguments obviously represent special pleading by those interest groups most likely to gain from the policy. Contractors, banks and lawyers (who will write contracts) will support competitive tendering, whilst left-wing city governments, public sector trade unions and voters who favour public production will be opposed. However, many of the arguments for and against competitive tendering can be resolved by empirical testing. Cost savings of some 20–25 per cent have been estimated, mostly reflecting productivity improvements but some reflecting private contractors requiring longer working hours, shorter holidays and reduced sickness and pension benefits (see Chapters 14 and 15). One study concluded that international evidence showed savings of 20 per cent were achievable without sacrificing the quality of service (Domberger and Jensen, 1997).

Economic theory offers some guidelines for an efficient competitive tendering policy. First, privatization and contracting-out are not sufficient for efficiency improvements. There is a need for genuinely competitive and contestable markets with opportunities for new entrants. But competitive tendering is likely to be associated with contractors and their trade associations lobbying for public sector business and for entry barriers to protect their existing markets (for example, claiming that only established members of a trade association have the reputation and competence to bid for public contracts). Second, there needs to be a competition for alternative levels and standards of service, aimed at achieving allocative efficiency. Here, though, there remains a principal–agent problem. Public sector procurement agents will make decisions on the optimal level of service on behalf of voter-consumers as principals. Elected representatives and their agents are unlikely to reflect the diversity of preferences of large numbers of individual voters and consumers in properly functioning markets. Third, there remains the treatment of successful 'in-house' units. Where public providers are allowed to bid for contracts, they need to be subject to the same contractual incentives and penalties as a private firm winning the contract (that is, a fixed price contract). Difficulties will arise in imposing 'hard' budget constraints on public providers. Finally, there is scope for experimentation aimed at determining the limits to competitive tendering and, ultimately, the optimal size of the public sector (see Chapter 14).

10.4 CONCLUSION

Typically, public ownership lacks incentives to control costs and to respond to market opportunities and changing consumer demands. Such enterprises are subject to soft budget constraints financed by taxpayers and to weak monitoring arrangements where government ministers, taxpayers and voters are required to act as substitutes for shareholders. In contrast, privately-owned companies are subject to hard budget constraints, to incentives provided by the profit motive and to monitoring by shareholders and by product market competition.

However, one leading authority has stated that

> It would be difficult to conclude from either the theoretical or empirical literature that there is any simple answer to whether private production is to be preferred to public production. The point of consensus is summarized by Yarrow: private production is preferred where markets are reasonably competitive and there are no other significant market failures . . . In general, competition and regulation are likely to be more important determinants of economic performance than ownership (Bailey and Pack, 1995, p. xix).

READING* AND REFERENCES

*Bailey, E.E. and J.R. Pack (eds) (1995), *The Political Economy of Privatization and Deregulation*, The International Library of Critical Writings in Economics 44, Aldershot, UK and Brookfield, US: Edward Elgar.

Boardman, A.E. and A.R. Vining (1989), 'Ownership and performance in competitive environments: A comparison of the performance of private, mixed and state-owned enterprises', *Journal of Law and Economics*, **XXXII**(1), April, 1–33.

Buxton, T., P. Chapman and P. Temple (1998), *Britain's Economic Performance*, London: Routledge.

Caves, D.W. and L.R. Christensen (1980), 'The relative efficiency of public and private firms in a competitive environment: The case of Canadian Railroads', *Journal of Political Economy*, **88**(5), October, 958–76.

Davies, D.G. (1971), 'The efficiency of public versus private firms: The case of Australia's two airlines', *Journal of Law and Economics*, **XIV**(1), April, 149–65.

*Domberger, S. and P. Jensen (1997), 'Contracting-out by public sector: theory, evidence and prospects', *Oxford Review of Economic Policy*, **13**, 67–78.

*Dunsire, A., K. Hartley and D. Parker (1991), 'Organisational status and performance: summary of findings', *Public Administration*, **69**(1), 21–40.

*Martin, S. and D. Parker (1997), *The Impact of Privatisation*, London: Routledge.

Ott, A.F. and K. Hartley (eds) (1991), *Privatization and Economic Efficiency: A Comparative Analysis of Developed and Developing Countries*, Aldershot, UK and Brookfield, US: Edward Elgar.

Szymanski, S. and S. Wilkins (1993), 'Cheap rubbish? Competitive tendering and contracting-out in refuse collection', *Fiscal Studies*, **14**(3).

QUESTIONS FOR REVIEW AND DISCUSSION

1. Does ownership matter? How would you prove your case?
2. Why might privately-owned firms be superior to state-owned enterprises?
3. What are the economic arguments for state ownership?
4. Critically evaluate the economic arguments for and against competitive tendering. What, if any, are the limits to competitive tendering?
5. Which groups gain and which lose from privatization?
6. How might privatized monopolies be regulated? Which is the 'best' method of regulation?
7. Is transaction cost economics relevant to understanding the debate about contracting-out?
8. Identify the various forms of public and private sector organizations. Formulate testable hypotheses about the efficiency of these various organizational forms.

PART D

Factor markets and policy

11. Labour markets

11.1   INTRODUCTION: THE SCOPE OF MANPOWER POLICY

Manpower policy embraces all aspects of government policy towards labour as a factor of production and in relation to the operation of the market for labour. While the list of potential policy issues is extensive, they can be classified around the broad demand, supply and relative wage variables in the market. Examples include state involvement in determining relative pay, particularly between the public and private sectors, as well as information provision and policies towards the unemployed, training and re-training, mobility, and regional development.

Governments might also make provision for special groups, such as the disabled, school-leavers, the long-term unemployed, the elderly, women and immigrants. Such policies often reflect a concern with both economic and social objectives. Indeed, labour markets are often regarded as 'different' since they involve transactions in people and their services. People are both consumers and workers, and the income obtained from work will clearly affect their consumption levels. Not surprisingly, governments aiming to reduce poverty and economic deprivation have frequently intervened to raise the wages of the low-paid through, for example, legislation on minimum wages and equal pay. Such policies can have perverse effects and they raise basic questions about the function of labour markets.

This chapter will outline the economic arguments which might justify government intervention in the labour market and the likely effects of intervention. Consideration will be given to the characteristics of labour markets, the behaviour of individuals in the market, and the predictive power of economic models. Emphasis will be placed on whether governments need a public policy towards the labour market and, if so, the possible form of such a policy. Specific examples to be considered will include job search, unemployment and legislation on discrimination. Governments are also major employers. Military conscription or the draft will be taken as an example of labour demand by the public sector. However, this chapter will not provide a detailed account of human capital theory and unions. The analysis of training and mobility as human investments and their implications for social policy will be presented in Chapter 12. Similarly, the appraisal of trade unions and their effects on relative wages and efficiency is given in Chapter 13.

11.2   THE FUNCTIONS AND ACHIEVEMENTS OF LABOUR MARKETS

In capitalist economies, the purpose of labour markets is to allow mutually advantageous trade and exchange between willing buyers and sellers of labour. In this context, the buyers consist of private and public sector firms, as well as non-profit organizations which employ labour, such as the armed forces, charities, churches, government bureaucracies, hospitals and schools. By bringing together buyers and sellers, labour markets contribute to the production of goods and services to satisfy consumer preferences, as well as providing incomes to workers. In fact, labour markets are a fascinating study of the complexity of allocative choices. Think of what they do. They provide a bewildering variety of jobs and relative incomes, for men and women, young and old, full- and part-time, both self-employed and employees. These jobs will require different skills and be located in different regions, in the private and public sectors, and in agriculture, mining, construction, manufacturing, and service industries. Even in a static world, this would be a complex allocative task for any central planner: change makes life even more difficult! Labour markets have to adjust to technical progress, new suppliers and changing consumer preferences. New firms emerge requiring labour, and existing enterprises substitute machinery for workers. Examples include computers, jet airliners, and microelectronics. Households have not escaped technical change, with servants and full-time housewives being replaced by machinery such as central heating, canned food, freezers, cookers and dishwashers. Change requires new skills, sometimes in different locations. Labour markets adapt to these changes through, for example, firms re-training their workers in new skills and through the movement of employers and labour between regions (and nations).

The end results of labour markets are expressed in observed outcomes which provide answers to a set of questions about pay and employment. What determines relative earnings and why are successful pop stars, soccer players, and cricketers paid much more than nurses? Why do accountants, judges, lawyers and university teachers generally receive more than workers involved in dirty, dangerous and disagreeable manual jobs, such as coal-mining, refuse collection, and deep-sea fishing? Why are men usually paid more than women, whites more than blacks? There are also questions about employment. What determines employment and unemployment, and what is full employment? Can workers price themselves into, as well as out of, jobs? But the fact that actual labour markets seem to answer these questions does not mean that the outcomes are 'socially desirable'. A clear distinction is required between positive economics which aims to explain facts and normative issues concerned with the desirability of the outcomes. Some criteria are required for assessing performance.

Performance Criteria

As a starting point, Paretian welfare economics would assess the performance of labour markets in terms of their conformity with the competitive model. In such markets, labour would receive the value of its marginal product. Converting these performance indicators into operational concepts would lead governments to assess labour markets in terms of their efficiency as clearing mechanisms. In particular, labour markets can be judged by criteria relating to unemployment and their adaptability to change. Inevitably, they will also be judged by the 'appropriateness' of their relative pay structures. Governments might dislike an income distribution based on marginal productivity and determined by market forces. Thus, distributional issues cannot be avoided. Why, for example, should nurses be paid less than successful pop stars? Should not the drivers of trains and buses be highly paid since they are 'responsible' for the safety of large numbers of people? And in the public sector, how is it possible to measure the marginal productivity of firemen, police-men and army tank commanders in peace-time? Critics of market solutions sometimes suggest that public sector pay should be determined on the basis of comparability. But what is the comparable reference group for an army tank commander, and who deter-mines the degree of comparability? What if tank commanders disagree with the results? In other words, economists can contribute to the formation of manpower policy by pre-dicting the effects of alternative pay structures and their relative conformity to the Pareto criterion. They can point to the shortages and surpluses which are likely to emerge if gov-ernments interfere with market-determined wage rates. And they can provide explana-tions of differences in relative pay. Such contributions do not require complex economic models. The competitive model provides an analytical basis for understanding behaviour and results in the labour market, but a preference for such an approach requires some justification (see Chapters 2 and 4).

Some Procedural Clarifications

The characteristics of a competitive market for labour provide a basis for examining some of the more significant possible imperfections in the way such manpower markets actu-ally operate. However, we do not begin from an exposition of these characteristics in the belief that a perfectly competitive market is likely to be created in our lifetime! The labour market has a number of unusual features, not least that the persons (labour force) offering services in it are also the community whose interests the market exists to serve. There is, for example, always a potential (though not a necessary) conflict between labour market policies concerned with economic efficiency, and particular views of the broader aims of social policy. Rather, the exposition provides a 'benchmark', or 'ideal type'. It facilitates an examination of the nature and practical significance of labour market imperfections, thereby identifying the potential opportunities for state intervention to correct market failures. Such an approach is also relevant for subsequent chapters since it outlines the market environment within which policies towards training, mobility and trade unions must be formulated and implemented.

11.3   THE COMPETITIVE LABOUR MARKET

A competitive labour market contains many buyers and sellers, each acting as a price-taker and possessing information on prices throughout the system, with free entry and exit from the market. In such a market, a firm's demand for labour will depend on the wage rate and the productivity of additional units of labour (marginal productivity). The supply of labour will depend on the wage rate, workers' preferences between income and leisure, the view taken of the non-pecuniary aspects of particular jobs, and the available job opportunities. In a competitive economy with full employment, wages and salaries in various markets will be determined by demand and supply, and prices will be the mecha-nism for allocating scarce labour between alternative uses. The model predicts that an increase in the demand for labour in an occupation, industry or area will normally result in a relative rise in wage rates. Workers will be attracted to the relatively high wage activ-ity, which is also the sector in which output, and hence their contribution to output, has come to be more highly valued. Similarly, a decrease in the demand for labour will result in a relative decline in real wage rates in that sector and a consequent reduction in labour employed. However, the downward adjustment in wage rates will offset some of the quantity reductions which would otherwise be required. Thus, in a competitive market, if other things remain constant, wage changes between activities will reflect changes in relative scarcities and so indicate the need for re-allocation of labour. The adjustment will take the form of labour moving from lower to higher paid occupations until the allocation required by market forces is achieved. As a result, in a system where prices allocate manpower and other resources between uses, prices (including wages) and outputs of products will always be changing in directions that respond to consumer preferences. Such adjustments will eliminate any 'shortages' or 'surpluses' generated by changes in consumer tastes or in the technical conditions of production. In other words, variations in relative wages will 'clear' the labour market, so removing vacancies and unemployment.

Why do Wages Differ?

In competitive markets differences in wage rates between occupations reflect the relative scarcity of various types of labour. Wage rates will differ because of variations in the monetary and non-monetary advantages of jobs, differences in the ability of labour, costs of training, and the geographical mobility of workers (see Chapter 12). Clearly, some sources of differences in relative wage rates will exist even in an economy not subject to change. People differ in ability, aptitudes and commitment to learning, and different skills and abilities are differentially scarce and hence would be differentially rewarded. Also, jobs differ in their security, cleanliness and safety, and workers may attach value to such job characteristics. To the extent that they do so, relative wages will reflect differences in these *non-monetary attributes*, even in an unchanging economy. Office jobs are relatively safe and pleasant compared with coal-mining, working as a steeplejack, trawling and serving as front-line combat troops in Afghanistan and Iraq. For example, in the UK's armed forces, the net disadvantages of the military employment contract are reflected in the X-factor which is used to determine military pay.

Other differences in relative wage rates at any time will result from changes in the patterns of labour demand in the economy, as explained above. In a competitive system, the response of labour to changes in market requirements will depend partly upon the time taken for the system to record and disseminate information about relative scarcities. Once the market signals its changing requirements for manpower, the degree of response of labour to a change in wage rates will depend on the costs of geographical and occupational mobility. Here, much depends not only on the costs of mobility and training but also on the extent to which individuals are able to obtain funds for worthwhile human investments (see Chapter 12). A competitive labour market requires that adjustments should be able to take place with reasonable freedom, unhindered either by cost and financing barriers or by other barriers to the entry of labour into particular occupations.

The nature of these obstacles to entry is complex. Apart from the simple cost obstacles, it has been argued that the labour market comprises a set of *non-competing groups*, the different markets being separated from one another by economic barriers, social prejudice and snobbery. Within each market, the wage-adjustment processes described above would operate, but not between the non-competing groups. The emphasis in this formulation has traditionally been upon the relation between social distinctions and entry barriers. However, there seems no reason to take so narrow a view: all barriers to entry not related to production requirements constitute market imperfections. Barriers related to sex, colour or religion, for example, are as much policy-relevant obstacles to the satisfactory operation of the market as are training and other obligations imposed by trade unions and professional associations with the purpose of restricting the supply of skilled labour rather than of ensuring competence. Such entry barriers are a further source of differences in relative pay. A variant of the non-competing groups model is the *dual labour market view* where the overall labour market is viewed as divided into two non-competing sectors, namely, a primary and a secondary sector. Jobs in the primary sector offer relatively high pay, stable employment, good working conditions and opportunities for promotion. In contrast, jobs in the secondary sector offer low pay, unstable employment and poor working conditions (that is, dead end jobs). Mobility between the two sectors is limited. Typically, a large proportion of women and minorities have been employed in the secondary sector, with associated claims of discrimination.

International labour mobility cannot be ignored. Often, nations impose barriers to entry for foreign workers with associated questions about the benefits and costs of immigration. For example, since 1998, net immigration into the UK has averaged over 150 000 a year (with substantial numbers from other EU states). A high proportion of immigrants are economically active and highly motivated workers (reflected in their willingness to travel large distances in search of work). They fill gaps in the labour market and allow the labour market to grow without 'overheating' the economy. For example, the UK Home Office estimated that a 1 per cent increase in the population from immigration was associated with a 1.25 to 1.5 per cent increase in per capita GDP (Shackleton, 2005, p. 37). But immigration is not costless. There are social problems reflected in access to housing, education and health, as well as racial tensions in parts of the country.

The Implications for Public Policy

The description of the ideal labour market provides guidance for policy-makers. If reality is to approach the competitive model, then governments will need to give attention to:

1. The number and size distribution of buyers and sellers in labour markets.
2. Entry conditions, both those imposed by trade unions and professional associations, and those which arise from the unwanted activities of other non-competing groups.
3. The conditions of geographical and occupational mobility (training and re-training) and the adaptability of the system to technological change.
4. The relation between detailed microeconomic policies and the need to provide an appropriate macroeconomic context. In particular, it will be necessary to adopt policies to deal with technological and cyclical unemployment.
5. The efficiency with which the system collects and transmits information.

This lengthy shopping list underlines the fact that labour market policy must necessarily be considered as an entity. As an illustration, take the frequent concern of governments with shortages of skilled manpower and their belief that more training is the *only* policy solution. The competitive model provides a useful framework for analysing the problem.

A permanent shortage of skilled labour suggests excess demand at the ruling wage rate, with wages either failing to adjust upwards or repeatedly settling below the market-clearing price (see Chapter 4 and Figure 4.3). Skill shortages can emerge for many reasons, related to such factors as entry conditions, training, mobility, information provision and government pay policies, together with difficulties in raising funds for human investments. For example, monopoly unions and professional associations can change the structure of relative wages, especially between skilled and unskilled tasks. Not surprisingly, any narrowing of wage differentials reduces the incentive of individuals to undertake training and bear some of its costs. Unions and professional associations can further contribute to skill shortages through entry restrictions for particular trades and lengthy apprenticeships. As a result, it is not surprising that supply responds only slowly and inadequately to changes in demand. Thus, if an efficiently operating labour market is required in which shortages will be absent, policy-makers need to consider the market as a whole and not simply one aspect of manpower, such as training. However, objection to the competitive model as a potential or approximate description of reality in any capitalist economy may be based upon the observations that barriers to entry exist, that some workers are immobile, and that the market is hampered by inadequate information. It may also be claimed that other policy objectives should, and do, override the objectives that can be served by a competitive market. These objections cannot be ignored.

Entry Barriers and Immobility

Critics of the competitive model point to the fact that most wage rates in capitalist economies are negotiated not between individual workers and their individual employers but between trade unions and employers' associations. Also, workers are believed to be immobile, either inherently because they attach a high value to their present location or because they are unable to finance worthwhile geographical movement or the acquisition of a new skill. Finally, it is said, workers normally have very poor information about current earnings from different jobs – much less about potential future changes which are characterized by uncertainty. If valid, these considerations seem sufficient to demand government intervention in the labour market, since they imply that the competitive pressures which are required for the allocation of labour between alternative uses are at least partly absent. But how important are these imperfections in practice?

There is, in fact, a substantial amount of evidence which is consistent with the predictions of the competitive model. In many capitalist economies, the net geographical movement of population is in the direction predicted by the theory: namely, from regions and countries of little opportunity, where long-run earnings are relatively low, to areas and nations of higher wages, more job opportunities, and relatively low unemployment rates (for example, international migration in the EU). In other words, movement is towards areas where there are expectations of higher lifetime earnings for the household. However, some critics have concluded that what appears to be a response to opportunities to increase earnings could be equally consistent with the attraction of employment possibilities and other non-wage factors. Such a conclusion is somewhat misleading since only when other things are held constant does the orthodox model explain geographical and occupational mobility in terms of variations in relative wage rates. When this is not so, movement is explained by differences in net advantages. Indeed, the model emphasizes that it is total net advantages and not merely wages which determine the occupational choices of workers and that relative wages only determine job choice in a framework in which other job properties are unchanged. There are obvious difficulties in obtaining evidence about these (expected) non-wage differences. Since they are not marketed, information must be sought about the subjective estimates of the workers who move between jobs – and, ideally, of workers who might have moved but did not! Elsewhere, instances of apparently irrational behaviour in decisions concerning occupations and skills become consistent with rationality once it is recognized that systematic job search and consideration of alternatives is not a costless process.

In total, there is some evidence to support the view that labour markets both within and between nations operate in the general direction that the competitive model would predict, albeit imperfectly. This is not to claim that the model is incapable of modification and that there are no alternative explanations of labour market behaviour. Some of the modern developments concerning search, households, uncertainty and internal labour markets will be outlined below, while subsequent chapters will introduce human capital and trade unions into the analysis. Nonetheless, if governments wish to achieve an optimum allocation of resources, there are opportunities for state intervention to remove or 'correct' identifiable labour market imperfections. Possibilities include anti-monopoly policies, unilateral tariff reductions to increase competitive pressures, measures to improve labour mobility and information flows, together with policies to prevent trade unions and professional associations from restricting the entry of qualified persons to any occupation. Critics, however, might claim that there are other, more important, policy objectives relating to labour markets.

The Importance of Other Policy Objectives

One argument for displacing the market can be dealt with quickly. This is the argument that the labour market generates an 'undesirable' distribution of income, which justifies state intervention in wage determination. To right-wing economists, this proposition rests on a misunderstanding of the function of markets. They are seen as mechanisms for allocating limited resources between many alternative users and providing signals about relative scarcities. Interference with this allocative process might be based upon the fact that the 'wrong' signals are being given because of market imperfections, which the intervention is designed to remove. On this view, correction of the distribution of income generated by the labour market is a matter for the tax system, which need not affect the functioning of specific labour markets and which can be related to incomes and responsibilities rather than to occupations.

A more substantial set of problems concerns policy towards full employment and economic growth. The discussion so far has proceeded on the assumption that there would be no overall demand deficiency which generated unemployment, much less simultaneous conditions of inflation and rising unemployment. Nor has account been taken of the fact that economic growth with technological change may raise average incomes, but does so at the price of an obligation to accept skill obsolescence and the need for job change, with the implied possibilities of workers needing to undertake retraining and/or experiencing unemployment. These are important and complex issues which cannot be ignored. There is, of course, scope for debate about the role of the state in unemployment policy. In so far as different occupations carry a different risk of unemployment (and high-risk occupations are frequently highly paid), there would seem to be sound reasons for requiring workers to insure themselves against unemployment at premiums that reflect such differential risks (perhaps by relating the premiums to past work experience?). If this were all, state involvement could be limited to legislation making unemployment insurance compulsory. But there are other considerations. First, macro-economic policy is a matter for the state, so that private insurers would be taking not only risks related to technological change (which might well be insurable in the aggregate) but also risks related to the government's management of the economy. These are not only difficult for the private insurer to deal with: they also support an argument of principle, that the state should bear at least part of the costs of unemployment as state policy is a major influence upon its size and character. Further, as mentioned above, the labour force is the *raison d'être* of the productive process as well as a part of it. If the labour market works in a fashion that produces what are thought to be conditions of unreasonable hardship for particular families, then the community will want to redistribute income towards those concerned. On this basis, whether unemployment insurance is provided by the state or by compulsory private arrangements, the state would carry a continuing residual obligation to provide for income deficiency due to unemployment (see Chapter 12).

To complete this unavoidably inadequate summary, there is the question of job change in a dynamic economy. Left to themselves, labour markets appear to operate imperfectly in this area because workers cannot provide adequate security for loans to facilitate job change. The essential similarity in this respect between geographical and occupational mobility (requiring finance for worthwhile training) will be apparent. Additionally, however, it must be recognized that state-supported policies to facilitate labour mobility may be a necessary precondition for acceptance by the community of dynamic change and its concomitant skill obsolescence. There is, of course, room for argument as to how far the state should intervene to influence the growth process, but there can be little doubt of the practical importance of the insecurity generated for workers by dynamic change. The policy options include redundancy pay as compensation for job loss, together with state assistance towards mobility, retraining, and job search. Mention of job search raises questions about the performance of labour markets in providing and transmitting information.

11.4   THE ECONOMICS OF INFORMATION

The competitive model assumes perfect information. But actual labour markets are not like agricultural commodities and stock exchanges where prices are clearly recorded. Labour is heterogeneous. People differ in their motivation and commitment to work, their abilities and skills, as well as in their tastes and preferences, and hence in their supply prices. Jobs also differ in their stability of employment, opportunities for overtime, training and promotion, together with general working conditions, all of which are reflected in the wage offered by employers. Given such diversity of workers and jobs, both buyers and sellers in the labour market have to search in order to obtain the 'best' terms. In other words, search provides information on the terms of trade in the labour market.

Information is not costless: resources with other valued uses have to be employed to obtain it. This fact alone casts some doubts upon the frequent assertion that 'labour is not a commodity' and consequently there should only be free or non-profit-making employment information services. In reply, it might be accepted that labour is not only a commodity, in that workers are also a major part of the community. Nevertheless, the community has as great an interest in the efficient use of labour resources, and hence in the efficient operation of the labour market, as it has in the efficient use of any other factor of production. If the provision of information involves costs, then, within the context of the competitive labour market model, it will be provided only if the anticipated benefits from having it justify the costs to be incurred. Workers will be willing to continue to 'buy' more information until its extra benefit is expected to be less valuable than the incremental cost of purchase. Thus, the model can be developed to incorporate a market in information. Trainees, for example, will require information on the costs of different training methods and the expected market value of the resulting skills. The 'information market' would be a complex one, since information can be acquired in a diversity of fashions. For example, learning by experience, by obtaining information based on the experience of parents and friends, or by reading advertisements in the newspapers and trade journals or by searching the Internet are all methods of searching the labour market. Such methods are not costless and frequently involve substantial time-costs, and the least-cost solution for the individual worker (or firm) might be to use none of them, but rather to purchase information from a specialist job agency. In other words, a competitive market will be characterized by a variety of information channels, including specialist agencies offering to sell information at a price.

Information, Job Search and Labour Market Decisions

The fact that information is not costless provides a basis for further understanding of behaviour in the labour market. Indeed, it is possible to combine information and job search with the ideas of human capital, the concept of the firm used by Coase (1937), and internal labour markets. And the analysis can be presented in the household context rather than that of the individual worker.

Consider the background against which individuals make labour market decisions. An individual might be aiming to maximize the present value of his or her expected lifetime earnings or expected utility over the life-cycle, where utility allows the inclusion of net advantages into the analysis. This is a standard optimization problem with the individual maximizing subject to a set of constraints in the form of available resources, the efficiency of resource use (which will also depend on technical progress), a limited amount of information, and uncertainty (no one can accurately predict the future). On the constraints side, the individual as a worker makes decisions in a household context. As a young worker, it will be his/her parents' household; with age, his/her own household. In other words, both the labour market and lifetime behaviour of the individual take place in a household setting. There are a number of features of households which can affect labour market behaviour:

1. Households possess a stock of monetary and physical assets in such forms as current and expected savings, goods and services. These form a wealth constraint for the

household which will usually exceed that available to an individual. This is often reflected in families acting as a 'cushion' and providing a source of internal funds and collateral for loans. Such funds might be a source of income during strikes, unemployment, job search and training.

2. Households possess a stock of human capital (see Chapter 12). In fact, the household can be regarded as an information agency. It has human capital in the form of information and knowledge about job opportunities and skills.

3. Households supply factor services, but an individual's offer decisions might be affected by the supply behaviour of other members of the household. For example, if a man loses his job, his wife or partner might go out to work, or if a man has a job, his wife or partner might not work – all of which affects participation or activity rates in an economy. These rates are measured by expressing the employed and registered unemployed as a percentage of the population of working age.

4. Households not only supply factor services but also produce goods and services (for example, housewives' services). Indeed, households add to the stock of factors (children). In this interpretation, a household is a firm. Using the Coase framework, the household is another island of central planning in a market system, and the existence and extent of the household is explained in terms of an organization for minimizing transactions costs. For example, with marriage contracts, the parties do not have to re-contract every meal-time, nor for every house-cleaning or car cleaning activity.

Within the household framework, individual workers make a continuous set of labour market decisions. For example, workers have to search for and to choose a job, some of which might require industrial training. They have to choose whether to stay in the job or to change it (to quit). A change of job involves a search for other work and the search can take place either on- or off-the-job. Or the choice might not be theirs and they might lose a job (redundancy and unemployment), in which case they have to search for another job. Searching for another job might require further investments in moving to a new location or acquiring a new skill. All these labour market decisions will be related to the worker's views about expected wage rates and incomes. At varying points in his/her working life, he/she might change his/her views about incomes in different jobs, and these views will determine his/her minimum offer price or his/her reservation wage. The offer price is also likely to change as the worker learns from experience, and household experience can be substituted for individual experience.

The labour market decisions outlined above form the *economics of job search*. This is a standard search process. Information is limited and costly to acquire and both workers and employers must search to find jobs and to fill vacancies. The analysis can be developed further by interpreting human capital theory in terms of information and knowledge embodied in human beings. On this basis, labour market decisions reflect a search process as workers and firms invest in acquiring additional information and knowledge about rates of exchange in the labour market, and in further reducing imperfections in knowledge by acquiring marketable skills. For example, in making career choices, individuals invest in themselves by acquiring information about different jobs. They also invest in themselves through education and training which represent 'knowledge-improving' investments. However, labour market decisions are made in a world of uncertainty. How do economic agents respond and adapt to uncertainty?

Uncertainty

Much depends on an individual's preferences and attitudes towards risks. Is he/she risk-averse or a gambler? Nonetheless, a worker can respond to uncertainty in various ways:

1. Savings can be acquired.
2. A general skill can be obtained which has value to a large number of employers.
3. Individuals can locate in areas of excess labour demand.
4. A person can join a trade union which might attempt to establish and to protect a worker's 'property rights' in his/her job and in his/her skills.
5. A group of workers in the community could persuade vote-conscious governments to introduce legislation establishing a worker's property rights in his/her job. Examples include legislation on employment protection, industrial democracy and redundancy payments.

Search is not confined to workers. Firms are also searching the labour market. They are searching for labour with minimum productivity requirements in relation to the agreed wage; or they are searching for manpower with specific characteristics, such as degrees; or they are searching for labour with characteristics which increase the probability that the worker will stay with the firm, so allowing it to recoup some of its investment in search, hiring, and possibly training the worker. For firms, a major uncertainty arises because labour is mobile. Unlike a machine, individuals can choose to leave a firm. How do firms respond to this uncertainty (that is, labour mobility)? Various methods are used:

1. Screening processes can be used to select labour which is more likely to be immobile and remain with a firm.
2. Fringe benefits can be 'tied' to the company and these might reduce mobility. Examples include company sports and health facilities, as well as cheap meals.
3. Fringe benefits can also be 'tied' to the length of service. Examples include paid holidays and occupational pensions.
4. Employment contracts. A firm's uncertainty about a new worker's ability, motivation and potential mobility might be reflected in the form of the employment contract. Typically, these vary and might take the form of sequential spot contracts or an authority relationship or provisions for incentive pay, training and pension rights. Some contracts require an individual to stay with the firm for a specified period, with premature departure involving repayment of part of the employer's hiring and training costs.
5. Firms can create internal labour markets. For example, firms might restrict entry to lower level jobs, obtain experience of the worker and promote from within on the basis of seniority. This policy both provides information on new entrants and 'ties' the interests of the worker to the firm in a continuing way, so increasing the firm's willingness to invest in training. For firms operating a seniority system, a voluntary 'quit' might involve a worker in substantial promotion costs (that is, forgone promotion opportunities in the firm which the employee has quit).

Internal Labour Markets

An internal labour market forms a non-competing group. It is a 'closed' labour market which is confined to the establishment, firm or industry, where there are a clear set of rules about entry, exit and movement within the internal labour market. In other words, the internal organization of a firm – its internal labour market – is an administered system with rules about wages and the allocation of labour. The result is a further entry barrier with existing members of a firm's work force in employment with jobs and representation in wage bargaining (insiders) and a group of outsiders without jobs and not represented in wage bargaining.

Internal labour markets contrast with the classical open, unstructured markets where there is no attachment between the worker and the employer other than the wage: workers do not have a claim on any job and employers do not have a hold over any person. Thus, internal labour markets can be regarded as a method of obtaining a return on a firm's investment in its workers (for example, search, hiring, screening, supervising and training). As such, they can be interpreted as a form of employment contract, in which case, there are clear interrelationships between human investments, employment contracts and internal labour markets. Indeed, internal labour markets might be an efficient solution for firms searching for information about the productivity of their manpower, while providing incentives and rewards for pursuing organizational goals and, at the same time, trying to obtain a return from investments in their workers. References to efficiency also raise questions about the possibilities of failure in information markets.

Should Governments Intervene in Information Markets?

The efficient operation of the labour market partly depends upon the transmission of information about relative scarcities in the economy. If, for example, labour is unaware of income and employment prospects in different jobs, this will impair the extent to which workers will respond by acquiring new skills and moving from the declining to the expanding regions and sectors of the economy. In the circumstances, both workers and firms in private enterprise economies find it worthwhile to invest in the acquisition of market information. The result is an extensive private sector information market embracing specialist job agencies, advertisements, certificates, licences, correspondence, phone calls, the Internet and informal contacts. Such methods can involve substantial money and time costs. Despite the willingness to pay for information, private competitive markets are not likely to provide as much of the commodity as consumers require. Some kinds of information are so general in character that it may be difficult to establish property rights in them with the consequent possibility of under-provision if information is left to be supplied by private markets. It is also a frequent characteristic of such information that it can be supplied to more people at very low additional cost, so that private provision might produce conditions of technical monopoly. Thus, state intervention in information markets can be rationalized on grounds of its public good characteristics and technical monopoly. There is a further general argument for government intervention. Through its macroeconomic policies, the state creates the context within which a competitive labour market might operate. This involves the state in the 'information business'. Information is required about its own plans, and about its inferences from those plans for the general development of the labour market. Any such information has to be hedged by qualifications, since state agencies have no special access to knowledge about an uncertain future. A major value of this type of information is that it can also be assessed by others. At the same time, the state's macroeconomic policy role might be argued to support some subsidization of information provision beyond the amounts individuals would want to pay for. This could be justified if the cost of the resultant information is less than the benefits in increased community output obtained by shortening the periods spent in unemployment or the lags in adjusting to changes in labour demand.

The existence of market failure does not, however, indicate the most appropriate policy solution. Various alternatives are possible, including the state subsidization of private information agencies, the state provision of grants and loans to individuals for investment in job search, as well as the public ownership or regulation of technical monopolies. Clearly, there will be differences of opinion about the appropriateness of private and state finance and state provision of information. Advocates of market solutions will claim that in a competitive labour market there is no reason or principle why workers should not pay for job information, but there must be access to funds for worthwhile investments. Such funds might take the form of loans or equities related to the marketability of the job information (see Chapter 12). Critics of market solutions might prefer state provision of information through a government employment agency offering its services to workers at zero price. Such an option could reflect a general community preference for public ownership of technical monopolies. Budget-maximizing bureaucracies are unlikely to oppose this policy! In addition, some state finance and provision of information could be justified because much labour market information is generated within government. Where there is a public social security system, it is likely that for certain kinds of information the state is potentially the lowest-cost organization for its collection and distribution. Finally, state finance and provision of job information is often defended in terms of 'helping the unemployed'. Similar arguments have been used for public policies towards training, retraining and mobility. Inevitably, distributional issues cannot be avoided. Economists can contribute to policy formulation by seeking clarification of government objectives, identifying potential conflicts and outlining the implications of alternative solutions. In view of its importance to labour market policy, some consideration has to be given to unemployment.

11.5   UNEMPLOYMENT

Unemployment is obviously a cause for concern. Usually, the policy problem embraces the numbers and percentages, as expressed in the recorded unemployment statistics, its duration, and regional distribution, as well as its impact on particular groups, such as school-leavers, immigrants and older workers. Unemployment also means lost output, it affects government expenditure and revenue, and it has social impacts. Moreover, there are dynamic effects. For example, while unemployment tends to cause some workers to withdraw from the labour force, the experience of unsuccessful job search might mean that the discouraged work effect 'spills over' into future years and future generations. Nor can unemployment be ignored by vote-sensitive governments (see Chapter 14). Clearly, the subject embraces both macro- and microeconomics, with the latter providing the material for this section. For simplicity, three policy issues will be assessed, relating to the reliability of unemployment statistics, the microeconomic causes of unemployment, and the likely effects of unemployment pay and labour market legislation.

Are the Official Unemployment Statistics Reliable Indicators of the State of the Labour Market?

Any answer to this question depends upon what ought to be measured. Theory provides a conceptual framework for an answer. The 'new' microeconomics approach suggests that there is a natural rate of unemployment reflecting labour adjustments and imperfections. This view resembles that of the classical economists where full employment occurs at the market-clearing real wage rate. In equilibrium, any unemployment is voluntary, reflecting a worker's preferred income–leisure position. Modern microeconomics also recognizes that in equilibrium there is likely to be some unemployment due to job search, movement between jobs, and labour market imperfections. Indeed, in this model, the existence of information costs means that unemployment, vacancies and flexible prices can co-exist, even where competitive markets are in equilibrium. There is a further possibility concerning the impact of the Internet on reducing the natural level of unemployment: it reduces both advertising and search costs. Such outcomes make life exceptionally difficult for governments trying to interpret the unemployment statistics as a guide to policy formulation!

Official unemployment figures are often used as an indicator of the state of demand and supply in the labour market. Usually, they are a record of those who actually register as unemployed with the state's manpower agency. The total might consist of those who are wholly and temporarily unemployed, as well as those who cannot find jobs or will not work at what they perceive as the ruling wages. But some of these groups might be voluntarily unemployed or using unemployment for job search (for example, some unemployed could be self-employed in job search). Other people might not be registered with the state's employment agency, even though they are willing to work and searching for a job. Between countries, differences in definition, coverage and accuracy make international comparisons difficult, if not misleading.

Proposals have been made for more accurate economic indicators of the state of the labour market. Some economists have argued that particular groups should be excluded from the official unemployment statistics. Examples might include school-leavers, those frictionally and structurally unemployed, the voluntarily unemployed and the unemployables. But what is the economic logic of excluding a specific group and how would the various categories be identified and measured? Alternative suggestions have been made for a more comprehensive measure of labour slack in an economy. Such a measure might embrace unemployment and activity rates, international migration, labour hoarding, and hours worked per annum. Interesting though these proposals might be, they are often aimed at providing macroeconomic indicators. Life at the micro-level is much more difficult. At this level, the more accurate official statistics often relate to unemployment in regional labour markets. Industry and occupational data can be less reliable indicators of surpluses and shortages. The former are usually based on an individual's previous industrial employer, even though the worker might be mobile between industries and possess skills which are transferable. Similarly, occupational data require a classification system based on skill categories and market groups which are separated by gaps in the chain of substitutes. Training policy, for example, cannot be divorced from data on current and forecast occupational unemployment rates. Policy-makers need to know whether the statistics provide an accurate indication of persistent skill shortages. They also require information on the education and training content of the skills which are in excess demand, together with the opportunities for substitution. In other words, without reliable microeconomic data on the state of labour markets and their efficiency, it is difficult for governments to formulate policy solutions. But there is a prior need to understand the causes of unemployment.

Search Unemployment

There is no shortage of microeconomic hypotheses to explain the apparent failure of labour markets to clear. Why does excess supply not lead to aggressive wage cutting by both buyers and sellers? Wage stickiness might be due to worker resistance to wage reductions, particularly where there are trade unions; or it might be due to market transaction costs. Or firms might be reluctant to cut wages if they feel that there would be costs in the form of antagonizing the remaining employees, so adversely affecting productivity, as well as making it costlier to recruit labour when sales improve. Or there could be widespread notions of fairness, together with social pressures and legislation which might prevent redundant workers from undercutting employed labour. Alternatively, unemployment even in competitive markets might be explained by information costs. In this model, workers might prefer search unemployment rather than accept a pay cut to retain a job.

Consider a situation where there is a decrease in the demand for a firm's product. Employers might respond by requiring a wage cut for labour to continue in employment. However, where knowledge of market opportunities is limited and costly to acquire, a worker might sensibly believe that a better offer could be obtained with some search. And if searching is more efficiently undertaken off-the-job, it might be worthwhile for a worker to refuse a wage cut, choose unemployment, and search the labour market. Choosing unemployment as a means of searching for a job is not 'costless'. Current consumption is sacrificed in return for expected future benefits which would make search unemployment worthwhile. Benefits take the form of a better paid job or one with greater non-monetary advantages. A simple model determining the average duration of search unemployment is shown in Figure 11.1. Workers lack perfect information and knowledge, so the longer they search for a job, the better the wage offers they discover. However, the longer they search, the more they are likely to revise downwards their reservation wage or supply price. As a result, the equilibrium period of search is determined where the reservation wage and wage offer curves intersect. There is a further possibility affecting the model. Increased periods of unemployment may send unfavourable signals to prospective employers suggesting some 'defect' in the unemployed person and existing skills may decay during unemployment.

Effects of State Unemployment Pay

A government concerned with both economic and social objectives will be interested in discovering whether state unemployment pay contributes to a rise in unemployment.

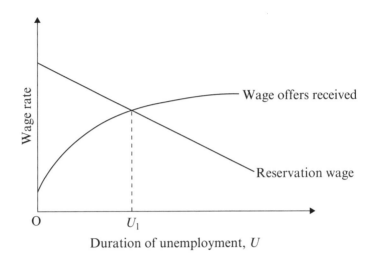

Figure 11.1   Search unemployment. Searching leads to the discovery of better wage offers. The wage offers curve represents the average of offers in general. At the same time, longer search leads workers to revise downwards their reservation wage (i.e. supply or offer price). The equilibrium period of search unemployment occurs where the curves intersect, at U_1, i.e. where at the margin the benefits of search are just equal to its costs. It is, of course, possible that after a point the wage offer received declines with the duration of unemployment (e.g. skills lose value if they are not used)

After all, unemployment payments are likely to reduce the costs of both unemployment and job search. The hypothesis can be derived from an income–leisure model and an example is shown in Figure 11.2. State unemployment pay results in a parallel shift in a worker's budget line and, if leisure is a normal good, more will be preferred, as shown in Figure 11.2(a). However, in testing for a relationship between unemployment and unemployment benefits, allowance has to be made for the effects of 'other influences'. Theory suggests an alternative hypothesis, namely that as people become richer they will demand more leisure, which is then reflected in voluntary unemployment! An example is shown in Figure 11.2(b) where a higher wage rate leads to income and substitution effects, resulting in the choice of more leisure and income. In other words, in testing for any disincentive effects of state unemployment pay, allowance has to be made for the impact of rising living standards on observed unemployment. The evidence suggests that state unemployment pay has disincentive effects; but there are doubts about its precise magnitude, with some studies estimating a relatively small impact on the level of unemployment. This is not the only example of a policy measure which results in conflicts between objectives. Other examples have occurred with labour market legislation, some of which has had unemployment effects.

11.6   LABOUR MARKET LEGISLATION

Labour markets are often characterized by differences in pay between men and women, whites and blacks, nationals and immigrants. They are also markets in which workers

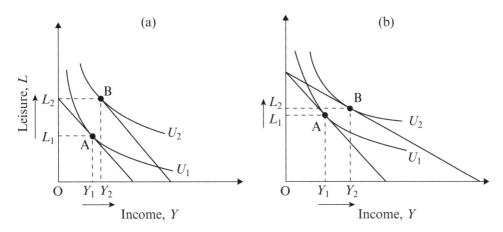

Figure 11.2 State unemployment pay. In diagram (a) the worker is initially in equilibrium at A. The introduction of state unemployment pay can be represented by a parallel shift in the budget line (income effect). The new equilibrium is at B. This example shows a corner solution, with the worker consuming the maximum available leisure, i.e. all his available time is allocated to leisure. In diagram (b), following a rise in the wage rate, the worker moves from an initial equilibrium at A to a new preferred combination at B (reflecting both income and substitution effects). Thus, with rising real incomes, people will demand more leisure, which is then observed as higher unemployment

might not have any rights of protection against unfair dismissal and where they might be subject to unhealthy and dangerous jobs. Understandably, vote-sensitive governments and budget-conscious bureaucrats believe that such characteristics are socially undesirable and can be eliminated through legislation and the establishment of state regulatory agencies. Examples include legislation on equal pay and minimum wages, as well as laws against discrimination on grounds of race and sex. Legislation has also been used to establish a worker's property rights in a job through laws relating to employment protection, contracts of employment, and health and safety at work. In each case, it is always a source of surprise to governments that legislation and attempts to administer markets through laws result in unexpected and undesirable side-effects and outcomes which differ from the original intentions. And yet, as shown throughout this book, microeconomics can predict some of these effects.

Differences in pay and employment opportunities are often related to race, religion and sex. Such differences are not necessarily an accurate indicator of labour market discrimination. Differences in pay between men and women, between nationals and immigrants, between different religious groups, or white and black people might be due to differences in relative scarcities related to variations in productivity, motivation, education and training, as well as hours of work and the non-monetary aspects of jobs. However, differential access to education and training together with occupational and union entry barriers based on race, religion or sex can create non-competing groups. As a result, the exclusion of minorities and women from particular occupations means that they 'crowd into' unrestricted occupations, so reducing relative wages in these jobs. In addition to such general explanations, specialist economic models of discrimination have been developed. These explain labour market discrimination in terms of imperfect information and prejudice by firms, workers or consumers. In searching for labour, firms will lack perfect information, so that they will develop 'rules of thumb' to screen applicants for jobs. Experience might lead employers to conclude that, on average, black people, women and minorities are less productive than whites and men. Such a conclusion will result in a firm discriminating against individual minorities and women who are more productive than their group average. Prejudice is a further explanation of discrimination. Employers might dislike particular groups and refuse to hire them, even at the expense of lost profits. For example, where there are no productivity differences between black people and white people, or between peoples of different religious gropus, an employer's utility function might contain a preference for whites and might favour some religious groups. In this situation, the employer's discrimination coefficient will determine how much cheaper black people and people from some religious groups will have to be before they are hired. But prejudice need not be restricted to firms. Employees might prefer not to work with minorities or women. Similarly, consumers might prefer particular types of labour, such discrimination being likely to arise in service industries (for example, accountancy, restaurants, hairdressing).

These explanations have been criticized. In particular, in the long run, competitive forces are likely to eliminate some types of discrimination. For example, non-discriminating firms will have lower labour costs so that they would outcompete discriminating firms, driving them out of business. Or the higher profits earned by non-discriminating firms would induce rivals to copy. Modern radical economists prefer alternative explanations of discrimination. They attribute the subordinate status of women in the labour market to the needs of capitalism and its institutions. According to the radical view, the nuclear family and the drive for male supremacy within the household have forced women into the specialized roles of child-rearing and family maintenance within a capitalist system designed primarily for the participation and benefit of men. Such views provide extensive opportunities for critical appraisal! Terms and concepts have to be defined, testable hypotheses have to be constructed, and some effort is required to deduce the critics' view of the 'ideal' world where these 'problems' would somehow be eliminated. Nor can empirical evidence be ignored. Where international data are available, this shows that, on average, women earn less than men in capitalist and other economies. But there might be non-economic explanations of such pay differences (for example, social and biological factors: child-bearing disrupts employment and productivity and often women are expected to be the main carers of others in the family). Questions arise as to whether legislation can solve the problem. Consider the case of legislation on equal pay for men and women doing the same jobs. The effects of the legislation are similar to those for minimum wage laws and can be predicted using demand and supply analysis (see Chapter 4). If the legislation is effective in raising wage rates above their market-clearing level, there will be a decline in female employment and the creation of unemployment. Profit-maximizing firms will respond to equal pay by replacing women with men and machines. Thus, equal pay will raise the wage rates of those women who remain employed; but the legislation leads to perverse results. Some of those who are supposed to benefit find themselves without jobs and there will be an increase in the demand for male substitutes! An example is shown in Figure 11.3. However, both the monopsony and shock effect cases provide possible exceptions to the unemployment impact of equal pay laws (see Chapter 13, Figure 13.7). Indeed, in defence of equal pay legislation, some economists have argued that monopsony is more likely to apply to

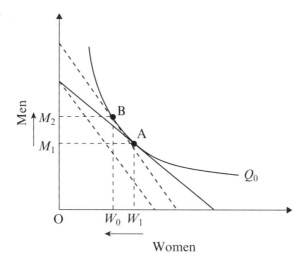

Figure 11.3   The substitution effects of equal pay. Consider a simplified production function with men and women as factor inputs. Prior to equal pay legislation, the firm is in equilibrium at A, producing output Q_0 (isoquant). The introduction of equal pay causes an inward shift in the isocost line and a change in relative factor prices. If the firm continues to produce Q_0, there will be a substitution effect, leading to a new equilibrium at B and the employment of more men. The analysis can be complicated by considering men and women as perfect substitutes or used in fixed-factor proportions

women, especially married women who tend to be immobile. Indeed, monopsony has been used to explain the lack of employment decline associated with UK equal pay legislation. There is a further possibility. Workers might break the law rather than accept the unemployment consequences of legal solutions. In other words, illegally low wages (black markets) might be preferred to unemployment and no wages.

Further insights into the effects of equal pay can be obtained by examining the evidence on the employment effects of minimum wage legislation. It has been shown that the competitive labour market model offers some clear predictions about the adverse employment effects of such legislation. The empirical evidence is less conclusive. One international survey concluded that

> we cannot be sure what the employment effects of a moderate minimum wage are likely to be. At modest levels . . . a minimum wage probably does not raise unemployment and might even reduce it. But at modest levels, the benefits of the minimum wage to those who remain in employment are modest too (Hyclak et al., 2005, p. 249).

A study of EU nations found no evidence that minimum wages cut adult employment but some evidence that they reduced youth employment reflecting the low productivity of young and unskilled labour (Begg et al., 2005, p. 178). Again some of these results could reflect monopsony labour markets and/or the incentive and shock effects of higher wages (efficiency wages).

Policy-makers might also focus on unemployment amongst specific groups, such as young people. For example, the UK introduced its New Deal programme (starting in

1998) initially aimed at reducing unemployment amongst young people aged 18 to 24. The New Deal involved a set of 'active labour market policies' for unemployed young people comprising retraining opportunities, subsidized work, interviews and work in the voluntary sector. A National Audit Office Report concluded that the first two years of the New Deal reduced youth unemployment by probably some 25 000 to 45 000 and increased youth employment by 8000 to 20 000. An academic study estimated that the scheme had raised employment by 17 000 a year. Although the scheme was not an outstanding success, its net costs were small as much of the published costs would have been incurred in paying unemployment benefits in the absence of the New Deal (Shackleton, 2005, p. 36). However, others have been more critical of the New Deal, claiming that it has been costly and that by 2007, the number of unemployed youngsters was higher than when the programme was launched (Field, 2007). Further problems arise in evaluating the New Deal because of deadweight loss, displacement and substitution effects. Deadweight loss arises where firms would have taken on young people anyway, regardless of the New Deal; displacement effects arise where young people involved in the scheme replace other groups not in the scheme; and similarly, substitution effects occur where firms hire subsidized groups at the expense of other non-subsidized groups.

Economists can also analyse the effects of laws relating to employment protection, contracts of employment, unfair dismissal and redundancy payments. Effectively, such laws establish or extend workers' property rights in their jobs. They make it more expensive for firms to employ and to dismiss labour. Inevitably, firms will adopt various responses to the legislation. Capital will be substituted for labour; there will be a greater use of subcontractors, overtime and temporary employment contracts; employers will be more selective in recruiting labour; and marginal firms in competitive export markets, where rivals might not be subject to such legislation, might have to close. As a result, the legislation will favour those who have jobs. Similar results arise with health and safety at work legislation. The costs of conforming to the legislation might lead to the elimination of marginal firms. Not surprisingly, workers and trade unions might oppose such laws, preferring unhealthy and dangerous work to healthy and safe unemployment. A further aspect of labour market legislation is often neglected by economists and this concerns the arrangements by which governments recruit labour for their armed forces.

11.7 MILITARY PERSONNEL

The recruitment of personnel for a nation's defence services is an example of public sector demand for labour where the government is a monopsonist (see Chapter 17: but there are markets for mercenaries). Governments have to choose between conscription (the draft or national service) and volunteer forces, or a mix of both. Conscription appears to be an attractive solution. A government simply passes a law requiring all young people to serve in the armed forces for a minimum period. Manpower is obtained cheaply at a price dictated by the government, with corresponding budgetary savings in achieving a given size of defence force. This is illustrated in Figure 11.4 where conscripts receive a wage considerably below their supply price. Conscription has also been advocated as a solution to a nation's unemployment problem. National service replaces unemployment, 'saves' state unemployment pay, and provides beneficial training, experience and discipline to young

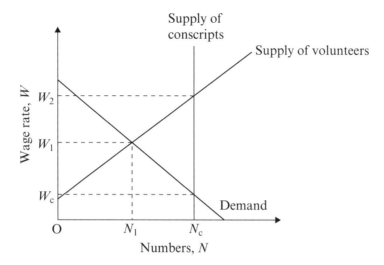

Figure 11.4   Conscription. An all-volunteer force of N_1 could be obtained at a wage rate of W_1. A conscript force of N_c could be obtained at a wage of W_c compared with W_2 if it were obtained on a voluntary basis. The difference W_2W_c shows the extent to which conscripts are underpaid, i.e. a budgetary saving of $W_2W_c \times ON_c$, although the state could choose to pay an even lower wage to the inelastic supply of conscripts

people. Such arguments require serious appraisal. What are the economic arguments against conscription and in favour of an all-volunteer force?

The first point to be stressed is that the budget outlays for a conscript force are not an accurate indicator of economic efficiency in resource use. They are not a true indicator of opportunity costs in the form of the forgone alternatives or society's valuation of the alternative uses of the conscript labour. For example, a trained doctor who is highly valued by the civilian economy would have to serve as a relatively cheap conscript where his military wage would not indicate the community's valuation of his services. Also, since manpower is relatively cheap, military commanders are encouraged to substitute labour for capital (weapons) and adopt labour-intensive military force structures. They will also have to maintain a substantial military training industry determined by the need to train conscripts. Thus, conscription is inefficient as well as being involuntary servitude or coercion.

Where exemptions operate, conscription has potential for inequity. For instance, rich children can avoid or delay conscription by undertaking higher education and lengthy training which might qualify for exemption. The employment and training argument for conscription is similarly suspect. It is not sufficient to argue that unemployed labour has no alternative-use value so that conscription would be costless (nothing is sacrificed). In such circumstances, *any* use of unemployed labour would be costless, including painting old people's homes, community service, restoring derelict land or working in a factory. Also, it must be remembered that conscription will not be restricted to the unemployed but will involve employed labour with its inevitable sacrifices. Finally, conscription is not the only nor necessarily the most efficient solution to unemployment. Other policy options include aggregate demand policies together with further education and training programmes as well as mobility of labour measures. Indeed, if the argument is that conscription would provide training to unemployed youths, the economic question is whether the armed forces or civilian training industries are the most efficient trainers in supplying skills which have value in *civilian* labour markets. Moreover, to use conscription as a *short-run* employment creator leads to questions about the proper objectives of national defence policy. Is it concerned with protection and security or employment creation?

Economic analysis predicts that the abolition of conscription and its replacement with an all-volunteer force will raise the relative cost of military personnel. This will encourage substitutions between capital (weapons) and labour as well as between skilled and unskilled, men and women, military personnel and civilians, and regulars and reserves. An example of the effects on manpower and weapons is shown in Figure 11.5. An all-volunteer force also allows the military to obtain a worthwhile return on their training investments. Conscription is a relatively costly method of training personnel to cope with the increasingly complex and rising skill requirements of modern weapons (for example, flying combat aircraft; operating nuclear-powered submarines). The more efficient solution requires highly-skilled, experienced and hence long-service regulars, able to maintain modern weapons, so providing the forces with a return on their substantial and rising training investments. This means that the services cannot ignore the relative efficiency of alternative employment contracts (for example, length of service) as a means of obtaining a return on their human investments. Different types of contract involve individuals sacrificing the 'rights' to their labour services and a related transfer of 'claims' to an employer in exchange for agreed payments and conditions of work. Clearly, an all-volunteer force relies upon voluntary exchange rather than the slavery-type contracts associated with conscription. But all employment contracts, even conscription, involve

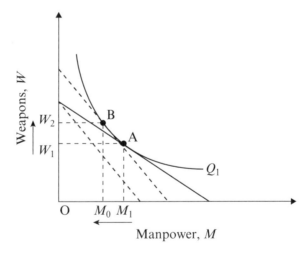

Figure 11.5   Manpower and weapons. With conscription, the least-cost combination of manpower and weapons to produce defence output Q_1 is shown at A. An all-volunteer force will raise the relative price of manpower, leading to an inward pivot of the isocost line (for a given expenditure). If defence output is to remain unchanged at Q_1, the new equilibrium will be at B, where there has been a substitution of weapons for manpower, together with increased defence expenditure

transaction costs in the form of search, negotiation, bargaining, hiring, training and retaining labour, as well as providing incentives and rewards and arrangements for monitoring and policing performance. Predictably, the military favours hierarchical and fixed-term employment contracts, which seem to be an attractive method of coping with uncertainty. They are, however, incomplete contracts frequently lacking any economic incentives. For example, compared with profit-maximizing firms, do military commanders have any incentives to substitute capital for labour as personnel becomes relatively more expensive? Or does the form of the military employment contract and the costs of enforcing it, allow and encourage individuals at all levels to be opportunistic, to hoard or distort information, and generally to pursue discretionary behaviour?

11.8 CONCLUSION

This chapter has shown how the competitive model can be used to explain labour market behaviour. The analysis was developed to include households, information costs, search, employment contracts and internal labour markets. Explanations have been offered for differences in relative pay, unemployment and discrimination. Policy solutions involving information provision, unemployment pay and labour market legislation have been assessed. It is not claimed that the treatment has been comprehensive. In particular, developments in human capital theory have to be considered, as well as the labour market impact of trade unions. These are the subject of the following chapters.

READING* AND REFERENCES

Begg, D., S. Fischer and R. Dornbusch (2005), *Economics*, 8th edn, London: McGraw-Hill.
*Coase, R. (1937), 'The nature of the firm', *Economica*, **4**, 386–405.
Ehrenberg, R.G. and R.S. Smith (2000), *Modern Labor Economics*, Reading, Massachusetts: Addison-Wesley.
Field, F. (2007), *New Deal for Young People*, London: Reform.
Griffiths, A. and S. Wall (2007), *Applied Economics*, Harlow: Prentice Hall, Pearson Education.
*Hyclak, T., G. Johnes and R. Thornton (2005), *Fundamentals of Labor Economics*, Boston: Houghton Mifflin.
Shackleton, J.R. (ed.) (2005), 'The labour market under "New Labour": the first two terms', *Economic Affairs*, **25**(3), 31–8.

QUESTIONS FOR REVIEW AND DISCUSSION

1. Are labour markets for economic or social functions?
2. Is the competitive model of the labour market capable of being tested and refuted? Explain and specify your empirical tests.
3. Why does relative pay differ? Are such differences socially desirable? What are the policy implications of your analysis?
4. Should top footballers be paid more than nurses?
5. Is international immigration socially desirable?

6. What are internal labour markets? Are they efficient?
7. Should governments provide labour market information at zero price through state-owned job agencies? Explain in relation to alternative policy options.
8. Does the search model provide a satisfactory explanation of unemployment in any market with which you are familiar?
9. Is military conscription (draft) an efficient solution to unemployment?
10. What are the likely impacts of the Internet on employment and unemployment in labour markets?

12.   Human capital and social policy

12.1   INTRODUCTION: THE SCOPE OF HUMAN CAPITAL THEORY

The economics of human resources offers explanations of individual and group (household) behaviour over the life-cycle. It provides a common analytical framework for apparently diverse issues such as:

1. Labour market behaviour, as reflected in job choice, training and retraining, wage determination, and age–earnings profiles, as well as job search and mobility (both domestically and internationally – brain drain), together with fringe benefits and employment contracts.
2. Compulsory schooling and voluntary education, as well as health care and retirement.
3. Income distribution and poverty.
4. Family decisions, including marriage (a search process) and the choice of the number of children.
5. Technical progress. Research and development leading to innovation involves the creation and dissemination (or the protection via patents) of the valuable information and knowledge which is initially embodied in human beings (for example, scientists).
6. Economic growth. Investment in human capital through formal education, training and on-the-job experience contributes to economic growth in both developed and developing nations. Human capital also contributes to growth through innovation resulting from the training of scientists, technologists and potential innovators (the knowledge-based economy). The Solow growth model found that a substantial part of US growth was not accounted for by inputs of capital and labour. This Solow residual was assumed to be caused by technical progress resulting from innovation (although other factors such as the business environment were also found to be important).

The common characteristic of these activities is that they involve human beings in an investment decision and the associated creation of human capital. They apply the standard economic theory of investment and capital where investment decisions are a sacrifice of present consumption in return for an expected higher income in the future. Human capital reflects the information, knowledge and skills embodied in people. For example, individuals who continue with formal education beyond the minimum compulsory level or who undertake additional training after entering a job (for example, apprenticeship) are effectively making an investment decision and bearing present costs in the expectation that they will acquire a productivity-raising investment which will improve their future

income stream. Similarly, job search and mobility can be analysed as investment decisions, with individuals investing in themselves. This 'non-separability' of human capital
is one of its distinguishing characteristics. With human capital, the property rights in the
investment reside in, and cannot be separated from, the individual. As a result, problems
arise in financing human investments since society usually rejects slavery-type employment contracts as illegal and contrary to the public interest. Policy-makers have to
decide whether private markets will under-invest in human beings, resulting in 'too little'
education and training and hence skill shortages, together with insufficient mobility and
information.

12.2   HUMAN CAPITAL, THE LIFE-CYCLE AND SOCIAL POLICY

The extensive nature of human resource studies is reflected in the range of potential economic and social policies. An indication of the scope of the subject and its corresponding policy implications is shown in Figure 12.1, which outlines the simplified life-cycle
behaviour of an individual.

Figure 12.1 shows some of the human investment decisions over the life-cycle from
birth through compulsory schooling to the labour market, and, ultimately, retirement.
Government social and economic policies can be related to the life-cycle, and may take
the form of payments-in-kind, subsidies, or cash. Thus, health policies offering 'free' or
subsidized hospital care and access to doctors might be available to all age groups.
Income-deficiency payments provide cash for the poor, large families, the unemployed, the
disabled, and the widowed. Emphasis might be placed upon special groups with payments
in cash and kind for children (for example, child cash benefits and 'free' schooling), and
state pensions for the retired. Payments-in-kind can also take the form of state-provided
and financed education, training and retraining courses, and information services (via
state employment offices), all of which are available to actual or potential workers and are
financed through the general tax system. Other policies might aim to control 'key' prices,
especially for so-called 'necessities' such as bread and housing, or minimum prices might
be imposed as in the case of minimum wage legislation and equal pay within labour
markets. Such an extensive range of policies, especially those with social objectives,
requires some explanation. Why do governments have such policies and which is the most
appropriate form of policy?

Does Economic Analysis Offer any Guidelines for Social Policy?

Government social policies often reflect distribution of income targets and the pursuit of
a more desirable distribution. While Paretian welfare economics offers no criterion for the
'best' income distribution, it can identify a class of optimal or efficient distributions. It
has been developed to suggest the desirability of individual decisions and the possibility
that institutions to promote voluntary exchange will undertake some redistribution
(Pareto-efficient redistribution). In other words, individuals can derive satisfaction from
their income and other people's. Examples include voluntary transfers through private
charities and special appeals for funds to help victims of natural disasters (for example,

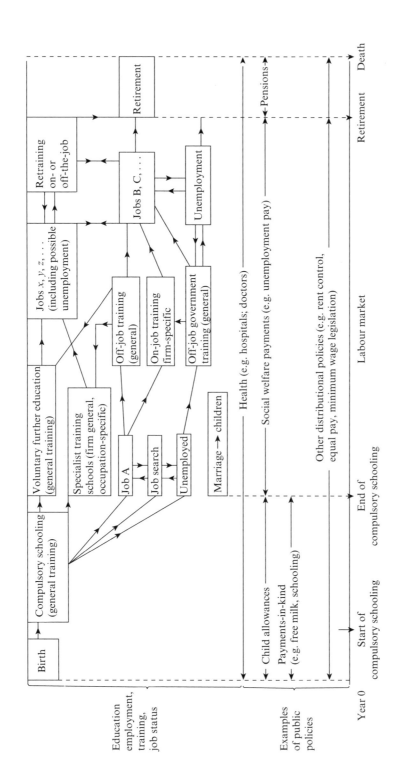

Figure 12.1   The life-cycle behaviour of an individual

flood, famine, earthquakes, explosions). Furthermore, it has been shown that under certain conditions, progressive income taxes can result in Pareto-optimal re-distribution (Hochman and Rodgers, 1969).

The compensation principle can also be applied to social policy. For example, technical change makes some education, information, training, and worker skills obsolete but, unlike old machinery, individuals cannot be scrapped. In this situation, society might agree that for economic growth to be worthwhile, the potential gainers should be able to overcompensate the potential losers. However, policy-makers have to define and identify the potential losers from a change and estimate the magnitude of their loss. The compensation principle suggests that the losers will be those who experience a reduction in utility. Unemployment from job loss due to new technology is a sufficient, but not a necessary, condition for inclusion in the losers' category; other losers who retain their jobs but experience utility losses are more difficult to identify operationally! Moreover, the compensation principle undertakes interpersonal comparisons of gains and losses in utility, using money as a measuring rod.

An alternative approach to social choice and policy has been provided by Rawls' (1973) concept of a just distribution. With this approach, individuals start from a hypothetical 'veil of ignorance' as to their initial position in society. The result is a social contract in which the primary goods of liberty, income and other sources of self-respect in society are distributed equally, except where inequality is to the benefit of the least-advantaged individuals and groups. Thus, to treat everyone equally (equality of opportunity) requires that society should favour those with fewer native assets and those born into the less-favourable social positions. For example, resources in education might be allocated to improve the long-term prospects of the least favoured, such as the less intelligent. On the Rawls criterion, no one would gain from basic inequalities in the social system except on terms which improve the situation of the less fortunate. According to Rawls (1973, p. 347), if governments and the law 'keep markets competitive, resources fully employed, property and wealth widely distributed over time, and ... maintain the appropriate social minimum, then if there is equality of opportunity underwritten by education for all, the resulting distribution will be just.' Social policy involving the state's obligation to protect individuals and groups over the life-cycle has a major role in such a society. However, the Rawlsian system requires a clear definition of the worst-off or least fortunate in society. These are unlikely to be restricted to the poor and might embrace the mentally and physically ill and handicapped. Moreover, once it is remembered that actual constitutions exist, problems can arise in implementing the Rawls principles, or any others. Society might be allowed to express its preferences on the acceptability of alternative social systems, assuming that they can be clearly defined. Majority voting does not always provide an unambiguous outcome, as shown in Table 12.1.

Consider a majority voting system, with three voters, confronted with three alternative social systems, say Rawls (X), the Pareto criterion (Y), and the compensation principle (Z). Table 12.1 shows that a majority prefers X to Y and Y to Z. A government might reasonably conclude that X is preferred to Z, but this would be incorrect. A majority prefers Z to X, which illustrates the difficulties of using a majority voting system to rank social choices. Of course, it might be argued that this outcome would not arise if the government's preferences were dominant or dictatorial. Further problems arise once it is recognized that social policies will be formed and implemented in the political market place.

Table 12.1   Voting and social choices: the paradox of voting

Voters	Rank in order of preference		
	First Choice	Second Choice	Third Choice
Mr 1	X	Y	Z
Mrs 2	Y	Z	X
Mrs 3	Z	X	Y

What 'rules' should be given to politicians and bureaucrats to achieve Rawls' just distri-bution, or any other? Take the simplest problem of a fair division: society has to divide a given cake between a set number of people. If a fair division is an equal one, the appro-priate rule would be to require the person dividing the cake to take the last piece. In this case, the cake would be divided equally since this would give the cutter the largest possible share. But how is such a simple rule applied to a complex set of social institutions admin-istered by politicians and bureaucrats who might be self-interested rather than impartial? Indeed, in the Downs model, social policies are explained by the vote-maximizing behav-iour of politicians, advised by budget-conscious bureaucracies. These might be further influenced by interest groups of consumers and producers seeking preferential treatment (for example, tax exemption for house-buyers, subsidies to regions). In the political market place, democratic governments are likely to redistribute income towards the median voter and hence towards the middle of the income distribution.

Which is the Most Appropriate Form of Policy?

Once a government has decided upon its income distribution objectives, it has to choose between alternative policy instruments to achieve its targets. The broad options include cash payments, subsidies (to products or factors), or payments-in-kind, involving private or public supply. Much depends upon the government's belief about the desirability of individual decisions and its general preference for market-improving or market-displacing policies. Right-wing politicians will favour market-improving measures which allow con-sumers and workers opportunities for individual choice. Examples include negative income taxes, cash bounties, and education vouchers. Left-wing politicians often favour public ownership and sometimes believe that individuals are not the best judges of their welfare. They will favour state schools, training centres and hospitals, free milk, rent control and publicly-owned housing. The effects of these alternative policies on consumer satisfaction and the quantities purchased are shown in Figure 12.2.

Governments might regard education as a 'socially desirable' commodity and wish to increase its consumption. Prior to any policy action, the individual is initially in equilib-rium at A in Figure 12.2. If the government subsidized the price of education, the con-sumer would move to a new equilibrium at B in Figure 12.2(a): she/he will be at a higher level of satisfaction or utility, namely U_2, purchasing more education, E_3, now that it is relatively cheaper. Alternatively, the state could offer the individual a lump sum cash payment equivalent to the price subsidy of $Y_2 Y_0$. Cash payments are equivalent to income effects, and for a normal good the consumer will move to a new equilibrium at C on the

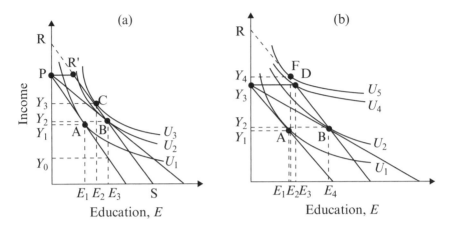

Figure 12.2   Alternative social policies. Governments might wish to increase the consumption of education. The analysis could be applied to other 'socially desirable' commodities such as health, housing or training. The diagrams show the effects on utility and amounts purchased of cash transfers (C and F), price subsidies (B), payments-in-kind and vouchers (C and D)

budget line RS in Figure 12.2(a): utility is higher than with a price subsidy, but less education is purchased and more is spent on other goods. Or the government could offer education vouchers. The voucher is a tied gift and, if it is non-tradable, it results in a new budget line $PR'S$. In Figure 12.2(a) both a voucher and cash payments give the same results, with equilibrium at C. Figure 12.2(b) shows a different case with a voucher and cash payments resulting in equilibria at D and F, respectively. Thus, if policy aims to maximize consumer satisfaction, then for a given state expenditure cash payments are preferable; but if society wishes to encourage education, price subsidies are superior.

12.3 INCOME DISTRIBUTION AND HUMAN CAPITAL THEORY

Before public policies can be formulated to improve income distribution, the causes of inequality have to be identified. Human capital theory is closely related to the study of income distribution, with earnings differentials and inequality explained by individual differences in human investments. For example, the human capital model predicts a concave age–earnings profile and simple examples are shown in Figure 12.3. These show that individuals who undertake additional years of education and/or training increase their lifetime earnings. In fact, a set of age–earnings profiles can be envisaged, reflecting the separate impact of different amounts of schooling, training and learning, each of which can occur at various points during the life-cycle. As a result, more educated and highly skilled workers will earn more than the less educated and unskilled. Thus, human capital in the form of different amounts of education and training might explain earnings differentials and inequality. Indeed, US studies have claimed that human capital explains two-thirds of annual earnings inequality, although other evidence suggests a lower contribution, perhaps around one-third. Such estimates encounter major problems

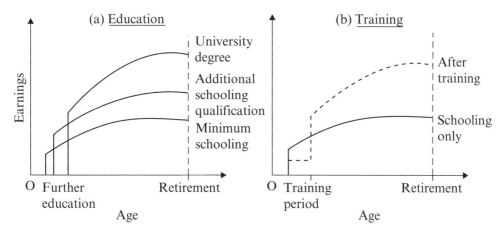

Figure 12.3 Age–earnings profiles. Diagram (a) shows that additional years of education beyond minimum schooling increases lifetime earnings. Three cases are shown: no qualifications (minimum schooling), an additional schooling qualification (e.g. certificate), and a university degree. Diagram (b) shows that individuals who undertake training after a certain number of years of schooling will receive a lower income during their training (apprenticeship), but a higher income with the acquisition of a skill

in isolating and measuring the contribution of other relevant variables such as ability, age, sex, family background and labour market imperfections. Nor must it be assumed that formal education is the only human capital input and hence the explanation of inequality. Figure 12.3 shows that industrial training cannot be ignored.

Education and Training: Are they Different?

Education and training are concerned with human investments. Both involve the acquisition of marketable skills which raise the present value of an individual's expected earnings. Skills are acquired in a variety of institutions. Compulsory schooling provides basic skills of reading, writing, numeracy and communication which are marketable throughout the economy. Thereafter, individuals can acquire further skills by continuing with formal education or by undertaking industrial or occupational training. Nor is skill acquisition confined to the younger age range. It can continue over an individual's lifecycle, although training investments will decline towards retirement since there is a shorter period for obtaining a return on the requisite human investment. The training of a typist illustrates the diversity of training arrangements. Typing skills can be acquired through self-teaching, or during compulsory schooling, or by full-time attendance at a private fee-paying college, or on-the-job, or through post-employment day release, or through evening classes in a public or private institution, or through state-sponsored retraining schemes for, say, the unemployed, or women re-entering the labour market after having children. In other words, industry and education establishments in the public and private sectors are involved in industrial training and retraining, so there is little to be gained from a refusal to recognize that these different institutions all contribute to skill acquisition.

12.4   TRAINING MARKETS: HOW ARE SKILLS OBTAINED?

Training is obtained in markets which are both varied and extensive. Training markets contain large numbers of buyers and sellers embracing a variety of courses, certificates, training methods and institutions in both the public and private sectors of the economy. In this form, the training market is the set of institutional and organizational arrangements for the purchase and sale of marketable skills through training, retraining and information acquisition over an individual's life-cycle.

The diversity of training supply arrangements reflects the varied demands of buyers, who consist of private individuals, firms and governments. Individuals have different preferences for training over their life-cycle, as well as differences in their willingness to pay to acquire skills through the use of work time or the sacrifice of leisure (consumption time). Firms also have varied demands for training, sometimes buying specialist training, including 'crash' courses from outside establishments or training workers within the plant. Governments behave in a similar way for their employees (for example, civil service, armed forces), training them within the work situation and sending them, for example, on day-release courses. Governments also affect training through intervention in the market for skill-acquisition (for example, by subsidy policy) and through direct provision (state training centres).

On the supply side, the training industry consists of private commercial establishments concerned with the profitability of training and public sector non-profit enterprises. In each sector, skills are acquired either in specialist training enterprises or in existing productive units. Various training methods are used. There is training undertaken in the work situation, through day release, evening classes, correspondence and sandwich courses, as well as through full-time further education. These training methods can be classified as learning-by-doing ('sitting-with-Nellie'), on- and off-the-job training. For many occupations the different methods offer alternative means of acquiring the necessary skills, so that there are possibilities of substitution. The combination of training methods used in practice to acquire a particular skill will depend on the preferences of trainees, occupational requirements, and the relative costs to those providing and acquiring the training. Often, the costs of training are shared in varying proportions between trainees, firms and the state.

In some nations, both private fee-paying and subsidized state training schools exist. Typically, public sector education and training courses are subsidized so that fees are less than costs or are made available at zero price and might also attract an earmarked grant (for example, university students) or a weekly training allowance. In these circumstances, questions arise about the continued existence of a substantial and specialist fee-based private training industry. A plausible explanation is that the public sector is 'failing' to fully and accurately satisfy the preferences of trainees, so that the private sector continues to exist as a viable entity in response to worthwhile market opportunities. In other words, the private sector is responding to market opportunities which are not being satisfied by the public sector. For example, the state education and training sector might limit the entry of potential trainees through various non-price rationing schemes (examination grades as an entry requirement for universities) or through a preference for specific age groups, such as the 16–21 range. Or, others might be deterred because courses are offered only on a full-time basis for a period determined by the institution when some individuals might prefer to acquire skills more quickly (crash courses) or on a part-time basis, using their leisure rather than work time and over a period chosen by the individual. And, of course, the public sector might be slow to respond to both changing skill requirements and new training methods. The result might be a viable private training industry, with fee-paying schools offering, say, language, secretarial and computing courses as well as courses in art, music, dancing and driving.

The time taken to acquire a skill varies according to the training methods and the occupation. Skills such as those of a waitress can be acquired in a relatively short time, usually measured in hours or a few days, whereas a craftsman might require a five-year apprenticeship beginning at 16. The training required for teachers, doctors and lawyers is measured in years. The successful completion of some training is recognized by the award of a certificate: Ordinary and Higher National Certificates, diplomas and university degrees. Where such certificates are treated as evidence of competence or are necessary for entry into particular labour markets, they enhance the earnings expectations of their owners. This distinguishes the markets for human and physical capital. With human capital, it is not possible to market the capital resource independently of its owner: skills can be marketed but not transferred. For this reason, certificates of skill proficiency (for example, degrees) are different from share certificates. Certificates of skill proficiency cannot be used to pass property in the skill to others, since transfer of the certificate does not transfer possession of the skill. An explanation is required of the human investment process. For simplicity, the analysis will concentrate on industrial training but the model can be extended to embrace other human investments such as further education, labour mobility and job search.

The Costs of Training: How are Training Costs Defined?

Training as an investment involves present costs. Three sets of economic agents can be distinguished, namely individuals, firms and the state, and each might be involved in training costs. Each will invest in training and retraining so long as it is expected to be worthwhile, and views on the expected benefits will depend upon labour market information on past, current and future relative scarcities.

For the individual, training costs are defined as all the direct money outlays incurred in skill acquisition, such as tuition fees, the purchase of books, materials and equipment, and any extra maintenance costs directly attributable to training. In addition, training costs include a major element which is frequently ignored, namely opportunity costs in the form of any forgone earnings which an individual incurs during the training process – that is, the difference between the trainee wage and earnings in the next-best alternative occupation. Of course, firms rather than individuals might bear the costs of training, and such costs would include the employment of training staff, buildings and equipment, any 'lost' output due to training, and the extent to which a trainee's wage exceeds the individual's current marginal productivity. Alternatively, the state might bear some or all the costs of training through, for example, 'free' or subsidized provision of education and training (for example, in universities, business schools, state skill centres). What are the likely benefits of training for these different agents?

Effectively, the returns to training investments accrue to individuals in the form of higher future income. Or, more generally, individuals benefit through the present value of the expected lifetime monetary and non-monetary gains from the sale of the acquired skill. Firms might benefit through the contribution to greater profits, and the community gains from any net social benefits such as greater output and 'education for citizenship'. However, competitive markets do not guarantee a skilled worker a higher income simply because he/she possesses a skill. The existence of pay differentials between skilled and unskilled workers depends on the relative scarcities of the different types of labour.

General and Specific Training: Who Pays for Training?

In the typist-training example given above, the costs of training are variously distributed. Individuals bear some or all of the cost (including sacrificed leisure) for 'self-teaching' and attendance at fee-paying schools and evening classes. On-the-job training costs might be borne by employers, whereas the costs of day release might be shifted to the trainee and the state, with the state bearing the costs of full-time training in government training units.

What determines the distribution of training costs between individuals, firms and the state? Here, the distinguishing feature of human capital is relevant. Although human investments are in principle similar to investment in physical capital, there is one major difference. In non-slave societies and in the absence of slavery-type contracts, the 'capital' resulting from training and skill-acquisition remains with the individual regardless of the source of finance. The property rights in training investments (and other human investments) are vested in the individual worker, so that human capital and workers cannot be separated. This has major implications for the distribution of training costs between individuals and firms and requires a distinction between two limiting cases, namely general and specific training.

General training provides a set of transferable skills which have value to a large number of firms in the economy. Specific skills are non-transferable and have value to only one firm, namely the initial training enterprise. Compulsory schooling with its provision of general competence in verbal and written skills is an example of general training. Examples of completely specific skills are hard to come by: they might include astronauts, military missile operatives, submariners and the basic induction course which most firms provide to introduce new workers to their management and organization procedures. Clearly, many skills contain a mixture of both general and specific elements (that is, transferable and non-transferable skills). For example, secretaries have a skill which is of value to a large number of employers, but each firm is likely to have a specific 'house-style'. Similarly, specific training usually contains a general element in the form of improved written and verbal skills and mathematical competence, some of which might contribute to 'education for citizenship' (with the state willing to bear some of the costs of such education).

The distinction between general and specific skills explains the distribution of training costs between workers and firms. In competitive markets, the costs of general training will usually be borne by workers, even in those cases where firms provide such training. Consider a firm which pays for the general training of its workers. To obtain a return on such training investments, it has to pay its newly skilled workers a wage less than their (current) marginal product. But rival firms who have not borne the costs of training will be willing to pay a market wage reflecting the productivity of the newly trained worker. Thus, if the training firm does not pay the market wage, it will lose its newly skilled workers to rivals, but if it pays the competitive wage it will fail to obtain a return on its training investments, which will therefore prove to be unprofitable. So, either way, the firm which pays for general training will suffer a loss.

In contrast, the costs of specific training will be borne by the firms. Such training has no value to rivals, so that the firm can pay a wage less than the marginal productivity of the newly trained labour. Similarly, without guaranteed job security, individuals have no incentive to bear such training costs, since the skills concerned cannot be marketed else-where. However, since labour is free to move, firms have an incentive to pay specifically-trained workers a wage greater than their next-best alternative in order to reduce the probability of labour turnover and so ensure that the firm captures a return on its specific human investments. The implications for age–earnings profiles are shown in Figure 12.4.

While the model is usually presented in terms of general and specific or transferable and non-transferable skills, the causal factor in the distribution of training costs is labour mobility. Predictably, firms attempt to protect any training investments through a variety of devices, some of which convert firm-general into firm-specific skills, so increasing a firm's willingness to finance what appears to be general training. The options available to firms include employment contracts, non-transferable company pensions, company houses, cars, sports, welfare and health facilities, subsidized meals, sick pay, holidays, and salaries – all related to length of service, as well as internal labour markets offering pro-motion through seniority. A local monopsony might also explain a firm's finance of general, as well as specific, training.

Slavery, the armed forces, footballers and entertainers provide examples of efforts to establish ownership, or property rights, in individuals, so increasing a firm's willingness to

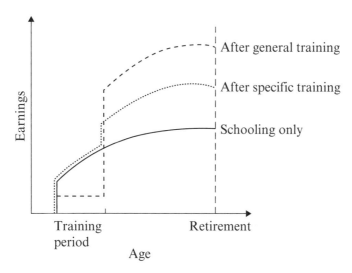

Figure 12.4   Earnings and skills. This is a simple example with only one training period and no
further training investments during the life-cycle. Generally-trained workers bear the
costs of training; hence their wage is below that paid to workers with schooling only.
Firms also finance specific training. The profile reflects the hypothesis that, ceteris
paribus, *specific trained workers earn less after training than those more*
generally-skilled.

invest in general training. But even slave societies find it costly to guarantee the productivity of labour inputs. Elsewhere, contracts might be limited or too costly to enforce. Football players are bought and sold for transfer fees, although movement to another industry means the loss of the club's asset. There are no transfer fees if a leading international footballer becomes a monk! Apprenticeships are probably the best-known example of the use of contractual arrangements to increase a firm's willingness to invest in general training. During training, the apprentice's productivity is likely to be less than the firm's training costs; once trained, the requirement to complete a specified period of apprenticeship enables the firm to recover its training investments by ensuring that the wage is less than the worker's productivity.

12.5   FINANCE FOR HUMAN INVESTMENTS: CAN INDIVIDUALS BORROW FOR HUMAN INVESTMENTS?

Firms will be willing to invest in training so long as it is expected to be worthwhile, taking into account the riskiness of human investments (due to labour mobility) and the costs of 'tying' labour to the training firm. Individuals will undertake a similar assessment of training, but they are likely to encounter a major restriction on the extent to which they can invest in themselves, namely the limitations of the capital market. Individuals have to incur present costs for expected future benefits but, in the absence of suitable collateral (for example, assets, insurance policies, property) or savings, how can they obtain funds for worthwhile training investments (or other human investments, such as job search or mobility)?

The capital market is the obvious source of finance, but problems arise because the potential trainee is unable to pledge the proposed investment as collateral (it cannot be marketed independently of him/herself) and *expected* future earnings are not a sufficiently attractive prospect to potential lenders. The market for physical capital is different since the purchaser of a new machine or a car can pledge the asset as collateral for the loan. Thus, the capital market could be a possible source of failure for human investments, the failure being more likely for worker-financed (general) training than for firm-financed (specific) training. In effect, capital market imperfections mean that workers might be unable to finance worthwhile training because the courts are likely to regard long-term slavery-type contracts as involuntary servitude; hence there are restrictions on individuals pledging future earnings as security for a loan. Perhaps the legal constraints on labour contracts should be classed not as a capital market imperfection (the market would really be failing if it ignored such legal constraints) but rather as a legal constraint on the property and exchange rights of individuals in their own skills. The result is likely to be under-investment in human capital. An example is shown in Figure 12.5.

A given skill, S_1, can be obtained with various combinations of cost (C) and time (T) inputs. A shorter training period requires greater resources and cheaper training implies a longer time-scale. A variety of iso-skill functions exist, each corresponding to different skill levels ($S_1, S_2, \ldots, S_n$). Economic agents, namely trainees, firms or the state, have to choose the optimal combination of skills, time and costs. The solution requires the ordering of these variables in terms of their expected market values to the investing agent. For simplicity, the analysis will concentrate on trainees, although it can be applied to any

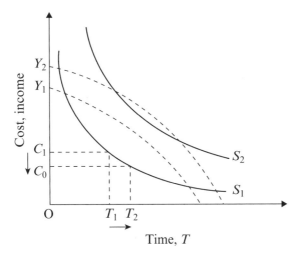

Figure 12.5 *Capital markets and training. Owing to capital market imperfections, individuals might not be able to finance their optimal training expenditures. As a result, skill S_1 might continue to be optimal, but the individual will have to substitute time for cost and select a longer training period which he can afford*

economic agent. For each skill, there will be an income or returns function showing the various present values of the expected lifetime incomes from the skill at different points in time over the individual's life-cycle. With a given discount rate, it is assumed that the expected value of the skill will decline over a person's life-cycle, tending to zero with retirement or death or obsolescence of the skill. In Figure 12.5, the present value functions Y_1 and Y_2 correspond to skill levels S_1 and S_2, respectively: $Y_2 > Y_1$ and $S_2 > S_1$ where S is measured in quality units (for example, certification). An income-maximizing trainee will aim to maximize the difference between the expected skill value and training costs ($Y - C$). In Figure 12.5, the optimal solution is to select skill S_1 with an optimal training period of T_1 at a cost of C_1. However, imperfections in the human capital market might restrict the extent to which individuals can raise funds for worthwhile training investments. If C_0 is the maximum training expenditure which an individual can finance, skill S_1 might continue to be optimal, but the individual will substitute time for cost and select a longer training period. The resort to time-intensive training methods ($T_2 > T_1$) is likely to be reflected in the use of a person's consumption time through attendance at, say, evening classes. If the capital market constraint is sufficiently great, the trainee might be obliged to select a lower level of skill, with implications for income distribution. In the circumstances, questions arise about the approximate magnitude of the under-investment in human capital and the most appropriate policy solution from alternatives such as state-guaranteed loan or equity finance to individuals, subsidies to firms, and legislative changes to permit individuals to trade the property in themselves as voluntary contracts of slavery.

Private capital markets might attempt a partial solution to the human investment problem through the use of voluntary contracts in which individuals would obtain funds for training and in return agree to repay willing lenders from future earnings. Labour mobility is a major obstacle to such a solution since it raises the transactions costs of enforcing such contracts. Transactions costs would not disappear with a state loans scheme administered through a state manpower bank. In comparing state and private financing solutions, much depends on the costs of administration, policing and enforcement for a voluntary contracts system. It has been argued that the state has a technical monopoly in this area since, if loan repayments were combined with income tax collection, the marginal costs of a state-operated loans scheme would be less than private solutions. Without quantitative evidence, this is by no means obvious. The state might have a potential cost advantage in administration and enforcement but, in the absence of competition, bureaucracies are unlikely to be X-efficient. Moreover, established public bureaucracies might lack the banking expertise required to assess individual loan applications, so that any scheme for a state manpower bank would require substantial 'set-up' costs, and it is unlikely to have the experience and comparative advantage of existing specialist financial institutions (for example, banks). Also, if a substantial private market in human investment finance were to develop, specialist debt-collection agencies are likely to emerge in an effort to minimize transactions costs. Once again there are no costless solutions.

12.6   THE PREDICTIONS OF HUMAN CAPITAL THEORY: WHAT ARE ITS IMPLICATIONS FOR TRAINING POLICY?

State intervention might be required whenever training markets are not working 'properly'. Market failure can arise because of monopolies, human capital financing problems, restrictive practices and entry barriers (for example, apprenticeships, professions). Or externalities might lead markets to provide 'too much' of some types of training and skills and 'too little' of others. For example, there might be 'too much' on-the-job specific training and 'too little' off-the-job general training; or too few engineers and scientists and too many economists. Policy could attempt to correct the situation by subsidizing 'desirable' training methods and skills. An example is shown in Figure 12.6. Governments might believe that firms are under-investing in off-the-job (general) training. In Figure 12.6 the firm's initial equilibrium is at A, where a combination of ON_1 on-the-job and OF_1 off-the-job training results in a given output of trained labour, Q_0. If the firm now receives a subsidy for off-the-job training, there will be a shift in the iso-cost line and new equilibrium at B. The movement to B comprises a substitution effect of F_1F_2 and a scale effect of F_2F_3, the net result being an expansion in off-the-job training and a larger output of trained labour.

Although private markets can fail, it has to be remembered that state solutions can also fail. Politicians are likely to be influenced by interest groups of trainers and educators who generally believe that all training is 'good' and more is 'desirable', regardless of cost. Bureaucrats might also be concerned with raising their budgets by exaggerating the demand for training and under-estimating its costs. This is most likely where specialist state agencies are established and given discretion in the formulation and operation of training policy, including the power to raise revenue by imposing taxes or levies on industry. The result could be a training policy which ignores consumer interests and which has potential for substantial inefficiency.

When applied to industrial training, human capital theory provides answers to a number of policy-relevant issues:

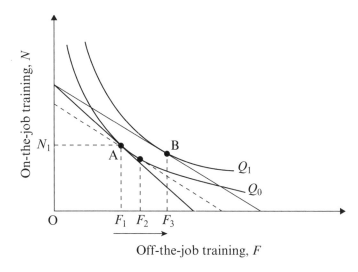

*Figure 12.6   Training methods and subsidies. Each isoquant shows the varying combinations of on-
and off-the-job training (substitutes) which can be used to produce given quantities of
trained or skilled labour (where $Q_1 > Q_0$). The subsidy to off-the-job training results in
a movement from A to B. The substitution effect $F_1 F_2$ leads to the substitution of off-
the-job for on-the-job training methods. If both training methods are normal factors,
the scale effect will reinforce the substitution effect and further increase off-the-job
training from F_2 to F_3*

*Table 12.2   A classification of training methods. Some skills can be general to a firm but specific to
an industry or an economy (e.g. linguists, lawyers), while other skills might be
marketable in many nations (e.g. doctors)*

General training	Specific training
Off-the-job training	Sitting-with-Nellie training
Schooling	On-the-job training within the plant
Further education	
Industrial training	
Economy-wide training	
State-owned training centres	

1.   Who pays for training? The costs of specific training will be borne by firms, whereas
general training will be worker- or state-financed. Table 12.2 shows different training
methods and institutions classified by their general or specific content. However, the
fact that human capital is embodied in individuals who retain the relevant property
rights during their lifetime (non-transferable at death, although information can be
transferred) is central to an understanding of the special character of the human
investment market. It is the fact that individuals are potentially mobile, rather than
the general or specific content of training, which determines the distribution of training costs between individuals, firms and the state. In other words, the general and
specific skills theorem is really a proposition about labour mobility and about the

costs of establishing (voluntary) property rights in human beings: the lower the labour turnover, the greater will be a firm's willingness to pay for training and hence the more all training resembles specific training (that is, training is treated as if it were specific).

2. How can firms avoid training costs? Firms can reduce or avoid training costs through various devices:
    (a) Training costs can be shifted to workers (general training) or to major suppliers.
    (b) Firms can substitute capital for labour – either at an existing technology or through a new technology.
    (c) Firms can recruit skilled labour.
    A firm's choice will depend partly on the relative costs of the alternatives, including any costs of transactions and search. For example, option (a) might involve bargaining, whereas (c) involves search costs which might rise, depending on the number of skilled workers demanded and the state of the labour market.

3. Are skill shortages due to poaching? Policy-makers often believe that poaching is a major cause of skill shortages. It is claimed that firms frequently poach skilled manpower from elsewhere rather than training for themselves, so that private markets under-provide training in general skills. But this interpretation of poaching assumes, incorrectly, that all training costs are borne by firms. Human capital theory shows that general or transferable skills will tend to be worker-financed, while specific or non-transferable training will be firm-financed. If poaching applies to specific skills and the training firm offers its specific trained labour a wage rate higher than the next-best alternative, how do rivals poach? Indeed, why do they poach since specific skills have no value to rival firms? If, as policy implies, poaching refers to general skills, doubts arise about the nature and extent of any loss which firms experience from the 'theft' (is it labour mobility?) of skilled labour. At the same time, under-investment in transferable skills can arise if individuals are unable to finance worthwhile training investments. But this suggests the need for a policy emphasis on the provision of finance for individual trainees!

4. What is the effect of training on earnings and income inequality? The human capital model predicts a concave age–earnings profile, reflecting the impact of schooling, general and specific training, and learning (experience). With learning-by-doing, individuals become more efficient the more frequently they perform a task, and this applies to both general and specific skills (see Figure 6.13). Learning has a number of implications for human capital theory. First, while training is expected to result in a higher future income, the income effects might be raised further and continuously (but at a decreasing rate) due to subsequent learning-by-experience. Where wages reflect marginal productivity (for example, incentive payments) the income benefits of learning tend to accrue to labour: this is likely with general skills. Second, learning means that the value of skills can appreciate with use since each application of the skill increases a worker's stock of knowledge. Third, learning shows that interruptions to production (including product changes or modifications) require workers to re-learn, and this has implications for the effects of unemployment on the market value of skills. For example, training policy which aims at short-run employment creation during the training process, regardless of the subsequent market value of the skills, is likely to have perverse results and be inefficient. If a newly-skilled worker

cannot obtain employment, he is likely to 'forget' quite quickly, with possible 'frustrated expectations' and adverse effects on both attitudes to work and the future value of government training schemes.
5. What are the implications for the education and training industry? The model predicts that the demand for post-compulsory schooling and for different types and methods of industrial training and work experience will be responsive to:
    (a) the direct and indirect costs of each of these activities;
    (b) expected variations in the earnings differentials associated with extra amounts of schooling and training; and
    (c) whether individuals can borrow for education and training investments.
    Most lending institutions require collateral for a loan but human investments cannot be separated from individuals. In the absence of suitable collateral, workers might not be able to finance worthwhile training investments. In other words, inequalities in the distribution of non-human wealth (collateral) will affect worker access to capital markets.
6. What is the relationship between training and unemployment? In a down-turn, firms will tend to 'lay off' untrained or even generally-trained workers (where no training costs are borne by the firm), while workers with specific training are less likely to be laid off (fixed or sunk employment costs, with labour as a quasi-fixed factor). The theory of labour as a quasi-fixed factor postulates that a profit-maximizing firm's sunk employment costs will be recouped through rents, represented by the difference between marginal revenue product and the wage rate. Figure 12.7 shows that the

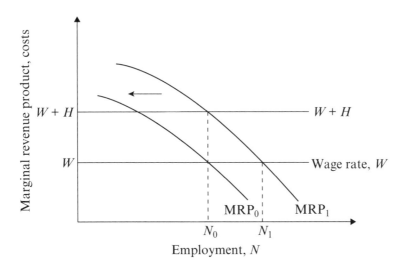

Figure 12.7   *Labour as a quasi-fixed factor where* W *is the wage rate;* H *represents fixed employment costs (sunk costs) such as search, hiring and training costs; MRP is the marginal revenue product. With sunk employment costs, the initial equilibrium is where* $MRP_1 = W + H$ *(= marginal labour costs, MLC); without fixed employment costs, equilibrium is where* $MRP = W$ *(= MLC). Consider an unexpected downturn in demand to* MRP_0. *Sunk costs are now irrelevant for short-run decisions; hence the firm with H costs will continue to employ* N_0 *(* $MRP_0 = W$ *). But where the wage rate is the only labour cost (e.g. unskilled; generally-trained workers) the firm will reduce employment from* N_1 *to* N_0

greater a firm's sunk employment costs, the smaller the reduction in employment for a decline in product demand.

12.7   CONCLUSION: HAS HUMAN CAPITAL THEORY BEEN SUCCESSFUL?

There have been major criticisms of human capital theory. Much of the research and empirical work has concentrated on education (mostly in the United States), with relatively little on training. Criticisms have been made of the failure to develop a theory of occupational choice, incorporating search behaviour (role of information). Moreover, is it really valid to maintain that human investment differs from physical capital investment? For example, although machines cannot walk, they can be bought and sold (cf. labour mobility and turnover) or even stolen (cf. poaching). Nor are a machine's performance certificates 'guaranteed' independently of labour cooperation. So caution is required in attempting to distinguish human investment from other kinds of capital investment. The essential difference lies in non-separability of human capital and the consequent problems of raising finance for education, training and other human investments.

At the policy level, some critics have concluded that education and training programmes have 'failed'. For example, it is asserted that the characteristics which economists had associated with productivity (schooling and training) appear to have had little effect on the employment and earnings prospects of large numbers of urban employees: unemployment, poverty and income inequality are still with us. Admittedly, we need to know much more about the success or failure of education and training policies and probably some of the initial claims for these policies were overstated: some studies used inadequate control groups and considered too short a post-training period.

The major criticism of human capital theory has come from the advocates of the *screening hypothesis*. The screening hypothesis asserts that education serves mainly as a screening or certification device. At the time of hiring, employers are uncertain about the potential employees' productivity, so education certificates and qualifications might be used as an initial screening device, with individuals selected on the basis of 'trainability' (rather than existing skill levels). If so, the observed correlation between earnings and length of schooling might conceal a more fundamental correlation between schooling and the attributes that characterize 'trainability' (that is, education certifies a worker's trainability). Thus, with the screening hypothesis, education simply provides a selection device for employers. In which case, is education the most efficient selection mechanism we can devise? The screening hypothesis implies waste in the system. For example, is a university degree required to signal to a potential employer that the holder of the degree possesses the personal characteristics to be a successful airline hostess? Part of the answer depends on whether education is state or privately financed. Subsidies make higher education worthwhile to students, so that labour is less available to employers at the school leaving stage. Otherwise, if education as a screening device is inefficient, the private sector might be expected to step in with superior alternatives.

Methodologically, the screening hypothesis is difficult to distinguish from the human capital model of schooling. Screening by educational qualifications means that such qualifications become worthwhile investments. Nor is it obvious whether, and how, the screening hypothesis applies to industrial training. Moreover, it is not too difficult to 'reconcile' the screening and human capital approaches by regarding education, training and other human investments as part of the economics of information and knowledge. Education and training are concerned with buying and selling information and knowledge (skills, some of which are associated with 'performance' certificates) and with the market value of information embodied in economic agents. For public policy purposes, the relevant question is whether information markets are working 'properly'.

READING* AND REFERENCES

*Ashton, D. and F. Green (1996), *Education, Training and the Global Economy*, Cheltenham, UK and Brookfield, USA: Edward Elgar.
*Becker, G.S. (1964), *Human Capital*, New York: NBER.
Blaug, M. (1970), *An Introduction to the Economics of Education*, London: Allen Lane.
Culyer, A.J. (1980), *The Political Economy of Social Policy*, London: Martin Robertson.
*Griffiths, A. and S. Wall (2007), *Applied Economics*, London: Prentice Hall, Pearson Education, chapters 13 and 14.
Hartley, K. (1974), 'Industrial training and public policy, in A.J. Culyer (ed.), *Economic Policies and Social Goals*, London: Martin Robertson.
Hartley, K. (1977), 'Training and retraining for industry', in *Fiscal Policy and Labour Supply*, London: Institute for Fiscal Studies, Conference Series 4.
Hochman, H.M. and J.D. Rodgers (1969), 'Pareto-optimal redistribution', *American Economic Review*, **59**, pp. 542–57.
Lamberton, D.J. (ed.) (1971), *Economics of Information and Knowledge*, London: Penguin, (for example, see chapters by Boulding, Stigler, Arrow, Demsetz).
O'Mahoney, M. (1992), 'Productivity levels in British and German manufacturing industry', *National Institute Economic Review*, **139**, 46–63.
Peacock, A.T. and J. Wiseman (1964), 'Education for democrats', Institute of Hobart Paper 25, London: Economic Affairs.
Rawls, J. (1973), 'Distributive justice', in E.S. Phelps (ed.), *Economic Justice*, London: Penguin.

QUESTIONS FOR REVIEW AND DISCUSSION

1. 'The test of whether a resource is an economic resource or a free resource is price: economic resources command a non-zero price, but free resources do not' (Mansfield). True or false? What are the implications of your answer for social policy?
2. What are the policy implications of a life-cycle approach to individual and group behaviour?
3. Does economic analysis offer any guidelines for social policy in the fields of education and health? Give examples.
4. What is a 'just distribution'? Has it any policy relevance?
5. Which do you regard as preferable: cash payments, subsidies (specify), or payments-in-kind? Explain your choice and illustrate with examples from (a) housing, (b) unemployment, and (c) poverty.
6. Are education and training different? Who pays for (a) education and (b) training? Are the financial arrangements for education and training efficient and equitable?

7. Does the capital market 'fail' to invest in human beings?
8. Do private enterprise economies 'over-invest' in on-the-job training and provide 'too little' off-the-job training?
9. Are student grants a product of imperfections in the human capital market? Are student loans preferable?
10. Are skill shortages due to poaching?

13. Trade unions

13.1 INTRODUCTION: WHAT IS THE PROBLEM?

Unions always arouse controversy. Critics point to union bargaining power, restrictive labour practices, overmanning, closed shops, strikes and picketing. Supporters stress their contribution to mitigating some of the less desirable aspects of free markets, such as monopsony, long hours of work, and dangerous working conditions (that is countervailing power). Marxists view wage levels as the outcome of a constant struggle between workers and capitalists (who are these groups?), with workers aiming to raise wages above the subsistence level and reduce the 'surplus value' accruing to capitalists. In fact, unions raise a set of microeconomic and public policy issues embracing efficiency in resource allocation and income distribution. Examples are:

1. The effects of unions on economic and technical efficiency. The popular belief is that unions adversely affect productivity and efficiency through restrictive practices, featherbedding, 'make-work', and barriers to labour mobility. Otherwise, if unions favourably affected productivity, there would be more instances of firms supporting the unionization of their workers.
2. Unions viewed as monopolists, with monopoly power enabling them to set wages above the competitive level. The hypothesis is that unions influence relative wages in favour of their members. This raises the empirical question of the magnitude of any wage differential compared with similar non-union labour.
3. The sources of a union's monopoly power. Unions adopt various methods to control the supply of labour. These include:
   (a) Entry restrictions in the form of lengthy apprenticeships, licences and professional qualifications (for example, doctors, lawyers).
   (b) Closed shops, where only union members are employed.
   (c) Strikes, which indicate the ability of a union to withdraw labour and to prevent labour being offered at terms less than the union wage rate (that is, to prevent undercutting or chiselling).
   (d) Lobbying governments to secure 'favourable or protective' legislation (for example, closed shops, licences; import controls for 'cheap' imports).
4. The policy implications of monopoly unions and restrictive labour practices. There are at least two issues. First, whether governments should treat monopoly unions and restrictive labour practices in the same way as they deal with monopolies, mergers and restrictive agreements in product markets. Or, is labour in some sense 'different'? Are the differences due to labour being voters in the political market? Second, questions arise about the appropriate role of the law in relation to trade union behaviour. Emphasis is often placed on industrial relations and collective bargaining and the law relating to the enforcement of contracts, the right to strike, picketing and closed

shops. Some governments use the law as an instrument for 'improving' industrial relations through, for example, the imposition of compulsory arbitration, strike ballots, and a 'cooling-off' period before a strike. Legislation might also prevent strikes in certain 'essential' services, such as the armed forces, gas supply and the police. Presumably, constraints on strike action will be reflected in the net advantages and disadvantages of a job and hence in relative wages. In total, the law affects the use of coercion by unions and the 'balance of power' between labour and capital in private enterprise economies.

The development of any public policy towards trade unions has to start from an understanding of their behaviour. Explanations are required of their existence and objectives. The sources of any monopoly power have to be identified and predictions are required about union behaviour in a bargaining context, including any constraints on their actions. Also, theory can offer a greater understanding of the efficiency implications of restrictive labour practices. Furthermore, these issues are relevant to anti-inflationary policy, particularly since the supporters of cost-push inflation models completely ignore the microeconomic foundations of union behaviour.

13.2   WHY DO UNIONS EXIST?

Trade unions and professional associations (for example, accountants, doctors, lawyers, solicitors) consist of groups of individual workers which can be compared with cartels in product markets. They can be viewed from a variety of perspectives, namely as clubs, information agencies, hedging devices, or organizations aiming to raise labour's share in the national product. It might be thought that individuals join a group or club because they expect membership to be worthwhile. In return for a membership fee, the union as a club offers a set of 'products', from information and legal services to collective agreements on wages and conditions of employment. But many of the club's products are collective goods, available to all workers, regardless of union membership. In that case, individuals have every incentive not to join a union, thereby 'free-riding' (see Chapter 2).

Public Goods and Free-riding: the Case for Coercion

Olson (1965) has argued that in so far as unions obtain any benefits, these are usually public goods. Any higher wages and improved conditions of employment negotiated by a union or professional body are available to everyone, including non-members. If so, self-interested individuals will not willingly and voluntarily contribute to the costs of a union since they will receive the benefits regardless of membership! Olson claims that large modern unions avoid collapse and remain in existence mainly through compulsion and coercion. This takes such forms as closed shops or compulsory membership as a condition of employment, together with private courts, picketing, violence, blacking and 'sending people to Coventry'. In addition, unions offer private benefits to members including insurance and welfare benefits, legal aid, assistance with job search, job protection, negotiation of seniority rights, grievance procedures and redundancy pay. For an individual, the relevant questions are the valuations which are placed on these private benefits and whether they could be obtained more efficiently in other ways. Nevertheless, Olson believes that compulsory membership and coercion are the major explanation for the continued existence of large unions.

The fact that unions provide collective benefits has sometimes been used to justify the closed shop as an acceptable form of coercion in a market economy. Like a firm, a union can be regarded as an organization for reducing transactions costs in situations where there are benefits to be obtained from exchange involving large numbers – that is, where the potential gains to exchange can be captured only with the agreement of a large number of workers. In these circumstances, union leaders claim that 'those who benefit should pay' and that coercion is required to obtain the available collective benefits and prevent 'free-riding'. This is not a completely convincing economic argument for the closed shop. There seems to be no technical or economic reason why unions could not negotiate employment contracts on behalf of their members, leaving others to reach individual bargains with their employers. In other words, exclusion is possible, but it would involve different transactions costs. Also, if a union failed to attract sufficient members, there would be an adverse effect on its monopoly power and hence its ability to obtain any collective benefits. Nor is it sufficient to claim that closed shops are justified because they are a legal requirement: the law can always be changed! However, legal support for the closed shop might be explained by the economics of politics. Vote-sensitive governments are likely to be influenced by unions combining to form a major interest group. Such groups will also oppose changes in legislation which would adversely affect their market power. Opposition might take the form of national strikes, increased militancy in wage negotiations, withdrawal from government agencies, demonstrations and the lobbying of politicians, together with newspaper and television advertisements presenting the union case. A classic example was the trade union opposition to the UK Conservative Government's 1971 Industrial Relations Act.

Unions: Information and Hedging

The analysis of unions as clubs is not unrelated to the view that they act as information agencies and hedging devices. Both information and hedging might be some of the goods provided by the club. As information agencies, unions can supply data to their members on the terms of trade in the labour market. Obviously, members will be interested in relative wage rates and the non-monetary aspects of various jobs, including the performance of rival unions. A union can also act as the workers' auditor of management, conveying information to employers about production methods and labour productivity, as well as monitoring and enforcing employment contracts. As information agencies, unions might have a market-improving function. Private competitive markets are likely to underprovide information, due to its public good aspects and the costs (difficulties) of establishing property rights in the commodity. Unions might correct some of this market failure by supplying additional information to club members. This aspect of behaviour has been further developed, with the suggestion that a union is a forum through which estimates of expected wage and price inflation are formulated and assessed. In this way, members can express their beliefs and expectations about future events, the result being a group judgement (cf. futures markets). Moreover, as agencies for formulating inflationary expectations, it has been suggested that unions and collective bargains are a technique for promoting monetary equilibrium under inflationary conditions.

Information and expectations are also related to uncertainty. In this context, a union can be regarded as a hedging device through which workers can respond to uncertainty. Given that no one can accurately predict the future, workers can respond in various ways. They can acquire a general skill or move to an area of excess labour demand. Or they can attempt to establish and protect the property rights in their job by joining a union. Nevertheless, information and hedging are not the generally accepted reasons for the existence of unions. Traditional explanations stressed the contribution of unions to raising wages. Once again, these are one of the collective goods available to club members.

Unions: Wages and Labour's Share

The standard view is that unions aim to raise labour's share in the national product and to achieve this at the expense of profits. This argument involves three stands. First, has labour's share increased? Second, do unions explain any increased share? Third, has any increased labour share been at the expense of profits? There are, of course, limits on the extent to which unions might successfully 'squeeze' profits in a capitalist economy. Firms can respond to higher wages by substituting capital for labour or raising product prices and, ultimately, capital requires a minimum return to induce it to remain in an activity. Neoclassical theory explains factor shares in terms of quantities employed and their relative prices or marginal productivities. In competitive markets, an increase in the relative price of labour will lead to its substitution by a relatively cheaper factor. Labour's share will depend upon the responsiveness of employment to the increase in relative wages, as determined by the elasticity of substitution. If this elasticity is less than unity, factor substitution will be difficult and, following a rise in wage rates, labour's share will increase. The general relationship between wage rates, labour income and total product is shown in Figure 13.1.

Traditionally, economists were impressed by the apparent historical constancy of the share of wages in national income. An explanation was provided by the Cobb–Douglas production function (1928):

$$Q = AK^a L^b$$

where Q is output, A refers to the state of technical knowledge, K measures the stock of physical capital, L is labour input, while a and b are constants representing the shares of capital and labour, respectively.

In this model, the elasticity of substitution is unity, which implies constant factor shares. In addition, with constant returns to scale, the sum of the marginal products exactly equals the total product (that is, the 'adding-up' problem is solved). Such a result is compatible with a perfectly competitive equilibrium so long as firms are operating at the minimum point of a U-shaped long-run average cost curve. Using this approach, labour's share was estimated historically, at between 60 and 75 per cent of national income and this seemed to 'fit the facts' in a number of countries, such as Australia, the United Kingdom and the United States. If, as the model suggests, the shares of labour and capital are constant, it implies that trade unions are unable to influence labour's aggregate share.

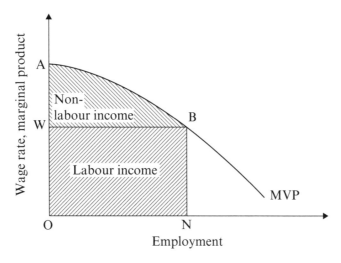

Figure 13.1 Labour's share. In a perfectly competitive economy in long-run equilibrium, wages will equal the value of the aggregate marginal physical product (MVP). The total value of output produced is the area OABN. Labour's income is OWBN and the income accruing to other factors is WAB (i.e. profit and other property incomes). Labour's share of the total product is OWBN/OABN. Readers are left to examine the short- and long-run effects on labour's share of an increase in wage rates with different slopes of the MVP curve

However, the Cobb–Douglas production function has been subject to both analytical and empirical criticisms. Doubts have been expressed about the concept of the aggregate production function for the whole economy and generalizations based on empirical results from manufacturing. There are difficulties of measuring and valuing the total stock of physical capital. Critics point to the limiting assumptions of a perfectly competitive equilibrium, constant returns to scale, and a unit elasticity of substitution. Further problems arise in measuring technical progress and adjusting for human capital inputs. In addition, since the mid-1960s, new evidence has emerged. This shows that in most Western nations labour's share of the national product actually increased for some time into the 1980s. Such estimates include both wages and salaries in determining the share of pay. Also, the rising share occurs regardless of whether or not the imputed earnings of the self-employed are included in the definition of labour's share.

Evidence for the United Kingdom is shown in Table 13.1. It can be seen that over the long run, labour's share in the United Kingdom has risen from 47 per cent for 1910–1914 (it was 45 per cent in the 1860s) to some 70 per cent in the 1970s, followed by a declining share in the 1980s (coinciding with the Thatcher Conservative Government). However, from the 1980s to 2002, there was a small increase in labour's share (an average of 64.3 per cent for 1981–89 and 67 per cent in 2002) and a corresponding fall in the profit share (an average of 29.3 per cent for 1981–89 compared with 24 per cent in 2002: Begg et al., 2005, p. 217). Simple arithmetic shows that for any nation a rising labour share must be accompanied by a fall in the share accruing to other non-labour groups (that is, property income). However, this does not necessarily mean that labour's rising share was achieved at the expense of the corporate profits component of national income. Other non-labour

318 *Factor markets and policy*

Table 13.1 Labour's share, United Kingdom

Years	Income shares of GNP (%)				
	Labour (wages and salaries)	Income from self-employment	Rent	Corporate profits	Net property income from abroad
1910–14	47.3	16.2	11.0	17.1	8.4
1921–24	58.5	17.2	6.8	13.0	4.5
1935–38	58.9	13.2	8.8	15.0	4.1
1946–49	65.3	12.3	4.0	16.8	1.7
1955–59	67.0	9.2	4.5	18.0	1.3
1964–68	67.6	8.0	6.4	16.8	1.2
1976	71.3	9.3	7.0	15.4	1.1
1981	67.9	8.7		23.4	
1989	63.8	9.1		27.1	
2005	64.7	10.3		25.0	

Notes:
(a) Due to the residual error of national income accounting, the 1976 data sum to more than 100.
(b) Some of the years were selected to show the possible impact of major wars.
(c) Data for 1981–2005 are based on a different series. They are based on factor shares as a percentage of gross value added at factor cost. For these data, three groups are shown, namely, compensation of employees (labour), gross operating surplus (profits) and other income. In the table, other incomes are shown under income from self-employment and are regarded as proxy variables for self-employment income (Griffiths and Wall, 2007, p. 264).

Sources: Burkitt and Bowers (1979, p. 61). Reproduced by permission of Macmillan, London and Basingstoke. Griffiths and Wall (2007, p. 264).

groups could have experienced a decline (for example, the self-employed and rent). This might be acceptable to trade unionists, especially if their objective is more widely interpreted as raising labour's share at the expense of property incomes in general. But do unions explain the periods when labour's share rose?

Why might Labour's Share Increase?

Consider a period when labour's share has increased. Various explanations have been offered, with unions forming only one of a number of explanatory variables. Part of the increase could reflect measurement biases. Structural changes in an economy might involve a shift towards labour-intensive sectors such as services and government, with the latter appearing to be especially labour-intensive due to the difficulties of valuing government capital assets (for example, roads, military bases and weapons). Studies show that, even after adjusting for these measurement problems, labour's share has increased substantially. Alternative theories of distribution have also emerged to explain the facts: these include a production function approach, macroeconomic theories, monopoly firms and bargaining models.

A generalized production function approach to factor shares concentrates on the roles of technical progress, relative factor prices, and the elasticity of substitution. Over the long-run, technical progress has been substantial, causing major shifts in production functions and affecting both physical and human capital. Technical progress in the capital goods industries could have contributed to a fall in the relative price of new capital goods. Also, it is possible that past innovation has depleted the opportunities for further labour-saving, relative to capital-saving, technical progress. If so, the resulting capital-saving innovation will lead to a smaller proportion of capital in the input mix and a corresponding rise in labour's share. At the same time, the rising share for labour has been accompanied by an observed increase in real wages and an associated fall in the relative price of capital. This suggests an elasticity of substitution of less than unity. Unions might have entered this process through any possible effects in raising relative wage rates and, also, through restricting the possibilities for factor substitution. Alternatively, some of the increase in labour's share might reflect greater inputs of human capital.

Some critics of the production function approach have formulated a macroeconomic model of distribution (for example, Kaldor, 1955). Such models show the contribution of aggregate demand and the different savings propensities of capitalists and workers. It is assumed that the propensity to save out of profits is greater than the savings propensity of wage-earners. In this model, total savings out of a given income form the adjustment mechanism. If planned investment exceeds intended savings, then the required increase in total savings will be achieved by raising profits relative to pay. For example, firms will eventually respond to excess aggregate demand with higher prices and profit margins, so increasing the profits share in national income and hence raising actual savings to the required level. Trade unions appear to have no direct influence in this macroeconomic model of distribution. Moreover, the model might be more appropriate as an explanation of cyclical, rather than long-run, variations in income distribution. Its lack of any microeconomic basis is a further cause for concern.

Other models of distribution are microeconomic and stress the contribution of monopoly firms and bargaining power. With profit-maximizing monopoly firms, it has been hypothesized that the share of pay will vary inversely with the degree of monopoly power (Kalecki, 1954). Monopoly firms can set prices to earn abnormal profits, so that the share of profits is likely to be higher as the amount of competition in an industry declines. After reviewing the international evidence, one economist concluded that 'the general drop in the share of profits between 1914 and the 1920s does not seem to have been accompanied by the heightened competition to which monopolistic pricing theory would attribute it' (Phelps-Brown, 1968, p. 28). Once again, this model has no direct role for unions. In contrast, bargaining theories of distribution recognize that both parties to a wage bargain have the ability to dictate the terms of exchange. Unions have, of course, attempted to acquire bargaining power through becoming monopoly suppliers of labour. Superficially, the international evidence seems impressive, with the long-run historical growth of unions and of militancy which seems to have coincided with labour's rising share. But correlation must not be confused with causation. Indeed, the reverse causation is plausible with higher wage rates resulting in increased union membership. And satisfactory tests of the quantitative effects of unions on labour's share require the specification of a model which incorporates other relevant explanatory variables. Some of these other influences have been outlined above, such as technical progress and relative factor prices. Additional explanatory variables might include the effects of major wars (see Table 13.1), international competition, globalization, a shift from manufacturing to services, and extensions in the role of the state, particularly in the adoption of full-employment policies. In total, the available evidence on the effects of unions ranges from zero to some impact on distributive shares. A sample of verdicts is:

1. 'No union influence on labour's share can be detected' (Rees, 1973, p. 220).
2. 'From the complex of influences affecting income distribution union activity does not appear to have been decisive, though it was significant in the UK under certain conditions at certain times' (Burkitt and Bowers, 1979, p. 72).

Finally, in assessing the evidence, a distinction might be made between the long- and short-run impact of unions on factor shares. For example, in the United Kingdom there was a substantial fall in the share of profits of manufacturing companies from 21 per cent of output in 1968 to under 4 per cent in 1976. Some economists (Bacon and Eltis, 1979) have explained this in terms of workers resisting further cuts in personal consumption. It is argued that between 1961 and 1969, market sector workers financed the growth of the non-market sector (for example, public sector; see Chapter 14) from their personal consumption. By 1969, workers' consumption was squeezable no more and they responded to extra taxes by successfully squeezing the share of profits. Apparently, this was achieved through negotiating prices and incomes policies with governments which were unfavourable to profits; through the introduction of new legislation which reinforced property rights (for example, employment protection); and through strengthening the influence of the militants in the trade union movement. The possibility that unions influence governments through their effects on labour market legislation and prices and incomes policies can also be related to the economics of politics. Tentative hypotheses have been developed suggesting that, *ceteris paribus*, money wage rates grow faster under left-wing governments. Nor can evidence on membership trends be ignored. In the UK, trade union membership rose in the 1970s reaching a peak in 1979, after which it fell substantially. UK trade union membership fell from over 13 million in 1979 to 7.5 million by 1997 (Shackleton, 2005, p. 32). The decline reflected the shift from manufacturing to services, reductions in the size of the public sector, including privatization and increased female participation in the labour force (with women in part-time jobs more difficult to organize in unions).

In addition to the possible contribution of unions to increasing labour's share, there is a further possibility. Unions might have obtained higher wages at the expense of unorganized labour, as well as at the expense of consumers and those who lose their jobs.

Unions: Relative Wages and Unorganized Labour

Monopoly unions might be expected to raise the wages of their members but such increases might be at the expense of unorganized labour, so resulting in a redistribution between different labour groups. The predicted effects of a union on relative wages and the allocation of labour are shown in Figure 13.2.

If wages rise in the union sector, employment falls and the labour released causes wages to fall in the unorganized industries. Once unions have fully exploited their monopoly power, the wage differential is likely to be a once-and-for-all effect. The resulting misallocation of labour and welfare losses as represented by lost output are shown by the shaded area in Figure 13.2.

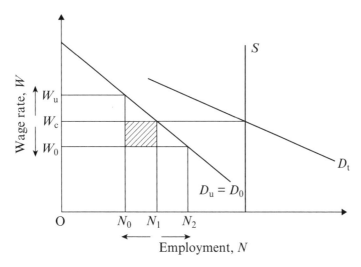

Figure 13.2 Union wage differentials. Consider an economy with a fixed supply of homogeneous labour, S. The demand curves for the union and unorganized sectors are identical and represented by $D_u = D_0$ (union and unorganized, respectively), giving a total demand curve of D_t. Initially, there is a competitive equilibrium with wage rate W_c, each sector employing N_1. Assume a union is formed which raises wages to W_u; employment in the union sector falls to N_0. If labour markets clear, supply in the unorganized sector will increase and wages will fall to W_0; employment in this sector rises to N_2. In this simplified model, the area under each demand curve up to the employment level represents the total product of each sector and the reduction in total output is shown by the shaded area, i.e. about one-half of the wage differential multiplied by the employment change

Evidence from UK and US studies confirms the historical existence of a union-non-union differential, but there are disagreements about the precise magnitude and whether it remains in the twenty-first century. In the USA, the union relative wage advantage is in the region of 10 to 20 per cent and is larger than for other countries. For example, for 1985–87, the union wage gap was estimated to be 18 per cent for the USA, compared with 10 per cent for the UK, 6 per cent for West Germany and 5 per cent for Austria (Ehrenberg and Smith, 2000, p. 508). For the UK, estimates suggest a union wage 'mark-up' of 9 per cent for males in 1991 and zero in 1999, and for women, the comparable figure was 16 per cent in 1991 falling to 10 per cent in 1999 (Shackleton, 2005). Estimation difficulties abound. The direction of causation might be from higher wages to greater unionization, rather than the opposite. Similarly, variables other than trade unions can result in higher wage rates. Examples include differences in labour quality (for example, skills, motivation, males–females) and in the non-monetary aspects of different jobs, as well as any increased demand for labour. Failure to incorporate these other influences in empirical work might lead to 'overestimates' of the wage effects of trade unions. More fundamental problems concern the 'counter-factual': what would happen to wage rates in the absence of unions? Without unions, pay would differ from the income accruing to unorganized labour simply because unions affect non-union wages by means of spillover effects (see Figure 13.2). Thus, while the evidence suggests that wage rates are higher where the labour force is covered by a collective bargain compared with a completely 'uncovered' industry, some caution is required before accepting the precise quantitative estimates. A further qualification is required. Much of the above analysis of the existence of unions assumed implicitly that they aim to raise wages. Is this a satisfactory specification of their objectives? If not, what are they trying to maximize?

13.3 THE OBJECTIVES OF UNIONS AND PROFESSIONAL ASSOCIATIONS

As with firms, various objective functions are plausible. Unions might be trying to maximize wage rates, or employment or membership (that is, growth and size of union), or the wage bill. Or they might be maximizing a general utility function containing both monetary and non-monetary aspects of employment. Such a generalized preference function might consist of wages, jobs, hours of work, fringe benefits, together with hiring, firing, training and promotion procedures, as well as agreements on working practices and discipline. Alternatively, unions might be satisficers, aiming at target levels of wage rates, membership and union funds. Some of these objectives are not easy to interpret. For example, it is sometimes suggested that unions act like profit-maximizing monopoly firms. An example is shown in Figure 13.3 where, acting like a profit-maximizing firm, the union raises wage rates

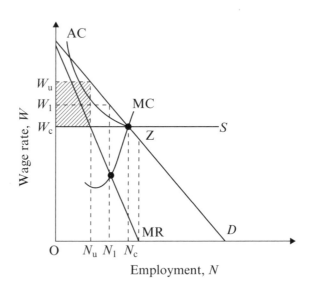

Figure 13.3   *A profit-maximizing union. Initially, the market is competitive, with* W_c *and* N_c *representing the equilibrium wage rate and employment. Assume that labour is unionized (costlessly) so that S now represents the supply curve of union labour to one firm. The marginal revenue curve (MR) shows the effect on the total wage bill of variations in wage rates. Acting like a profit-maximizing monopolist, the union would equate MR and the supply price of labour (= marginal labour cost), setting the wage at* W_u*. But if monopolization involves costs, the appropriate average and marginal cost curves for a monopoly union might be AC and MC. If so, the new equilibrium combination is* W_1N_1*. In contrast, point Z maximizes the wage bill*

above the competitive level. But what is the meaning of the shaded area in Figure 13.3? The surplus could be distributed to the union, or to its members, or shared between both parties. It could be appropriated by the union in the form of membership fees, so that the union acquires funds, or it might be distributed as windfall gains to members.

Similar analysis is required of alternative objective functions. A desire to maximize the wage bill would involve setting employment where marginal revenue is zero, corresponding to point Z in Figure 13.3. Whether the resulting wage rate is above or below the competitive level will depend on the elasticity of labour demand at the competitive position. Clearly, if this objective involves setting a wage below the competitive non-union level, the union is unlikely to survive! Difficulties also arise where a union adopts a simple objective such as maximizing wage rates. With this objective, the logical implication is to continue raising wage rates until the union has only one member. Such behaviour would be costly to police, since the union would have to prevent increasing numbers of unemployed members from 'undercutting'. Nor is it clear how, with falling employment, the union would retain its monopoly power. Indeed, once voting, political and bureaucratic elements are incorporated into the analysis, it is unlikely that such a simple objective would be pursued.

The Internal Organization of Unions

Trade unions usually consist of elected officials operating in a political market place determined by the union's constitution. The voting arrangements, together with the period of tenure and the employment contract for union leaders, will influence their motivation and behaviour. For example, where skilled and unskilled workers are members of the same union but the latter form the majority, then the median voter model predicts that union policy will favour the unskilled. However, where union officials are elected for life, they have greater opportunities for discretionary behaviour and the pursuit of 'goods' which enter more directly into their utility functions. Examples might include salary, luxury offices, expense accounts, union cars, secretarial staff, on-the-job leisure, and the prestige from negotiating with governments (for example, political honours). Even in this situation, there are constraints on the independent, discretionary behaviour of union officials. Members can express their preferences through lobbying or forming opposition groups within the union, or they can resort to unofficial action (for example, unofficial strikes). As a result, a utility function might emerge (how; whose?) reflecting a concern with, say, employment as well as wage rates; an example is shown in Figure 13.4. But simple propositions about unions raising wage rates require an examination of the sources of their monopoly power.

13.4 UNIONS AS MONOPOLIES

Theory would define a monopoly union as a single seller of labour with no close substitutes (see Figure 13.3). Since these are the characteristics which define a monopoly union, it has to be presumed that they can be readily identified and observed in actual labour markets. Consider the definition in more detail, beginning with the concept of a single seller. Are single sellers prevalent in actual labour markets?

Once it is recognized that there is a multiplicity of union types, the concept of a single seller is by no means straightforward. Nor is the identification of the relevant labour

Factor markets and policy

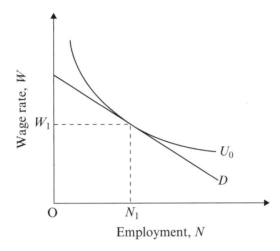

Figure 13.4   A utility-maximizing union. A union is faced with a downward-sloping labour demand function, D. Higher wage rates result in lower employment. If it has a utility function, $U = U(W,N)$, its utility-maximizing combination will be W_1N_1

market. For example, in the United Kingdom there are few industrial unions which are the sole suppliers of labour to one industry. Elsewhere, there are professional associations and craft unions which attempt to regulate the supply of certain categories of skilled labour; there are white collar unions; and there are general unions which recruit all workers, particularly semi-skilled and unskilled. But the general union tends to resemble a conglomerate firm which is large in absolute or aggregate terms. If this is the case, there are worries about using aggregate unionization as an indicator of monopoly power in an individual labour market.

Questions also arise about the process through which any monopoly union emerges. After all, if individual workers have different preferences, there would appear to be opportunities for a competitive number of unions in a market. Paretians might regard large numbers and diversity as 'socially desirable', but from the viewpoint of an individual union, competition and competitive wages are unattractive! They are likely to respond with inter-union agreements to avoid competition (for example, no poaching agreements). Mergers between unions are a further possibility and will occur so long as each party regards a merger as worthwhile and mutually beneficial. Such developments might even be supported by governments. Politicians and bureaucrats might believe that a merger movement will reduce transactions costs or the costs of 'doing business' with the unions (for example, negotiations on industrial relations legislation, the welfare state, and prices and incomes policies). A reduction in the number of recognized bargainers might also contribute to the desire for a 'quiet life and on-the-job leisure' by governing politicians and bureaucrats. Monopoly power also depends upon the possibilities of substitution which face unions. Here, there are extensive possibilities, all of which create problems for unions seeking to establish and maintain their monopoly position:

1.   Non-union labour might be substituted for union labour.
2.   Capital can be substituted for labour.

3. Technical progress can result in labour-saving innovations as well as extending the possibilities for replacing skilled with unskilled labour. An emphasis on de-skilling might result in the extinction of a single-skill craft union whose skills become obsolescent. Examples include locomotive firemen and Glenn Miller-type dance bands whose music is replaced by that provided by pop groups with electronic aids.
4. Firms can substitute foreign locations for domestic locations (for example, direct investment overseas; globalization; outsourcing overseas).
5. Consumers can buy close substitute products, either from domestic or foreign sources of supply. As a result, there is a higher probability that unionized firms will become bankrupt in the short or long run.

To maintain their monopoly power, trade unions and professional associations respond to these substitution possibilities. They can introduce restrictions on factor substitution. Examples include the use of firemen on diesel locomotives, minimum manning requirements on new machinery (for example, for 'safety'), a minimum period of training, apprenticeships, requirements for nationality, certification, and professional qualifications, as well as the introduction of a closed shop. In other words, to maintain its monopoly, a union can try to raise the costs to the firm of factor substitution (that is, it can try to make it relatively costly to replace union labour). In addition, unions can support tariff protection and import controls, restrictions on overseas investment, state subsidies for domestic industries, together with public ownership. Furthermore, the union movement as a whole can form a major interest group to influence vote-sensitive governments. For example, as a collective body, the union movement can lobby for legislation which establishes and protects a worker's property rights in his/her job (for example, legislation on closed shops, employment protection and redundancy pay). Unions can also support the extension of the public sector. After all, public sector output is often difficult to measure (for example, health, safety, defence) and activities are not subject to competition from rival firms. Bureaucrats and managers of state industries do not have any income incentives to resist union demands. And the costs of public sector wage increases can always be distributed among large numbers of taxpayers, where specific labour outlays form only a small component of public expenditure (see Chapter 14). Given that unions have monopoly power, how are they likely to behave in a bargaining situation?

13.5   UNION BARGAINING AND CONSTRAINTS

Typically, unions bargain in a bilateral monopoly situation where a firm as a sole buyer faces a union as a single seller of labour services. Often, bargains occur at the national level and embrace employer and union representatives. Economic models of wage bargaining under bilateral monopoly usually give indeterminate outcomes (see Chapter 2 on the Edgeworth box and Chapter 9 on game theory). An example is shown in Figure 13.5, where the union wage demand exceeds the employer's offer. The result is collective bargaining, with the outcome depending on such factors as bargaining skill, learning-by-experience, bluff, game strategy, and the expected costs and benefits of strikes and lockouts. As a result, wages appear to be determined by bargaining factors rather than market forces.

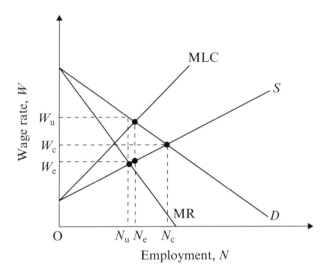

Figure 13.5   A bargaining model. Labour demand and supply curves are represented by D *and* S,
respectively, and the competitive equilibrium is W_cN_c*. A profit-maximizing union will
equate marginal revenue (MR) and marginal cost as represented by the union's labour
supply curve,* S; *it will aim to sell* N_u *at* W_u*. If the employer's group is a monopsony it
will equate marginal labour cost (MLC) with marginal revenue product, requiring* N_e
labour at a wage rate of W_e*. Thus, the union wants* W_u *and the employer's offer is* W_e

Strikes

In a bilateral monopoly bargaining situation, each party has to assess the expected costs
and benefits of agreeing or disagreeing. Strikes and the threat of strikes are the major elements in a union's bargaining power. In principle, a union will strike if it is expected to be
worthwhile (that is, if the present value of the expected gain over the contract period
exceeds the expected costs). Gains will take the form of a higher wage rate or the monetary equivalent of improved job conditions, while the costs will consist of the income
losses associated with a stoppage. Some of these income losses might be reduced if strik-
ers or their relatives can obtain state welfare payments, or support from union funds, or
if other members of the household (for example, wives/partners) enter the job market.
Strikes are, of course, designed to impose costs on employers through lost profits, liquid-
ity problems, and a loss of consumer goodwill.

When bargaining, both unions and employers have to guess the other's aims, valuations
and sticking points (that is, their preference functions). Although information emerges
during the bargaining process, some of the signals and messages can be deliberately distorted as each party struggles for an advantage. Threats of strikes and lockouts are
obvious tactics. However, it is significant that in the real world collective agreements pre-
dominate. In other words, determinate outcomes are typical. In such circumstances, some
economic models suggest that strikes are mistakes. Strikes can occur through accidents
and miscalculations, where one or other party is overoptimistic and incorrectly assesses
the other's preference function and sticking points. Some strike activity might also be
required to remind management of the effectiveness of union threats. Typically, collective

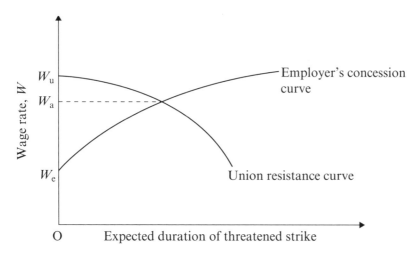

Figure 13.6   Bargaining and strikes. The Hicks model is based on union resistance and employer concession curves dependent upon the expected length of a strike. The employer's initial offer is W_e and the union's first claim is W_u (see Figure 13.5). Skilful bargaining results in a wage W_a, which is greater than the employer's initial offer but less than the union's first claim

bargaining starts with a union claim which exceeds the employer's initial offer (see Figure 13.5). Collective bargaining involves each party adjusting its initial bid until an agreement is reached. Consider a model in which the adjustment process depends on the expected length of a strike. Unions can be viewed as having a resistance curve showing the minimum wage rate which they would accept rather than undergo a strike of a given duration. This curve slopes downwards, indicating that a union will accept a lower wage rate the longer the expected length of a strike. Similarly, employers will have a concession curve reflecting the highest wage rate which they will be willing to pay rather than accept a strike. The shape of the curve will be determined by the costs of agreeing to a union wage demand compared with the costs of resistance as reflected in a strike. The firm's concession curve slopes upwards, showing that the employer will be willing to pay higher wages in order to prevent increasingly lengthy strikes. An example is presented in Figure 13.6. Interestingly, using simplifying assumptions, one economic model (Hieser, 1970) has estimated that a determinate outcome of the bargaining process will be achieved at a wage rate corresponding to an elasticity of labour demand of minus 5/3!

Empirical work on strikes has to start with an appropriate definition of strike activity. Possible measures include the number of stoppages, the number of workers involved, or the number of working days lost, each within the year, with appropriate adjustments for total employment (for example, number of stoppages a year per 100 000 workers employed). Much of the resulting empirical work is ad hoc. Equations are estimated containing a variety of plausible economic explanatory variables, such as unemployment, profits and plant size, together with money and real wages as well as inflation rates. Some of the results suggest that unemployment has a negative effect and increasing plant size a positive impact on strike records. But strikes are not the only option for unions. They can 'work to rule', ban overtime, 'go slow', and resist new working procedures. Such behaviour has implications for public policy towards strikes. Where strikes are made less attractive, unions can respond by substituting other forms of action and behaviour. Such responses are also likely where employers attempt to protect themselves through the creation of private strike insurance schemes.

The Employment Effects of Union Wage Increases

Are there any limits on the ability of monopoly unions to raise wage rates? Labour demand curves are a major constraint since higher wage rates for some members will be achieved at the expense of lost jobs for others. The magnitude of any adverse employment effects resulting from a higher wage will depend upon the elasticity of demand for union labour. As originally developed by Marshall (1890), this elasticity is determined by four conditions:

1.   the elasticity of demand for the product (that is, the good being produced);
2.   the importance of union labour in production costs;
3.   the ease of substituting other factors of production, including non-union labour, for union workers (i.e. the elasticity of substitution); and
4.   the elasticity of supply of the cooperating factors of production.

   In general, the greater is each of these four conditions, the larger will be the elasticity of demand for union labour. As a result, the greater will be the adverse employment effect of a union wage increase. It follows that union power to raise wage rates without major job losses requires an inelastic product demand plus labour forming a relatively small part of total production costs, together with difficulties in substituting other factors for union labour and an inelastic supply of cooperating factors. Such conditions are also likely to explain the growth of unions, since they indicate the potential benefits from collective action (but the costs of organizing should not be neglected). Airline pilots, doctors, lawyers, teachers, and maintenance workers in capital-intensive industries are examples of groups where conditions are potentially favourable to union power. In the case of certain essential public services, where demand is inelastic, the state might constrain union power through 'no strike' legislation. Examples might include the armed forces in wartime, police and gas workers. Elsewhere, unions can attempt to create these favourable conditions. For instance, in an oil crisis miners in a state-owned coal industry can increase their bargaining power in a strike through picketing and so prevent supplies reaching coal-fired electricity generating stations. Also, they can obtain the support of dockers in 'blacking' coal imports. In this way, a miner's union can impose substantial costs not only on coal consumers but also on the rest of the community (for example, via disruption of national electricity supplies to firms and households). However, such action might only result in short-run gains. Nuclear power might eventually replace coal as a source of electricity. Governments can also respond through stockpiling coal at electricity stations and changing the law on picketing.
   Where the elasticity conditions favour a union or professional association, the resulting wage increase will represent a windfall gain for those who retain their jobs. But the higher wage rate will attract other workers and new entrants to the labour force. Entry restrictions will exist. As a result, queues will develop of workers willing to pay the costs of entry, whether in money or time. Bribes and lobbying costs might be required to secure

preferential treatment in the market. Eventually, the costs of entry will be 'bid up' until the successful entrant secures no higher return than could be obtained elsewhere. In other words, the higher income in the union-restricted occupation is required to compensate for the entry costs. This does, of course, add a further qualification to the interpretation of the observed wage differential between union and non-union labour. It also means that once a person is successful in entering the restricted occupation, he/she will support the union and its existing practices for life: otherwise they will earn less than normal profits on their investment in securing entry (see Chapter 12).

Are there any Exceptions to the Adverse Employment Effects of a Union Wage Increase?

In addition to the conditions outlined above, there are three further cases where higher union wages do not necessarily result in job losses. These are associated with imperfect markets and embrace the 'shock effect', monopsony and oligopoly (see Chapter 11 on minimum wage laws). The shock effect depends on the existence of organizational slack or X-inefficiency in firms. Inefficiency is likely to arise in imperfect markets where there are no competitive or environmental influences forcing firms to minimize costs. In this situation, it is argued that a union wage increase might shock the firm into greater efficiency, with no job losses. Such possibilities are not unlimited and will be exhausted once a firm reaches its efficient production function. At the policy level, government prices and incomes policies can have a shock effect. Where slack exists, a state prices and pay board might approve union wage increases but prevent firms from raising prices.

In monopsony markets, there exists a range over which wages might be increased without any adverse employment effects. An example is shown in Figure 13.7: a union

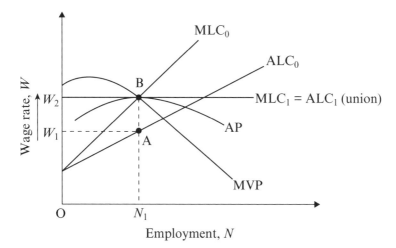

Figure 13.7   *Unions and monopsony. A profit-maximizing monopsonist will equate marginal labour cost with marginal value product (for simplicity, assume a competitive product market). Employment will be N_1 and the wage paid W_1. Monopsony profit is shown by $W_1 ABW_2$. If labour is now unionized, wages can rise to W_2 and employment remains unchanged. Effectively the union insists that all labour be sold at a uniform wage, so ending the difference between marginal and average labour cost*

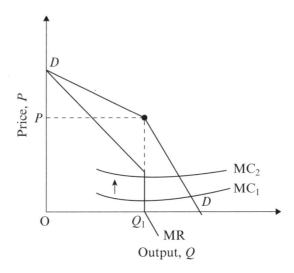

Figure 13.8   Unions and oligopoly. A profit-maximizing oligopolist will produce Q_1. If a union wage increase raises marginal costs from MC_1 to MC_2, price and output, and hence employment, will remain unchanged

ensures that labour is only sold at a uniform wage where marginal and average labour costs are identical. In practice, the opportunities for such wage increases depend on the existence and extent of monopsony in labour markets. Possibilities are airline pilots, teachers and nurses where there exist state-owned airlines and state-run education and health services, respectively. Other examples include one-company towns, professional sport, astronauts and military manpower. Such examples are by no means universal. In Western economies, labour markets are characterized by alternative employers and by mobility, so that the monopsony case can be exaggerated.

Finally, oligopoly markets provide further opportunities for union wage increases without job losses. The kinky demand model results in a range of indeterminacy in an oligopolist's price-output decisions (see Chapter 9). Over this limited range, it is possible for an oligopolist's marginal cost curve to shift upwards (for example, due to union wage increases), without any effect on price and output. An example is shown in Figure 13.8. However, while oligopoly is often believed to be a typical market form, their price-output behaviour will depend upon the objective function. Even if the kinky demand model is accepted, unions are unlikely to have sufficient knowledge to enable an accurate estimation of the magnitude of the range of indeterminacy.

13.6   UNIONS: RESTRICTIVE LABOUR PRACTICES AND EFFICIENCY

The popular view is that unions impose restrictive labour practices which adversely affect productivity and result in allocative and technical inefficiencies. Governments wishing to achieve an optimal allocation of resources have to be aware of the extent of such practices in an economy, the union rationale for their existence, and their likely effect on firm behaviour and the operation of labour and product markets. Union-created restrictive labour practices are often extensive, ranging from entry requirements to rules relating to working conditions and, ultimately, dismissal. They affect the hiring, utilization and dismissal of labour, as well as its mobility. Well-known examples are lengthy apprenticeships, certification requirements, closed shops, demarcation, featherbedding or make-work, together with seniority and redundancy rules. Explanations for the existence of unions and professional associations have already been provided, including the contribution of such practices to maintaining monopoly power. But what are the likely effects of such practices on firm behaviour and labour markets? Two examples will be analysed, namely featherbedding and the effects of unions on labour supply.

The Economics of Featherbedding

Featherbedding can be defined as a labour working rule which causes a firm to hire or retain more labour of a certain type than it would otherwise at the ruling wage rate. Unions often introduce featherbedding rules in response to the threat of a decline in employment resulting from, say, technical progress or a decrease in demand. Firemen in diesel locomotives are a classic example; others occur in printing, dockwork and airline pilots. Consider the simple case where a union secures a wage increase and the firm wants to respond by reducing employment, as shown in Figure 13.9. Assume that the union insists that employment remains unchanged. A profit-maximizing firm will be prevented from achieving a tangency position. As a result, the firm will incur higher costs to achieve a given output and this will be represented by an upward shift in its average cost curve. In

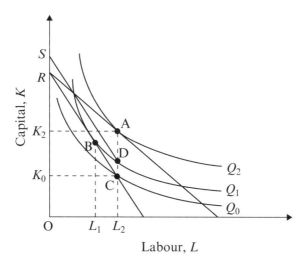

Figure 13.9   Featherbedding. The diagram shows isoquants and isocost lines. Initially, a profit-maximizing firm is in equilibrium at A. When wage rates rise, the firm's long-run equilibrium will adjust from A to B and employment will decline from L_2 to L_1 with the new output at Q_1. The union insists that employment remains at L_2. If the firm's expenditure is unchanged, it will locate at C, with K_0 capital and output falling to Q_0 (corner solution). To produce Q_1, the firm has to raise its expenditure (by RS), locating at point D, which is not a tangency position

addition, the increased wage rates will raise marginal costs, so leading to higher prices. Such restrictive labour practices are an obvious source of X-inefficiency. They are likely to be prevalent in monopoly industries and in markets which are protected from foreign competition, including the public sector (see Chapter 14). Furthermore, the economics of politics suggests that in public enterprises and firms receiving state assistance, there could be government and bureaucratic complicity in featherbedding. It might be too costly for politicians and bureaucrats to 'attack' overmanning, particularly in high-unemployment areas. Costs will be incurred in the form of lost votes, less leisure, and smaller budgets for the affected bureaucracy. Even so, governments with an interest in the efficiency of resource allocation cannot ignore the extent and magnitude of featherbedding in an economy. Unfortunately, few quantitative economic studies are available. One historical estimate concluded that unionization adversely affected productivity in the UK coal industry (Pencavel, 1977). A totally unionized coalfield produced some 20 per cent less output than a completely non-unionized field. It was also suggested that in the mid-1970s, output losses due to unionism in the rest of the UK economy were likely to be greater!

Union Restrictions on Labour Supply

Unions can also affect the labour supply of their members through imposing constraints on hours worked. This can affect the utility levels of workers. Two examples are presented in Figure 13.10. In case (a), individuals are not allowed to work more than a specific number of hours, so effectively imposing an income limit. Case (b) shows a situation where a union requires a reduction in hours worked following an increase in wage rates: the individual is unable to respond by supplying more effort. Both examples in Figure 13.10 result in workers being unable to achieve their preferred combinations. Unionists

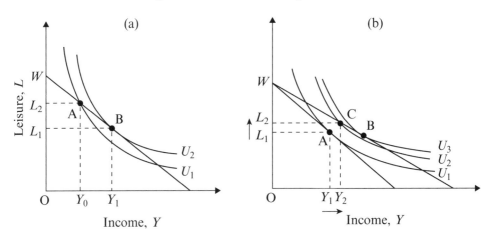

Figure 13.10   *Unions and hours worked. In diagram (a) the union prevents an individual from working more than WL_2 hours. Thus, he is constrained to position A when his preferred position is B, i.e. at A he has to accept lower income, more leisure, and hence lower utility (U_1) compared with B. In diagram (b) the individual is initially in equilibrium at A. Assume a union achieves a wage increase and requires a reduction in hours worked to WL_2. Thus, the individual moves to position C which results in higher utility, but his preferred position is B*

would, of course, reply that collective action results in the attainment of a higher budget line and greater utility than could otherwise be obtained, even though some individuals cannot achieve preferred combinations of income and leisure.

13.7   CONCLUSION: IS THERE A NEED FOR GOVERNMENT INTERVENTION?

Nations differ in their policies towards trade unions. At one extreme there is a preference for a comprehensive legal framework governing collective bargaining, strikes, picketing and closed shops. An alternative is a system of voluntary collective bargaining with the state supporting reforms through publicity and persuasion. Instead of examining specific solutions, this section will show how the methodology of economic policy can be used to appraise any government policy towards trade unions. The policy problem has to be defined, its causes identified, and a solution chosen from a set of alternatives.

The market failure paradigm suggests that governments aiming at optimum resource allocation will intervene wherever there are substantial imperfections or externalities. Monopoly and oligopoly unions, restrictive labour practices, and mergers between unions are obvious examples of imperfections. Similarly, significant externalities can arise through strikes and picketing, particularly where the actions involve firms, workers and consumers not directly involved in a dispute. Explanations of such union behaviour and its predicted effects have been outlined in this chapter. Such understanding is obviously central to the formulation of any public policy. If a government wishes to improve the operation of labour markets it needs to intervene to correct these failures. Union-created imperfections can be removed through some form of discretionary or non-discretionary anti-monopoly policy which could also embrace union mergers and restrictive labour practices. Externalities can be internalized through legislative changes making it unlawful for unions to use secondary picketing, blacking and sympathy strikes to inflict damages upon parties who have nothing to do with a dispute. Such policies are, in fact, often used in product markets. For example, state regulatory agencies frequently criticize monopoly and oligopoly firms for excessive profits, entry barriers, restrictive agreements, inefficiency and a failure to innovate. Applying similar competitive criteria to unions and professional associations would require consideration of the rate of return on union membership, entry conditions, featherbedding, and other restrictive labour practices as well as a union's contribution to technical progress. However, in some instances, particularly with professional associations, it will be claimed that a restrictive agreement is required to protect the public against injury, damage, dishonesty and incompetence. Examples include accountants, doctors, lawyers, solicitors and teachers. Such arguments require critical appraisal. Are consumers rather than suppliers not the best judges of what is in their own interests? Also, some economic models of regulation suggest that the beneficiaries are likely to be suppliers rather than consumers. Regulation protects an established group from competition from so-called 'quacks, cowboys, and inferior suppliers offering services for gain and reward'. But are professional groups not motivated by gain and reward? There are also worries about competition within an established profession. Some groups restrict advertising, thereby making it difficult for consumers (who are supposed to benefit?) to obtain information on alternative suppliers. Further restrictions on competition occur through the fixing of standard fees, the failure to publicize charges, and resistance to new ideas and technical change. Claims are sometimes made that professional groups employ non-professionals to undertake their work, often without supervision. Examples might include conveyancing work for houses, the preparation of accounts, and the treatment of sick patients (for example, doctors' receptionists make judgements about the urgency of telephone calls for attention and appointments; see Chapters 5 and 8).

Why might a government be unwilling to subject trade unions and professional associations to the type of anti-monopoly policy it operates in product markets? There are at least three interrelated possibilities. First, governments are usually concerned with distributional objectives and not solely allocative efficiency. Unions might be seen as agencies for achieving a desirable redistribution of income between labour and other groups. This objective is likely to differ between right- and left-wing governments. It also raises questions about the role of taxation as a redistributive instrument. Second, policy-makers might regard unions as second-best constraints, so that the standard rules for a Pareto optimum are no longer appropriate. With this argument, difficulties arise in determining whether current policy is achieving a second- or nth-best solution. Questions also arise about the nature of the union constraint. If the constraint is policy-created and supported, it implies a preferred outcome. An unwillingness to change policy raises questions about the aims of the government, and leads to a third possibility. Third, policy might be explained by the economics of the political market place. Unions as a whole represent a major interest group with substantial votes. They are also attractive to politicians and bureaucrats because of the opportunities they seem to offer for negotiating vote-winning anti-inflationary pay policies and a 'quiet life'. But if a vote-sensitive government accepts unions as a policy-created constraint, are there any options for state intervention?

One possibility would be to implement an active pro-competition policy in product markets. Competition could be used as a policing mechanism to induce management and employees to reduce X-inefficiency (complete elimination might be too costly). Further opportunities exist for the use of indirect policies. Labour market measures, designed to improve resource re-allocation, might contribute to the acceptance of change, particularly if they reduced the costs imposed on workers. Examples include state income-deficiency payments and training and mobility policies. Alternatively, the state could 'buy out' restrictive labour practices. Such a policy might be rationalized in terms of the compensation principle (see Chapter 2). A related possibility would give state subsidies to firms to guarantee job security, the belief being that this would eliminate restrictive practices. But in the case of restrictive labour practices, why is state intervention required? Why can firms not buy out restrictions through, for example, productivity bargaining? Moreover, these policies focus on restrictive practices which form only one dimension of the trade union 'problem'.

Governments are also concerned with the environment for collective bargaining and the procedures for solving industrial disputes, particularly strikes. Legal solutions are sometimes advocated. These involve the enforcement of contracts and compensation for damages due to breach of contract, including damages arising from secondary picketing and sympathetic strikes (Veljanovski, 2006). Problems arise where such solutions are introduced into a system of voluntary collective bargaining. Unions view legal changes as an attack on their traditional powers. In addition, difficulties arise in determining the responsibility for a strike and its consequences; whether any damages and fines should be paid by the union or individual officials; and whether breaches of the law constitute criminal acts with the possibility of imprisonment. Given such problems, industrial democracy solutions have been proposed. These can take various forms, including worker directors, supervisory boards, joint consultation, and labour-managed firms (see Chapter 7). The supporters of industrial democracy believe that it will reduce industrial conflict and raise productivity by removing restrictive labour practices. Critics claim that it will have adverse effects on private investment as investors will require a higher return to compensate for the perceived greater risks. There are also fears of adverse effects on labour-saving technical progress and great inflationary pressure in labour markets (due to greater union bargaining power). Clearly, there are opportunities for microeconomists to examine the causal relationships in these competing hypotheses and to determine their empirical validity.

READING* AND REFERENCES

Bacon, R. and W. Eltis (1979), 'Britain's economic problem: an interchange', *Economic Journal*, June, 402–15.
*Begg, D., S. Fischer and R. Dornbusch (2005), *Economics*, Eighth edition, London: McGraw-Hill.
Burkitt, B. and D. Bowers (1979), *Trade Unions and the Economy*, London: Macmillan.
Cobb, C.W. and P.H. Douglas (1928), 'A theory of production', *American Economic Review*, **8**, March, 139–65.
*Ehrenberg, R.G. and R. Smith (2000), *Modern Labor Economics*, Reading, Mass: Addison-Wesley.
Griffiths, A. and S. Wall (2007), *Applied Economics*, London: Prentice-Hall.
Hieser, R.O. (1970), 'Wage determination with bilateral monopoly in the labour market', in J.E. King (ed.) (1980), *Readings in Labour Economics*, Oxford: Oxford University Press.
*Hyclak, T., G. Johnes and R. Thornton (2005), *Fundamentals of Labor Economics*, Boston: Houghton Mifflin.
Kaldor, N. (1955), 'Alternative theories of distribution', *Review of Economic Studies*, **23**, 94–100.
Kalecki, M. (1954), *The Theory of Economic Dynamics*, London: Allen and Unwin.
Marshall, A. (1890), Principles of Economics, 8th edn, London: Macmillan.
Olson, M. (1965), *The Logic of Collective Action*, Cambridge, Mass: Harvard University Press.
Pencavel, J. (1977), 'The distributional and efficiency effects of trade unions in Britain', *British Journal of Industrial Relations*, July, pp. 137–56.
Phelps-Brown, E.H. (1968), *Pay and Profits*, Manchester: Manchester University Press.
Rees, A. (1973), *The Economics of Work and Pay*, New York: Harper.
Shackleton, J.R. (2005), 'The labour market under "New Labour": the first two terms', *Economic Affairs*, **25**(3), 31–8.
Veljanovski, C. (2006), 'The economics of law', Hobart Paper 157, Institute of Economic Affairs, London.

QUESTIONS FOR REVIEW AND DISCUSSION

1. Why do unions and professional associations exist? Should public policy treat unions and professional groups differently?
2. Which models of trade union and firm behaviour 'best' explain any recent strike with which you are familiar? Does the same model(s) explain why collective agreements emerge without strikes?

3. Predict the effect of the formation of a trade union on a firm's pricing, employment, and investment behaviour. Explain how you would test the predictions of your model.

4. What are the sources of union monopoly power? Does your analysis suggest that public policy should treat union monopolies differently from private monopolies in product markets? Do professional associations merit special treatment?

5. Does labour deserve 100 per cent of the national product?

6. Explain the decline in UK trade union membership since 1979.

7. (a) Have unions and professional associations raised the wages of their members?
   (b) If so, how and at whose expense?

8. (a) Are closed shops in the 'public interest'?;
   (b) Are licensing and certification desirable for some professional groups? Explain why and which groups, if any.

9. How many monopoly unions can you name? Carefully explain the economic criteria used in your selection and identify the sources of each union's monopoly power.

10. Are restrictive labour practices and strikes 'undesirable'? Is state intervention required to solve these problems? Why and, if so, what is the most appropriate form of state intervention?

PART E

Public choice

14. Do votes determine policies? A public choice perspective on policy

14.1 INTRODUCTION

In Western economies, governments perform many activities ranging from the management of aggregate demand, incomes and prices to the direct provision of goods and services such as defence, police, education and roads. Economists often try to explain and justify the extent of government activities in terms of market failure. In this context, a concern with the 'public interest' or maximizing community welfare might require governments to intervene to reduce monopoly power in product and factor markets, to provide public goods, and to correct externalities (see Chapter 2). Ideally, governments should undertake activities in which they have a comparative advantage. For example, even in private enterprise economies, governments are required to create 'law and order' for the enforcement of contracts enabling mutually advantageous trade and exchange in private markets. But it is not obvious that the market failure analysis satisfactorily explains the whole range of any government's activities at the federal, central, state or local levels. Why, for example, do governments often supply goods and services which could be *provided* by private firms (for example, arms; refuse collection; transport; R&D establishments)? While there might be a case for *state finance* of some socially desirable activities (which?), it does not necessarily require government supply. Nor can it be assumed that government services will be operated by public spirited officials, devoid of self-interest, responding to the public will and dedicated to the achievement of the public interest. Indeed, it is paradoxical that economists were willing to apply the self-interest utility-maximizing postulate to private markets, but seemed to assume that individual behaviour somehow changed in public office! Developments in the economics of politics and bureaucracies provide an alternative explanation of the extent and form of state intervention in Western economies. How are behaviour, and ultimately choices and decisions, affected by the political market place? Are public policies determined by voters or by producer groups and bureaucracies; and what are the implications of the political market place for the size and efficiency of the public sector?

The economics of politics is an example of the application of standard microeconomics to the political market place and the problem of collective choice. In this model, policies are the result of a process involving a search for votes by political parties, further influenced by the budget aims of bureaucracies supported by interest groups with a monetary involvement in the outcomes.

This analysis concludes that governments *can fail*. It is especially relevant since the political mechanism is often advocated as an alternative to markets as an allocative device (for example mixed economies; socialism). In addition, the public sector influences and affects the operation of private markets (for example, procurement policy, regulation: see

Chapters 8 and 15). Thus, we need to know how the public sector works and the efficiency of its operations.

14.2   A TAXONOMY

The political market place can be analysed like any other market. It contains buyers and sellers undertaking mutually advantageous exchange within the constraints determined by the constitution. And even the constitutional constraints can be changed through, for example, the electoral process or dictatorial edict. In democracies, the market is one where political contracts are negotiated and revised. Voting can be regarded as a contract and the political market can be analysed in terms of the contractual process, its specification, and associated commitments. For any analysis, we need to know:

1. the agents in the market place;
2. the objectives of the agents; and
3. the market structure in which the agents operate.

The Agents

Political markets contain voters, parties, bureaucracies and interest groups. Voters, like consumers, demand goods, services and policies from the governing party and they supply factors of production directly (for example, public sector employment) or indirectly via taxation. Political parties can be regarded as firms: each party is a potential supplier of policies, with taxes representing prices. The winning party in an election becomes the actual supplier and its plans are implemented by the bureaucracies responsible for such products as defence, education and roads. As a result, the governing party demands factors of production from households and supplies goods and services. Policies might, however, be influenced by interest groups of producers and consumers. Examples include employers and professional associations, trade unions, high unemployment areas, low profit industries, large government contractors, the education, farming, health, old age pensions and road lobbies, as well as environmental groups and consumer protection movements. Nor are interest groups confined to national entities. International organizations, such as the EU, IMF, NATO and the UN, can be elements in the domestic political market place.

The Objectives of Agents

Any analysis of behaviour requires a specification of the objective function of the relevant decision-makers. Like consumers, voters are assumed to maximize the expected satisfaction or utility to be obtained from alternative policies, taking into account their prices through direct charges and taxation. In principle, voter preferences are determined by the same influences which affect consumer tastes and preferences in the theory of demand (see Chapter 5). Citizens will vote for the party which they believe will provide them with a higher utility from government activity. But voters are subject to knowledge and information constraints. They have to acquire information which involves search costs, and they have a limited capacity to store knowledge. This provides an opportunity for producers and other interest groups to influence policy. Producer groups, for example, can use their specialist knowledge to provide detailed and persuasive information, showing political parties that their activities are in the 'national interest' and make a 'socially desirable' contribution to jobs, advanced technology and the balance of payments (and hence votes). Questions also arise as to why individuals vote (where voting is voluntary). After all, the direct benefits of voting are relatively small in that one vote is unlikely to affect the outcome and the transaction costs are not trivial. Information has to be acquired about alternative candidates, and resources (time and possibly spending) are required for a visit to the polls. Presumably, individuals vote because the costs of voting are relatively small, especially if voters do not acquire much information about the candidates or if a visit to the polls is combined with other activities, or the perceived benefits of voting could make it worthwhile (for example, voting might be enjoyable; see also Chapter 5).

Political parties offer policies in exchange for votes; hence, it is often assumed that parties are vote-maximizers. Politicians are assumed to be self-interested, using policies to achieve the rewards and satisfactions of office, rather than seeking office to implement preconceived policies. Of course, vote-maximization is a simplifying assumption which can be modified to reflect different constitutions, collective decision rules and the costs of attracting voters. Parties might aim to maximize the number of elected representatives or a majority of seats. Similarly, in a winner-takes-all election, each candidate might plan to obtain 51 per cent of the votes or simply more votes than his greatest rival, always assuming that a candidate knows the number of votes for his rivals! Expressed more generally, it is assumed that the governing party will be seeking re-election and the opposition will be striving for office. Clearly, at an election, competing parties have to choose how to allocate their available resources and candidates between different constituencies where the probabilities of success range from almost zero to 100 per cent. The larger parties might gain scale economies in, for example, advertising, fund-raising, and the employment of specialist research and information staffs. Even so, parties are likely to find it too costly (and not worthwhile) to aim for 100 per cent of the votes! Similarly, a party might regard it as worthwhile to contest a seat where it has little chance of winning. The marginal cost might be relatively low and there are possible benefits in continuing to demonstrate a national presence and in using such constituencies as a training ground for new candidates.

Once elected, the policies of the governing party are implemented through the bureaucracy. However, a government can find that it is costly to achieve compliance with its objectives. How can a President, a Prime Minister, a Cabinet or a Secretary of State ensure that their wishes are actually implemented? Problems arise because bureaucrats are experts on the possibilities of varying output, as well as on the opportunities for factor substitution. Although some of these substitution possibilities can result in perverse outcomes for a government (assuming that they have a clear idea of their policy objectives), they might be too costly for any individual minister to monitor, police and eliminate completely. In this way, bureaucracies can affect the quantity and efficiency of public sector output. Government bureaucracies are defined as non-profit organizations in the public sector and they embrace ministries, departments and other state agencies (including international organizations such as the UN and IMF). Economists have now developed economic models of bureau behaviour which offer testable propositions. A starting point was the assumption that bureaucrats are budget-maximizers. Such an objective enables bureaucrats to satisfy their preferences for salary, power, patronage, public regulation and the perquisites of office. This behavioural assumption can relate to either the absolute or relative size of the bureau (that is, the bureau's budget relative to the government's total budget). Further modifications have been based on a more general utility function in which bureaucrats exhibit a preference for staff *inputs* and organizational slack, as well as output. In total, the economic models suggest that bureaucrats have incentives and opportunities for satisfying their own preferences rather than those of the voters. They will obviously favour bureaucratic solutions in the belief that all such solutions are 'good' and more are desirable, regardless of cost. Examples include support for the public regulation of private industry, for administrative procedures to control inflation, for economic planning, and for redistribution in kind rather than cash. Predictably, bureaucrats will oppose 'hiving off' their activities to the private sector. However, the situation is complicated by the fact that government employees are voters and thereby constitute a substantial interest group.

Interest or pressure groups try to influence government policy in their favour. For example, producer groups might try to 'buy' monopoly rights by 'purchasing' protection from competition. They lobby for tariffs and import controls, or the regulation of prices and restrictions on the entry of 'unreliable' firms offering 'inferior and unsafe' products (for example, pharmaceutical products or drugs). Producers are the beneficiaries rather than consumers (cf. air fares). Effectively, there is trade and exchange between governments and interest groups (a negotiations democracy?). In this situation, governments can be regarded as supplying favourable legislation to groups which outbid their rivals. A group will be willing to pay a 'price' which reflects the expected value of the protective legislation to its members. Payment may take the form of cash contributions to the governing party, votes, bribes, or the supply of persuasive information, including advertisements and specialist consultancy reports, as well as payments-in-kind through the provision of campaign speakers and accommodation for political meetings. Information is especially important in explaining the role of interest groups. Vote-sensitive politicians have to be well informed of public opinion. Where voter preferences are diverse and uncertain, politicians are likely to incur substantial costs in collecting information. In comparison, interest groups are well informed in their specialist areas, so providing a low cost source of expertise to vote-conscious politicians. This is most attractive if the group has a large membership. Moreover, legislation promising benefits to an interest group is likely to attract the support of group members. But if interest groups appear so influential, why are there not more of them? Presumably, the number and size of groups is partly explained by the transaction costs of forming and maintaining them. If these costs were reduced, more groups would be formed. Costs are incurred in establishing the organization to obtain collective goods, such as favourable legislation. There are costs of identifying potential group members, communicating between them, bargaining about the distribution of benefits, as well as the outlays for staffing and policing the group. Free-riding is a major problem, particularly for large groups.

Since the benefits of government policies are available to all (public goods; see Chapter 2), no individual has an inducement to be a member of a specialist group – in which case, groups would not exist! This led Olson (1965) to conclude that unless the group is small or there is coercion or some incentive to make individuals act in their common interest, then self-interested individuals will not act to achieve their common or group interests. Certainly it cannot be concluded that *groups* will be self-interested simply because *individuals* are self-interested. A lobbying organization, a trade union, a professional association, or any other body working in the interests of a large group of firms, or workers in an industry, would receive no assistance from self-interested individuals in the industry. But if this is the case, how do we explain the existence of large groups (for example, trade unions, doctors)? According to Olson, large and powerful lobbying groups are usually the *by-products* of organizations which obtain their support and income either through coercion or by offering private (that is, non-collective) benefits to individual members. For example, there might be legal requirements that practising lawyers must be members of the appropriate bar association (cf. a closed shop). Other professional bodies such as doctors, accountants and architects have the authority to govern themselves by specifying minimum standards and qualifications for practitioners, as well as the power to discipline members who fail to maintain the requisite ethical standards. Membership of a professional body might also provide valuable private benefits through access to insurance on favourable terms, professional support in the event of negligence and malpractice suits, and the provision of technical journals and conferences. Thus, both coercion and inducements are used to maintain large organizations which can then act as a lobby and pressure group.

Market Structure

Finally, analysis of the political market requires consideration of the market structure in which each agent operates. Both political and economic factors will influence structure. A nation's constitution will determine its voting and collective choice rules and, within such constraints, the costs of transactions will further affect market structure (see Chapter 7). An assessment of structure involves consideration of:

1. The number of voters and political parties in the market (that is, buyers and sellers). Are there large or small numbers?
2. The size distribution of voters and parties in the market. Is any party or voter large in relation to the size of the market?
3. Entry conditions. Can new voters and parties enter the market or are there entry barriers? If there are entry restrictions, why do they exist and what form do they take? For example, only registered citizens over the age of, say, 18 might be allowed to vote. There might also be barriers to the entry of new political parties through, say, legal restrictions on access to television.
4. The form of competition in the market. Do political parties compete in price or in non-price forms? Changes in taxation and direct charging are the major price variables. Other forms of competition and product differentiation include public expenditure, subsidies and policies to improve or replace the operation of private markets (see Chapter 2).

A structural analysis enables markets to be classified according to their degree of competition or the lack of it. Questions then arise about the performance of the political market place and the extent to which it results in a Pareto optimum. How do political markets compare with private markets and competition?

14.3 THE PERFORMANCE OF POLITICAL MARKETS

Political markets can be compared with the perfectly competitive model. Like firms, parties offer policies to voters in exchange for votes. If political markets were perfectly competitive, parties would compete and eliminate abnormal political 'profits', where these take the form of discretionary behaviour reflected in the pursuit of supplier interests rather than those of the voter. Thus, with large numbers of relatively small voters and political parties and no entry restrictions, the political market would result in a competitive solution (Pareto optimal), with parties responding to the wishes of voters. But, just as private markets can 'fail', so too can political markets. Various imperfections exist in the political process which affect adversely the extent to which the system fully and accurately satisfies voter preferences. Some of these imperfections are also points of contrast with private competitive markets and they include:

1. Competition in democratic political markets is infrequent and discontinuous. Usually, voters make a binding decision resulting in the election of government for a fixed or maximum term of office. In other words, voters cannot re-contract daily (cf. shopping at supermarkets).
2. Competition in the political market is of the 'all-or-nothing' type. The majority party obtains the *entire* market, whereas in private markets, buyers who are in a minority might still be able to purchase from their preferred firm.
3. The nature of contracts in political markets. Voters cannot 'bind' politicians to an agreed, and clearly specified, set of policies; hence elected representatives have discretion. They can choose when to implement their election promises, they can rank policies, and they can select people who might never be subject to direct electoral representation (for example, judges, bishops, police and defence chiefs). Moreover, the actual revelation of voter preferences can be affected (distorted) by the electoral system. Votes are often for a package of policies rather than specific issues (for example, general elections compared with a single issue referendum). A voter might prefer one party's views on social welfare spending but a rival party's views on taxation, privatization and defence. Which should be chosen and what does the choice reflect about a voter's true preference ordering? Further opportunities for discretionary behaviour arise because a majority voting system can fail to establish a clear, unambiguous ordering of society's preferences or its social welfare function (see Chapter 12, Table 12.1).
4. The supply side is imperfect. In some democracies, there are only two or three effective parties so that political competition is imperfect. Significantly, in private markets, the presence of duopoly or oligopoly would be regarded as a source of market failure. Also, once elected, the governing party becomes a monopoly supplier for its term of office.

In assessing the political process, a major methodological difficulty arises in that *actual* political markets are compared with *ideal* competitive solutions in private markets. This has led to the criticism that comparisons are being made between muddle and model when it would be more appropriate and accurate to compare *actual* institutional arrangements (that is, imperfect political processes and imperfect private markets; imperfect private markets and imperfect state enterprises). Constitutions can, of course, differ in providing varying opportunities for the political process to reflect and satisfy voter preferences. For example, alternative voting rules are possible, such as unanimity, proportional representation, or majority voting; there could be general and primary elections, or referenda, together with opportunities for voting at federal or central as well as state and city or local elections. Economists can contribute in this area by analysing the implications of different voting rules. Consider the unanimity rule. It seems particularly attractive for Pareto optimal solutions. A society which has a public sector and tax policy which is Pareto optimal will be unable to alter such a policy if a change requires unanimous support. With a Pareto optimal solution, any change must make at least one person worse off, so that one citizen will vote against the change, hence preventing it. Similarly, any public policy which receives unanimous support must result in an actual Pareto improvement. But a unanimity rule is likely to result in the status quo: policy is unlikely to change. In contrast, majority voting allows policy changes which are *potential* Pareto improvements. A change which makes three individuals better by £100 each and one worse off by £3, would have a majority in its favour, and the potential gainers would be able to overcompensate the potential loser. But this is not always the outcome. Majority rules can accept policy changes in which the potential gainers could not overcompensate the losers. In such a case, the potential losers might then find it worthwhile to bribe the potential gainers to vote against the change!

Political markets also generate other devices allowing voters to register their preferences and so overcome any apparent deficiencies in the community's voting rules. The possibilities including log-rolling, political participation, interest groups, private provision and mobility. Log-rolling is a vote-trading arrangement whereby individuals exchange their less urgent for their more urgent desires. Legislator A might offer to support B's favourite policy in return for similar support from B when A's preferred policy is being considered. In this way, the intensity of preferences can be registered and there are opportunities for mutually advantageous trade and exchange. This raises the possibility of introducing more specific and complete contractual arrangements into the political market place. Attractive though such contracts might seem (cf. private markets where you agree to pay a firm £x for painting your house at a specific time and an agreed quality), they are likely to be extremely costly to write, execute and enforce.

Where citizens are dissatisfied with the existing parties, they could respond by increased political participation. This might involve starting a new party or trying to change the position of an existing party, depending on the relative costs of the alternatives. Or, interest groups might enable individuals to achieve gains which would be too costly to obtain through the voting mechanism. Or, individuals might respond to government deficiencies by seeking the private provision of goods and services, and the formation of voluntary clubs (for example, swimming, tennis, golf). In the last resort, people can always move to a different locality or country, or they can organize a revolution (all of which are costly).

Further understanding of political markets can be acquired by analysing the behaviour of parties and bureaucracies. What are the predictions of the economists' models of politics and bureaucracies? Are these predictions consistent with the facts?

14.4   ECONOMIC MODELS OF POLITICS

A major contribution to developing economic models of politics was Anthony Downs' *An Economic Theory of Democracy* (1957). It assumes that voters are utility-maximizers and that political parties are vote-maximizers. Voters will compare the present value of the expected satisfaction from the re-election of the present government with that which might be obtained if the rival parties were in office. Citizens will vote for the party which they believe will provide them with the highest utility. Voters might reach their decisions about *future* performance by considering a government's *past* record in relation to its original promises and the beliefs about how well the opposition would have performed in the same period.

In seeking votes required for office, vote-maximizing political parties have the task of identifying the preferences of citizens. The median voter theorem provides a starting point for the analysis of party behaviour. Assume a decision is required on a single major issue and that opinion can be represented on a political spectrum ranging from left to right (socialist to conservative). Each voter has single-peaked preferences, such that he/she votes for the candidate closest to this preferred position. Voters are assumed to be normally distributed across the political spectrum, as shown in Figure 14.1. With two parties and majority voting, both parties will adopt the policy favoured by the median voter. In other words, two-party competition and majority voting satisfies voters in the middle or the centre rather than voters at either extreme of the political spectrum. The problem for political parties is to identify the exact location of the middle of the distribution! For economists, there are also questions concerning the *determinants* of the distribution of voters across the political spectrum and the long-run stability of the distribution.

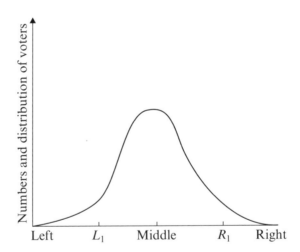

Figure 14.1   Consensus politics. Vote-maximizing parties, seeking office, will not locate at the extremes of the political spectrum, say L_1 and R_1. Each can gain more votes by moving towards the centre. Just like oligopolists, parties will tend to cluster towards the centre of almost any distribution of demand (see Chapter 9, Figure 9.9). Marginal cost functions could be imposed on the diagram, showing the costs which each party has to incur to acquire extra votes and reach the centre

Alternative distributions are possible. For example, the mass of voters might be almost equally divided between each of the political extremes; or voters might be fairly evenly distributed across the whole political spectrum, so resulting in a multi-party system. But are such distributions determined by economic factors in the form of information and transactions costs for voters and parties, or by history, or by ideology, or by sociological factors such as the 'balance of class forces'?

The Predictions of the Models, Examples and Evidence

The economics of politics models give a number of predictions which are relevant in explaining microeconomic policy:

1. In a two-party democracy, both parties agree on any issues favoured by a majority of voters. Consensus politics tends to emerge, with both parties offering similar and vague policies which are less directly linked to an ideology than in a multi-party system.
2. Where the median voter is decisive, redistribution will be towards the *middle* of the income distribution.
3. The voters who are best informed on any policy issue are those whose income is directly affected by it (that is the income-earners in the area likely to affected by policy changes). Such voters are likely to be less informed on policies that affect them as consumers. As a result, the policies of democratic governments tend to favour producers more than consumers.

  In two-party systems, there are numerous examples of consensus politics. Parties might adopt similar policies towards discrimination in the labour market, minimum wage legislation and training, as well as towards rent control, support for domestic defence industries and monopolies, mergers and restrictive practices policy. However, parties will try to differentiate their policies; otherwise they would be identical and non-rival (they behave like duopolies in, say, the soap powder business). A socialist party will tend to favour more public ownership and state solutions, while conservatives will prefer more privatization and laissez faire policies. Neither party will move to the extremes of the political spectrum, namely complete socialism or unbridled free enterprise: such extremes are prevented by the potential losses of moderate voters. Nor is the evidence on this hypothesis restricted to casual empiricism. A study of the UK Conservative and Labour Parties in the elections between 1924 and 1966 concluded that both parties had tended to move nearer to each other and that a process of convergence had taken place over time (Robertson, 1976). However, convergence in the UK formally ended in 1979 with the election of a Conservative Government (led by Margaret Thatcher) which implemented a range of market-type policies (for example, privatization; de-regulation) and was able to do so because the rival Labour Party shifted from the centre ground to the extreme left of the political spectrum.
  Alternative predictions about income distribution have been formulated from different models. Altruists and normative theories of redistribution usually suggest that redistribution ought to be from the rich to the poor (see Chapter 12). Alternatively, Marxists and socialists would allege that redistribution is from the poor to the rich and others in 'power'. But the economics of politics predicts that the median voter is in power, so that

redistribution is towards the *middle* of the income distribution. In contrast, interest group theories predict that targeted government expenditures, regulations, tax measures and subsidies can best be explained as the rewards to organization and lobbying by special interest groups (for example, farm groups; licensing requirements for doctors, opticians and plumbers). Overall, 'normative theories of redistribution envisage impartial or altruistic individuals unanimously agreeing to programs that redistribute income from themselves. These theories seem romantic and naïve alongside the pragmatic public choice theories, which predict that the organizationally and numerically strong grab from unorganized minorities' (Mueller, 1989, pp. 455–6).

A distinctive feature of the Downs model is its prediction that government policies will be pro-producer and anti-consumer (cf. Chapter 2). This prediction emerges because of substantial transactions and information costs in political markets. Given that information is costly to acquire and that there are gains from specialization and division of labour, people are best informed in the area of their speciality, namely their producing or income-earning activity. Producer groups embrace firms and unions. In addition:

1.   They can afford the substantial investments in information to influence government policy. Producer groups have to show governments that they are more knowledgeable than the best-informed voters. To be influential, interest groups have to be specialists in their preferred policy area, whereas voters are generalists. Specialization demands expert knowledge and information which can be costly to acquire. Since producer groups are already knowledgeable about their area, the costs to them of acquiring information can be relatively low; there might be scale economies in the collection and distribution of information and, in the case of firms and trade unions, some of the information costs can be charged to the enterprise. Moreover, with only small numbers, the costs of creating a group and avoiding the 'free-rider' problem can be more readily, and cheaply, solved.
2.   They find it worthwhile to invest in information. The potential returns from purchasing information to influence policy are sufficiently large to make costly investments worthwhile. Income-earners are most likely to gain directly and significantly from influencing policy in their favour. Since voters usually earn their income in one activity (that is, a firm, a union and in one locality) but spend in many, the area of earning or producing is much more vital to them than their spending or consuming activities (Downs, 1957).

It might seem surprising that vote-sensitive governments ignore large numbers of consumers and are influenced by small numbers of producers. Vote-maximizing governments will be concerned about the income and utility of voters only in so far as these affect votes. If a government knows that a citizen's income is affected by its policies, and the citizen is aware of this, then the government will carefully assess the effect of its policies on the voter. The less a citizen knows about policy options and their effects on his income and utility, the more likely he will be ignored by a government, hence increasing the governing party's opportunities for discretionary behaviour. Certainly there are numerous examples of policies which favour producers rather than consumers. Tariffs and import controls favour domestic firms and create domestic jobs, while the consumer pays in the form of higher prices (see Chapter 4, Figure 4.14). Similar results occur with policies supporting agricultural prices (for example, the European Union's Common Agricultural Policy), influencing the location of industry, subsidizing lame duck firms, favouring domestic firms in allocating government contracts, and supporting prestige high technology projects (for example, Airbus). Governments might also be ambiguous and inconsistent in their treatment of monopolies and mergers. They might adopt an anti-monopoly and pro-competition policy and then fail to implement it. Or vague elements (for example, an undefined 'public interest') might be introduced into the legislation and the task of interpretation might be given to an independent agency, with further opportunities for discretionary behaviour.

But if such policies are detrimental to consumers (and there are numerous examples in this book), why are they adopted? Why do consumers not protect themselves by forming an interest group to influence government policy in their favour? The answer is that such groups are costly to form. There are large numbers of consumers which have to be located, and negotiations and bargaining are required to share the burdens and benefits over the group. Without a group, an individual consumer will find it costly to acquire information on the price effects of agricultural support schemes, monopolies, regional policy and tariffs; and any resulting benefits to an *individual* consumer are likely to be small although large numbers of free-riders will *each* derive relatively small gains. The result is that governments will tend to *oversupply* special interest legislation favouring *producer* groups. Such legislation helps to create, increase or protect a group's monopoly position and its associated monopoly rents. Examples of government policies which favour producers include a monopoly airline route between two cities, regulation, tariffs and quotas and the award of government contracts. These government policies offer prizes in the form of monopoly rents and their pursuit is known as rent-seeking. It might be expected that rent-seeking firms will be willing to invest resources in lobbying and other related policies to an amount similar to the expected monopoly rents from the special interest legislation. Efforts to eliminate wasteful rent-seeking will inevitably be opposed by those interest groups likely to suffer income losses from such changes (for example, farmers; protected industries).

Political Business Cycles

Once elected, the governing party becomes a monopoly supplier of goods and services. As such, it has the opportunity to use its policies to influence voter preferences directly. It can, for example, offer subsidies and award contracts to major firms (producer groups) in marginal constituencies or introduce import controls for low-profit industries concentrated in such constituencies. The government can also use aggregate demand policies to increase its chances of re-election. To increase its popularity, it can embark on expansionary policies prior to an election. Such use of aggregate demand management as a potential vote-winner raises the possibility of politically-created business cycles. Indeed, the management of aggregate demand and 'stop-go' policies might appear attractive to vote-sensitive politicians, since a government can be seen to be involved in 'controlling' the economy. But much depends on the success of such demand management, its relationship to voter preferences, and the memory of voters.

The political business cycle assumes that voters are myopic and focus on the current election period, tending to forget the past. Following an election victory, the government will aim to control inflation by deflating the economy, so raising unemployment. This will occur in the politically safe period after an election victory. Such a policy might be presented and interpreted as an investment in the future to 'squeeze inflation out of the system and create permanent jobs' (inflation–unemployment trade-off). Over the government's term of office, unemployment is steadily reduced, and if voters are myopic they will assess the government on its performance at the time of the election (for example, during the current election year). *After the election*, there is a significant increase in inflation and the cycle is repeated. In these circumstances, traditional Keynesian fiscal policy seemed especially appropriate. Budget deficits allow politicians to spend their way out of a recession without raising taxes or charges; hence their attraction as potential vote-winners. In contrast, budget surpluses to combat inflation require reduced spending and/or higher taxes: both are unattractive to voters and there is also opposition from bureaucrats who dislike their budgets being cut. Consequently, government manipulation of the economy for votes results in a preference for budget deficits, increased public expenditure and inflationary pressures.

Voters are often criticized for being myopic. But the political business cycle model also suggests that politicians can be short-sighted. The public sector can be as myopic or even more so than individuals, with adverse consequences for efficiency in resource allocation. After all, private markets are often condemned for 'failing' to take a long view! Nor is it necessarily valid to assume that voters have limited memories and that they do not learn from experience. For example, after repeated experience of the political business cycle, voters might learn of a subsequent deflation following an election victory and so favour a rival party offering a better, and apparently costless, solution (for example, a policy to avoid 'boom and bust'). However, the acceptability of the political business cycle model also depends on its empirical validity. Considerable evidence exists showing that voters judge governments and presidents on their macroeconomic performance reflected in low levels of unemployment and inflation and high levels of income. The results are consistent across a variety of countries such as France, Germany, Japan, Sweden, the UK and the USA, showing that a government's popularity is affected by macroeconomic variables, and that there is support for a political-economic cycle in these countries. The equations for testing the model are of the general form:

$$P = P(U, p, y, R)$$

where P = a measure of the governing party's popularity (for example, percentage lead over its main rival)
   U = national unemployment rate
   p = inflation rate
   y = growth of real disposable income
   R = other relevant variables (for example, expected time to the next election, depreciation of the government's lead over its term of office).

The evidence indicates that increases in both unemployment and inflation adversely affect a government's popularity (a negative relationship), while higher real income has a favourable effect (a positive relationship). But such results are not beyond criticism. It is far from clear whether the equations represent demand or supply side variables, equilibria or disequilibria in political markets. Moreover, if a governing party knows the effect of economic variables on its popularity, why does it lose elections? Modern Austrian economists would not be surprised at election defeats since the school maintains that there are no constant relations in economics, so that no measurement is possible. Finally, the political business cycle model contains only *macroeconomic* influences and neglects their microeconomic foundations. If a government pursues an expansionary policy to increase its popularity prior to an election, are the microeconomic effects of higher aggregate demand completely irrelevant? For example, public expenditure can be increased through alternative public works programmes favouring defence, hospitals, roads or schools, each with different industrial and regional implications; or state-owned industries could be required to increase investment; or more subsidies could be offered to clearly identifiable groups, such as large firms in marginal constituencies or training programmes for unemployed school-leavers. Nor does the model consider the role of bureaucrats in determining government policies.

14.5 ECONOMIC MODELS OF BUREAUCRACY

Bureaucracies are public sector non-profit organizations which are responsible for advising federal, central, state, city and local governments on the extent and form of microeconomic policy, including any opportunities for new initiatives. Their responsibilities range from the provision of public goods, such as defence, to purchasing goods and services from the private sector; they are involved in regulating private firms and industries, collecting taxes, and administering redistribution policies. Examples have dominated this book! But how do such non-profit organizations behave and do they perform efficiently?

Bureaucracies supply information, goods and services to the governing political party and, ultimately, to the community. They are usually monopoly suppliers, protected from possible public and private sector rivals through a governing party's allocation of property rights and restrictions on new entrants. Normally, each government department tends to specialize (for example, defence, education, employment, highways, housing, transport), there being no competition or rivalry between different parts of the *public* sector for the provision of specific services. This applies both within and between cities, within and between state or local governments, as well as between local and federal or central administrations. For example, within a city, the municipal passenger transport and fire departments are not generally invited to bid for the refuse collection service, and vice versa. Similarly, the housing repairs and highways maintenance departments are not normally rivals for government building contracts. Nor are private firms invited to tender for some of the traditional functions of government (for example, careers advice and job search, schooling, refuse collection, fire services). The absence of competition and rivalry means that bureaucrats have opportunities for discretionary behaviour. They are interest groups of experts and specialists and, in the absence of alternative sources of information and comparative cost data, the government as buyer and sponsor might not be sufficiently well informed to question a bureau's budget requests. Not surprisingly, bureaucrats are often supporters of increased 'coordination, rationalization and centralization' within the public sector, so creating larger departments: such reorganization is reputed to eliminate the alleged 'duplication and wastes' of competition! The outcome is bilateral monopoly with bureaux acting as monopolists and the governing party as a monopsonist, purchasing desired levels of service in return for an agreed budget. There are, however, limitations on the extent to which the wishes of the governing party will be implemented. Such limitations mean that bureaucrats have opportunities to further their own ends.

Opportunities for discretionary behaviour arise in large organizations in non-competitive markets and where objectives and end-outputs are vague and ill-defined. Large organizations encounter difficulties of coordination, so resulting in control loss. In such organizations, both ministers and senior bureaucrats will find it costly to achieve complete compliance with their wishes. Each level in an hierarchy increases the chances that an order will be changed, either deliberately or accidentally. Consider an organization with four hierarchical levels and all subordinates executing 80 per cent of their orders: at the fourth level, only about 40 per cent of a minister's orders will be effective. Orders might be misunderstood, incapable of being executed, or subordinates might be unwilling to cooperate. In these circumstances, opportunities arise for bureaucrats to deliberately distort or hoard information to further their own ends. Various measures can be used to reduce such distortions, including independent audits and the appointment of external advisers. Or, incentives might be offered for the release of valuable information: new ideas could be rewarded with prizes, promotion or attendance at international conferences. While control loss arises in all large organizations, both public and private, the opportunities for discretion are reinforced in non-competitive markets. As monopolists, bureaucrats can pursue self-interest, with implications for economic decisions and policy outcomes. The situation is reinforced by the bureaucrat's employment contract which is often incompletely specified and lacking in efficiency incentives, so giving further opportunities for exercising discretion. Of course, it might be claimed that large organizations, monopolies, and incompletely-specified employment contracts also exist in *private* markets. If so, there are opportunities for improving performance in both sectors. However, in the private sector, there are consumers, rival firms, a more clearly defined output, a takeover mechanism, the risking of private funds and employment contracts which provide monetary rewards for increased efficiency: all these act as 'policing' mechanisms. Such controls are absent in the political market place. Voters might not be able to express their views on a specific issue, such as a state support for new civil jet aircraft (for example, Airbus A380) or similar projects. Nor is it a simple task for a politician at the ministerial or city council level to challenge a bureaucracy's information, advice and budget requests, especially where ministers have a relatively short tenure in a post. All of which raises questions about the behaviour of bureaucracies.

Predictions, Examples and Evidence

A starting point is Niskanen's (1971) model in which bureaucrats as utility-maximizers have every incentive to maximize their budgets. Larger budgets enable bureaucrats to satisfy their preferences for salary, perquisites of office, public regulation, job opportunities, power and patronage. The model assumes that bureaucrats can operate as perfect price discriminating monopolists, extracting the available consumer surplus from the purchasing government (bilateral monopoly). Effectively, a bureau offers a total output in exchange for a budget, an example of which is shown in Figure 14.2. A department will offer an output which provides the largest possible budget consistent with covering total costs. Output will exceed the social optimum (Q_c), hence the prediction that bureaux 'overproduce', giving too large an output. On this basis, it is likely that industries and services supported by monopoly ministries and state agencies will be too large. Figure 14.2 also compares public and private monopolies, showing that the latter will produce at Q_m,

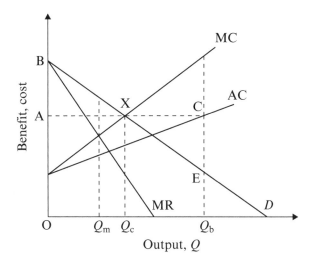

*Figure 14.2   A budget-maximizing bureaucracy. The community's demand for the government
service (the demand function of the median voter) is represented by D, with MR as
marginal revenue and marginal and average costs as MC and AC, respectively. A
budget-maximizing bureaucrat will produce at Q_b where the largest possible budget is
obtained, subject to the constraint that total revenue equals total cost. At Q_b the
budget is $OACQ_b$ which equals $OBEQ_b$. Consumer surplus of ABX at Q_c is used to
increase output to Q_b (ABX = XCE). For comparative purposes, the competitive
output or social optimum is Q_c and the output for the private profit-maximizing
monopolist is Q_m. The welfare losses at Q_m are smaller than at Q_b*

giving 'too little' output, but the private profit-maximizing monopolist results in smaller
welfare losses than a budget-maximizing bureaucracy.

Budget maximization can affect the behaviour of bureaucracies. In aiming to raise their
budgets, departments have every incentive to overestimate or exaggerate the demand for
their preferred policies and to underestimate the costs of policies and projects. This can
affect the ways in which bureaucrats present information to politicians. Bureaux can stress
the social benefits of a project in the form of jobs, high technology, and its contribution
to the balance of payments. In the defence field, where they have a monopoly of information, the armed forces and the defence department can exaggerate the threat from a
potential enemy and point to the numbers of its troops, tanks, aircraft, ships and nuclear
warheads; and they can exaggerate the threat from terrorism and from rogue states (for
example, Iraq and its weapons of mass destruction). Bureaux can formulate programmes
which will be supported by producer groups likely to benefit from contracts and they can
suggest policies which are potential vote-winners for a government. Departments can also
hire independent consultants to provide further expertise supporting their case. After all,
the case for a new public expenditure programme can be enhanced if it has the approval
of reputable, independent consultants which have assessed the scheme using all the latest
cost–benefit, statistical, econometric and survey techniques of appraisal. Possible vote
losses from any increased taxation and inflation required to finance greater public expenditure will be widely diffused among the electorate, so that the adverse effects are likely to
be quite small.

While bureaucracies and interest groups are usually enthusiastic about social benefits, they are understandably silent on the reliability of a project's cost estimates and on any external costs. A ministry might deliberately underestimate the costs of a project in order to 'buy into' a new programme. Cost estimates which are 'too low' can lead a government to buy 'too much' of a project which appears to be relatively cheap. Once started, public sector projects are difficult to stop. Agents in the political market place have an interest in continuation and the costs are borne by the taxpayer. Projects create interest groups of architects, engineers, scientists, surveyors, contractors and unions, each with relative income gains from the continuation of the work. Such groups are likely to support the bureaucracy with a budgetary involvement in the project. Bureaucrats can easily show vote-conscious politicians that a project is in the 'national interest' and will produce substantial social benefits. Such behaviour is not unknown in the public sector. Examples of cost estimates which were substantially less than actual expenditures have occurred with weapons, high technology work, and major construction programmes (see cost escalation in Chapter 15). Although cost escalation occurs on private commercial projects, it raises different issues for efficiency. Market-based organizations are less likely to persist with unproductive or obsolete projects since the necessary support will be removed by the market. Budget-conscious departments will also be reluctant to recognize and estimate any external costs. Examples include noise from new airports and new, state-financed, jet engines, as well as the pollution and environmental effects from the establishment of coalfields, off-shore oil drilling, and the possible hazards and risks associated with nuclear power stations. It is in a department's interest to ignore or underestimate such social costs. Thus, to raise their budgets, bureaucracies have an incentive to underestimate costs and exaggerate demands. In the process, they can also justify their preferred output by creating an impression of allocative efficiency, as shown in Figure 14.3.

The model has numerous applications. Examples from the fire service, state high technology programmes and city building projects are sufficient to illustrate its potential and show how it can be combined with the economics of politics. Many fire services are bureaucracies operated by city, regional or state authorities. In bargaining about budgets, fire departments will aim to supply protection to meet all possible contingencies. They will insist that an 'adequate' cover requires the purchase of the latest sophisticated equipment, ignoring its costs and the probability of its use. A fire officer's employment contract provides no inducements to respond to economic incentives: the officer does not share in any savings. Indeed, any savings might accrue to rival departments or even to the Treasury. Thus, the system creates incentives to *spend*. In the circumstances, there is every incentive to provide cover to meet the worst-possible contingency or catastrophe. Also, callers requesting the fire service are judged incapable of assessing the extent of any fire. Consequently, the service insists that the minimum response to any emergency requires, say, two vehicles. Think of the cases where most of the local fire brigade turns out to extinguish a small cooker fire! In addition, en route to any emergency, the fire service creates sufficient externalities (noise) to remind the local community of its existence and 'performance'. Finally, in bargaining with politicians for its budget, the fire department can always use its ultimate 'weapon' and point to the possible political (that is, vote) consequences of any loss of life due to 'inadequate' fire protection following budget cuts. The result is likely to be expensive solutions providing 'too much' fire protection (that is, over-insurance).

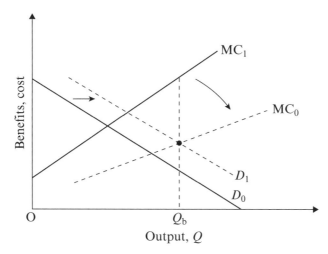

Figure 14.3   Bureaucracy behaviour. Assume that Q_b is the budget-maximizing output; see Figure 14.2. Bureaux can create an impression of allocative efficiency by overestimating demand – D_1 instead of D_0 – and underestimating costs – MC_o instead of MC_1.

High technology projects are particularly attractive to bureaucrats and interest groups of scientists, engineers and technologists interested in expanding the frontiers of knowledge at the taxpayer's expense. Examples include state involvement in computers, microelectronics, nuclear power stations, space satellites and in major weapons projects. Median preference voters are likely to be uncertain about the benefits and costs of government support for advanced technology: they will be attracted by its potential benefits, but wary of the likely costs and possibilities of failure. In the circumstances, vote-sensitive politicians are likely to be influenced by those who are best informed, namely interest groups of experts. Such groups, which are likely to benefit from a ministry's increased spending, will have every incentive to support the bureaucracy's exaggerated claims of major social benefits. References will be made to the need to keep a nation in the forefront of technology, to the valuable (but difficult to quantify) fall-out for the rest of the economy, to the provision of the next generation of jobs, to the possibility of a new technological revolution, and the need to avoid 'undue' dependence on foreign technology. Vote-conscious politicians might be attracted by such alleged benefits, especially if state support for new technology appears to offer a means of 'solving' a nation's economic problems. Where such projects have to be undertaken in collaboration with other nations (for example, European space satellites: see Chapter 15), bureaucrats further benefit from the opportunities for international travel and its associated amenities. Thus, the high technology example shows the possible range of beneficiaries in the political market place. Domestic industry, scientists and jobs will be favoured. Politicians will expect to gain votes through the allocation of government funds to clearly identifiable groups. Bureaucrats benefit from a larger budget, the discretionary power in allocating contracts, and the need for monitoring and policing the work to ensure that the 'best value for money is obtained' and the public interest is protected. Rarely is it asked whether the resources used in government-supported high technology work would make a greater contribution to employment, balance of payments, and technology objectives and, ultimately, to human satisfaction, if they were used elsewhere in the economy.

Further insights into how bureaucrats obtain a larger budget can be obtained by examining the information which they present to the governing party. Consider the case for a new city-financed building, such as an arts, conference or sports centre. Or, take the case which might be used to persuade a city to bid for the Olympic Games. It can be argued that the project is 'vital' to prevent a city 'sliding down the league table' and for regeneration of a region and that we must 'go ahead and subsidize the scheme because our rivals have done so'. References will be made to social benefits in the form of extra local spending from the new project which, together with existing business, will give a 'substantial' total benefit: note the potential confusion between *marginal* and *total* benefits. It will, of course, be argued that the social benefits are difficult to quantify, but nonetheless they are believed to be substantial! On the cost side, estimates might not be presented on a consistent price basis with, say, 2001 expenditures simply added to 2007 outlays. This, plus the omission of interest charges, the neglect of life-cycle costs, displacement effects (for example, loss of tourists) and external costs (for example, noise, pollution), understates the true opportunity cost of a project. Further 'pressure'can be placed on city decision-makers if the scheme is presented with a 'keenly competitive price' determined by selective tendering, providing a 'unique and final opportunity' to proceed. And, after all, if the project does not 'go ahead', all the previous expenditure will be 'wasted'. Indeed, completion for its own sake sometimes becomes a point of honour. It is not unknown for city politicians and officials to argue that, having embarked on a scheme and having been fully committed to it for some time, it is the city's view that it must be carried through to its conclusion, despite the heavily inflated costs.

While these arguments *appear* persuasive, they are often emotional, lacking in economic analysis and devoid of empirical support. For example, use of the word 'vital' invites questions of vital to whom, and is it vital regardless of cost? The 'rivals are subsidizing' argument is dubious since if they wish to offer free gifts, a local community could respond by accepting them and specializing elsewhere. Indeed, in appraising any scheme, the likely costs and benefits of alternative projects have to be considered, including a 'do nothing' option (for example, why not 'slide down the league table'?). Nor is the 'substantial benefits' argument convincing in the absence of evidence showing that the benefits are greater than could be obtained from alternative uses of the resources. At its most general, the benefits argument simply suggests that *any* new local project will have multiplier effects. By itself, this is not a convincing case for choosing an arts centre rather than, say, new houses, schools or roads. Moreover, it is possible that the difficulties of quantifying social benefits might reflect the fact that there is nothing to be measured! As for costs, references to a 'keenly competitive price' are misleading for decision-making if the project design has not been 'frozen' and a firm fixed-price contract cannot be awarded. Indeed, examples have arisen where two to three years after the start of a major building project, city officials have declared that its cost estimates will become more reliable as the contract proceeds towards completion! Arguments about cancellation are also confusing, since previous expenditures are 'sunk' costs where the sacrifices have already been incurred. Nor is cancellation necessarily 'wasteful'; it may be cheaper than continuing with the project, and past expenditures can provide benefits in the form of valuable information and knowledge.

While the Niskanen (1971) model is persuasive at the level of casual empiricism, there are limitations. Its prediction that the public sector will be 'too large' is difficult to subject to direct empirical test. The model also assumes that bureaucracies are technically efficient. Modifications have been introduced to allow bureaucrats to maximize a utility function containing both output and a preference for discretionary expenditures (that is, the pursuit of other goals, such as on-the-job leisure; see Chapter 7 and below). Such modifications result in the prediction that bureaucracies are both technically and allocatively inefficient. There are studies showing that for airlines, fire services and refuse collection, private firms are lower-cost suppliers than public agencies – hence the suggestion that there is considerable X-inefficiency or slack in the public sector. The addition of X-inefficiency to the model also results in further examples of behaviour which are intuitively attractive. Paperwork has been introduced into the analysis. Paperwork is a characteristic of bureaucracies, both in their internal organization and in their dealings with the private sector. Understandably, private industry is critical of the numerous demands it receives to complete official forms, a process which can be costly. But paperwork is attractive to utility-maximizing bureaucrats when negotiating with politicians for a larger budget. Paperwork is an output indicator which can be used to inflate a bureau's costs in a way which the government sponsor cannot easily check. And the harder it is to measure a bureaucracy's output, the easier it will be to deceive the sponsor. Once a bureau has obtained its budget, it can shift some of the costs of paperwork onto private firms. And bureaucrats can 'consume' the cost 'savings', namely the difference between the original *estimate* of total costs at the budget-bargaining stage and the new 'lower' costs after a budget has been allocated. A simplified example is shown in Figure 14.4. There are,

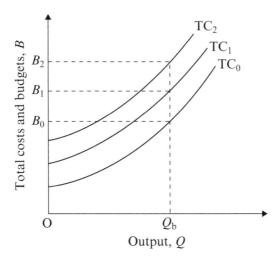

Figure 14.4 *Bureaucratic behaviour and costs. For simplicity, assume that the government requires an output of Q_b from the bureaucracy and that it will pay the total costs of producing the output. The true minimum total cost curve is represented by TC_1, resulting in a budget of OB_1. However, the bureau will try to persuade the government that TC_2 is the appropriate cost curve; if successful, the bureau will receive a budget of OB_2. The difference between B_2 and B_1 represents the bureaucrats' discretionary expenditures. Once a budget of OB_2 has been received, the bureaucracy can increase its discretionary expenditures by shifting some of its costs (e.g. paperwork, tax collection) onto private industry. As a result of such shifting, the bureau's new total cost curve might be TC_0, so raising its discretionary expenditures to B_2B_0*

however, limits on a bureaucracy's ability to shift some of its costs onto private industry. Firms will eventually respond by lobbying politicians and pressing for less bureaucracy and for the work to be 'hived-off' to the more efficient private sector. Nonetheless, these aspects of bureaucracy behaviour raise general questions about the optimum size of the public sector and its efficiency.

14.6   THE OPTIMUM SIZE OF THE PUBLIC SECTOR

Does Economic Theory Offer any Guidelines?

This section focuses on whether the public sector is 'too large'. A starting point is to consider whether economic theory offers any policy guidelines. It will be shown that economic models of politics and bureaucracies offer predictions about the size and efficiency of the public sector. Consideration will also be given to possible solutions to reduce size and improve efficiency in the public sector.

Governments are often involved in policies towards the agricultural, manufacturing and service sectors, as well as towards regions and high technology. Paretian welfare economics suggests that an optimal economic and industrial structure can be left to market forces in the form of domestic and foreign consumer preferences, and the competitiveness of domestic and foreign firms. In this way, properly working competitive markets will determine the optimal allocation of resources between agriculture, manufacturing and services and between regions, as well as the optimum size of both firms and the manufacturing sector. However, private markets might fail to work 'properly'. Some goods and services desired by society might not be provided by private markets or might be underprovided. Examples include public goods such as national defence, basic research and development, law and order, and arrangements for regulating and administering the operation of markets such as state agencies for competition, the environment and health policies (see Chapter 2). Such sources of market failure provide an economic justification for state intervention in market economies. In principle, the optimum size of the public sector is achieved when, at the margin, the expected benefits and costs of additional state intervention are equal. But there are alternative *forms* of state intervention, each with their different costs and benefits. For example, private monopolies might be controlled by reducing tariffs, by de-mergers, by regulating prices and profits, or by state ownership. Similarly, even if the arguments for *state finance* of some activities were accepted (which activities and why?), there remain extensive possibilities for the *private provision* of services which are often publicly-provided. Examples might include government training centres, arms firms, road and air transport, public utilities, education, health and city services, such as refuse collection and house building (see Chapters 10 and 15). In principle, activities such as defence, law and protection could also be contracted-out to private suppliers, namely mercenaries and private protection and law enforcement agencies. The fact that such functions are normally government-supplied often reflects 'wider considerations', such as a concern with democracy, the distribution of power within society, and its potential for abuse and the possibilities of corruption. Where public provision is accepted, should it be supplied by national, regional, state, city or local governments? People might prefer smaller authorities with local autonomy and be willing to pay a premium where this involved sacrificing any scale economies which would be available to larger units. Inevitably, in assessing alternative forms of state intervention, problems arise in identifying and valuing costs and benefits. In particular, whose valuations are to be used in any decision? Nor does Pareto optimality necessarily require private ownership; given certain conditions, it can be achieved under perfect socialism (cf. perfect competition). Nevertheless, the existence of market failure does not imply that the existing public sector in any market economy is of optimal size. Interesting questions also arise in selecting the most appropriate indicators for measuring the size of the public sector. Should we use government expenditure or employment, absolute amounts, or proportions of totals, and how are state assets to be valued? But indicators of size do not measure the efficiency of public provision.

The Benefits and Costs of State Intervention

In the Paretian model, state intervention is expected to result in net benefits through the achievement of an optimal allocation of resources. Allocative improvements arise from the removal of significant imperfections in factor and product markets, from the provision of public or collective goods in amounts which would not otherwise be provided, and through 'correcting' externalities. Examples include consumer protection and environmental policies (Chapters 5 and 16). But state intervention is not costless. Direct costs arise from the creation of a bureaucracy which is required to produce public sector output, including regulatory activities. For this purpose, resources have to be bid away from alternative uses in the private sector. The bureaucracy is financed either through general taxation or through direct charging for its services. There are also possible indirect, unexpected and sometimes perverse effects from state intervention and these have to be included in any cost–benefit calculus. Regulation is an example.

The Economics of Regulation

Regulation is not costless. For the EU, it has been estimated that regulatory costs represent about 4 per cent of the EU's GDP and that the cost of EU-generated red tape was about double the economic benefits generated by the Single European Market (Mandelson, 2004). Standard economic theory justifies state regulation as a means of correcting for market failures reflecting externalities, information asymmetries and market imperfections. Examples include regulation affecting financial services, health, utilities, air, land and sea transport, postal services and pension schemes.

Pharmaceutical products are often subject to regulation. In an apparent effort to protect patients and improve safety, many governments have imposed restrictions (for example, licences) on the introduction of new drugs developed by private industry (see Chapter 5). This involves direct costs in the form of the staff and resources used in the state's regulatory agency, as well as the costs imposed upon private industry in conforming to the regulatory requirements. Governments might require specific tests to be undertaken and passed satisfactorily before a new drug can be tested on humans in a clinical situation, followed by additional tests and satisfactory performance before a product licence is awarded. As a result, it will take longer to develop and market new drugs, with fewer being marketed, so that some patients are likely to suffer! Economists can contribute to policy formulation by quantifying some of the direct and indirect costs of regulation, leaving society to decide upon the desirable amount. We need to know how many people and resources are involved in regulation; how much longer it takes to develop a new drug and the magnitude of the extra development costs; and whether regulation has had any observable effects on patient safety.

Critics of state regulation argue that it is not possible to conceive of a omniscient, beneficent regulator whose actions can perfect an imperfect market. Public choice economics recognizes that we do not have a choice between imperfect markets and the same markets as perfected by state regulators. Instead, we have a choice between two imperfect market and institutional arrangements, namely, unregulated imperfect markets and markets regulated by governments. There is also the law of the unintended consequences of state regulation: regulation can have unintended and undesirable consequences and regulatory failure might be worse than market failure. In some cases, the regulatory agency might be 'captured' by industry interest groups seeking to influence the agency's policy to favour industry rather than consumers (for example, on industry pricing and profit controls). Even regulatory impact assessments might not address the problem of government and regulatory failures. Such assessments are vulnerable to bureaucratic or government pressures to provide results which support the prior conclusions preferred by a bureaucrat or politician. Finally, it has to be recognized that it is neither possible nor desirable to control every risk. Diminishing returns suggests that the smaller a risk, the greater the cost of removing it (Boyfield, 2006).

Taxation and Incentives

Part of the debate about the costs and benefits of government activity and the optimum size of the public sector involves taxation and its effects on incentives. It has been argued that a large public sector requires correspondingly high taxation. As a result, there are reputed to be adverse effects on incentives to enterprise and effort, with corresponding implications for an economy's competitiveness and its growth rate. Thus, some governments have claimed that incentives must be improved by allowing people to keep more of what they earn.

Theory shows that incentives can operate through their effects on labour supply. Lower income taxes are equivalent to an increase in wage rates and the effect on the supply of effort will depend on the relative strengths of the income and substitution effects (see Chapter 11). For the incentive argument to work, the substitution effect has to be dominant. However, theory offers no *a priori* predictions about the relative strengths of the income and substitution effects. Thus, the relationship between income taxes and effort has to be resolved through empirical testing. One possible approach involves the estimation of a Laffer curve for an economy.

A Laffer curve shows the relationship between tax rates and tax revenue, with the latter being zero at the extreme tax rates of 100 per cent and zero. Between these two extremes, there is assumed to be some point of maximum tax revenue, as shown in the Laffer curve in quadrant I of Figure 14.5. A trade-off between GDP and the tax rate is shown in quadrant III. As tax rates rise (for example, for distributional objectives), the operation of net disincentive effects is likely to result in a fall in GDP. A similar trade-off between GDP and tax revenue is outlined in quadrant IV. Higher tax revenue requires higher tax rates,

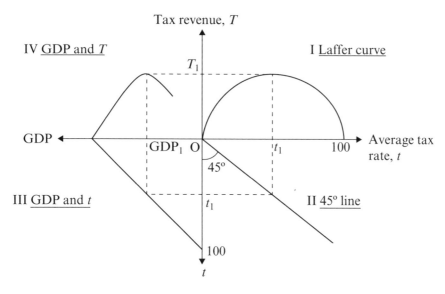

Figure 14.5   The Laffer curve analysis. This is illustrative only and assumes other things are constant (e.g. economic growth can shift the schedules). A simplified (smooth) Laffer curve is shown in quadrant I. Tax revenue is maximized (T_1) at an average tax rate of t_1. Quadrant III shows the relationship between GDP and average tax rates, with t_1 associated with GDP_1. Quadrant IV shows the relationship between GDP and tax revenue, with T_1 associated with GDP_1. The peak in the schedule in quadrant IV shows that points to the right of GDP_1 are inefficient; the same revenue could be raised with a higher GDP. The actual shape of the various schedules might be much more complex

with adverse effects on GDP. However, policy-makers interested in incentive effects require evidence on the precise shapes and slopes of the various schedules shown in Figure 14.5.

The Displacement Effect and the Size of the Public Sector

Arguments about taxation and its incentive effects also involve the size of the public sector. Taxation can act as a constraint on government expenditure. Wagner's Law is an empirically observed relationship by which as the national economy grows, the public sector will grow at a faster rate than the private sector (Peacock, 2006). In this model, there is a complementarity between the growth of the economy and the growth of public services (for example, the need for road, rail and telecommunications networks). The Law also raises questions about the public finance (tax) implications of an increasing public sector and whether there is a limit to the burdens of taxation: suggestions have been made that today's limit might be about 40 per cent of private incomes (Peacock, 2006).

In a model developed by Peacock and Wiseman (1967), government and bureaucrats prefer to spend more money, but voters do not like to pay higher taxes, and vote-sensitive politicians cannot ignore voter preferences. In normal times, public expenditure would show a gradual upward trend, reflecting the higher tax revenue from rising real incomes and a constant tax rate. However, during periods of crisis and social upheavals, such as

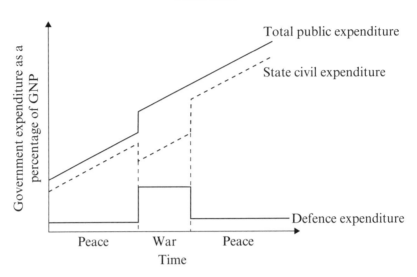

*Figure 14.6   A permanent displacement effect. The trend in government expenditure during the war
continues into the post-war years. In this example, there are upward shifts in both
defence and state civil expenditures*

wars, public expenditure would rise much more rapidly, with an associated increase in the
levels of taxation. Electorates will accept higher taxation during a crisis. The resulting
upward displacement in public expenditure and in the size of the public sector is called
the 'displacement effect'. Following the crisis, public expenditure and taxation do not
fall to their original, pre-crisis, levels. There is a public choice explanation of the displacement effect: voters are likely to become more tolerant of the higher taxation, and
budget-maximizing bureaucracies will always find ways of spending additional funds (for
example, on 'essential' social welfare and transport infrastructure programmes). An
example of the displacement effect is shown in Figure 14.6.

Some of the policy issues about the size of the public sector are now clearer. Taxation
and public expenditure are related elements in the controversy. Displacement effects result
in a larger public sector. In contrast, policies to improve incentives through reduced
income taxes will involve reductions in public expenditure and a smaller public sector.
How, then, can economists assess the efficiency of government expenditure?

Is the Public Sector Inefficient?

Inefficiency can be defined to embrace both allocative and technical aspects. Paretian
welfare economics suggests that state intervention can contribute to the achievement of an
optimum allocation of resources by improving the operation of markets through removing the sources of market failure and such an outcome would *not* be inefficient. But actual
public sectors do not operate in a Paretian world where all the marginal conditions for an
optimum are satisfied. Certainly, the market failure paradigm does not explain the whole
range of activities undertaken by modern governments, both nationally and locally.
Instead, the public sector in market economies operates in the political market where there
is potential for government failure: hence, some functions of government are more likely

to be explained by the economics of politics and bureaucracies. This provides an analytical framework for assessing the claims often made by right-wing politicians that the public sector is 'too large'. Usually, these claims embrace budgets, outputs and factor inputs.

Consider a government which wishes to reduce public expenditure and enforce cash limits on spending departments, while improving efficiency and reducing waste (it might be too costly to eliminate waste completely). At the same time, the government could be committed to reducing public sector manpower, with an associated desire to change the labour mix by economizing on the numbers of central government civil servants, reducing local government manpower, and restricting the numbers of managers and administrators in its state health and education services. Such a government will soon discover that it is costly to achieve compliance with its objectives. How can a Cabinet and individual ministers, with limited knowledge and time, ensure that their wishes are actually implemented? If it is costly to achieve compliance, there will be an optimal amount of non-compliance or control loss and the possibility of perverse outcomes. Problems arise because bureaucrats are experts on public sector production functions. They are experts on the opportunities for varying output and for factor substitution in response to budgetary cuts. Take, as an example, behaviour in state-owned hospitals where the government might be trying to 'economize' through imposing 'cash limits' on spending. How might such cash limits affect the purchase of, say, new high-technology medical equipment?

Every year, doctors and specialist groups will submit bids for new capital equipment, such as scanners, X-ray equipment, or a new computerized cardiac arrest unit. Usually, there will be excess demand. Assume that it is Dr D's turn in the 'queue' and that he is allowed to acquire new X-ray equipment on condition that he finances its running costs from his annual recurrent budget, which is subject to cash limits. Motivation and behaviour within this framework has four significant features:

1. No administrator has the competence to question the doctor's professional judgement on the need for the equipment. Nor can specialist supplies officers question whether a cheaper item might be as effective. The usual story is that a doctor colleague in a nearby hospital has recently acquired some Japanese equipment with all the latest technical aids and gadgets, and his friend wants the same or even better!
2. A doctor's employment contract provides no inducements to respond to economic incentives: he does not share in any savings and economies. Indeed, any savings might accrue to rival departments within the hospital or to the local hospital authority or even to the central government treasury. Moreover, a failure to spend an allotted budget or a refusal to bid for an allocation might incur the opprobrium of staff within the doctor's unit, as well as from colleagues in other spending departments. Thus, the system creates incentives to spend.
3. Doctors can respond to cash limits on spending by using their specialist knowledge and discretion to reduce output in *their preferred areas*. An obvious strategy is to reduce output in those areas, which will increase a doctor's chances of obtaining a larger budget in the future. For example, he could lengthen the queue for X-rays by making short-run economies in cooperating labour inputs (for example, clerical staff might be reduced, so increasing the waiting time for an X-ray!)
4. Performance indicators are not necessarily an inducement to efficiency. A classic example is where the doctor reports that the operation was a success but the patient died!

Such examples of behaviour are not unique to state-owned hospitals: they are likely to occur in other parts of the public sector. Analysis and critical evaluation requires a model which offers explanations and testable predictions about the behaviour of public bureaucracies. Also, the model has to address itself to the issues which often dominate debates about the size of the public sector. Does theory predict that the public sector will be 'too large' and will be characterized by waste and inefficiency? Can the models be developed to include manpower as well as showing the response of bureaux to budget cuts?

14.7 ECONOMIC MODELS OF BUREAUCRACY AND THE SIZE OF THE PUBLIC SECTOR

The economics of politics would explain the size of the public sector as a response of vote-maximizing governments to the preferences of the median voter. At the same time, the model recognizes that the voters who are best informed on a policy issue are those whose incomes are directly affected by it, with democratic governments responding to such interest groups. In the public sector, this means government employees or bureaucrats. The Niskanen model predicts that budget-maximizing bureaucrats will 'overproduce', the result being allocative inefficiency in the public sector. This model can be developed to include X-inefficiency, budgets and manpower, as shown in Figures 14.7 and 14.8.

Figure 14.7 incorporates manpower into the Niskanen model of bureaucrats as budget-maximizers (see Figure 14.2). Four sectors are shown, namely output, total budgets, manpower and real wages. Initially, bureaucrats are assumed to be X-efficient. Quadrant I shows the bureau's output (Q_b) exceeding the social optimum (Q_c), and the implications for total budgets and total costs are shown directly in quadrant II. The manpower implications of the bureau's output can be derived from the bureaucracy's X-efficient production function relating output and employment, as shown in quadrant III. The real wage required to attract and retain a bureaucracy labour force of N_b is shown by the labour supply function in quadrant IV (W_b/P). One further implication of the model is relevant to the public sector debate. It is often claimed that many state activities are justified by decreasing costs (see Chapter 8). However, this might be the result of bureaucrats trying to estimate the governments' demand curve for the bureau's output. A downward-sloping demand curve would mean that a bureau would offer a larger output at a lower unit price (at least up to Q_c in Figure 14.7), even though the true underlying costs were constant or increasing! Nevertheless, in debates about 'inefficiency and waste' in the public sector, the model in Figure 14.7 is limited to allocative inefficiency.

In the Niskanen model, budget maximization is equivalent to maximizing output subject to the budget constraint: bureaux do not derive any satisfaction from discretionary expenditures. Figure 14.8 modifies the model to incorporate discretionary expenditures, technical inefficiency and a preference for staff inputs. Panel I in Figure 14.8 assumes that bureaux are utility-maximizers, where utility depends on both output and discretionary expenditures (U_0). Also, panel I shows the surplus curve which represents discretionary expenditures or a fiscal residual. This is the difference between the total budget for a bureau and its *minimum* costs of production. A utility-maximizing bureaucrat with a preference for output and surplus will choose the combination QuS_1. The surplus provides bureaucrats with opportunities for discretionary expenditures on salary,

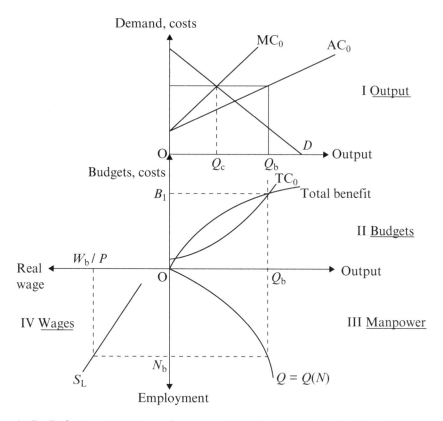

Figure 14.7 *Budget maximization and manpower. Quadrant I is identical to Figure 14.2 with Q_b as the bureau's output and Q_c as the competitive output. Quadrant II shows total budgets and total costs directly, with the bureau maximizing its budget subject to the constraint that total revenue (budget) equals total costs (Q_b). It should be emphasized that the total benefit schedule assumes perfect price discrimination, with bureaux extracting the available consumer surplus. The employment implications of budget maximization are shown in quadrant III (N_b), and the resulting real wage is derived in quadrant IV (W_b/P)*

promotions, new offices, additional staff, on-the-job leisure, and payments to consultants and interest groups supporting the bureau. As a result, bureaux will be technically inefficient and costs will rise above the minimum level (from TC_0 to TC_1). In other words, output Q_u involves 'waste' in the sense of X-inefficiency. Next, let it be assumed that the bureau has a preference for staff. In this case, discretionary expenditures will be used to buy labour inputs. An example is shown in panel II of Figure 14.8, where the bureaucracy chooses an inefficient production function resulting in the employment level N_u. The implications for real wages are shown in panel III.

The analytical framework outlined in Figure 14.8 suggests that the public sector will be 'too large' as well as technically inefficient and will contain 'too many' civil servants. Ultimately, the acceptability of such a model of behaviour and performance depends on its explanatory power and predictive accuracy. There remain extensive opportunities for empirical testing and, in the absence of satisfactory tests, the model has some tentative

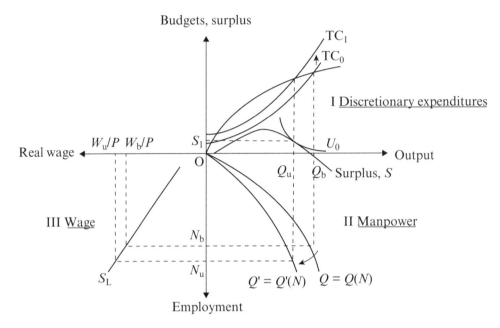

Figure 14.8   Utility maximization. Panel I is the same as panel II in Figure 14.7. For simplicity, the diagram of demand and marginal-average cost schedules has been omitted. In panel I, Q_b is the output of Niskanen budget-maximizing bureaucracy, with TC_0 as the minimum cost of production. A bureau which maximizes a more general utility function (U = U(Q,S) where S is surplus) – will produce at Q_u and consume inefficiency in the form of a higher cost schedule, namely TC_1. If it is assumed that bureaucrats prefer to use their surplus on staff, the result might be a higher level of employment N_u where $N_u > N_b$ as shown in panel II. Strictly, this implies a utility function U = U(Q,L) where L is labour input. The real wage implications of N_u are shown in panel III

support from casual empiricism. Examples include criticisms of city governments and local authorities for overstaffing and operational inefficiency, especially in direct labour organizations; for the proliferation of departments and chief officer posts, and the upgrading of posts and internal promotion following city government reorganization; for unnecessarily high standards in building and equipment; for defective incentive bonus schemes; and for a spate of new city halls (for example, Layfield, 1976).

The Effects of Budget Cuts

Will cuts in a bureaucracy's budget improve efficiency, reduce waste and release man-power? The model in Figure 14.8 predicts that a budget cut is likely to reduce output, with a possible move towards the social optimum! After all, the government and the bureaucracy will be operating in a bilateral monopoly bargaining situation with the former lacking expert and independent information on the bureau's efficient production function. What is the likely behaviour of the production function in such a situation, and especially in an environment of budget cuts? Civil servants and officials might respond to a cut by labour hoarding. They might try to protect jobs by shifting the bureaucracy's production

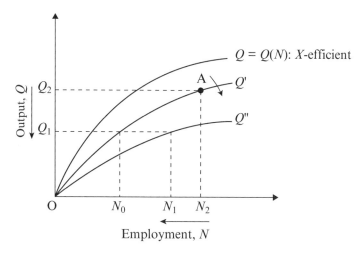

Figure 14.9   Labour hoarding. A utility-maximizing bureaucrat is initially in equilibrium at point A with output–employment Q_2N_2, as derived in Figure 14.8. A budget cut results in a reduction in output from Q_2 to Q_1, but, if the bureaucracy can shift its production function to Q'', employment will fall to N_1 rather than N_0

function and offering only token manpower savings. After all, in the absence of alternative suppliers and cost-comparisons, bureaucrats can shift a department's production function at their discretion and in their favour. An example is shown in Figure 14.9. However, it might be argued that productivity increases in the public sector are low relative to the private sector and that this is a source of rising relative costs of government-supplied services. But is low productivity an inherent characteristic of the technology involved in state-supplied services or does it reflect the behavioural framework within which bureaucrats operate? These alternative hypotheses could be tested by allowing extensive experiments in competitive bidding for some of the functions traditionally undertaken by national, state, city and local governments.

14.8   IMPROVING EFFICIENCY WITHIN THE PUBLIC SECTOR

Various proposals have been made to improve both the technical and allocative efficiency of the public sector. New management techniques have been suggested to assist governments in resource allocation and to improve rational analysis in policy-making. The number and variety of so-called 'rational' evaluation techniques is ever expanding and includes cost–benefit analysis, evaluation research, impact assessment, futures research, social indicator research, performance indicators and competitive tendering. Cost–benefit analysis involves the monetary valuation for society of all the expected costs and benefits (including externalities) of a policy or project in relation to the alternative choices. The aim is to select the policy or project which is most worthwhile to society. A related technique is evaluation research which aims at assessing the performance of government programmes. What are the policy objectives? How can they be measured? Were the objectives achieved, and at what cost? Planning Programming Budgeting Systems (PPBS) is an example of this approach. Other variants include Management by Objectives (MBO) and Zero-Based Budgeting which, through annual evaluations of programmes, aims to eliminate or reduce activities which have become 'dubious'. Indeed, public sector budgeting systems are an alternative means by which politicians and society can assess the efficiency with which government departments use scarce resources. Here, further examples include Management Budgeting where top level managers are given fixed budgets to achieve specific objectives; and Resource Accounting and Budgeting (RAB) which replaces cash budgeting and introduces private sector accounting techniques, including depreciation and cost of capital charges, into the public sector.

Environmental and social impact assessments were a response to the alleged deficiencies of cost–benefit analysis and the apparent neglect of non-economic criteria in judging the worth of a project. Environmental analysis assesses all the direct and indirect environmental effects of an activity such as air pollution, the disposal of nuclear waste, or earth moving – for example, the effects on present and future vegetation growth, fresh water, farming, forestry, fishing and tourism. Similarly, social impact assessment identifies the effects of policies, including new technology, on all dimensions of living conditions including demographic, social and economic aspects. Futures research tries to provide governments with some picture of the future in terms of both what might happen and what will happen. Social indicators research provides measures of socioeconomic well-being or welfare. Examples range from crime rates to efforts at measuring the 'quality of life'.

Performance indicators are another means of assessing and comparing government departments and various parts of the public sector against targets which aim to measure output. Hospitals can be assessed and compared by using mortality rates and by waiting times for various treatments (for example, cancer screening; hip surgery); schools can be assessed by comparing examination results; universities can be compared using teaching and research assessments; and railways can be assessed against the percentage of trains arriving on time.

All these evaluation techniques have a number of common problems:

1. Confusion often arises between allocative and technical efficiency and effectiveness. A programme might be effective in achieving its objectives, but at what cost? Similarly, technical efficiency is a necessary, but not a sufficient, condition for allocative efficiency, which is much more difficult to assess. Technical efficiency requires identification of the least-cost method of supplying an output, whereas allocative efficiency requires that the socially-desirable output be selected (that is the equality of marginal social costs and benefits: see Chapter 2). It should not be assumed that targets for public sector organizations represent allocatively efficient outcomes.

2. There are principal–agent problems. In the public sector, the principals are voters, and agents are elected politicians and their civil servants. Voters as principals are only able to make general expressions of their preferences, leaving agents with the discretion to interpret these preferences. Typically, policy decisions are not made by one individual but are the outcome of a search and bargaining process involving a variety of individuals and groups. Some fascinating problems arise in identifying the various agents in public sector decision-making and in modelling their behaviour (that is, what are the various groups trying to maximize and for whose benefit?).

3. Since policy-making is about politics, particularly distributional equity, value judgements cannot be avoided. The task is to identify what, and whose, value judgements are part of the allegedly 'rational policy analysis'.

4. There is a preference for quantification and a tendency to ignore qualitative data. One view maintains that 'if it cannot be measured, ignore it'. Alternatively, it seems reasonable to require the analyst to specify and list those aspects of any policy evaluation which are regarded as relevant, but which cannot be quantified.

5. There is a real danger that evaluation techniques in policy analysis will be used to support, serve and reinforce the budget-maximizing aims of bureaucracies. And, in the last resort, administrators can refuse to cooperate where it is not in their personal interests to have programmes examined in great depth. Efforts to measure a bureaucracy's performance lead to the inevitable response that output cannot be measured, that there is no truth in numbers, that our activities are 'priceless', and that vulgar notions of cost–benefit analysis do not apply to us!

6. There is a view that 'better analysis and information are not a general solution to the problem of bureaucracy. The superior performance of market institutions is not due to their use of more or better analysis. The primary difference in the performance of different organizations are due . . . to differences in their structure and in the incentives of their managers' (Niskanen, 1971). If so, how can society control bureaucracies and their propensity to spend?

14.9 METHODS OF CONTROLLING BUREAUCRACIES

Ideally, a starting point is the need to specify a clear, unambiguous objective function for government activities, reflecting community preferences and minimizing opportunities for discretionary behaviour. If such an objective function could be specified (which is highly unlikely!), governments would have to ensure compliance. Governments can try to achieve their objectives through hiring, firing and promoting senior personnel; through bargaining about budgets and offering funds for preferred policies; through organizational changes to promote competition and rivalry; through introducing new information and budgetary systems; through value for money audits by public sector audit agencies; and by appointing independent outside experts to provide alternative sources of advice. Some solutions are not always successful. Organizational changes to promote competition between bureaux, say between the army, navy and air force, might result in collusion rather than rivalry. Departments experiencing budget cuts might respond with 'savings' based on future reductions in long-term spending plans; by threatening to cancel projects located in high unemployment areas and marginal constituencies; and by offering 'token-paper' savings, while protecting their 'prestige' projects (for example, those which offer satisfaction to civil servants rather than consumer/voters).

Research assessment exercises designed to monitor and assess the quality of research undertaken by university staff are open to abuse. Where funds follow a university's research rating, there are incentives to hire staff with established research records and to offer them research-only contracts whilst shifting non-research active staff to teaching-only contracts or any other method of ensuring that such staff do not enter the research returns (for example, by allocating them to fictitious departments or to the library or administration). World experts from foreign universities might be hired at attractive pay rates on a visiting basis to be entered in the university's staff return for assessment. With such incentives, research is preferred to teaching. The system also ensures that producer interests (university academics) determine the criteria for assessing research quality. Typically, so-called independent assessment panels will seek to minimize their transaction costs and in the interests of transparency will specify research quality in terms of publications in the world's top academic economics journals with their focus on game theory, econometrics and mathematical economics (the system penalizes book publications). This will ensure that current and future generations of economics researchers will direct their research into these areas, hence creating barriers to new entry in the research domain. Nor does such a system guarantee that the resulting research will make a genuine contribution to social welfare. Most of the research is of interest and relevance to only a small field of economists specializing in these areas. Very few publications are empirical and of policy relevance dealing with society's most urgent problems (for example, energy; the environment; poverty; the future of civilization threatened with terrorism and nuclear/biological/chemical weapons).

Ultimately, the behaviour of bureaucrats and the efficiency with which they provide services will be determined by the prevailing form of the employment contract. For example, in the armed forces, schools, universities and hospitals, do employment contracts provide inducements and rewards for staff to respond to economic incentives and substitute between capital and labour and between various types of personnel as relative factor prices change? Alternatively, are public sector employment contracts incomplete and extremely difficult and costly to monitor, so allowing individuals and groups at all levels opportunities for hoarding and distorting information and pursuing discretionary behaviour, the result being substantial organizational slack? If, however, modified public sector employment contracts (that is, more completely specified, with more economic incentives) are rejected as 'impossible' (why?), there is an alternative solution. Governments can sell or 'hive off' state activities to the private sector, they can abolish legislative barriers to new entrants, and private firms can be invited to compete for contracts to supply state services (for example, via competitive tendering: see Chapter 15). One survey of some 50 studies comparing the efficiency of public and private provision found only two cases where public firms were more efficient than their private sector equivalents; and in over 40 studies public firms were found to be significantly less efficient than private firms supplying the same service. 'The evidence that public provision of a service reduces the efficiency of its provision seems overwhelming' (Mueller, 1989, p. 266).

14.10   CONCLUSION: VOTES, POLICY AND METHODOLOGY

The economics of politics and bureaucracies are attractive in that they seem to describe real world events. But description and appearances plus casual empiricism are insufficient for the acceptance of a theory. Much more work is required in clarifying public choice concepts, such as producer groups. Is a producer group a large firm located in a high unemployment area or a firm in a marginal constituency? Do governments actually favour such groups? Similar questions need to be asked about economic models of bureaucracy.

How can the output of bureaucracies be measured and how can the predictions of these models be tested?

Questions also need to be asked as to whether there are alternative explanations of government policy? If so, it is necessary to identify differences in the predictions offered by alternative models and assess their relative empirical validity. Marxists, for example, would explain policy in terms of the 'struggle of class forces' and the need for public expenditure and subsidies to 'lame duck' firms to maintain capitalism. Applied to a nation's military spending, Marxists would assert that defence expenditure is necessary for the maintenance of capitalism as a viable international system. In contrast, standard economic theory would start with the concept of a public good and analyse defence spending as an optimization problem. Defence output in the form of 'protection' is then maximized subject to constraints of resources, efficiency, technology and information. Alternatively, the economics of politics and bureaucracies would explain military spending in terms of the vote-maximizing behaviour of governments and politicians, and utility-maximizing actions of bureaucracies supported by producer groups in the form of weapons firms (that is, the military–industrial–political complex). Advocates of other explanations of military power might, of course, claim that 'class forces' underlie the economics of politics model. Analysts have the task of identifying alternative predictions from these various 'explanations'. Otherwise, 'explanation' becomes a matter of choice between deities: Chicago, Moscow, Peking, Mecca or Rome?

In summary, the economics of politics has resulted in economists including political and bureaucratic variables in their models. It provides an explanation of the extent and form of state intervention, including the size and growth of the public sector in Western economies. The analysis is obviously applicable to the whole range of microeconomic policies (for example, see the chapters in this book). A general conclusion is that government solutions can also 'fail'. But if both private markets and governments can fail, what is left?

READING* AND REFERENCES

Borcherding, T. and D. Lee (2006), 'The supply side of democratic government: a brief survey', in A. *Ott and R.J. Cebula (eds), *The Elgar Companion to Public Economics*, Cheltenham, UK and Northampton, MA, USA: Edward Elgar.

Boyfield, K. (2006), 'Better regulation without the state', *Economic Affairs*, June, **26**(2), 2–37.

Breton, A. (1974), *The Economic Theory of Representative Government*, Chicago: Aldine.

Buchanan, J.M. and G. Tullock (1962), *The Calculus of Consent*, Ann Arbor: University of Michigan Press.

*Buchanan, J.M. et al. (1978), *The Economics of Politics,* IEA Readings No. 18, London: Institute of Economic Affairs.

Cebula, R.J. and G. Tullock (2006), 'An extension of the rational voter model', in A. Ott and R.J. Cebula (eds), *The Elgar Companion to Public Economics*, Cheltenham, UK and Northampton, MA, USA: Edward Elgar.

*Downs, A. (1957), *An Economic Theory of Democracy*, New York: Harper and Row.

Downs, A. (1967), *Inside Bureaucracy*, Boston: Little, Brown.

Dunleavy, P. (1991), *Democracy, Bureaucracy and Public Choice*, Hemel Hempstead: Harvester Wheatsheaf.

Frey, B.S. and F. Schneider (1978), 'A politico-economic model of the UK', *Economic Journal*, June, pp. 243–53.

Layfield, F. (1976), *Local Government Finance*, Cmnd 6453, London: HMSO.

Mandelson, P. (2004), 'Mandelson comes out fighting on state aid', *Financial Times*, 9th November, London.

*Mueller, D.C. (1989), *Public Choice II*, Cambridge: Cambridge University Press.

Niskanan, W.A., Jr. (1971), *Bureaucracy and Representative Government*, Chicago: Aldine-Atherton.

Niskanen, W.A., Jr. (1973), *Bureaucracy: Servant or Master?*, Hobart Paperback 5, London: Institute of Economic Affairs.

Olson, M., Jr. (1965), *The Logic of Collective Action*, Cambridge, Mass: Harvard University Press.

Orzechowski, W. (1977), 'Economic models of bureaucracy: survey, extensions and evidence', in T.E. Borcherding (ed.), *Budgets and Bureaucrats: The Sources of Government Growth* North Carolina: Duke University Press.

Peacock, A. (1992), *Public Choice Analysis in Historical Perspective*, Cambridge: Cambridge University Press.

Peacock, A. (2006), 'Wagner's Law of increasing expansion of public activities', in A. Ott and R.J. Cebula (eds), *The Elgar Companion to Public Economics*, Cheltenham, UK and Northampton, MA, USA: Edward Elgar.

Peacock, A. and J. Wiseman (1967), *The Growth of Public Expenditure in the UK*, London: Allen and Unwin.

Robertson, A. (1976), *A Theory of Party Competition*, Chichester: Wiley.

*Tullock, G. (1976), *The Vote Motive*, London: Hobart Paperback 9 Institute of Economic Affairs.

QUESTIONS FOR REVIEW AND DISCUSSION

1. Why do people vote?
2. Which economic model(s) best explains the extent and form of state intervention in your country?
3. What is a producer interest group? Give examples of such groups, explaining your choices. Construct an economic model to explain the behaviour of any producer interest group with which you are familiar.
4. Carefully explain how you would test any economic model of government bureaucracy.
5. The critics of government bureaucracy often:
   (a) ignore bureaucracies in large corporations and
   (b) compare actual bureaucracies with perfect markets (i.e. muddle with model).
   Evaluate these two criticisms. What is your response to them?
6. Would a perfectly competitive solution in the political market place be socially desirable?
7. What determines the distribution of voters across the political spectrum?
8. Does the evidence on political business cycles confuse correlation with causation?
9. Does the economics of politics provide a satisfactory explanation of (a) government subsidy policy or (b) government defence expenditure?
10. What is rent-seeking and why does it exist? Suggest policy measures to control and remove rent-seeking.
11. Is the public sector inefficient? How would you test such a proposition?
12. Predict the response of a bureaucracy to a 20 per cent cut in its budget. Illustrate your answer with examples from central, state or local government.
13. Do economic models of politics and bureaucracy predict a displacement effect?

15. The contract state

15.1 INTRODUCTION: CONTROVERSY AND THE CHOICE SET

Government purchasing is big business and represents a significant proportion of economic activity in most countries. It involves governments at various levels (national, state, local, city) buying goods and services from private firms. In some markets, governments are major or even monopsony buyers. Public procurement policy involves governments in a set of choices about what to buy, who to buy it from, and how. In other words, decisions are required on the type of goods and services to be purchased, the choice of contractor, and the form of contract. Uncertainty increases the problem of choice. Questions arise about the most appropriate market, institutional and contractual arrangements for coping with uncertainty.

At one extreme, uncertainty is absent and the competitive model is applicable. The government as a buyer knows what it wants; the products exist and are being bought and sold in something resembling a competitive market (for example, office furniture, buildings, houses, vehicles). In such circumstances, the state simply acts as a competitive buyer, specifies its requirements, and invites competitive tenders. The lowest bid is selected and a fixed-price contract is awarded.

At the other extreme, governments are not always certain about the type of product that they wish to buy, as with high technology goods (for example, weapons, electronics, nuclear power and telecommunications). Moreover, within the domestic market, there might be relatively few potential suppliers and no other buyers (for example, defence, UK Post Office). In this case, uncertainty occurs in a bilateral monopoly bargaining situation where both buyer and seller have opportunities for exercising bargaining power and discretionary behaviour in a non-competitive or imperfect market. The buyer might have to choose a contractor and select a contract for a project which does not exist and which might involve a substantial jump in technology or the 'state of the art'. For example, a modern combat aircraft might take 10 or more years to develop and will remain in service for a further 30 years, so that the buyer has to anticipate a variety of technical developments as well as economic and political changes among both allies and likely enemies over a 40-year time horizon. Such advanced technology projects are often associated with cost escalation and overruns, time slippages and major modifications, leading to allegations of contractor inefficiency, especially where the work is undertaken on a cost-based contract with no incentive provisions. Sometimes projects are cancelled, giving rise to further allegations of 'waste and incompetence' by both the buyer and the contractor.

Protection of something called the 'public interest' is a recurring theme. One interpretation requires the negotiation of 'fair and reasonable' prices on non-competitive government contracts and the achievement of 'good value for money'. A wider interpretation of the 'public interest' starts from the magnitude of government expenditure and the range of goods and services acquired from the private sector and raises issues of power, control and democracy involved in the partnership between the state and industry. Further complications arise because the objectives of procurement policy frequently embrace 'ends' additional to the actual acquisition of goods and services. Considerations of the 'national interest' might be used to justify government purchase from a higher-cost domestic supplier. The 'need to protect' a nation's technology, its jobs, the balance of payments, or its 'strategic and key' industries are some of the 'ends' which typically are purchased by the state.

Government procurement policy is a controversial subject area, relatively unexplored by economists. It can be analysed with the methodology of economic policy. There are questions about the scope and objectives of procurement policy, the relevant analytical framework, and the appropriateness of alternative competitive and contractual policies.

15.2   THE SCOPE OF PUBLIC PROCUREMENT POLICY: SOME DIFFICULTIES OF DEFINITION

The extensive nature of government contracting policies creates problems of definition. Broadly, procurement policy consists of the allocation of various types of government contracts for the purchase of consumption and investment goods and services from private sector firms both domestically and overseas. Government or the public sector includes central or federal government departments, state, local and city authorities, publicly-owned firms and industries, and other state agencies. Through these organizations the output purchased by the public sector can range from such standard items as food, furniture, cars, housing, general building (schools, hospitals, factories), and civil engineering (roads, bridges, harbours, sewerage) to more complex products like airliners, communications systems, computers, drugs, motorways, nuclear power stations, railway systems, space satellites and weapons. Services purchased might include design and technical advice, consultancy, management, research, training, financial and legal advice. In this way, the scope and extent of public procurement policy is defined by the existing organization and range of goods and services bought by the public sector from private firms.

The Make or Buy Decision: Contracting-out

A starting point in analysing public procurement requires governments to choose which goods and services are to be purchased from external suppliers or contractors rather than being produced 'in-house'. This is the make-or-buy decision. Often governments make or supply a range of 'in-house' activities such as health and education through state-owned hospitals and schools; defence through national armies, navies and air forces; prisons for criminals and terrorists; and such local services as leisure facilities, refuse collection, road repairs and street cleaning. In many states over the last twenty-five years, there has been a trend towards the outsourcing of services and activities that were formerly undertaken within government. Examples of activities which have been contracted-out include catering, cleaning and laundry facilities within hospitals; catering, training, transport and some management activities for the armed forces; prison management and security guarding; and local refuse collection, street cleaning and the management of leisure facilities. Such outsourcing has been known variously as competitive tendering, contractorization and contracting-out and involves the private provision of activities previously undertaken 'in-house' by national or local governments (but with continued state finance of such activities). Cost savings of around 20 per cent have been reported from contracting-out (Domberg et al., 1986).

The trend towards outsourcing and contracting-out reflects a search by governments for efficiency savings, innovation and private sources of finance for the public sector. Efficiency problems arise since government-provided 'in-house' activities are effectively monopolies which are not subject to competition. Compared with competition, monopolies are characterized by higher prices, monopoly profits, inefficiency and a poor record on innovation. Furthermore, some forms of outsourcing involve the private sector both financing and providing assets and services to government in return for annual rental payments on long-term contracts (known as the private finance initiative in the UK). The benefits claimed for such private finance forms of outsourcing include cost savings from lower construction costs and lower life-cycle costs; the transfer of risks from the public to the private sector and the opportunity for private firms to be innovative in project design, construction, operation and maintenance.

Economists explain an organization's choice between outsourcing and internal provision in terms of transaction costs (pioneered by Oliver Williamson: Williamson, 1979). Various forms of organization are explained as efforts to economize on the total of both production and transaction costs. Where transaction costs are negligible, buying rather than making will usually be the most cost-effective means of procurement. In contrast, where external procurement results in small production cost economies and/or high transaction costs, then alternative supply and organizational arrangements such as in-house provision (or vertical integration in the private sector) are likely.

Outsourcing is not without its critics. Where outsourcing takes the form of private finance initiatives, the simple transfer of resources from the public to the private sector has no effect on efficiency if identical resources are used. Moreover, governments can always borrow more cheaply than the private sector: hence, if private finance initiatives are to result in cost savings, the extra financing costs for the private sector must be offset by savings elsewhere on the project (that is, over the life-cycle). Further problems and transaction costs arise in writing, negotiating, monitoring and enforcing long-term contracts which have to deliver services of approved quality: often such contracts require trust, commitment and partnership between both parties to the contract and they provide opportunities for corruption in public administration. Once awarded a long-term contract, firms have incentives to exploit their monopoly power and earn monopoly profits: for example, by economizing or defaulting on those parts of the contract which have not been specified completely (for example, aspects of quality). Also, when a government agency contracts out, it may lose learning opportunities and the expertise needed to monitor contracts, especially those which are complex and involve large firms with expert teams of lawyers (Tisdell, 2004). Finally, large value and long-term contracts often require large firms, and the supplying industry might be monopolistic rather than competitive. Even where competition is possible, a major loser can always take over the winning firm. But within nations, public procurement markets are often characterized by protectionism and raise wider aspects of competition.

Openness in Public Markets: the Example of the Single European Market

In choosing between make or buy, governments can protect their 'in-house' activities by preventing private firms from bidding for such work. Competitive tendering is a means of opening such markets to rivalry. Similarly, within nations, government can use preferential public purchasing to protect their 'national champions' (for example, defence, pharmaceutical, IT and telecommunications firms). Economists usually focus on anti-competitive behaviour by suppliers; but public procurement highlights the possibilities and opportunities for anti-competitive behaviour by governments acting as buyers. The Single European Market is a good example of efforts to open up public markets.

Before the introduction of the Single European Market, public purchasing in member states was characterized by preferential purchasing, protectionism, support for national champions and discriminatory practices favouring domestic over foreign suppliers. Generally, only part of public purchasing was put out to tender; only limited information was provided on public contracts; and restricted or negotiated tenders were preferred to open competitions. Tenders were not advertised in the Official Journal of the European Communities; bidders from other member states were excluded; governments subsidized some activities; there were widely different national or exclusive standards; and discrimination occurred in assessing the technical and financial capabilities of the rival bidders.

Estimates showed that opening up or liberalizing civil public procurement markets would lead to substantial savings in the region of 0.5 per cent of Community GDP over the medium to long term and the creation of some 350 000 jobs. These savings were expected to arise from two sources. First, from the competition effect, whereby opening up national public procurement markets would allow state procurement agencies to buy from the lowest-cost suppliers, including foreign firms. Increased competition would also mean that domestic firms in previously protected national markets would reduce prices and profit margins to compete with foreign rivals as new entrants. Second, from the scale effect, whereby increased competition over the long run would mean that industries would be rationalized and restructured, enabling the surviving firms to achieve economies of scale and learning.

The task of opening up national public procurement markets in the EU is an example of the problems of translating economic models into a set of legally enforceable rules (directives). The legislation for the Single European Market aimed to create open, liberalized public procurement markets often expressed in terms of non-discriminatory purchasing and a 'level playing field'. The Single Market directives for public purchasing specified:

i.   Contract thresholds above which all contracts must be advertised on an EU-wide basis in the Official Journal;
ii.   Awards procedures, comprising open, restricted and negotiated procedures. There was a preference for open or restricted tendering with negotiated tendering regarded as exceptional;
iii. Transparency and time limits, requiring contracting authorities to provide minimum time-periods for firms to respond to advertised contracts so ensuring a 'level playing field';
iv.   Technical standards, with the aim of applying EU-wide technical standards thereby reducing opportunities for applying special national standards which might be discriminatory;

v. Awards criteria which specify that contracts must normally be awarded to the lowest-priced or 'most economically advantageous tender' which allows non-price factors to be included in tender evaluations (for example, artistic and technical merit; delivery dates; after-sales service).

vi. Compliance with the directives is achieved through two routes. First, aggrieved parties can take action through their national courts. Second, the European Commission can take a member state to the European Court of Justice for infringement of the EU rules on public procurement.

The Single Market is an example of rigorous efforts to introduce competition into public procurement markets. However, by the late 1990s, a study concluded that the results were disappointing, with the objectives achieved in only a few markets. The reasons for failure included the problem of enforcement, a lack of clarity in the rules, a lack of response on the supply side and imperfect competition in supplying industries.

Buying Power

Once governments have decided to buy rather than make, they acquire buying power. Where a government is a monopsonist or a major buyer, its procurement decisions can determine technical progress, as well as industry size, structure, conduct and performance. The type of product demanded affects technical progress: for example, governments might demand an advanced computer system or space satellite communication system, where some of the technology might 'spill-over' into other sectors of the economy (for example, military aircraft engines and radar applied to civil airliners). Its buying power determines the size of a national industry: buying from national firms creates and supports national employment. Government purchasing also determines industry structure reflected in the size of firms (for example, by allowing mergers), as well as entry and exit conditions (for example, by allowing or preventing foreign firms to bid for national contracts). Government can also determine market conduct through specifying the form of competition (that is, price versus non-price competition); and it can use its buying power and regulation to determine performance as reflected in efficiency, prices, profits and exports (for example, via export licences). In these circumstances, procurement embraces other policy objectives which cannot be ignored in assessing the purchased 'product'.

Similar difficulties of definition and scope arise in relation to government subsidy policy. Using a production function approach, subsidies can be classified into those for output and for factor inputs of labour, capital and research and development (technical progress). Constraints usually exist such that subsidies might be limited to certain regions (for example, high unemployment areas), a specific sector of the economy (for example, manufacturing rather than services), to one industry (for example, shipbuilding), or to an individual firm. Similarly, factor subsidies can be constrained to 'approved' investments (for example, plant and machinery), to specified research and development work (for example, Concorde), to 'approved' training methods and skills, as well as to clearly identified groups such as the unemployed, school-leavers, older workers and 'approved' worker cooperatives. Time constraints might be imposed (for example, a temporary employment subsidy) and the subsidies can be in cash, or kind, or earmarked. Examples include federal or central government cash grants to state or local authorities, free factory space in high unemployment localities, and grants designated for training unskilled, unemployed workers. Inevitably, questions arise about the economic logic of subsidy policy, especially its relationship to the Paretian model, as well as its internal consistency. Who, for example, is maximizing what for the benefit of whom? Nevertheless, subsidies to private firms enable governments to achieve desired objectives. As such, subsidy policy and the role of public money in the private sector can be included in a wider interpretation of procurement policy. Other forms of state intervention which affect procurement policy include preferential purchasing, tariffs and import quotas. For example, government purchasing departments might give preferential treatment to firms in high unemployment areas. Alternatively, a highly-localized industry which is declining because of import competition might receive tariff protection (see Chapter 4, Figure 4.14).

The extensive nature of government procurement has usually been reflected in a state's organizational and regulatory arrangements. Changes often occur in the number and size distribution of government departments, with new entrants and exits. Such changes can result from:

1. Growth or decline in the size of the public sector. Examples include more state ownership or the desire of vote-sensitive governments to be seen to be searching for solutions to a nation's economic problems. For instance, an energy or technology problem or a terrorist threat might lead to the creation of a new government department (for example, homeland security). Alternatively, privatization transfers procurement from the public to the private sectors; or government might prefer to shift from undertaking activities 'in-house' to awarding contracts to private firms (contracting-out).
2. A desire to rationalize departments, to centralize public sector purchasing, and to introduce more accountable management units. For example, specialist procurement agencies might be created for defence and health, for the purchase of all government stationery requirements, and for the acquisition of buildings, equipment and transport for public clients.

Government procurement also raises issues of regulation and public accountability. With non-competitive contracts, government departments might be required to negotiate 'fair and reasonable' prices. Specialist regulatory agencies might be established for monitoring and policing non-competitive contracts. Such bodies might have the powers to investigate and re-negotiate contracts where profits are found to be 'excessive'. However, some models of regulation suggest that this arrangement might benefit industry rather than society! Public accountability might also be reinforced by specialist constitutional committees with the specific function of assessing each government department's expenditure plans and their outcomes.

15.3   POLICY OBJECTIVES: WHAT ARE THE AIMS OF GOVERNMENT PROCUREMENT POLICY?

The immediate aim of public procurement policy is to secure the 'best value for money spent', which is usually interpreted as the 'most suitable goods at the most satisfactory price'. Where a government wishes to buy an existing product, a 'satisfactory' price can

be obtained through competitive tendering. Price criteria are used for the choice of contractor, and a firm or fixed-price contract is allocated to the lowest bidder. Provided the
market is competitive, the process is impersonal and requires no arbitrary judgement
about what is 'reasonable'. However, there is a view on contractor selection which maintains that competition is a useful, but not necessarily essential, means to the end of achieving value for money. Policy-makers often prefer selective to open competition. Critics
claim that open competition raises the costs of abortive tendering for an industry and
increases the risks of contractor bankruptcy. Selective competition is believed to avoid
these alleged disadvantages by restricting tendering to a limited number of firms (possibly
5 to 10 firms) from an approved list and of known reliability. The underlying economic
models for these alternative views are clearly a matter for critical appraisal. What assumptions are being made about firm behaviour? Is it assumed that firms are profit-, sales-, or
utility-maximizers, or satisficers, and what are the price-output and efficiency implications
of different behaviour? And central to the arguments about open versus selective competition must be whether the various hypotheses are consistent with the facts.

Discretionary behaviour by governments and bureaucrats becomes possible with non-
competitive contracts and where non-price criteria (quality, delivery, and so on) are major
elements in value for money. With non-competitive contracts, the aim of policy is to pay
'fair and reasonable' prices. These are usually prices based on either actual or estimated
costs plus a 'reasonable' profit rate defined by the state's profit formula. Of course, even
where there is 'equality of information' and post-costing, there can be no presumption
that in an imperfect market a contractor's cost levels will be X-efficient. Moreover, so long
as a 'fair and reasonable' price is negotiated, a concern with 'value for money, suitable
goods and satisfactory prices' provides opportunities for governments to satisfy wider
policy targets. The most 'suitable goods' might be domestic rather than foreign, or supplied by a 'lame duck' firm in a high unemployment region, or provided by a firm which
observes the government's pay guidelines or its anti-discrimination and equal pay legislation. Contracts can also be used to encourage mergers and so re-structure industries (for
example, contract awards being dependent on a merger). In the circumstances, import
saving, domestic technology, jobs and price stability might be part of the 'product' being
bought; they are often elements in a government's objective function.

In some instances, the arguments used to justify state support of an industry reveal the
underlying policy aims and provide an indication of the valuations being placed upon
chosen objectives. For example, an industry might be supported because it is claimed to
be a high-skill, high-value-added sector which makes an important contribution to the
balance of payments and which, without state support, would decline, so leading to substantial job losses. Such arguments for state support tend to be presented in emotional
terms, using catastrophe language and gross numbers which ignore completely the
alternative-use value of resources. Indeed, using these arguments, are there any firms and
industries which would not qualify for state support? The relevant question is whether the
resources used in the industry would make a greater contribution to employment, technology, the balance of payments, and, ultimately, human welfare or satisfaction, if they
were used elsewhere in the economy. Moreover, once wider policy 'ends', such as jobs and
technology, become part of the procurement choice and the purchased 'product', they
accentuate the problems of public accountability. Choices and decisions are always subjective and in the absence of a clearly specified objective function, how is it possible to

evaluate the efficiency of government procurement? There might also be a potential conflict between 'value for money' and the requirements of public accountability. Public accountability might inhibit innovation and lead to a preoccupation with the lowest tender price and lower priority to completion on time. The system of incentives for civil servants and their general attitude towards risk could be a causal factor. Critics sometimes claim that civil servants tend to be judged by failure and this inevitably conditions their approach to work, leading to delays in decision-making and the blurring of responsibility (that is, a lack of entrepreneurship).

15.4   THEORY AND PROCUREMENT POLICY: THE CONCEPTUAL FRAMEWORK

Explanations of government procurement behaviour require the construction of the underlying policy model. This can be deduced from government behaviour and its perception of the policy problem, its choice of the preferred solution and the standard criticisms of procurement policy. Usually, public procurement authorities are concerned with reducing escalation in cost, time and quality while preventing excessive prices and profits, and providing contractors with efficiency incentives. Such features are most prevalent with uncertainty and non-competitive contracts. For example, uncertainty affects both buyers and sellers. It might take the form of unexpected technical problems, modifications, and changing requirements, all of which contribute to escalation in development and production costs and delays in delivery. On the supply side, it is recognized that in non-competitive markets, firms might not be X-efficient: hence, criticisms are made if incentive contracts are not used in such markets or if contractors are reluctant to risk private funds, and if the buyer fails to enforce penalty clauses in contracts (for example, for delays or poor performance).

The criticisms of contracting and the various recommendations for 'solving' the problems can be used to deduce a government's optimal purchasing policy. Where some form of competitive tendering is possible, there is usually a presumption that competitive pressures together with fixed-price contracts provide the appropriate efficiency incentives and policing arrangements for 'fair and reasonable' prices. With non-competitive work, where prices have to be negotiated, there is often a preference for clearly-specified contracts with constraints on the buyer's financial liability, together with regular progress reports to the sponsoring department and to society's elected representatives. To stimulate efficiency in imperfect markets, there might be a general dislike of cost-plus contracts and a preference for incentive and fixed-price arrangements, with prices determined at the start of the work and the contractor subject to regulatory review (for example, a review board for post-costing and re-negotiation of government contracts).

The underlying policy model contains a mixture of positive and normative propositions offering extensive opportunities for critical evaluation. There are propositions about 'fair' prices (what is 'fair'?) and the desirability of avoiding escalation (regardless of transaction costs?). Potential conflicts are likely between some of the procurement objectives, such as reducing escalation in both cost and time, as well as regulating profits without adversely affecting efficiency. Various economic models can be used to analyse procurement policy. The market structure–conduct–performance paradigm can be used to assess the allocative efficiency of different market structures, ranging from competitive tendering to non-competitive situations. A concern with broader policy aims such as jobs, technical 'fall-out', and the balance of payments suggests externalities and the use of market failure analysis. Alternatively, governments might not be social welfare-maximizers, in which case the economics of politics and bureaucracies might provide more accurate explanations of procurement policy. In this context, vote-maximizing governments are likely to favour producer interest groups (for example, major contractors) while bureaucracies aiming to maximize budgets have every incentive to underestimate the costs of policies and overestimate their alleged benefits. Indeed, bureaucracies and politicians might enjoy the 'discretionary power' associated with the allocation of non-competitive contracts; this might explain the attractions of a selective tendering policy and the official opposition to a truly competitive solution.

Further analytical difficulties arise in formulating policy rules for improving *ex ante* decision-making under uncertainty. There are alternative methods of coping with uncertainty, and economists are interested in identifying the costs and benefits of the various options. Information and knowledge is not costless and it can be purchased at different points in the life-cycle of a project, ranging from the initial design and development stage to the construction of a prototype and, ultimately, a production decision. Advanced technology projects are the classic example of public sector choice under uncertainty (for example, modern weapons, nuclear power stations, microelectronics). They can be bought 'off the drawing board', with only paper or design competition and the successful bidder receiving a contract for development and production work. This is believed to reduce the costs of competition but, at the same time, there are higher risks of technical failure as well as the removal of competitive pressure from the successful contractor. Alternatively, competition could be continued beyond the design stage through, say, the government purchase of relatively cheap competing prototypes. In this way, a government might postpone its final choice until it has more information on the actual performance of competing designs. An example was the US experiment with a 'fly-before-you-buy' policy which was used to choose between competing prototype combat aircraft (for example, Boeing and Lockheed Martin competing prototypes for the US Joint Strike Fighter competition which was won by Lockheed Martin). However, such a policy is frequently rejected because it is believed to lead to delays and to involve higher development costs through competitive 'duplication'. But the critics implicitly compare an actual competitive procurement policy with an ideal (but never achieved) project, ordered off the drawing board, which never encounters any technical problems, cost escalation, or delays! The general point remains. In buying advanced technology projects, a government has to choose the point in the development cycle at which competition should cease and selection occur. And economists can make a contribution by showing that alternative policies involve different costs and benefits and, where possible, offering evidence on orders of magnitude.

Economists can also contribute to the evaluation of procurement policy by analysing its positive economics content. There are hypotheses about firm behaviour in imperfect markets and the expected reaction of enterprises to different contractual incentives and regulatory constraints. However, firms in imperfect and regulated markets have opportunities to pursue non-profit objectives, so that procurement and regulatory policy formulated on the assumption of profit-maximizing behaviour under competition

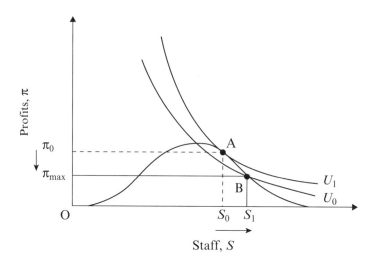

Figure 15.1   *Profit regulation and firm behaviour. Utility depends on profits and staff expenditures*
S (e.g. number of secretaries). In the absence of profit restrictions, utility is
maximized at point A. The introduction of a government profit constraint will restrict
the firm to B, where utility is lower and increased staff expenditures are substituted for
profits

might not produce the expected outcomes. An example is shown in Figure 15.1 where a
utility-maximizing contractor is subject to a state-determined limit on its profits. As a
result, the firm has an incentive to substitute staff or other discretionary expenditures
for profits.

Economic models also provide a framework for analysing the causes of escalation in
costs, time and quality which are common sources of concern in public procurement.
It is not unknown for public projects to cost more than their original estimates, to be
considerably delayed, and to be 'gold plated', built to unnecessarily high standards,
and lavishly equipped. Nor is such escalation unique to defence and government-
financed high technology projects. There are examples of cost escalation in civil as
well as defence sectors, in central or federal and local or state government, in construction as well as research and development, and in private industry. Cost escalation
can be defined as the relationship between the original cost estimate on a specific
development, construction or production task and the actual outlays, expressed in
constant prices. If, say, actual expenditure is twice the initial estimate, the cost escalation factor is 2.0. Escalation, slippages, or overruns also apply to time-scales and the
performance of a project. Some examples of cost escalation and delays are shown in
Table 15.1.

The causes of escalation can be shown using a 'trade-off' between costs and the time
required to develop or construct a given type of project. For example, the development of
a new supersonic airliner, a moon landing, or the exploitation of a new oil-field can be
achieved with varying combinations of cost and time inputs. Faster development is costlier, and an example of the trade-off is shown in Figure 15.2. Consider a public project
such as a new sports complex, conference centre, opera house, or an advanced combat aircraft. Initially, the construction or development of a project involves a set of plans about

Table 15.1   Examples of cost escalation and delays

Project	Cost escalation (constant prices)	Delays
Eurofighter Typhoon	14%	54 months (33%)
UK Nimrod MR4	35%	89 months (110%)
UK Astute submarine	35%	43 months (43%)
US F-22 Raptor	189%	117 months (101%)

UK public sector construction projects:
– 55% delivered to budget and 63% delivered on time
– average cost escalation of 6.5%

UK government procurement of IT projects:
– characterized by overspends, delays, performance shortfalls and cancellations at major cost

UK large public procurement projects (MacDonald):
– government projects with average of 47% cost overruns and average of 17% time overruns;
– private finance initiative projects with 1% cost overruns and −1% time overruns

US defence projects: 26 major weapons programmes (GAO):
– development cost escalation of 37%
– average delays of 26 months or 17%

Transport infrastructure projects in 20 nations (n=258 projects: Flyberg):
– For rail, average cost escalation of 45%
– For bridges and tunnels, average cost escalation was 34%
– For roads, average cost escalation was 20%
– Cost escalation appears more pronounced in developing nations than in North America and Europe.

Sources: National Audit Office (2004; 2005a,b); Flyvbjerg et al. (2004); MacDonald (2002); GAO (2006).

its performance, cost and time-scale, between which there are possibilities of substitution. Figure 15.2 provides an analytical framework which explains escalation in terms of urgency, modifications and unforeseen technical problems, together with contractor optimism and performance.

In Figure 15.2, a given quality or performance Q_0 might be initially estimated to cost C_2, requiring T_2 years to complete (position A). Actual costs can exceed estimates if a project is required earlier than planned. Urgency can lead to 'crash' programmes with more resources being required if the project (Q_0) is needed earlier at, say, T_1 (position B). Furthermore, urgency might cause inefficiency in a government's procurement agency, so further contributing to escalation. There could be 'hasty' decision-making, 'inadequate' project specification, and relatively 'poor' government financial control and estimation. Escalation can also be caused by unexpected project changes with modifications, alterations or improvements resulting in Q_1 being purchased at cost C_4 and time T_4 (position C). Or, a project might encounter unforeseen technical problems, especially if it involves a 'jump' in technical knowledge and hence substantial uncertainty; for example Q_0 in Figure 15.2 might be a band rather than a well-defined single line. This is a likely source of cost escalation if contractors and the bureaucracy tend to respond to uncertainty by

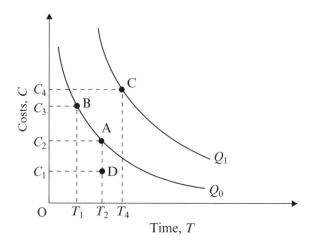

*Figure 15.2   The causes of cost escalation. Different levels of quality or performance are
represented by Q_0 and Q_1, with Q_1 reflecting a higher quality or performance (e.g. a
faster aircraft) than Q_0. The model shows that the planned quality of a project
depends on inputs of costs and time or duration (cf. Figure 12.5); it is also assumed
that the technology is given and that Q_0 and Q_1 are efficient frontiers*

submitting a minimum or most-optimistic cost estimate rather than a central point
estimate from a range of feasible outcomes. Indeed, consideration has to be given to contractor behaviour as a possible source of escalation. With a given quality Q_0, escalation
might be due to the deliberate underestimation of costs, say, C_1 instead of C_2 for duration
T_2 (position D). Such behaviour might reflect the efforts of an income-maximizing contractor to 'buy into' an attractive new programme by offering optimistic cost, time, and
quality estimates, thereby establishing a temporary monopoly. In competitive markets
with firm or fixed-price contracts, this optimism, especially in costs, would result in losses
and possibly bankruptcy. But in non-competitive markets with cost-based contracts, a
firm's optimism will be financed by the purchasing government, so that the penalties for
underestimation might be absent. The situation could be reinforced by any budget-
maximizing aim of bureaucracies sponsoring the project, supported by interest groups of
scientists, architects and planners with a preference for new technology and new designs:
they would have an incentive to underestimate costs. Once a contractor has been selected,
then cost-based contracts are unlikely to deter modifications, ambitious technical proposals, or X-inefficiency. As a result, firms might behave as though the *actual* (*ex post*)
time–cost relationship is positive, which will be reflected in both cost and time slippages,
with extra time being costlier. Clearly, this analysis of the microeconomics of escalation
raises questions about the extent of competition for public procurement and the type of
contract which finances overruns.

15.5   POLICY INSTRUMENTS: PERFORMANCE AND RESULTS

Once the government has determined the optimal point in a product's life-cycle at which
to terminate competition and select a project, there remains the choice of both contractor

and contract type. The former involves a choice between competitive tender and negotiation; the latter requires a choice between cost-reimbursement and fixed-price contracts, or some intermediate incentive arrangement.

The Choice of Contractor

The application of the competitive model to tendering requires open competition with large numbers of bidders, the absence of entry restrictions, and a clear product specification so that seller rivalry and buyer choice can be restricted to the price domain. In this model, the buyer simply has to select the lowest bidder and award a firm or fixed-price contract. Discretionary behaviour, including favouritism and corruption, is less likely. Departures from the model arise where non-price criteria, such as technical characteristics, quality, delivery, and 'wider policy aims', enter into the buyer's choice set.

Public authorities often prefer selective to open competition. Since open competition is likely to result in lower prices, some explanation is required for the general opposition to this method. One possibility is that public buyers regard open competition as 'too costly': it involves substantial transactions costs for the buyer and it is believed to raise the costs of tendering for industry. Consider the transactions costs involved in organizing an open competition and acting as a competitive buyer. The public agency will have to search for the 'best buy', which will be the lowest price, assuming there is a clearly-defined product. Search is not costless and it will require the public buyer to specify a product or at least outline a broad requirement, so that contractors can submit meaningful bids. Lower prices might be obtained by approaching more firms, but searching will cease when its expected savings through lower prices equal the costs of obtaining the extra information (that is, optimal search). The details of the competition have to be advertised, printed and distributed to potential bidders and enquiries have to be handled. When submitted, each bid has to be carefully assessed and checked, a selection procedure is required, and the bidders have to be informed of the outcome. Selective competition is believed to reduce some of these search and transactions costs since only a limited number of firms from an approved list and of known reliability are invited to tender. Also, since contracts are often imperfect and cannot be completely specified, the use of 'reputable' firms might minimize the procurement agency's transactions costs. The successful contractor is the lowest bidder from the group of invited firms. Not only does this appear to reduce buyer search costs but it is believed to avoid the 'wasteful duplication' of estimating and tendering resources. Usually, only a few firms on the approved list will be invited to bid for a contract, the aim being to ensure that in the long run all firms on the list have an opportunity to tender.

The supporters of selective competition claim that it is the simplest way of demonstrating that regard has been paid to the 'public interest'. But simplest to whom – society, taxpayers, or the bureaucracy acting as the government's agent – and whose interpretation of the public interest is being used? What are the price implications and resource costs of selective, compared with open, competition? What about new entrants, X-inefficiency, and the probability of collusion? Select lists might remain unchanged, so that there is neither new entry nor exit. It is also likely that the criteria required for entry onto an approved list will reflect a *bureaucrat's* preference for avoiding and minimizing risks: hence governments as buyers are unlikely to be presented with information on the price implications of alternative risks associated with different contractors, including innovators. Nor can it be assumed that firms will be cost-minimizers when only a small group of approved enterprises are invited to tender and the buyer determines the invitation list. Indeed, selective competition resembles oligopoly with entry restrictions. It shows how governments can determine the extent of the market, so that any market failure is policy-created and policy-preferred. However, there are no costless solutions. The choice is between open competition with lower prices and a belief of a greater risk of bankruptcy, or selective tendering which is believed to reduce the risks of default, but at a higher price. In each case evidence is required on the probability of bankruptcy and the magnitude of price differences. But open and selective competition are not the only methods for contractor selection. Non-competitive and negotiated contracts are common.

Negotiation occurs if a monopoly exists or if competition is 'inappropriate' (for example, emergency repairs of damaged sewers). Or policy-makers might exclude competition by allocating more profitable production contracts to the firm which has undertaken the less profitable development work. Once again, this is not the only solution. Development and production could be separated, with contracts for each stage allocated on a competitive basis and research and development rewarded at market rates. However, if development and production work were undertaken by different contractors, there would be problems of establishing and protecting property rights in new ideas and the associated costs of transferring technology.

Contractor selection also involves wider choice issues which are often highlighted with the purchase of defence equipment and advanced technology items such as airliners, computers, microelectronics, nuclear power stations and space satellites. For developed nations with an established manufacturing base, the choice set can be illustrated by considering two limiting policy options. At one extreme, a nation could adopt the nationalist or complete independence solution and purchase all its military and high-technology equipment domestically. This would involve sacrificing the gains from international specialization and trade. At the other extreme, a nation could 'shop around', acting as a competitive buyer, and purchase its weapons and technology from the lowest-cost suppliers within the world market. For many countries, this would probably mean buying more abroad, especially from the United States, with the attendant worries of 'undue' dependence on one nation and the fear of an American monopoly of the world's high-technology goods (for example, Boeing airliners). Opposition to such a policy would also arise from domestic interest groups of national producers and trade unions, supported by bureaucrats with a preference for domestic suppliers, and vote-sensitive governments might believe that there are more votes in allocating contracts to national firms rather than foreign firms located overseas. Between these extremes, there are various intermediate policies. A nation could undertake the licensed manufacture or co-production of foreign equipment. This is likely to be costlier than purchasing 'off-the-shelf' from the established supplier. But there are believed to be benefits through domestic jobs, the saving of both foreign exchange and research and development resources, together with access to new technology. Alternatively, a country could participate in a joint project with other nations. European examples have occurred with aircraft, missiles and space satellites, including the Anglo-French Concorde, the French–German–UK–Spain collaboration in Airbus and the UK–German–Italian–Spain Eurofighter Typhoon combat

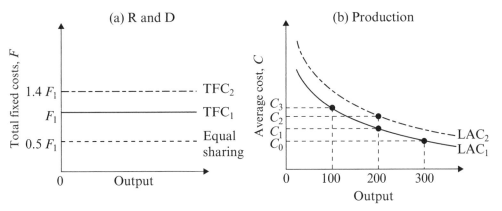

Figure 15.3 The costs of alternative policies. Research and development costs are shown as TFC in diagram (a). Unit production costs are shown by long-run average cost curves, LAC, in diagram (b). Initially costs are based on TFC_1 and LAC_1, but, with inefficiencies, the relevant cost curves could be TFC_2 and LAC_2, or even higher cost curves. For example, comparing a national venture with a joint project, the latter might lead to savings in unit production costs of $C_3 - C_2$, instead of $C_3 - C_1$ in the ideal case

aircraft. Joint projects involve two or more nations sharing the R&D costs of a project and combining their production orders. In this way, a nation can retain a domestic industry while being involved in high-technology work which would be 'too costly' to undertake alone.

Cost functions can illustrate the costs of alternative government procurement options, so allowing policy-makers to compare expenditures with expected benefits. Figure 15.3 shows a simplified example which can be developed to incorporate more realistic assumptions and complications. Development and production cost curves are shown separately, each based initially on X-efficient behaviour. For simplicity, it is assumed that prices depend on unit costs and that a government wishes to purchase 100 units of a given product, say an aircraft or a computer. Research and development is a fixed cost which is required independently of the number to be manufactured. If a nation prefers to be independent, it cannot avoid incurring all the required R&D costs, namely F_1 in Figure 15.3(a). For 100 units, the average manufacturing costs are C_3, as in Figure 15.3(b). Alternatively, two nations each requiring 100 units could combine to share equally the R&D costs, so halving each nation's development bill ($0.5F_1$). Compared with an independent solution, a doubling of output for a collaborative project should also reduce unit production costs to C_1 (see the learning curve in Figure 6.13). In contrast, a direct buy 'off the shelf' from a foreign manufacturer already producing, say, 200 units of the item will result in average production costs of C_0. Licensed production of 100 units will involve manufacturing costs of at least C_3. With this option and a direct buy from abroad, there could be an additional negotiated contribution (royalty) towards the innovator's development expenditures. For licensed manufacture, this must be less than F_1 in Figure 15.3(a), otherwise independence is cheaper. But these are only simplified examples, based on the assumption of given and efficient cost functions. For example, international collaborative military projects might result in higher development and production costs, compared with a one-nation venture. Higher R&D costs might be caused by duplication, especially if each partner government attempts to establish and protect its property rights in advanced technology. For example, on collaborative military aircraft projects, each partner will demand a share in the high technology work in the airframe, engine and avionics parts of the aircraft which is not the most cost-efficient way to build an aircraft. In other words, national and equity requirements for work-sharing will mean that work is allocated on political criteria rather than on the basis of relative costs. Some studies have suggested that total R&D costs on joint military projects might be equal to the square root of the number of nations involved: hence for two countries the actual fixed outlays could be $1.4F_1$ in Figure 15.3(a). For the four-nation Eurofighter Typhoon, estimates show that its total development costs were almost twice those of a national alternative (NAO, 2001, p. 16). However, since total development costs are shared between the partners, each partner continues to achieve cost savings compared with a national alternative. On production, collaborative military projects can lead to higher costs, reflecting increased coordination and transport, together with duplicate final assembly lines. Thus, the collaborative premium shown by LAC_2 might mean average manufacturing costs of C_2 for the joint output, so that there are some savings compared with a national venture but less than in the ideal case. Evidence shows that collaborative military programmes might achieve economies of scale in the region of half of those on national projects (for example, 5 per cent unit cost savings compared with 10 per cent on national projects: NAO, 2001, p. 17). Finally, international collaborative military projects are characterized by time delays resulting from the programme management and cooperative industrial arrangements, from changes in requirements and from partner budget constraints. Typically, for the UK, average delays on collaborative military programmes averaged 11 months (NAO, 2001, p. 19). However, these cost inefficiencies and delays are characteristic of *collaborative military projects*. In contrast, the Airbus programme of collaboration on civil aircraft has created a successful and internationally-competitive company as a major rival to the American Boeing company (forming a duopoly in large civil aircraft).

Contract Types: Fixed Prices

With the selection of a contractor, there remains the choice of contract type. There are two limiting cases, namely fixed-price and cost-plus contracts, with various intermediate types. Fixed prices are in two variants, namely, firm and fixed. Governments frequently favour firm or fixed prices and these can be determined by open or selective competition, or by negotiation. Firm prices are generally used for contracts of relatively short duration (for example, up to two years), such as building and civil engineering projects. Such contracts allow no variation of price for inflation with the bidder required to estimate inflation in the bid price. Where the work is long-term, fixed-price contracts contain provisions for inflation through agreed variations in the prices of labour and materials based on official inflation indices. In other words, firm and fixed prices are distinguished by their allowance for price variations based on inflation of input costs. In this context, though, there are no obvious market failures preventing firms from bearing risks and estimating likely inflation rates over the period of the contract, whatever the length. Someone in the economy either in the private or the public sector has to bear risks, and the process is not costless.

Generally, fixed-price contracts are used where the work required can be clearly specified and the uncertainties are removed (for example, production as opposed to R&D work). The aim is to place the contractor at risk and provide the maximum efficiency incentives, both of which require the price to be agreed before the work begins. If the contractor beats a competitively-determined fixed price, he retains the whole of any extra profits or, in the opposite case, bears all the losses. However, problems arise with non-competitive fixed-price contracts, especially where a government is a monopsonist and negotiates with a single supplier. Since competition is absent, the market cannot be used to determine prices, to provide competitive pressures for efficiency, and to 'regulate' profits through entry and exit. Instead, in non-competitive situations, prices and profits have to be negotiated. Government buying agents are concerned with minimizing the taxpayers' liability, so they aim to negotiate 'fair and reasonable' prices. For non-competitive fixed-price contracts, these are prices based on estimated costs plus a state-determined profit margin. Such contracts assume that firms are profit-maximizers and that governments can estimate X-efficient costs (see Figure 15.1). The state's profit rules for non-competitive contracts might be based on a target rate of return on capital or costs, designed to provide contractors with a return equal to the average earned by the whole of manufacturing industry. Higher profit rates might be awarded for risk work and for contractor performance and there can be upper and lower limits on the profitability of non-competitive government contracts. Indeed, regulatory agencies might be created to police and monitor the returns on such contracts and to re-negotiate any cases of 'excessive' profits. But how do 'excessive' profits arise?

Fixed-price contracts specify the price to be paid for an agreed quantity and quality of product, together with delivery dates. A typical non-competitive fixed-price contract is shown as follows:

$$P_f = E_0 + \pi_g \qquad (15.1)$$

Where E_0 = total *estimated* outlays or expenditures for the required output. This total comprises direct labour, materials and bought-out parts (variable costs) and fixed outlays or overheads (fixed costs). Direct labour costs might be estimated by using a labour learning curve (Figure 6.13) and an agreed wage rate. Fixed outlays might be recovered by applying an overhead recovery rate to estimated direct labour costs.

   π_g = the government-determined profit margin, calculated as a rate of return ($r\%$) on capital employed (rK) or costs (rC).

With fixed-price contracts, profits will exceed the government-determined margins whenever a firm's actual costs are below the original estimates. For example, if costs are estimated to be £100 million and the state allows a profit margin of 10 per cent on costs, the firm will receive a lump sum payment of £110 million on completion of the work. An example is shown in Figure 15.4. If actual costs are, say, £90 million, its realized profits will be £20 million, which represents a return of some 22 per cent on cost.

Firms can reduce actual costs below the estimated level through two sources. First, they can raise efficiency. Second, there might be errors in the government's cost estimates, so that the negotiated price is not based on X-efficient behaviour. As a result, the actual profits earned on fixed-price contracts will be 'excessive' in the sense of exceeding the

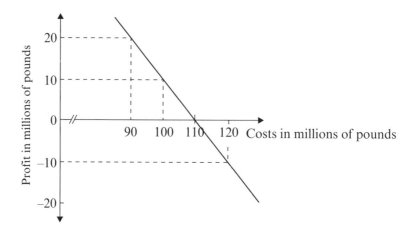

*Figure 15.4   Profits and fixed-price contracts. Estimated costs are £100m, on which the state allows
a profit or fee of £10m. If the final cost is £110m, the profit received is zero and further
cost increases result in losses*

state-determined profit rates. Equation (15.2) shows the determinants of a firm's actual
profits on fixed-price work:

$$\pi = \pi_g + s(E_0 - A_0) \qquad (15.2)$$

where π = actual profits received by the contractor
            π_g = profit sum negotiated and agreed by the government and the firm
            s = the rate at which any difference between E_0 and A_0 will be shared between
                   the firm and the government
            E_0 = estimated outlays
            A_0 = actual expenditures

   With fixed-price contracts where $s = 1$, so that the firm retains the whole of any
difference between estimated and actual outlays, $\pi > \pi_g$ when $E_0 > A_0$. This provides a
basis for defining and determining excessive profits, especially if $E_0 > A_0$, not as a result
of increased efficiency but due to inaccuracies in the state procurement agency's cost estimates. Such inaccuracies can result from the estimating techniques used by the government, differences in the information available to both parties (information asymmetries),
and their behaviour in the bargaining process (cf. wage bargaining, Chapter 13). During
negotiations for non-competitive fixed-price contracts, a firm wishing to increase its
profits above the state-determined level has every incentive to maximize its estimated, and
minimize its actual, outlays.

Cost-plus Contracts

Advanced technology projects confront state procurement authorities with the classic
problem of choice under uncertainty. They have to determine the optimal distribution of
risks between the buyer and the contractor. In these circumstances, some form of cost-
reimbursement contract is usually adopted with the state bearing most, if not all, of the

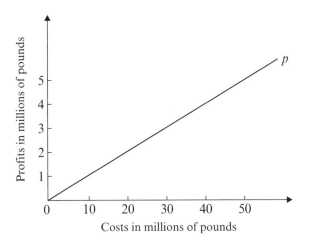

*Figure 15.5   Profits and cost-plus a percentage profit contracts. With this form of cost-plus
contract, profits (π) depend directly on the percentage profit rate (p) to be applied to
costs (C), that is π = pC. In this example, p = 10 per cent (0.1), so that an increase in
costs from £20m to £50m raises profits or the fee from £2m to £5m*

risks. Under a cost-plus a percentage profit contract (for example, research and development for military aircraft or space systems), the firm recovers all its actual outlays regardless of their level, plus a government-determined percentage profit. Such contracts are
believed to offer little or no efficiency incentives: they have been called 'blank cheque' contracts. Since the profit sum is directly related to costs, the contractor is almost encouraged
to incur higher costs and to search for perfection! An example is shown in Figure 15.5.

It is likely that cost-plus pricing in non-competitive markets provides contractors with
the financial framework for cost escalation and labour hoarding. Economists can contribute to policy by formulating these propositions into testable hypotheses. Cost escalation has already been analysed (Figure 15.2). The labour-hoarding hypothesis provides a
further example of the problems in applied economics. Hypotheses have to be specified
clearly and related to an established theoretical framework so that appropriate empirical
tests can be undertaken. For example, in weapons markets, it is believed that defence contractors follow a labour-retention policy financed by cost-based government contracts.
These beliefs arise from the frequent observation that the cancellation of weapons contracts leads to employment reductions, but usually by much less than the numbers
involved on the project (see Figure 12.7). Thus, the central hypothesis is that cost-plus
defence contracts result in excess employment which is reflected in a sluggish employment
response to cancellations of projects and a relatively labour-intensive reaction to an
increase in sales. In other words, it is predicted that employment behaviour in weapons
markets will differ from that in a normal commercial environment. Empirical tests of this
hypothesis require a model which identifies the major determinants of employment. The
standard approach starts from a production function (for example, Cobb–Douglas) and
derives an employment model as shown in equation (15.3). In this model, employment is
determined by output, technology and capital:

$$L = f(Q,A,K) \tag{15.3}$$

where L = employment
        Q = output
        A = state of technology
        K = capital stock

This employment model can be estimated by assuming that capital and technology can be represented by a time-trend and that actual employment adjusts to its desired level with a lag: hence, the estimating equation only requires data on real output and employment. The labour-hoarding hypothesis can be tested by estimating the relationship between employment and output, *ceteris paribus*. For cancellations and reductions in output, the resulting elasticity of employment with respect to variations in output is predicted to be lower for defence contractors compared with civilian enterprises. In other words, the hypothesis can be tested by estimating employment elasticities for defence industries compared with other industries not dependent on government defence contracts. But empirical work is not without its analytical and statistical problems. There could be alternative explanations of sluggish employment behaviour by defence contractors. For example, the announced redundancy figures associated with the cancellations of weapons might be deliberate exaggerations, reflecting an attempt by producer interest groups supported by budget-conscious bureaucracies to influence the decisions of vote-maximizing governments. Also, data might not be available and there are difficulties in obtaining accurate and reliable indicators of technology and the capital stock (see Figure 12.7). Not surprisingly, criticisms of cost-plus a percentage profit contracts have led to the introduction of incentive contracting for government R&D work. A simple form is the cost-plus a fixed fee, where the fee is based on estimated costs. While the firm recovers all of its allowable costs, its fixed fee remains constant regardless of actual expenditures. An example is shown in Figure 15.6(a).

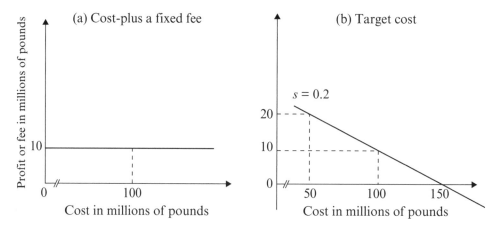

Figure 15.6   *Incentive contracts. In both cases, costs are estimated at £100m. With a cost-plus a
            fixed fee, the firm receives a fee of £10m based on estimated costs, and this fee remains
            constant regardless of actual costs (s = 0; see equation 15.2). With a target cost
            contract and a sharing ratio of 80:20 (s = 0.2), the firm's profits will be £20m if its
            actual costs are £50m, while losses are incurred when actual costs exceed £150m.
            Additional constraints can be introduced into target cost contracts, such as a maximum
            and/or minimum fee*

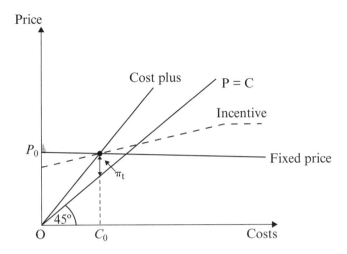

Figure 15.7   Three contract types. Price $P_0 = C_0 + \pi_t$ and the 45° line shows all points where price equals cost and the intersection of this line with the fixed price and incentive lines shows the points beyond which losses are incurred

Alternatively, a target cost contract might be negotiated. This is based on estimates and consists of an agreed target cost, a profit rate based on the target, and a sharing ratio whereby cost savings or losses are shared in a specified proportion between the government and the contractor. For example, the target cost could be £100 million, the target fee £10 million, and the sharing ratio 80:20. If the actual cost *equals* the target, the firm receives the target fee of £10 million. If actual costs *exceed* the target, the firm bears 20 per cent of the extra cost, with adverse effects on its fee; and vice versa where actual costs are *below* target. An example is shown in Figure 15.6(b). Of course, with a target cost contract and a bilateral monopoly bargaining situation, a contractor has an incentive to bargain for the maximum possible target cost, a favourable sharing ratio and the highest possible maximum price liability. As a result, a firm's observed performance on an incentive contract might reflect its relative success in the bargaining process where there are extensive opportunities for 'game-playing'!

The relationship between fixed price, cost-plus and target cost incentive contracts is shown in Figure 15.7. In the figure, price is based on estimated costs (C_0) and a target profit, Π_t. Fixed price contracts are represented by the horizontal price line; cost-plus by a positive slope with profits as a mark-up on the 45° line and incentive contracts are intermediate between the two with the slope reflecting the sharing ratio and the horizontal section shows the government's maximum price liability.

15.6   CONCLUSION

Government procurement raises an array of analytical, empirical and policy issues to which microeconomics can contribute. It embraces the study of government and firm behaviour in various market and bargaining situations and the choice of the most appropriate contractual arrangements for coping with uncertainty. It also involves economics

and law. Economists often formulate rules for efficient public procurement and government contracting policy. However, such policy guidelines have to be converted into a set
of legally-enforceable rules and contracts. Public procurement is a classic example of a
field which combines the skills of economists and lawyers. It also raises another related
issue, namely the opportunities and incentives for criminal activity. Bribery can be used
to influence contract awards; fraudulent claims can arise during the execution of contracts; and contractors will seek to conceal 'excessive profits'. Indeed, there are potential
market failures on both the supplying and buying sides of public procurement markets.
Suppliers might be involved in cartels and collusive tendering; they have incentives to bid
low to win contracts which might then lead to bankruptcy; and they might not behave
efficiently. Similarly, governments as buyers might focus on transparency at the expense
of efficiency; they might be involved in complex strategic interactions with bidders and
their procurement choices might be influenced by broad public choice factors (for
example, vote-winning).

One fundamental issue remains. Why do governments undertake some work themselves
rather than 'contract-out'; is there 'too much or too little' contracting-out; and what are
the limits to contracting-out? For example, are there any economic arguments for undertaking research and development in state-owned establishments rather than in the private
sector? And if research and development were government supplied, how would society
ensure that such units satisfied voter preferences rather than the desires of scientists, technologists, bureaucrats and other interest groups? Such questions are part of the study of
the public sector (see Chapter 14).

READING* AND REFERENCES

*Arrowsmith, S. and K. Hartley, (eds) (2002), *Public Procurement*, The International Library of
    Critical Writings in Economics, 144, Cheltenham, UK and Northampton, MA, USA: Edward
    Elgar.
Domberg, S. S.A. Meadowcroft and D.J. Thompson (1986), 'Competitive tendering and efficiency:
    the case of refuse collection', *Fiscal Studies*, **7**(4), 69–87.
*Domberger, S. and S. Rimmer (1994), 'Competitive tendering and contracting in the public sector:
    a survey', *International Journal of the Economics of Business*, **1**(3), 439–53.
Emerson, M. et al. (1988), *The Economics of 1992*, Oxford: Oxford University Press.
Flyvbjerg, B., M.K.S. Holm and S.L. Buhl (2004), 'What causes cost overrun in transport infra-
    structure projects?', *Transport Reviews*, **24**(1), 3–18.
GAO (2006), 'Defense acquisitions: Assessment of selected major weapon programs', US
    Government Accountability Office, GAO-06-391, Washington DC.
MacDonald, M. (2002), *Review of Large Public Procurement in the UK*, London: HM Treasury.
NAO (2001), *Maximising the benefits of defence equipment co-operation*, National Audit Office,
    HCP 300, London: The Stationery Office.
NAO (2004), *Improving IT procurement*, National Audit Office, HCP 877, London: The Stationery
    Office.
NAO (2005a), *Major Projects Report 2005*, National Audit Office, HCP 595-II, London: The
    Stationery Office.
NAO (2005b), *UK Public Sector Construction Projects*, National Audit Office, HCP 364, London:
    The Stationery Office.
*Tisdell, C. (2004), 'Efficient public provision of commodities: transaction costs, bounded ratio-
    nality and other considerations', *International Review of Economics and Business*, **LI**(2),
    177–91.

*Williamson, O.E. (1979), 'Transaction-cost economics: The governance of contractual relations', *Journal of Law and Economics*, **XXII**(2), 233–61 (also reprinted in S. Arrowsmith and K. Hartley (eds) (2002).

QUESTIONS FOR REVIEW AND DISCUSSION

1. What should the objectives of government procurement policy be?
2. What are the 'best' contractual, organizational and institutional arrangements for government procurement of high-technology items? What are the efficiency implications of your proposals?
3. Which models of firm, bureaucratic and government behaviour 'best' explain cost escalation on government projects? Is cost escalation undesirable?
4. Should a nation purchase all its defence equipment from domestic firms? Evaluate in relation to alternative policies.
5. What are the economic arguments for contracting-out? Are there any limits to contracting-out? What are these limits and why do they exist?
6. What are the economic benefits of a Single European Market for the public procurement of civil goods and services? Have such benefits been achieved; and if not, why not? Should the Single Market rules for civil public procurement be extended to defence procurement?
7. Compare and evaluate the efficiency and profitability implications of fixed price, target cost incentive and cost-plus contracts.

PART F

Global applications

16. The state of the environment and the availability of natural resources

16.1 INTRODUCTION

Because of long-term economic growth, the volume of global production is now very large. Economic growth has altered natural environments and continues to do so, and it also impacts on the availability of natural resources. Consequently, the state of the natural environment is not independent of economic activity, and vice versa. Economic growth has resulted in concerns about the continuing availability of clean air and water, the disappearance of natural and semi-natural landscapes, loss of biodiversity, and increasing greenhouse gas emissions (for example, from the combustion of fossil fuels), sparking fears of considerable climate change and sea-level rises (Stern, 2006; BBC, 2006; Anon, 2006). In addition, there are periodic concerns that important natural resources, such as oil reserves and natural fish stocks, are being depleted and that this will result in shortages which will eventually reduce standards of living.

Microeconomic analysis can help us assess such issues. Furthermore, if there are socially unwanted environmental changes, including unwanted natural resource depletion, as a result of economic activity, often appropriate microeconomic policies can be adopted to alleviate such problems. This is not, however, to suggest that microeconomics on its own and microeconomic solutions can solve all environmental problems. Generally, the study of environmental problems calls for an interdisciplinary approach. Furthermore, the adoption of particular public policies has social impacts and almost always has ethical or normative objectives. Individuals may disagree about the appropriateness of such objectives. Should human wishes be paramount in deciding on policies, or should the preferences of humans be taken into account subject to ethical constraints, such as the possible right of other species to exist or to be free from undue molestation by humans? Do animals or other species have rights independently of human wishes? Different ethical perspectives often result in disagreements about choice of economic policies.

Mainstream economics is based on the view that only human welfare counts. It is, therefore, anthropocentric. However, it does allow the (perceived) welfare of non-human entities to be taken into account if this affects the utility of humans. For example, if some individuals are distressed by the harvesting of whales, then their willingness to pay to prevent whale harvesting would be taken into account in trying to determine an optimal economic solution to the harvesting of whales (Tisdell, 2005, p. 115). Therefore, even the relatively anthropocentric approach of economics to policy displays some sensitivity to changing human values about non-human species.

Because the available literature on environmental and natural resource economics is now very extensive, this chapter should be regarded as only an introduction to the subject. It is developed by first briefly considering aggregate relationships between economic growth, the state of the environment and the availability of natural resources because much of the theory involved is based on microeconomics. Then important economic concepts for environmental analysis and policy such as environmental externalities or spillovers, public goods and bads are introduced. Microeconomic policies designed to remedy environmental problems arising from the presence of externalities, of public goods or bads and inadequate systems of property rights are also outlined and examined.

16.2 ECONOMIC GROWTH, THE ENVIRONMENT AND NATURAL RESOURCE AVAILABILITY: MACRO-PERSPECTIVES

Concerns have emerged in the last few decades that continuing economic growth of the type experienced in the past may prove to be unsustainable because of environmental pollution associated with it and the depletion of non-renewable natural resources, such as fossil fuels. For example, because of their rapid economic growth, China and India have become major users of natural resources and emitters of greenhouse gases. However, many higher income countries, particularly the USA, although showing less current economic growth, continue to be major users of natural resources and emitters of greenhouse gases. Much of the discussion is based on the use of microeconomic concepts. The purpose of this section is to illustrate this and provide a broad backdrop to environmental issues.

It is now widely recognized that natural resource stocks are economic assets. They contribute to human productivity and often directly to human welfare in a similar way to man-made capital and assets. They are essential to human survival and they play an important role in sustaining economic productivity and human welfare. The following question has arisen: given that natural capital or assets complement the productivity of man-made capital and contribute to the bundle of commodities that individuals want to consume, such as clean air or natural landscapes, to what extent can the natural resource stock be degraded or depleted and economic productivity and welfare be sustained?

To some extent, the answer to this question depends on how easily, and to what extent, man-made commodities can be substituted for natural commodities. For illustrative purposes, the set of available commodity possibilities could be represented by a product or commodity transformation function. Most, if not all, man-made commodities rely, either directly or indirectly, on the use of some natural resources.

Given available technology and knowledge of the availability of natural resources, the economy's product or commodity possibility function might be represented by curve ABCD in Figure 16.1. The economy can be envisaged as a global one or as a more localized one. This indicates that if production of man-made commodities is on a relatively low scale, say less than Y_1 per period, little availability of natural commodities has to be forgone, but as production of man-made commodities per period rises above Y_1, greater availability of natural resources has to be forgone for each unit increase in production of man-made commodities. This means that the marginal opportunity cost of producing man-made commodities rises in terms of natural commodities forgone, as man-made production increases. If attempts are made to increase man-made production to very high levels, the availability of natural commodities may be reduced to such an extent that the

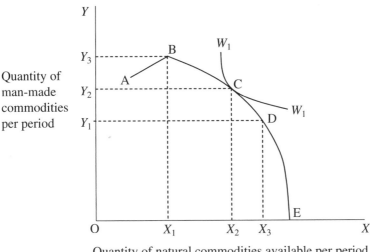

Quantity of natural commodities available per period

Figure 16.1   Man-made production relies to a large extent on the use of natural resources. This can result in increasing natural resource scarcity with economic growth and socially excessive use of natural resources. Technological change and the discovery of new natural resources stave off this problem

level of man-made production cannot be sustained. For example, attempts to increase the level of man-made production beyond Y_3 may prove to be counterproductive. It could result in both man-made production falling as well as the availability of natural commodities, that is, a movement along the segment AB of the commodity-possibility curve in Figure 16.1.

In Figure 16.1, point B corresponds to the maximum level of available man-made commodities. However, this is not necessarily the ideal combination from a social point of view because many natural resources are themselves valued by individuals, for example, beaches and natural scenery. Consequently, the socially ideal combination of commodities is likely to be to the right of B, for example at point C, assuming that the social welfare indifference curve marked $W_1 W_1$ is the highest attainable one. Because of market failures, there is a risk that an economy can move to a point left of C, such as B or even move to point A.

If the economy is at a point on the transformation function well to the right of C, there should be little or no concern about reducing the amount of natural commodities in order to produce more man-made commodities. As C is approached, more concern is needed because the risk increases of the economic system moving to the left of C. Therefore, weak restrictions might be placed on economic growth when the economy is well to the right of C and natural resources are abundant. However, stronger restrictions on economic growth (which transforms natural resources) become appropriate as the availability of natural resources dwindles.

Nevertheless, with the passing of time, two factors can reduce the natural resource constraints to the production of man-made goods. Technological progress could reduce the amount of natural resources needed to produce man-made goods. This would cause the transformation function to move to the right with point E, the known availability of natural commodities remaining fixed. In other words, the function would rotate clockwise on the fixed joint, E. Secondly, new natural resources may be discovered. This effectively moves point E to the right. Both technological progress and the discovery of new natural resource stocks stave off the problem of natural resource scarcity. Nevertheless, opinions differ about how effective they are likely to be in the long term in overcoming economic problems associated with natural resource depletion and environmental degradation associated with increasing production of man-made commodities.

It can be seen that production function concepts developed in microeconomics underlie the above simplified exposition of the problem of natural resource scarcity and this illustration of environmental constraints to sustaining growth of economic production. Consider another application of microeconomic concepts.

The environmental Kuznets curve (EKC) relates the intensity of the emission of pollutants to the level of Gross Domestic Product (GDP) of a nation. The intensity of the pollution is measured by the amount of a pollutant emitted per unit of GDP and is therefore an average concept. It is believed that typically environmental Kuznets curves are of a reversed U-shape, as indicated in Figure 16.2 by curve OBC. This curve has similarities to per-unit production functions in microeconomics. The EKC has associated with it a marginal curve indicated in Figure 16.2 by curve DBF. This is above EKC, when EKC is rising, and below EKC when EKC is falling.

The EKC implies that as economic growth occurs, pollution intensities rise at first, and with sufficient economic growth will eventually decline. However, it should be observed that the maximum intensity of pollution emission (which occurs at B for a level of GDP of X_1 in Figure 16.2) does not indicate the maximum amount of pollution emission per unit of time. This corresponds to the level at which marginal emissions equal zero, a level

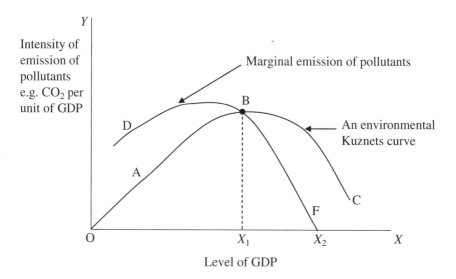

Figure 16.2 *Environmental Kuznets curves are believed to be typically of a reversed U-shape. With sufficient economic growth, it is therefore possible that pollution levels could fall. There is, however, a risk of being too optimistic in this regard, as explained in the text*

of GDP equal to X_2 in Figure 16.2. This could be well in excess of the level for which pollution intensity reaches its maximum.

Secondly, it should be observed that the EKC relates to the flow of pollutants, not their stock. The natural environment may not be able to neutralize or absorb all pollutants, especially as their volume of emission rises. Therefore, the stock of pollutants may accumulate, such as has happened with CO_2 emissions. It is possible that even if current emissions begin to fall, stocks of pollutants in the environment can continue to rise. In Figure 16.2, even if marginal emission of the relevant pollutant becomes negative (GDP $> X_2$), its total emission may still be so large that the stock of the pollutant in the environment continue to rise. A very large reduction in emissions may be needed before the level of emissions of some pollutants can be absorbed by natural processes and can no longer add to stocks of pollutants.

Furthermore, emissions of all pollutants may not have the reversed U-shape of the EKC, and pollution emissions or levels of accumulation beyond some thresholds may trigger massive environmental changes (Tisdell, 2001). The latter is not accounted for by environmental Kuznets curves. However, it is a concern in relation to emissions of greenhouse gases. The accumulation of these is predicted to bring about significant global warming and climate change as well as a rise in sea levels.

16.3 ENVIRONMENTAL EXTERNALITIES, SPILLOVERS AND RELEVANT MICROECONOMIC POLICIES

Externalities or spillovers have been discussed in Chapters 2 and 6. It was pointed out that an externality or a spillover exists when economic activity engaged in by one party harms or benefits another, and no payment is made by the originator of the activity to compensate the damaged party or no payment is made by the beneficiary for the benefit recorded. This can result in market failure because some of the costs or benefits associated with economic activity are not priced. The originator of an activity causing an adverse externality does not pay the full marginal (social) cost associated with the activity. Similarly, the originator of a favourable economic spillover does not obtain the full marginal (social) benefit from this activity. Therefore, an activity generating unfavourable externalities is liable to be overextended from a social point of view and an activity having favourable spillovers is likely to be on a smaller scale than is socially optimal.

Many types of economic externalities or spillovers are associated with shared environments. Such environmental spillovers can include water, air and soil pollution of various forms, changes in hydrology (water systems) and alterations in local, regional or global climate. Variations in scenery, impediments to views and to light or air movements caused by buildings may have external effects; loss of shared and wanted species of wildlife or ecosystems (reduced biodiversity) can have adverse external effects. On the other hand, reduced population of species, such as mosquitoes and rats, which create health hazards may be viewed as having a positive externality. Activities generating radiation can potentially or actually give rise to negative spillovers. The 'melt-down' of the Chernobyl nuclear power plant for example led to severe adverse externalities and even now the site continues to pose some environmental risks. The range of possible environmental spillovers is very large. The above just gives an indication of the range.

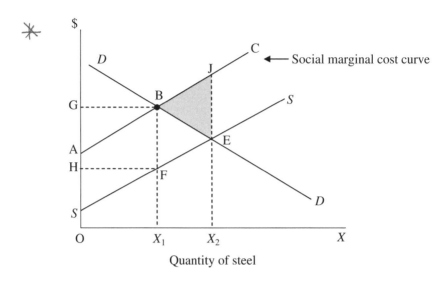

Figure 16.3   An illustration of Pigou's approach to the regulation of environmental spillovers

Arthur Pigou (1932) was the first economist to consider market failures that may arise from economic externalities. He proposed taxing the production of industries that gave rise to adverse externalities and subsidizing those generating favourable externalities. His approach can be illustrated by the example given in Figure 16.3. While this example relates hypothetically to the steel industry, it can be adapted to apply to other industries which generate negative environmental spillover. The air transport industry, for example, has negative environmental externalities as a result of its noise and carbon dioxide emissions.

In Figure 16.3, the line marked *DD* represents the market demand for steel, and the line marked *SS* is the supply curve of steel. The latter represents the marginal private cost of producing steel. The steel industry is assumed for illustrative purposes to be a perfectly competitive industry. Consequently, market equilibrium is established at point E. However, steel production may cause unfavourable environmental spillovers as a result of emissions of particulate matter (smoke), carbon dioxide, sulphur dioxide and other gases. Particulate matter may, for example, increase the incidence of lung diseases and emissions of sulphur dioxide may contribute to the occurrence of acid rain. When this is taken into account, the social marginal cost of steel production may be as indicated by the line ABC. The difference between line *SS* and line ABC, FB, represents marginal environmental spillover costs from steel production.

These externalities will not be taken into account by profit-maximizing steel producers. Hence, they produce X_2 units of steel and the social marginal cost of this production corresponding to point J exceeds its private marginal value, corresponding to point E on the demand curve. A social deadweight loss equivalent to the area of triangle BEJ occurs. Pigou (1932) suggested that this might be remedied by placing a tax of BF on each unit of steel production. As a result, after payment of this tax, the private marginal costs of steel production would be aligned with the social marginal cost of steel production, and the industry would come into equilibrium at point B, with its level of production being reduced from X_2 to X_1. At point B, the social marginal cost of steel production equals the extra value placed on it by buyers. There is no social economic loss, so it seems. However, this assumes that the technology and input requirements for steel production are fixed. If this is not so, it may be more efficient to place a tax (or taxes) directly on unfavourable emissions of pollutants, or to charge polluters for these by other policy mechanisms, such as by using a system of tradeable pollution rights, discussed below.

To make the polluter pay directly for offending pollution emissions can be more efficient for several reasons. First, it provides an incentive for the polluter to use inputs that are less polluting if there is a choice. For example, in the above case, low sulphur coal may be substituted for high sulphur coal if there is a charge on sulphur dioxide emissions. This will not happen if steel production is taxed. Secondly, it may encourage the installation of technology that reduces pollution emission. For example, if there is a charge for emission of a particulate matter, scrubbers may be installed on smoke stacks, which reduce such emissions. Thirdly, this policy provides an economic incentive for inventions, innovations and adoption of technologies that will reduce relevant emissions. It provides pollution reduction with private economic value. The Pigovian tax on products does not have these effects.

On the other hand, the monitoring and enforcement costs of charging fees on actual emissions can be high. These costs are likely to be lowest where emissions can be measured at a single point or a few points. However, this system of regulation can become impractical when there are non-point emissions. For example, the nitrogen and phosphorus run-off from fertilizer and animal manure on farms has negative environmental spillover consequences but can be very difficult to measure. Therefore, 'second-best' policy solutions may have to be adopted, such as limiting fertilizer use or the type of agriculture permitted, or stocking rates of farm animals. Run-off of nitrates and phosphorus causes nutrient-enrichment of water which often promotes excessive weed and algal growth. This may choke water bodies, making these unfit for many conventional uses, such as swimming, fishing and boating. Fish stocks may be reduced or altered in favour of less palatable species. Water quality is likely to deteriorate and it may become unsuitable for drinking by humans and livestock.

The analysis introduced by means of Figure 16.3 can be extended to consider several alternative microeconomic policy options that can be used to regulate pollution emissions. Systems of pollution taxes, levies or fees and of tradable pollution permits use pricing systems to bring about desired levels of pollution emission. In principle, they can lead to the same level of pollution control but there are practical differences.

The similarities between pollution taxes or fees and systems of tradable permits can be visualized by means of Figure 16.4. There, line DBF represents the marginal benefit to polluters of being able to pollute, and line ABC represents the marginal cost to victims of the pollution and is a spillover cost. No external costs are imposed until pollution emissions exceed the threshold OA. OABC may, for example, be the estimated marginal cost of increased morbidity and mortality as a result of the pollutant emitted. In the absence of any restrictions on pollution spillovers, polluters will maximize their economic benefit by emitting E_2 of the pollutant and a social deadweight loss equal to the area of triangle BFC will occur. The most economic level of emissions, applying the Kaldor–Hicks criterion, is E_1. This can, in principle, be achieved by means of a number of alternative economic policies.

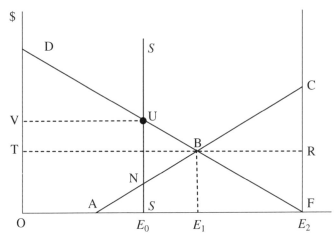

Quantity of pollutant, E_2 emitted per unit of time

Figure 16.4   Illustration of alternative microeconomic policies for controlling pollution emissions

One possible policy measure is to impose a tax or charge of OT on pollution for each unit of the pollutant emitted. This reduces the private benefit obtained from polluting. For levels of pollution emissions beyond E_1, the marginal benefit to polluters, shown by BF in Figure 16.4, is less than the marginal tax (or marginal charges imposed) as shown by BR. Therefore, polluters maximize their profits by reducing their pollution emissions from E_2 to E_1.

Alternatively, pollution permits or certificates giving rights to the holders to emit pollutants may be issued. Often these are issued in proportion to the past level of emissions of each existing polluter. This allocation is often free of charge, a practice sometimes called 'grandfathering'. The property rights bestowed on existing polluters provide them with a marketable asset and help purchase their political support for regulation of pollution. To achieve the optimal economic result, enough permits should be issued to allow an aggregate level of emissions of E_1. If these pollution rights are marketable and if perfect competition exists, a vertical line located on E_1 represents their supply, and line DBC indicates the demand for the permits. Hence, the market for rights comes into equilibrium at B and the market price of each permit is OT. Thus, the same level of emission emerges as in the case where a tax or levy of OT is imposed on each unit of pollutant emitted.

In practice, however, the marginal cost and benefit curves shown in Figure 16.4 may not be known or may be poorly known, and/or be subject to controversy. Or again special interest groups may exert political pressures and an 'optimal' economic solution may not be adopted by the government. It may adopt a standard that differs from the economic ideal. For example, in the case illustrated in Figure 16.4, the government may opt for a standard that only allows E_0 of pollutants per unit of time to be emitted. It may achieve this goal efficiently by either imposing a tax or fee of OV on each unit of the pollutant emitted or by issuing tradable pollution permits allowing a volume of emissions equal to E_0. In the latter case, the supply of permits corresponds to the vertical line marked SS, and the demand curve for those rights is shown by line DF. Assuming perfect competition, market equilibrium is established at U and the price of each permit is OV. In this simplified theoretical case, both policies result in the same level of emissions of the pollutant.

Note that although the standards approach is not ideal from a social economic point of view, it can be socially better than no intervention at all. For example, in the case just discussed, the social deadweight loss when a pollution standard adopted is equal to the area of triangle NBU. This is less than the area of triangle BFC which represents the social deadweight loss from pollution in the absence of government intervention.

There has been considerable discussion of whether taxing pollution is a superior approach to a system at tradable pollution rights. In a dynamic situation both involve challenges because the marginal curves shown in Figure 16.4 may shift with the passage of time. For example, the marginal costs for the victims of pollution may shift upward. This may occur because the level of population in the polluted area increases, for instance. Other things being equal, this would call for a reduction in emissions. This might be achieved by either raising the pollution tax or fee or reducing the number of pollution permits.

However, depending on the political processes involved, changing the level of the pollution tax may be slow and difficult. Furthermore, if permits have been issued, they are a type of property right. Whether and how the entitlements to emit pollution can be reduced depends upon the conditions of their issue. If the pollution permits are rights in perpetuity, then the government may have to purchase some to reduce their number. This can be costly. If on the other hand, the rights only give permit-holders a proportionate slice of the total allowed level of emissions, this provides the government with more flexibility to alter the aggregate level of emissions.

An important policy consideration is how to provide holders of pollution permits with some security of property rights and yet allow some flexibility for the government to adjust to changes in the public interest without its incurring large financial outlays. A variety of pollution permit schemes can achieve this. For example, apart from schemes giving permit-holders rights to a fixed share of the total allowable level of emission of a pollutant, schemes are possible in which a proportion of permits revert to the government with the passage of time. The government could then decide to freeze these, or reissue all or part of these, or even issue extra permits, depending on the circumstances. In doing this it needs to balance the security of property rights of permit-holders against changes in the public interest. Some of the issues involved are discussed, for example, by Tisdell (2003, Chapters 17 and 18).

The Stern Report to the UK Government (Stern, 2006) concluded on economic grounds and on the basis of evidence from natural science, that urgent global policy action is required to reduce the rate of growth in global greenhouse gas emissions, stabilize the level of such emissions, and then reduce it. Stern found that the economic benefit of taking action now, or in the near future, will exceed the cost of doing so. The economic benefit of speedy action is estimated as the economic costs (economic losses) averted which would occur with global warming and associated environmental change if business continues as 'usual'. One of the report's recommendations is that the European Union's Emission Trading Scheme be extended globally to include such countries as the United States, China and India.

This scheme is intended to stabilize the total levels of carbon emissions but its total allowable level of emissions would need to be reduced in the future. A stumbling block could be disputes about the relative allocation of initial permitted levels of emissions to countries not already in the EU scheme; that is the initial distribution of rights to emit greenhouse gases. China and India might argue or believe that it is equitable for them to have the lion's share of rights, because the countries that have already developed have been the major contributors to rising levels of greenhouse gases and have a smaller population.

A different property rights approach to regulating environmental externalities has been suggested by Coase (1960). He is of the view that many economic failures attributed to environmental externalities occur because property rights are uncertain or not defined. He believes that many economic failures due to externalities would disappear if property rights were more precisely defined and were to be legally enforceable. He predicts that in ideal circumstances, this would promote bargaining between those responsible for an externality and those subject to it and result in a Paretian optimal outcome being negotiated by the parties, that is an agreement in which no party to the negotiations can be made better off without making another worse off. Furthermore, Coase claims that the negotiated solution conditions will be the same (in terms of the amount of pollution emitted) whether the rights are given to the polluter or the victims of the pollution. This has been dubbed the Coase theorem. However, the income distribution consequences are very different depending on whether rights are assigned to polluters or their victims. If polluters have the right to pollute, then real income will be redistributed in favour of polluters given Coase's approach. On the other hand, if the victims of the pollution have the right to a pollution-free environment, real income will be redistributed in their favour if Coase's negotiated solution applies. This is illustrated by Figure 16.5, which is the same as Figure 16.4 with a minor modification to improve exposition. OBC in Figure 16.5 now represents the marginal spillover costs of pollution to victims and as before, DBF is the marginal benefit to polluters of being able to pollute.

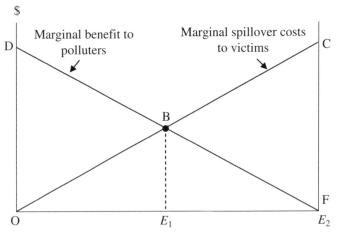

Figure 16.5   *An illustration of Coase's theorem*

Now if ideal conditions exist and property rights are clearly defined, the Coase Theorem implies that negotiations will result in an outcome corresponding to point B in Figure 16.5 and a level of emissions equal to E_1. If polluters have the right to pollute, they could, in the absence of bargaining, emit E_2 of the pollutant. However, they would be willing to accept a payment equal to the area of triangle E_1BF to reduce this level of pollution emissions to E_1. In principle, victims could be willing to pay this amount and with this payment would be better off as a result of the reduced level of emissions by an amount equivalent to the area of triangle BFC. Income will be transferred in favour of polluters. However, a bilateral bargaining situation may emerge. Polluters may demand a transfer of more than the area of triangle BE_1F because the maximum victims could be willing to pay for a reduction in pollution emissions is an amount equal to the area of quadrilateral BE_1FC. Thus, the negotiated income transfer could be at or between those extremes.

Similarly, if those subject to pollution have the right to a pollution-free environment, they can make an economic gain by permitting some pollution in exchange for compensation by polluters. The maximum marginal amounts that polluters are willing to pay are shown by line DBF and the minimum marginal compensation that victims are willing to accept is shown by line OBC. In Coase's ideal world, bargaining by the parties would result in emissions at E_1. Polluters would transfer income to victims and the amount transferred would be at a minimum equal to the area of triangle OE_1B and at a maximum equal to the area of quadrilateral OE_1BD.

While clearly defined property rights to either polluters or victims results in this idealized world in a Paretian efficient outcome, the income distribution consequences are very different. Ethical or moral issues would need to be taken into account in deciding which parties should be given the property rights. It is also possible that bargaining uncertainties and frictions could prevent a negotiated solution being achieved.

In practice, the ideal conditions required for Coase's solution are rarely satisfied. It assumes that bargaining costs are absent, and that the legal enforcement of property rights is costless and certain. In addition, any bargained outcome negotiated is supposed to be binding. In practice, those conditions are rarely satisfied. If they were, externalities would be rare.

Also barriers to bargaining often differ between the parties. For example, if there are many victims and each is damaged by a small amount by the emission of a pollutant, no one may wish to bargain because the cost to initiators of the bargaining process may exceed their potential benefits. While class legal actions in some countries can be initiated by lawyers to help circumvent this problem, Coase's property rights solution is much less effective than the exposition of the idealized case suggests. That is not to suggest that a clear definition of environmental rights is unimportant. However, often government (public) action is required to ensure that these rights are respected. Private negotiations do not always result in an ideal economic outcome, even when property rights in the environment are clearly defined. Nevertheless, private negotiations do sometimes work. For example, recreational anglers in the United Kingdom who value river fishing for salmon have, in some areas, bought out net fishermen based in estuaries so as to increase their availability of salmon stocks for recreational fishing.

Zoning and separation of activities provides another means of dealing with externalities. For example, smoking areas may be separated from non-smoking areas, industrial areas may be separated from residential areas and so on. This can be an economical policy measure when externalities have localized effects.

In discussing pollution taxes and tradable pollution permits, it was assumed that the marginal externalities generated were independent of the geographical location of the activities involved. However, this is not always so. This can require pollution taxes or fees to be varied according to geographical location of a pollution emission in order to take into account differences in the marginal benefits and marginal spillover costs to each locality (Tisdell, 1993, Chapter 4). If a system of tradable permits is used, the supply of permits needs to be specific to each region. This can make the market for permits 'thin' in some regions because there may be few firms with permits in some areas and the market for pollution permits may become imperfect.

It should also be noted that it is by no means easy to measure accurately the cost and benefits associated with environmental externalities. Nevertheless, several alternative methods are available. While these may provide differing estimates, this in itself should not be an excuse for policy inaction. For example, take the case shown in Figure 16.6. There ABC is the marginal economic benefit to polluters of emitting a pollutant. DBF represents the marginal damage to victims according to one estimate and D'B'F' according to another estimate. If these are the range of estimates, it will be socially preferable to reduce emissions from E_2 to E_1 rather than to do nothing in each case.

A reduction in emissions from E_2 to E_1 will ensure an aggregate economic gain equivalent to, at least, the area of triangle BFC. In this case, even a reduction in emissions to E_0 is bound to yield an aggregate economic gain. It ensures a gain equal to, at least, the area of triangle BFC less the area of triangle BSB', and the latter triangle is smaller in area than the former.

Line DBF might represent the marginal costs of ill-health caused by a pollutant and may consist of victims' medical and hospital expenses and their loss of earnings due to

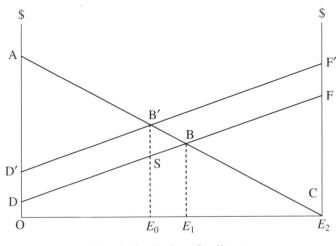

Level of emission of pollutant

Figure 16.6   Uncertainty about the costs and benefits of pollution control can rarely be used as a sound reason for policy inaction

ill-health. Line D′B′F′ might provide an additional allowance for their pain and suffering and earlier mortality than usual. Even if this additional consideration is ignored, it will be socially beneficial to reduce pollution emissions to at least E_1.

In some cases, the willingness to pay for the avoidance of an unfavourable externality by those subject to it is used as an estimate of spillover costs, and in other cases, willingness to accept compensation to allow the spillover is the basis of the estimates. Estimates based on the latter approach (Knetsch, 1990; Perman et al., 2003, Chapter 12) have been found empirically to exceed significantly those based on the former approach. However, in line with the above argument, this difference should not rule out all public intervention to regulate environmental externalities. For example, if in Figure 16.6, D′B′F′ represents the marginal willingness to accept compensation to allow pollution, and if DBF represents the marginal willingness to pay to avoid pollution, a reduction in the level of pollution from E_2 to any level in the region $E_0 \leq E \leq E_1$ will be socially preferable to no reduction in the level of pollution, if the Kaldor–Hicks criterion is applied. The Kaldor–Hicks criterion regards an economic change to be a social improvement if those gaining from it could at least compensate those losing from it and be better off than before the change. Thus, no matter whether DBF or D′B′F′ is considered to be the appropriate measure of marginal externality cost of the emission of the pollutant, it is socially more economical to ensure that pollution emission is in the above-mentioned range than not to regulate it at all.

This result does, however, undermine the 'neatness' of Coase's theorem. This is because if, for instance, victims have the right to a pollution-free environment, the relevant marginal damages function from their point of view would be based on their willingness to accept compensation. On the other hand, if polluters have the right to pollute, it will be based on the willingness of victims of pollution to pay to avoid it. In the former case, a marginal damages function like DBF will apply and in the latter case, one like D′B′F′. Thus, the amount of pollution that will be Paretian optimal will depend on the allocation of property rights.

16.4 ENVIRONMENTAL EFFECTS AS PUBLIC GOODS OR BADS

Public goods are goods that once supplied can be enjoyed by all (their consumption cannot be made dependent on a payment) and their consumption by one individual does not reduce their availability to others (see Chapter 2). These attributes have been described in the relevant literature as non-excludability and non-rivalry. Public bads involve environmental effects from which no one can be excluded and which are not reduced by any individual being affected by them.

Greenhouse gas emissions, emissions of substances that destroy the ozone layer, and loss of biodiversity are often viewed as public bads. The self-interest of nations may drive them to contribute to these bads and lead to a situation in which all or many nations are damaged. Global international agreements, such as the Kyoto Protocol and its prospective successor as signalled by the G8 nations at their meeting in June, 2007, are intended to try to avoid mutually damaging environmental outcomes.

This matter can be illustrated by a simple game of strategy which shows that individuals or nations, by following their own self-interest, can damage their common good. For

Table 16.1   An environmental example (the case of greenhouse gas emissions) of how pursuit of individual self-interest may damage the common good

	Strategies of Nation II →	
Strategies of Nation I	Restrict emissions	Do not restrict emissions
↓	β_1	β_2
Restrict emission	α_1 (10,10)	(3,15)
Do not restrict	α_2 (15,3)	(4,4)

simplicity, assume two nations and that each has two strategies: reduce greenhouse gas emissions, and not to reduce greenhouse gas emissions. Let these strategies for nation I be represented by α_1 and α_2 respectively and for Nation II be represented by β_1 and β_2 respectively. The economic payoffs to the nations from these strategies depend on their joint strategies. The numbers in the matrix in Table 16.1 display the assumed payoffs. The first entry in each cell represents the payoff to Nation I and the second entry is the payoff to Nation II.

It can be seen from Table 16.1 that no matter what the other nation does, it pays each nation not to restrict its emissions of greenhouse gases if it acts in its own self-interest. For example, if Nation II restricts its emissions, Nation I increases its gains from 10 to 15 by not restricting its emissions. If Nation II does not restrict its emissions, Nation I will gain 4 rather than 3 by doing likewise. Thus, there is a high probability that neither nation will restrict its emissions. Hence, each will be worse off than if they had all restricted their emissions. This problem (sometimes called the prisoners' dilemma problem) can only be overcome if both parties enter into an agreement to restrict their greenhouse gas emissions and act in good faith to carry out the agreement. Regulation of many global environmental problems requires international agreements of this type, that is international collective action.

In the absence of government intervention, public goods (which include reductions in public bads) are liable not to be supplied or to be under-supplied compared to the demand for these. To take an example from environmental health, the control of mosquitoes carrying malaria is likely to be under-supplied in economies where malaria is present if public measures to control these mosquitoes are absent. Owners of swampy land where such mosquitoes breed are likely to find that the cost to them of controlling the population of these mosquitoes on their land exceeds their benefits. But when the benefit of others in the region is also taken into account, the total economic benefit of this control may exceed the cost. Because a public good is involved (one for which a high external benefit exists), the government may have to supply the good to bring about a social optimum, or at least, finance its supply.

Consider another example involving the conservation of a wild species, such as the northern hairy-nosed wombat in Australia. The remaining population of this species occurs only in a small area in Queensland where efforts are being made by government wildlife officers to increase its number. This area is not open to the public and the species is not allowed in zoos. The species appears to have no economic use value. Its total economic value consists of non-use value such as its existence value or its bequest value.

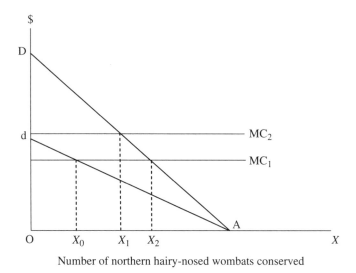

Figure 16.7   When an environmental commodity has public goods characteristics, it is likely to be under-supplied

Tisdell and Swarna Nantha (2007) discuss this case specifically. Many wildlife species have high non-use economic values but low or zero economic use values. Their populations are, therefore, pure public goods or nearly such goods. In the absence of government intervention, the conservation of their populations is likely to be less than socially optimal.

This can be illustrated by Figure 16.7. Assume, for simplicity, a society consisting of just two individuals and that each has the demand curve dA for conserving populations of the northern hairy-nosed wombat, taking into account its public good characteristics, such as its existence and its bequest value. The aggregate demand curve for conserving population of this species is then as shown by line DA. For example, if each individual is willing to pay $150 to conserve the first of the wombats, the aggregate value or demand for conserving these is $300, and is equal to the distance OD in Figure 16.7. The line DA also represents this society's marginal valuation of additional wombats.

If the marginal cost of conserving this species of wombat is as shown by the horizontal line marked MC_1, it is socially optimal to conserve X_2 wombats. For this level of population, society's marginal valuation of population of this species just equals the marginal cost of conserving them. In the absence of government intervention, one individual might conserve X_0 wombats and wombats will be insufficiently conserved. Should the marginal cost of conserving wombats be MC_2, no individual will conserve them, although the socially optimal number to be conserved is X_1. Thus, when environmental goods possess attributes of public goods, they are likely to be under-supplied in the absence of public intervention. For example, there is likely to be insufficient conservation of wildlife species and ecosystems that have little use value but that have high non-use economic values or public goods characteristics. This is so even though some individuals and voluntary organizations such as the Royal Society for the Protection of Birds, may help to conserve such species.

16.5   TOTAL ECONOMIC VALUE, MIXED GOODS AND THE ENVIRONMENT

Some commodities are mixed goods in the sense that they have some attributes that give them economic use value as well as other attributes that give them non-use economic value. Commodities with use value are normally marketable whereas those with non-use value are not. Hence, the use component (private good component) of mixed goods may find a market whereas the non-use component (public good element) cannot be marketed. If a commodity or resource has attributes that provide it with both types of values, then in a market system, marketed use value is likely to dominate decisions about its conservation and use. The outcome may not be optimal from a social economic point of view.

According to one classification of economic values, the total economic value (TEV) of a commodity or resource is equal to its economic use value (TUV) plus its total non-use value (TNUV), that is TEV = TUV + TNUV.

Total use value can consist of consumptive value (for example, consumption of African elephants for their meat, leather and ivory) and non-consumptive value (such as the use of elephants for viewing by tourists). Non-use values reflect the fact that some individuals value the existence of resources independently of whether they intend to use them (for example, they may value the continuing existence of African elephants and be prepared to contribute to their conservation independently of any intention to use them) or they might wish to ensure that a resource continues to exist so that it is available to future generations (bequest value). Non-use values are usually important in relation to environmental goods.

The total non-use value of a resource or commodity can either be regarded as a public good attribute or an element generating an externality. If decisions about resource allocation are made purely on the basis of economic use value (as is normal in a free market system), misallocation of resources is liable to occur. This can be illustrated by some examples.

Consider a land area consisting of a natural forest that has no other economic alternative use but which can be logged for timber. The net economic value of its timber production represents a part of its economic use value. If the forested area is also used for outdoor recreation, this would be an additional use value. But, for simplicity, suppose its only economic use value is for logging. Its logging could threaten the population of a rare wild species for example, the orangutan, and this threat might increase with the amount of land logged. Suppose that this species has no use value, but that its existence is highly valued. As the extent of logging of the area increases, the marginal expected non-use value of the species will decline. This will not be taken into account by owners of the forested land. Because owners of the forested land do not appropriate any income from the non-use value of their forested land, an excessive amount of logging is likely to occur from a social economic point of view.

This is illustrated by Figure 16.8. There, line CAD represents the marginal economic return from logging different percentages of the forested area. Line OAB indicates the marginal reduction in expected non-use value that occurs as a result of the logging. From a Kaldor–Hicks economic point of view, the optimal degree of logging of the area corresponds to point A and involves x_1 of the area being logged. However, landholders will find it profitable to log all of the forested land because they obtain no economic returns

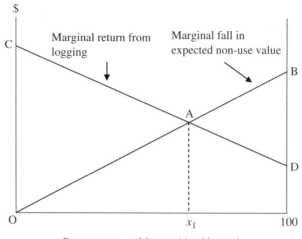

Figure 16.8   Illustration of how the presence of non-use value of resources can result in failure to maximize economic welfare

from non-use values. This would result in a deadweight economic social loss equal to the area of triangle ADB.

Consider another mixed good case, namely whaling. Whales have consumptive use value for some Japanese and Norwegians, for example. They also have non-consumptive use value for whale watching, and they have non-use economic values for many conservationists. Whales are, therefore, a very complex mixed economic resource. There is economic conflict between those who wish to use whales for consumption and those who obtain greater economic value if they are not consumed. Those who oppose the killing of whales for consumption may do so for several different reasons. For example, they may be opposed to killing large intelligent mammals because they believe it is cruel to kill them; they may believe that whaling will endanger some whale species or reduce their existence value; and for those who like to view whales, whaling is likely to reduce their chances of seeing whales.

Some of the issues involved can be illustrated by Figure 16.9. There the curve marked *DD* represents the demand for whales for meat and the curve marked A*S* represents the supply curve of whales for meat. The curve marked ABC represents the marginal social cost of whaling. For example, the difference between curve BE*S* and ABC might indicate the marginal willingness to pay to prevent whaling of those opposed to it and can be regarded as a marginal externality cost. Although the market would result in X_1 whales being harvested annually, the socially optimal level of harvest is less. It is X_0 if the Kaldor–Hicks criterion is adopted. It is likely to be much smaller if those opposed to whaling have to be bribed (compensated) to allow whaling rather than pay (hypothetically) to have it stopped or reduced. As discussed above, willingness to pay for retention of an environmental good is usually less than willingness to accept compensation for its loss.

Note that it is possible that the social marginal cost curve of whaling may exceed the demand curve for whales for meat. Then even if private harvesting were profitable, no whaling would be socially optimal from a Kaldor–Hicks point of view.

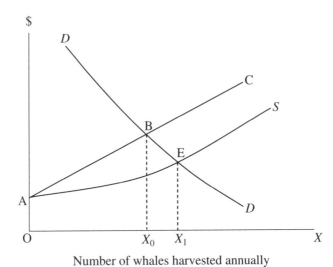

Number of whales harvested annually

Figure 16.9   An illustration of how an excessive level of whaling may occur if spillover costs from whaling, some of which may be associated with reduction in their non-use values, are important

Actually, the whaling case is even more complicated because whales are an internationally shared resource. This is partly because whales travel long distances. In the past, they were also open-access resources and their over-harvesting brought several species close to extinction. Let us, therefore, consider the economics of the use of open-access and common property resources.

16.6   OPEN-ACCESS AND COMMON PROPERTY RESOURCES

The types of property rights that exist in resources are important for their economic use. In a perfectly operating market system, individual private ownership will promote efficient resource use in a wide range of circumstances, which include the absence of externalities and of monopoly power. However, the right to use resources is often shared. Individuals in such cases do not have exclusive use of the resources. In various circumstances, this can be a source of economic inefficiency.

An extreme case involves the economic use of open-access resources. These resources are open to all to use but their products become private property once taken by individuals from the open area. Thus if there is open-access to a forest, all can use it, but once individuals gather products from it, these become their private property. Similarly, if there is open-access fishing, all have access to it, but once fish are caught by individuals they become their private property.

A number of economic inefficiencies occur in the use of open-access resources. In a market system, too many resources are liable to be employed in exploiting open-access resources. Secondly, those exploiting an open-access resource fail to take account of user costs, that is, the benefits of conserving and husbanding such resources for future use.

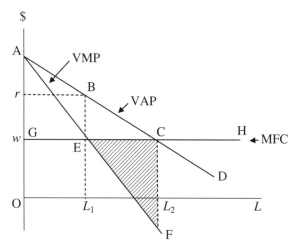

Quantity of labour (fishers) harvesting fish in an open-access area

Figure 16.10   An illustration of how an excessive amount of resources may be allocated to harvesting an open-access resource

Because user costs are ignored, those harvesting an open-access resource are likely to react in a perverse manner to market signals (such as rising prices) which indicate that the resource is becoming scarce. As a result, instead of conserving the resource, suppliers intensify its use and reduce its stocks. These are not the only possible inefficiencies but they are important ones (Tisdell, 2005, Chapter 6).

In an economy in which some resources are mobile between uses, an excessive amount of resources (from an economic efficiency point of view) will be allocated to exploitation of open-access resources compared to those used in industries in which private property is the dominant ownership regime. This can be illustrated by Figure 16.10. This assumes open-access to a fishery in a particular region but that private ownership of resources prevails elsewhere and perfect competition exists throughout the economy. It is assumed that the mobile resource is labour (or labour plus a fixed proportion of other resources). The quantity of labour allocated to exploiting the open-access resource is designated by L. The wage-rate available to labour in the rest of the economy is w. This is the marginal factor cost of labour and is also equal to value of the marginal product of labour when used elsewhere in the economy.

Suppose that the supply of fish from the open-access region does not influence the price of fish, and let line AEF represent the value of the marginal product of fish from the open-access region. The corresponding value of average product curve is as indicated by line ABCD.

If the uncaptured fish in the open-access region happened to be private property, then owners of these could charge each fisher $r - w$ to fish. This would result in L_1 labourers (fishers) fishing in the area, and would ensure that the value of the marginal product from labour fishing in the area is equal to the value of the marginal product of labour when used elsewhere in the economy.

However, in the absence of the private ownership of fish in the area, no access fee is payable. Labour will find it economic to catch fish in the area as long as the value of its average catch (VAP) exceeds the going wage rate elsewhere in the economy. Therefore, L_2 units of labour are engaged in fishing in the open-access area. This allocation is excessive by $L_2 - L_1$ from an economic efficiency point of view. It results in a deadweight economic loss equivalent to the area of triangle EFC.

A second type of economic inefficiency occurs because users of an open-access resource consider only their current benefits from using it and take no account of future benefits that may be forgone because of the nature and amount of its present use; they fail to take account of user costs. They do this because if an individual conserves an open-access resource or husbands it, others are likely to benefit rather than the conservationist because anyone is free to take an open-access resource. The problem can be illustrated by Figure 16.11. There, curve ABC represents the marginal net benefit to users of their current harvesting of an open-access resource and curve OBF represents the marginal user costs of this activity. Users of the open-access resource will harvest X_2 of it, whereas a harvest-level of X_1 is optimal when account is taken of user costs. Failure to take account of user costs results in an economic benefit being lost equivalent to the triangular area, BCF.

If the future value of a resource is expected to rise considerably because the future price of its produce is expected to escalate, this will provide a strong economic incentive to conserve the resource if it is privately owned. However, this is not the case if the resource is an open-access one. The use of an open-access resource is only sensitive to the current price of its produce, not the future price of its produce. If its current price should rise, then the current exploitation of the resource will increase (other things constant), even if the economic ideal is to reduce current production so as to increase or sustain future supply. In such circumstances, a species being harvested as an open-access resource may be driven to extinction even when its conservation is optimal from an economic point of view.

Such problems can, however, sometimes be avoided if the use of common property is subject to communal or social rules governing its use. However, as the group or community subject to such rules becomes larger, enforcement of the rules may become more

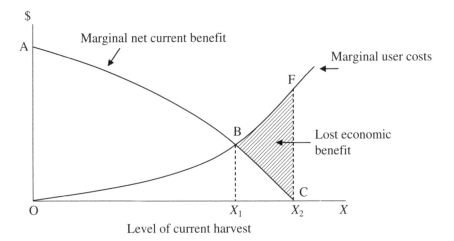

Figure 16.11   Those exploiting open-access resources fail to take account of user costs as illustrated. This is inefficient and adds to future resource scarcity

difficult. If the social rules are habitually flouted, the situation becomes in effect one of open-access.

16.7 CONCLUDING OBSERVATIONS

Some advocates of private property regimes seem to believe that the key to solving inefficiencies in the use of environmental and natural resources is to have them fully covered by a private property regime. However, this view may be unrealistic because it ignores the economics of establishing and maintaining private property rights.

A system based on the institution of private property rights involves costs. These include the costs of identifying ownership of resources and the expenses of excluding others from using resources illegally as well as obtaining compensation from illegal use. These costs will generally be lower in societies where it is customary to respect private property rights. These costs have to be weighed against the economic benefit that owners can obtain by having exclusive use of their property.

The costs of exclusion of those intent upon the illegal use of private property may fall as new technologies are developed that make it easier to enforce exclusion and detect illegal use, and the less costly are legal remedies available to owners who have had their private property rights violated. Furthermore, the economic incentive to enforce private property rights will be greater the higher are the economic benefits expected from such rights. If the costs of establishing and maintaining private property rights are high in relation to the anticipated economic benefits, then it will be uneconomic to have a private property regime. Nevertheless, with economic development there is a tendency for more and more resources to become private property. This is partly a result of technological advances and increasing economic returns from such resources. However, social innovations, for example, in the legal system, which make it less costly to enforce private property rights may also contribute to this result.

It has been observed that some property rights regimes (such as those involving open-access and significant externalities) can add to the scarcity of environmental and natural resources. This problem cannot always be economically solved by extending private property regimes: Coase's preferred option. Therefore, other policies such as resource-use taxes or fees or tradable-use permits must be considered. In the case of resources including a large public good element, public funding of their provision needs considering. Therefore, it is clear that while extension of private property regimes may solve some environmental and natural resource problems, it is not the key to the solution of all such problems.

Furthermore, while private property rights may help to conserve resources in areas where those rights can be established, it is by no means clear that they will result in an ideal level of conservation of resources in practice, even if externalities and so on are ignored. This is because the future is uncertain, and individuals and businesses may have a strong preference for short-term economic gains rather than long-term gains. This reduces their incentive to conserve resources. At the same time, economic agents may be unduly optimistic about the possibility that continuing scientific and technological programmes will overcome any resource shortages that otherwise would increase with economic growth. The more strongly and widely this belief is held by economic agents the greater is their incentive not to worry about the future state of the environment and natural resource availability and to base their resource-use decisions on very short-term economic benefits. Consequently, user costs may play only a small role in economic decision-making, even in an economy dominated by private property regimes.

READING* AND REFERENCES

Anon (2006), 'Stern Review', Wikipedia the free encyclopaedia, http://wikipedia.org/wiki/Stern_ Review. Accessed 8 December, 2006.
*BBC (2006), 'At a glance: The Stern Review', http://new.bbc.co.uk/2/hi/business/6098362.stm.
Coase, R. (1960), 'The problem of social waste', *The Journal of Law and Economics*, **3**, 1–14.
*Isor, S., S. Pecke and S. Wall (2002), *Environmental Issues and Policies*, Harlow, UK: Pearson Education.
*Kahn, J.K. (2005), *The Economic Approach to Environmental and Natural Resources*, 3rd edn, chapters 1–5, Mason, Ohio: South-Western.
Knetsch, J. (1990), 'Environmental policy implications of disparities between willingness to pay and compensation demanded', *Journal of Environmental Economics and Management*, **18**, 227–37.
*Perman, R., Y. Ma, J. McGilvray and M. Common (2003), *Natural Resource and Environmental Economics*, 3rd edn, Part I, chapters 6–7 and Harlow, UK: Pearson Education.
Pigou, A.C. (1932), *The Economics of Welfare*, 4th edn, London: Macmillan.
Stern, N. (2006), *Stern Review. The Economics of Climate Change*, http://www. hm-treasury.gov.uk/independent_review/stern_review_economies_climate_change/stern_review_index -report.cfm.
Tisdell, C.A. (1993), *Environmental Economics*, Cheltenham, UK and Northampton, MA, USA: Edward Elgar.
Tisdell, C.A. (2001), 'Globalisation and sustainability: environmental Kuznets curve and the WTO', *Ecological Economics*, **39**, 449–62.
*Tisdell, C.A. (2003), *Ecological and Environmental Economics*, chapters 17 and 18, Cheltenham, and Northampton, MA, USA: Edward Elgar.
*Tisdell, C.A. (2005), *Economics of Environmental Conservation*, 2nd edn, chapters 1, 3, 11 and 12, Cheltenham, UK, and Northampton, MA, USA: Edward Elgar.
Tisdell, C. and H. Swarna Nantha (2007), 'Comparison of funding and demand for the conservation of the charismatic koala with those for the critically endangered wombat, *Lasiorhinus kreffti*', *Biodiversity and Conservation*, **16**, 1261–81.

QUESTIONS FOR REVIEW AND DISCUSSION

1. The values underlying social decision-making in economics are anthropocentric or human-centred. Explain. Does this mean that the welfare of other species is ignored? Explain how, given the above approach, the amount of weight given in social choice to the welfare of non-human species, might alter with the passage of time.
2. Illustrate and explain why the conservation of natural resources (including environmental resources) is essential for sustaining economic welfare.
3. What is an environmental Kuznet's curve? What shape is it believed to have typically? Why could it give a misleading impression of the ability of economic growth to reduce pollution levels?
4. Show how unfavourable environmental externalities or spillovers arising from the production of a commodity can lead to a social economic loss. Use a diagram to identify the social deadweight loss that could arise.

5. Pigou suggested that the production of commodities giving rise to negative externalities might be taxed in order to increase economic efficiency. Illustrate his approach, identifying the optimal level of tax given his approach and explain why it leads to increased economic efficiency.
6. The Pigovian approach of taxing the production of a commodity that creates a negative environmental spillover may after all be less efficient than directly taxing a pollution emission or attribute that causes the externality. Why?
7. A system of emission taxes or charges can yield identical economic results to a system of tradable pollution permits. To what extent is this so? Explain and discuss these alternative approaches to environmental management.
8. Why are standards often used to control pollution? How and what economic instruments can be used to achieve environmental standards? Illustrate.
9. Tradable pollution or resource-use rights give their holders property rights. Many different types of rights are possible. In deciding on an appropriate system of tradable resource-use, governments need to determine an appropriate balance between the security of the holders of rights and the government's flexibility in altering aggregate environmental resource-use. Discuss.
10. The Stern Report (Stern, 2006) favours a global system for trading in carbon emission rights. Outline the possible merits and difficulties that could arise in trying to implement and arrange such a system.
11. What is Coase's theorem? What are its limitations?
12. Uncertainty about environmental spillovers is not always a sufficient justification for lack of their public control. Explain and illustrate.
13. Some environmental phenomena involve public goods or bads and this can result in socially sub-optimal choice of environmental resources. Explain and illustrate.
14. Explain the concept of total economic value. Relate it to the concept of mixed goods. Why are whales mixed goods? Explain and illustrate how mixed goods may not be used in a socially optimal manner.
15. What are open-access resources? Outline ways in which their presence can add to resource scarcity. In doing so, take account of user costs.
16. It has been claimed that the key to reducing resource scarcity and ensuring resource conservation and environmental protection is the extension of private ownership of resources. Discuss this view, taking into account its merits and its limitations.

17.   Defence, disarmament and conflict

17.1   INTRODUCTION: THE SCOPE OF DEFENCE ECONOMICS

Defence economics is relatively new. One of the first specialist contributions in the field was by Hitch and McKean, *The Economics of Defense in the Nuclear Age* (1960). This book applied basic economic principles of scarcity and choice to national security. It focused on the resources available for defence and the efficiency with which such resources were used by the military. Like all economic problems, choices cannot be avoided. Scarce resources allocated to defence means that these resources are not available for alternative uses such as social welfare spending (for example, missiles versus education and health trade-offs). But further choices are needed. Within a limited defence budget, resources have to be allocated between equipment and personnel, between nuclear and conventional forces and between air, land and sea forces. Military commanders have to use their limited resources efficiently, combining their inputs of arms, personnel and bases to 'produce' security and protection. Within such a military production function, there are opportunities for substitution. For example, capital (weapons) have replaced military personnel, and nuclear forces have replaced large standing armies. Defence economics is about the application of economic theory to defence-related issues.

   Of course, the standard trade-off analysis and the need for choices assumes that an economy's resources are fully and efficiently employed. Where there is involuntary unemployment (for example, the Depression years of the 1930s) there may be no or little immediate economic trade-off. Hitler's large military spending prior to World War II helped to reduce mass unemployment and enabled the German people to return to work, so increasing his popularity. However, defence spending is not the only, nor the most cost-effective nor the most desirable method of pump-priming an economy with large-scale unemployment. There is also a further opportunity cost even in a depression, namely, that some of the resources used for the war or defence effort are lost to future generations.

   Developments in defence economics have reflected current events. During the Cold War, there was a focus on the superpower arms races, alliances (NATO and the Warsaw Pact), nuclear weapons and 'mutually-assured destruction'. The end of the Cold War resulted in research into disarmament, the opportunities and challenges of conversion and the availability of a peace dividend. But the world remains a dangerous place, with regional and ethnic conflicts (for example, Bosnia; Kosovo; Afghanistan; Iraq), threats from international terrorism (for example, terrorist attacks on USA: 11 September 2001), rogue states and weapons of mass destruction (that is, biological, chemical and nuclear). NATO has accepted new members (for example, former Warsaw Pact states) and has developed new missions. The European Union has also developed a European Security and Defence Policy.

   Changing threats and new technology require the Armed Forces and defence industries to adjust to change and new challenges. Globalization involves greater international transactions in goods, services, technology and factors of production which brings new security challenges for nation states and the international community. Defence firms have become international companies with international supply networks. Globalization also highlights the importance of international collective action to respond to new threats such as international terrorism and to maintain world peace (for example, via international peace-keeping missions under UN, NATO or EU control). But international collective action experiences the standard problems of burden-sharing and free-riding (Hartley, 2008).

This chapter shows how economics can be applied to issues of defence, disarmament and conversion. It starts by explaining the defence economics problem and then considers the economic aspects of disarmament. Defence economists have also developed models to analyse conflict and terrorism.

17.2 DEFENCE CHOICES

Definitions

Defence economics studies all aspects of war and peace and embraces defence, disarmament and conversion. The definition includes studies of both conventional and non-conventional conflict such as civil wars, revolutions and terrorism. It involves studies of the armed forces and defence industries and the efficiency with which these sectors use scarce resources in providing defence output in the form of peace, protection and security. Cuts in defence spending (for example, following the end of World War II and the Cold War) result in disarmament, which requires resources to be re-allocated from defence to the civilian sector with the aim of achieving a peace dividend. This raises questions about the impact of disarmament on the employment and unemployment of both military personnel and defence industry workers; the possibilities for converting military bases and arms industries to civil uses (for example, the Biblical swords to ploughshares); and the role of public policies in assisting the transition and minimizing the adjustment costs involved in the re-allocation of resources.

There are two distinctive economic characteristics of the defence sector. First, both defence and peace are public goods which are non-rival and non-excludable. For example, my consumption of a city's air defence is not at the expense of you being protected; and if I live in the city, you cannot prevent me from being protected by the city's air defence. However, not all citizens view defence in this way: conscientious objectors such as Quakers take a different and critical view of defence. Nor do voting systems in democracies usually provide a means of expressing voter preferences about defence budgets and policy. Second, governments are major buyers of both equipment (weapons) and military personnel (in some cases, they are monopsony buyers) and their procurement choices affect defence industries and labour markets. Inevitably, agents in political markets seek to influence government purchasing in their favour. The armed forces will lobby for larger budgets; defence firms and industries will seek to be awarded contracts; and politicians will demand contracts be awarded to firms in their constituencies and that military bases be retained (i.e. the role of the military–industrial–political complex: see Chapters 14 and 15).

Table 17.1   World military spending and armed forces

World military expenditure	US$ billion, 2005
World total	*1118*
NATO	779
USA	507
UK	58
France	54
China	44
Germany	36
Russia	29

Defence share of GDP	Percentage (%), 2004
Developed nations	
USA	4.0
UK	2.8
France	2.6
Germany	1.4
Less Developed Nations	
Eritrea	19.6
Oman	12.0
Israel	8.7
Jordan	8.2
Burundi	6.3
Morocco	4.5
Pakistan	3.4
India	3.0
Sudan	2.4

Defence Research and Development	US $ billions, 2004 (2001 prices and PPP rates
USA	67.5
Russia	6.1
UK	4.7
USA and EU total	80.9
Estimated world total of defence R&D	**90.0+**

World Armed Forces	Number of military personnel, 1999 (000s)
World	**21 300**
Developed nations	6 550
Developing nations	14 700
NATO	4 580
China	2 400
USA	1 490
UK	218
Eritrea	215

Table 17.1 (continued)

World Arms Trade	US$ millions, 2001–2005 (2005 prices)
Major importers	
China	19 948
India	13 986
Greece	9 127
UAE	7 276
UK	4 376
Egypt	4 337
Israel	4 295
World total	**139 806**
Major exporters	
Russia	43 328
USA	42 213
France	12 817
Germany	8 377
UK	5 880
World total	**139 806**

Notes: (i) Defence share data for Eritrea and Sudan are for 2003. (ii) Defence R&D data are for government-funded defence R&D. PPP are Purchasing Power Parity rates.

Sources: DoS, 2002; OECD, 2004; SIPRI, 2006.

World Military Spending

There is a belief that few data are available on a nation's defence spending. In fact, as Table 17.1 shows, there are substantial data available, especially on world military spending, the world's Armed Forces and the arms trade. The USA accounted for 45 per cent and NATO accounted for some 70 per cent of total world military spending. Similarly, in 2004, the USA dominated defence R&D spending, accounting for some 75 per cent of the world total. Table 17.1 also shows examples of defence shares of GDP to illustrate the burdens of defence spending, especially for developing nations such as Eritrea, India and Pakistan (an arms race situation) and for the Middle East (a conflict region). Burundi and Sudan have similar or greater defence burdens than the UK and Germany. Table 17.1 shows other measures of the economic burdens of defence for the world's poorer nations (for example, nations which cannot feed, house or educate their populations and which have poor health records). Developing nations accounted for 70 per cent of the world total of 21.3 million military personnel. Similarly, developing nations are major importers of arms whilst the developed nations are the major arms exporters, with Russia and the USA each accounting for 30 per cent of world arms exports (Table 17.1).

Data based for the largest arms-producing companies and employment in national defence industries are shown in Table 17.2. It can be seen that the USA has six of the world's top ten arms companies and that the American firms have a substantial scale

Table 17.2   Defence companies and industries

Major Defence Companies	Arms Sales, 2003 (US$ millions)
Lockheed Martin (USA)	24 910
Boeing (USA)	24 370
Northrop Grumman (USA)	22 720
BAE Systems (UK)	15 760
Raytheon (USA)	15 450
General Dynamics (USA)	13 100
Thales (France)	8 350
EADS (Europe)	8 010
United Technologies (USA)	6 210
Finmeccanica (Italy)	5 290
Major Defence Industries	**Employment Numbers, 2003 (000s)**
World Total	**7 479**
Industrialized	4 710
Developing	2 769
NATO	3 452
USA	2 700
China	2 100
Russia	780
EU	645
France	240
UK	200

Sources: BICC (2005); SIPRI (2005).

advantage over their European rivals: the average size of a US firm from the top ten is almost twice the corresponding average for the European companies. The industrialized nations also accounted for over 60 per cent of total employment in the world's defence industries; with the developing countries accounting for the remaining 37 per cent. The USA, China and Russia have the largest defence industries by employment, accounting for 75 per cent of the world total. Overall, the world military–industrial complex employed almost 29 million personnel in the armed forces and defence industries, reinforcing its role as a major employer of labour, including some highly-qualified R&D staff and other highly-skilled workers. Such scarce labour has alternative uses in the civilian sector, raising questions as to whether defence spending 'crowds-out' valuable civil investment and diverts scientific manpower from civil research projects. Such issues are addressed by the defence economics problem.

The Defence Economics Problem

At the outset, there is the challenge of achieving 'top level' efficiency in defence provision. Economic theory solves this challenge as a standard optimization problem involving the maximization of a social welfare function subject to resource or budget constraints (where

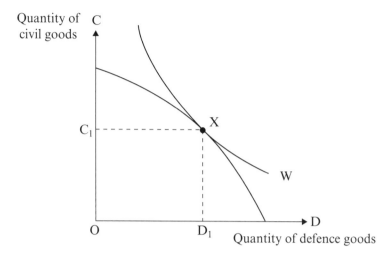

Figure 17.1 Society's preferred output is shown by the point of tangency between the production possibility boundary and the welfare function at point X with OD_1 of defence goods and OC_1 of civil goods

welfare is dependent on civil goods and security, with security provided by defence). Figure 17.1 shows a solution to the classic 'guns versus butter' or missiles versus education and health trade-off. The production possibility boundary shows all points where an economy's resources are fully and efficiently employed so that increases in defence spending involve cuts in civilian output.

Society's preferred combination of military and civil goods is shown at point X.

Implementing this apparently simple optimization rule is much more difficult. Individual preferences for defence are subject to its public good characteristics and free-riding problems. Defence output is difficult to define and subject to security problems. Also, in democracies, society's preferences are usually expressed through voting at elections. However, elections are a limited mechanism for obtaining an accurate indicator of society's preferences for defence and its willingness to pay. Elections occur infrequently; they are usually for a range of policies of which defence is only one element in the package (for example, policies on education, health, transport, the environment, foreign policy and taxation); and the 'voting paradox' shows the difficulty of deriving a society's preferences using the voting system. Nor do voters have reliable information on the output of defence spending. In these circumstances, society's decisions on defence output are made by governments acting as society's agents (that is, a principal–agent problem) influenced by specialist interest groups with information and knowledge on defence. Such specialist interest groups include the military–industrial–political complex comprising the armed forces, defence industries and politicians with a defence interest in their constituency; but other groups opposed to defence spending will also lobby government (for example, CND; environmental groups).

Once society has decided on its defence budget, there are further defence choices to be made. The limited defence budget has to be allocated between capital (weapons) and labour (military personnel), between nuclear and conventional forces, between air, land and sea forces and between different regions within a country and between different parts

Global applications

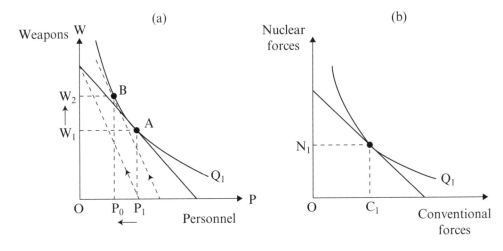

Figure 17.2a   shows the choice of the capital–labour mix. A cost-minimizing defence ministry and
its armed forces will use inputs OW_1 of weapons and OP_1 of military personnel for a
defence output of OQ_1. This figure also shows the impacts of a shift from a draft to
an all-volunteer force. Figure 17.2b shows the optimal combination of nuclear forces
for a given defence output

of the world. Examples of these choices and how they can be represented by economic
models are shown in Figure 17.2. These figures use standard iso-quant and iso-cost curves
to represent the choice set and the optimal solution.

Figure 17.2a shows the impact of a shift from a draft to an all-volunteer force (AVF).
An AVF involves costlier labour inputs which are represented by the iso-cost line pivoting
inwards (shown by the broken line in Figure 17.2a). The substitution effect of the change
means that capital (weapons) are substituted for labour (military personnel). If society
wishes to maintain defence output at OQ_1 then there will be a move from point A to point
B with weapons replacing personnel but at the cost of a higher defence budget (shown by
the parallel shift in the iso-cost line and the move to point B with OW_1 of weapons and
OP_1 of military personnel). Alternatively, if the defence budget remains unchanged, the
shift to an AVF will involve a reduced defence output but a change in relative factor prices.

Following the end of the Cold War, defence budgets have been either constant or falling
in real terms, and these limited budgets are faced with rising input costs of both capital
and labour. Equipment costs have been rising at some 10 per cent per annum in real terms
which means a long-run reduction in the numbers of weapons acquired for the armed
forces (for example, the USAF original requirement for F-22 combat aircraft was 750
units, later reduced to some 180 aircraft). Similarly, with an all-volunteer force, the costs
of military personnel have to rise faster than wage increases in the civil sector. This wage
differential is required to attract and retain military personnel by compensating them for
the net disadvantages of military life. Here, the military employment contract is unique
in that armed forces personnel are subject to military discipline; they are required to
deploy to any part of the world at short notice; they could remain overseas indefinitely;
and some might never return (that is, death and injury are a feature of this contract). This
combination of constant or falling defence budgets and rising input costs means that

governments and defence policy-makers cannot avoid the need for difficult choices in a world of uncertainty (that is, where the future is unknown and unknowable and no one can accurately predict the future). Can economics help to resolve this defence choice problem?

Economics offers three broad policy guidelines for formulating an efficient defence policy, namely, final outputs, substitution and competition. First, the principle of *final outputs*. Measuring defence output is notoriously difficult, but it can be expressed in such general terms as peace, security and threat reduction. A nation might solve this problem by committing (and funding) its armed forces to fighting independently, say, two major regional conflicts without international support or three small to medium conflicts (for example, Bosnia; Kosovo). This focus on military capability is a departure from the traditional concern with inputs in terms of the numbers of infantry regiments, warships, tanks and combat aircraft. Such a focus fails to address the key issue of the contribution of these inputs to final defence output in the form of peace and protection. A focus on inputs also fails to address the marginal contribution of each of the armed forces: what would the implications for defence output be if, say, the air force were expanded by 5 to 10 per cent, or the navy was reduced by 5 to 10 per cent?

The second economic principle is that of *substitution*. There are alternative methods of achieving protection, each with different cost implications. Possible examples of partial substitutes include reserves replacing regular personnel; civilians replacing regulars (for example, police in Northern Ireland replacing army personnel); attack helicopters replacing tanks; ballistic and cruise missiles and UCAVs replacing manned strike and bomber aircraft; air power replacing land forces; and nuclear forces replacing conventional forces (see Figure 17.2b). Some of these substitutions might alter the traditional monopoly property rights of each of the armed forces. For example, surface-to-air missiles operated by the army might replace manned fighter aircraft operated by the air force; and maritime anti-submarine aircraft operated by the air force might replace frigates supplied by the navy.

The third economic principle is that of *competition* as a means of achieving efficiency. Standard economic theory predicts that compared with monopoly, competition results in lower prices, efficiency, competitively-determined profits and innovation in both products and industrial structure. For equipment procurement, competition means allowing foreign firms to bid for national defence contracts and awarding fixed price contracts rather than cost-plus contracts; it also means ending any 'cosy' relationship between the Defence Ministry and its national champions; and ending preferential purchasing and guaranteed home markets.

Competition can be extended to activities provided by the armed forces. Here, there is a public sector monopoly problem where the armed forces have traditionally supplied a range of activities 'in-house' without being subject to any rivalry. Military outsourcing allows private contractors to bid for and provide such 'in-house' activities. Examples include accommodation, catering, maintenance, repair, training, transport and management tasks (for example, managing stores/depots and firing ranges). In some cases, outsourcing involves private finance initiatives where the private sector finances the activity (for example, new buildings; an aircrew simulator training facility) and then enters into a long-term contract with the Defence Ministry to provide services to the armed forces in return for rental payments. Another variant is a public–private partnership where the private sector finances an activity or asset in return for rental payments from the Defence Ministry, but the contractor is allowed to sell any peace-time spare capacity to other users (for example, tanker aircraft capacity which when not needed in peace-time can be rented to other users).

Application of the policy guidelines for an efficient defence policy requires that individuals and groups in the military–industrial–political complex are provided with sufficient incentives to behave efficiently. There are the inevitable principal–agent problems where agents have considerable opportunities to pursue self-interest which will depart from the objectives of their principals (for example, a quiet life rather than bearing the costs of change). Individuals and groups in the armed forces and Defence Ministries will be reluctant to apply the substitution principle if there are no personal or group incentives and rewards for achieving efficient substitution (that is, interest groups as barriers to change). In contrast, in the private sector there are market and institutional arrangements which promote efficiency through rivalry between suppliers, through the profit motive and through the capital market as a 'policing and monitoring' mechanism with the threats of takeovers and bankruptcy. Such market arrangements are absent in the armed forces (and elsewhere in the public sector).

17.3   DISARMAMENT

The Peace Dividend

The end of the Cold War resulted in a disarmament race replacing the superpowers' arms race. There was much talk of a peace dividend with its prospects of an increased output of civilian goods and services (economic growth). Indeed, a number of myths emerged, namely, that the peace dividend would be large; that it would solve a nation's economic, social and environmental problems and that adjustment problems could be ignored. Reality was different and there are some clear economic principles of disarmament.

Principle I: Disarmament as an investment
Disarmament can be analysed as an investment process. This approach regards disarmament as involving both costs and benefits. Adjusting to cuts in defence spending is not costless and involves a re-allocation of resources from the military–industrial complex to the civilian sector. But such re-allocation takes time and involves costs (we do not live in a world of magic wand economics). Adjustment costs take the form of unemployment and under-employment of labour, capital and other resources affecting both armed forces and defence industries. On this basis, disarmament resembles an investment process involving short-run costs to achieve long-run benefits. These benefits include peace (which is a public good) and a peace dividend in the form of a greater output of civilian goods and services (UNIDIR, 1993).

The economic adjustment to disarmament is complex. For the armed forces, there will be cuts in personnel and base closures with impacts on local economies (including rural areas). Similarly, for defence firms and industries, there will be job losses and plant closures with impacts on industry supply chains and city and regional economies. The achievement of a peace dividend involves both supply and demand sides of factor and product markets. Disarmament releases resources from the military sector, but in the short run the achievement of a peace dividend requires that these resources are re-employed in the production of civil goods and services. For example, some released labour resources

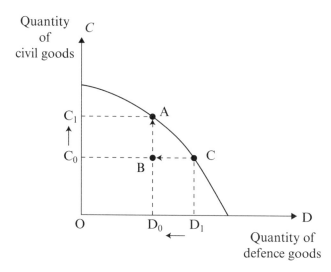

Figure 17.3   Disarmament reduces defence spending from D_1 to D_0 allowing the output of civil goods to rise from C_0 to C_1, where the increased output of civil goods is the peace dividend. However, adjustment costs mean that the adjustment path is from C to A via B

might remain unemployed, emigrate or might exit the labour market (retirement). In the long run, disarmament will create a new set of labour and factor market signals indicating that there are reduced employment prospects in the armed forces and defence industries. Figure 17.3 shows the adjustment costs of disarmament. With a reduction in defence spending, the economy moves from position C to A via position B (that is, the adjustment path does not remain on the production possibility frontier).

Principle II: Adjustment paths
Viewed as an investment, society's aim is to maximize the returns from disarmament. This requires that reductions in military spending should be gradual and predictable, so allowing smooth economic and social adjustments to cuts in defence spending. The aim should be to avoid major, rapid and unexpected reductions in defence spending, especially in recessionary conditions and where markets are failing to work properly and there is no state intervention to correct for market failure. Figure 17.4 shows two scenarios of a successful and a failed adjustment. Scenario I is a successful disarmament with relatively low costs and substantial economic benefits. This is the case where disarmament occurs slowly and predictably in an expanding economy with government intervening to ensure that markets are working properly. Scenario II is a failed disarmament involving massive costs and relatively small benefits. Here, there are large-scale cuts in defence spending occurring in an economy in recession and moving further into recession with markets failing to work properly and government not intervening to correct for such market failure.

Principle III: Uniqueness
The disarmament following the end of the Cold War was unique in that it occurred without a prior major war. Also, in several countries disarmament occurred simultaneously with a shift from a centrally-planned to a market economy (for example, former

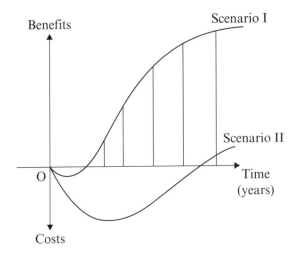

Figure 17.4   Disarmament as an investment process. Scenario I is a successful disarmament whilst Scenario II is a failed disarmament

Warsaw Pact states). Such economies were subject to two major shocks, so increasing their adjustment problems.

Principle IV: Conversion can be costly
Converting resources from military to civilian use is not costless. Examples include converting tank factories to tractor plants; nuclear weapons plants to car factories; and military bases to housing estates. There are economic, technological and environmental costs and constraints on conversion. Typically, removing these constraints on conversion requires finance, managerial innovation, retraining for personnel and capital re-tooling. For example, there are environmental clean-up costs for redundant military bases and nuclear research plants to ensure that the sites are safe for alternative civilian uses. There are costs of entering civil markets, including the costs of converting defence plants and retraining the work force and management. Costs arise in changing a firm's culture from dependency on military contracts to enterprise with its culture of risk-taking and profit-seeking based on entrepreneurship. Furthermore, there is the challenge of identifying civil markets which are expected to be profitable (that is, competing with established civil firms who are experts on production technology and market opportunities with reputations in the field). A taxonomy for analysing conversion is presented in Figure 17.5. Two variable are shown, namely, dependence on defence sales and dependence on defence-led and defence-specific technology and assets. Firms in box D which are highly dependent on defence sales (for example, 100 per cent defence-dependent) and which are wholly-dependent on defence-specific technology and assets will encounter the greatest conversion problems. In contrast, firms in box A are readily able to move between defence and civil markets.

Conversion raises issues about the transferability and specificity of resources (labour and capital). Some resources are readily and easily transferred almost at low cost from military to civilian use. Examples include military personnel with marketable civilian skills such as air force transport aircraft pilots, air traffic controllers, computer operatives, systems

		Dependence on defence sales	
		Low	High
Dependence on defence-led and defence-specific technology and assets	Low	A	B
	High	C	D

Figure 17.5 Conversion

engineers and lorry drivers. Similarly, redundant air force bases can be used as civilian airports and redundant naval bases as sea ports. Other military personnel have highly defence-specific skills such as parachutists, tank gunners and submariners which have no obvious civil market opportunities. The same problems arise with redundant defence industry workers and plants. Some workers and plants in sectors such as military aerospace can be immediately used for manufacturing civil aircraft and engines whereas other resources in sectors such as the nuclear submarine construction and repair industry have little alternative use value. On this basis, public policies are needed to assist the re-allocation of resources from defence to civil production (for example, training and mobility policies; R&D policies). But there remains a problem. The physical conversion of some military facilities and defence plants can be technically difficult and costly (for example, nuclear weapons research and manufacturing plants; nuclear submarine construction and repair yards).

The end of the Cold War released substantial resources from the military–industrial complex especially in NATO and the former Warsaw Pact nations. Table 17.3 shows examples based on defence spending, military personnel and defence industry employment over the period 1990 to 2000. There were major resources released in the former Warsaw Pact nations. However, these data show only the supply-side and do not indicate whether the resources were re-employed in the civilian sector. Also, the end of the Cold War did not signal a period of continued world peace. There were conflicts in the Gulf, Middle East, Bosnia and the terrorist attacks of 11 September 2001 (9/11) on the USA. The world remained a dangerous place with new conflicts and new threats.

17.4 CONFLICT AND TERRORISM

Traditionally, conflict and terrorism have been the preserve of disciplines other than economics. For example, debates and decisions about war involve political, military, moral

Table 17.3   The peace dividend

	1990	1999/2000	Size of reductions 1990–2000
Military expenditures ($ billion, 1999 prices)			
World	1 280	852	428
NATO	578	475	103
Warsaw Pact (former)	394	62	332
Defence share of GNP (%)			
World	4.5	2.4	2.1
NATO	4.1	2.6	1.5
Warsaw Pact (former)	9.7	3.2	6.5
Armed forces personnel (000s)			
World	27 700	21 300	6 400
NATO	5 780	4 580	1 200
Warsaw Pact (former)	4 400	2 170	2 230
Employment in arms production (000s)			
World	16 241	8 080	8 161
NATO	4 706	3 180	1 526
Soviet Union/CIS	5 920	1 170	4 750
East Europe	6 481	1 320	5 161

Sources: BICC (2002); DoS (2002)

and legal judgements. But conflict has an economic dimension, namely, its costs. Wars are not costless: they can involve massive costs (for example, World War II). Economics has also made further contributions in analysing the causes of conflict and in identifying potential targets during conflict (for example, the World War II target selection of aircraft and ball-bearing factories, dams, submarine yards and oil fields for allied bombing raids on Germany; similarly for the conflicts in Iraq and Kosovo).

Conflict

Comparisons can be made between standard microeconomics and conflict. Microeconomics focuses on market transactions based on voluntary trade and exchange. Within markets, resources are allocated and re-allocated via the price mechanism. There is a focus on markets, their equilibrium and the creative power of economies leading to a greater output of goods and services.

Economic models start by analysing wars and conflict as the use of military force to achieve a re-allocation of resources within and between nations (that is, civil wars and international conflict). Nations invade to capture or steal another nation's property rights over its resources (for example, land; minerals; oil; population; water). Conflict destroys markets leading to disequilibrium and chaos. There is a further distinctive feature of conflict: it destroys goods, factors of production and civilian infrastructure (for example, bridges; communications; roads) and it is easier to destroy than to create. In peace-time, civilian economies aim to create more goods and services through growth and expanding a nation's production possibility frontier. Conflict uses military force and destructive power to enable a nation to acquire resources from another state, so expanding its production boundary through military force (Vahabi, 2004). However, occupied populations and slave labour are not willing suppliers and cooperative of effort. As a result, occupying powers incur substantial policing and enforcement costs.

Conflict and terrorism provide opportunities for applying game theory. They involve strategic behaviour, interactions and interdependence between adversaries ranging from small groups of terrorists, rebels and guerrillas to nation states. Strategic interaction means that conflict can be analysed as games of bluff, chicken and 'tit-for-tat' with first-mover advantage and possibilities of one-shot or repeated games. For example, first-mover advantage might be achieved through a pre-emptive strike (for example, Pearl Harbour, 1941; Kuwait, 1990). There are, though, other non-economic explanations of conflict. These include religion, ethnicity and grievance (for example, Germany after World War I); the desire for a nation state (for example, Palestine); the absence of democracy; and mistakes and mis-judgement. Alternatively, political leaders might suffer from megalomania (Napoleon I?) or try to use wars to gain political support; or wars might arise from pressure and interest groups pursuing their own agenda aiming to benefit from conflict.

The costs of war are a relatively neglected dimension of conflict. War involves both one-off and continuing costs. One-off costs are those of the actual conflict, and continuing costs are any post-conflict costs including occupation, peace-keeping and reconstruction costs. A further distinction is needed between military and civilian costs. In principle, the military costs of conflict are the marginal resource costs arising from the conflict (that is, those costs which would not otherwise have been incurred and which are additional to the annual defence budget). Examples include the costs of preparation and deployment prior to a conflict; the costs of the conflict, including the costs of basing forces overseas and the use of ammunition, missiles and equipment, including human capital and equipment losses in combat; the post-conflict occupation and peace-keeping missions and the costs of returning armed forces to their home nation.

There are further costs of conflict in the form of impacts on the civilian economies of the nations involved in the war. For example, the US and UK involvement in the Iraq war had possible short- and long-term impacts for both economies. There were possible impacts on oil prices, share prices, the airline business, tourism, defence industries, private contractors, aggregate demand and future public spending plans. Further substantial costs were imposed on the Iraq economy in the form of deaths and injuries of military and civilian personnel, together with the damage and destruction of physical assets, including antiquities. Wars also involve environmental costs (for example, destruction and degradation of natural resources such as oil spills in Lebanon resulting from the Israeli–Hezbollah conflict). Some costs are long-term such as injuries and health problems (for example, from the atomic bombs used on Hiroshima and Nagasaki in 1945) and the lasting consequences of land mines, cluster bombs and the use of Agent Orange in Vietnam. Institutional assets may be destroyed and costly reorganization of social structures may be required at the end of a major war (for example, Germany and Japan in 1945; Iraq after 2003).

Table 17.4 gives some examples of the costs of various conflicts for the UK and USA (based on immediate budgetary costs only). The general point remains that wars are costly and require scarce resources which have alternative uses (that is, wars involve the sacrifice of

Table 17.4   Costs of conflict

UK: Conflict	Military costs to UK (US$ billions, 2005 prices)
World War I	357
World War II	1175
Gulf War	6.0
Bosnia	0.7
Kosovo	1.7
Iraq	6.5+

USA: Conflict	Military costs to USA (US$ billions, 2005 prices)
World War I	208
World War II	3148
Korea	365
Vietnam	537
Gulf War	83
Iraq	440

Estimated civilian costs: Iraq war	Civilian costs (US$ billion, 2005 prices)
Costs to US economy from Iraq war	557
Costs to world economy from Iraq war	1183

Iraq war: costs to Iraq	US$ billion (2005 prices)
Deaths of military and civilian personnel	(??)
Reconstruction costs	20–300

Notes:
(i)   US civilian costs are of lost GDP over the period 2003–2010.
(ii) Cost to world economy is lost GDP for period 2003–2010.
(iii) Iraq costs are for the period to 2006.

Source: Hartley (2006).

hospitals, schools and social welfare programmes). Questions then arise as to whether the benefits of conflict exceed its costs. Ideally, such a benefit–cost calculation needs to be undertaken before the conflict (*ex ante*) although critics with the benefit of hindsight usually focus on the outcomes (*ex post*). Analysts also need to recognise the counter-factual, namely, what would have happened in the absence of the conflict. For example, in the case of the Iraq war, what would have happened to oil prices without the war, and what would have happened to Iraq with and without Saddam Hussein and with and without international sanctions?

Terrorism

Defence economists have also contributed to the analysis of terrorism using both choice theoretic and game theory models. Terrorism is a form of non-conventional conflict which is also costly. The attacks on 11 September 2001 in the USA resulted in almost 3 000 deaths and economic losses of \$80–90 billion (Barros *et al.*, 2005). Other terrorist-related costs include nations spending on homeland security measures, on terrorist-related intelligence, on security measures in airports, the increased waiting time at airports to clear security, disruption to travel, the losses of liberty and freedoms and the general war on terror (for example, Afghanistan; Iraq). However, some commentators have referred to the general war on terrorism as 'doublespeak' (Lynch, 2006). This is language that pretends to communicate but which makes the bad seem good, the negative becomes positive and the unpleasant is presented as at least tolerable. Public choice models predict that if politicians offer funding to prevent terrorism, then bureaucracies will spend that money on anything remotely resembling homeland security and the need to protect its citizens from any form of terrorist threats.

Choice-theoretic models of terrorism apply standard consumer choice theory with terrorists maximizing a utility function subject to budget constraints. The utility function can be specific, such as a choice between attack modes, say, skyjackings and bombings, or more generally involving a choice between terrorist and peaceful activities. The approach offers some valuable insights into terrorist behaviour and possible policy solutions. The model shows that terrorist behaviour and activities can be influenced by governments acting to reduce terrorist funds (that is, an income effect); by changing relative prices (that is, promoting a substitution effect); and by efforts to change terrorist preferences towards more peaceful activities (for example, Northern Ireland). The substitution effect is an especially powerful insight showing that policies which increase the relative price of one attack mode, such as skyjackings, will encourage terrorists to substitute an alternative and lower-cost method of attack such as assassinations, bombings and kidnappings. Similarly, there are externalities in government policy responses whereby strong airport security in one nation might persuade terrorists to shift their attentions to other nations with weak airport security. The analysis also involves a collective action problem and predicts that nations will free-ride on any nation (for example, USA) which actively pursues international terrorists. Finally, deterrence and retaliation policies can be viewed as measures to increase the costs of terrorism, thereby reducing its activity. For example, costs can be imposed on nations supporting terrorist groups through, for example, international sanctions or invasion as in the case of Afghanistan after 9/11 (Frey and Luechinger, 2003; Anderton and Carter, 2005).

Examples of the choice theoretic models of terrorism are shown in Figure 17.6. In Figure 17.6a, an increase in the cost of assassinations (or bombings) leads terrorists to choose more skyjackings. Figure 17.6b shows the choice between terrorism and peaceful activities. Reductions in the cost of peaceful activity lead to less terrorism (for example, Northern Ireland). The models can also be used to show the effects of government policies which reduce terrorist access to funds (an income effect) and measures to shift tastes and preferences away from terrorism to more peaceful activities (that is, changing tastes and preferences). Figure 17.6c shows the case of a suicide terrorist where the only argument in the utility function is the number of deaths of an enemy (for example, Middle East).

17.5 CONCLUSION

Defence economics is now established as a reputable sub-discipline of economics. It shows how economic theory and methods can be applied to the defence sector embracing the

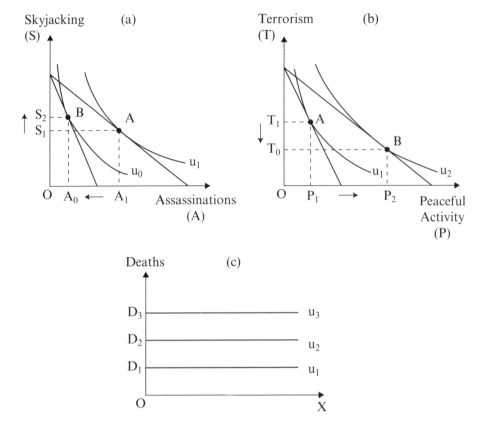

Figure 17.6   *shows various applications of indifference curve analysis to terrorism. Figure 17.6a*
shows the choice between alternative attack modes. An increase in the cost of
assassinations leads to a move from A to B comprising both income and substitution
effects. Figure 17.6b shows the choice between peaceful and terrorist activity and the
effect of a reduction in the 'price' of peaceful activity leading to a shift from A to B.
Figure 17.6c shows the utility function for a suicide terrorist where only deaths enter
into the utility function

armed forces, defence industries and the political–institutional arrangements for making
defence choices. But opportunities remain for further research in the field. Changes in
threats, new technology, globalization and continued budget constraints will require
further adjustments in armed forces and defence industries and will generate a new set of
research problems. Examples include space warfare, the economics of nuclear weapons
policy, assessing the internal efficiency of armed forces, improving the efficiency of military alliances and developing more efficient solutions for international governance and
international collective action, including peacekeeping operations.

There is also a need for caution. Economic theory has its uses in relation to defence
policy but it is only one element in the total picture. It has its limits and achieving the right
balance in an uncertain and grey world is not easy. Textbook models suggest that achieving an optimum and efficient solution is simply a matter of applying the standard marginal

conditions for such a maximum. The real world is much more difficult and challenging. Defence choices have to be made in a world of uncertainty where the future is unknown and unknowable and where there is asymmetry of information in society when it comes to matters of defence, war and conflict. Politicians may exploit this asymmetry to their advantage (for example, prior to the conflict, claims about Iraq's weapons of mass destruction). Wars always involve at least one loser, but often it is not known in advance who it will be.

READING* AND REFERENCES

Anderton, C.H. and J.R. Carter (2005), 'On rational choice theory and the study of terrorism', *Defence and Peace Economics*, **16**(4), 275–82.

Barros, C.P., C. Kollisa and T. Sandler (2005), 'Security challenges and threats in a post-9/11 world', *Defence and Peace Economics*, **16**(6), 1–3.

BICC (2002), *Conversion Survey, 2002*, Bonn: Bonn International Centre for Conversion.

BICC (2005), *Conversion Survey, 2005*, Bonn International Centre for Conversion, Baden-Baden: Nomos Verlagsgellschaft.

DoS (2002), *World Military Expenditures and Arms Transfers, 1999–2000*, Washington DC: US Department of State; Bureau of Verification and Compliance.

Frey, B.S. and S. Luechinger (2003), 'How to fight terrorism: alternatives to deterrence', *Defence and Peace Economics*, **14**(4), 237–49.

*Hartley, K. (2006), 'The economics of conflict', in A. Ott and R.J. Cebula (eds), *The Elgar Companion to Public Economics: Empirical Public Economics*, Cheltenham, UK and Northampton, MA, USA: Edward Elgar.

Hartley, K. (2008), 'Defence economics', in L. Blume and S.N. Durlauf (eds), *The New Palgrave Dictionary of Economics*, 2nd edn, London: Macmillan.

Hitch, C.J. and R. McKean (1960), *The Economics of Defense in the Nuclear Age*, Cambridge, USA: Harvard University Press.

Kennedy, P. (1988), *The Rise and Fall of the Great Powers*, London: Fontana Press.

Lynch, T. (2006), *Doublespeak and the War on Terrorism*, CATO Briefing Paper No. 98, Washington DC: Cato Institute.

OECD (2004), *Main Science and Technology Indicators*, Paris: OECD.

*Sandler, T. and K. Hartley (1995), *The Economics of Defense*, Cambridge Surveys of Economic Literature, Cambridge: Cambridge University Press.

Sandler, T. and K. Hartley (eds) (2007), *Handbook of Defense Economics, volume 2*, Amsterdam: Elsevier.

SIPRI (2005), *SIPRI Yearbook 2005*, Stockholm International Peace Research Institute, Oxford: Oxford University Press.

SIPRI (2006), *SIPRI Yearbook 2006*, Stockholm International Peace Research Institute, Oxford: Oxford University Press.

UNIDIR (1993), *Economic Aspects of Disarmament: Disarmament as an Investment Process*, Geneva: United Nations Institute for Disarmament Research.

Vahabi, M. (2004), *The Political Economy of Destructive Power*, Cheltenham, UK and Northampton, MA, USA: Edward Elgar.

QUESTIONS FOR REVIEW AND DISCUSSION

1. How do economists analyse the defence sector?
2. What is the military production function? What are the problems in operationalising this function?

3. What are the distinctive features of defence markets?
4. Do you believe that your country spends too much on defence? Explain the economic model used in deriving your answer.
5. What is the peace dividend? Estimate the size of this dividend for NATO and former Warsaw Pact states.
6. Identify the economic problems of conversion for both the military sector and defence industries. Does your analysis suggest the need for public policies to achieve conversion? If so, which are your preferred policies and why?
7. Does economic analysis explain the causes of conflict? Illustrate with reference to the conflicts in Afghanistan and Iraq.
8. Using cost-benefit analysis identify and estimate both the costs and benefits of the Iraq war.
9. Does economic analysis explain the causes of terrorism, including suicide terrorism? What are the public policy implications of your analysis?
10. Identify and estimate the economic impacts of the terrorism attacks of 11 September 2001 on the US and UK economies.

Index